Christian Omnibus Vol. 2
Six Books on Victorious Living

TABLE OF CONTENTS

How To Succeed In The Christian Life

~ ※ ~

By *R. A. Torrey*

~ ※ ~

Dedicated to the many thousands in many lands
who have professed Christ in our meetings.

Introduction

I have for years felt the need of a book to put in the hands of those beginning the Christian life that would tell them just how to make a complete success of this new life upon which they were entering. I could find no such book, so I have been driven to write one. This book aims to tell the young convert just what he most needs to know. I hope that pastors and evangelists and other Christian workers may find it a good book to put in the hands of young converts. I hope that it may also prove a helpful book to many who have long been Christians but have not made that headway in the Christian life that they long for.

Chapter I. Beginning Right

There is nothing more important in the Christian life than beginning right. If we begin right we can go on right. If we begin wrong the whole life that follows is likely to be wrong. If any one who reads these pages has begun wrong, it is a very simple matter to begin over again and begin right. What the right beginning in the Christian life is we are told in John 1: 12, "But as many as received Him, to them gave He power to become the sons of God, even to them that believe on His name." The right way to begin the Christian life is by receiving Jesus Christ. To any one who receives Him, He at once gives power to become a child of God. If the reader of this book should be the wickedest man on earth and should at this moment receive Jesus Christ, that very instant he would become a child of God. God says so in the most unqualified way in the verse quoted above. No one can become a child of God in any other way. No man, no matter how carefully he has been reared, no matter how well he has been sheltered from the vices and evils of this world, is a child of God until he receives Jesus Christ. We are "sons of God through faith in Christ Jesus" (Gal. 3: 26), and in no other way.

What does it mean to receive Jesus Christ? It means to take Christ to be to yourself all that God offers Him to be to everybody. Jesus Christ is God's gift. "For God so loved the world that He gave His only begotten Son that whosoever believeth in Him should not perish but have everlasting life" (John 3: 16). Some accept this wondrous gift of God. Every one who does accept this gift becomes a child of God. Many others refuse this wondrous gift of God, and every one who refuses this gift of God perishes. He is condemned already. "He that believeth on the Son is not condemned, but he that believeth not is condemned already because he hath not believed in the name of the only begotten Son of God" (John 3: 18).

What does God offer His Son to be to us?

1. First of all, *God offers Jesus to us to be our sin-bearer*. We have all sinned. There is not a man or woman or a boy or a girl who has not sinned (Romans 3: 22, 23). If any of us say that we have not sinned we are deceiving ourselves and giving the lie to God (1 John 1: 8, 10). Now we must each of us bear our own sin or some one else must bear it in our place. If we were to bear our own sins, it would mean we must be banished forever from the presence of God, for God is holy. "God is light and in Him is no darkness at all" (1 John 1:5). But God Himself has provided another to bear our sins in our place so that we should not need to bear them ourselves. This sin-bearer is God's own Son, Jesus Christ, "For He hath made Him to be sin for us who knew no sin that we might be made the righteousness of God in Him" (2 Cor. 5:21). When Jesus Christ died upon the cross of

Calvary He redeemed us from the curse of the law by being made a curse in our stead (Gal. 3:13). To receive Christ then is to believe this testimony of God about His Son, to believe that Jesus Christ did bear our sins in His own body on the cross (1 Pet. 2:24), and to trust God to forgive all our sins because Jesus Christ has borne them in our place. "All we like sheep have gone astray; we have turned every one to his own way; and the Lord hath laid on Him the iniquity of us all" (Is. 53:6). Our own good works, past, present or future have nothing to do with the forgiveness of our sins. Our sins are forgiven, not because of any good works that we do, they are forgiven because of the atoning work of Christ upon the cross of Calvary in our place. If we rest in this atoning work we shall do good works, but our good works will be the outcome of our being saved and the outcome of our believing on Christ as our sin-bearer. Our good works will not be the ground of our salvation, but the result of our salvation, and the proof of it. We must be very careful not to mix in our good works at all as the ground of salvation. We are not forgiven because of Christ's death *and our good works*, we are forgiven solely and entirely because of Christ's death. To see this clearly is the right beginning of the true Christian life.

2. *God offers Jesus to us as our deliverer from the power of sin.* Jesus not only died, He rose again. To-day He is a living Savior. He has all power in heaven and on earth (Matt. 28: 18). He has power to keep the weakest sinner from falling (Jude 24). He is able to save not only from the uttermost but "to the uttermost" all that come unto the Father through Him. (Wherefore He is able to save to the uttermost them that draw near unto God through Him, seeing that He ever liveth to make intercession for them.—Heb. 7: 25) "If the Son therefore shall make you free, ye shall be free indeed" (John 8: 36). To receive Jesus is to believe this that God tells us in His Word about Him, to believe that He did rise from the dead, to believe that He does now live, to believe that He has power to keep us from falling, to believe that He has power to keep us from the power of sin day by day, and just trust Him to do it.

This is the secret of daily victory over sin. If we try to fight sin in our own strength, we are bound to fail. If we just look up to the risen Christ to keep us every day and every hour, He will keep us. Through the crucified Christ we get deliverance from the guilt of sin, our sins are all blotted out, we are free from all condemnation; but it is through the risen Christ that we get daily victory over the power of sin. Some receive Christ as a sin-bearer and thus find pardon, but do not get beyond that, and so their life is one of daily failure. Others receive Him as their risen Savior also, and thus enter into an experience of victory over sin. To begin right we must take Him not only as our sin-bearer, and thus find pardon; but we must also take Him as our risen Savior, our Deliverer from the power of sin, our Keeper, and thus find daily victory over sin.

3. But *God offers Jesus to us, not only as our sin-bearer and our Deliverer from the power of sin, but He also offers Him to us as our Lord and King.* We read in Acts 2: 36, "Let all the house of Israel know assuredly, that God hath made that same Jesus, whom ye have crucified, both Lord and Christ." Lord means Divine Master, and Christ means anointed King. To receive Jesus is to take Him as our Divine Master, as the One to whom we yield the absolute confidence of our intellects, the One whose word we believe absolutely, the One whom we will believe though many of the wisest of men may question or deny the truth of His teachings; and as our King to whom we gladly yield the absolute control of our lives, so that the question from this time on is never going to be, what would I like to do or what do others tell me to do, or what do others do, but the whole question

is what would my King Jesus have me do? A right beginning involves an unconditional surrender to the Lordship and Kingship of Jesus.

The failure to realize that Jesus is Lord and King, as well as Savior, has led to many a false start in the Christian life. We begin with Him as our Savior, as our sin-bearer and our Deliverer from the power of sin, but we must not end with Him merely as Savior, we must know Him as Lord and King. There is nothing more important in a right beginning of the Christian life than an unconditional surrender, both of the thoughts and the conduct to Jesus. Say from your heart and say it again and again, "*All* for Jesus." Many fail because they shrink back from this entire surrender. They wish to serve Jesus with half their heart, and part of themselves and part of their possessions. To hold back anything from Jesus means a wretched life of stumbling and failure.

The life of entire surrender is a joyous life all along the way. If you have never done it before, go alone with God to-day, get down on your knees and say, "All for Jesus," and mean it. Say it very earnestly; say it from the bottom of your heart. Stay there until you realize what it means and what you are doing. It is a wondrous step forward when one really takes it. If you have taken it already, take it again, take it often. It always has fresh meaning and brings fresh blessedness. In this absolute surrender is found the key to the truth. Doubts rapidly disappear for one who surrenders all (John 7: 17). In this absolute surrender is found the secret of power in prayer (1 John 3: 22). In this absolute surrender is found the supreme condition of receiving the Holy Ghost (Acts 5: 32).

Taking Christ as your Lord and King involves obedience to His will as far as you know it in each smallest detail of life. There are those who tell us that they have taken Christ as their Lord and King who at the same time are disobeying Him daily in business, in domestic life, in social life and in personal conduct Such persons are deceiving themselves. You have not taken Jesus as your Lord and King if you are not striving to obey Him in everything each day. He Himself says, "Why call ye Me 'Lord, Lord!' and do not the things that I say?" (Luke 6: 46).

To sum it all up, the right way to begin the Christian life is to accept Jesus Christ as your sin-bearer and to trust God to forgive your sins because Jesus Christ died in your place; to accept Him as your risen Savior who ever lives to make intercession for you, and who has all power to keep you, and to trust Him to keep you from day to day; and to accept Him as your Lord and King to whom you surrender the absolute control of your thoughts and of your life. This is the right beginning, the only right beginning of the Christian life. If you have made this beginning, all that follows will be comparatively easy. If you have not made this beginning, make it now.

Chapter II. The Open Confession of Christ

Having begun the Christian life right by taking the proper attitude towards Christ in a private transaction between Himself and yourself, the next step is an open confession of the relationship that now exists between yourself and Jesus Christ. Jesus says in Matt. 10: 32, "Whosoever therefore shall confess Me before men, him will I confess also before My Father which is in heaven." He demands a public confession. He demands it for your own sake. This is the path of blessing. Many attempt to be disciples of Jesus and not let the world know it. No one has ever succeeded in that attempt. To be a secret disciple means to be no disciple at all. If one really has received Christ he cannot keep it to himself. "For out of the abundance of the heart the mouth speaketh" (Matt. 12: 34). So important is the public confession of Christ that Paul puts it first in his statement of the conditions of salvation. He says, "If thou shalt *confess with thy mouth* the Lord Jesus and shalt believe in thine heart that God hath raised Him from the dead, thou shalt be saved. For with the heart man believeth unto righteousness; and with the mouth confession is made unto salvation" (Rom. 10: 9, 10). The life of confession is the life of full salvation. Indeed, the life of confession is the life of the only real salvation. When we confess Christ before men down here, He confesses us before the Father in heaven and the Father gives us the Holy Spirit as the seal of our salvation.

It is not enough that we confess Christ just once, as, for example, when we are confirmed, or when we unite with the church, or when we come forward in a revival meeting. We should confess Christ constantly. We should not be ashamed of our Lord and King. We should let people know that we are on His side. In the home, in the church, at our work, and at our play, we should let others know where we stand. Of course, we should not parade our Christianity or our piety, but we should leave no one in doubt whether we belong to Christ. We should let it be seen that we glory in Him as our Lord and King.

The failure to confess Christ is one of the most frequent causes of backsliding. Christians get into new relationships where they are not known as Christians and where they are tempted to conceal the fact; they yield to the temptation and they soon find themselves drifting. The more you make of Jesus Christ, the more He will make of you. It will save you from many a temptation if the fact is clearly known that you are one who acknowledges Christ as Lord in all things.

Chapter III. Assurance of Salvation

If one is to have the fullest measure of joy and power in Christian service, he must know that his sins are forgiven, that he is a child of God, and that he has eternal life. It is the believer's privilege to *know* that he has eternal life. John says in 1 John 5: 13, "These things have I written unto you, *that ye may know* that ye have eternal life, even unto you that believe on the name of the Son of God." John wrote this first epistle for the express purpose that any one who believes on the name of the Son of God *might know* that he has eternal life.

There are those who tell us that no one can know that he has eternal life until he is dead and has been before the judgment seat of God, but God Himself tells us that we may know. To deny the possibility of the believer's knowing that he has eternal life is to say that the First Epistle of John was written in vain, and it is to insult the Holy Spirit who is its real author. Again Paul tells us in Acts 13: 39, "By Him (that is by Christ) every one that believeth *is justified* from all things." So every one that believeth in Jesus may know that he is justified from all things. He may know it because the Word of God says so. Again John tells us in John 1: 12, "But *as many as received Him* (that is Jesus Christ) to them gave He the right to become children of God, even to them that believe on His name." Here is a definite and unmistakable declaration that every one who receives Jesus becomes a child of God. Therefore every believer in Jesus may know that he is a child of God. He may know it on the surest of all grounds, *i. e.*, because the Word of God asserts that he is a child of God.

But how may any individual know that he has eternal life? He may know it on the very best ground of knowledge, that is through the testimony of God Himself as given in the Bible. The testimony of Scripture is the testimony of God. What the Scriptures say is absolutely sure. What the Scriptures say God says. Now in John 3: 36 the Scriptures say, "He that believeth on the Son *hath* everlasting life." Any one of us may know whether we believe on the Son or not. Whether we have that real faith in Christ that leads us to receive Him. If we have this faith in Christ we have God's own written testimony that we have eternal life, that our sins are forgiven, that we are the children of God. We may feel forgiven, or we may not feel forgiven, but that does not matter. It is not a question of what we feel but of what God says. God's Word is always to be believed. Our own feelings are oftentimes to be doubted. There are many who are led to doubt their sins are forgiven, to doubt that they have everlasting life, to doubt that they are saved, because they do not feel forgiven, or do not feel that they have everlasting life, or do not feel that they are saved. Because you do not feel it is no reason why you should doubt it.

Suppose that you were sentenced to imprisonment and that your friends secured a pardon for you. The legal document announcing your pardon is brought to you. You read it and know you are pardoned because the legal document says so, but the news is so good and so sudden that you are dazed by it. You do not realize that you are pardoned. Some one comes to you and says, "Are you pardoned?" What would you reply? You would say, "Yes, I am pardoned." Then he asks, "Do you feel pardoned?" You reply, "No, I do not feel pardoned. It is so sudden, it is so wonderful, I cannot realize it." Then he says to you, "But how can you know that you are pardoned if you do not feel it?" You would hold out the document and you would say, "This says so." The time would come, after you had read the document over and over again and believed it, when you would not only know you were pardoned because the document said so but you would feel it. Now the Bible is God's authoritative document declaring that every one that believeth in Jesus is justified; declaring that every one that believeth on the Son hath everlasting life; declaring that every one who receives Jesus is a child of God. If any one asks you if your sins are all forgiven, reply, "Yes, I know they are because God says so." If they ask you if you know that you are a child of God, reply, "Yes, I know I am a child of God because God says so." If they ask you if you have everlasting life, reply, "Yes, I know I have everlasting life because God says so. God says, 'He that believeth on the Son hath everlasting life.' I know I believe on the Son, and therefore I know I have eternal life—because God says so." You may not feel it yet but if you will keep meditating upon God's statement and believing what God says, the time will come when you will feel it.

For one who believes on the Son of God to doubt that he has eternal life is for him to make God a liar. "He that believeth on the Son of God hath the witness in him. He that believeth not God, hath made Him a liar because he hath not believed in the witness that God hath borne concerning His Son and the witness is this, that God gave unto us eternal life, and this life is in His Son. He that hath the Son hath the life: he that hath not the Son of God hath not the life" (1 John 5: 10-12). Any one who does not believe God's testimony that He has given unto us eternal life and that this life is in His Son and that he that hath the Son hath the life, makes God a liar.

It is sometimes said "it is presumption for any one to say that he knows he is saved, or to say that he knows that he has eternal life." But is it presumption to believe God? Is it not rather presumption not to believe God, to make God a liar? When you who believe on the Son of God and yet doubt that you have eternal life, you make God a liar. When Jesus said to the woman who was a sinner, "Thy sins are forgiven" (Luke 7: 48), was it presumption for her to go out and say, "I know my sins are all forgiven"? Would it not have been presumption for her to have doubted for a moment that her sins were all forgiven? Jesus had said that they were forgiven. For her to doubt it would have been for her to give the lie to Jesus. Is it then any more presumption for the believer to-day to say, "My sins are all forgiven, I have eternal life," when God says in His written testimony to every one that believeth, "You are justified from all things" (Acts 13: 39), "You have eternal life" (John 3: 36; 1 John 5: 13)?

Be very sure first of all that you really do believe on the name of the Son of God; that you really have received Jesus. If you are sure of this then never doubt for a moment that your sins are all forgiven, never doubt for a moment that you are a child of God, never doubt for a moment that you have everlasting life. If Satan comes and whispers, "Your sins are not forgiven," point Satan to the Word of God and say, "God says my sins are forgiven and I know they are." If Satan whispers, "Well perhaps you don't believe on Him," then say, "Well if I never did before I will now." And then go out rejoicing, knowing that your sins are forgiven, knowing that you are a child of God, knowing that you have everlasting life.

There are doubtless many who say they know they have eternal life who really do not believe on the name of the Son of God, who have not really received Jesus. This is not true assurance. It has no sure foundation in the Word of God who cannot lie. If we wish to get assurance of salvation we must first get saved. The reason why many have not the assurance that they are saved is because they are not saved. They ought not to have assurance. What they need first is salvation. But if you have received Jesus in the way described in the first chapter, YOU ARE SAVED, you are a child of God, your sins are forgiven. Believe it, know it. Rejoice in it.

Having settled it, let it remain settled. Never doubt it. You may make mistakes, you may stumble, you may fall, but even if you do, if you have really received Jesus, know that your sins are forgiven and rise from your fall and go forward in the glad assurance that there is nothing between you and God.

Chapter IV. Receiving the Holy Spirit

When the Apostle Paul came to Ephesus, he found a little group of twelve disciples of Christ. There was something about these twelve disciples that struck Paul unfavorably. We are not told what it was. It may be that he did not find in them that overflowing joyfulness that one learns to expect in all Christians who have really entered into the fullness of blessing that there is for them in Christ. It may be that Paul was troubled at the fact that there were only twelve of them, thinking that if these twelve were what they ought to be, there would certainly have been more than twelve of them by this time. Whatever it may have been that impressed Paul unfavorably, he went right to the root of the difficulty at once by putting to them the question, "Did ye receive the Holy Ghost when ye believed?" (Acts 19: 2). It came out at once that they had not received the Holy Ghost, that in fact they did not know that the Holy Ghost had been given. Then Paul told them that the Holy Ghost had been given, and also showed them just what they must do to receive the Holy Ghost then and there, and before that gathering was over the Holy Ghost came upon them. From that day on there was a different state of affairs in Ephesus. A great revival sprang up at once so that the whole city was shaken, "So mightily grew the Word of God and prevailed" (Acts 19: 20). Paul's question to these young disciples in Ephesus should be put to young disciples everywhere, "Have ye received the Holy

Ghost?" In *receiving the Holy Spirit* is the great secret of joyfulness in our own hearts, of victory over sin, of power in prayer, and of effective service.

Every one who has truly received Jesus must have the Holy Spirit dwelling in him in some sense; but in many believers, though the Holy Spirit dwells in them, He dwells way back in some hidden sanctuary of their being, back of consciousness. It is something quite different, something far better than this, to receive the Holy Spirit in the sense that Paul meant in his question. To receive the Holy Spirit in such a sense that one knows experimentally that he has received the Holy Spirit, to receive the Holy Spirit in such a sense that we are conscious of the joy with which He fills our hearts different from any joy that we have ever known in the world; to receive the Holy Spirit in such a sense that He rules our life and produces within us in ever increasing measure the fruit of the Spirit, love, joy, peace, long-suffering, gentleness, goodness, faith, meekness, temperance; to receive the Holy Spirit in such a sense that we are conscious of His drawing our hearts out in prayer in a way that is not of ourselves; to receive the Holy Spirit in such a sense that we are conscious of His help when we witness for Christ, when we speak to others individually and try to lead them to accept Christ, or when we teach a Sunday-school class, or speak in public, or do any other work for the Master. Have you received the Holy Spirit? If you have not, let me tell you how you may.

1. First of all in order to receive the Holy Spirit, one must be resting in the death of Christ on the cross for us as the sole and all-sufficient ground upon which God pardons all our sins and forgives us.

2. In order to receive the Holy Spirit we must put away every known sin. We should go to our heavenly Father and ask Him to search us through and through and bring to light anything in our life, our outward life or our inward life, that is wrong in His sight, and if He does bring anything to light that is displeasing to Him, we should put it away, no matter how dear it is to us. There must be a complete renunciation of all sin in order to receive the Holy Spirit.

3. In the third place, in order to receive the Holy Spirit, there must be an open confession of Christ before the world. The Holy Spirit is not given to those who are trying to be disciples in secret, but to those who obey Christ and publicly confess Him before the world.

4. In the fourth place, in order to receive the Holy Spirit, there must be an absolute surrender of our lives to God. You must go to Him and say, "Heavenly Father, here I am. Thou hast bought me with a price. I am Thy property. I renounce all claim to do my own will, all claim to govern my own life, all claim to have my own way. I give myself up unreservedly to Thee—all I am and all I have. Send me where Thou wilt, use me as Thou wilt, do with me what Thou wilt—I am Thine." If we hold anything back from God, no matter how small it may seem, that spoils it all. But if we surrender all to God, then God will give all that He has to us. There are some who shrink from this absolute surrender to God, but absolute surrender to God is simply absolute surrender to infinite love. Surrender to the Father, to the Father whose love is not only wiser than any earthly father's, but more tender than any earthly mother's.

5. In order to receive the Holy Spirit there should be definite asking for the Holy Spirit. Our Lord Jesus says in Luke 11: 13, "If ye then, being evil, know how to give good gifts unto your children: how much more shall your heavenly Father give the Holy Spirit to them that ask Him?" Just ask God to give you the Holy Spirit and expect Him to do it, because He says He will.

6. Last of all, in order to receive the Holy Spirit, there must be faith, simply taking God at His Word. No matter how positive any promise of God's Word may be, we enjoy it personally only when we believe. Our Lord Jesus says, "All things whatsoever ye pray and ask for, believe that ye have received them, and ye shall have them" (Mark 11: 24). When you pray for the Holy Spirit you have prayed for something according to God's will and therefore you may know that your prayer is heard and that you have what you asked of Him (1 John 5: 14, 15). You may feel no different, but do not look at your feelings but at God's promise. Believe the prayer is heard, believe that God has given you the Holy Spirit and you will afterwards have in actual experience what you have received in simple faith on the bare promise of God's Word.

It is well to go often alone and kneel down and look up to the Holy Spirit and put into His hands anew the entire control of your life. Ask Him to take the control of your thoughts, the control of your imagination, the control of your affections, the control of your desires, the control of your ambitions, the control of your choices, the control of your purposes, the control of your words, the control of your actions, the control of everything, and just expect Him to do it. The whole secret of victory in the Christian life is letting the Holy Spirit who dwells within you, have undisputed right of way in the entire conduct of your life.

Chapter V. Looking Unto Jesus

If we are to run with patience the race that is set before us, we must always keep looking unto Jesus (Heb. 12: 1-3). One of the simplest and yet one of the mightiest secrets of abiding joy and victory is to *never lose sight of Jesus*.

1. First of all *we must keep looking at Jesus as the ground of our acceptance before God*. Over and over again Satan will make an attempt to discourage us by bringing up our sins and failures and thus try to convince us that we are not children of God, or not saved. If he succeeds in getting us to keep looking at and brooding over our sins, he will soon get us discouraged, and discouragement means failure. But if we will keep looking at what God looks at, the death of Jesus Christ in our place that completely atones for every sin that we ever committed, we will never be discouraged because of the greatness of our sins. We shall see that while our sins are great, very great, that they have all been atoned for. Every time Satan brings up one of our sins, we shall see that Jesus Christ has redeemed us from its curse by being made a curse in our place (Gal. 3: 13). We shall see that while in ourselves we are full of unrighteousness, nevertheless in Christ we are made the righteousness of God, because Christ was made to be sin in our place (2 Cor. 5: 21). We will see that every sin that Satan taunts us about has been borne and settled forever (1 Pet. 2: 24; Is. 53: 6). We shall always be able to sing,

> *"Jesus paid my debt,*
> *All the debt I owe;*
> *Sin had left a crimson stain,*
> *He washed it white as snow."*

If you are this moment troubled about any sin that you have ever committed, either in the past or in the present, just look at Jesus on the cross; believe what God tells you about Him, that this sin which troubles you was laid upon Him (Is. 53: 6). Thank God that the sin is all settled; be full of gratitude to Jesus who bore it in your place and trouble about it no more. It is an act of base ingratitude to God to brood over sins that He in His infinite love has cancelled. Keep looking at Christ on the cross and walk always in the sunlight of God's favor. This favor of God has been purchased for you at great cost. Gratitude demands that you should always believe in it and walk in the light of it.

2. In the second place, *we must keep looking at Jesus as our risen Savior, who has all power in heaven and on earth and is able to keep us every day and every hour.* Are you tempted to do some wrong at this moment? If you are, remember that Jesus rose from the dead, remember that at this moment He is living at the right hand of God in the glory; remember that He has all power in heaven and on earth, and that, therefore, He can give you victory right now. Believe what God tells you in His Word that Jesus has power to save you this moment "to the uttermost" (Heb. 7: 25). Believe that He has power to give you victory over this sin that now besets you. Ask Him to give you victory, expect Him to do it. In this way by looking unto the risen Christ for victory you may have victory over sin every day, every hour, every moment. "Remember Jesus Christ risen from the dead" (2 Tim. 2: 8).

God has called every one of us to a victorious life, and the secret of this victorious life is always looking to the risen Christ for victory. Through looking to Christ crucified we obtain pardon and enjoy peace. Through looking to the risen Christ we obtain present victory over the power of sin. If you have lost sight of the risen Christ and have yielded to temptation, confess your sin and know that it is forgiven because God says so (1 John 1: 9) and look to Jesus, the risen One, again to give you victory now and keep looking to Him.

3. In the third place, *we must keep looking to Jesus as the One whom we should follow in our daily conduct.* Our Lord Jesus says to us, His disciples to-day, as He said to His early disciples, "Follow Me." The whole secret of true Christian conduct can be summed up in these two words "Follow Me." "He that saith he abideth in Him ought himself so to walk *even as He walked*" (1 John 2: 6). One of the commonest causes of failure in Christian life is found in the attempt to follow some good man, whom we greatly admire. No man and no woman, no matter how good, can be safely followed. If we follow any man or woman, we are bound to go astray. There never has been but one absolutely perfect Man upon this earth—the Man Christ Jesus. If we try to follow any other man we are more sure to imitate his faults than his excellencies. Look at Jesus and Jesus only as your Guide.

If at any time you are in any perplexity as to what to do, simply ask the question, What would Jesus do? Ask God by His Holy Spirit to show you what Jesus would do. Study your Bible to find out what Jesus did do and follow Jesus. Even though no one else seems to be following Jesus, be sure that you follow Him. Do not spend your time or thought in criticizing others because they do not follow Jesus. See that you follow Him yourself. When you are wasting your time criticizing others for not following Jesus, Jesus is always saying to you, "What is that to thee; follow THOU Me" (John 21: 22). The question for you is not what following Jesus may involve for other people. The question is what does following Jesus mean for you?

This is the really simple life, the life of simply following Jesus. Many perplexing questions will come to you, but the most perplexing question will soon become as clear as day if you determine with all your heart to follow Jesus in everything. Satan will always be ready to whisper to you, "Such and such a good man does it," but all you need to do is to answer, "It matters not to me what this or that man may do or not do. The only question to me is, What would Jesus do?" There is wonderful freedom in this life of simply following Jesus. This path is straight and plain. But the path of the one who tries to shape his conduct by observing the conduct of others is full of twists and turns and pitfalls. Keep looking at Jesus. Follow on trustingly where He leads. This is the path of the just which shineth more and more unto the perfect day (Prov. 4: 18). He is the Light of the World, any one who follows Him shall not walk in darkness, but shall have the light of life all along the way (John 8: 12).

Chapter VI. Church Membership

No young Christian and no old Christian can have real success in the Christian life without the fellowship of other believers. The church is a divine institution, built by Jesus Christ Himself. It is the one institution that abides. Other institutions come and go; they do their work for their day and disappear, but the church will continue to the end. "The gates of hell shall not prevail against it" (Matt. 16: 18). The church is made up of men and women, imperfect men and women, and consequently is an imperfect institution, but none the less it is of divine origin and God loves it, and every believer should realize that he belongs to it and should openly take his place in it and bear his responsibilities regarding it.

The true church consists of all true believers, all who are united to Jesus Christ by a living faith in Himself. In its outward organization at the present time, it is divided into numberless sects and local congregations, but in spite of these divisions the true church is one. It has one Lord, Jesus Christ. It has one faith, faith in Him as Savior, Divine Lord and only King; one baptism, the baptism in the one Spirit into the one body (Eph. 4: 4, 5; 1 Cor. 12: 13). But each individual Christian needs the fellowship of individual fellow believers. The outward expression of this fellowship is in membership in some organized body of believers. If we hold aloof from all organized churches, hoping thus to have a broader fellowship with all believers belonging to all the churches, we deceive ourselves. We will miss the helpfulness that comes from intimate union with some local congregation. I have known many well-meaning persons who have held aloof from membership in any specific organization, and I have never known a person who has done this, whose own spiritual life has not suffered by it. On the day of Pentecost the three thousand who were converted were at once baptized and were added to the church (Acts 2: 41, 47), and "They continued steadfastly in the apostle's doctrine and fellowship, and in breaking of bread and in prayers." Their example is the one to follow. If you have really received Jesus Christ, hunt up as soon as possible some company of others who have received Jesus Christ and unite yourself with them.

In many communities there may be no choice of churches, for there is only one. In other communities one will be faced with the question, "With what body of believers shall I unite?" Do not waste your time looking for a perfect church. There is no perfect church. If you wait until you find a perfect church before you unite with any, you will unite with none, and thus you will belong to a church in which you are the only member and that is the most imperfect church of all. I would rather belong to the most imperfect Christian church I ever knew than not to belong to any church at all. The local churches in Paul's day were very imperfect institutions. Let one read the epistles to the Corinthians and see how imperfect was the church in Corinth, see how much there was that was evil in it, and yet Paul never thought of advising any believer in Corinth to get out of this imperfect church. He did tell them to come out of heathenism, to come out from fellowship with infidels (2 Cor. 6: 14-18), but not a word on coming out of the imperfect church in Corinth. He did tell the church in Corinth to separate from their membership certain persons whose lives were wrong (1 Cor. 5: 11, 12), but he did not tell the individual members of the church in Corinth to get out of the church because these persons had not yet been separated from their fellowship.

As you cannot find a perfect church, find the best church you can. Unite with a church where they believe in the Bible and where they preach the Bible. Avoid the churches where words are spoken open or veiled that have a tendency to undermine your faith in the Bible as a reliable revelation from God Himself, the all-sufficient rule of faith and practice. Unite with a church where there is a spirit of prayer, where the prayer-meetings are well kept up. Unite with a church that has a real active interest in the salvation of the lost, where young Christians are looked after and helped, where minister and people have a love for the poor and outcast, a church that regards its mission in this world to be the same as the mission of Christ, "to seek and to save the lost." As to denominational differences, other things being equal, unite with that denomination whose ideas of doctrine and of government and of the ordinances are most closely akin to your own. But it is better to unite with a live church of some other denomination than to unite with a dead church of your own. We live in a day when denominational differences are becoming ever less and less, and oftentimes they are of no practical consequence whatever; and one will often feel more at home in a church of some other denomination than in any accessible church of his own denomination. The things that divide the denominations are insignificant compared with the great fundamental truths and purposes and faith that unite them.

If you cannot find the church that agrees with the pattern set forth above, find the church that comes nearest to it. Go into that church and by prayer and by work try to bring that church as nearly as you can to the pattern of what you think a church of Christ ought to be. But do not waste your strength in criticism against either church or minister. Seek for what is good in the church and in the minister and do your best to strengthen it. Hold aloof firmly, though unobtrusively, from what is wrong and seek to correct it. Do not be discouraged if you cannot correct it in a day or a week or a month or a year. Patient love and prayer and effort will tell in time. Drawing off by yourself and snarling and grumbling will do no good. They will simply make you and the truths for which you stand repulsive.

Chapter VII. Bible Study

There is nothing more important for the development of the spiritual life of the Christian than regular, systematic Bible study. It is as true in the spiritual life as it is in the physical life that health depends upon what we eat and how much we eat. The soul's proper food is found in one book, the Bible. Of course, a true minister of the gospel will feed us on the Word of God, but that is not enough. He feeds us but one or two days in the week and we need to be fed every day. Furthermore, it will not do to depend upon being fed by others. We must learn to feed ourselves. If we study the Bible for ourselves as we ought to study it, we shall be in a large measure independent of human teachers. Even if we are so unfortunate as to have for our minister a man who is himself ignorant of the truth of God we shall still be safe from harm.

We live in a day in which false doctrine abounds on every hand and the only Christian who is safe from being led into error is the one who studies his Bible for himself daily. The Apostle Paul warned the elders of the church in Ephesus that the time was soon coming when grievous wolves should enter in among them not sparing the flock and when of their own selves men should arise speaking perverse things to draw away the disciples after them, but he told them how to be safe even in such perilous times as these. He said, "I commend you to God and to the Word of His grace, which is able to build you up and to give you an inheritance among them which are sanctified." Through meditation on the Word of God's grace they would be safe even in the midst of abounding error on the part of the leaders in the church (Acts 20: 29-32). Writing later to the Bishop of the church in Ephesus Paul said, "But evil men and impostors shall wax worse and worse, deceiving and being deceived" (2 Tim. 3: 13) but he goes on to tell Bishop Timothy how he and his fellow believers could be safe even in such times of increasing peril as were coming. That way was through the study of the Holy Scriptures, which are able to make wise unto salvation (2 Tim. 3: 14, 15). "All Scripture," he adds, "is given by inspiration of God and is profitable for doctrine, for reproof, for correction, for instruction in righteousness that the man of God may be perfect, thoroughly furnished unto all good works." That is to say, through the study of the Bible one will be sound in doctrine, will be led to see his sins and put them away, will find discipline in the righteous life and attain unto complete equipment for all good works. Our spiritual health, our growth, our strength, our victory over sin, our soundness in doctrine, our joy and peace in Christ, our cleansing from inward and outward sin, our fitness for service, all depend upon the study of the Word of God. The one who neglects his Bible is bound to make a failure of the Christian life. The one who studies his Bible in the right spirit and by a true method is bound to make a success of the Christian life.

This brings us face to face with the question, "What is the right way to study the Bible?"

1. First of all, we should *study it daily* (Acts 17: 11). This is of prime importance. No matter how good the methods of Bible study that one follows may be, no matter how much time one may put into Bible study now and then, the best results can only be secured when one makes it a matter of principle never to let a single day go by without earnest Bible study. This is the only safe course. Any day that is allowed to pass without faithful Bible study is a day thrown open to the advent into our hearts and lives of error or of sin. The writer has been a Christian for more than a quarter of a century and yet to-day he would not dare to allow even a single day to pass over his head without listening to the voice of God as it speaks to him through the pages of His Book. It is at this point that many fall away. They grow careless and let a day pass, or even several days pass, without going alone with God and letting Him speak to them through His Word. Mr. Moody once wisely said, "In prayer we talk to God. In Bible study, God talks to us, and we had better let God do most of the talking."

A regular time should be set apart each day for the study of the Bible. I do not think it is well as a rule to say that we shall study so many chapters in a day, for that leads to undue haste and skimming and thoughtlessness, but it is well to set apart a certain length of time each day for Bible study. Some can give more time to Bible study than others, but no one ought to give less than fifteen minutes a day. I set the time so low in order that no one may be discouraged at the outset. If a young Christian should set out to give an hour or two hours a day to Bible study, there is a strong probability that he would not keep to the resolution and he might become discouraged. Yet I know of many very busy people who have given the first hour of every day for years to Bible study and some who have given even two hours a day. The late Earl Cairns, Lord Chancellor of England, was one of the busiest men of his day, but Lady Cairns told me a few months ago that no matter how late he reached home at night he always arose at the same early hour for prayer and Bible study. She said, "We would sometimes get home from Parliament at two o'clock in the morning, but Lord Cairns would always arise at the same early hour to pray and study the Bible." Lord Cairns is reported as saying, "If I have had any success in life, I attribute it to the habit of giving the first two hours of each day to Bible study and prayer."

It is important that one choose the right time for this study. Wherever it is possible, the best time for this study is immediately after arising in the morning. The worst time of all is the last thing at night. Of course, it is well to give a little while just before we retire to Bible reading, in order that God's voice may be the last to which we listen, but the bulk of our Bible study should be done at an hour when our minds are clearest and strongest. Whatever time is set apart for Bible study should be kept sacredly for that purpose.

2. We should *study the Bible systematically*. Much time is frittered away in random study of the Bible. The same amount of time put into systematic study would yield far larger results. Have a definite place where you are studying and have a definite plan of study. A good way for a young Christian to begin the study of the Bible is to read the Gospel of John. When you have read it through once, begin and read it again until you have gone over the Gospel five times. Then read the Gospel of Luke five times in the same way; then read the Acts of the Apostles five times, then 1 Thessalonians five times, then 1 John five times, then Romans five times, then Ephesians five times.

By this time you will be ready to take up a more thorough method of Bible study. A good method is to begin at Genesis and read the Bible through chapter by chapter. Read each chapter through several times and then answer the following questions on the chapter:

(1) What is the principal subject of the chapter? (State the principal contents of the chapter in a single phrase or sentence.)

(2) What is the truth most clearly taught and most emphasized in the chapter?

(3) What is the best lesson?

(4) What is the best verse?

(5) Who are the principal people mentioned?

(6) What does the chapter teach about Jesus Christ? Go through the entire Bible in this way.

Another and more thorough method of Bible chapter study, which cannot be applied to every chapter in the Bible, but which will yield excellent results when applied to some of the more important chapters of the Bible, is as follows:

(1) Read the chapter for to-day's study five times, reading it aloud at least once. Each new reading will bring out some new point.

(2) Divide the chapter into its natural divisions and find headings for each division that describes in the most striking way the contents of that division. For example, suppose the chapter studied is 1 John 5. You might divide it in this way: First division, verses 1-3, The Believer's Noble Parentage. Second division, verses 4, 5, The Believer's Glorious Victory. Third division, verses 6-10, The Believer's Sure Ground of Faith. Fourth division, verses 11, 12, The Believer's Priceless Possession. Fifth division, verse 13, The Believer's Blessed Assurance. Sixth division, verses 14, 15, The Believer's Unquestioning Confidence. Seventh division, verses 16, 17, The Believer's Great Power and Responsibility. Eighth division, verses 18, 19, The Believer's Perfect Security. Ninth

division, verse 20, The Believer's Precious Knowledge. Tenth division, verse 21, The Believer's Constant Duty.

(3) Note the important differences between the Authorized Version and the Revised.

(4) Write down the leading facts of the chapter in their proper order.

(5) Make a note of the persons mentioned in the chapter and of any light thrown upon their character.

(6) Note the principal lessons of the chapter. It would be well to classify these. For instance lessons about God; lessons about Christ, lessons about the Holy Spirit, etc.

(7) Find the central truth of the chapter.

(8) The key verse of the chapter, if there is one.

(9) The best verse in the chapter. Mark it and memorize it.

(10) Write down what new truth you have learned from the chapter.

(11) Write down what truth already known has come to you with new power.

(12) What definite thing have you resolved to do as a result of studying this chapter. It would be well to study in this way, all the chapters in Matthew, Mark, Luke, John and Acts; the first eight chapters of Romans; 1 Cor. 12, 13 and 15; first six chapters of 2 Corinthians; all the chapters in Galatians, Ephesians, Philippians, First Thessalonians and First Epistle of John. It would be well at times to vary this by taking up other methods of study for a time.

Another profitable method of Bible study is the topical method. This was Mr. Moody's favorite method of study. Take up the great topics of which the Bible teaches such as, the Holy Spirit, Prayer, the Blood of Christ, Sin, Judgment, Grace, Justification, the New Birth, Sanctification, Faith, Repentance, the Character of Christ, the Resurrection of Christ, the Ascension of Christ, the Second Coming of Christ, Assurance, Love of God, Love (to God, to Christ, to Christians, to all men), Heaven, Hell. Get a Bible text-book and go through the Bible on each one of these topics. (Other methods of Bible study, and more thorough methods for the advanced student, will be found in the author's book "How to Study the Bible for Greatest Profit.")

3. We should *study the Bible comprehensively*—the whole Bible. Many who read their Bibles make the great mistake of confining all their reading to certain portions of the Bible that they enjoy, and in this way they get no knowledge of the Bible as a whole. They miss altogether many of the most important phases of Bible truth. Begin and go through the Bible again and again—a certain portion each day from the Old Testament and a portion from the New Testament. Read carefully at least one Psalm every day.

It is well oftentimes to read a whole book of the Bible through at a single sitting. Of course, with a few books of the Bible this would take one or two hours, but with most of the books of the Bible it can be done in a few minutes. With the shorter books of the Bible they should be read through again and again at a single sitting.

4. *Study the Bible attentively.* Do not hurry. One of the worst faults in Bible study is haste and heedlessness. The Bible only does good by the truth that it contains. It has no magic power. It is better to read one verse attentively than to read a dozen chapters thoughtlessly. Sometimes you will read a verse that takes hold of you. Don't hurry on. Linger and ponder that verse. As you read, mark in your Bible what impresses you most. One does not need an elaborate system of Bible marking, simply mark what impresses you. Meditate upon what you mark. God pronounces that man blessed who "meditates" in God's law day and night (Ps. 1: 2). It is wonderful how a verse of Scripture will open

if one reads it over and over again and again, paying attention to each word as he reads it, trying to get its exact meaning and its full meaning. Memorize the passages that impress you most (Ps. 119: 11). When you memorize a passage of Scripture, memorize its location as well as its words. Fix in your mind chapter and verse where the words are found. A busy but spiritually-minded man who was hurrying to catch a train once said to me, "Tell me in a word how to study my Bible." I replied, "Thoughtfully."

5. *Study your Bible comparatively.* That is compare Scripture with Scripture. The best commentary on the Bible is the Bible itself. Wherever you find a difficult passage in the Bible, there is always some passage elsewhere that explains its meaning. The best book to use in this comparison of Scripture with Scripture is "The Treasury of Scripture Knowledge." On every verse in the Bible this book gives a large number of references. It is well to take up some book of the Bible and go through that book verse by verse, looking up carefully and studying every reference given in "The Treasury of Scripture Knowledge." This is a very fruitful method of Bible study. It is also well in studying the Bible by chapters to look up the references on the more important verses in the chapter. One will get more light on passages of Scripture by looking up the references given in "The Treasury of Scripture Knowledge," than in any other way I know.

6. *Study your Bible believingly.* The Apostle Paul in writing to the Christians in Thessalonica says, "For this cause also thank we God without ceasing, because, when ye received the Word of God which ye heard of us, ye received it not as the Word of men, but as it is in truth, the Word of God, which effectually worketh also in you that believe" (1 Thess. 2: 13). Happy is the one who receives the Word of God as these believers in Thessalonica received it, who receives it as what it really is, the Word of God. In such a one it "works effectually." The Bible is the Word of God and we get the most out of any book by studying it as what it really is. It is often said that we should study the Bible just as we study any other book. That principle contains a truth, but it also contains a great error. The Bible, it is true, is a book as other books are books, the same laws of grammatical and literary construction hold here as in other books, but the Bible is a unique book. It is what no other book is, the Word of God. This can be easily proven to any candid man.[1] The Bible ought then to be studied as no other book is. It should be studied as the Word of God. This involves five things:

(1) A greater eagerness and more careful and candid study to find out just what it teaches than is bestowed upon all other books. It is important to know the mind of man. It is absolutely essential to know the mind of God. The place to discover the mind of God is the Bible. This is the book in which God reveals His mind.

(2) A prompt and unquestioning acceptance of, and submission to its teachings when definitely ascertained. These teachings may appear to us unreasonable or impossible, nevertheless we should accept them. If this book is the Word of God, how foolish it is to submit its teachings to the criticism of our finite reasoning. A little boy who discredits his wise father's statements simply because to his infant mind they appear unreasonable, is not a philosopher, but a fool. But the greatest of human thinkers is only an infant compared with the infinite God. And to discredit God's statements found in His Word because they appear unreasonable to our infantile minds is not to act the part of the philosopher, but the

---

[1] The author has given some of the proofs that the Bible is the Word of God in his book, "Talks to Men."

part of a fool. When we are once satisfied that the Bible is the Word of God, its clear teachings must be for us the end of all controversy and discussion.

(3) Absolute reliance upon all its promises in all their length and breadth and depth and height. The one who studies the Bible as the Word of God will say of any promise, no matter how vast and beyond belief it appears, "God who cannot lie has promised this, so I will claim it for myself." Mark the promise you thus claim. Look each day for some new promise from your infinite Father. He has put "His riches in glory" at your disposal (Phil. 4: 19). I know of no better way to grow rich spiritually than to search daily for promises, and when you find them appropriate them to yourself.

(4) Obedience. Be a doer of the Word and not a hearer only deceiving your own soul (James 1: 22). Nothing goes farther to help one understand the Bible than the purpose to obey it. Jesus said, "If any man willeth to do His will, he shall know of the teaching" (John 7: 17). The surrendered will means the clear eye. If our eye is single (that is, our will is absolutely surrendered to God) our whole body shall be full of light. But if our eye be evil (that is, if we are trying to serve two masters and are not absolutely surrendered to one Master, God) our whole body shall be full of darkness (Matt. 6: 22-24). Many a passage that looks obscure to you now would become as clear as day if you were willing to obey in all things what the Bible teaches. Each commandment discovered in the Bible that is really intended as a commandment to us should be obeyed instantly. It is remarkable how soon one loses his relish for the Bible and how soon the mind becomes obscured to its teachings when we disobey the Bible at any point. Many a time I have known persons who have loved their Bibles and have been useful in God's service and clear in their views of the truth who have come to something in the Bible that they were unwilling to obey, some sacrifice was demanded that they were unwilling to make, and their love for the Bible has rapidly waned, their faith in the Bible began to weaken, and soon they were drifting farther and farther away from clear views of the truth. Nothing clears the mind like obedience; nothing darkens the mind like disobedience. To obey a truth you see prepares you to see other truths. To disobey a truth you see darkens your mind to all truths.

Cultivate prompt, exact, unquestioning, joyous obedience to every command that it is evident from its context applies to you. Be on the lookout for new orders from your King. Blessing lies in the direction of obedience to them. God's commands are but sign-boards that mark the road to present success and blessedness and to eternal glory.

(5) Studying the Bible as the Word of God involves studying it as His own voice speaking directly to you. When you open the Bible to study realize that you have come into the very presence of God and that now He is going to speak to you. Realize that it is God who is talking to you as much as if you saw Him standing there. Say to yourself, "God is now going to speak to me." Nothing goes farther to give a freshness and gladness to Bible study than the realization that as you read God is actually talking to you. In this way Bible study becomes personal companionship with God Himself. That was a wonderful privilege that Mary had one day, of sitting at the feet of Jesus and listening to His voice, but if we will study the Bible as the Word of God and as if we were in God's very presence, then we shall enjoy the privilege of sitting at the feet of God and having Him talk to us every day. How often what would otherwise be a mere mechanical performance of a duty would become a wonderfully joyous privilege if one would say as he opens the Bible, "Now God, my Father, is going to speak to me." Oftentimes it helps us to a realization of the presence of God to read the Bible on our knees. The Bible became in some measure a new book to me when I took to reading it on my knees.

7. *Study the Bible prayerfully.* God, who is the author of the Bible, is willing to act as interpreter of it. He does so when you ask Him to. The one who prays with earnestness and faith the Psalmist's prayer, "Open Thou mine eyes that I may behold wondrous things out of Thy law" (Ps. 119: 18) will get his eyes opened to see new beauties and wonders in the Word of God that he never dreamed of before. Be very definite about this. Each time you open the Bible to study it, even though it is but for a few minutes, ask God to give you an open and discerning eye, and expect Him to do it. Every time you come to a difficulty in the Bible, lay it before God and ask an explanation and expect it. How often we think as we puzzle over hard passages, "Oh, if I only had some great Bible teacher here to explain this to me!" God is always present. He understands the Bible better than any human teacher. Take your difficulty to Him and ask Him to explain it. Jesus said, "When He the Spirit of Truth is come, He shall guide you into all the truth" (John 16: 13). It is the privilege of the humblest believer in Christ to have the Holy Spirit for his guide in his study of the Word. I have known many very humble people, people with almost no education, who got more out of their Bible study than most of the great theological teachers that I have known; simply because they had learned that it was their privilege to have the Holy Spirit for their teacher as they studied the Bible. Commentaries on the Bible are oftentimes of great value, but one will learn more of real value from the Bible by having the Holy Spirit for his teacher when he studies his Bible than he will from all the commentaries that were ever published.

8. *Improve spare moments for Bible study.* In almost every man's life many minutes each day are lost, while waiting for meals, riding on trains, going from place to place in street-cars and so forth. Carry a pocket Bible or Testament with you and save these golden moments by putting them to the very best use, listening to the voice of God.

9. *Store away the Scripture in your mind and heart.* It will keep you from sin (Ps. 119: 11); from false doctrine (Acts 20: 29, 30, 32; 2 Tim. 3: 13-15). It will fill your heart with joy (Jer. 15: 16); and peace (Ps. 85: 8). It will give you victory over the evil one (1 John 2: 14); it will give you power in prayer (John 15: 7); it will make you wiser than the aged and your enemies (Ps. 119: 98, 100, 130); it will make you "complete, furnished completely unto every good work" (2 Tim. 3: 16, 17). Try it. Do not memorize at random but memorize Scripture in a connected way; memorize texts bearing on various subjects in proper order; memorize by chapter and verse that you may know where to put your finger on the text if any one disputes it. You should have a good Bible for your study. One of the best is "The Oxford Two Version Bible, Workers' Edition."

Chapter VIII. Difficulties in the Bible

Sooner or later every young Christian comes across passages in the Bible which are hard to understand and difficult to believe. To many a young Christian, these difficulties become a serious hindrance in the development of their Christian life. For days and weeks and months oftentimes faith suffers partial or total eclipse. At just this point wise counsel is needed. We have no desire to conceal the fact that these difficulties exist. We rather desire to frankly face and consider them. What shall we do concerning these difficulties that every thoughtful student of the Bible will sooner or later encounter.

1. *The first thing we have to say about these difficulties is that from the very nature of the case difficulties are to be expected.* Some people are surprised and staggered because there are difficulties in the Bible. I would be more surprised and more staggered if there

were not. What is the Bible? It is a revelation of the mind and will and character and being of the infinitely great, perfectly wise, and absolutely holy God. But to whom is this revelation made? To men and women like you and me, to finite beings. To men who are imperfect in intellectual development and consequently in knowledge, and in character and consequently in spiritual discernment.

There must, from the very necessities of the case, be difficulties in such a revelation made to such persons. When the finite tries to understand the infinite there is bound to be difficulty. When the ignorant contemplate the utterances of one perfect in knowledge there must be many things hard to be understood and some things which to their immature and inaccurate minds appear absurd. When sinful beings listen to the demands of an absolutely holy being they are bound to be staggered at some of His demands, and when they consider His dealings they are bound to be staggered at some of His dealings. These dealings will necessarily appear too severe, stern, harsh, terrific. It is plain that there must be difficulties for us in such a revelation as the Bible is proven to be. If some one should hand me a book that was as simple as the multiplication table and say, "This is the Word of God, in which He has revealed His whole will and wisdom," I would shake my head and say, "I cannot believe it. That is too easy to be a perfect revelation of infinite wisdom." There must be in any complete revelation of God's mind and will and character and being, things hard for a beginner to understand, and the wisest and best of us are but beginners.

2. *The second thing to be said about these difficulties is that a difficulty in a doctrine, or a grave objection to a doctrine, does not in any wise prove the doctrine to be untrue.* Many thoughtless people fancy that it does. If they come across some difficulty in the way of believing in the divine origin and absolute inerrancy and infallibility of the Bible, they at once conclude that the doctrine is exploded. That is very illogical. Stop a moment and think and learn to be reasonable and fair. There is scarcely a doctrine in science commonly believed to-day that has not had some great difficulty in the way of its acceptance. When the Copernican theory, now so universally accepted, was first proclaimed, it encountered a very grave difficulty. If this theory were true the planet Venus should have phases as the moon has. But no phases could be discovered by the best glass then in existence. But the positive argument for the theory was so strong that it was accepted in spite of this apparently unanswerable objection. When a more powerful glass was made, it was discovered that Venus had phases after all. The whole difficulty arose, as all those in the Bible arise, from man's ignorance of some of the facts in the case. According to the common sense logic recognized in every department of science, if the positive proof of a theory is conclusive, it is believed by rational men, in spite of any number of difficulties in minor details. Now the positive proof that the Bible is the Word of God, that it is an absolutely trustworthy revelation from God Himself of Himself, His purposes and His will, of man's duty and destiny, of spiritual and eternal realities, is absolutely conclusive. Therefore every rational man and woman must believe it in spite of any number of difficulties in minor details. He is a shallow thinker who gives up a well-attested truth because of some facts which he cannot reconcile with that truth. And he is a very shallow Bible scholar who gives up the divine origin and inerrancy of the Bible because there are some supposed facts that he cannot reconcile with that doctrine.

3. *The third thing to be said about the difficulties in the Bible is that there are many more and much greater difficulties in the way of a doctrine that holds the Bible to be of human origin, and hence fallible, than are in the way of the doctrine that holds the Bible to be of divine origin and hence altogether trustworthy.* A man may bring you some

difficulty and say, "How do you explain that if the Bible is the Word of God?" and perhaps you may not be able to answer him satisfactorily. Then he thinks he has you, but not at all. Turn on him and ask him how do you account for the fulfilled prophecies of the Bible if it is of human origin? How do you account for the marvelous unity of the Book? How do you account for its inexhaustible depth? How do you account for its unique power in lifting men up to God? How do you account for the history of the Book, its victory over all men's attacks, etc., etc., etc. For every insignificant objection he can bring to your view, you can bring many deeply significant objections to his view, and no candid man will have any difficulty in deciding between the two views. The difficulties that confront one who denies that the Bible is of divine origin and authority are far more numerous and weighty than those that confront the ones who believes it is of divine origin and authority.

4. *The fourth thing to be said about the difficulties in the Bible is the fact that you cannot solve a difficulty does not prove that it cannot be solved, and the fact that you cannot answer an objection does not prove at all that it cannot be answered.* It is passing strange how often we overlook this very evident fact. There are many who, when they meet a difficulty in the Bible and give it a little thought and can see no possible solution, at once jump at the conclusion that a solution is impossible by any one, and so throw up their faith in the reliability of the Bible and in its divine origin. A little more of that modesty that is becoming in beings so limited in knowledge as we all are would have led them to say, "Though I see no possible solution to this difficulty, some one a little wiser than I might easily find one." Oh! if we would only bear in mind that we do not know everything, and that there are a great many things that we cannot solve now that we could easily solve if we only knew a little more. Above all, we ought never to forget that there may be a very easy solution to infinite wisdom of that which to our finite wisdom—or ignorance—appears absolutely insoluble. What would we think of a beginner in algebra who, having tried in vain for half an hour to solve a difficult problem, declared that there was no possible solution to the problem because he could find none? A man of much experience and ability once left his work and came a long distance to see me in great perturbation of spirit because he had discovered what seemed to him a flat contradiction in the Bible. It had defied all his attempts at reconciliation, but in a few moments he was shown a very simple and satisfactory solution of the difficulty.

5. *The fifth thing to be said about the difficulties in the Bible is that the seeming defects in the book are exceedingly insignificant when put in comparison with its many and marvelous excellencies.* It certainly reveals great perversity of both mind and heart that men spend so much time expatiating on the insignificant points that they consider defects in the Bible, and pass by absolutely unnoticed the incomparable beauties and wonders that adorn and glorify almost every page. What would we think of any man, who in studying some great masterpiece of art, concentrated his entire attention upon what looked to him like a fly-speck in the corner. A large proportion of what is vaunted as "critical study of the Bible" is a laborious and scholarly investigation of supposed fly-specks and an entire neglect of the countless glories of the book.

6. *The sixth thing to be said about the difficulties in the Bible is that the difficulties in the Bible have far more weight with superficial readers of it than with profound students.* Take a man who is totally ignorant of the real contents and meaning of the Bible and devotes his whole strength to discovering apparent inconsistencies in it, to such superficial students of the Bible these difficulties seem of immense importance; but to the one who has learned to meditate on the Word of God day and night they have scarce any weight at

all. That mighty man of God, George Müller, who had carefully studied the Bible from beginning to end more than a hundred times, was not disturbed by any difficulties he encountered. But to the one who is reading it through carefully for the first or second time there are many things that perplex and stagger.

7. *The seventh thing to be said about the difficulties in the Bible is that they rapidly disappear upon careful and prayerful study.* How many things there are in the Bible that once puzzled us and staggered us that have been perfectly cleared up, and no longer present any difficulty at all! Is it not reasonable to suppose that the difficulties that still remain will also disappear upon further study?

How shall we deal with the difficulties which we do find in the Bible?

1. First of all, *honestly.* Whenever you find a difficulty in the Bible, frankly acknowledge it. If you cannot give a good honest explanation, do not attempt as yet to give any at all.

2. *Humbly.* Recognize the limitations of your own mind and knowledge, and do not imagine there is no solution just because you have found none. There is in all probability a very simple solution. You will find it some day, though at present you can find no solution at all.

3. *Determinedly.* Make up your mind that you will find the solution if you can by any amount of study and hard thinking. The difficulties in the Bible are your heavenly Father's challenge to you to set your brains to work.

4. *Fearlessly.* Do not be frightened when you find a difficulty, no matter how unanswerable it appears upon first glance. Thousands have found such before you. They were seen hundreds of years ago and still the Old Book stands. You are not likely to discover any difficulty that was not discovered and probably settled long before you were born, though you do not know just where to lay your hand upon the solution. The Bible which has stood eighteen centuries of rigid examination and incessant and awful assault, is not going under before any discoveries that you make or any attacks of modern infidels. All modern infidel attacks upon the Bible are simply a revamping of old objections that have been disposed of a hundred times in the past. These old objections will prove no more effective in their new clothes than they did in the cast-off garments of the past.

5. *Patiently.* Do not be discouraged because you do not solve every problem in a day. If some difficulty defies your best effort, lay it aside for awhile. Very likely when you come back to it, it will have disappeared and you will wonder how you were ever perplexed by it. The writer often has to smile to-day when he thinks how sorely he was perplexed in the past over questions which are now as clear as day.

6. *Scripturally.* If you find a difficulty in one part of the Bible, look for other Scripture to throw light upon it and dissolve it. Nothing explains Scripture like Scripture. Never let apparently obscure passages of Scripture darken the light that comes from clear passages, rather let the light that comes from the clear passage illuminate the darkness that seems to surround the obscure passage.

7. *Prayerfully.* It is wonderful how difficulties dissolve when one looks at them on his knees. One great reason why some modern scholars have learned to be destructive critics is because they have forgotten how to pray.

Chapter IX. Prayer

The one who would succeed in the Christian life must lead a life of prayer. Very much of the failure in Christian living to-day, and in Christian work, results from neglect of prayer. Very few Christians spend as much time in prayer as they ought. The Apostle James told believers in his day that the secret of the poverty and powerlessness of their lives and service was neglect of prayer. "Ye have not," says God through the Apostle James, "because ye ask not." So it is to-day. Why is it, many a Christian is asking, that I make such poor headway in my Christian life? Why do I have so little victory over sin? Why do I accomplish so little by my effort? and God answers, "You have not because you ask not."

It is easy enough to lead a life of prayer if one only sets about it. Set apart some time each day for prayer. The rule of David and of Daniel is a good one; three times a day. "Evening and morning and at noon," says David, "will I pray and cry aloud and He shall hear my voice" (Ps. 55: 17). Of Daniel we read, "Now when Daniel knew that the writing was signed, he went into his house; and his windows being open in his chamber towards Jerusalem, he kneeled upon his knees three times a day, and prayed, and gave thanks before his God as he did aforetime" (Dan. 6: 10). Of course, one can pray while walking the street, or riding in the car, or sitting at his desk, and one should learn to lift his heart to God right in the busiest moments of his life, but we need set times of prayer, times when we go alone with God, shut to the door and talk to our Father in the secret place (Matt. 6: 6). God is in the secret place and will meet with us there and listen to our petitions.

Prayer is a wonderful privilege. It is an audience with the King. It is talking to our Father. How strange it is that people should ask the question, "How much time ought I to spend in prayer?" When a subject is summoned to an audience with his king, he never asks, "How much time must I spend with the king?" His question is rather, "How much time will the king give me?" And with any true child of God who realizes what prayer really is, that it is an audience with the King of Kings, the question will never be, "How much time must I spend in prayer," but "How much time may I spend in prayer with a due regard to other duties and privileges?"

Begin the day with thanksgiving and prayer. Thanksgiving for the definite mercies of the past, prayer for the definite needs of the present day. Think of the temptations that you are likely to meet during the day; ask God to show you the temptations that you are likely to meet and get from God strength for victory over these temptations before the temptations come. The reason why many fail in the battle is because they wait until the hour of battle. The reason why others succeed is because they have gained their victory on their knees long before the battle came. Jesus conquered in the awful battles of Pilate's judgment hall and of the cross because He had the night before in prayer anticipated the battle and gained the victory before the struggle really came. He had told His disciples to do the same. He had bidden them "Pray that ye enter not into temptation" (Luke 22: 40), but they had slept when they ought to have prayed, and when the hour of temptation came they fell. Anticipate your battles, fight them on your knees before temptation comes and you will always have victory. At the very outset of the day, get counsel and strength from God Himself for the duties of the day.

Never let the rush of business crowd out prayer. The more work that any day has to do, the more time must be spent in prayer in preparation for that work. You will not lose time by it, you will save time by it. Prayer is the greatest time saver known to man. The more the work crowds you the more time take for prayer.

Stop in the midst of the bustle and hurry and temptation of the day for thanksgiving and prayer. A few minutes spent alone with God at midday will go far to keep you calm in the midst of the worries and anxieties of modern life.

Close the day with thanksgiving and prayer. Review all the blessings of the day and thank God in detail for them. Nothing goes farther to increase faith in God and in His Word than a calm review at the close of each day of what God has done for you that day. Nothing goes further towards bringing new and larger blessings from God than intelligent thanksgiving for blessings already granted.

The last thing you do each day ask God to show you if there has been anything in the day that has been displeasing in His sight. Then wait quietly before God and give God an opportunity to speak to you. Listen. Do not be in a hurry. If God shows you anything in the day that has been displeasing in His sight, confess it fully and frankly as to a holy and loving Father. Believe that God forgives it all, for He says He does (1 John 1: 9). Thus at the close of each day all your accounts with God will be straightened out. You can lie down and sleep in the glad consciousness that there is not a cloud between you and God. You can arise the next day to begin life anew with a clean balance sheet. Do this and you can never backslide for more than twenty-four hours. Indeed, you will not backslide at all. It is very hard to straighten out accounts in business that have been allowed to get crooked through a prolonged period. No bank ever closes its business day until its balance is found to be absolutely correct. And no Christian should close a single day until his accounts with God for that day have been perfectly adjusted alone with Him.

There should be special prayer in special temptation—that is when we see the temptation approaching. If you possibly can, get at once alone somewhere with God and fight your battle out. Keep looking to God. "Pray without ceasing" (1 Thess. 5: 17). It is not needful to be on your knees all the time but the heart should be on its knees all the time. We should be often on our knees or on our faces literally. This is a joyous life, free from worry and care. "In nothing be anxious; but in everything by prayer and supplication with thanksgiving, let your request be made known unto God, and the peace of God which passeth all understanding shall guard your hearts and thoughts in Christ Jesus" (Phil. 4: 6, 7).

There are three things for which one who would succeed in the Christian life must especially pray. 1. For wisdom. "If any of you lack wisdom (and we all do) let him ask of God" (James 1: 5). 2. For strength. "For they that wait upon the Lord shall renew their strength" (Is. 40: 31). 3. For the Holy Spirit. "Your heavenly Father shall give the Holy Spirit to them that ask Him" (Luke 11: 13). Even if you have received the Holy Spirit, you should constantly pray for a new filling with the Holy Spirit and definitely expect to receive it. We need a new filling with the Spirit for every new emergency of Christian life and Christian service. The Apostle Peter was baptized and filled with the Holy Spirit on the Day of Pentecost (Acts 2: 1-4) but he was filled anew in Acts 4: 8 and Acts 4: 31. There are many Christians in the world who once had a very definite baptism with the Holy Spirit and had great joy and were wonderfully used, but who have tried to go ever since in the power of that baptism received years ago, and to-day their lives are comparatively joyless and powerless. We need constantly to get new supplies of oil for our lamps. We get these new supplies of oil by asking for them.

It is not enough that we have our times of secret prayer to God alone with Him, we also need fellowship with others in prayer. If they have a prayer-meeting in your church attend it regularly. Attend it for your own sake; attend it for the sake of the church. If it is a prayer-meeting only in name and not in fact, use your influence quietly and constantly (not obtrusively) to make it a real prayer-meeting. Keep the prayer-meeting night sacredly for that purpose. Refuse all social engagements for that night. A major-general in the United States army once took command of the forces in a new district. A reception was arranged for him for a certain night in the week. When he was informed of this public reception he replied that that was prayer-meeting night and everything else had to give way for prayer-meeting, that he could not attend the reception on that night. That general had proved himself a man that can be depended upon. The Church of Christ in America owes more to him than to almost any other officer in the American army. Ministers learn to depend upon their prayer-meeting members. The prayer-meeting is the most important meeting in the church. If your church has no prayer-meeting, use your influence to have one. It does not take many members to make a good prayer-meeting. You can start with two but work for many.

It is well to have a little company of Christian friends with whom you are in real sympathy and with whom you meet regularly every week simply for prayer. There has been nothing of more importance in the development of my own spiritual life of recent years than a little prayer-meeting of less than a dozen friends who have met every Saturday night for years. We met and together we waited upon God. If my life has been of any use to the Master, I attribute it largely to that prayer-meeting. Happy is the young Christian that has a little band of friends like that that meet together regularly for prayer.[2]

Chapter X. Working for Christ

One of the important conditions of growth and strength in the Christian life is work. No man can keep up his physical strength without exercise and no man can keep up his spiritual strength without spiritual exercise, *i. e.*, without working for his Master. The working Christian is the happy Christian. The working Christian is the strong Christian. Some Christians never backslide because they are too busy about their Master's business to backslide. Many professed Christians do backslide because they are too idle to do anything but backslide. Jesus said to the first disciples, "Follow Me and I will make you fishers of men" (Matt. 4: 19). Any one who is not a fisher of men is not following Christ. Bearing fruit in bringing others to the Savior is the purpose for which Jesus has chosen us and is one of the most important conditions of power in prayer. Jesus says in John 15: 16, "Ye have not chosen Me, but I have chosen you and ordained you *that ye should go and bring forth fruit*, and that your fruit should remain, *that whatsoever ye shall ask of the Father in My name He may give it you*." These words of Jesus are very plain. They tell us that the one who is bearing fruit is the one who can pray in the name of Christ and get what he asks in that name. In the same chapter Jesus tells us that bearing fruit in His strength is the condition of fullness of joy. He says, "These things have I spoken unto you (that is, the things about abiding in Him and bearing fruit in His strength) that My joy might remain in you and that your joy might be full" (John 15: 11). Experience abundantly

---

[2] If any reader desires more full and definite instruction on the subject of prayer he is referred to the author's book, "How to Pray."

proves the truth of these words of our Master. Those who are full of activity in winning others to Christ are those who are full of joy in Christ Himself.

If you wish to be a happy Christian; if you wish to be a strong Christian, if you wish to be a Christian who is mighty in prayer, begin at once to work for the Master and never let a day pass without doing some definite work for Him. But how can a young Christian work for Him? How can a young Christian bear fruit? The answer is very simple and very easy to follow. You can bear fruit for your Master by going to others and telling them what your Savior has done for you, and by urging them to accept this same Savior and showing them how to do it. There is no other work in the world that is so easy to do, so joyous, and so abundant in its fruitfulness, as personal hand to hand work. The youngest Christian can do personal work. Of course, he cannot do it so well as he will do it later, after he has had more practice. But the way to learn how to do it is by doing it. I have known thousands of Christians all around the world who have begun to work for Christ, and to bring others to Christ, the very day that they were converted. How often young men and young women, yes, and old men and old women too, have come to me and said, "I accepted Jesus Christ last night as my Savior, my Lord and my King, and to-night I have led a friend to Christ." Then the next day they would come and tell me of some one else they had led to Christ. When we were in Sheffield, a young man working in a warehouse accepted Christ. Before the month's mission in Sheffield was over he had led thirty others to Christ, many of them in the same warehouse where he himself worked. This is but one instance among many. There are many books that tell how to do personal work.[3]

But one does not need to wait until they have read some book on the subject before they begin. One of the commonest and greatest mistakes that is made is that of frittering one's life away in getting ready to get ready to get ready. Some never do get ready. The way to get ready is to begin at once. Make up your mind that you will speak about accepting Christ to at least one person every day. Early in his Christian life Mr. Moody made this resolution that he would never let a day pass over his head without speaking to at least one person about Christ. One night he was returning late from his work. As he got near home it occurred to him that he had not spoken to any one that day. He said to himself, "It is too late now. I will not get an opportunity. Here will be one day gone without my speaking to any one about Christ." But a little ways ahead of him he saw a man standing under a lamp-post. He said, "Here is my last opportunity." The man was a stranger to him, though he knew who Mr. Moody was. Mr. Moody hurried up to him and asked him, "Are you a Christian?" The man replied, "That is none of your business. If you were not a sort of a preacher I would knock you into the gutter." But Mr. Moody spoke a few faithful words to him and passed on. The next day this man called on one of Mr. Moody's business friends in Chicago in great indignation. He said, "That man Moody of yours over on the Northside is doing more harm than he is good. He has zeal without knowledge. He came up to me last night, a perfect stranger, and asked me if I was a Christian. He insulted me. I told him if he had not been a sort of preacher I would have knocked him into the gutter." Mr. Moody's friend called him in and said to him, "Moody, you are doing more harm than good. You have zeal without knowledge. You insulted a friend of mine on the street last night." Mr. Moody went out somewhat crestfallen, feeling that perhaps he was doing more harm than good, that perhaps he did have zeal without knowledge. But some weeks after,

---

[3] The author has written a little book on this line named "How to Bring Men to Christ" that has proved helpful to many.

late at night, there was a great pounding on his door. Mr. Moody got out of bed and rushed to the door supposing that the house was on fire. That same man stood at the door. He said, "Mr. Moody, I have not had a night's rest since you spoke to me that night under the lamp-post and I have come around for you to tell me what to do to be saved." Mr. Moody had the joy that night of leading that man to Christ. It is better to have zeal without knowledge than to have knowledge without zeal, but it is better yet to have zeal with knowledge, and any one may have this. The way to get knowledge is by experience, and the way to get experience is by doing the work. The man who is so afraid of making blunders that he never does anything, never learns anything. The man who goes ahead and does his best and is willing to risk the blunders, is the man who learns to avoid the blunders in the future. Some of the most gifted men I have ever known have never really accomplished anything, they were so fearful of making blunders. Some of the most useful men I have ever known were men who at the outset were the least promising, but who had a real love for souls and went on, at first in a blundering way, but they blundered on until they learned by experience to do things well. Do not be discouraged by your blunders. Pitch in and keep pegging away. Every honest mistake is but a stepping-stone to future success. Try every day to lead some one else to Christ. Of course, you will not succeed every day, but the work will do you good any way, and years after you will often find that where you thought you have made the greatest blunders, you have accomplished the best results. The man who gets angriest at you, will often turn out in the end the man who is most grateful to you. Be patient and hope on. Never be discouraged.

Make a prayer list. Go alone with God. Write down at the top of a sheet of paper, "God helping me, I promise to pray daily and to work persistently for the conversion of the following persons." Then kneel down and ask God to show you who to put on that list. Do not make the list so long that your prayer and work become mechanical and superficial. After you have made the list keep your covenant, really pray for them every day. Watch for opportunities to speak to them—improve these opportunities. You may have to watch long for your opportunities with some of them, and you may have to speak often, but never give up. I prayed about fifteen years for one man, one of the most discouraging men I ever met, but I saw that man converted at last, and I saw him a preacher of the gospel, and many others were converted through his preaching, and now he is in the Glory.

Learn to use tracts. Get a few good tracts that are fitted to meet the needs of different kinds of people. Then hand these tracts out to the people whose needs they are adapted to meet. Follow your tracts up with prayer and with personal effort.

Go to your pastor and ask him if there is some work he would like to have you do for him in the church. Be a person that your pastor can depend upon. We live in a day in which there are many kinds of work going on outside the church, and many of these kinds of work are good and you should take part in them as you are able, but never forget that your first duty is to the church of which you are a member. Be a person that your pastor can count on. It may be that your pastor may not want to use you, but at least give him the chance of refusing you. If he does refuse you, don't be discouraged, but find work somewhere else. There is plenty to do and few to do it. It is as true to-day as it was in the days of our Savior, "The harvest truly is plenteous but the laborers are few" (Matt. 9: 37), "Pray therefore the Lord of the harvest that He will send forth laborers into His harvest," and pray that He will send you (Matt. 9: 38). The right kind of men are needed in the ministry. The right kind of men and women are needed for foreign mission work, but you may not be the right kind of a man or woman for foreign missionary work, but none the less there is work for you to do just as important in its place as the work of the minister or the missionary is. See that you fill your place and fill it well.[4]

Chapter XI. Foreign Missions

In order to have the largest success in the Christian life one must be interested in foreign missions. The last command of our Lord before leaving this earth was, "Go ye therefore, and make disciples of all the nations, baptizing them into the name of the Father, and of the Son and of the Holy Ghost: teaching them to observe all things whatsoever I have commanded you: and lo, I am with you alway even unto the end of the world" (Matt. 28: 19, 20). Here is a command and a promise. It is one of the sweetest promises in the Bible. But the enjoyment of the promise is conditioned upon obedience to the command. Our Lord commands every one of His disciples to go and "make disciples" of all the nations. This command was not given to the apostles alone, but to every member of Christ's church in all ages. If we go, then Christ will be with us even unto the end of the age; but, if we do not go, we have no right to count upon His companionship. Are you going? How can we go? There are three ways in which we can go, and in at least two of these ways we must go if we are to enjoy the wonderful privilege of the personal companionship of Jesus Christ every day unto the end of the age.

1. First, *many of us can go in our own persons*. Many of us ought to go. God does not call every one of us to go as foreign missionaries, but He does call many of us to go who are not responding to the call. Every Christian should offer himself for the foreign field and leave the responsibility of choosing him or refusing him to the all-wise One, God Himself. No Christian has a right to stay at home until he has gone and offered himself definitely to God for the foreign field. If you have not done it before, do it to-day. Go alone with God and say, "Heavenly Father, here I am, Thy property, purchased by the precious blood of Christ. I belong to Thee. If Thou dost wish me in the foreign field, make it clear to me and I will go." Then keep watching for the leading of God. God's leading is clear leading. He is light and in Him is no darkness at all (1 John 1: 5). If you are really willing to be led, He will make it clear as day. Until He does make it clear as day, you need have no morbid anxiety that perhaps you are staying at home when you ought to go to the foreign field. If He wants you, He will make it clear as day in His own way and time. If He does make it clear, then prepare to go step by step as He leads you. And when His hour comes, go, no matter what it costs. If He does not make it clear that you ought to go in your own person, stay at home and do your duty at home and go in the other ways that will now be told.

2. *We all can go, and all ought to go to the foreign field by our gifts.* There are many who would like to go to the foreign field in their own person, but whom God providentially prevents, but who are still going in the missionaries they support or help to support. It is possible for you to preach the Gospel in the remotest corners of the earth by supporting or helping to support a foreign missionary or a native worker in that place. Many who read this book are able financially to support a foreign missionary out of their own pocket. If you are able to do it, do it. If you are not able to support a foreign missionary, you may be able to support a native helper—do it. You may be able to support one missionary in Japan

---

[4] The author's book, "How to Work for Christ," is a large work describing at length many ways of working for our Master.

and another in China, and another in India and another in Africa and another somewhere else—do it. Oh! the joy of preaching the Gospel in lands that we shall never see with our own eyes. How few in the church of Christ to-day realize their privilege of preaching the Gospel and saving men and women and children in distant lands by sending substitute missionaries to them, that is, by sending some one that goes for you where you cannot go yourself. They could not go but for your gifts by which they are supported and you could not go but for them, by their going in your place. You may be able to give but very little to foreign missions, but every little counts. Many insignificant streams together make a mighty river. If you cannot be a river, at least be a stream.

Learn to give largely. The large giver is the happy Christian. "The liberal soul shall be made fat" (Prov. 11: 25). "He which soweth sparingly shall reap also sparingly, and he which soweth bountifully shall reap also bountifully," and "God is able to make all grace abound towards you, that ye, always having all sufficiency in all things may abound to every good work" (2 Cor. 9: 8, 9). Success and growth in the Christian life depend upon few things more than upon liberal giving. The stingy Christian cannot be a growing Christian. It is wonderful how a Christian man begins to grow when he begins to give. Power in prayer depends on liberality in giving. One of the most wonderful statements about prayer and its answers is 1 John 3: 22. John says there that, whatsoever he asked of God he received; and he tells us why, because he on his part, kept God's commandments and did those things which were pleasing in His sight, and the immediate context shows that the special commandments he was keeping were the commandments about giving. He tells us in the twenty-first verse that when our heart condemns us not in the matter of giving then have we confidence in our prayers to God. God's answers to our prayers come in through the same door that our gifts go out to others, and some of us open the door such a little ways by our small giving that God is not able to pass in to us any large answers to our prayers. One of the most remarkable promises in the Bible is that found in Phil. 4: 19, "My God shall supply, (fulfill, that is fill full) all your need according to His riches in glory by Christ Jesus," but this promise was made to believers who had distinguished themselves above their fellows by the largeness and the frequency of their giving (Cf. vs. 14-18). Of course, we should not confine our giving to foreign missions. We should give to the work of the home church: we should give to rescue work in our large cities. We should do good to all men as we have opportunity, especially to those who are of the household of faith (Gal. 6: 10). But foreign missions should have a large part in our gifts.

Give systematically. Set aside for Christ a fixed proportion of all the money or goods you get. Be exact and honest about it. Don't use that part of your income for yourself under any circumstances. The Christian is not under law, and there is no law binding on the Christian that he should give a tenth of his income, but as a matter of free choice and glad gratitude a tenth is a good proportion to begin with. Don't let it be less than a tenth. God required that of the Jews and the Christian ought not to be more selfish than a Jew. After you have given your tenth, you will soon learn the joy of giving free will offerings in addition to the tenth.

3. But there is another way in which we can go to the foreign field, that is by our prayers. We can all go in this way. Any hour of the day or night you can reach any corner of the earth by your prayers. I go to Japan, to China and to Australia and to Tasmania and to New Zealand and to India and to Africa and to other parts of the earth every day, by my prayers. And prayer really brings things to pass where you go. Do not make prayer an excuse for not going in your own person if God wishes you, and do not make prayer an

excuse for small giving. There is no power in that kind of prayer. If you are ready to go yourself if God wishes you, and if you are actually going by your gifts as God gives you ability, then you can go effectually by your prayers also. The greatest need of the work of Jesus Christ to-day is prayer. The greatest need of foreign missions to-day is prayer. Foreign missions are a success, but they are no such success as they ought to be and might be. They are no such success as they would be if Christians at home, as well as abroad, were living up to the full measure of their opportunity in prayer.

Be definite in your prayers for foreign missions. Pray first of all that God will send forth laborers into His harvest, the right sort of laborers. There are many men and women in the foreign field that ought never to have gone there. There was not enough prayer about it. More foreign missionaries are greatly needed, but only more of the right kind of missionaries. Pray to God daily and believingly to send forth laborers into the harvest.

Pray for the laborers who are already on the field. No class of men and women need our prayers more than foreign missionaries. No class of men and women are objects of more bitter hatred from Satan than they. Satan delights to attack the reputation and the character of the brave men and women who have gone to the front in the battle for Christ and the Truth. No persons are subjected to so numerous and to such subtle and awful temptations as foreign missionaries. We owe it to them to support them by our prayers. Do not merely pray for foreign missionaries in general. Have a few special missionaries of whose work you make a study that you may pray intelligently for them.

Pray for the native converts. We Christians at home think we have difficulties and trials and temptations and persecutions, but the burdens that we have to bear are nothing to what the converts in heathen lands have to bear. The obstacles oftentimes are enormous and discouragements crushing. Christ alone can make them stand, but He works in answer to the prayers of His people. Pray often, pray earnestly, pray intensely and pray believingly for native converts. How wonderfully God has answered prayer for native converts we are beginning to learn from missionary literature. It is well to be definite here again and to have some definite field about whose needs you keep yourself informed and pray for the converts of that field. Do not have so many that you become confused and mechanical. Pray for conversions in the foreign field. Pray for revivals in definite fields. The last few years have been years of special prayer for special revival in foreign fields and from every corner of the earth tidings have come of how amazingly God is answering these prayers. But the great things that God is beginning to do are small indeed in comparison with what He will do if there is more prayer.

Chapter XII. Companions

Our companions have a great deal to do with determining our character. The companionships that we form create an intellectual, moral and spiritual atmosphere that we are constantly breathing, and our spiritual health is helped or hindered by it. Every young Christian should have a few wisely chosen friends, intimate friends, with whom he can talk freely. Search out for yourself a few persons of about your own age with whom you can associate intimately. Be sure that they are spiritual persons in the best sense. Persons who love to study the Bible, persons who love to converse on spiritual themes, persons who know how to pray and do pray, persons who are really working to bring others to Christ.

Do not be at all uneasy about the fact that some Christian people are more agreeable to you than others. God has made us in that way. Some are attracted to some persons and some to others, and it proves nothing against the others and nothing against yourself that you are not attracted to them as you are to some people. Cultivate the friendship of those whose friendship you find helpful to your own spiritual life.

On the other hand avoid the companionships that you find spiritually and morally hurtful. Of course, we are not to withdraw ourselves utterly from unconverted people, or even of very bad people. We are to cultivate oftentimes the acquaintance of unspiritual people, and even of very bad people, in order that we may win them for Christ; but we must always be on our guard in such companionships to bear always in mind to seek to lift them up or else they will be sure to drag us down. If you find in spite of all your best effort that any companionship is doing harm to your own spiritual life, then give it up. Some people are surrounded with such an atmosphere of unbelief or cynicism or censoriousness or impurity or greed or some other evil thing that it is impossible to associate with them to any large extent without being contaminated. In such a case, the path of wisdom is plain; stop associating with them to any large extent. Stop associating with them at all except in so far as there is some prospect of helping them.

But there are other companionships that mold our lives besides the companionships of living persons. The books that we read are our companions. They exert a tremendous influence for good or for evil. There is nothing that will help us more than a good book, and there is nothing that will hurt us more than a bad book. Among the most helpful books are the biographies of good men. Read again and again the lives of such good and truly great men as Wesley and Finney and Moody. We live in a day in which good biographies abound. Read them. Well written histories are good companions. No study is more practical and instructive than the study of history, and it is not only instructive but spiritually helpful if we only watch to see the hand of God in history, to see the inevitable triumph of right and the inevitable punishment of wrong in individuals and in nations.

Some few books of fiction are helpful, but here one needs to be very much on his guard. A large portion of modern fiction is positively pernicious morally. Books of fiction that are not positively bad, at least give false views of life and unfit one for life as it really is. Much reading of fiction is mentally injurious. The inveterate novel reader ruins his powers of close and clear thinking. Fiction is so fascinating that it always tends to drive out other reading that is more helpful mentally and morally. We should be on our guard in even reading good literature, that the good does not crowd out the best; that is that the best of man's literature does not crowd out the very best of all—God's Book. God's Book, the Bible, must always have the first place.

Then there is another kind of companionship that has a tremendous influence over our lives, that is the companionship of pictures. The pictures that we see every day of our lives, and the pictures that we see only occasionally, have a tremendous power in the shaping of our lives. A mother had two dearly loved sons. It was her dream and ambition that these sons should enter the ministry, but both of them went to sea. She could not understand it until a friend one day called her attention to the picture of a magnificent ship in full sail careening through the ocean that hung above the mantel in the dining-room. Every day of their lives her boys had gazed upon that picture, had been thrilled by it, and an unconquerable love for the sea and longing for it had thus been created and this had determined their lives. How many a picture that is a masterpiece of art, but in which there is an evil suggestion, has sent some young men on the road to ruin. Many of our art collections are so polluted with improper pictures that it is not safe for a young man or a young woman to visit them. The evil thought that they suggest may be but for a moment, and yet Satan will know how to bring that picture back again and again and work injury by it. Don't look for a moment at any picture, no matter how praised by art critics, that taints your imagination with evil suggestion. Avoid as you would poison every painting, or engraving, every etching, every photograph that leaves a spot of impurity on your mind, but feast your soul upon the pictures that make you holier, kinder, more sympathetic and more tender.

Chapter XIII. Amusements

Young people need recreation. Our Savior does not frown upon wholesome recreation. He was interested in the games of the children when He was here upon earth. He watched the children at their play (Matt. 12: 16-19), and He watches the children at their play to-day, and delights in their play when it is wholesome and elevating. In the stress and strain of modern life older people too need recreation if they are to do their very best work. But there are recreations that are wholesome, and there are amusements that are pernicious. It is impossible to take up amusements one by one, and it is unnecessary. A few principles can be laid down.

1. *Do not indulge in any form of amusement about whose propriety you have any doubts.* Whenever you are in doubt, always give God the benefit of the doubt. There are plenty of recreations about which there can be no question. "He that doubteth is condemned: for whatsoever is not of faith is sin" (Rom. 14: 32). Many a young Christian will say, "I am not sure that this amusement is wrong." Are you sure it is right? If not, leave it alone.

2. *Do not indulge in any amusement that you cannot engage in to the glory of God.* "Whether therefore ye eat or drink, or whatsoever ye do, do all to the glory of God" (1 Cor. 10: 31). Whenever you are in doubt as to whether you should engage in any amusement ask yourself, Can I do this at this time to the glory of God?

3. *Do not engage in any amusement that will hurt your influence with anybody.* There are amusements, which perhaps are all right in themselves, but which we cannot engage in without losing our influence with some one. Now every true Christian wishes his life to tell with everybody to the utmost. There is so much to be done and so few to do it that every Christian desires every last ounce of power for good that he can have with everybody, and, if any amusement will injure your influence for good with any one, the price is too great. Do not engage in it. A Christian young lady had a great desire to lead others to Christ. She made up her mind that she would speak to a young friend of hers about coming to Christ, and while resting between the figures of a dance she said to the young man who was her companion in the dance, "George, are you a Christian?" "No," he said, "I am not, are you?" "Yes," she replied, "I am." "Then," he said, "what are you doing here?" Whether justly or unjustly the world discounts the professions of those Christians who indulge in certain forms of the world's own amusements. We cannot afford to have our professions thus discounted.

4. *Do not engage in any amusement that you cannot make a matter of prayer*, that you cannot ask God's blessing upon. Pray before your play just as much as you would pray before your work.

5. *Do not go to any place of amusement where you cannot take Christ with you, and where you do not think Christ would feel at home.* Christ went to places of mirth when He was here upon earth. He went to the marriage feast in Cana (John 2), and contributed to the joy of the occasion, but there are many modern places of amusement where Christ would not be at home. Would the atmosphere of the modern stage be congenial to that holy One whom we call "Lord"? If it would not, don't you go.

6. *Don't engage in any amusement that you would not like to be found enjoying if the Lord should come.* He may come at any moment. Blessed is that one whom when He cometh, He shall find watching and ready, and glad to open to Him immediately (Luke 12: 36, 40). I have a friend who was one day walking down the street thinking upon the return of his Lord. As he thought he was smoking a cigar. The thought came to him, "Would you like to meet Christ now with that cigar in your mouth?" He answered honestly, "No, I would not." He threw that cigar away and never lighted another.

7. *Do not engage in any amusement, no matter how harmless it would be for yourself, that might harm some one else.* Take for example card playing. It is probable that thousands have played cards moderately all their lives and never suffered any direct moral injury from it, but every one who has studied the matter knows that cards are the gamblers' chosen tools. He also knows that most, if not all, gamblers took their first lessons in card playing at the quiet family card table. He knows that if a young man goes out into the world knowing how to play cards and indulging at all in this amusement that before long he is going to be put into a place where he is going to be asked to play cards for money, and if he does not consent he will get into serious trouble. Card playing is a dangerous amusement for the average young man. It is pretty sure to lead to gambling on a larger or a smaller scale, and one of the most crying social evils of our time is the evil of gambling. Some young man may be encouraged to play cards by your playing who will afterwards become a gambler and part of the responsibility will lie at your door. If I could repeat all the stories that have come to me from broken-hearted men whose lives have been shipwrecked at the gaming table; if I could tell of all the broken-hearted mothers who have come to me, some of them in high position, whose sons have committed suicide at Monte Carlo and other places, ruined by the cards, I think that all thoughtful and true Christians would give them up forever.

For most of us the recreations that are most helpful are those that demand a considerable outlay of physical energy. Recreations that take us into the open air, recreations that leave us refreshed in body and invigorated in mind. Physical exercises of the strenuous kind, but not over-exercise, is one of the great safeguards of the moral conduct of boys and young men. There is very little recreation in watching others play the most vigorous game of football but there is real health for the body and for the soul in a due amount of physical exercise for yourself.

Chapter XIV. Persecution

One of the discouragements that meets every true Christian before he has gone very far in the Christian life is persecution. God tells us in His Word that "All that will live godly in Christ Jesus shall suffer persecution" (2 Tim. 3: 12). Sooner or later every one who surrenders absolutely to God and seeks to follow Jesus Christ in everything will find that this verse is true. We live in a God-hating world and in a compromising age. The world's hatred of God in our day is veiled. It does not express itself in our land in the same way that it expressed itself in Palestine in the days of Jesus Christ, but the world hates God to-day as much as it ever did, and it hates the one who is loyal to Christ. It may not imprison him or kill him but in some way it will persecute him. Persecution is inevitable for a loyal follower of Jesus Christ. Many a young Christian when he meets with persecution is surprised and discouraged and not a few fall away. Many a one seems to run well for a few days but like those of whom Jesus spoke, "They have no root in themselves, but endure for a while; then when tribulation or persecution ariseth because of the Word straightway they stumble" (Mark 4: 17). I have seen many an apparently promising Christian life brought to an end in this way. But if persecution is rightly received, it is no longer a hindrance to the Christian life but a help to it.

Do not be discouraged when you are persecuted. No matter how fierce and hard the persecution may be, be thankful for it. Jesus says, "Blessed are they which are persecuted for righteousness' sake: for theirs is the kingdom of heaven. Blessed are ye, when men shall revile you, and persecute you, and shall say all manner of evil against you falsely, for My sake. Rejoice, and be exceeding glad: for great is your reward in heaven: for so persecuted they the prophets which were before you" (Matt. 5: 10-12). It is a great privilege to be persecuted for Christ and for the truth. Peter found this out and wrote to the Christians of his day: "Beloved, think it not strange concerning the fiery trial which is to try you, as though some strange thing happened unto you. But rejoice, inasmuch, as ye are partakers of Christ's suffering; that, when His glory shall be revealed, ye may be glad also with exceeding joy. If ye be reproached for the name of Christ, happy are ye; for the spirit of glory and of God resteth upon you: on their part He is evil spoken of, but on your part He is glorified" (1 Peter 4: 12-14). Be very sure that the persecution is really for Christ's sake and not because of some eccentricity of your own, or because of your stubbornness. There are many who bring upon themselves the displeasure of others because they are stubborn and cranky and then flatter themselves that they are being persecuted for Christ's sake and for righteousness' sake. Be considerate of the opinions of others and be considerate of the conduct of others. Be sure that you do not push your opinions upon others in an unwarrantable way, or make your conscience a rule of life for other people. But never yield a jot of principle. Stand for what you believe to be the truth. Do it in love, but do it at any cost. And if when you are standing for conviction and principle you are disliked for it and slandered for it and treated with all manner of unkindness because of it, do not be sad but rejoice. Do not speak evil of those who speak evil of you, "because Christ also suffered for us, leaving us an example, that ye should follow His steps: who, when He was reviled, reviled not again, when He suffered, He threatened not; but committed Himself to Him that judgeth righteously" (1 Peter 2: 21, 23).

At this point many a Christian makes a mistake. He stands loyally for the truth, but he receives the persecution that comes for the truth with harshness, he grows bitter, he gets to condemn every one but himself. There is no blessing in bearing persecution in that way. Persecution should be borne meekly, lovingly, serenely. Don't talk about your own persecutions. Rejoice in them. Thank God for them, and go on obeying God. And don't forget to love and pray for them who persecute you (Matt. 5: 44).

If at any time the persecution seems harder than you can bear, remember how abundant the reward is, "If we suffer, we shall also reign with Him. If we deny Him, He also will deny us" (2 Tim. 2: 12). Every one must enter into the kingdom of God through much tribulation (Acts 14: 22), but do not go back on that account. Remember always however fiercely the fire of persecution may burn, "That the sufferings of this present time are not worthy to be compared with the glory which shall be revealed in us" (Rom. 8: 18). Remember too that your light affliction is but for the moment, and that it worketh out for you "a far more exceeding and eternal weight of glory" (2 Cor. 4: 17). Keep looking, not at the things which are seen, but at the things which are not seen, for the things which are seen are but for a time, but the things which are not seen are for eternity (2 Cor. 4: 18). When the apostles were persecuted, even unto imprisonment and stripes, they departed from the presence of the council that had ordered their terrible punishment, rejoicing that they were counted worthy to suffer shame for the name of Jesus, and they continued daily in the temple and every house teaching and preaching Jesus Christ (Acts 5: 40-42).

The time may come when you think that you are being persecuted more than others, but you do not know what others may have to endure. Even if it were true,—that you were being persecuted more than any one else, you ought not to complain but to humbly thank God that He has bestowed upon you such an honor. Keep your eyes fixed upon "Jesus, the Author and Finisher of our faith; who for the joy that was set before Him endured the cross, despising the shame, and is set down at the right hand of the throne of God. For consider Him that endured such contradiction of sinners against Himself, lest ye be wearied and faint in your mind" (Heb. 12: 2, 3). I was once talking with an old colored man who in the slave days had found his Savior. The cruel master had him flogged again and again for his loyalty to Christ but he said to me, "I simply thought of my Savior dying on the cross in my place, and I rejoiced to suffer persecution for Him."

Chapter XV. Guidance

I have met a great many who are trying to lead a Christian life who are much troubled over the question of guidance. They wish to do the will of God in all things, but what puzzles them is to tell what the will of God may be in every case. When any one starts out with the determination to obey God in everything and to be led by the Holy Spirit, Satan seeks to trouble him by perplexing him as to what the will of God is. Satan comes and suggests that something is the will of God that is probably not the will of God at all, and then when he does not do it, Satan says, "There you disobeyed God." In this way, many a conscientious young Christian gets into a very morbid and unhappy state of mind, fearing that he has disobeyed God and has lost His favor. This is one of the most frequent devices of the devil to keep Christians from being cheerful.

How may we know the will of God?

First of all let me say that a true Christian life is not a life governed by a whole lot of rules about what one shall eat, and what one shall drink, and what one shall do, and what one shall not do. A life governed by a lot of rules is a life of bondage. One is sure sooner or later to break some of these man-made rules and to get into condemnation. Paul tells us in Rom. 8: 15, "Ye have not received the spirit of bondage again to fear; but ye have received the spirit of adoption (placing us a son), whereby we cry, Abba, Father." The true Christian life is the life of a trusting, glad, fear-free child; not led by rules, but led by the personal guidance of the Holy Spirit who dwells within us. "As many as are led by the Spirit of God these are sons of God" (Rom. 8: 14). If you have received the Holy Spirit, He dwells within you and is ready to lead you at every turn of life. A life governed by a multitude of rules is a life of bondage and anxiety. A life surrendered to the control of the Holy Spirit is a life of joy and peace and freedom. There is no anxiety in such a life, there is no fear in the presence of God. We trust God and rejoice in His presence just as a true child trusts his earthly father and rejoices in his presence. If we make a mistake at any point, even if we disobey God, we go and tell Him all about it as trustfully as a child and know that He forgives us and that we are restored at once to His full favor (1 John 1: 9).

But how can we tell the Holy Spirit's guidance that we may obey Him and thus have God's favor at every turn of life? This question is answered in James 1: 5-7, "But if any of you lacketh wisdom, let him ask of God, who giveth to all liberally and upbraideth not; and it shall be given him, but let him ask in faith, nothing doubting: for he that doubteth is like the surge of the sea driven by the wind and tossed. For let not that man think that he shall receive anything of the Lord." This is very simple. It includes five points.

(1) That you recognize your own ignorance and your own inability to guide your own life—that you lack wisdom.

(2) The surrender of your will to God, and a real desire to be led by Him.

(3) Definite prayer to Him for guidance.

(4) Confident expectation that God will guide you. You "ask in faith, nothing doubting."

(5) That you follow step by step as He guides. God may only show you a step at a time. That is enough. All you need to know is the next step. It is here that many make a mistake. They wish God to show them the whole way before they take the first step. A university student once came to me over the question of guidance. He said, "I cannot find out the will of God. I have been praying but God does not show me His will." This was in the month of July. I said, "About what is it that you are seeking to know the will of God?" "About what I should do next summer." I said, "Do you know what you ought to do to-morrow?" "Yes." "Do you not know what you ought to do next autumn?" "Yes, finish my course. But what I want to know is what I ought to do when my university course is over." He was soon led to see that all he needed to know for the present was what God had already shown him. That when he did that, God would show him the next step. Do not worry about what you ought to do next week. Do what God shows you you ought to do to-day. Next week will take care of itself. Indeed, to-morrow will take care of itself. Obey the Spirit of God for to-day. "Be not therefore anxious for the morrow; for the morrow will be anxious for the things of itself. Sufficient unto the day is the evil thereof" (Matt. 6: 34). It is enough to live a day at a time, if we do our very best for that day.

God's guidance is clear guidance, "God is light and in Him is no darkness at all" (1 John 1: 5). Do not be anxious over obscure leadings. Do not let your soul be ruffled by the thought, "Perhaps this obscure leading is what God wants me to do." Obscure leadings are not divine leadings. God's path is as clear as day. Satan's path is full of obscurity and uncertainty and anxiety and questioning. If there comes some leading of which you are not quite sure whether it is the will of God or not, simply go to your Heavenly Father and say, "Heavenly Father, I desire to know Thy will. I will do Thy will if Thou wilt make it clear. But Thou art light and in Thee is no darkness at all. If this is Thy will make it clear as day and I will do it." Then wait quietly upon God and do not act until God makes it clear, but the moment it is made clear, act at once.

The whole secret of guidance is an absolutely surrendered will, a will that is given up to God and ready to obey Him at any cost. Many of our uncertainties about God's guidance are simply because we are not really willing to do what God is really guiding us to do. We are tempted to say, "I cannot find out what God's will is," when the real trouble is we have found out His will and it is something we do not wish to do and we are trying to make ourselves think that God wants us to do something else.

All supposed leadings of God should be tested by the Word of God. The Bible is God's revealed will. Any leading that contradicts the plain teaching of the Bible is certainly not the leading of the Holy Spirit. The Holy Spirit does not contradict Himself. A man once came to me and said that God was leading him to marry a certain woman. He said that she was a very devoted Christian woman and they had been greatly drawn towards one another and they felt that God was leading them to be married. But I said to the man, "You already have a wife." "Yes," he said, "but we have never lived happily and we have not lived together for years." "But," I replied, "that does not alter the case. God in His Word has told us distinctly the duty of the husband to the wife and how wrong it is in His sight for a husband to divorce his wife and marry another." "Yes," said the man, "but the Holy Spirit is leading us to one another." I indignantly replied that "Whatever spirit is leading you to marry one another, it is certainly not the Holy Spirit but the spirit of the evil one. The Holy Spirit never leads any one to disobey the Word of God."

In seeking to know the guidance of the Spirit always search the Scriptures, study them prayerfully. Do not make a book of magic out of the Bible. Do not ask God to show you His will and then open your Bible at random and put your finger upon some text and take it out of its connection without any relation to its real meaning and decide the will of God in that way. This is an irreverent and improper use of Scripture. You may open your Bible at just the right place to find right guidance, but if you do, it will not be by some fanciful interpretation of the passage you find. It will be by taking the passage in its context and interpreting it to mean just what it says as seen in its context. All sorts of mischief has arisen from using the Bible in this perverse way. I knew an earnest Christian woman once who was somewhat concerned about the predictions made by a false prophetess that Chicago was to be destroyed on a certain day. She opened her Bible at random. It opened to the twelfth chapter of Ezekiel, "Son of man, eat thy bread with quaking, and drink thy water with trembling and with carefulness.… And the cities that are inhabited shall be laid waste, and the land shall be desolate" (Ezek. 12: 18, 20). Now this seemed to exactly fit the case and the woman was considerably impressed, but if the verses had been studied in their connection, it would have been evident at once that God was not speaking about Chicago and that they were not applicable to Chicago. It was not an intelligent study of the Word of God and therefore led to a false conclusion.

To sum up, lead a life not led by rules but by the personal guidance of the Holy Spirit. Surrender your will absolutely to God. Whenever you are in doubt as to His guidance, go to Him and ask Him to show you His will, expect Him to do it, follow step by step as He leads. Test all the leadings by the plain and simple teachings of the Bible. Live free from anxiety and worry lest in some unguarded moment you have not done the right thing.

After you have done what you think God led you to do, do not be always going back and wondering whether you did the right thing. You will get into a morbid state if you do. If you really wished to do God's will and sought His guidance, and did what you thought He guided you to do, you may rest assured you did the right thing, no matter what the outcome has been. Satan is bound that we shall not be happy, cheerful Christians if he can prevent it, but God wishes us to be happy, cheerful, bright Christians every day and every hour. He does not wish us to brood but to rejoice (Phil. 4: 4). A most excellent Christian man came to me one Monday morning in great gloom over the failures of the work of the preceding day. He said to me, "I made wretched work of teaching my Sunday-school class yesterday." I said, "Did you honestly seek wisdom from God before you went to your class?" He said, "I did." I said, "Did you expect to receive it?" He said, "I did." "Then," I said, "in the face of God's promise what right have you to doubt that God did give you wisdom?" (James 1: 5-7). His gloom disappeared and he looked up with a smile and said, "I had no right to doubt." Let us learn to trust God. Let us remember that if our wills are surrendered to Him He is ever more willing to guide us than we are to be guided. Let us trust that He does guide us at every step and even though what we do does not turn out as we expected, let us never brood over it but trust God. Let us walk in the light of simple trust in God. In this way we shall be glad and peaceful and strong and useful at every turn of life.

How To Live The Victorious Life

~ ※ ~

By *Unknown Christian*

(Assumed today to be Albert Richardson)

The 1921 Edition

~ ※ ~

Author's Preface

Most men hesitate to speak of their own spiritual experiences. They are deterred by the fear of making "self" too prominent, or are ashamed to confess how much practical unbelief and half-hearted allegiance to their Lord exist in their lives.

The writer of this book knows his own unworthiness; but he humbly believes that he also knows something of the worthiness of an All-sufficient Savior.

The manner in which this knowledge came — through an apparently trivial incident — is itself remarkable.

The immediate result was a joy which no bridling could restrain. But whenever this Victorious Life was spoken of, requests were made for "something in print." After much pressure from many directions, and with much hesitation on the part of the writer, he ventured to put down his reflections.

These appeared in the columns of *THE LIFE OF FAITH*, through the kindness of the Editor.

They are here republished with practically no alterations. These chapters show the pathway by which one seeking soul found its way from "life" to "life more abundant."

They endeavor to reveal the helps and the hindrances which a seeker after the Victorious Life should know.

The writer owes much to the lives of four men, but the great "CRISIS" in his spiritual life took place, not in the uplift of a great convention, but in the quietude of his own study.

He believes that his experience is that of tens of thousands of Christian men and women — who have LIFE, and are earnest and devoted workers, yet who long for some Power which will conquer the so-called "little sins."

That POWER is the Lord Jesus Christ — and HE offers Himself to us (John 1:12).

So this book goes forth with much earnest prayer that others may be helped by the things which have been such an unspeakable inspiration to the writer, who — lest any shadow of self should fall upon these pages — humbly craves to be allowed to remain

— An Unknown Christian

Chapter One: Is It Possible?

Is there such a Life? St. John plainly says that every child of God "overcometh the world."

Now *that* is Victory! And he tells us how Victory is secured: "This is the VICTORY that overcometh the world — even our faith" (1 John 5:4) — and then most of us give up in despair!

It all seems too vague — too indefinite. Besides, isn't our faith too small or too weak? Or perhaps we don't possess the "right kind of faith" to get the Victory.

With many of us there is a sneaking idea that the schoolboy was very near the mark when he said "Faith is believing what ain't." But of this we are sure: to most Christians the Victorious Life is a beautiful mirage which vanishes into thin air, or recedes into the distance as we try to approach it. And so we look forward to finding it in heaven!

Now St. John isn't speaking about Victory in heaven — for *there*, "faith is *lost* in sight."

So there must be a Victory here on earth, in some way the result of faith. The writer would gladly give all he had in the world if in exchange he could have seen this way of Victory 25 years ago! After many years of Bible study; after many fears of futile "struggling with temptation" which, with monotonous regularity, tested him, he at last saw a way out — or rather a way IN. It was to him a new way — a LIVING way — and eagerly he entered in. He now sees there is such a thing as Victory, and he marvels how he missed his way before. In the joy of — to him — a wonderful discovery he longs for others to share the blessing — in these "last days." And is there not a real heartfelt yearning amongst Christians today to lay hold — not on *life*, for they have that — but on "*life more abundant?*"

The Victorious Life! The words ring with hope. Moreover, wherever an announcement is made that such a topic is to be talked about, men and women flock to discover the secret of such a life. For they *know* intuitively that when *Victory* comes defeat goes! Those shameful betrayals of the Master, which are so discouraging, will vanish away.

With Victory will come PEACE — a peace which really passeth all understanding.

With Victory will come JOY — a rejoicing with joy unspeakable and full of glory (1 Peter 1:8).

With Victory will come POWER — the very "power of God." The Victorious Life — a life of Peace, and Joy, and Power. Would not *such* a life satisfy any man?

Can we ask for anything better? And Christ offers *this*.

The writer proposes to try to make it plain and clear to the simplest mind, what the Bible says about this Life. We shall ask: How can it be obtained and retained? What are its difficulties and its dangers? Can it be lost? If so, can it be regained? We shall speak of real Victory and *false*. We hope to tell of its Triumphs and its Testings. Now we wish…

TO GIVE A WARNING

It is this: Satan will do his utmost to cloud your mind. He will bring all sorts of doubts and difficulties to light. Why is this? Just because he is eager to prevent you from gaining Victory! Believe me, the devil does not mind your being "religious," and he does not mind how much *powerless* work you attempt so long as you fall short of the Victorious Life.

So long as you go to the world for your pleasures, and so long as you fall into the usual sins of respectable people, *the more you attempt for Christ* the more the *devil is pleased*. He simply revels in seeing defeated, worldly Christians desperately busy for Christ. But the devil will do his level best to discredit Victorious Life teaching and to keep you from even *seeking* to understand it. He is quite an adept in using — *i.e.,* misusing — Scripture.

But be confident of this very thing — that the teaching is striking home and striking him — the devil — when difficulties are suggested to your mind or some verse of Scripture "comes" to you, which seems to contradict some statement made in these chapters.

No one is more anxious than the writer that only the truth as it is in Christ shall be heard. If any statement is not true to Scripture or to experience, none will be more delighted to have this pointed out than the writer, who is possessed with a consuming desire that every Christian shall be "filled with all the fullness of God."

Chapter Two: Can "Little" Sins Be Conquered?

The Victorious Life is a Life of Victory over Sin. Is such a thing possible? It is not a question of absolute sinlessness like that of Christ, or that of Adam before the Fall. There will always remain the clear declaration of St. John. "If we say that we have no sin, we deceive ourselves."

IS VICTORY PROMISED US?

The question we are facing is this — Can we obtain Victory over known, voluntary sin? Is any such hope of victory taught in the Bible? Is it ever experienced — lived out — by men today? If so, can *any* believer in Jesus Christ have Victory over all known sin — say, for one whole day — or is such Victory only for our spiritual leaders?

Surely these questions are often in men's minds. We *want* such Victory and even the Church of England teaches us to pray daily, "Vouchsafe, O Lord, to keep us this day, *without sin*." "Grant that this day we fall into *no sin*." Our Lord Himself taught us to pray, "Deliver us from evil" — or the evil one — *i.e.,* sin, or the author of sin. In the Church Catechism we teach our children that in this prayer we are asking God to "keep us from all sin and wickedness." Does Christ or any branch of His Church bid us ask for an impossibility? If these prayers are not mockery, then a Victorious Life is possible.

But come down to everyday life. Can we think of any *one sin* over which Victory has never been won? We have seen drunkards turning to Christ, and *in a moment* getting absolute Victory over strong drink. Such men often declare not only that they have never fallen again, but that *the very desire* for alcohol has been entirely taken away. This is miraculous. So with other great besetting sins — God has given instantaneous and complete Victory.

If then we can get Victory over some deep-rooted, besetting sin, cannot our Savior make us Victorious over the sins we sometimes regard as "little"? Christian people, as a rule, *i.e.,* in the great majority of cases, are *not* drunken, or vicious, or immoral.

But this can also be said of very many worldly and irreligious people. Isn't it true that there is little to choose between the average Christian and the ordinary moral "worldly" man? So the latter says, "What will it profit me to become a Christian?" And what can we say in reply? What would the worldly man gain? And what would others benefit by the change in him?

UNDER THE TYRANNY OF SIN

Do we see any signs of the Victorious Life in the majority of professing Christians? In any flourishing Church, how many of its members exhibit a glowing love of souls and a burning zeal for Christ? We merely ask the question.

In how many do we see Victory over so-called *respectable* sins? — bad temper, irritability, pride, jealousy, backbiting, unlove, *anxiety*?

Now we ask in all humility, Is there any remedy? Is there any hope of getting the Victorious Life? That is, a life of habitual Victory over sins ("small" as well as great) — a life of constant and conscious fellowship with God?

If such a hope can be found, it will be in God's Holy Word. Is it there?

"Victory over known sin! Can I get it?" What a momentous question! If we can get it for an hour — or a day — then why not *habitually*? Dare we ask every reader to put aside all ideas of his own on such a question? Will you approach it with an unprejudiced and unbiased mind? For the time being just shelve any preconceived ideas you may have on this subject. Forget all your own failures — and the faults of other Christians. Yes — and forget all *theories* of holiness. Simply allow God's written Word to speak for itself. Surely this is not an unfair demand?

A PROMISE AND A COMMAND

What does the New Testament talk about chiefly? By far the greatest part of it is devoted to telling Christians how to live after they have found Christ as their Savior, rather than how to *get salvation* from the penalty of sin.

Before our Lord was born, the Angel of the Lord said of Him, "Thou shalt call His name Jesus for He shall save His people *from their sins*" (Matthew 1:21).

Quite early in His ministry, Christ Himself said to His disciples, "Be ye therefore perfect even as your Father which is in heaven is perfect" (Matthew 5:48).

This must mean *something*. The Savior would never command an impossibility. Here He definitely bids us possess some sort of "perfection" — in fact a perfection in *some way* like that of God the Father.

It is very wonderful and at first sight it seems impossible — incomprehensible. But *there is the command*.

Peter, speaking by the Holy Spirit, gives a very similar exhortation: "But LIKE as He which called you is holy, be ye yourselves also holy in all manner of living; because it is written 'Ye shall be holy, for I am holy'" (1 Peter 1:15).

We are then definitely commanded to possess some sort of "holiness" — in fact a holiness like that of Jesus Christ.

The writer of the Epistle to the Hebrews shows how important this is. "Follow peace," says he, "with all men, and holiness, *without which no man can see the Lord*" (Hebrews 12:14).

John tells us plainly that he is writing his first Epistle so that its readers "may not sin" (1 John 2:1).

May we very humbly ask whether it is presumption on our part to inquire into the meaning of these words?

WHERE PRESUMPTION LIES

It surely *would be presumption* to doubt the possibility of our carrying out any command of Jesus Christ or the Holy Spirit? Ought not every sincere follower of the Lord Jesus to try to discover what these verses of Scripture mean?

Are you looking for the Return of Jesus Christ? Is that your hope? Well, more than 1,900 years ago, John said, "Everyone that hath this hope set on Him, purifieth himself, *even as He is pure*" (1 John 3:3).

St. John expects to find in Christians a purity somehow like Christ's!

"Whosoever is begotten of God doeth no sin... he cannot sin..." (1 John 3:9).

We have not referred to Paul's declarations on the same subject. "Reckon ye yourselves to be dead unto sin..." "sin shall *not* have dominion over you" (Romans 6:11 and 14).

He tells us how it is done. "The shield of faith wherewith ye shall be able to quench ALL the fiery darts of the Evil one" (Ephesians 6:16).

Do not our hearts burn within us at the very *thought* of such a life as is held out here?

Now whatever we may think about these words from Scripture — whatever our prejudices, whatever our past failures — however impossible it all seems — we cannot deny the following facts. In the Bible — God's Word: —

1. There is a perfection commanded, in some way like that of God the Father.
2. There is a holiness enjoined like that of God Himself.
3. There is a purity offered, like that of Jesus Christ.
4. There is a *possibility* shown of resisting every attack of the evil one.

The life which such "perfection," such holiness, such purity, and such power would produce would surely be a Victorious Life. Are we willing to study the question further? We are absolutely certain that God would not mock us by commanding an impossible standard, or by offering us something He is not able to give.

The question is NOT "Can *I* live a Victorious Life?" (We all know what the answer to that question is.) No! The thing which concerns me, is just this: "Can Jesus Christ *make* me holy — *keep* me holy —*give* me Victory?" If He can — shall we not get it? And then, shall we not cry out with St. Paul — in all exultation and yet withal, in all humility and adoration —

Thanks be unto God which giveth us the VICTORY through our Lord Jesus Christ (1 Corinthians 15:57).

Chapter Three: God's Love Never Faileth

What is the Victorious Life? It is the life of holiness, or the "perfect" life which is so often referred to by Paul in his Epistles.

Surely then the very first thing for us to do is to find out just what is commanded us, and promised us, in the New Testament. Two very definite things have been already spoken of — HOLINESS and PERFECTION. What do these words mean? And is "Holiness" the same thing as "Perfection?"

Now it is a very singular fact that really devoted — yet *defeated* — Christians gladly aim at "holiness," but are frightened of "perfection." "There is no such thing as 'perfection'" is a common remark on the lips of Christian people. Our reply is, that our Lord *commanded* it, whatever it is.

"PERFECTION" HERE AND NOW

"Perfection," said a Professor of Theology, "is an unrealizable ideal towards which we progress through all eternity." Yet Christ demands some sort of "perfection" *here* and *now*. If we are really sincere we shall try to see what the Savior means. "Be ye therefore 'perfect,'" said Christ.

"That's a bewildering command," was the comment made on this verse, by a modern preacher, "but when our Lord adds, 'as your heavenly Father is perfect' we are simply staggered, and in despair give up attempting to obey!" Yet these added words are the key to the solution of the difficulty! For at once we can cut out all false ideas of "perfection."

How is our Heavenly Father "perfect"? Surely in everything. But He is *God* and we are *men*. He does not command us to be 'perfect' as God. The FATHER is "perfect" in absolute sinlessness; in Majesty, in Glory, in Power, in Wisdom. Such "perfection" cannot be attained by mortal man. In what then are *we* to be "perfect"? "Be ye *therefore* perfect." That word "therefore" evidently refers to what has been said just before. What is that? Simply a command to be full of love. Godless men love their friends: the followers of Christ are to *love their enemies* as well. Our Lord is commanding perfect LOVE. This thought came to me with overwhelming power. The Victorious Life is simply a life of *perfect love*.

OUR LORD'S "NEW COMMANDMENT"

Towards the end of His earthly life, our Lord said, "A new commandment I GIVE unto you, that ye *love* one another; even AS *I* HAVE LOVED YOU, that ye also love one another. By this shall all men know that ye are My disciples, if ye have love one to another" (John 13:34). There is the standard and there is the command to reach it.

As Christ loved — that is the standard; and that is perfect love. And this is commanded *us*. And St. Paul reminds us that "love" is the only thing which can enable us to obey God. "Love is the fulfilling of the Law." (Romans 13:10).

"The point is, can an imperfect man or woman have 'perfect' love?" That was the opening sentence of an address on this subject. But surely that is not the way to approach this question? It is the blessed Master Who commands. It is not for me to cast even the shadow of a doubt on the possibility of what He bids. But, do we not feel constrained to cry out, like a seeker of old, "How CAN these things be?" Is there such a thing as "perfect love?"

Assuredly there is. The Father's love is "perfect." The love wherewith Christ loved us is perfect. Human love is imperfect and always will be. But does not the Bible say, "The love of God hath been shed abroad in our hearts?" (Romans 5:5). Would you believe it, if you were told that this was the reason why Jesus Christ revealed God the Father? Yet it is so. We have His own words for it.

Our Lord said, "I have made known unto them Thy name, and will make it known" — that includes you and me — "that the *love* wherewith Thou lovest Me, may be IN THEM, and I in them" (John 17:26).

THE SECRET — "PERFECT LOVE"

Here, then, is the secret of it all. "Perfect love" is surely possible, but only possible when Jesus Christ Himself — God Himself Who is love — comes to dwell in our hearts.

St. John, the Apostle of love, told us this long ago. "If we LOVE one another God abideth IN US, and His love is perfected *in us*" (1 John 4:12).

"We *know* and have believed the love which God hath IN US. God is love: and he that abideth in love, abideth in God, and God abideth in him. Herein is love made PERFECT with us" (1 John 4:16-17). It is, therefore, as clear as day, that if we desire "perfect love," we *can get it* by having Jesus Christ — Who is love — filling our whole being. Then, and then only, can we understand that stupendous comparison of John: "because as He is, even so are WE in this world" (ver. 17).

No wonder St. Paul cried out exultantly — defiantly? — "Who shall separate us from the love of God?" (Romans 8:39). No wonder he bursts out in triumphant faith, when he prays for the Ephesians "that Christ may dwell *in your hearts* by faith; to the end that ye being rooted and grounded in LOVE, may be strong to apprehend with all the saints, what is the breadth, and length and height and depth, and to know the LOVE OF CHRIST, which passeth knowledge, that ye may be filled unto all the fullness of God" (Ephesians 3:17).

Before we go on to ask, not doubtingly, but in a spirit of joyous expectation, "*How can these things be?*" may we just answer the questions which are in the minds of some. "And *is* love *alone* really enough?" "Does 'love' indeed banish sin from my life?" "Does 'perfect love' mean 'holiness'?"

To answer such questions, we need only just look at that wonderful 13th chapter of 1 Corinthians in order to realize what Divine Love can work in us.

"Love suffereth long" — it drives away all impatience.

"Love is kind" — it leaves room for no unkindness.

"Love envieth not" — all jealousy is banished.

"Love vaunteth not itself" — boasting and self-assertion disappear.

"Is not puffed-up" — pride finds no place in the heart.

"Does not behave itself unseemly" — folly goes.

"Seeketh not its own" — "self" is dead — selfishness will be unknown.

"Is not provoked" — anger and wrath will not be seen.

"Taketh no account of evil" — brooding over so-called "wrongs" will be no more. Malice and all uncharitableness are not found in the heart.

"Beareth all things" — complainings will never be heard.

"Hopeth all things" — despair, anxiety, despondency go.

"LOVE NEVER FAILETH."

No wonder Paul adds, "When that which is PERFECT is come…" What *is* it that is "Perfect?" — why, just the love of God — shed abroad in our hearts.

If "perfect love" casts out this great procession of sins, and fills our entire being, we might well cry out in an ecstasy of thankfulness and delight, "To me to live is Christ"

— and Christ is love. If we have not done so before, we must surely set ourselves the task of finding out how this great Possession can be secured.

How can we get this Perfect Love — and keep it?

Chapter Four: How Sin Is Overcome

SIN IS OVERCOME ONLY BY THE INDWELLING CHRIST.

We have now been led into a very definite position in Christian experience. It cannot be doubted that the Bible commands and expects some kind of "perfection," some kind of "holiness," without which no man can see the Lord.

But we long to see Him. We long to know, not only about Him, but to know HIM. This holiness cannot possibly be reached by man by his own efforts — no, nor by a man merely "helped" by God. "All our righteousnesses are as filthy rags" (Isaiah 64:6).

But we have seen that Jesus Christ has promised to come and make His abode in our hearts: bringing His own "perfect love" and pure holiness into our very being.

When "HE is our LIFE," then we indeed know HIM. "And this is life eternal, that they might know Thee, the only true God, and Jesus Christ Whom Thou hast sent" (John 17:3). And Jesus Christ is "perfect love." And perfect love casteth out, not only fear, but all sin.

All this we have seen — perhaps for many years. Now it is easy enough to write such things, and — in some sort of way — believe such things. But we want more than that. The question is, "How can I, a struggling sinner, though saved by grace, get this 'perfect love'? How can I get victory over all known sin, and live the Victorious Life?"

WHAT GOD CAN DO

God gives great and open sinners instant victory over great and open sins, and rescues such men from the clutches of such sins. We want to know how *we* can get instantaneous deliverance from little sins (so-called). The Loving Savior and Almighty Redeemer CAN do it, we know — *but* how is it done?

This is the most momentous question any Christian man can ask. Most Christians have made many and frequent attempts to get victory over sin: and most of them have failed in the attempt. The great majority of believers reach a certain level in Christian experience, and then gradually slip back to lower levels. Why is this? Is it not probably because their method of attempt was wrong?

This is such an important matter that we hope the reader will patiently examine the following criticisms. We say "patiently," because so much will be said which cuts right across the usual advice given to seekers after sanctification. The writer knows full well what he is talking about. He has himself sadly trodden all the paths described, and has tasted both their joys and their sorrows. And today as he looks back, he realizes why they failed to lead him into the Victorious Life.

THE POPULAR WAY

Fight your temptations. You have accepted Jesus Christ as your personal Savior, yet you find your sinful passions still remain, and often break out into actual sin. You want victory over those temptations, for tempted we always shall be here on earth. Very well

— make a victorious struggle (by God's help, or course) against these evil passions and desires, and in this way overcome them.

This idea appeals to us, and seems so good and wise. And God does indeed help us to conquer after a determined fight — if our will-power lasts out. The writer has tried it (who has not?), and has often at length gained a victory. But again, he has often tried it only to fail miserably after a struggle: because Satan is stronger than man!

The popular way is a doubtful way! Where can you find anything in the Bible to support us in the belief that we are to fight or to struggle with *temptation*? We are told to "flee" from sin, from youthful lusts, from idolatry, and such like. Are we ever told to fight *temptation*?

If so, where? It is true that St. Paul exhorts us to "fight the good fight" — hut he hastens to add "of faith." Now a "fight of faith" cannot be a struggle. It is true that James said, "Resist the devil" (James 4:7). How? With your hands? Surely not. "Whom resist, steadfast in the faith" (1 Peter 5:9).

We are to "STAND," not struggle. "Having done all things, stand." The shield of FAITH is able to quench all the fiery darts of the evil one (Ephesians 6). "Faith does nothing; faith lets God do it all."

JESUS CHRIST HAS WON...

the victory for us. "I live," says Paul, "yet not I, Christ LIVETH IN ME." "Ye are of God," says John, "and have overcome them." How? Why? "Because greater is HE that is *in you*, than he that is in the world" (1 John 4:4). So we come back to the some theme: The secret of Victory is the Indwelling-Christ. Victory is in trusting, not in trying. "This is the Victory that overcometh the world" — and SIN — "even our faith" (1 John 5:4).

A man who tries by strenuous effort to resist or struggle against sin till it is frequently conquered, is said to be "growing in grace." Yet all growth takes place without effort. "No man by taking thought can add one cubit to his stature," said our Lord. And this is true of our spiritual stature.

THEORY AND PRACTICE

How is growth secured? Air, food and exercise insure growth when there is life. If our spiritual life is sustained by the Holy Spirit, within and around us; if it is nourished by Jesus Christ Himself "the bread of God" (John 6:33), it will exercise itself in "good works," and there will be "growth." There is a wondrous "growth in grace" — but there is no growth into grace. Sin hinders this growth, and *struggling* against sin cannot help the growth.

Now, this is all theoretical. How does it work out in practice? The writer heard a sermon recently on our Lord's command, "Be ye therefore perfect." The preacher was a man of holy and humble heart. The gist of the address was that perfection was a thing we were to aim at but never reach. But we could get nearer and nearer to the goal. How? By tackling one sin at a time, subdue it, suppress it. Then another sin was to be resolutely dealt with until at last, some day, all our sins would be mastered. We were told that a piano could not be tuned all at once — a note at a time was taken.

Very well. Have you ever known such a method to succeed? Sin is sin, and all "sins" have their root in SIN in the heart. Sin has been conquered by Christ. Are we to spend our time cutting off branches, or are we to destroy the root of the tree? If Jesus Christ is not able to conquer any known sin in me today, will He be stronger in five months' — or five years' — time? After all is said and done, I can do nothing of myself in the matter. It is Jesus Christ Himself Who gives the victory. All I can do is to look to Christ in faith and let *Him* overcome for me.

AN ILLUSTRATION WITH A POINT

A pick-pocket once strolled into a rescue mission — so the story goes — and was converted. He saw in Christ pardon for his sins and power against them. Rejoicing in a new life, he went on his way planning for the future. "In my unregenerate days," said he to himself, "I used to pick quite twenty pockets a day. But now I am a Christian man, and I know that to pick pockets is to sin. So I must give it up — gradually, of course. Tomorrow I'll make a start and for the rest of this month by striving and struggling against this sin, I'll cut it down to five a day — for I'm a Christian man now. By the end of the year by constant endeavor (and the help of God) I hope to give up picking pockets altogether."

Do you believe that story? The writer does not. But have we not all been guilty of this very thing in our dealings with bad temper, pride, irritability, jealousy, unlove? We expect a pick-pocket, or a drunkard, or a gambler to give up his sin once for all — the very moment of his conversion. We tell him — and tell him truly — that Christ is able to give him complete and instant victory. Is God unable to give us a similar victory over what we deem to be lesser sins? He is able to make us "more than conquerors."

Victory over sin is a gift of God and not a growth. Paul recognized this. He did not say, "Thanks be unto God, which gives us a gradual victory," but "giveth us the victory through Jesus Christ our Lord" (1 Corinthians 15:57). There is no such thing as a gradual victory over sin — although we may think there is. God's gifts are perfect. The fact is, He gives us Jesus Christ Himself to dwell in our hearts by faith. And Jesus Christ keeps us. "He is able to keep us from stumbling" (Jude 24). "We know that whosoever is born of God sinneth not," says the Holy Spirit — and He gives the reason — "for He that is begotten of God (Jesus Christ) KEEPETH him, and that wicked one toucheth him not" (1 John 5:18). Can we trust Christ to do it?

An old colored man in America saw this truth — that is, the wonderful power of the indwelling Christ, and his life became incarnate joy. "So, Sam, you've got the mastery of the devil, they tell me?" said a scoffing white man. "No, sah!" replied Sam, "But I've got de MASTER of de devil." And is not this what we all want?

Chapter Five: None Can Imitate Christ

NOT THE IMITATION OF CHRIST BUT HIS INDWELLING PRESENCE IS THE REAL SECRET OF CONSTANT TRIUMPH

Have we grasped the fact that the Victorious Life is not secured *gradually*, nor by effort and striving on our part? We know that a partial self-control can be obtained and IS obtained for a time by men who give no thought to pleasing God. An athlete will "flee youthful lusts" and to a great degree "keep himself unspotted from the world" simply to gain Victory in the world of sport. A business man or a shop-assistant will "control" his temper merely to secure orders, or keep a situation. A society lady will remain "sweet" even if you ruin her smartest dress by upsetting your tea over it. A Christian man may "school" himself in the same manner — but this is not necessarily the Victorious Life.

Do not misunderstand me. There IS a fight — and a strenuous fight — against a world of sin. But to fight against sin *in the heart* is to mistrust Christ and is sure of failure in the long run. What then *can* we do to get this Victorious Life? Many of us have tried the *Imitation of Christ*. We may call this...

THE PROMISING WAY

because it looks so attractive and right; and so likely to succeed. Surely it is a splendid thing to imitate Christ. But can you do it? "Oh, well," you reply, "I can try." As a matter of fact, no one ever lived who imitated Christ. It cannot be done. Nor are we told to attempt it.

CHRIST OUR LIFE

One of the world's masterpieces of religious literature is called *The Imitation of Christ*. Most of us know it well. It is, indeed, a delightful book, and has helped countless thousands — but not to imitate Christ! John Newton, the blaspheming slave raider, was led to Christ by reading this book. Read it again, for your soul's good, and you will notice that from beginning to end there is nothing about imitating Christ. It is full of helpful counsels and advice, of meditations, and prayers and exhortations. The title well might be *The Appropriation of Christ*, or *The Absorption of Christ*.

Christ is to be more than an example — He is *our life*. Someone has gone so far as to have declared that the "idea of imitating Christ is a hoax of the devil"! And he is really right in his strong assertion, For although no harm, but only good, can come from attempting to imitate the Lord Jesus, failure is certain to be the result. Good is always the enemy of "best." We know how hopeless it is to try to imitate the holy men and women whose friendship we value. How much more difficult it would be to imitate Christ!

THE BIBLE ON IMITATORS

But we must not rely upon human opinions. What does the Bible say about this question? Has it ever struck you that nowhere in the New Testament are we told to be like Jesus Christ — or to strive to be like Him — or to pray that we may be like Him? Is it not so? This is very startling. The nearest approach you get to such an idea is found in Romans 8:29, "Whom He foreknew He also fore-ordained to be conformed to the image of His Son." In his wonderful commentary on the Epistle to the Romans, Dr. Moule, the late Bishop of Durham, says, "The Greek here is literally 'conformed ones of the image' — as if their similitude made them *part* of what they resembled."

Paul also says, "Ye became imitators of us, and of the Lord" (1 Thessalonians 1:6). But in what way? In the matter of being afflicted for the Gospel's sake. The servant is not above his Lord. If the world persecuted Christ, it will persecute us.

The same idea is brought out in 1 Peter 2:21. "For even hereunto were ye called: because Christ also suffered for you, leaving you an example that ye should follow His steps" — *i.e.*, in suffering patiently (even though He was sinless) the contradiction of sinners against Himself. "But," you ask, "does not St. Paul tell us to be 'imitators' of God?" Yes, but always and only in this matter of showing a forgiving spirit. (See Ephesians 4:32 and 5:1.) We may and can and should imitate some acts of Jesus Christ

— but to imitate HIM is impossible. And, moreover, when we think we are "imitating" Him, it is in reality Christ Himself working IN US. One day we *shall be* like Him — but not by any attempt at imitation on our part. "When He shall appear we shall be *like* Him for we shall see Him as He is" (1 John 3:2).

CHRIST IN OUR HEARTS

There would be little harm in trying to imitate Christ, if such an endeavor did not hide from us what our Lord really desires; and so keep us back from "life more abundant." He wants to come Himself into our lives, to dwell in our hearts and live His life in us. What a wonderful thing this is! We should despair if Christ simply left us an example to "follow" or "imitate."

But He says He will come and dwell in our hearts by faith. Surely this is much better than having Christ as my helper, or than getting "power" from Christ. Paul sums up this great privilege in a sentence. "For," says he, "it is God which worketh IN YOU both to will and to work, for His good pleasure" (Philippians 2:13). The word means "work mightily, effectively." Remember it is not an "influence" or a "spiritual force" — it is God Himself dwelling in the heart of the believer.

We are sometimes urged to "possess our possessions," but we would rather invite all true believers to possess their POSSESSOR — Jesus Christ Himself, "Who is all and in you all." In fact, the word "imitate" really means "a going into." In this sense there is imitation indeed: for we enter into Christ, and Christ enters into us. So that we can say with Paul, "For me to live is Christ" (Philippians 1:21); "Christ Who is our life" (Colossians 3:4).

We must remember that Christ IS already in the heart of every believer. But unless He has FULL possession, and FULL control, we cannot have Victory.

Forgive a homely illustration which the writer used in speaking to lads. He asked the question, "Would you like to play football as well as B——?" (a celebrated professional center-forward). "Yes, sir," "Well, it's quite simple — imitate him." "We can't do it, sir." "But if I could endow you with all the strength of B——, would you not play as well?" "No, sir, for we should still lack his skill." "But suppose that with his strength I could also impart his mind — the mind which controls and guides his play and which gives him his skill?" "Then we'd play as well as he," they broke in. Now, that is just what our Lord wishes to do for every one of His children. He does not say, "Imitate Me." But He does say, "Let Me come into your very being and think IN you good thoughts; and work IN you, and enable you to put those thoughts into deeds."

"Ye shall be endued with power form on high." Yes, but that very Power is the Holy Spirit of God Himself. "Who shall be IN you," says Christ. So that St. Paul boldly says, "We have the mind of Christ" (1 Corinthians 2:16). But if we have the mind of Christ in us, and "Power from on high" to fulfill the purposes of that mind, "Holiness" becomes, not second nature, but our very life.

KNOWING AND DOING

You may be saying to yourself, "There is nothing new in this." No, indeed; but have you acted upon it? For years the writer read all these things in the Bible and believed them — yes, and spoke about them in addresses. Then came a day when he resolutely faced his failure to conquer so many "little" sins — these sad betrayals of his Lord and Savior. Was there no "better thing" than this in store? Again he knelt and surrendered himself fully to Christ and in simple faith claimed Jesus Christ as his indwelling Savior. Then he rose from his knees and took it for granted that the Lord Jesus Christ was filling his entire life. That is, he simply BELIEVED God's Word.

What a wonderful consciousness of His Presence was secured. Christ is no longer simply One Who inhabiteth eternity — Someone to Whom to turn in times of difficulty; no longer Someone Who comes to one's aid and helps from without. He has come to make His abode in the whole heart — taking full possession of my very being; body, soul and spirit. So that the first thought in the morning and the frequent recollection during the day is just this: "To me to live is Christ."

A little girl once heard such teaching from God's Holy Word, and hurried home with joyful heart. Her mother, on entering the house, heard the child's voice in the dining-room. "Lord Jesus," said she, "they tell me You are willing to come and dwell in my heart. Forgive me all my sins. Make my heart clean. And now, Lord Jesus, come into the *whole* of my heart." Then the child stood up and looking up to heaven said simply, "He's IN."

Cleansing, Surrender; Faith.

It is as simple as that. Yet the very "Power which raised Jesus Christ from the dead" is involved in it (Ephesians 1:19-20). "Power from on high."

Chapter Six: How To Enter In

HOW TO BE WHOLLY POSSESSED BY CHRIST AND THUS ENTER INTO AND ENJOY THE LIFE OF HOLINESS

If, then, we are unable to become holy by struggling against our sins; and if we cannot imitate Christ so as to become like Him, what hope is left us?

Hope? The writer soon discovered that there was not only no hope, but miserable failure in struggling and trying to "imitate."

THE QUEST FOR GOD'S PRESENCE

But there came a bright star on his spiritual horizon. It was hailed with all the joy of the wise men of old when they "saw the star." Surely this wondrous light would lead him into the very presence of the Lord — and there he would find victory? A little book was given him by a fellow-worker. It was called, *The Practice of The Presence of God*, by Brother Lawrence. It made a profound impression on his life.

Brother Lawrence found that books of devotion and religious "exercises" did not help him — but were rather hindrances to his spiritual life, so he set himself to work to secure at all times a sense of God's presence. He endeavored always to walk as in the presence of God. The result was a communion with God so close and uninterrupted that set times of prayer were not different from other times. "The time of business," said he, "does not with me differ from the time of prayer; and in the noise and clatter of my kitchen, while several persons are at the same time calling for different things, I POSSESS GOD in as great tranquility as if I were on my knees at the Blessed Sacrament."

Now, is not that the spirit we want? "In Thy presence is fullness of joy," says the Psalmist (Psalm 16:11). But is this the Victorious Life? It certainly seemed so to Brother Lawrence.

The booklet was inspiring. Never before had the writer experienced such a wonderful uplift of soul: such an inspiration for service.

Not only the knowledge that "Thou, God, seest me," but the habitual consciousness, "I am now in the very presence of God." The mind went back to Zacharias in the Temple and the words of the Archangel, "I am Gabriel, that stand in the presence of God" (Luke 1:19). Ah! that's the thought. His feet may tread the temple courts, but he never forgets that he stands in the very presence of God. "Take heed," said the Lord Jesus Christ, "that ye despise not one of these little ones... for their angels do always BEHOLD THE FACE OF MY FATHER which is in heaven."

IN THE PRESENCE OF GOD

That, then, is the secret of the angels' service — they are always conscious of being in the presence of God. Was it not so with Elijah? When he suddenly emerges from obscurity and springs into our view he cries, "As the Lord God of Israel liveth before Whom I STAND!" (1 Kings 17:1; 18:5). When he refused "to stand" in the presence of God, he begged that he might die; and God could not use him again till he "stood" once more in His presence. "Go forth," said God to the despondent prophet, "and STAND upon the mount before the Lord" (1 Kings 19:11). But he hid in the cave. Then came wind, and earthquake and fire — but all in vain. They did not drive him forth from his hiding-place from God. After the fire there was a sound of gentle stillness (ver. 12, RV, marg.). Did the prophet fear that God had deserted him? Had God departed? Elijah wrapped his face in his mantle and went out and STOOD in the entering in of the cave. Once more he "stands" before God, and God could speak to him and use him.

Yes. All this is Scriptural. Oh, what resources of help and strength and comfort lie in this thought, "I... stand in the presence of God." When some unwelcome duty, some unpleasant task, or some "big thing" had to be faced the writer has again and again steadied himself, nerved himself by quietly repeating the words, "I... stand in the presence of God."

WHAT OUR LORD DESIRES

We thank God with unfeigned gratitude for this help by the way. But it is not the Victorious Life. A *heathen* may use such help.

During the war a troopship was torpedoed in the Mediterranean and was fast sinking. A British soldier in great terror hurried hither and thither bewildered. A Hindu put his hand on the shoulder of the terrified man and pointing upward said, "Johnnie" (their equivalent of Tommy); "God!" And this steadied the lad. Helpful; but not sufficient. It may be the source of strength for angels, and for saints *before the day of Pentecost*. But we need something more than this.

And the Lord Jesus has promised us this "something more."

Is, then, the Way of the Presence right or wrong? Surely it is right as far as it goes. No one will ever know what a help the writer found it. After all, we are "IN Christ" and to remind ourselves of His presence around us — near us — must be helpful.

THE CHRIST DWELLING WITHIN

But our Lord's great desire is that we shall realize His presence within us. He tried to get His disciples to believe (and to know) that the Father was in Him and He in the Father (John 10:38). That He could do nothing of Himself — but that the Father was working in and through Him (John 5:19, 30). And that in the same way we are sent by Him. That without Christ we can do nothing — but He would come and dwell IN us and work in and through us. Christ Jesus says this with the utmost plainness.

"As Thou hast sent Me into the world," says our Lord in His prayer, "even so have I also sent them" — the apostles (John 17:18). "At that day," (Pentecost) said Christ, "Ye shall KNOW that I am in My Father, and ye in Me, and I IN YOU" (John 14:20).

How can we get this Indwelling of Christ? And how know we have Him and thus "know Him and the power of His Resurrection"? How did Brother Lawrence get his blessing? How did he keep it? He just surrendered himself entirely to God. Without such surrender one cannot really practice the presence of God. "I know," said he, "that for the right practice of it, the heart must be empty of all other things; because God will possess the heart ALONE. And as He cannot possess it alone without emptying it of all besides, so neither can He act there and do in it what he pleases unless it be left vacant to Him."

This was his Prayer: "My God, here I am, all devoted to Thee. Lord, make me according to Thy heart."

And what was the result? He had such a joy in God that for 30 years his soul was so elated and exultant that he had to repress his raptures so as to hinder them appearing outwardly.

"Were I a preacher," he used to say, "I should above all other things preach the practice of the presence of God: so necessary do I think it and so easy too."

But one does not fully appropriate that life merely by accepting Christ as the Savior from the guilt of sin. Many sincere Christians are living defeated lives. Their sinful passions — yes, and sinful desires — are not entirely gone. So there is failure, and such lives are little different from those of the worldlings around them.

There must be an entire surrender of self — a real yearning desire to be free from all known sin: a looking to Jesus Christ by faith to destroy sin in us; and a taking of Christ to be our whole life — literally our life.

"You will never have the Victorious Life," said Wilbur Chapman, "until Jesus Christ has all there is of you — never!" When He comes and takes entire possession of our being, He brings the Victorious Life, and we can say, "I live, and yet no longer I, but Christ liveth in me."

When He possesses us wholly, then we shall be holy. Are we willing to take the step? Are we willing to put ourselves unreservedly into His hands?

To do so is to secure Heaven on earth!

Chapter Seven: Buried With Christ

WHAT IT MEANS TO BE BAPTIZED INTO CHRIST JESUS

"One of the bitterest moments of my life," said a missionary recently, "was when an earnest young Buddhist boy said to me, 'I want to believe in Christ, but I have never seen Him in those who profess Him. How can I believe in someone Whom I have not seen?'"

Would that lad have spoken in the same way had he known us? At all costs we must have the fullness of the indwelling Christ.

THE HOLY SPIRIT'S CHIEF WORK

The chief work of the Holy Spirit is to reveal Christ. How often we have prayed, "O God fill us with Thy Holy Spirit." We hear the prayer again and again at prayer meetings with little apparent result. Why is it? Is God to blame? Are *we* to blame?

"He shall glorify ME," said Christ, "for He shall receive of Mine and show it unto you." So then it is the work of the Holy Spirit to see that Christ is "formed within" us (Galatians 4:19). If then God answers our prayer and fills us with His Holy Spirit, we shall indeed be wonderfully conscious of the indwelling Christ. So will others be!

Now let the writer confess that he has often spoken about this doctrine and has read the Gospel and Epistles of St. John again and again without really appropriating this indwelling of Christ. The Lord Jesus has been within the heart for many years, "for if any have not the Spirit of Christ, he is none of His" (Romans 8:9). But the Lord Jesus was not filling the whole heart. There must be many believers in a like condition. Many have told me by letter and lip how they have agonized for this Victorious Life for 20, 30, even 40 years, without getting it. "For years I have agonized for this," wrote a clergyman to me. "What a difference it would make to my ministry! What a blessing it would prove to my people! Tell me how I can get it." How then can this fullness of blessing be secured? Only by letting Jesus Christ do what all our strugglings and strivings have failed to do.

We cannot overcome any sin by trying to do so. Christ only has conquered sin. He conquered it not for Himself — the devil had nothing in Him. He conquered it for you — for me! He doesn't ask me to do what He has already done. He does ask me to enter into His victory. We cannot grow by trying to grow. We cannot grow in grace by trying to grow in grace. It is all of Christ. How?

A DIVINE SECRET REVEALED

St. Paul says that there was a great secret hidden from age to age, but which it pleased God to reveal to him. What is it? "Christ IN YOU the hope of glory" (Colossians 1:27). "God was pleased to make known what is the riches of the glory of this mystery" — that He "may present every man perfect in Christ Jesus" (Colossians 1:28). Heathen religions have tried to bring their gods down to man — with the passions and vices of humanity! Our Lord came Himself and lived as a man: Emmanuel, "God with us"! Isn't it a stupendous thought that the high and lofty One that inhabits eternity, Whose Name is HOLY, should dwell not only in the high and holy place, but also "with him that is of a contrite and humble spirit — to revive [give new life to] the humble"? (Isaiah 57:15). Christ came to take us into Himself, and He Himself comes into us. He the Head; we His body. He the Vine: we the branches. Thus His life is IN US.

This is the "overcoming life," the life more abundant, the Victorious Life. How do Christians come to understand how to enter in? Many, like the writer himself, found the "secret" entrance through careful and prayerful study of Romans 6:3-11. "Are ye ignorant that all we who are baptized into Christ Jesus…?" What is it to be baptized into Christ Jesus? Again and again Paul reminds believers that they are "in Christ" — that they have "put on Christ." When does this happen? It takes place the moment a man, woman or child accepts Jesus Christ as Savior. Water baptism is a rite ordained by Christ which expresses baptism into Jesus Christ.

WHEN CHRIST IS RECEIVED

This new life — the life from above, the regenerate life — is a miraculous life, and it is the result of our being taken into Christ. The instant we received Christ as Savior, we were made part of Him. In Paul's day, a man was apparently baptized immediately he believed in Christ. So Paul takes baptism to illustrate or even prove the fact that a believer is taken into Christ. We are made "members" of Christ — a part of His body. So that Christ's life becomes our life, and we can say, "Christ Who is our life" (Colossians 3:4). Get hold of this truth.

An old lady who, late in life, accepted Christ as her Savior, was always praising God and talking about her Savior. One day a friend said, "You seem pretty confident about this Savior of yours! I wouldn't be too sure about it, if I were you. Suppose the Lord should let you slip through His fingers?" "But," said the old lady, "I am one of His fingers." Now she was perfectly right — she was indeed a member of Christ. We dare not say such a thing if it were not openly told us in Scripture.

It is all too wonderful for words. I, a poor sinner saved by grace, have been made a member of the Lord Jesus Christ Himself.

"I hope," said a critic of an address on this subject by the writer, "I hope the speaker is not making out that we are all little gods!" Far from it. But we do "make out" that we have a great God living in us and making us members of Himself.

BAPTIZED INTO CHRIST

"Are ye ignorant that all we who were baptized into Christ Jesus were baptized into His death?" Are we "ignorant" as to what this means? Here, again, the writer must plead guilty of failing for years to grasp the import of these words.

"In Adam all die" — yes, we are conscious enough of that — "who is a figure of Him that was to come" (Romans 5:14). This surely means that we must in some way share the death of Christ? Every believer went to death with Christ on the Cross. "I have been crucified with Christ," says Paul.

"We were buried, therefore, with Him through baptism into death" (Romans 6:4). St. Paul is thinking of baptism by immersion. This is a symbol of burial (which means *a previous death*). As the believer went right under the water, he realized that he was dead and buried. Dead as regards the old life — dead to sin. Sin has no power over a dead man. No "dominion" over him. "For he that is dead is freed from sin…. Reckon ye yourselves to be dead indeed unto sin… Sin shall not have dominion over you" (Romans 6:7).

But death could not "hold" Christ, nor can it hold us, if we are in Christ. After death and burial — what? "That like as Christ was raised from the dead through the glory of the Father, so we also might walk in newness of life" (Romans 6:4). Jesus Christ did not raise Himself: God raised Him. Over and over again we are told this: God raised Him from the dead. And all the mighty power which God exercised in raising Christ from the dead is at our disposal. And to think that we should for a moment imagine that our feeble struggles are also needed!

St. Paul longed that believers in his day should realize this. He prays for them that "having the eyes of your heart enlightened, ye may know what is the hope of His calling, what the riches of the glory of His inheritance in the saints, and what the exceeding greatness of His POWER TO US-WARD who believe." What power? "According to the working of the strength of His might which He wrought in Christ when He raised Him from the dead" (Ephesians 1:18). THAT POWER GOD OFFERS YOU.

A GIFT TO BE TAKEN

Isn't it wonderful? Can we grasp it? Paul, seeing the stupendous nature of this gift, cries, "I count all things but refuse, that I may gain Christ: …that I may know Him, and the power of His resurrection" (Philippians 3:8, 10). This mighty power in Christ is a gift to be "gained" by the removal of all hindrances.

How can we "know Him and the power of His resurrection"? Simply by being buried with Christ — being dead unto sin. That is, not only claiming forgiveness of our sins, but by God's help renouncing the world, the flesh and the devil — by forsaking all sin — and then looking to God in faith to raise us up to walk in newness of life.

Try to understand what death and resurrection meant to our Lord. There He is perfect God and perfect man nailed to the Cross. The sins of the world came upon Him. God cannot die, nor can He remain in contact with sin. So the Spirit of God in the perfect man "Jesus" forsook that body of clay. He "yielded up His spirit". And a dead *man* hangs upon the Cross. That perfect body is buried; and on the third day God raised Him from the dead. What happened? The Spirit of Christ came back into that dead human body and Christ Jesus rose again — once more perfect God and perfect man.

That is what God wishes to do for every man. When we can indeed "reckon ourselves to be dead unto sin" and "buried with Him by baptism into death"; then we can look to Christ *to put His Spirit into us* and to raise us up "to walk in newness of life." Then "our life" is no longer ours but is the Christ-Life. Not an imitation of Christ, but Christ Himself dwelling in our hearts by faith. Then we can humbly say with Paul, "I have been crucified with Christ, yet I live, and yet no longer I, but Christ liveth in me" (Galatians 2:20).

What a glorious privilege! What a tremendous responsibility! "It pleased God to reveal His Son IN me"! (Galatians 1:16).

WHEN SELF IS DEAD

Is all this difficult to understand? It is all there on the page of Scripture. But praise be to God, it is not necessary for us to understand *how* God works — but just to believe that He will (and does) perform this work in us.

The question is just this: Am I willing to give up all known sin and to put myself absolutely at the disposal of the Savior? — myself, my talents, my possessions, my work, my future? Am I willing to surrender myself entirely to Him? Dr. Wilbur Chapman for some time hesitated to trust his future career to Christ, although he was then a noted missioner. Dr. Meyer said, "Are you willing to be made willing?" Dr. Chapman told Christ he was *willing to be made willing.* At once every difficulty was removed. Yes, we must even surrender our surrender to Christ. Our Lord did not crucify Himself — nor bury Himself — nor can we crucify ourselves. But when we have emptied ourselves of "self," Christ will crucify us — and will "raise us up to walk in newness of life." The Cross for you and me is just I (self) crossed out.

The surrender must be absolute and entire. You remember the story of the goddess who, wishing to make her child Achilles immortal, dipped him beneath the waters of the river Styx. She succeeded with the exception of his ankles, by which she held him, thus preventing the water from laving that spot. His ankles were vulnerable and there he became mortally wounded. That fable has a moral truth.

There must be no part of us left unsurrendered in our burial with Christ through baptism unto death.

When Satan sees a man accept Christ as his Savior, he tries his level best to keep his hand upon some small part of him. He wants to have just a *little* control over us, so that he can bring about our downfall. He knows that if he can prevent full surrender, he will also prevent a Victorious Life.

HOW TO BE FILLED

A man "full of the Holy Spirit" is a mighty power — which power almost vanishes when even a little of our surrender is withdrawn. That power is also impossible when a little of our surrender to Christ is withheld. But if with "full and glad surrender" we yield ourselves to our blessed Master, He will come and fill us wholly with His Divine Presence.

Can we trust our all to Him, so that He may become "all in all" to us? "Jesus Christ is the Savior of *all* the life as well as the Savior of every life."

Chapter Eight: Surrender All To Christ

WHAT "ABSOLUTELY SURRENDERED TO GOD" REALLY MEANS, AND THE RESULTS THAT FOLLOW THIS ATTITUDE OF FAITH

We have again and again declared that before anyone can enter into the Victorious Life, two things are necessary — surrender and faith: man's part and God's part.

First of all, we must be willing to give up all known sin and all self-will and surrender ourselves entirely into God's hands. Then we must in faith look to God to sanctify us. So the entrance in may be summed up in two simple mottoes: —

LET GO AND LET GOD

Now it is extraordinary how difficult it is to make people understand what "surrender" is. And when they *do* understand, it is still more difficult to persuade them that it is for their good!

The writer sent a business letter to a Christian friend a week ago and in it put this question: "May I ask if you are entirely surrendered to Christ?" He called round the following day. He had just taken offense because of the conduct of a fellow-Christian (who had been both courteous and right — but firm).

Irritation, censure and divergence from the truth were all exhibited in five minutes. Then as he left the room, he turned and said in a surprised tone, "By the way, what did you mean by that hint in your letter that I am not entirely surrendered to God? I *am* entirely surrendered to Him." It was quite obvious that he knew little about surrender. Yet he seemed perfectly satisfied with himself.

WHAT SURRENDER MEANS

Many readers of this paper may be equally satisfied. But many, we know, are yearning for a victory they do not possess, although they have sought it for many years.

Will you examine your surrender? What does it mean? If we wish to be entirely yielded up to Christ, we must leave three things with Him: the Past, the Future and the Present.

This involves the surrender of SELF — not merely of things. "Surrender your very selves unto God" (Romans 6:13, Weymouth). A cleric in the USA once said, "Do you know that Campbell Morgan came to this country and preached one sermon that destroyed 40 years of my sermons? For 40 years I had been preaching on the duty of sacrifice — the denying things to ourselves; giving up this and that. We practiced it in our family. We would give up butter one week and try to use the money in some way that God might bless. Another week we would give up something else, and so on. Campbell Morgan said that what we needed to give up, was not things but *self*: and that was the only thing we had not given up in our home. We had given up everything under the sun, but self. We were giving up so many things that we had become proud of our humility!" So let us look at self. Am I willing to surrender it entirely to God, and just "Let go"?

THERE IS THE PAST

1. "But," you exclaim, "the past is dead and gone." Oh, no; far from it! "The sins of the past are forgiven, but oh, what a weight they are about our necks!" said a worker for Christ. This ought not to be. Are we willing to let the past go?

A lady missionary who longed for Victory through Christ and confessed her deep yearning for it, was just broken-hearted over the matter. Why? "Because of the sins of the past," she replied. "But God has forgiven your past sins. They are blotted out. How can they hinder you?" "But you do not know the sort of failures I have made!" she moaned. "No — the past is too awful."

When she had surrendered her past, the blessing came. There is a hymn which runs, "When God forgives, He forgets." "For I will be merciful to their iniquities and their sins will I remember no more" (Hebrews 8:12; 10:17). Why, then, should *I* remember my past sins? Surely no good can possibly come of it?

THINGS THAT MAR SERVICE

A momentary recollection of what God has saved us from may add to our praise of Him. But haven't we enough to bless and praise His glorious name for, even without such backward glances? It is bad enough to have sinned in the past: but it is surely a terrible thing to allow past sins to mar present service.

When you have forgiven your child some wrong-doing, do you wish him to grieve over it — to be miserable over it for days, weeks, months, years? Yet many children of God are doing this. Self-examination has its place, but to wreck the present by mourning over the past is sin.

Look at Simon Peter. He denied our Lord with oaths and curses. Our Lord forgave him, reinstated him, and used him. The one of the eleven who fell the lowest was the very one chosen to be spokesman on the day of Pentecost. Nor did Peter allow his past fall to hamper him, for he accuses the Jews of the very sin he had himself committed.

"You denied Him," he cried. "You denied the Holy and Righteous One" (Acts 3:14). O let us thank God that the sins of the past are blotted out, and let us never grieve Him by spoiling the present by reproaching ourselves for the sad past. "Looking unto Jesus" must be our attitude. "Forgetting the things that are behind;… I press on toward the prize of the high calling of God in Christ Jesus" (Philippians 3:13).

THERE IS THE FUTURE

2. Are we willing to leave that entirely in God's hands? Many people seem to think that God will take advantage of them! That if they agree to obey all God's wishes, God will make them miserable. They cannot trust God to fill their lives with joy — so they seek their pleasures from the world, and sometimes from deliberate sin.

The Lord Jesus said to His disciples, "These things have I spoken unto you that My joy might remain in you, and that your joy might be full" (John 15:11). What things had He been speaking about? Why, just abiding in Christ and keeping His commandments. His joy — the very joy of God!

Could we desire anything more than that — better than that? Of course, if He dwells in us, and lives His life in us, we have His joy.

FROM TONIGHT, LORD

A wayward little boy climbed onto his father's knees one evening and said, "Father, from tonight I'm going to do all you ask of me." How did the father act? Did he think to himself, "Now I have that boy in my power. Now I have the chance of making his life miserable!" It is unthinkable. He drew the laddie closer to him and silently vowed he would do everything in his power to make that boy happy.

Is a God of Love going to take advantage of us, if we surrender our all to Him? Will He deign to remain in our debt? Remember, God has not only the will, but the power to make us supremely happy. There are our future plans. Does not God know what is best for us? Yet how unwilling believers often are to trust Him to do what is best.

When addressing a party of missionaries home on furlough last summer, the writer was struck by the miserable face of an elderly man. "Why is he so miserable?" "Oh," replied the chairman, "he longs to return to China to die in harness, but the committee refused to allow him to go back." A devoted servant of God — yet unwilling to leave his future in God's hands. The result was not fullness of joy — but misery. We might well pray, as one dear saint did, "Oh, God! do not let anyone here be afraid of Thee."

Are you afraid of God? Yes — if you know of anything you are not willing to give up, should God show you that it was His will you should do so.

> God knows, He loves, He cares;
> Nothing this truth can dim;
> He does the very best for those
> Who leave the choice to Him.

THEN THERE IS THE PRESENT

3. How will this be affected? All unlove, bitterness, irritability, pride, jealousy, resentment, censoriousness — all must go, really go. An active lady worker said to the writer, "That's easy enough for me, for I haven't an enemy in the world!" The next day she was limping. "I've fallen down," she explained. "I saw that horrid Miss K—— coming along and I didn't want to acknowledge her, and in looking the other way, I slipped off the curb and fell in the gutter!"

Now we may be sure that if there is anyone against whom we harbor any ill- feeling or resentment, or "owe a grudge" — anyone to whom we could not show Christian love and kindliness — we are not living the Victorious Life. Dr. Schofield once said, "If you have a sin in your life which you cannot let go, bring it to Jesus and let Him kill it." It may be some habit which others regard as harmless.

"Whenever you talk of surrender," said a man to the writer, "I always think of my pipe." Not a word had been said about smoking — but the pipe went. Forgive this remark — it is true or it would not be recorded here: You will find very few fully surrendered Christians whose consciences allow them to smoke.

One word of warning: Do not allow any fear of the future to rob you of present victory. "I've surrendered all to Christ," said a missionary at Keswick last summer, "And I am so happy. But I'm fearful what will happen when I get home." Do you see, the future was not really surrendered.

Dr. A. T. Pierson in his last address at Mildmay said, "Believe me as a dying man, no one ever obtained as much as he might have obtained from God." Why? Because God cannot give all He would until we surrender all we have — and are. If you find any difficulty in this matter — then just surrender your surrender to the Lord Jesus.

NOW IS THE DAY OF VICTORY

The present is the time for Victory. Let your aim ever be to glorify the Lord Jesus now. So many Christians let present opportunities slip by unused, because their minds are fixed upon something they are going to do *tomorrow* or next Sunday. School yourself to live in the present. How can Christ Jesus manifest forth His glory — Himself through me today — now, this very moment?

Perhaps the secret of Victory in Christ lies just here. God gives needed grace just when it is needed.

"Have you dying grace?" a lady asked Charles Spurgeon. "No, madam, and I do not want it now — but praise God, I have living grace," was his reply.

Surrender. Let go. Then look to Christ in faith. Let GOD ——.

Ask the Lord Jesus Christ to crucify you and to give you His Resurrection Life. In that delightful little book, *The Christian's Secret of a Happy Life*, there is a chapter on…

"HOW TO ENTER IN"

The way suggested is to pray, "Lord Jesus, I believe that Thou art able and willing to deliver me from all the care and unrest and sin of my Christian life. Thou didst die to set me free, not only in the future, but here and now. I believe that Thou art stronger than sin and canst keep me from yielding to it. Lord, I am going to trust Thee to keep me. I have tried keeping myself and have failed grievously. I am also helpless. So now I will trust Thee. I give myself to Thee. I keep nothing back. … And now I AM Thine.

"I believe that THOU dost accept this poor, weak, foolish heart; and that it has been taken possession of by Thee; and that Thou hast at this moment begun to work in me to will and to do of Thy good pleasure. I trust Thee utterly, I trust Thee now."

But be careful to remember that surrender is not simply making a promise to God to forsake sin and always to do His will. That would be living under the Law. Surrender is just turning over to God all that we are and have, *for Him to do with us* whatever He wishes. Surrendered Christians are often defeated, because they think they can carry out their good resolutions by God's help. No! Just hand yourself over to God, and then trust Christ to do His part. "He is able to keep."

It is not our surrender that gives us the victory. It is not even our faith! It is CHRIST HIMSELF — the Faithful One.

Surrender and trust, and Christ will never fail you.

Chapter Nine: Real Victory And False

REAL VICTORY AND ITS COUNTERFEIT

The Victorious Life is simply a life fully surrendered to God, with Christ dwelling within and in complete control — a life in which the only desire is to bring glory to Jesus Christ. It is the only truly happy life, yet Christians refuse to enter in, lest their lives should be made miserable!

THE JOY OF PERFECT TRUST

But is it a life filled with "crosses"? That is the idea that many Christians have — that where there is the choice between things agreeable and disagreeable, the unpleasant one must, of course, be chosen! Can we find anything of this in the Bible?

Paul is never tired of talking about the wonderful joy in his life. "Rejoice evermore!" "In everything give thanks." Yet what hardship and bitter persecution were his lot! If you love God and fully trust Him, the place in which you are is the happiest place in which you can possibly be; and the work you are doing is the very best for you. Of course, God may move you elsewhere or give you other work. That can be left to Him. But let Him be glorified in us NOW.

Crosses? Nowhere in the Bible do we read of crosses. Yet when our plans are upset, or the weather "spoils" our day, or sickness or bereavement alters our prospects, we are apt to say sadly (or cheerfully), "Well, I suppose this is my cross for today." It may not be murmuring, but merely what we call "resignation." There should be no such word as "resignation" in the vocabulary of the Christian. If God has complete control over us, nothing can happen contrary to His will. And is not His will the very best for us? Instead of resignation there should be glad acceptance. The feeling of our hearts should ever be, "I delight to do Thy will, O my God!" (Psalm 40:8). There can be no such thing as disappointment in the life of a man really living the Victorious Life. "My meat is to do the will of Him that sent me," (John 4:34) said our Lord. Can we say the same?

When we are transformed by the renewing of our mind, we shall prove every day that God's will is good and perfect; shall it not therefore be acceptable? (Romans 12:2.) How eagerly, how joyfully we should embrace it! Believers are nowhere called upon to bear crosses.

TAKING UP THE CROSS

We know, however, that Jesus Christ said: "If any man would come after Me, let him deny himself and take up his cross and follow Me" (Matthew 16:24); "Whosoever does not bear his cross and come after Me cannot be My disciple" (Luke 14:27). It is, then, our duty to take up the cross, but not to carry crosses. There is one cross for every one and for every day.

If you had seen a man in our Lord's day carrying a cross, you would know that it meant death to someone — probably for the man himself. The cross is always a sign of death. Before anyone can really follow Christ — really be a disciple, that is, a learner —

he must be dead with Christ and risen with Him. That is what Paul meant when he said, "I have been crucified with Christ: yet I live, yet no longer I, but Christ liveth in me" (Galatians 2:20). Someone has said, "It is one thing to be saved from the penalty of sin; it is another thing to follow Christ."

Dr. Griffith Thomas says that some Christians are monstrosities. They are no more like Christ twenty years after their conversion than they were when they began the Christian life. They are not "learning" of Him. They have not taken up the cross: have not been crucified with Christ. "The taking up of the cross is the end of crosses and the beginning of discipleship," said Mr. C. G. Trumbull.

Do let us get hold of this fact: that our Lord wishes us always to be full of joy — always, everywhere, under all circumstances.

A gloomy, miserable-looking Christian stood outside a mission. "Will you come into our service tonight?" he asked of a passer-by. The stranger gave him one swift glance, and replied (as he hurried off), "No, thank you! I've troubles enough of my own!" Are we surprised?

A life of Victory is a life of Trust; and must be always full of Joy. Such a life glorifies Christ.

WHAT REAL VICTORY MEANS

But let us be quite clear as to what the Victorious Life is. For the devil does all he can to entice us to accept a counterfeit Victory — that is, a "victory" which we think we are getting ourselves by our own efforts.

Take the question of bad temper or irritability. Many Christians pride themselves on the fact that they exercise such self-control that their temper "never gets the better of them." By this they mean that they never *show* it. Now the Victorious Life is not one which merely makes our outward actions right. It is a life which gives victory in the inner realm of the heart, so that our very desires are right. To want to do wrongful things and to restrain from doing them is not real victory. The wonderful thing is that God takes the "want to" out of our very hearts, and we long only to do His will.

No doubt most of our readers have heard the story of the old Quaker lady who apparently never lost her temper. Under the most trying circumstances she was quite unruffled. A friend once commented on this, and said to her, "I cannot for the life of me understand how you always keep so delightfully sweet. Why, if the things happened to me which happen to you, I should just boil over with rage; but *you* never do." The old Quaker lady quietly replied, "Perhaps I do not boil over, my dear, but thou dost not know what boiling is going on inside." Now that is not victory. There is no victory in keeping our sinful feelings from expressing themselves. We may do that simply because we are ashamed to let others know how sinful we are. Moreover, it does not require the grace of God to enable a man to hide his temper. A shop assistant in a drapery establishment will do that all day long — or he might lose his job. A business man will do it to get an order. A "gentleman" will do it to avoid "bad form." A Society lady does it for social reasons. But this is not the Victorious Life.

WHEN THE MIRACLE HAPPENS

An American speaker tells the following story to illustrate real victory. A lady missionary who had surrendered all to Christ but had never looked to Him for complete victory, found her temper not improved by the Tropics. She was much distressed about her failures, and her struggles against them seemed in vain. However, a friend showed her that there was victory through simple faith in Christ, and she claimed this victory as a gift from God. Writing to this friend some time afterwards, she told of the wonderful thing that had happened in her spiritual life. "I wanted to write to you at first, but I was afraid it would not last," said she. "But it has lasted. Do you know that for three months not only have I not once slammed the door in the face of any of these stupid Indian servants that used to get on my nerves so, but *I have not even wanted to* — not once." Now that is victory.

We must recognize it as a miracle. No good resolutions, no will-power, can alter our likes and dislikes. But God can. He can take away from us all desire to do sinful things. Bad temper is not the only sin of Christian people, and many Christians have the sweetest of dispositions. The best test of all is in the matter of love. Do we love our "enemies" — those who despitefully use us or persecute us? Do we nevertheless love them? "If you want him to love you, you must knock him down," said a worker to the writer, speaking about a friend. What is your first feeling when men injure you or oppose you? Is it a spontaneous outflowing of love towards them? Or do we first find it necessary to shoot up an urgent, earnest prayer that we *may* love them, and may not feel resentment? Do we eagerly welcome opposition, unkindness, rudeness, discourtesy (and suchlike) towards us, as opportunities of showing that the love of Christ is filling our hearts? It is in small matters that we are tested.

UNDER THE LOVE OF CHRIST

How often we hear earnest Christian people saying, "I cannot love the unlovable." No; it is humanly impossible for human love to do this. We cannot make ourselves love another. Human love is kindled only by what it thinks is lovable. The love of God — Christ's love — embraces all and sees everyone to be lovable. When Christ dwells richly in our hearts, we shall love even our enemies. There is victory when "the love of God is shed abroad in our hearts" (Romans 5:5), to the expulsion of all unlove — then and then only. There we have a definition of real victory.

FACTS THAT HELP LOVE

At first such a thing seems beyond our highest hopes. Many regard it as an impossibility. So it is to man. But with God this thing is possible. It is a miracle, and God works miracles every day. Fellow-Christian, do not give up the idea of living the Victorious Life because it seems impossible to you. Just yield yourself to Christ, and trust Him to work in you both to will and to do His good pleasure (Philippians 2:13).

Many reply that their faith is not strong enough. Why, faith the size of a grain of mustard seed is enough if you will exercise it. May we give you two FACTS to help your love and faith? Remember that:

1. The Lord Jesus dearly loves all those whom we might regard as unlovable: loves them every bit as much as He loves us. Can we not see them with the eyes of Christ?

"Do not be afraid of me, mum," said a filthy, wild-looking tramp to a lady who crossed the road to avoid meeting him. "Do not be afraid of me, mum. My mother was a woman." "Do not refuse to love me," the unlovable might exclaim. "The Lord Jesus LOVES ME."

2. The most unlovable person — the most loathsome and repulsive creature — becomes lovable even in *our* eyes when the love of God is shed abroad in HIS heart. If

you really want to love him, pray earnestly for him and try to save his soul. If he is a Christian — but "nastily saved," as the Lancashire man put it — pray that he may get the Victorious Life; send him this book and continue in prayer. The writer has had the joy of pointing to Christ as their Savior most revolting men and women, in whom every vestige of beauty appeared to be stamped out by drunkenness and vice. He has met them a week after, new creatures in Christ Jesus. A miraculous transformation has taken place in an incredibly short time. Is he — she — unlovable in your eyes? Then just think what that one may become when the love of God reaches him or her.

LIBERATING THE ANGEL

Michael Angelo lingered before a rough block of marble so long that his companion remonstrated. In reply, Michael Angelo said with enthusiasm, "There's an angel in that block and I'm going to liberate him!" Ah, what unbounding love would manifest itself in us towards the most unlovable — the most vile — if only we saw what they might become, and in our enthusiasm for souls we cried out, "There's the image of Christ — marred, scarred, well-nigh obliterated — in that dear fellow, and I'm going to make that man conscious of it."

A fable declares that a gallant prince kissed a serpent and it became a lovely princess. Fact shows us that when "kissed" by love, the vilest may become beautiful; the "serpent" become a saint.

"What are the outward and visible signs of the Victorious Life?" asked a young evangelist of the writer. The answer to that question would describe real victory. Briefly we would say: Everything contrary to love is expelled from the heart and life. Read the closing words of Chapter Three, and you will see what Divine LOVE can do — or rather, what LOVE DOES in scores and hundreds of lives. It drives out impatience, unkindness, jealousy, envy, boasting, self-assertion, pride, folly, selfishness, self-seeking, anger, irritability, bad temper, fretfulness, malice, uncharitable remarks, complaining, censoriousness, despair, anxiety, despondency, backbiting, repeating damaging information even if it is true. ALL THESE WE CALL RESPECTABLE SINS — or ever refuse to regard them as sins at all! God help us! So long as any of these — even one of these — remains, there is no victory for us. When a fully surrendered Christian looks in simple faith to Christ and asks Him to fill the whole heart, HE, CHRIST, who is love, "perfect love," banishes every one of these vile "respectable" sins, which we have been regarding as LITTLE sins, but which mar our work and hinder our usefulness. Are we willing to allow the Lord Jesus to do this for us?

Chapter Ten: This Life Is A Gift

THE VICTORIOUS LIFE IS ALL A GIFT RECEIVED IN FAITH AND IS NOT OBTAINED BY STRIVING AND STRUGGLING

This victorious life is a *gift* and is not to be secured by any struggling or striving on our part. It is not a thing to be attained to by long and laborious effort. It is not a thing we can reach gradually by growing more and more like Christ. This must be clearly seen.

All life comes as a gift. Our physical life — we just receive it. Our spiritual life is "the gift of God" (Romans 6:23). The life "more abundant" is a gift. We cannot receive a gift *gradually*. There may be hesitation or delay in taking it, there may be a struggle before we are willing to receive it. But a gift is accepted not gradually, but in a moment. It is obtained not attained.

The Victorious Life, then, can be received by a definite act. There is, of course, a "growth in grace" in the man who is wholly sanctified — a going on to perfection as his capacity increases.

But "this life is in His Son" (1 John 5:11). When we accept the Son as the Lord of all our being, we receive (as a gift) the LIFE. It is something God does for us — IN US. There is, however, often a long struggle before surrender. Many a Christian has a terrific struggle before he is willing to yield himself wholly to Christ.

But this is before the Victorious Life begins. Victory begins only when struggling ceases. The moment you surrender yourself entirely to Christ and look to Him in faith to dwell in your entire heart, that moment He comes and takes control of you.

TAKING CHRIST AT HIS WORD

This indwelling is quite independent of any feeling on your part. It is independent of any ideas of your own as to how He should manifest His presence. You must just take Him at His word and rest upon that — not upon any feeling. You may feel a wonderful thrill of joy. You may feel nothing unusual. Can you trust His promise? Every Christian has to decide whether he will be wholly consecrated to God, or whether he will remain content to live the Christian life on a low level — which is ALWAYS a powerless one, and a perilous one.

THE CRISIS AND THE PROCESS

This DECISION FOR HOLINESS is a crisis in a Christian's life. With it comes an instantaneous revelation of God to him, that Christ can be all in all; that Christ can and does give Victory over all known sin: not gradually but INSTANTANEOUSLY. "Having therefore these promises let us cleanse ourselves from all defilement of the flesh and spirit perfecting holiness in the fear of the Lord" (2 Corinthians 7:1). The tense in the Greek shows that this is done at once as a definite and decisive act. This is the *crisis* of sanctification.

But after this definite step of whole-hearted dedication of one's self to God, there comes a life-long process of sanctification — a going on from strength to strength, from glory to glory. A *process* under which the believer becomes more and more conformed to the life and character of Christ.

WHERE MANY BLUNDER

We have dwelt long on this point because the mistake the writer made (and which many of his readers have probably made) was to try to experience the process without first experiencing the crisis of sanctification. There is little — if any — growth in grace until we have claimed by surrender and faith the "life that is Christ." Have you experienced the crisis? Have you obeyed the command, "Sanctify in your hearts Christ as Lord"? (1 Peter 3:15.) Christ is in the heart of every believer as "JESUS" — Savior. But is He indeed Lord? It is not a question of re-conversion, it is just a question of recognizing the indwelling Christ as Master in His own house — my heart.

Remember, however, that surrender alone, that is, "decision," is not enough. That is only our part in giving up all hindrances to blessing. If surrender sufficed, then we should make sanctification to be a mere act of the *will*. We are neither saved nor sanctified by what we give up, but by what we receive. It is "the very God of peace Who sanctifies us wholly." After surrendering ourselves, we must look to Christ to crucify us and to raise us from the death to sin to live the resurrection life.

Let go — surrender: then "let God" do His part. But God will not allow any effort or struggle on your part to help Him. Salvation is entirely a gift of God: entirely of grace.

Now salvation is a threefold work: Past, Present and Future. Justification, sanctification and glorification.

ETERNAL LIFE A GIFT

And it is all by faith. You cannot earn, or get, any part of it by your own efforts or struggles. "For by grace have ye been saved through faith; and that not of yourselves; it is the gift of God: not of works, that no man should glory" (Ephesians 2:8-9. See Romans 11:6). Paul goes even further than this. "Ye are severed from Christ, ye who would be justified by the law" (*i.e.*, effort) (Galatians 5:4). When a man accepts Christ as a Savior from the penalty of sin, he learns that Christ's forgiveness is absolutely and entirely through faith. Sorrow for sin, good resolutions, and tears, often accompany repentance. But repentance does not save a man. We have to leave that to Christ. Justification is entirely the work of Christ; and faith in Him secures this salvation. We can do nothing whatever to gain or merit it. We accept it as a gift.

When Christ shall come again, we shall be glorified. This is the future of salvation. In this work of glorification, we know we can do absolutely nothing. It is all of Christ.

LIFE MORE ABUNDANT — A GIFT

What about the present? That is, our sanctification (which is first a crisis and then a process). We have called this the Victorious Life.

When we claim it by faith, there is the crisis. When we live it day by day, there is the process.

Our Blessed Savior justified us, and will glorify us by His own power entirely. Does He need or demand our help in the matter of sanctification? How much will our struggling and striving or agonizing avail against the devil? Absolutely nothing. He is far stronger than we are. Does Christ, the Almighty Savior, need my struggles to assist Him? Remember, our weakness will never be made strong. A dear Christian lady in an address on this subject said, "*Is* not the Christian life a long struggle? But thank God He gives us power to struggle!" Exactly the reverse is true. While we struggle, He cannot help us as He would, we limit and restrain His power.

The Victorious Life is simply salvation in the present; and all salvation is entirely of grace — entirely of Christ — a GIFT. "As therefore ye received Christ Jesus the Lord, *so* walk in Him" (Colossians 2:6). How did we receive Him? By simple faith. How are we to walk in Him; that is, live a Victorious Life? By simple FAITH. "If we live by the Spirit (*i.e.*, eternal life is ours as a gift by the power of the Spirit), by the Spirit let us also walk" (Galatians 5:25). Do get hold of this truth: we may not, cannot in the smallest degree, share with Christ the work of accomplishing any part of our salvation. Yet so many of us imagine that in the matter of sanctification we must "paddle our own canoe."

TRUST, NOT STRUGGLE

Blaze it out in letters of fire, that Christ can, and will, save us from the power of sin every day and every hour without struggling, striving and agonizing. If you struggle, you do not trust.

Have not most of us learned from our own experience how useless our struggles are? Some besetting sin gets the better of us. How we struggle against it! How we agonize in prayer over it — even "standing on the promises of God" as we think. Yet we get up from our knees only to fall again and again into sin! Christ's promises cannot give us power. Even faith cannot save us. Only Jesus Christ can do it.

Are we willing to look to Him and trust Him to conquer our sin for us? He has conquered sin and Satan. HE — the Conqueror — is willing to come and fill our hearts and be OUR LIFE. "Sin shall NOT have dominion over you," says God's Word (Romans 6:14). We may be "more than conquerors" — not by struggling, but entirely "through HIM that loved us" (Romans 8:37). What does it mean? Not only that the besetting sin will be conquered — but the very *desire* to sin will be taken away.

Only Christ can do this. It is a wonderful *miracle*. Some of us have proved this.

A well-known character in London has recently passed to the life beyond the grave. He was a notorious drunkard, but marvelously saved by Christ. For weeks after his conversion he had an intense desire to drink coming upon him with almost overwhelming power. He fought and struggled against the temptation. Although an untutored man, he felt that God had a better way than this. Kneeling in a field in North London, he cried out, "O God, can't you make a better job of me than this?" And God at once took away all desire to drink and the craving never returned.

The saintly Bishop Moule confessed in an address to confirmation candidates that a severe and terrible temptation assailed him in the street. He added, "I stopped dead and said quickly, 'Holy Spirit, come it.' Then I said to myself, 'The evil spirit, who is strong, is here. But I have the Holy Spirit, Who is Almighty, and I can leave Him to deal with the temptation.'"

Christ does not give us power apart from Himself. "All power is given unto ME" said Christ. "And lo! I am *with you* all the days" (Matthew 28:18, 20).

"For if while we were yet enemies we were reconciled to God through the death of His Son, much more being reconciled shall we BE SAVED BY HIS LIFE" (Romans 5:10) —*i.e.*, by the living Christ living in us. He will keep us safe from the power of sin, if we will let Him. Christ can do this. He will do it. He does it in every life that trusts Him to do it.

SELF-EFFORT MEANS FAILURE

We have proved by our own experience that we cannot be good by self-effort. Stop trying to be good. Stop struggling, and let the Savior do the great work for you. He came "to save His people from their sins" (Matthew 1:21). We can reckon on Him. "The promise is to him that worketh not, but believeth" (Romans 4:5). "It is GOD that worketh in you both to will and to do" (Philippians 2:13).

"My God shall supply all your need according to His riches in glory in Christ Jesus" (Philippians 4:19). Dear Christian, is your most urgent NEED just deliverance from this awful sin? How you have struggled and agonized! Yet the supply is IN YOU!

"Ah," you cry, "but you do not know how weak I am." No — but we thank God for your weakness. "My grace is sufficient for you — for My POWER is made perfect in weakness" (2 Corinthians 12:9). Your weakness, which has been your lament, shall be your highest glory.

"Most gladly therefore will I glory in my weakness, that the power of Christ may cover me" (2 Corinthians 12:9). We can be kept *only* "by the power of God through faith" (1 Peter 1:5). "Thanks be unto God which giveth us the Victory through our Lord Jesus Christ" (1 Corinthians 15:57).

PRESSING TOWARDS THE GOAL

Does this mean, then, that we need do nothing but sit down and sing psalms? Far, far from it! We have been speaking only of the matter of our own personal salvation — past, present, future. ALL of this must be accepted as a gift. But when Christ comes into the heart, He comes with power. "Ye shall be endued with power [Greek: *dynamis*, like 'dynamite' or 'dynamo'] from on high" (Luke 24:49). Power is a thing which makes itself felt. "Woe is unto me if I preach not the Gospel!" (1 Corinthians 9:16) says Paul, whose teaching we have given above.

"We cannot but speak the things which we saw and heard" (Acts 4:20). Struggling and agonizing play no part in our personal salvation. They merely hinder and hamper it. But we are in the midst of a wicked generation. The devil is strongly entrenched in the lives of men and women around us. They encourage temptation and welcome it. They find their greatest enjoyment in sin. They do not want to conquer sin. So Paul, who declares that salvation is all of faith, also warns us that we have a fight to wage, a race to win, a wrestling to engage in. "The God of peace shall bruise Satan" says Paul: but it is under OUR FEET (Romans 16:20). The enemy's Conqueror working in you will make the struggle short and decisive. He Who made peace FOR you, works peace IN you. All our powers of body, soul and mind are to be brought to bear upon this great task. In this "race" Paul presses on towards "the goal for the prize of the upward calling of God in Christ Jesus" (Philippians 3:14). What *is* this prize? Certainly not forgiveness of sin, or power over temptation, or the gift of eternal life. The "runner" has already laid aside "every weight and sin" (Hebrews 12:1), or he would not be in the race at all. No! The "prize" is not eternal life — that is a gift. The race, the fight, the wrestling (against the rulers of the darkness of this world — Ephesians 6:12) is what we experience when we are fellow-workers with Christ, who came to destroy the works of the devil. (See Galatians 5:19-21 for some of them.) Never forget that even in all this outward activity, it is fruitful only as Christ inspires *it* and empowers *us*.

OUR LORD'S EXAMPLE

Our Lord Himself "strove" in this way. He it was Who resisted unto blood, striving against sin (Hebrews 12:4). But HE had not to struggle against any inward desire or any temptation to sin. HE did not find it hard to be good.

To sum up — there may be fierce conflicts in a Christian man's heart before he is willing to surrender himself entirely to Christ. And there IS a great conflict to be waged against the devil, in our efforts to snatch others out of his bondage. But the Victorious Life, as it concerns our own souls, in one free from all struggle. "He is able to keep."

When the writer was a boy, he spent much time walking on stilts. He gained considerable freedom in their use. But although he "walked" it required constant effort, and sometimes struggle, to keep from falling. A little thing brought collapse. Contact with anyone usually meant a fall. That is a picture of the "walk" of many a Christian. Effort, struggle, slow progress, constant falls and new starts, and an almost total inability to help anyone else.

It is an unnatural "walk." Claim the Victorious Life — Victory through the Indwelling Christ — and the Christian walk will be found as easy as "walking on our feet."

Some shell-shocked soldiers with normal limbs believe that they are unable to walk — and they cannot. The skillful physician makes them *believe* they can walk — and they do. The power of Christ to "walk by faith" is at our disposal. Can we not trust Him?

A little girl of 13 was asked what difference the Victorious Life meant to her in times of temptation. After a little pause she replied, "Before I saw this truth, I used to argue with the tempter, and he usually got the better of me. But now, when he knocks at the door of my heart, I say, 'Lord Jesus, will you answer the door for me?' And when Satan sees the Lord Jesus within, he says, 'I'm sorry; I think I've come to the wrong house' — and he flees."

HOW THE VICTORY COMES

And what is true of our Victory over temptation through Christ alone is also true of the warfare we wage with the "works of the devil" around us. It is Christ — and not we ourselves — Who wins the Victory.

"What do you consider the most dangerous heresy of today?" was a question asked of the Editor of the *Sunday School Times*. He passed by Christian Science, spiritism, higher criticism and other "isms," and gave this answer: "The most dangerous heresy is the emphasis that is being given by professing Christians on *what we do for God*, instead of on *what God does for us*."

In our work for the Master let us remember that it is not we who are doing His work, but HE Who is working through us.

This being so, every Christian who is living the Victorious Life will be much in prayer and in communion with God over the pages of His Holy Word.

Before we bring this chapter to a close we ought just to ask what effect the Victorious Life in us will have on others. So far, we have been dealing with ourselves. If we stopped there, we should still exclaim, "It's worth having." But we are saved to serve. And every one of the many letters sent to the writer asking for help has come from Christians; from men and women trying to work for Christ, yet not equipped for service.

Dr. Temple, the new Bishop of Manchester, said at his enthronement, a few weeks ago, "Remember that the converting power of the Church does not depend chiefly on the eloquence of its preachers, or the perfectness of its organization. It depends on the degree in which men see in the lives of Christians the evidence of the power of the love of Christ." That is it. And when men see that "the love of Christ shed abroad in our hearts" has such power that it has killed those sins in us which were so distressing to our friends, then they begin to think.

LOVE, THE CONQUEROR

No one is beyond the reach of love. The power of Divine Love is infinite. In the days of the American war, there lived at Ephrata, a plain Baptist minister, Peter Miller, who enjoyed the friendship of Washington. There also dwelt in that town one Michael Wittman, an evil-minded man who did all in his power to abuse and oppose that minister. But Michael Wittman was involved in treason and was arrested, and sentenced to death. The old preacher started out on foot and walked the whole seventy miles to Philadelphia that he might plead for that man's life! He was admitted into Washington's presence and begged the life of the traitor. "No, Peter," said Washington, "I cannot grant you the life of your friend." "My friend!" exclaimed the preacher, "he is the bitterest enemy I have!" "What?" cried Washington. "You have walked seventy miles to save the life of an enemy? That puts the matter in a different light. I will grant the pardon." And he did. And Peter Miller took Michael Wittman from the very shadow of death, back to his own home in Ephrata — but he went no longer as an enemy but as a friend. And so it came to pass that LOVE brought a reviler from the foot of the gallows to the foot of the cross.

Christian worker, listen! Are you getting the success you would like to see in your work for Christ? Are you getting *any* apparent success? If not, is it not worthwhile — for your own sake, for your work's sake, for the Savior's sake, for lost sinners' sake — to enter the life of Victory?

Surrender: Faith: Taking: Praising the Giver.

Chapter Eleven: Not Sinless Perfection

HOW THE DEVIL USES THE BOGEY OF "SINLESS PERFECTION" TO SCARE AWAY MANY SINCERE SOULS FROM SEEKING A LIFE OF HOLINESS

Have we really grasped the fact that the Victorious Life is a gift from God? We may think of it as "the fullness of the Holy Spirit," or we may think of it as Jesus Christ dwelling in the heart. Personally, the writer finds the greatest help from the fact of the indwelling Christ, and the consciousness of this indwelling.

After all, the Holy Spirit's chief work is to take of the things of Christ, and show them to us.

HOW TO GET A GIFT

But however we may regard it, the Victorious Life is a gift. "If ye being evil know how to give good gifts to your children, how much more shall your Heavenly Father give the Holy Spirit to them that ask Him?"

"If thou knewest the gift of God," said our Lord to a sinful woman, "and Who it is that saith to thee, 'Give Me to drink,' thou wouldest have asked of Him and He would have given thee living water" (John 4:10).

Now what must I do to secure a gift? Just take it. If a gift is offered me for the asking, will it please the giver if, instead of taking the gift, I spend long weeks, or months, or years begging and praying and agonizing for it?

Would it give pleasure to a father and mother if their children sat up all night agonizing in prayer for the Christmas gift they had promised to give them?

If they did such a thing, their "agonizing" would have absolutely nothing to do with their receiving the gifts. One could well imagine the distressed father telling his children that if they didn't cease their petitions and get to bed and trust him, they should get no gifts at all!

Jesus Christ is the great Christmas Day Gift. "Thanks be unto God for His unspeakable gift" (2 Corinthians 9:15). That gift is ours. Someone has said, "Our Lord wants our lives on earth to be one long Christmas Day of receiving His gift of Himself as our victory."

We do not need to "agonize" about it; we do not need to work for it. Provided we are wholly surrendered to God, we have simply to "receive," "take" the Gift of Christ Himself.

But did not Jesus Christ tell His disciples "to tarry in Jerusalem until [they were] endued with power from on high"? Yes, He did. "Wait," said He, "for the promise of the Father." But that was *before* Pentecost.

READY FOR OUR ACCEPTANCE

We never hear of the disciples after Pentecost telling believers to "wait" for this gift. In fact, we read in the 10th chapter of the Acts that the gift of the Holy Spirit fell upon "all them that heard the word," while St. Peter was yet speaking to the household of Cornelius, although none of them was yet baptized. The Holy Spirit was given to Gentiles without delay, on simple faith in Jesus Christ. There is no need today to wait at all. If we fulfill the conditions, we can claim the gift.

The earliest disciples did not at first appreciate the value and necessity of this gift. Our Lord seems to have told "more than 500 brethren" to "tarry ye in the city, until ye be clothed with power from on high." Yet only 120 obeyed the command, and consequently only 120 received the gifts on the day of Pentecost — the gift meant for all.

Let us today make no mistake about this. Our Lord is longing to fill every believer with His Holy Spirit. Christ is desirous of dwelling in our entire hearts by faith. Not until we have surrendered our wills to Him and have yielded our bodies to Him as well as our souls can He fill us with Himself.

This is what St. Paul means when he prays "that He would grant you to be strengthened by His Spirit with power penetrating to your inmost being" (Ephesians 3:16, Weymouth). "That ye may be filled unto all the fulness of God" (Eph. 3:19), "till we all attain unto the measure... of the fullness of Christ" (4:13), "the fullness of Him that filleth all in all" (1:23).

CHRIST IN HIS FULLNESS

It is very wonderful that He should be willing to come. But it is a glorious thing that He should be willing to take absolute responsibility in our lives, because He cannot make a mistake, and He cannot fail.

It seems incredible that any believer should refuse such a gift. Again we urge you — receive Him in His fullness by faith. Do not wait for or expect any "thrill," any "ecstasy." You may feel one, and you may not. But take Christ at His word, and believe that He has come into your heart to be your life. Then rely upon Him to supply all your need.

"Behold, I stand at the door and knock; if any man hear My voice and open the door, I will come in to him" (Revelation 3:20).

Bear in mind that Christ is already in the heart of every believer — even in the heart of one who is only following afar off. But in so many cases He is not filling the *whole* heart. He has only partial possession; He has not complete control. There are often chambers of the heart which are shut against Him. And not only closed, but with a lodger within, and that lodger a burglar waiting his time to gain entrance to other rooms within. "If any man… open the door."

We Christians sometimes sing:

> *O Jesus, Thou art standing*
> *Outside the fast closed door,*
> *In lowly patience waiting*
> *To pass the threshold o'er:*
> *Shame on us, CHRISTIAN brothers,*
> *His name and sign who bear:*
> *Oh, shame — thrice shame upon us,*
> *To keep Him standing there.*

And with the great majority of believers this is true of some part of the heart.

But it isn't so much the "shame" as the utter folly of it. For we know that He wishes to gain access to the whole of our hearts simply to bring richest blessing.

Paul implores the Roman Christians, "Yield yourselves unto God." He himself did so, and "heard His voice," with no closed door between — words unutterable; he felt joy unspeakable and full of glory, and in the fullness of his heart he cries, "Thanks be unto God for His unspeakable gift."

TEMPTATION AND FAILURE

"Is it possible to lose the Victorious Life?" is a question often asked. Indeed, it is possible. Temptation will certainly come, and failure may occur. A great Christian leader of men told the writer, a few days ago, how he had sometimes temporarily lost the victory. "But," said he, "whenever I've failed, it has always been through the sin of worrying." Yet there *need* be no failure. We have a perfect Savior. When we look back upon a break in this wonderful communion with Christ, we shall always have to confess that the failure need not have occurred.

SINLESS PERFECTION?

There are many saintly souls who openly declare that they never sin. They claim sinless perfection. They also claim that St. John teaches such a thing.

"We know that whosoever is begotten of God sinneth not, but He that was begotten of God (*i.e.*, Jesus Christ) keepeth him, and the evil one toucheth him not" (1 John 5:18). "Whosoever is begotten of God doeth no sin, because His seed (Jesus Christ) abideth in Him, and he cannot sin, because he is begotten of God" (1 John 3:9).

These statements refer not to single acts of sin, but to habitual sin. The tense used in the Greek does not imply that he cannot commit one definite act of sin, but that he cannot continue sinning; he cannot make a practice of sinning, or frequently repeat acts of sin; it is not his habit to sin. John is here speaking of known and voluntary sins, not of sins of infirmity or the falling short of the glory of God.

TENDENCY OR POSSIBILITY

Any man can sin. Any man can tell a lie. But we know what we mean when we say "An honest man cannot lie." We do not accuse George Washington of untruth when he declared "I cannot tell a lie!"

Every sin is against a good man's nature. We say the "wood cannot sink." this is true. The tendency of wood is always to float. Yet there is always the possibility of its sinking. The hand of a child may submerge it; when sodden with water it will lie on the bottom. When the child releases it, it floats again. When a man is living the victorious life — a life maintained and actually lived for him by the indwelling Christ — there is no tendency to sin. He desires always to do those things which are pleasing to God. But there is always the awful possibility of his sinning. He may become absorbed in the "world;" he may allow temptation to gain entrance and the hand of Satan upon him may drag him down. So long, however, as a man is fully surrendered to Christ and in full communion with Him, he cannot sin. But such a life is a moment by moment victory through a moment by moment faith. At any time he can partially withdraw his surrender or break his communion.

IN THE FATHER'S HANDS

A railway coach attached to a moving locomotive cannot stop. But at any moment the coupling may break and a stoppage ensue. Let us, however, repeat the statement that no man need commit any known and voluntary sin. "He is able to keep (guard) that which I have committed unto Him." The marginal reading is, "He is able to guard that which He hath committed unto me" (2 Timothy 1:12).

Both statements are true — praise be to God. "He is able to keep you from stumbling" (Jude 24).

Moreover our Lord Himself says of His followers, "No man shall snatch them out of My hand" … "And no one is able to snatch them out of the Father's hand" (John 10:28-29). And it is evident that our Savior has made every provision for guarding us lest we snatch ourselves out of His hand. The victory over sin which is secured from faith in Christ is, however, a moment by moment victory, and we must ever be "looking unto Jesus, the Beginner and Finisher of our faith" (Hebrews 12:2).

But thanks be to God, it isn't our "looking unto Jesus" that gives us the victory, but "His looking unto us." Peter could see the Lord despitefully used, and whilst looking at Him could curse and deny that he knew Him. But when our Savior "turned and looked upon Peter", no further denial was possible. Not our faith, but His faithfulness, is our safeguard.

The indwelling Christ is more than equal to all emergencies. So long as we trust Him fully and obey His smallest behest — so long shall we continue in victory. Why then should a man ever commit any voluntary sin? And why are we surprised when a fully sanctified Christian man tells us he never sins knowingly?

THE CAUSE OF FAILURE

The reason why even fully consecrated Christians are sometimes "overtaken in a fault" is because the majority of believers are not fully surrendered to the will of God. It would be safe to say that most Christians think very little of such sins as pride, anger, irritability, impatience, jealousy, self-seeking, un-love and suchlike. It is, therefore, such an easy thing for a man living the Victorious Life to fall into any of these sins; so many of his fellow- Christians do so unblushingly. And should he fall probably no one is in the least surprised at it! Moreover, no one but a wholly sanctified man can reprove such a one, or he will get the reply, "Physician, heal thyself," or even be referred to the "beam" and the "mote." In fact, only a "spiritual" man can help him. As St. Paul says, "If a man be overtaken in a fault, ye which are spiritual restore such a one" (Galatians 6:1).

Yet how easy it is to live the life of victory when in the company of wholly sanctified men and women! Oh, that there were many more such!

Why are we surprised when a man says he has reached a state of "sinless perfection"? Well, as a rule it is perfectly obvious to anyone but himself that he has not reached such an ideal. Sooner or later he is "overtaken in a fault." A saintly Christian man was recently arguing this point at a big luncheon party, and he claimed "sinless perfection" for himself. A fellow guest quietly said, whether in sincerity or as a test I know not, "Forgive me for saying so, but I was thinking you were a little greedy over your food!" "I've never yet been accused of greed over anything," flashed out the reply, "nor will I allow *you* to accuse me!" The warmth with which the retort was made raised a smile on the faces of all who heard it; practice and profession so evidently disagreed.

This little story proves both the statements made above. The "sinlessly perfect" man is sometimes irritable and angry, and when he is "overtaken in a fault" the average Christian is both amused and pleased!

SINS OR "INFIRMITIES"

The writer has had the privilege of meeting believers who claim "sinless perfection." He sat at a table with one at every meal for a week. To be quite frank he must acknowledge that he saw no outward trace of any sin. But this dear child of God took the writer to task in a kindly way for not preaching sinless perfection. This led to a long chat on the subject. My critic declared that a violent temper had been completely eradicated by the Lord Jesus. But he confessed to occasional feelings of impatience, irritability, and un-love. "These, however, I regard as *infirmities* and not as sins," said he.

My experience is that when men who profess sinless perfection are tackled about it, they always maintain that "little" things which *we* call sins are only infirmities. Brothers, take your infirmities to Christ, and let the "strength of Christ rest upon you" (2 Corinthians 12:9).

Sometimes, alas! great harm is done to the cause of Christ by men professing "sinless perfection," and boasting about it, even while allowing things in their lives which give the lie to their profession.

One such came to a friend of the writer to consult him on a business question. It was such an obvious case of sharp practice, if not of downright dishonesty, that my friend said in surprise, "How does such an act fit in with your profession of sinless perfection?" "Oh, business is business," came the impatient reply. "And I will have nothing to do with this piece of business, then," answered my friend.

We have dealt at length on this point because the devil uses the bogey of "sinless perfection" to scare away many sincere souls from seeking a life of holiness.

Our position is just this: So long as a fully surrendered believer simply trusts the Lord Jesus to keep him and to conquer his temptations for him, he need not commit willful sin. It is, therefore, quite legitimate and right and fitting that we should pray every morning, "Grant that this day we fall into no sin." "Vouchsafe, O Lord, to keep us this day without sin." And Christ is able to keep us even from stumbling (Jude 24, RV). And He does keep us just so long as we trust Him to do so.

Yet at any moment we may fall into sin. It is a moment by moment victory. Many who read this will gladly confess to have experienced this freedom from known sin for five minutes, for ten minutes, for an hour, and for a much longer time. But we shall all sadly confess that at times we willfully harbor a sinful thought and sometimes even commit knowingly some sinful act, falling under some sudden temptation. As we look back upon it, we are confident that we need not have sinned. It was "our own most grievous fault." Moreover, we find that the majority of such slips are due to unchristian acts or words of other believers. They are more often due to the low level of spiritual life in fellow-Christians than to the opposition of the world.

Do not condemn us, but claim victory for yourself and so raise the standard around us.

Claim victory for yourself, and show us by practical demonstration what a glorious life can be lived by one who is wholly Christ's.

Chapter Twelve: The Perils Of This Life

SOME OF THE PERILS THAT BESET A LIFE OF HOLINESS AND HOW THEY MAY BE MET AND CONQUERED

The Victorious Life is not something which is obtained once for all — a summit reached from which nothing can dislodge us. This victory is secured from moment to moment by a moment-by- moment faith. There is constant victory for the believer so long as he trusts Christ entirely — and only so long.

The moment that simple faith is lost, that moment the victory over sin is broken. That is why our Lord seems to sum up "sin" in the one word "unbelief." "The Holy Spirit when He is come shall convict the world of sin… of sin, because they believe not on Me" (John 16:8). And this is why St. John says, "This is the victory that overcometh the world, even our FAITH (1 John 5:4).

Since, then, there is no such thing as a once-for-all victory, it is evident that this life is beset with perils, and we must be constantly on our guard. Or, to be strictly accurate, we must ever allow "the peace of God to guard our hearts." An earnest laboring man used to insist upon quoting that verse as "A piece of God shall guard your hearts" — and his idea was right. For it is the indwelling Christ, the Son of God, Who does this for us.

THE ABIDING CHRIST

What are some of the dangers that beset a life of holiness? To be forewarned is to be forearmed. Nor need we fear to face any danger. "For in all these things we are more than conquerors through Him that loved us" (Romans 8:37).

There is, first of all —

1. *Self-effort.*

In the first flush of joy at realizing the possibility of such a life of victory, there is a tendency to attempt to hug our possession — to make a continuous and conscious effort to cling to it. A feeling that if we do not strenuously concentrate our thoughts upon the indwelling Christ, we shall lose Him. Perhaps this comes from regarding the Victorious Life as a blessing — a possession we can forfeit or lose. Satan always tries to get us to regard it as such. It may slip from our grasp. No. It is a Person, not a "thing." It is the Lord Jesus Christ Himself, Who comes not so much for us to possess Him, but that He may possess us. He cannot slip from our grasp. He holds us. He has promised, "I will never leave thee nor forsake thee" (Hebrews 13:5). That is why the writer likes to dwell upon the abiding Christ rather than the "fullness of the Spirit."

> *Once it was the blessing,*
> *Now it is the Lord;*
> *Once it was the feeling,*
> *Now it is His Word.*
> *Once His gifts I wanted.*
> *Now the Giver own;*
> *Once I sought for healing,*
> *Now Himself alone.*

He keeps us — it is not we who keep Him, and "He is able to keep." Of course, we must allow the Lord Jesus to be "the home of our thoughts." But "looking unto Jesus" in faith and love does not mean strenuous effort to retain Him — a willing guest. Our "look" of faith is not with strained eyes, but with a restful gaze.

IN THE PLACE OF SAFETY

"Abide in Me," says our Lord. Just rest peacefully in Him so far as your life of victory is concerned. At every alarm, at every approach of temptation, just "hide in Him," the Rock of Ages, just as the coney takes cover in his rock of defence. "Consider the lilies of the field, how they grow" — not by self-effort, toiling or striving. They just abide in the sunshine and drink in its life. "Which of you by being anxious can add one cubit to his stature?" asks our Lord in the Sermon on the Mount. And in His mind was something more than physical stature.

It is not our faith but His faithfulness that maintains the Victorious Life. "Trust in the Lord," and then "do good; so shalt thou dwell in the land and verily thou shalt be fed" (Psalm 37:3).

We may remark in passing that even in our conflict with evil around us our trust must be entirely in Him, and not in our own power and effort. How remarkably this is brought out in our Lord's instructions to His Apostles. "Behold, I send you forth as sheep amidst wolves," says He. Now how does He proceed? "Be ye therefore armed to the teeth?" NEVER. "Be ye therefore harmless as doves" (Matthew 10:16). Why? Because *He* is our defence and our shield.

2. *No Freedom From Temptation.*

The Victorious Life is not an untempted life. Only *one* Man has ever lived an unbroken Victorious Life, and that was our Lord Himself. And "He was tempted in all points like as we are, yet without sin." The sinless angels were tempted, and some fell. Adam and Eve in their sinless state were tempted, and also fell. So let us not be surprised when the devil tempts us. He will do all in his power to drag us down, because the

Victorious Life is the only one that really counts. Every child of God will be tempted, but we can "count it all joy," for we are told that the shield of faith is "able to quench ALL the fiery darts of the evil one" (Ephesians 6:16).

A CONSTANT ATTITUDE OF FAITH

3. If We Fall.

There is always the possibility of sinning, and there is the provision for it. "'If the anointed priest shall sin so as to bring guilt on the people, then let him offer for his sin…' (Leviticus 4:3). Doesn't this prove that sin is inevitable?" asked an inquirer. Surely not. Every ship that sails is provided with a supply of lifeboats, lest there should be a shipwreck or a collision.

This does not imply that it is the captain's intention to wreck his ship; nor does it mean that therefore every ship must be wrecked.

So, then, it is possible for both priest and people to sin.

The Victorious Life is secured by an act of faith: and it is only maintained by a constant attitude of faith. Suppose, then, there is a momentary failure and we fall into some sin. What then? Why, Satan immediately tries to follow up his victory by trying to persuade us that there is no such thing as the Victorious Life; or that if there is, then we never had the blessing; or if we had — well, it is gone forever: we've lost it. And our fellow-Christians who have never seen the only way of victory will gladly back him up in his assertions. Even devout and earnest believers will assure us that such teaching is a dangerous heresy.

Do not listen either to Satan or them. We have seen that the Bible is full of Victorious Life teaching. This "dangerous heresy" was taught by Christ, and shows itself again and again in St. Paul's Epistles and those of St. John.

Remember that God gave us the Victorious Life after many, many falls. Will He then withhold it forever because of one more fall? Surely not!

SATAN'S WHISPERINGS

But if Satan fails in dissuading you from again attempting to live a life of victory, he will try to delay your recovery. He will whisper that after such a grievous failure you must lie low for a while; it will take a long time for you to get back again into the life of victory; there must be an arduous climb, a tedious and humbling process of recovery. What answer will you give him?

Now we have conclusively shown that no striving or struggling on our part will ever bring us victory in the first place.

It must, therefore, be obvious that such effort and struggling will never reinstate us! If we fall into any sin, our Savior wishes us at once to turn to Him in faith for forgiveness.

Instant forgiveness and instant restoration. Even in the Old Testament dispensation this was so. "I have sinned against the Lord," said the penitent king David. "The Lord also hath put away thy sin," replied the prophet Nathan immediately (2 Samuel 12:13).

"If we confess our sins, He is faithful and just to forgive us our sins, and to cleanse us from all unrighteousness" (1 John 1:9). Your fall does not weaken Christ. "He is (still) able to keep." HE has not failed. Nor will He fail you. And once you are forgiven, turn your thoughts away from that sin and try never to think of it again. "One thing I do," said Paul, "forgetting the things [he might well have said "sins"] that are behind … I press on toward the goal" (Philippians 3:13).

A HINDRANCE TO HOLINESS

This is not minimizing or under- rating the sin. No one has such a horror of sin as he who is living the Victorious Life. Nor does it mean complacency under defeat.

But we feel strongly that the recollection of past sins is one of the greatest hindrances to present holiness and usefulness. Such recollection weakens our confidence, prevents our usefulness, and reminds us of the "pleasures of sin": so there follow feeble witness, fruitless work, and fresh falling into sin.

Moreover, remorse, or agony of feeling, or self-condemnation, cannot do aught to heal the wound. The atoning blood of Christ is sufficient for that. In fact, so sufficient — if one may use such an expression — that after the gift of the Holy Spirit at Pentecost Christians are nowhere told to pray for the forgiveness of their sins. The command is simply to confess them to God, and their forgiveness is assured.

The reason is obvious. When the Holy Spirit of Christ dwells in the heart, sin is abhorrent, and a longing for forgiveness always accompanies confession.

4. *Do Not Presume.*

"The truth about the indwelling Christ, or rather the consciousness of His indwelling, gives you such wonderful confidence," said a venerable cleric to the writer, "that the danger is that you get *too* confident." We see his point. But we cannot be too confident! What this man of God meant is this: There is a danger of relying upon past victory to keep us safe in the present. We may have — and Christ desires us to have — a long period of unbroken victory.

But the longer the period, the safer and stronger we are apt to *feel* ourselves to be. Paul knew the danger full well, "Let him that thinketh he standeth take heed lest he fall" (1 Corinthians 10:12). We must bear in mind that *our* weakness is never made strong. "Our sufficiency is from God." We are NEVER sufficient of ourselves to account anything as from ourselves (2 Corinthians 3:5).

It is "All of Christ" and always of Christ.

"It is God that worketh in you both to will and to do" (Philippians 2:13). As Mr. C. G. Trumbull puts it, in his *Perils of the Victorious Life*:

"Christ and Christ alone is our victory. Ten years of unbroken record does not add a particle to the strength of our Lord Jesus Christ; it does not increase the sufficiency of His grace, for that sufficiency is infinite. The assurance of our continuance in victory is not our good record, but the grace of our Lord. Our continued record in victory adds nothing to our assurance of victory."

THE NECESSITY OF OBEDIENCE

Moreover our victory for any length of time does not weaken Satan. *He* is just as powerful and active and spiteful, and just waits his opportunity. And *his* opportunity is any over-confidence or spiritual pride in us.

5. *Disobey Not Our Lord's Command.*

A radiantly happy couple wished to speak to me after an address on the indwelling Christ. "We have known and experienced the truth of the Victorious Life for many months now," said the husband, "and it has completely revolutionized our lives. All this time we have been staying away from the Lord's Table. We never go to the Holy Communion now. But are we right in keeping away?" "What is your *reason* for absenting yourselves?" I asked. "Because Paul tells us there is no further need of the Holy Communion when once Christ has come to dwell in the heart," was the astonishing reply. With much curiosity the writer asked for the reference to such a command. And this was the answer: "Paul said, 'As oft as ye eat this bread and drink this cup ye proclaim the Lord's death *till He come*' (1 Corinthians 11:26). Well, now that he *has* come to abide *in* us, we have refrained from partaking of the Holy Communion." That godly man and woman were delighted to learn that those words "Till He come" evidently refer to the Second Coming of our Lord. Paul himself was then living and preaching the Victorious Life, but he still partook of the Holy Communion. "We *all* partake of the one bread," says he (1 Cor. 10:17). We must never disobey any command of our Lord.

Yet how gracious our Lord is! The dear people mentioned above were radiantly happy and were bringing forth "the fruit of the Spirit," although they were disobeying God. They "did it ignorantly," but not in unbelief, and the Savior graciously blessed them and in due time showed them the "better way."

INDWELT BY THE HOLY TRINITY

The writer has met advanced Churchmen of the Anglo-Catholic school — holy and humble men of God — who have been thrilled by talks on the Victorious Life, but who have expressed a fear that such teaching would "do away with the need of the Sacrament." No such fear need ever disturb their minds.

This teaching is entirely Scriptural, as we have shown.

Space forbids us to enter fully into the relationship between the indwelling of Christ through the Holy Spirit and our Lord's definite declaration, "Except ye eat the flesh of the Son of Man and drink His blood, ye have not life in yourselves" (John 6:53).

Let us remind ourselves that all the Persons of the Trinity dwell in us. Christ said, "If a man love Me he will keep My word: and My Father will love him, and WE will come unto him, and make our abode with him" (John 14:23). We know that the Holy Spirit dwells in us "that He may abide with you for ever" (14:16).

It may be that God the Father, God the Son, and God the Holy Spirit "sanctify us wholly" — soul, body and spirit.

But we do believe that no victory ever admits of disobedience to any of our Lord's commands. And when He says "Do this" we must obey. If we love Him we shall keep His commandments.

Chapter Thirteen: Other Perils

SOME MORE OF THE PERILS THAT BESET THE PATH
OF THE TRUE SEEKER AFTER HOLINESS

There are other perils in the path of holiness in addition to those already dealt with. Let us look at them.

WHERE MANY BLUNDER

6. *Do Not Assume Infallibility.*

We can picture many of our readers smiling at such a ridiculous counsel. But this is a real danger! There is such a joy in unbroken communion with our Lord, and often such a consciousness of power — not our power, but that of the indwelling Christ — that there is a danger of our supposing that we always know God's will in any matter — that we are always right.

The writer once had occasion to live with four consecrated men of God — all of them far more experienced in holy living than himself. One of them was, indeed, deeply taught of God and used to spend long hours in prayer. But in our deliberations he always quietly assumed that he had the mind of Christ, and that any proposal which conflicted with his ideas must necessarily be wrong; and this, even if four of us felt led another way to that suggested by him. Not infrequently, subsequent events showed that we were right and he was wrong.

One morning our leader quietly and kindly remarked, "My dear ——, some of us think that we also are led to God." Do not misunderstand me. The reference here is not to an obstinate, dogmatic, self-opinionated man who wished to have his own way. Our friend in question was holy, humble, and unselfish to a degree — but was "infallible." He always assumed that he was absolutely guided by God in all his proposals. The best of us is not a little deaf spiritually, and we do not always catch God's message; just as a deaf person does not always catch the right message through a telephone. There must be a perfect "doing of God's will" before there is a perfect "knowing of the doctrine" (John 7:17).

Let us recognize that we are fallible. We may be mistaken. This does not mean that the majority is always right. Ten men once said, "We are not able to go up against the people, for they are stronger than we." While only two men urged, "Let us go up at once and possess it: for we are well able to overcome it" (Numbers 13:30). The people sided with the ten and years of misery and rebellion ensued, because the two were right and had the mind of God.

THE WORLD AND ITS CLAIMS

7. Do Not Ignore This World.

A consecrated man of God lives in a house called "Torthorwold." His neighbors say that is what he lives for: "T'other world." But all who know him are aware that he leads a most strenuous life trying to make this world and its inhabitants better. We live in two worlds at the same time and have a duty to each.

"Do you think it is wrong of me to play marbles with my little boy of four?" asked a white-haired saintly father. We wonder what answer our readers would give.

How it would delight the heart of Satan if he could persuade all wholly sanctified people that all pleasures were sinful! Dear man of God, by all means play marbles — if you are not tempted to cheat!

We are living not only a spiritual life, but a bodily life, and whether we like it or not, a very large part of our time and interests is taken up with things which concern the body. Moreover, we are placed in communities. God never meant man to live alone. God made two statements about the first man, Adam, right at the beginning of his existence.

The first was that he was "very good." The next remark was this, "it is not good that the man should be alone" (Genesis 2:18). Every man is born into a family — every man has his human relationships. Each of us is to show love to all men. All the little social amenities of life are points of contact with those around us. Love manifests itself in deeds, and we must be human as well as "divine." We can only show our love to God by deeds of love to our fellow-men. By all means romp with the little ones and play with the big ones!

HAPPY AND "HUMAN"

Men living the Victorious Life are the happiest and "humanest" of people, overflowing with the joy of the Lord — bubbling over with innocent fun and mirth. We are here to make this world a happier world. "The joy of the Lord is your strength" (Nehemiah 8:10). We are to "rejoice evermore," and that means we are to begin now, here on earth.

A mother sat searching her Bible, trying to probe the secrets of a life of holiness. She spent so much time seeking spiritual help that the duties of her household became irksome and were either hurried through or neglected. The "homeliness" of the home was gone. One day, as she was deep in study, her little girl toddled up to her side with a broken doll. "Mummy, please mend dolly for me." With an impatient gesture, the mother brushed the little one aside. "I've more important things to do than trouble about dolly!" The little one turned sadly away, and the mother continued her search for holiness.

But the search was a fruitless one, and the mother closed her book with a sigh, and sought the little child. She was lying on the hearthrug clutching her darling doll, and with the tears still wet on her pretty face. The mother's heart was smitten. God spoke to her then and there. Tenderly stooping over the little one, she woke her with her kisses. Then taking her into her arms, she breathed a prayer to God for forgiveness. She saw that holiness could not thrive on neglected duties. Her devotion to her Lord was henceforth seen in her care of the household, and shone out even in mending broken toys! Home became home again. And the very page of Scripture was lighted up with a fresh glory.

Yes, and victory shone in the mother's radiant face.

THE CHRISTIAN HERITAGE

We believe that the Lord Jesus, Who watched the children at their play, and the fishermen and farmers at their work, Who worked Himself and yet made time to be present at a wedding feast, wishes us to take a real and lively interest in all the concerns of life — our own and those of our friends. He has given us a capacity for pleasure, and He longs to see us enjoy His gift of life.

He has given us a physical frame which needs food, and work, exercise, and relaxation. He wishes us to enjoy our meals, our work, and our recreation. The marvelous realm of nature, the wonderful infinitude of space peopled with suns, the cadence of music and the color of sky and sea and landscape are for our enjoyment.

> *All things bright and beautiful,*
> *All creatures great and small,*
> *All things wise and wonderful,*
> *The Lord God made them all*

for our pleasure as well as for His glory.

The world is so full of a number of things
I'm sure we should all be as happy as kings.

says the child's poet. God expects His children to be careful about their dress and manners. Surely, He desires us to be attractive Christians? The King's business requires haste, but it never requires discourtesy or lack of proper attentiveness to our fellows.

IS RELIGION MISERY?

The writer met a godly major on a voyage to India. He had been converted from a life of dissolution, and was now ever engrossed in his Bible. He avoided every kind of amusement — even deck quoits. Writing to me from a public school in England, a son of the dear major said, "I *am so* glad you have met my father. Do try to convert him to the Church of England, his religion makes him so miserable."

No wonder the high-spirited lad found little happiness in his father's company, and was a little shy of "religion."

God's religion never yet made a man miserable! Nor does the Lord Jesus delight in misery! Did not the Savior say, "These things have I spoken unto you that My joy might remain in you, and that your joy might be full"? (John 15:11) There is a *right* way of "making the most of both worlds."

NOT TRUSTING TO THRILLS

8. *Do Not Rely On Thrills.*

It often happens that when a believer enters upon a life of victory over voluntary sin that he experiences a joy, and an ecstasy and a thrill which make him feel as if he were treading on air. But this is not always the case, and we must not suppose that an absence of thrills is a proof that Christ has not come in His fullness.

God wants us to trust Him and His Word, and not to rely upon feelings. He would save us from the peril of testing our victory, or testing His indwelling, by any preconceived notions of ours as to *how* His presence shall be felt or manifested. Think less of the victory, less of the blessing, and more of the Blesser.

You remember Spurgeon's apt remark, which is worth repeating just here. "I looked at Jesus, and the dove of peace flew into my heart. I looked at the dove of peace, and she flew away."

Do not then be examining or testing your victory. Maintain a simple and constant trust in Christ — *He* cannot fail.

It is really better to enter into the Victorious Life by simple faith unaccompanied by ecstasy or thrill.

For when the thrill subsides, and life seems humdrum and commonplace, we may be tempted to think that the victory has vanished with the thrill! Fact — faith — feeling: that is the order.

9. *Do Not Be Surprised If Others Fail To See Our Victory.*

Only One Man ever lived a sinless life — a really Victorious Life all through — and that is the Man Christ Jesus.

But the leaders of religion in His days on earth were so blinded that they failed to see the Victorious Life in Him. They called Him a "wine-bibber."

"We know that this man is a sinner," said they of Christ. So we must not be surprised if men fail to recognize the Victorious Life in us.

We must be very humble, and when others thwart us or oppose us, and deny our sincerity or orthodoxy, no spirit of un-love or root of bitterness must come in; no holier-than-thou feeling must be entertained for a moment — or our victory is broken.

We are certain to be misunderstood, and our greatest opponents will be not the world, but the Church!

The devil has sown tares in the field of the Church, and only God Himself knows what is tares and what is wheat. It is from these — the children of the wicked one in the Church — that the greatest opposition is to be expected. [Our Lord never calls mere unbelievers "children of the devil," but only "religious" unbelievers (see Matthew 13:25, 38; 23:15; John 8:38-44). It is an awful thought, but must be noted.] The servant is not greater than his Lord. If Christ received opposition from "religious" people, so shall we.

But every such act of opposition is an opportunity for us to show, not by our lip, but by our life, the Christ-life; to prove that there *is* victory through the Lord Jesus Christ.

And even if some oppose and criticize and condemn, many around us, seeing our victory through Christ, will be glad thereof and rejoice; because they will see the mighty power of God — mighty to the overthrowing of strongholds.

THE MOMENT OF VICTORY

10. *Now — Not Tomorrow.*

May we remind our readers of a very simple fact, and yet one so often forgotten. It is this: The only time you can live the Victorious Life is Now.

The only way to have Victory through Christ is to get it Now — at this very moment. This life is not merely one for emergencies. So many dear people are waiting for future opportunities to manifest the indwelling Christ.

They wait for a prayer meeting, or an open-air, or for a conversation with another congenial spirit.

But Now is the only moment of victory.

God is Light as well as Love. And our Lord said, "*Let* your light shine" — not *make* it shine as occasion arises. LET IT shine always, everywhere.

When you spring out of bed each day and say joyously to yourself and your God, "To me to live is Christ," make up your mind to manifest something of the glory of Christ to everyone you meet that day. Keep a watch over yourself.

Let the people in the home see the light — the victory. Let your fellow- workers in the office or yard, in the shop or the ship, the factory or the school, see that Christ is dwelling in your heart. Why should not the tradesman, the postmen, the bus- conductors detect your secret? Be epistles of Christ, "known and read of all men" (2 Corinthians 3:2).

A dear friend of the writer's — a cultured man brought literally to the gutter through drink — was converted at a tramps' mission. The day following, he boarded a tram. The conductor was mystified, for the passenger's clothes told of beggary, while his face reflected heaven! "Why, mate," he exclaimed, "you look as if someone's died and left you a fortune!" "You are right there," came the quick reply. "Jesus Christ has died for me and has given me His riches in glory." "Well, he might dress you better," was the sneer — and HE DID.

Shall not even strangers be attracted by our joy?

IN COMMUNION WITH CHRIST

But do not wait for the future. Let victory be yours NOW.

Just live in such communion with Christ that He can always show forth His glory through you.

"Unto me was this grace given, to preach unto the Gentiles the unsearchable riches of Christ, to make ALL MEN see what is the mystery which from all ages hath been hid in God … that NOW might be made known through the Church [*i.e.*, through you and me] the manifold wisdom of God" (Ephesians 3:9-10).

Yes — and His wondrous life and ineffable glory.

Chapter Fourteen: "Highest" Criticism

THE HIGHEST CRITICISM THAT PREVENTS MANY CHRISTIANS FROM BELIEVING AND ACCEPTING THEIR RICH HERITAGE IN CHRIST

The most extraordinary thing about the Victorious Life is that although it is so clearly taught in Scripture, yet it is so frequently unrecognized by Bible students. Many who have a thorough knowledge of their Bibles know nothing of this truth experimentally. The writer himself had been a careful student of the Scriptures for many years before the glory of this life lighted up his soul. Again and again clergy have confessed, "We do not preach this truth because we do not know it experimentally."

How is it that we are so slow of heart to understand? Probably the best way to put the case is to describe at some length the inner experiences of two men who had long been devoted to the service of God. Hudson Taylor, then a missionary in China, was one of these men. He has left in a letter to his sister a record of his search for holiness and his total inability to see how to get it, although the way lies so clearly on the page of Scripture. This is his confession: —

HUDSON TAYLOR'S CONFESSION

"I prayed, fasted, agonized, strove, made resolutions, read the Bible more diligently, sought more time for retirement and meditation — but all without effect. Every day — almost every hour — the consciousness of sin oppressed me. Then came the question: 'Is there no rescue? Must it be this to the end — constant conflict, and instead of Victory, too often defeat?' I hated myself, I hated my sin, and yet I gained no strength against it. I felt I was a child of God, but how to rise to my privileges as a child I was utterly powerless to see. I thought that holiness, practical holiness, was to be gradually attained by a diligent use of the means of grace. I felt there was nothing I so much desired in the world, nothing I so much needed. When my agony of soul was at its height, a sentence in a latter was used to remove the scales from my eyes, and the Spirit of God revealed the truth of our oneness with Jesus."

What was this letter? What was the sentence? The letter runs: "By faith a channel is formed by which Christ's fullness plenteously flows down. The barren branch becomes a portion of the fruitful stem. He is most holy who has most of Christ within. It is defective faith which clogs the feet and causes many a fall. Abiding — not struggling or striving: looking off to Him; trusting Him for present power; trusting Him to subdue all inward corruption; resting in the conscious joy of a complete salvation; a salvation from all sin: willing that He should be truly supreme. That is NOT NEW, YET IT IS NEW TO ME. I seem to have got to the edge only, but to the edge of a sea that is boundless. Christ literally ALL seems to me now the power —the only power— for service; the only ground for unchanging joy. Now, then, is this faith increased? Only by thinking of all that JESUS is and all that He is for us: His life, His death, His work, HIMSELF, as revealed to us in His Word, to be the subject of our constant thoughts. *Not a striving to have faith*, or to increase our faith, *but a looking off to the* FAITHFUL ONE seems all we need — a resting in the Loved One entirely for time and eternity. IT DOES NOT APPEAR TO ME ANYTHING NEW — only formerly misapprehended."

FROM FAILURE TO TRIUMPH

That was the letter, and the sentence which arrested Hudson Taylor's attention was the last one — "Not a striving to have faith, but a looking off to the Faithful One seems all we need."

We have quoted these letters at length, partly because they sum up all we have been trying to teach in these pages; but chiefly because both these men of God confess that such teaching is NOT NEW, yet both have failed to apprehend it, although they were simply yearning for a life of Victory.

As the writer looks back on his past life, nothing so surprises him as the fact that he failed to see, or grasp, or apprehend this Victorious Life teaching, although it is not new, although it is so plainly taught in Scripture.

Why is this? Why do so many devout scholars fail to claim, or even seek, a life of Victory? We cannot help feeling that it is because many read the Bible critically —yes, and devoutly and reverently— but without really claiming the illumination of the Holy Spirit. Many scholars will indignantly deny this. But we feel that it is so. We do not accuse anyone of deliberately rejecting the help of the Holy Spirit — but of deceiving themselves, or at least of being deceived.

Even the saintly Bishop Moule confessed that although he was Principal of a Theological College, he not only failed to grasp the meaning of this teaching, but was confident that it was wrong — unscriptural — until the light dawned. Many of our readers will remember how Bishop Moule came to see these truths when on a visit to Scotland. And all the world knows how full of it his books are.

UNDER THE SPIRIT'S POWER

The writer would like to suggest the following as an explanation of some of our blindness. Paul says, "The letter killeth: it is the Spirit that giveth life" (2 Corinthians 3:6). Unless then the Holy Spirit illuminates the Word, it is not life-giving and no Victorious Life can result. Our Lord once said, "Man shall not live by bread alone, but by every word that proceedeth out of the mouth of God" (Matthew 4:4). Not by every word that proceeded. The word is in the present tense, "proceedeth." Now the word is always proceeding. That is to say, the Holy Spirit takes the "letter that killeth" and brings it home with power and life to the hearts of those who rely upon Him to do so.

The disciples had heard many things they could not understand — hard sayings — but Christ said, "When He, the Spirit of truth is come, He shall guide you into all the truth; for He shall not speak from Himself, but what things soever He shall bear, these shall He speak" (John 16:13). Now we live by the same written word which the Lord *is speaking* to us through the Holy Spirit — the word which, through the Spirit, is still "proceeding" out of the mouth of God.

The Holy Spirit is called in the Nicene Creed "The Lord and Giver of Life." it is He Who gives us the Victorious Life. But He does it by revealing to us the WORD OF GOD — not only the meaning of the written word, but by giving us the indwelling Christ — The "Word." Christ is born in us, as it were, and lives in us "by the operation of the Holy Spirit."

One is often asked the question: "Is the Victorious Life the same thing as the fullness of the Holy Spirit?" Well, what is the work of the Holy Spirit? He comes in all His fullness not to speak for Himself, but to reveal the Lord Jesus Christ, and to lead us into all truth. "He shall glorify Me," says Christ, "for He shall take of Mine and shall declare it unto you."

WHERE SO MANY FAIL

"There is nothing new in all this!" is the impatient, well-nigh querulous comment so often made concerning this teaching. But the very tone of voice betrays an unwillingness to attempt to really assimilate this ancient teaching.

The real trouble is that so many people who deplore higher criticism, themselves indulge in what we venture to call Highest criticism. They must acknowledge that this Victorious Life is scriptural, but they openly declare that it is impossible. They do not deny the truth of the Word of God, but they tacitly believe that it is unworkable. Oh, if we could only just take Christ at His word! If we only had a simple childlike faith in God!

> *If our faith were but more simple*
> *We should take Him at His word;*
> *And our lives would be all sunshine*
> *In the glory of the Lord.*

Let us explain what we mean by highest criticism. We mean absolutely refusing to believe that it is possible to obey all God's commands. Now the joy which is inseparable from the Victorious Life is from just taking God at His word.

Take such a definite command as Philippians 4:6, "In nothing be anxious." Do we obey it? Do we believe it is God's will that we should never have an anxious thought? Many Christian people must sadly confess that their experience is that they are anxious about everything. The writer a few years back consulted an eminent physician, who expressed an opinion — wrongly, as events proved — that the heart was overstrained and that a long rest was imperative. Anxiety was clearly noted by the doctor, for he said, "May I make a remark about you clergy? Many people consult me, but I find that you leaders of religion are *just as anxious* about your bodies as men who profess no religion at all." What a rebuke! The writer stood condemned — and felt condemned; but his anxiety still remained! Why? Simply because he did not know the secret of the indwelling Christ.

SURE OF THREE THINGS

He was not acting up to what he professed to believe. He had often quoted to others the God-given command, "Cast thy burden upon the Lord and He shall sustain THEE" (Psalm 55:22). "Casting ALL your ANXIETY upon Him, for He careth for you" (1 Peter 5:7). Yet here he was, anxious and troubled over his physical condition, when God's very plain and definite command is "In nothing be anxious."

There was clearly something wrong with the spiritual life. What was it? Not blind unbelief, but blank unbelief!

"We may be quite sure of three things," says Francis Ridley Havergal. "First, that whatever our Lord commands us, He really means us to do.

"Secondly, that whatever He commands us is 'for our good always.'

"And thirdly, that whatever He commands, He is able and willing to enable us to do, for 'all God's biddings are enablings.'"

Now is there any reason for the slightest anxiety in one wholly surrendered to God? Dare we ever doubt His love or His ability to provide for us? Why, if a believer only obeys this one command of God, "In nothing be anxious," he finds heaven begun on earth below. But it is impossible for *me* to keep that command.

So Christ just comes to dwell in my heart, to live His life in me, and to do what I myself cannot do.

> *Said the sparrow to the robin:*
> *"I should really like to know*
> *Why these anxious human beings*
> *Rush about and worry so."*
> *Said the robin to the sparrow:*
> *"Friend, I think that it must be*
> *That they have no Heavenly Father*
> *Such as cares for you and me."*

Now we *do* know our Heavenly Father, Who gave us His own SON. "Shall He not also with Him freely give us all things?" (Romans 8:32). Then why be anxious?

If you really desire the Victorious Life, you must "Cast — 'roll off' the word means — all your anxiety upon Him." For if you keep any of your worry, there is something wrong with your spiritual life and you cannot enjoy the life more abundant; for you fail to trust God.

Now Christ, living in you, can alone give you miraculous power to obey His command, "In nothing be anxious."

DO WE BELIEVE GOD'S WORD?

We were speaking a little time back about the possibility of freedom from sinning. There are two very definite statements in Scripture which show that Christians need not commit known sins. One is in Ephesians 6:16, "Taking the shield of faith, wherewith ye shall be able to quench all the fiery darts of the evil one." The other is this: "God is faithful, Who will not suffer you to be tempted above that we are able; but will with the temptation make also the way of escape, that ye may be able to endure it" (1 Corinthians 10:13).

These are really very wonderful statements. What a glorious possibility is here held out to us! For this includes the great root sin of unbelief. Every sorrow comes through sin — every worry comes through sin. And there is a possible Victory over every sin through Jesus Christ our Lord.

The question is, do we believe God's Word or do we not? The usual up-and-down experience of the Christian is not God's plan for him. If we really believe that the indwelling Christ can do this thing for us, then let us trust Him to do it.

There is another comforting *fact* given in the Bible. God says, "My grace is sufficient for thee" (2 Corinthians 12:9). This is not a promise; it is a FACT — an unchangeable, unmoving fact. The writer made this remark at a meeting, and a lady came up to him immediately afterwards and said, "But you left out the condition." "What condition?" "Why, there must be faith before God's grace can be sufficient," said she. But, dear reader, whether you have faith or whether you have not, does not and cannot alter a FACT! "God's grace is sufficient for you," whether you believe it or not. There was always "bread enough and to spare" in the Father's house, even when the prodigal was in a far country desiring to be fed upon the husks the swine did eat! Always enough and to spare: he had only to go and share it.

God's grace is always sufficient. God Himself has declared it to be so. When sudden temptation comes upon you unawares, do you stop to pray for deliverance from it — or do you look to Christ for victory over it? Someone has said, "When tempted, do not begin to ask '*how* can I get out of it?', but '*what* can I get out of it?' "The peace of God, which passeth all understanding, shall guard your hearts and YOUR THOUGHTS in Christ Jesus" (Philippians 4:7 RV). The Lord Jesus is dwelling in the heart to banish even the thought of evil before it can become sin.

If you are troubled with evil thoughts, claim this promise — that the indwelling Christ can indeed guard our "thoughts."

It was this verse, "My grace is sufficient for thee," which led that veteran Christian warrior, Preb. Webb-Peploe, into the Victorious Life. After the crushing sorrow of losing a beloved child, he tried to prepare a sermon with this as his text. But he could not "cast his burden upon the Lord." Rising to his feet he cried out to God in his agony, "Oh, God, it is not true. I do not find Thy Grace sufficient for me in this heavy sorrow that has befallen me. But, oh, *make* it sufficient."

A GREAT EXPERIENCE

Falling on his knees, he repeated this prayer. Then through his tears he saw over the mantelpiece an illuminated textacard, "My grace is sufficient." In a flash he saw his mistake! "What a fool I am," he cried. "How dare I ask God to *make* what is! I will get up and trust Him." And he did trust Him. We all know what the entrance into the Victorious Life meant for Webb-Peploe, and through him, for the whole world! So also Paul, who knew that God's grace was sufficient, could promise this: "My God shall fulfill every need of yours according to HIS RICHES IN GLORY (what a treasury!) IN CHRIST JESUS (what a Savior!)" (Philippians 4:19).

Fellow-Christian, can you conceive any greater promise?

This supply is moment by moment. The manna just fell day by day. As one dear saint has said, "God gave me a great fortune — placed thousands and millions to my credit. But gave me a cheque-book with this one condition, 'You never can draw more than you need at the time.'"

We have to learn to take from Him our spiritual life every second.

Just one other command — as binding as "thou shalt not steal." It is this. "Rejoice in the Lord." Have you thought out what these words mean? It is not a call to rejoice in our oneness with Him; or in the means of grace given us; or His work in us; or in our fellowship with Him. We are not bidden so much to rejoice in what He is to us, or what He is working in us, but just to rejoice in HIM in HIM HIMSELF — to rejoice in what He is and has in Himself.

Do you not see what a wonderful cause of rejoicing this is? If our joy consists in His giving us victory over sin, our joy goes if we are overtaken in a fault. If our joy rests upon His work in and through us, we may not always be conscious of just what He is accomplishing, and we may be exalted or cast down unduly.

But if our joy is in HIM and what HE is, that cannot change or fluctuate, and we can always abound in joy. Rejoice in the Lord: "Jesus Christ, Whom having not seen ye love; in Whom, though now ye see Him not, yet believing, ye rejoice greatly with joy unspeakable and full of glory" (1 Peter 1:8); "He that glorieth let him glory in the Lord" (1 Corinthians 1:31); "O magnify the LORD with me!" Think often of Him. Let His wondrous glory be the theme of your thoughts and your songs. Ever recollect that it is HE — This glorious One — Who dwells in your heart by faith. And if He is supreme, then you can say, "I live, yet not I, but Christ liveth in me," and joyfully add, TO ME TO LIVE IS CHRIST.

Chapter Fifteen: Days Of Heaven On Earth

FROM THE GLOOM AND DISAPPOINTMENT OF THE WILDERNESS EXPERIENCE TO THE GLORY AND ABUNDANCE OF THE PROMISED LAND

There is only one thing now to be considered, and that is the sort of life God expects His children to live.

FOR OUR ADMONITION

Before we look at that ideal — a POSSIBLE ideal — we must just give a glance at the wonderful object-lesson given us in the redemption of God's people, Israel. Paul tells us that the experiences of the children of Israel, in their deliverance from Egypt and their journey to the Promised Land, and are "examples," or types, and that they are written for our admonition (1 Corinthians 10:11). They are full of instruction. God means us to study the failures and failings of His chosen people, and to take warning lest we also suffer for having an evil heart of unbelief.

Egypt is a type of the world — Sin. Canaan, the land of promise, is a type of Sanctification — the Victorious Life here below.

No Egyptian taskmaster was ever more merciless and cruel than sin is. The Israelites could not save themselves. The more they struggled to get free, the harder their burdens became. So likewise the sinner cannot save himself. His struggles and efforts avail nothing. Salvation is all of grace.

Then came God's deliverance through the shedding of blood. That Passover Lamb was a type of Christ. "Christ our Passover is sacrificed for us" (1 Corinthians 5:7). The lamb was slain and the blood shed. That was substitution. "That lamb dies instead of me," a Jew might have truly said.

Yet that blood *shed* saved no one. To effect salvation, it must be sprinkled upon the door-posts and upon the lintel. That is to say, there must be an individual claiming and acceptance of that substitutionary sacrifice. Only the blood *sprinkled* saved anyone. "Christ died for the ungodly." But if I am not to die for my sins, I must accept Christ's death in my stead. "As many as received Him, to them gave He the right to become the sons of God" (John 1:12).

THE RED SEA. — Then came that miraculous passage through the Red Sea, which Paul likens unto baptism. "Our fathers were baptized into Moses in the cloud and in the sea" (1 Corinthians 10:2), although neither the waters of the sea nor the cloud touched them, and not until the passage of the Jordan did they become fully sanctified.

What did the Red Sea accomplish for the Israelites? Before they crossed it they were redeemed by the shed blood appropriated, but were still living and moving amongst their foes.

TWO ASPECTS OF CHRIST'S DEATH

They were subjected to a merciless pursuit and a determined attempt to drag them back into bondage. When once they had passed through the sea, however, they were delivered from all dominion, all control of their foes. They never again had trouble from them or conflict with them. Their oppressors lay DEAD on the seashore.

What does this mean for us? Remember that there are two aspects of Christ's death. He died for our sins. He died for us — substitution. But then Paul tells us that we are also to die with Him. "I have been crucified WITH CHRIST" (Galatians 2:20); "Reckon ye yourselves to be dead indeed unto sin" (Romans 6:11). The Israelites in bondage were delivered by the blood shed and sprinkled. But they are pursued by certain of their foes. These foes are slain at the Red Sea, but they themselves escape and are free. Egypt stands for the world of sin. Christ found us in "Egypt," and by His death in our stead delivered us from the penalty of sin. But even after our conversion some of these sins followed us and harassed us — temper, pride, jealousy, lust, worry, avarice — causing discomfiture and misery, and occasionally temporary defeat. Where is there any escape, any real victory? Only through the Red Sea — baptism, or what baptism implies; *i.e.*, a death to sin and a rising again to righteousness. That is a crucifixion with Christ, so as to be able to "reckon ourselves dead indeed unto sin."

WHERE MANY CHRISTIANS FAIL

The Egyptians were seen DEAD upon the seashore. An Israelite might have gone back and have recognized his old taskmaster lying there. "There he is *dead*: he will never trouble me any more." Another might have said, "Yes, and there is my taskmaster; no more will he oppress me!"

Now it is just as true that when we enter into death with Christ we are dead to sin. We can, indeed, reckon ourselves "dead indeed unto sin" (Romans 6:11) — to temper, pride, jealousy, avarice, lust. Hitherto such sins have been our taskmasters.

But notice that Paul does not say, "Sin is dead unto you." Those pursuing Egyptians were slain, but Egypt — sin — as a nation was still in evidence. "My personal sins I may count as 'slain' but SIN back of them all is very much alive," says one.

The reason why many Christians are constantly falling into sin is because they try to obey only one-half of Paul's injunctions. "Neither yield ye your members as instruments of unrighteousness unto sin," says St. Paul. Many attempt to act up to that. But he also says, "but yield yourselves unto God, as those alive from the dead" (Romans 6:13). That was what Christ's death meant to our Lord Himself. He submitted His will absolutely unto God. "Lo, I come to do Thy will" (Hebrews 10:9), "I do always those things that please Him," said our Lord (John 8:29). When, and so long as there is the unconditional surrender of my life to God, then "sin has NO dominion over me" (Romans 6:14).

DELIVERANCE FROM SIN

The Pass-over means deliverance from the PENALTY of SIN.

The Pass-through (the Red Sea) means deliverance from the POWER of sin.

But even in the wilderness those children of God needed to learn that in God and in Him alone they had ALWAYS ALL sufficiency in ALL things (2 Corinthians 9:8).

BITTER WATERS

After the children of Israel were delivered from both the bondage and power of the Egyptians, they arrive — thirsty and weary — at Marah, the bitter waters. These are at once made sweet by the WOOD thrown in. So it is still: the *wood* — the Cross — that is, the *Christ* of the cross — takes the bitterness out of everything that would be otherwise galling.

But these pilgrims go on from strength to strength. From the bitter waters of Marah — that need to be sweetened — they pass on to the sweet and plenteous waters of Elim, and then on to that miraculous water which flowed out of the Rock — and "that rock was Christ" (1 Corinthians 10:4); and that water a type of the Blessed Spirit.

MANNA

And food was provided as well as drink. Manna — bread from heaven. Again we are taken to the cross. For Christ is our Bread from heaven — His Body broken on the cross is indeed the "bread of God… which cometh down from heaven and giveth life unto the world" (John 6:33).

So those pilgrims were led and fed entirely by God. The water — a type of the Holy Spirit — did not *give* life; it only sustained it. The Manna — a type of the "Bread of life" — did not *give* life, it only maintained it. The Holy Spirit, however, is "the Lord and *giver* of life." Jesus Christ is the Bread of Life — Who GIVES life, as well as sustains it.

Yet with all their manifold privileges and blessings, the children of Israel "provoked God in the wilderness." Think of it! They were miraculously delivered; miraculously led; miraculously fed; miraculously preserved from sickness — for "there was not one feeble person amongst their tribes" (Psalm 105:37). Yet there were murmurings and disobedience. Their lives were not full of joy and victory.

AT THE CRISIS OF LIFE

But THAT was God's ideal for them — an ideal only possible *in the Promised Land.*

THE CRISIS OF LIFE

So they came to Kadesh-Barnea — and there lay the land of promise before them; typical of the Victorious Life which we have outlined before the eyes of our readers.

As we read the story we expect to learn they rushed forward with joy in their hearts and songs on their lips — vying with each other as to who should be the first to enter in. Moses called the people together. "Ye are come to the mountain which the Lord our God doth GIVE unto us. Behold the Lord thy God hath set the land before thee; go up and possess it, as the Lord God of thy fathers hath said unto thee; fear not, neither be discouraged" (Deuteronomy 1:20, 21). Then the amazing thing happened: the people refused to go! "Let us first send men before us and they shall search out the land!" said they.

And Moses assented. Those people COULD NOT TRUST GOD. We all know the result. The spies return with a wonderful story and wonderful fruit. Two of their number — the two surely who carried that bunch of grapes? — said, "Let us go up AT ONCE and possess it, for we are well able to overcome it." But the other ten cried, "We are not able to go up against the people, for they are stronger than we! (Numbers 13:31). Again the faithful two spoke up. "If the Lord delight in us then HE will bring us into the land and GIVE IT TO us. Only rebel not ye against the Lord, neither fear ye the people of the land; for they are bread for us: their defence is departed from them; and the Lord is with us: fear them not."

THE WILDERNESS WANDERINGS

But the people sided with the ten and refused to obey the living God: refused to enter the land to which GOD had led them, and which GOD had promised to GIVE them. And God never gave them another chance. Not one of those people over twenty years of age, except Joshua and Caleb, ever saw the land again.

Now what does it all mean? For them it was a time of crisis. Behind them was Egypt, that gave them garlic, and leeks, and onions — and bondage. Before them was the promised land with milk and honey and luscious fruits — and FREEDOM. Which shall they choose? Thank God, they did not go back to Egypt (sin)! But, alas! they refused to enter the land of promise, where there was rest and communion with God. So they wandered for forty years in the wilderness, amid snares and noisome pestilences, and the destruction that wasteth at noonday.

What is there of "example" in all this? The Promised Land is the Victorious Life. We have tried in these articles to lead our readers right up to its borders, and we have "looked in." Have we entered in? This is God's will for everyone who is trusting Him as Savior. He wishes us to enter now, and to abide there forever. The difficulties of such a life, free from known sin, seem gigantic and insuperable. They are like the people occupying Canaan, "Nations greater and mightier than thyself" (Deuteronomy 9:1).

We believe that God's command to us is, "Go up and possess it: fear not, neither be discouraged" (Deuteronomy 1:21). Many believers declare the Victorious Life to be impossible: to be beyond them. "We are unable to enter in," they cry. Now God calls us to live this life in His STRENGTH, and not in our own. "If the Lord delight in us then will He bring us into the land." It means an absolute surrender of all we have and are, and a simple faith in Christ's ability to do all He has promised. Our Lord bids us go in and possess it. For, remember that "God's omnipotence is at our disposal for *keeping* as well as for service."

WHAT THE EXPERIENCE MEANT

The life of most Christians is simply a wilderness experience which is far removed from the rest and joy of the Promised Land.

The wilderness experience means:

1. *Restlessness.*

No settled home — no abiding-place — no possessions. At any moment they had to move on, should the cloud lift from off the tabernacle. It means discontent and murmuring against God and His providential dealings with us; murmurings against the leaders whom God has chosen; murmurings against our lot which WE have chosen (for the wilderness wanderings are really rebellion against God, and contrary to His wishes). It means, sometimes, a longing to be back in Egypt — a life of sin; and sometimes a going back.

2. *It Means Fruitlessness.*

The children of Israel fought in the wilderness, but they gained nothing by their fighting except the right to go on their way unhindered. They gained no possessions. That is the ordinary life of every Christian who has not claimed the Victorious Life. It is a life made up of "not doing things." He does not dance, or play cards, or attend theatres; he, perhaps, does not even drink or smoke. But his Christian life consists of not doing wrongful or harmful things. The *fruit* of the Promised Land — the fruit of the Spirit — is not there: love, joy, peace. There is no growth in grace, and little —if any— "fruit" in service. What *seeming* results there are do not last. In the main, it is only of the one living the Victorious Life in whom Christ's desire is fulfilled — that His "fruit should abide" (John 15:16). Many Christians have renounced the pleasures of sin — but not sin itself. They have not entered the Promised Land where true joy is found. This alone is lamentable. But the saddest part of their failure is this:

THEY KEEP OTHERS OUT

Joshua and Caleb had a right to enter in. So had Moses. Yet the two were shut out for forty years because of the unwillingness of others to enter in! And Moses soon forfeited the right to enter in at all!

Oh, that Joshua and Caleb had refused to go with the majority! Had they but boldly marched in — they two only — we believe that God would have honored their faith, and have conquered their foes before them. Yes, and thousands would have followed in their steps. GOD CAN DO SUCH THINGS.

Jonathan and his armor-bearer knew that (1 Samuel 14:6). Moreover God offered to do it for Moses alone. "Let me alone, that I may destroy them…; and I will make of THEE a nation mightier and greater than they" (Deuteronomy 9:14).

FOUR THINGS TO REMEMBER

We have put before YOU the land of promise — the Victorious Life which God can give you. Christian — are you willing to enter in? Remember four things:

1. God has promised some better thing for us than a wilderness life of failure and discontent and doubt. He offers victory over known sin, and the enjoyment of wonderful communion with Him.
2. Our struggling and striving *cannot* give us that which God only can give.
3. We may and should bring our sins — the sins of Christian people — our doubts, our fears, our anxieties, our defeats, our weaknesses to Him, and trust the Lord Jesus to kill them; and then claim by faith Victory through Christ.
4. Then we can confidently say, "I now by faith *take* the life of Victory, with all its rest and joy and fruitfulness.

"If ye be WILLING and obedient ye shall eat the good of the land."

Take another good look at that "land" — that LIFE — if you still hold back.

1. *It is a life of perfect rest.* "COME unto Me… I will give you rest. Take My yoke upon you and LEARN OF ME —be My disciple— and ye shall find REST to your souls" (Matthew 11:28-29). All unrest dishonors Christ.
2. *It is a life of perfect peace.* "Peace I leave with you; My peace I give unto you" (John 14:27). To experience anything but peace — even under opposition, oppression, loss, bereavement, or perplexity — is to dishonor Christ and His Word.

VICTORY FOLLOWS OBEDIENCE

3. *It is a life of power.* "Ye shall receive power" (Acts 1:8). If we do not *possess* power, we are dishonoring Christ. We are not waiting for God; GOD IS WAITING FOR US.
4. *It is a fruitful life.* "I can do all things through Christ Who strengtheneth me" (Philippians 4:13). A life of failure is dishonoring to Christ.
5. *It is a life lived by the Christ dwelling in us*, and therefore a life of perfect JOY.

In the wilderness, God led His people — disobedient, rebellious, murmuring people — by a pillar of cloud and fire.

No sooner had they entered the land of promise than the Lord Jesus Christ Himself appeared to Joshua, not as one fighting for him, but as the Victorious Leader winning Victory so long as the people obeyed Him.

"Art thou for us or for our adversaries?" asks Joshua.

"Nay, but as captain of the host of the Lord am I NOW come" (Joshua 5:13-14). He was unable to come before. He could not come in this manner so long as the people wandered in the wilderness.

So with us. Christ will guide us — as with a cloud — even when our lives are but a wilderness experience.

But when we are fully surrendered to Him, He fills our hearts with His presence and takes complete control, and wins all our Victories for us — He, the captain of the host of the Lord.

Such a life is a Victorious Life — a life of constant miracle.

May every reader of these lines enter in and they too will get a vision of Christ Jesus, the Captain of the host of the Lord. And the JOY OF THE LORD which He Himself brings shall be their strength.

O Spirit of God and Jesus,
Blessed Trinity, come and possess
My body, my soul, and my spirit,
And fill me with Thy holiness.
Come in, come in, Holy Spirit,
Thy work of great blessings begin.
By faith I lay hold of Thy promise,
And claim complete victory o'er sin.

Waiting on God

Daily Messages for a Month

~ ※ ~

By *Andrew Murray*

The 1897 Edition

'My soul, wait thou only upon God.' —Ps. 62:5

'Wait Thou only upon God.'

'A God… which worketh for him that waiteth for Him.' —Isa. 64:4 (R.V.)

'WAIT only upon God;' my soul, be still,
And let thy God unfold His perfect will,
Thou fain[1] would'st follow Him throughout this year,
Thou fain with listening heart His voice would'st hear,
Thou fain would'st be a passive instrument
Possessed by God, and ever Spirit-sent
Upon His service sweet—then be thou still
For only thus can He in thee fulfil
His heart's desire. Oh, hinder not His hand
From fashioning the vessel He hath planned.
'Be silent unto God,' and thou shalt know
The quiet, holy calm He doth bestow
On these who wait on Him; so shalt thou bear
His promises, and His life and light e'en where
The night is darkest, and thine earthly days
Shall shew His love, and sound His glorious praise
And He will work with head unfettered, free
His high and holy purposes through thee.
First on thee must that hand of power be turned,
Till in His love's strong fire thy dross is burned,
And thou come forth a vessel for thy Lord,
So frail and empty, yet, since He hath poured
Into thine emptiness His life, His love
Henceforth through thee the power of God shall move
And He will work *for* thee. Stand still and see
The victories thy God will gain for thee;
So silent, yet so irresistible,
Thy God shall do the thing impossible.
Oh, question not henceforth what thou canst do;
Thou canst do *naught*. But He will carry through
The work where human energy had failed
Where all thy best endeavors had availed
Thee nothing. Then, my soul, wait and be still;
Thy God shall work for thee His perfect will.
If thou will take no less, *His best* shall be
Thy portion now and through eternity.

—FREDA HANBURY

---

[1] Fain: 'with pleasure'

Extract from Address in Exeter Hall

May 31st 1895

I HAVE been surprised at nothing more than at the letters that have come to me from missionaries and others from all parts of the world, devoted men and women, testifying to the need they feel in their work of being helped to a deeper and a clearer insight into all that Christ could be to them. Let us look to God to reveal Himself among His people in a measure very few have realized. Let us expect great things of our God. At all our conventions and assemblies too little time is given to waiting on God. Is He not willing to put things right in His own divine way? Has the life of God's people reached the utmost limit of what God is willing to do for them? Surely not. We want to wait on Him; to put away our experiences, however blessed they have been; our conceptions of truth, however sound and scriptural we think they seem; our plans, however needful and suitable they appear; and give God time and place to show us what He could, what He will do. God has new developments and new resources. He can do new things, unheard of things. Let us enlarge our hearts and not limit Him. 'When Thou camest down, Thou didst terrible things we looked not for; the mountains flowed down at Thy presence.'

—A. M.

Preface

PREVIOUS to my leaving for England last year, I had been much impressed by the thought of how, in all our religion, personal and public, we need more of God. I had felt that we needed to train our people in their worship more to wait on God, and to make the cultivation of a deeper sense of His presence, of more direct contact with Him, of entire dependence on Him, a definite aim of our ministry. At a 'welcome' breakfast in Exeter Hall, I gave very simple expression to this thought in connection with all our religious work. I have already said elsewhere that I was surprised at the response the sentiment met with. I saw that God's Spirit had been working the same desire in many hearts.

The experiences of the past year, both personal and public, have greatly deepened the conviction. It is as if I myself am only beginning to see the deepest truth concerning God, and our relation to Him, center in this waiting on God, and how very little, in our life and work, we have been surrounded by its spirit. The following pages are the outcome of my conviction, and of the desire to direct the attention of all God's people to the one great remedy for all our needs. More than half the pieces were written on board ship; I fear they bear the marks of being somewhat crude and hasty. I have felt, in looking them over, as if I could wish to write them over again. But this I cannot now do. And so I send them out with the prayer that He who loves to use the feeble may give His blessing with them.

I do not know if it will be possible for me to put into a few words what are the chief things we need to learn. In a note at the close of the book on Law I have mentioned some. But what I want to say here is this: The great lack of our religion is, *we do not know God.* The answer to every complaint of feebleness and failure, the message to every congregation or convention seeking instruction on holiness, ought to be simply, What is the matter: *Have you not God?* If you really believe in God, He will put all right. God is willing and able by His Holy Spirit. Cease from expecting the least good from yourself, or the least help from anything there is in man, and just yield yourself unreservedly to God to work in you: He will do all for you.

How simple this looks! And yet this is the gospel we so little know. I feel ashamed as I send forth these very defective meditations; I can only cast them on the love of my brethren, and of our God. May He use them to draw us all to Himself, to learn in practice and experience the blessed art of Waiting only upon God. Would God that we might get some right conception of what the influence would be of a life given, not in thought, or imagination, or effort, but in the power of the Holy Spirit, wholly to waiting upon God.

With my greeting in Christ to all God's saints it has been my privilege to meet, and no less to those I have not met, I subscribe myself, your brother and servant,

ANDREW MURRAY.

Wellington

3rd March 1896

Day 1: The God of Our Salvation.

'My soul waiteth only upon God[1]; from Him cometh my salvation.' —Ps. 62:1.

IF salvation indeed comes from God, and is entirely His work, just as our creation was, it follows, as a matter of course, that our first and highest duty is to wait on Him to do that work as it pleases Him. Waiting becomes then the only way to the experience of a full salvation, the only way, truly, to know God as the God of our salvation. All the difficulties that are brought forward as keeping us back from full salvation, have their cause in this one thing: the defective knowledge and practice of waiting upon God. All that the Church and its members need for the manifestation of the mighty power of God in the world, is the return to our true place, the place that belongs to us, both in creation and redemption, the place of absolute and unceasing dependence upon God. Let us strive to see what the elements are that make up this most blessed and needful waiting upon God: it may help us to discover the reasons why this grace is so little cultivated, and to feel how infinitely desirable it is that the Church, that we ourselves, should at any price learn its blessed secret.

The deep need for this waiting on God lies equally in the nature of man and the nature of God. God, as Creator, formed man, to be a vessel in which He could show forth His power and goodness. Man was not to have in himself a fountain of life, or strength, or happiness: the ever-living and only living One was each moment to be the Communicator to him of all that he needed. Man's glory and blessedness was not to be independent, or dependent upon himself, but dependent on a God of such infinite riches and love. Man was to have the joy of receiving every moment out of the fulness of God. This was his blessedness as an unfallen creature.

When he fell from God, he was still more absolutely dependent on Him. There was not the slightest hope of his recovery out of his state of death, but in God, His power and mercy. It is God alone who began the work of redemption; it is God alone who continues and carries it on each moment in each individual believer. Even in the regenerate man there is no power of goodness in himself: he has and can have nothing that he does not each moment receive; and waiting on God is just as indispensable, and must be just as continuous and unbroken, as the breathing that maintains his natural life.

It is, then, because Christians do not know in their relation to God of their own absolute poverty and helplessness, that they have no sense of the need of absolute and unceasing dependence, or of the unspeakable blessedness of continual waiting on God. But when once a believer begins to see it, and consent to it, that he by the Holy Spirit must each moment receive what God each moment works, waiting on God becomes his brightest hope and joy. As he appreciates how God, as God, as Infinite Love, delights to impart His own nature to His child as fully as He can, how God is not weary of each moment keeping charge of his life and strength, he wonders that he ever thought otherwise of God than as a God to be waited on all the day. God unceasingly giving and working; His child unceasingly waiting and receiving: this is the blessed life.

'Truly my soul waiteth upon God; from Him cometh my salvation.' First we wait on God for salvation. Then we learn that salvation is only to bring us to God, and teach us to wait on Him. Then we find what is better still, that waiting on God is itself the highest

---

[1] Or, 'is silent unto God'

salvation. It is the ascribing to Him the glory of being All; it is the experiencing that He is All to us. May God teach us the blessedness of waiting on Him.

'My soul, wait thou only upon God!'

Day 2: The Keynote of Life.

'I have waited for Thy salvation, O Lord!' —Gen. 49:18.

IT is not easy to say exactly in what sense Jacob used these words, in the midst of his prophecies in regard to the future of his sons. But they do certainly indicate that both for himself and for them his expectation was from God alone. It was God's salvation he waited for; a salvation which God had promised and which God Himself alone could work out. He knew himself and his sons to be under God's charge. Jehovah the Everlasting God would show in them what His saving power is and does. The words point forward to that wonderful history of redemption which is not yet finished, and to the glorious future in eternity. They suggest to us how there is no salvation but God's salvation, and how waiting on God for that, whether for our personal experience, or in wider circles, is our first duty, our true blessedness.

Let us think of ourselves, and the inconceivably glorious salvation God has wrought for us in Christ, and is now purposing to work out and to perfect in us by His Spirit. Let us meditate until we somewhat realize that every participation of this great salvation, from moment to moment, must be the work of God Himself. God cannot part with His grace, or goodness, or strength, as an external thing that He gives us, as He gives the raindrops from heaven. No; He can only give it, and we can only enjoy it, as He works it Himself directly and unceasingly. And the only reason that He does not work it more effectively and continuously is, that we do not let Him. We hinder Him either by our indifference or by our self-effort, so that He cannot do what He would. What He asks of us, in the way of surrender, and obedience, and desire, and trust, is all comprised in this one word: waiting on Him, waiting for His salvation. It combines the deep sense of our entire helplessness of ourselves to work what is divinely good, and the perfect confidence that our God will work it all in His divine power.

Again, I say, let us meditate on the divine glory of the salvation God purposes working out in us, until we know the truth it implies. Our heart is the scene of a divine operation more wonderful than Creation. We can do as little towards the work as towards creating the world, except as God works in us to will and to do. God only asks of us to yield, to consent, to wait upon Him, and He will do it all. Let us meditate and be still, until we see how appropriate and right and blessed it is that God alone do all, and our soul will of itself sink down in deep humility to say: 'I have waited for Thy salvation, O Lord.' And the deep blessed background of all our praying and working will be: 'Truly my soul waiteth upon God.'

The application of the truth to wider circles, to those we labor among or intercede for, to the Church of Christ around us, or throughout the world, is not difficult. There can be no good but what God works; to wait upon God, and have the heart filled with faith in His working, and in that faith to pray for His mighty power to come down, is our only wisdom. Oh for the eyes of our heart to be opened to see God working in ourselves and in others, and to see how blessed it is to worship and just to wait for His salvation!

Our private and public prayer are our chief expression of our relation to God: it is in them chiefly that our waiting upon God must be exercised. If our waiting begin by quieting the activities of nature, and being still before God; if it bows and seeks to see God in His universal and almighty operation, alone able and always ready to work all good; if it yields itself to Him in the assurance that He is working and will work in us; if it maintains the place of humility and stillness and surrender, until God's Spirit has quickened the faith that He will perfect His work: it will indeed become the strength and the joy of the soul. Life will become one deep blessed cry: 'I have waited for Thy salvation, O Lord.'

'My soul, wait thou only upon God!'

Day 3: The True Place of the Creature.

'These wait all upon Thee;

That Thou mayest give them their meat in due season.

That Thou givest unto them, they gather;

Thou openest Thine hand, they are satisfied with good.' —Ps. 104:27, 28 (R.V.).

THIS Psalm, in praise of the Creator, has been speaking of the birds and the beasts of the forest; of the young lions, and man going forth to his work; of the great sea, wherein are things creeping innumerable, both small and great beasts. And it sums up the whole relation of all creation to its Creator, and its continuous and universal dependence upon Him in the one word: 'These all wait upon Thee!' Just as much as it was God's work to create, it is His work to maintain. As little as the creature could create itself, is it left to provide for itself. The whole creation is ruled by the one unalterable law of—*waiting upon God!*

The word is the simple expression of that for the sake of which alone the creature was brought into existence, the very groundwork of its constitution. The one object for which God gave life to creatures was that in them He might prove and show forth His wisdom, power, and goodness, in His being each moment their life and happiness, and pouring forth unto them, according to their capacity, the riches of his goodness and power. And just as this is the very place and nature of God, to be unceasingly the supplier of every want in the creature, so the very place and nature of the creature is nothing but this—to wait upon God and receive from Him what He alone can give, what He delights to give. (See note on Law, *The Power of the Spirit.*)

If we are in this little book at all to appreciate what *waiting on God* is to be to the believer, to practice it and to experience its blessedness, it is of consequence that we begin at the very beginning, and see the deep reasonableness of the call that comes to us. We shall understand how the duty is no arbitrary command. We shall see how it is not only rendered necessary by our sin and helplessness. It is simply and truly our restoration to our original destiny and our highest nobility, to our true place and glory as creatures blessedly dependent on the All-Glorious God.

If once our eyes are opened to this precious truth, all Nature will become a preacher, reminding us of the relationship which, founded in creation, is now taken up in grace. As we read this Psalm, and learn to look upon all life in Nature as continually maintained by God Himself, waiting on God will be seen to be the very necessity of our being. As we think of the young lions and the ravens crying to Him, of the birds and the fish and every insect waiting on Him, until He give them their meat in due season, we shall see that it is the very nature and glory of God that He is a God who is to be waited on. Every thought of what Nature is, and what God is, will give new force to the call: 'Wait thou only upon God.'

'These all wait upon Thee, that thou may *give*.' It is God who gives all: let this faith enter deeply into our hearts. Ere yet we fully understand all that is implied in our waiting upon God, and ere we ever have been able to cultivate the habit, let the truth enter our souls: waiting on God, unceasing and entire dependence upon Him, is, in heaven and earth, the one only true religion, the one unalterable and all-comprehensive expression for the true relationship to the ever-blessed One in whom we live.

Let us resolve at once that it shall be the one characteristic of our life and worship, a continual, humble, trustful waiting upon God. We may rest assured that He who made us for Himself, that He might give Himself to us and in us, that He will never disappoint us. In waiting on Him we shall find rest and joy and strength, and the supply of every need.

'My soul, wait thou only upon God!'

Day 4: For Supplies.

'The Lord upholdeth all that fall,

And raiseth up all those that be bowed down.

The eyes of all wait upon Thee;

And Thou givest them their meat in due season.' —Ps. 145:14, 15.

PSALM 104 is a Psalm of Creation, and the words, *'These all wait upon Thee,'* were used with reference to the animal creation. Here we have a Psalm of the Kingdom, and *'The eyes of all wait upon Thee'* appears especially to point to the needs of God's saints, of all that fall and them that be bowed down. What the universe and the animal creation does unconsciously, God's people are to do intelligently and voluntarily. Man is to be the interpreter of Nature. He is to prove that there is nothing more noble or more blessed in the exercise of our free will than to use it in waiting upon God.

If an army has been sent out to march into an enemy's country, and tidings are received that it is not advancing, the question is at once asked, what may be the cause of delay. The answer will very often be: 'Waiting for supplies.' All the stores of provisions or clothing or ammunition have not arrived; without these it dare not proceed. It is no otherwise in the Christian life: day by day, at every step, we need our supplies from above. And there is nothing so needful as to cultivate that spirit of dependence on God and of confidence in Him, which refuses to go on without the needed supply of grace and strength.

If the question be asked, whether this be anything different from what we do when we pray, the answer is, that there may be much praying with but very little waiting on God. In praying we are often occupied with ourselves, with our own needs, and our own efforts in the presentation of them. In waiting upon God, the first thought is of *the God upon whom we wait*. We enter His presence, and feel we need just to be quiet, so that He, as God, can overshadow us with Himself. God longs to reveal Himself, to fill us with

Himself. Waiting on God gives Him time in His own way and divine power to come to us.

It is especially at the time of prayer that we ought to set ourselves to cultivate this spirit.

Before you pray, bow quietly before God, just to remember and realize who He is, how near He is, how certainly He can and will help. Just be still before Him, and allow His Holy Spirit to waken and stir up in your soul the childlike disposition of absolute dependence and confident expectation. Wait upon God as a Living Being, as the Living God, who notices you, and is just longing to fill you with His salvation. Wait on God until you know you have met Him; prayer will then become so different.

And when you are praying, let there be intervals of silence, reverent stillness of soul, in which you yield yourself to God, in case He may have aught He wishes to teach you or to work in you. Waiting on Him will become the most blessed part of prayer, and the blessing thus obtained will be doubly precious as the fruit of such fellowship with the Holy One. God has so ordained it, in harmony with His holy nature, and with ours, that waiting on Him should be the honor we give Him. Let us bring Him the service gladly and truthfully; He will reward it abundantly.

'The eyes of all wait upon Thee, and Thou givest them their meat in due season.' Dear soul, God provides in Nature for the creatures He has made: how much more will He provide in Grace for those He has redeemed. Learn to say of every want, and every failure, and every lack of needful grace: I have waited too little upon God, or He would have given me in due season all I needed. And say then too—

'My soul, wait thou only upon God!'

Day 5: For Instruction.

'Shew me thy ways, O Lord; Teach me Thy paths.

Teach me Thy paths.

Lead me in Thy truth, and teach me;

For Thou art the God of my salvation;

On Thee do I wait all the day.' —Ps. 25:4, 5.

'I SPOKE of an army, on the point of entering an enemy's territories, answering the question as to the cause of delay: *'Waiting for supplies.'* The answer might also have been: *'Waiting for instructions,'* or, *'Waiting for orders.'* If the last dispatch had not been received, with the final orders of the commander-in-chief, the army dared not move. Even so in the Christian life: as deep as the need of *waiting for supplies*, is that of *waiting for instructions.'*

See how beautifully this comes out in Ps. 25. The writer knew and loved God's law exceedingly, and meditated in that law day and night. But he knew that this was not enough. He knew that for the right spiritual apprehension of the truth, and for the right personal application of it to his own peculiar circumstances, he needed a direct divine teaching.

The psalm has at all times been a very favorite one, because of its reiterated expression of the felt need of the Divine teaching, and of the childlike confidence that that teaching would be given. Study the psalm until your heart is filled with the two thoughts—the absolute need, the absolute certainty of divine guidance. And notice, then, how entirely it is in this connection that he speaks, *'On Thee do I wait all the day.'* Waiting for guidance, waiting for instruction, all the day, is a very blessed part of waiting upon God.

The Father in heaven is so interested in His child, and so longs to have his life at every step in His will and His love, that He is willing to keep his guidance entirely in His own hand. He knows so well that we are unable to do what is really holy and heavenly, except as He works it in us, that He means His very demands to become promises of what He will do, in watching over and leading us all the day. Not only in special difficulties and times of perplexity, but in the common course of everyday life, we may count upon Him to teach us *His* way, and show us *His* path.

And what is needed in us to receive this guidance? One thing: waiting for instructions, waiting on God. 'On Thee do I wait all the day.' We want in our times of prayer to give clear expression to our sense of need, and our faith in His help. We want definitely to become conscious of our ignorance as to what God's way may be, and the need of the Divine light shining within us, if our way is to be as of the sun, shining more and more unto the perfect day. And we want to wait quietly before God in prayer, until the deep, restful assurance fills us: It will be given—'the meek will He guide in the way.'

'On Thee do I wait all the day.' The special surrender to the Divine guidance in our seasons of prayer must cultivate, and be followed up by, the habitual looking upwards 'all the day.' As simple as it is, to one who has eyes, to walk all the day in the light of the sun, so simple and delightful can it become to a soul practiced in waiting on God, to walk all the day in the enjoyment of God's light and leading. What is needed to help us to such a life is just one thing: the real knowledge and faith of God as the one only source of wisdom and goodness, as ever ready, and longing much to be to us all that we can possibly require—yes! this is the one thing we need. If we but saw our God in His love, if we but believed that He waits to be gracious, that He waits to be our life and to work all in us,—how this waiting on God would become our highest joy, the natural and spontaneous response of our hearts to His great love and glory!

'My soul, wait thou only upon God!'

Day 6: For all Saints.

'Let none that wait on Thee be ashamed.' —Ps. 25:3.

LET us now, in our meditation of today, each one forget himself, to think of the great company of God's saints throughout the world, who are all with us waiting on Him. And let us all join in the fervent prayer for each other, 'Let none that wait on Thee be ashamed.'

Just think for a moment of the multitude of waiting ones who need that prayer; how many there are, sick and weary and solitary, to whom it is as if their prayers are not answered, and who sometimes begin to fear that their hope will be put to shame. And then, how many servants of God, ministers or missionaries, teachers or workers, of various name, whose hopes in their work have been disappointed, and whose longing for power and blessing remains unsatisfied. And then, too, how many, who have heard of a life of rest and perfect peace, of abiding light and fellowship, of strength and victory, and who cannot find the path. With all these, it is nothing but that they have not yet learned the secret of full waiting upon God. They just need, what we all need, the living assurance that waiting on God can never be in vain. Let us remember all who are in danger of fainting or being weary, and all unite in the cry, 'Let none that wait on Thee be ashamed'!

If this intercession for all who wait on God becomes part of our waiting on Him for ourselves, we shall help to bear each other's burdens, and so fulfil the law of Christ.

There will be introduced into our waiting on God that element of unselfishness and love, which is the path to the highest blessing, and the fullest communion with God. Love to the brethren and love to God are inseparably linked. In God, the love to His Son *and to us* are one: 'That the love wherewith Thou hast loved Me, may be in them.' In Christ, the love of the Father to Him, and *His love to us,* are one: 'As the Father loved me, so have I loved you.' In us, He asks that His love to us shall be *ours* to the brethren: 'As I have loved you, that ye love one another.' All the love of God, and of Christ, are inseparably linked with love to the brethren. And how can we, day by day, prove and cultivate this love otherwise than by daily praying for each other? Christ did not seek to enjoy the Father's love for Himself; He passed it all on to us. All true seeking of God and His love for ourselves, will be inseparably linked with the thought and the love of our brethren in prayer for them.

'Let none that wait on Thee be ashamed.' Twice in the psalm David speaks of his waiting on God for himself; here he thinks of *all* who wait on Him. Let this page take the message to all God's tried and weary ones, that there are more praying for them than they know. Let it stir them and us in our waiting to make a point of at times forgetting ourselves, and to enlarge our hearts, and say to the Father, *'These all wait upon Thee,* and Thou givest them their meat in due season.' Let it inspire us all with new courage—for who is there who is not at times ready to faint and be weary? 'Let none that wait on Thee be ashamed' is a promise in a prayer, 'They that wait on Thee shall not be ashamed'! From many and many a witness the cry comes to everyone who needs the help, brother, sister, tried one, 'Wait on the Lord; be of good courage, and He shall strengthen your heart; wait, I say, on the Lord. Be of good courage, and He shall strengthen your heart, all ye that wait on the Lord.'

Blessed Father! we humbly beseech Thee, Let none that wait on Thee be ashamed; no, not one. Some are weary, and the time of waiting appears long. And some are feeble, and scarcely know how to wait. And some are so entangled in the effort of their prayers and their work, they think that they can find no time to wait continually. Father! teach us all how to wait. Teach us to think of each other, and pray for each other. Teach us to think of Thee, the God of all waiting ones. Father! let none that wait on Thee be ashamed. For Jesus' sake. Amen.

'My soul, wait thou only upon God!'

Day 7: A Plea in Prayer.

'Let integrity and uprightness preserve me; for I wait on Thee.' —Ps. 25:21.

FOR the third time in this psalm we have the word wait. As before in ver. 5, 'On Thee do I wait all the day,' so here, too, the believing supplicant appeals to God to remember that he is waiting on Him, looking for an answer. It is a great thing for a soul not only to wait upon God, but to be filled with such a consciousness that its whole spirit and position is that of a waiting one, that it can, in childlike confidence, say, Lord! Thou knowest, I wait on Thee. It will prove a mighty plea in prayer, giving ever-increasing boldness of expectation to claim the promise, 'They that wait on Me shall not be ashamed'!

The prayer in connection with which the plea is put forth here is one of great importance in the spiritual life. If we draw near to God, it must be with a true heart. There must be perfect integrity, wholeheartedness, in our dealing with God. As we read in the next Psalm (26:1, 11), 'Judge me, O Lord, for I have walked in my integrity,' 'As for me, I will walk in my integrity,' there must be perfect uprightness or single-heartedness before God. As it is written, 'His righteousness is for the upright in heart.' The soul must know that it allows nothing sinful, nothing doubtful; if it is indeed to meet the Holy One, and receive His full blessing, it must be with a heart wholly and singly given up to His will. The whole spirit that animates us in the waiting must be, 'Let integrity and uprightness'— Thou seest that I desire to come so to Thee, You know I am looking to Thee to work them perfectly in me;—let them 'preserve me, for I wait on Thee.'

And if at our first attempt truly to live the life of fully and always waiting on God, we begin to discover how much that perfect integrity is wanting, this will just be one of the blessings which the waiting was meant to work. *A soul cannot seek close fellowship with God, or attain the abiding consciousness of waiting on Him all the day, without a very honest and entire surrender to all His will.*

'For I wait on Thee': it is not only in connection with the prayer of our text but with every prayer that this plea may be used. To use it often will be a great blessing to ourselves. Let us therefore study the words well until we know all their bearings. It must be clear to us *what we are waiting for*. There may be very different things. It may be waiting for God in our times of prayer to take his place as God, and to work in us the sense of His holy presence and nearness. It may be some special petition, to which we are expecting an answer. It may be our whole inner life, in which we are on the lookout for God's putting forth of His power. It may be the whole state of His Church and saints, or some part of His work, for which our eyes are ever toward Him. It is good that we sometimes count up to ourselves exactly what the things are we are waiting for, and as we say definitely of each of them, 'On Thee do I wait,' we shall be emboldened to claim the answer, '*For* on Thee do I wait.'

It must also be clear to us, *on Whom we are waiting*. Not an idol, a God of whom we have made an image by our conceptions of what He is. No, but the living God, such as He really is in His great glory, His infinite holiness, His power, wisdom, and goodness, in His love and nearness. It is the presence of a beloved or a dreaded master that wakens up the whole attention of the servant who waits on him. It is *the presence of God, as He can in Christ by His Holy Spirit make Himself known*, and keep the soul under its covering and shadow, that will awaken and strengthen the true waiting spirit. Let us be still and wait and worship until we know how near He is, and then say, '*On Thee do I wait.*'

And then, let it be very clear, too, that *we are waiting*. Let that become so much our consciousness that the utterance comes spontaneously, 'On Thee *I do wait* all the day; I *wait* on Thee.' This will indeed imply sacrifice and separation, a soul entirely given up to God as its all, its only joy. This waiting on God has hardly yet been acknowledged as the only true Christianity. And yet, if it be true that God alone is goodness and joy and love; if it be true that our highest blessedness is in having as much of God as we can; if it be true that Christ has redeemed us wholly for God, and made a life of continual abiding in His presence possible, nothing less ought to satisfy than to be ever breathing this blessed atmosphere, 'I wait on Thee.'

'My soul, wait thou only upon God!'

Day 8: Strong and of Good Courage.

'Wait on the Lord: be strong,

And let your heart take courage:

Yea, wait thou on the Lord.' —Ps. 27:14 (R.V.)

THE psalmist had just said, 'I had fainted, unless I had believed to see the goodness of the Lord in the land of the living.' If it had not been for his faith in God, his heart had fainted. But in the confident assurance in God which faith gives, he urges himself and us to remember one thing above all,—to wait upon God. 'Wait on the Lord: be strong, and let your heart take courage: yea, wait on the Lord.' One of the chief needs in our waiting upon God, one of the deepest secrets of its blessedness and blessing, is a quiet, confident persuasion that it is not in vain; courage to believe that God will hear and help; that we are waiting on a God who never could disappoint His people.

'Be strong and of good courage.' These words are frequently found in connection with some great and difficult enterprise, in prospect of the combat with the power of strong enemies, and the utter insufficiency of all human strength. Is waiting on God a work so difficult, that, for that too, such words are needed, 'Be strong, and let your heart take courage'? Yes, indeed. The deliverance, for which we often have to wait, is from enemies, in presence of whom we are impotent. The blessings for which we plead are spiritual and all unseen; things impossible with men; heavenly, supernatural, divine realities. Our souls are so little accustomed to hold fellowship with God, the God on whom we wait so often appears to hide Himself. We who have to wait are often tempted to fear that we do not wait aright, that our faith is too feeble, that our desire is not as upright or as earnest as it should be, that our surrender is not complete. Our heart may well faint and fail. Amid all these causes of fear or doubt, how blessed to hear the voice of God, 'Wait on the Lord! Be strong, and let your heart take courage! Yea, wait thou upon the Lord! Let nothing in heaven or earth or hell—let nothing keep you from waiting on your God in full assurance that it cannot be in vain.

The one lesson our text teaches us is thus, that when we set ourselves to wait on God, we ought beforehand to resolve that it shall be with the most confident expectation of God's meeting and blessing us. We ought to make up our minds to this, that nothing was ever so sure, as that waiting on God will bring us untold and unexpected blessing. We are so accustomed to judge of God and His work in us by *what we feel*, that the great probability is that when we begin more to cultivate the waiting on Him, we shall be discouraged, because we do not find any special blessing from it. The message comes to us, 'Above everything, when you wait on God, do so in the spirit of abounding hopefulness. It is God in His glory, in His power, in His love longing to bless you that you are waiting on.'

If you say that you are afraid of deceiving yourself with vain hope, because you do not see or feel any warrant in your present state for such special expectations, my answer is, it is God, who is the warrant for your expecting great things. Oh, do learn the lesson. You are not going to wait on yourself to see what you feel and what changes come to you. You are going to WAIT ON GOD, to know *first*, WHAT HE IS, and then, after that, what He will do. The whole duty and blessedness of waiting on God has its root in this, that He is such a blessed Being, full, to overflowing, of goodness and power and life and joy, that we, however wretched, cannot for any time come into contact with Him, without that life and power secretly, silently beginning to enter into us and blessing us. God is Love! That is the one only and all-sufficient warrant of your expectation. Love seeks not its own: God's love is just *His delight to impart Himself and His blessedness* to His children. Come, and however feeble you feel, just wait in His presence. As a feeble, sickly invalid is brought out into the sunshine to let its warmth go through him, come with all that is dark and cold in you *into the sunshine of God's holy, omnipotent love*, and sit and wait there, with the one thought: Here I am, in the sunshine of His love. As the sun does its work in the weak one who seeks its rays, *God will do His work in you.* Oh, do trust Him fully. 'Wait on the Lord! Be strong, and let your heart take courage! Yea, wait on the Lord'!

'My soul, wait thou only upon God!'

Day 9: With the Heart.

'Be strong, and let your heart take courage,

All ye that wait for the Lord.' —Ps. 31:24. (R.V.).

THE words are nearly the same as in our last meditation. But I gladly avail myself of them again to press home a much-needed lesson for all who desire to learn truly and fully what waiting on God is. The lesson is this: It is *with the heart* we must wait upon God. 'Let *your heart* take courage.' All our waiting depends upon the state of the heart. As a man's heart is, so is he before God. We can advance no further or deeper into the holy place of God's presence to wait on Him there, than our heart is prepared for it by the Holy Spirit. The message is, 'Let *your heart* take courage, all you that wait on the Lord.'

The truth appears so simple, that some may ask, Do not all admit this? where is the need of insisting on it so specially? Because very many Christians have no sense of the great difference between the religion of the mind and the religion of the heart, and the former is far more diligently cultivated than the latter. They know not how infinitely greater the heart is than the mind. It is in this that one of the chief causes must be sought of the feebleness of our Christian life, and it is only as this is understood that waiting on God will bring its full blessing.

Proverbs 3:5 may help to make my meaning plain. Speaking of a life in the fear and favor of God, it says, 'Trust in the Lord with all your heart, and lean not upon your own understanding.' In all religion we have to use these two powers. The mind has to gather knowledge from God's word, and prepare the food by which the heart with the inner life is to be nourished. But here comes in a terrible danger, of our leaning to our own understanding, and trusting in our understanding of divine things. People imagine that if they are occupied with the truth, the spiritual life will as a matter of course be strengthened. And this is by no means the case. The understanding deals with conceptions and images of divine things, but it cannot reach the real life of the soul. Hence the command, 'Trust in the Lord with all your heart, and lean not upon your own understanding.' It is with the heart man believes, and comes into touch with God. It is in the heart God has given His Spirit, to be there to us the presence and the power of God working in us. In all our religion it is the heart that must trust and love and worship and obey. My mind is utterly impotent in creating or maintaining the spiritual life within me: the heart must wait on God for Him to work it in me.

It is in this even as in the physical life. My reason may tell me what to eat and drink, and how the food nourishes me. But in the eating and feeding my reason can do nothing: the body has its organs for that special purpose. Just so, reason may tell me what God's word says, but it can do nothing to the feeding of the soul on the bread of life—this the heart alone can do by its faith and trust in God. A man may be studying the nature and effects of food or sleep; when he wants to eat or sleep he sets aside his thoughts and study, and uses the power of eating or sleeping. And so the Christian needs ever, when he has studied or heard God's word, to cease from his thoughts, to put no trust in them, and to awaken his heart to open itself before God, and seek the living fellowship with Him.

This is now the blessedness of waiting upon God, that I confess the impotence of all my thoughts and efforts, and set myself still to bow my heart before Him in holy silence, and to trust Him to renew and strengthen His own work in me. And this is just the lesson of our text, 'Let *your heart* take courage, all you that wait on the Lord.' Remember the difference between knowing with the mind and believing with the heart. Beware of the temptation of leaning upon your understanding, with its clear strong thoughts. They only help you to know what the heart must get from God: in themselves they are only images and shadows. 'Let *your heart* take courage, all ye that wait on the Lord.' Present it before Him as that wonderful part of your spiritual nature in which God reveals Himself, and by which you can know Him. Cultivate the greatest confidence that, though you cannot see into your heart, God is working there by His Holy Spirit. Let the heart wait at times in perfect silence and quiet; in its hidden depths God will work. Be sure of this, and just wait on Him. Give your whole heart, with its secret workings, into God's hands continually. He wants the heart, and takes it, and as God dwells in it. 'Be strong, and let your heart take courage, all ye that wait on the Lord.'

'My soul, wait thou only upon God!'

Day 10: In Humble Fear and Hope.

'Behold, the eye of the Lord is upon them that fear Him,

Upon them that hope in His mercy;

To deliver their soul from death,

And to keep them alive in famine.

Our soul hath waited for the Lord;

He is our help and our shield.

For our heart shall rejoice in Him,

Because we have trusted in His holy name.

Let thy mercy, O Lord, be upon us,

According as we wait for thee.' —Ps. 33:18-22 (R.V.).

GOD'S eye is upon His people: their eye is upon Him. In waiting upon God, our eye, looking up to Him, meets His looking down upon us. This is the blessedness of waiting upon God, that it takes our eyes and thoughts away from ourselves, even our needs and desires, and occupies us with our God. We worship Him in His glory and love, with His all-seeing eye watching over us, that He may supply our every need. Let us consider this wonderful meeting between God and His people, and mark well what we are taught here of those on whom God's eye rests, and of Him on whom our eye rests.

'The eye of the Lord is on them that fear Him, on them that hope in His mercy.' Fear and hope are generally thought to be in conflict with each other; in the presence and worship of God they are found side by side in perfect and beautiful harmony. And this because in God Himself all apparent contradictions are reconciled. Righteousness and peace, judgment and mercy, holiness and love, infinite power and infinite gentleness, a majesty that is exalted above all heaven, and a condescension that bows very low, meet and kiss each other. There is indeed a fear that has torment, that is cast out entirely by perfect love. But there is a fear that is found in the very heavens. In the song of Moses and the Lamb they sing, 'Who shall not fear Thee, O Lord, and glorify Thy name?' And out of the very throne the voice came, 'Praise our God, all His servants, and ye that fear Him.' Let us in our waiting ever seek 'to fear the glorious and fearful name, The Lord thy God.' The deeper we bow before His holiness in holy fear and adoring awe, in deep reverence and humble self-abasement, even as the angels veil their faces before the throne, the more will His holiness rest upon us, and the soul be fitted to have God reveal Himself; the deeper we enter into the truth 'that no flesh glory in His presence,' will it be given us to see His glory. 'The eye of the Lord is on them that fear Him.'

'On them that hope in His mercy.' So far will the true fear of God be from keeping us back from hope, it will stimulate and strengthen it. The lower we bow, the deeper we feel we have nothing to hope in but His mercy. The lower we bow, the nearer God will come, and make our hearts bold to trust Him. Let every exercise of waiting, let our whole habit of waiting on God, be pervaded by abounding hope—a hope as bright and boundless as God's mercy. The fatherly kindness of God is such that, in whatever state we come to Him, we may confidently hope in His mercy.

Such are God's waiting ones. And now, think of the God on whom we wait. 'The eye of the Lord is on them that fear Him, on them that hope in His mercy; to deliver their soul from death, and to keep them alive in famine.' Not to prevent the danger of death and famine—this is often needed to stir up to wait on Him—but to deliver and to keep alive. For the dangers are often very real and dark; the situation, whether in the temporal or spiritual life, may appear to be utterly hopeless; there is always one hope: *God's eye is on them.*

That eye sees the danger, and sees in tender love His trembling waiting child, and sees the moment when the heart is ripe for the blessing, and sees the way in which it is to come. This living, mighty God, oh, let us fear Him and hope in His mercy. And let us humbly but boldly say, 'Our soul waiteth for the Lord; He is our help and our shield. Let Thy mercy be upon us, O Lord, according as we wait for Thee.'

Oh, the blessedness of waiting on such a God! a very present help in every time of trouble; a shield and defense against every danger. Children of God! will you not learn to sink down in entire helplessness and impotence, and in stillness to wait and see the salvation of God? In the utmost spiritual famine, and when death appears to prevail, oh, wait on God. He does deliver, He does keep alive. Say it not only in solitude, but say it to each other—the psalm speaks not of one but of God's people—'Our soul waits on the Lord: He is our help and our shield.' Strengthen and encourage each other in the holy exercise of waiting, that each may not only say it of himself, but of his brethren, 'We have waited for Him; we will be glad and rejoice in His salvation.'

'My soul, wait thou only upon God!'

Day 11: Patiently.

'Rest in the Lord, and wait patiently for Him.

Those that wait upon the Lord, they shall inherit the land.' —Ps. 37:7, 9 (R.V.).

'IN patience possess your souls.' 'Ye have need of patience.' 'Let patience have its perfect work, that ye may be perfect and entire.' Such words of the Holy Spirit show us what an important element in the Christian life and character patience is. And nowhere is there a better place for cultivating or displaying it than in waiting on God. There we discover how impatient we are, and what our impatience means. We confess at times that we are impatient with men and circumstances that hinder us, or with ourselves and our slow progress in the Christian life. If we truly set ourselves to wait upon God, we shall find that it is with Him we are impatient, because He does not at once, or as soon as we could wish, do our bidding. It is in waiting upon God that our eyes are opened to believe in His wise and sovereign will, and to see that the sooner and the more completely we yield absolutely to it, the more surely His blessing can come to us.

'It is not of him that wills, nor of him that runs, but of God that shows mercy.' We have as little power to increase or strengthen our spiritual life, as we had to originate it. We 'were born not of the will of the flesh, nor of the will of man, but of the will of God.' Even so, our willing and running, our desire and effort, avail nought; all is 'of God that showeth mercy.' All the exercises of the spiritual life, our reading and praying, our willing and doing, have their very great value. But they can go no farther than this, that they point the way and prepare us in humility to look to and to depend alone upon God Himself, and in patience to await His good time and mercy. The waiting is to teach us our absolute dependence upon God's mighty working, and to make us in perfect patience place ourselves at His disposal. They that wait on the Lord shall inherit the land; the promised land and its blessing. The heirs must wait; they can afford to wait.

'Rest in the lord, and wait patiently for Him.' The margin gives for 'Rest in the Lord,' 'Be silent to the Lord,' or R.V., 'Be still before the Lord.' It is resting in the Lord, in His will, His promise, His faithfulness, and His love, that makes patience easy. And the resting in Him is nothing but being silent unto Him, still before Him. Having our thoughts and wishes, our fears and hopes, hushed into calm and quiet in that great peace of God which passeth all understanding. That peace keeps the heart and mind when we are anxious for anything, because we have made our request known to Him. The rest, the silence, the stillness, and the patient waiting, all find their strength and joy in God Himself.

The needs be, and the reasonableness, and the blessedness of patience will be opened up to the waiting soul. Our patience will be seen to be the counterpart of God's patience.

He longs far more to bless us fully than we can desire it. But, as the husbandman has long patience until the fruit be ripe, so God bows Himself to our slowness and bears long with us. Let us remember this, and wait patiently: of each promise and every answer to prayer the word is true: 'I the Lord will hasten it *in its time*.'

'Rest in the Lord, and wait patiently for Him.' Yes, for Him. Seek not only the help, the gift, you need; seek Himself; wait for Him. Give God His glory by resting in Him, by trusting him fully, by waiting patiently for Him. This patience honors Him greatly; it leaves Him, as God on the throne, to do His work; it yields self wholly into His hands. It lets God be God. If your waiting be for some special request, wait patiently. If your waiting be more the exercise of the spiritual life seeking to know and have more of God, wait patiently. Whether it be in the shorter specific periods of waiting, or as the continuous habit of the soul; rest in the Lord, be still before the Lord, and wait patiently. 'They that wait on the Lord shall inherit the land.'

'My soul, wait thou only upon God!'

Day 12: Keeping His Ways.

'Wait on the Lord, and keep His way,

And He shalt exalt thee to inherit the land.' —Ps. 37:34.

IF we desire to find a man whom we long to meet, we inquire where the places and the ways are where he is to be found. When waiting on God, we need to be very careful that we keep His ways; out of these we never can expect to find Him. 'Thou meetest him that rejoices and worketh righteousness; those that remember *Thee in Thy ways*.' We may be sure that God is never and nowhere to be found but in His ways. And that there, by the soul who seeks and patiently waits, He is always most surely to be found. 'Wait on the Lord, and keep His ways, and He shall exalt thee.'

How close the connection between the two parts of the injunction. 'Wait on the Lord,'—that has to do with worship and disposition; 'and keep His ways,'—that deals with walk and work. The outer life must be in harmony with the inner; the inner must be the inspiration and the strength for the outer. It is our God who has made known His ways in His Word for our conduct, and invites our confidence for His grace and help in our heart. If we do not keep His ways, our waiting on Him can bring no blessing. The surrender to a full obedience to all His will, is the secret of full access to all the blessings of His fellowship.

Notice how strongly this comes out in the psalm. It speaks of the evildoer who prospers in his way, and calls on the believer not to fret himself. When we see men around us prosperous and happy while they forsake God's ways, and ourselves left in difficulty or suffering, we are in danger of first fretting at what appears so strange, and then gradually yielding to seek our prosperity in their path. The psalm says, 'Fret not thyself; trust in the Lord, and do good. Rest in the Lord, and wait patiently for Him; cease from anger, and forsake wrath. Depart from evil, and do good; the Lord forsakes not His saints. The righteous shall inherit the land. The law of his God is in his heart; none of his steps shall slide.' And then follows—the word occurs for the third time in the psalm—'Wait on the Lord, and keep His ways.' Do what God asks you to do; God will do more than you can ask Him to do.

And let no one give way to the fear: I cannot keep His ways; it is this robs us of our confidence. It is true you have not the strength yet to keep all His ways. But keep carefully those for which you have received strength already. Surrender yourself willingly and trustingly to keep all God's ways, in the strength which will come in waiting on Him. Give up your whole being to God without reserve and without doubt; He will prove Himself God to you, and work in you that which is pleasing in His sight through Jesus Christ. Keep His ways, as you know them in the Word. Keep His ways, as nature teaches them, in always doing what appears right. Keep His ways, as Providence points them out. Keep His ways, as the Holy Spirit suggests. Do not think of waiting on God while you say you are not willing to walk in His path. However weak you feel, only be willing, and He who has worked to will, will work to do by His power.

'Wait on the Lord, and keep His ways.' It may be that the consciousness of shortcoming and sin makes our text look more like a hindrance than a help in waiting on God. Let it not be so. Have we not said more than once, the very starting-point and groundwork of this waiting is utter and absolute impotence? Why then not come with everything evil you feel in yourself, every memory of unwillingness, unwatchfulness, unfaithfulness, and all that causes such unceasing self-condemnation? Put your trust in God's omnipotence, and find in waiting on God your deliverance. Your failure has been owing to only one thing: you sought to conquer and obey in your own strength. Come and bow before God until you learn that He is the God who alone is good, and alone can work any good thing. Believe that in you, and all that nature can do, there is no true power. Be content to receive from God each moment the inworking of His mighty grace and life, and waiting on God will become the renewal of your strength to run in His ways and not be weary, to walk in His paths and never faint. 'Wait on the Lord, and keep His ways' will be command and promise in one.

'My soul, wait thou only upon God!'

Day 13: For More Than We Know.

'And now, Lord, what wait I for? My hope is in Thee. Deliver me from all my transgressions.' —Ps. 39:7, 8.

THERE may be times when we feel as if we knew not what we are waiting for. There may be other times when we think we do know, and when it would just be so good for us to realize that we do not know what to ask as we ought. God is able to do for us exceeding abundantly above what we ask or think, and we are in danger of limiting Him, when we confine our desires and prayers to our own thoughts of them. It is a great thing at times to say, as our psalm says: 'And now, Lord, what wait I for?' I scarce know or can tell; this only I can say—'My hope is in Thee.'

How we see this limiting of God in the case of Israel! When Moses promised them meat in the wilderness, they doubted, saying, 'Can God furnish a table in the wilderness? He smote the rock that the water gushed out; can He give bread also? Can He provide flesh for His people?' If they had been asked whether God could provide streams in the desert, they would have answered, Yes. God had done it: He could do it again. But when the thought came of God doing something new, they limited Him; their expectation could not rise beyond their past experience, or their own thoughts of what was possible. Even so we may be limiting God by our conceptions of what He has promised or is able to do.

Do let us beware of limiting the Holy One of Israel in our very prayer. Let us believe that every promise of God we plead has a divine meaning, infinitely beyond our thoughts of them. Let us believe that His fulfilment of them can be, in a power and an abundance of grace, beyond our largest grasp of thought. And let us therefore cultivate the habit of waiting on God, not only for what we think we need, but for all His grace and power are ready to do for us.

In every true prayer there are two hearts in exercise. The one is your heart, with its little, dark, human thoughts of what you need and God can do. The other is God's great heart, with its infinite, its divine purposes of blessing. What think you? To which of these two ought the larger place to be given in your approach to Him? Undoubtedly, to the heart of God: everything depends upon knowing and being occupied with that. But how little this is done. This is what waiting on God is meant to teach you. Just think of God's wonderful love and redemption, in the meaning these words must have to Him. Confess how little you understand what God is willing to do for you, and say each time as you pray 'And now, what wait I for?' My heart cannot say. God's heart knows and waits to give. 'My hope is in Thee.' Wait on God to do for you more than you can ask or think.

Apply this to the prayer that follows: 'Deliver me from all my transgressions.' You have prayed to be delivered from temper, or pride, or self-will. It is as if it is in vain. May it not be that you have had your own thoughts about the way or the extent of God's doing it, and have never waited on the God of glory, according to the riches of His glory, to do for you what has not entered the heart of man to conceive? Learn to worship God as the God who does wonders, who wishes to prove in you that He can do something supernatural and divine. Bow before Him, wait upon Him, until your soul realizes that you are in the hands of a divine and almighty worker. Consent not to know what and how He will work; expect it to be something altogether godlike, something to be waited for in deep humility, and received only by His divine power. Let the, 'And now, Lord, what wait I for? My hope is in Thee' become the spirit of every longing and every prayer. He will in His time do His work.

Dear soul, in waiting on God you may often be ready to be weary, because you hardly know what you have to expect. I pray you, be of good courage—this ignorance is often one of the best signs. He is teaching you to leave all in His hands, and to wait on Him alone. 'Wait on the Lord! Be strong, and let your heart take courage. Yea, wait on the Lord.'

'My soul, wait thou only upon God!'

Day 14: The Way to the New Song.

'I waited patiently for the Lord, and He inclined unto me, and heard my cry… And He hath put a new song in my mouth, even praise unto our God.'
—Ps. 40:1-3.

COME and listen to the testimony of one who can speak from experience of the sure and blessed outcome of patient waiting upon God. True patience is so foreign to our self-confident nature, it is so indispensable in our waiting upon God, it is such an essential element of true faith, that we may well once again meditate on what the word has to teach us.

The word patience is derived from the Latin word for suffering. It suggests the thought of being under the constraint of some power from which we want to be free. At first we submit against our will; experience teaches us that when it is vain to resist, patient endurance is our wisest course. In waiting on God it is of infinite consequence that we not only submit, because we are compelled to, but because we lovingly and joyfully consent to be in the hands of our blessed Father. Patience then becomes our highest blessedness and our highest grace. It honors God, and gives Him time to have His way with us. It is the highest expression of our faith in His goodness and faithfulness. It brings the soul perfect rest in the assurance that God is carrying on His work. It is the token of our full consent that God should deal with us in such a way and time as He thinks best. True patience is the losing of our self-will in His perfect will.

Such patience is needed for the true and full waiting on God. Such patience is the growth and fruit of our first lessons in the school of waiting. To many a one it will appear strange how difficult it is truly to wait upon God. The great stillness of soul before God that sinks into its own helplessness and waits for Him to reveal Himself; the deep humility that is afraid to let its own will or its own strength work aught except as God works to will and to do; the meekness that is content to be and to know nothing except as God gives His light; the entire resignation of the will that only wants to be a vessel in which His holy will can move and mold: all these elements of perfect patience are not found at once. But they will come in measure as the soul maintains its position, and ever again says: 'Truly my soul waiteth upon God; from Him cometh my salvation: He only is my rock and my salvation.'

Have you ever noticed what proof we have that patience is a grace for which very special grace is given, in these words of Paul: 'Strengthened with all might, according to His glorious power, unto all'—what? 'patience and long-suffering with joyfulness.' Yes, we need to be strengthened with all God's might, and that according to the measure of His glorious power, if we are to wait on God in all patience. It is God revealing Himself in us as our life and strength, that will enable us with perfect patience to leave all in His hands. If any are inclined to despond, because they have not such patience, let them be of good courage; it is in the course of our feeble and very imperfect waiting that God Himself by His hidden power strengthens us and works out in us the patience of the saints, the patience of Christ Himself.

Listen to the voice of one who was deeply tried: 'I waited patiently for the Lord, and He inclined unto me, and heard my cry.' Hear what he passed through: 'He brought me up also out of an horrible pit, out of the miry clay, and set my feet upon a rock, and established my goings. And He has put a new song in my mouth, even praise unto our God.' Patient waiting upon God brings a rich reward; the deliverance is sure; God Himself will put a new song into your mouth. O soul! be not impatient, whether it be in the exercise of prayer and worship that you find it difficult to wait, or in the delay in respect of definite requests, or in the fulfilling of your heart's desire for the revelation of God Himself in a deeper spiritual life—fear not, but rest in the Lord, and wait patiently for Him. And if you sometimes feel as if patience is not your gift, then remember it is God's gift, and take that prayer (2 Thess. 3:5 R.V.): 'The Lord direct your hearts into the patience of Christ.' Into the patience with which you are to wait on God, He Himself will guide you.

'My soul, wait thou only upon God!'

Day 15: For His Counsel.

'They soon forgot His works: they waited not for His counsel.' —Ps. 106:13.

THIS is said of the sin of God's people in the wilderness. He had wonderfully redeemed them, and was prepared as wonderfully to supply their every need. But, when the time of need came, 'they waited not for His counsel.' They thought not that the Almighty God was their Leader and Provider; they asked not what His plans might be. They simply thought the thoughts of their own heart, and tempted and provoked God by their unbelief. 'They waited not for His counsel.'

How this has been the sin of God's people in all ages! In the land of Canaan, in the days of Joshua, the only three failures of which we read were owing to this one sin. In going up against Ai, in making a covenant with the Gibeonites, in settling down without going up to possess the whole land, they waited not for His counsel. And so even the advanced believer is in danger from this most subtle of temptations—taking God's word and thinking his own thoughts of them, and not waiting for His counsel. Let us take the warning and see what Israel teaches us. And let us very specially regard it not only as a danger to which the individual is exposed, but as one against which God's people, in their collective capacity, need to be on their guard.

Our whole relation to God is rooted in this, that His will is to be done in us and by us as it is in heaven. He has promised to make known His will to us by His Spirit, the Guide into all truth. And our position is to be that of waiting for His counsel, as the only guide of our thoughts and actions. In our church worship, in our prayer-meetings, in our conventions, in all our gatherings as managers, or directors, or committees, or helpers in any part of the work for God, our first object ought ever to be to ascertain the mind of God. God always works according to the counsel of His will; the more that counsel of His will is sought and found and honored, the more surely and mightily will God do His work for us and through us.

The great danger in all such assemblies is that in our consciousness of having our Bible, and our past experience of God's leading, and our sound creed, and our honest wish to do God's will, we trust in these, and do not realize that with every step we need and may have a heavenly guidance. There may be elements of God's will, applications of God's word, experiences of the close presence and leading of God, manifestations of the power of His Spirit, of which we know nothing as yet. God may be willing, no, God is willing to open up these to the souls who are intently set upon allowing Him to have His way entirely, and who are willing in patience to wait for His making it known. When we come together praising God for all He has done and taught and given, we may at the same time be limiting Him by not expecting greater things. It was when God had given the water out of the rock that they did not trust Him for bread. It was when God had given Jericho into his hands that Joshua thought the victory over Ai was sure; he now knew what God could do, and waited not for counsel from God. And so, while we think that we know and trust the power of God for what we may expect, we may be hindering Him by not giving time, and not definitely cultivating the habit of waiting for His counsel.

A minister has no more solemn duty than teaching people to wait upon God. Why was it that in the house of Cornelius, when 'Peter spoke these words, the Holy Ghost fell upon all that heard him'? They had said, 'We are here *before God* to hear all things that are commanded you *of God.*' We may come together to give and to listen to the most earnest exposition of God's truth with little spiritual profit if there be not the waiting for

God's counsel. In all our gatherings we need to believe in the Holy Spirit as the Guide and Teacher of God's saints when they wait to be led by Him into the things which God has prepared, and which the heart cannot conceive.

More stillness of soul to realize God's presence; more consciousness of ignorance of what God's great plans may be; more faith in the certainty that God has greater things to show us; more longing that He Himself may be revealed in new glory: these must be the marks of the assemblies of God's saints, if they would avoid the reproach, 'They waited not for His counsel.'

'My soul, wait thou only upon God!'

Day 16: For His Light in the Heart.

'I wait for the Lord, my soul doth wait,

And in His word do I hope.

My soul waiteth for the Lord

more than they that watch for the morning:

More than they that watch for the morning.' —Ps. 130:5, 6.

WITH what intense longing the morning light is often waited for. By the mariners in a shipwrecked vessel; by a benighted traveler in a dangerous country; by an army that finds itself surrounded by an enemy. The morning light will show what hope of escape there may be. The morning may bring life and liberty. And so the saints of God in darkness have longed for the light of His countenance, more than watchmen for the morning. They have said, 'More than watchmen for the morning, my soul waiteth for the Lord.' Can we say that too? Our waiting on God can have no higher object than simply having His light shine on us, and in us, and through us, all the day.

God is Light. God is a Sun. Paul says: 'God has shined in our hearts to give the light.' What light? 'The light of the glory of God, in the face of Jesus Christ.' Just as the sun shines its beautiful, life-giving light on and into our earth, so God shines into our hearts the light of His glory, of His love, in Christ His Son. Our heart is meant to have that light filling and gladdening it all the day. It can have it, because God is our sun, and it is written, 'Your sun shall no more go down forever.' God's love shines on us without ceasing.

But can we indeed enjoy it all the day? We can. And how can we? Let nature give us the answer. Those beautiful trees and flowers, with all this green grass, what do they do to keep the sun shining on them? They do nothing; they simply bask in the sunshine, when it comes. The sun is millions of miles away, but over all that distance it sends its own light and joy; and the tiniest flower that lifts its little head upwards is met by the same exuberance of light and blessing as flood the widest landscape. We have not to care for the light we need for our day's work; the sun cares, and provides and shines the light around us all the day. We simply count upon it, and receive it, and enjoy it.

The only difference between nature and grace is this, that what the trees and the flowers do unconsciously, as they drink in the blessing of the light, is to be with us a voluntary and a loving acceptance. Faith, simple faith in God's word and love, is to be the opening of the eyes, the opening of the heart, to receive and enjoy the unspeakable glory of His grace. And even as the trees, day by day, and month by month, stand and grow into beauty and fruitfulness, just welcoming whatever sunshine the sun may give, so it is the very highest exercise of our Christian life just to abide in the light of God, and let it, and let Him, fill us with the life and the brightness it brings.

And if you ask, but can it really be, that even as naturally and heartily as I recognize and rejoice in the beauty of a bright sunny morning, I can rejoice in God's light all the day? It can, indeed. From my breakfast-table I look out on a beautiful valley, with trees and vineyards and mountains. In our spring and autumn months the light in the morning is exquisite, and almost involuntarily we say, How beautiful! And the question comes, Is it only the light of the sun that is to bring such continual beauty and joy? And is there no provision for the light of God being just as much an unceasing source of joy and gladness? There is, indeed, if the soul will but be still and wait on Him, will only let God shine.

Dear soul! learn to wait on the Lord, more than watchers for the morning. All within you may be very dark; is that not the very best reason for waiting for the light of God? The first beginnings of light may be just enough to discover the darkness, and painfully to humble you on account of sin. Can you not trust the light to expel the darkness? Do believe it will. Just bow, even now, in stillness before God, and wait on Him to shine into you. Say, in humble faith; God is light, infinitely brighter and more beautiful than that of the sun. God is light. The Father, the eternal, inaccessible, and incomprehensible light. The Son, the light concentrated, and embodied, and manifested. The Spirit, the light entering and dwelling and shining in our hearts. God is light, and is here shining on my heart. I have been so occupied with the rushlights of my thoughts and efforts, I have never opened the shutters to let His light in. Unbelief has kept it out. I bow in faith: God's light is shining into my heart. The God of whom Paul wrote, 'God hath shined into our heart,' is my God. What would I think of a sun that could not shine? what shall I think of a God that does not shine? No, God shines! God is light! I will take time, and just be still, and rest in the light of God. My eyes are feeble, and the windows are not clean, but I will wait on the Lord. The light does shine, the light will shine in me, and make me full of light. And I shall learn to walk all the day in the light and joy of God. My soul waits on the Lord, more than watchers for the morning.

'My soul, wait thou only upon God!'

Day 17: In Times of Darkness.

'I will wait upon the Lord, that hideth His face from the house of Jacob; and I will look for Him.' —Isa. 8:17.

HERE we have a servant of God, waiting upon Him, not on behalf of himself, but of his people, from whom God was hiding his face. It suggests to us how our waiting upon God, though it commences with our personal needs, with the desire for the revelation of Himself, or of the answer to personal petitions, need not, may not, stop there. We may be walking in the full light of God's countenance, and God yet be hiding His face from His people around us; far from our being content to think that this is nothing but the just punishment of their sin, or the consequence of their indifference, we are called with tender hearts to think of their sad estate, and to wait on God on their behalf. The privilege of waiting upon God is one that brings great responsibility. Even as Christ, when He entered God's presence, at once used His place of privilege and honor as intercessor, so we, no less, if we know what it is really to enter in and wait upon God, must use our access for our less favored brethren. 'I will wait upon the Lord, who hides His face from the house of Jacob.'

You worship with a certain congregation. Possibly there is not the spiritual life or joy either in the preaching or in the fellowship that you could desire. You belong to a Church, with its many congregations. There is so much of error or worldliness, of seeking after human wisdom and culture, of trust in ordinances and observances, that you do not wonder that God hides His face, in many cases, and that there is but little power for conversion or true edification. Then there are branches of Christian work with which you are connected—a Sunday school, a gospel hall, a young men's association, a mission work abroad—in which the feebleness of the Spirit's working appears to indicate that God is hiding His face. You think, too, you know the reason. There is too much trust in men and money; there is too much formality and self-indulgence; there is too little faith and prayer; too little love and humility; too little of the spirit of the crucified Jesus. At times you feel as if things are hopeless; nothing will help.

Do believe that God can help and will help. Let the spirit of the prophet come into you, as you take his words, and set yourself to wait on God, on behalf of His erring children. Instead of the tone of judgment or condemnation, of despondency or despair, realize your calling to wait upon God. If others fail in doing it, give yourself doubly to it. The deeper the darkness, the greater the need of appealing to the one only Deliverer. The greater the self-confidence around you, that knows not that it is poor and wretched and blind, the more urgent the call on you who profess to see the evil and to have access to Him who alone can help, to be at your post, waiting upon God. As often as you are tempted to complain, or to sigh and say ever afresh: 'I will wait on the Lord, who hides His face from the house of Jacob.'

There is a still larger circle—the Christian Church throughout the world. Think of Greek, Roman Catholic, and Protestant churches, and the state of the millions that belong to them. Or think only of the Protestant churches with their open Bible and orthodox creeds. How much nominal profession and formality! how much of the rule of the flesh and of man in the very temple of God! And what abundant proof that God does hide His face!

What are those to do who see and mourn this? The first thing to be done is this: 'I will wait on the Lord, who hides His face from the house of Jacob.' Let us wait on God, in the humble confession of the sins of His people. Let us take time and wait on Him in this exercise. Let us wait on God in tender, loving intercession for all saints, our beloved brethren, however wrong their lives or their teaching may appear. Let us wait on God in faith and expectation, until He shows us that He will hear. Let us wait on God, with the simple offering of ourselves to Himself, and the earnest prayer that He would send us to our brethren. Let us wait on God, and give Him no rest until He make Zion a joy in the earth. Yes, let us rest in the Lord, and wait patiently for Him who now hides His face from so many of His children. And let us say of the lifting up of the light of His countenance we desire for all His people, 'I wait for the Lord, my soul doth wait, and my hope is in His word. My soul waits for the Lord, more than the watchers for the morning, the watchers for the morning.'

'My soul, wait thou only upon God!'

Day 18: To Reveal Himself.

'And it shall be said in that day, Lo, this is our God; we have waited for Him, and He will save us: THIS IS THE LORD; we have waited for Him, we will rejoice and be glad in His salvation,' —Isa. 25:9.

IN this passage we have two precious thoughts.

The one, that it is the language of God's people who have been unitedly waiting on Him; the other, that the fruit of their waiting has been that God has so revealed Himself, that they could joyfully say, Lo, this is our God: this is the Lord. The power and the blessing of united waiting is what we need to learn.

Note the twice repeated, 'We have waited for Him.' In some time of trouble the hearts of the people had been drawn together, and they had, ceasing from all human hope or help, with one heart set themselves to wait for their God. Is not this just what we need in our churches and conventions and prayer-meetings? Is not the need of the Church and the world great enough to demand it? Are there not in the Church of Christ evils to which no human wisdom is equal? Have we not ritualism and rationalism, formalism and worldliness, robbing the Church of its power? Have we not culture and money and pleasure threatening its spiritual life? Are not the powers of the Church utterly inadequate to cope with the powers of infidelity and iniquity and wretchedness in Christian countries and in heathendom? And is there not in the promise of God, and in the power of the Holy Spirit, a provision made that can meet the need, and give the Church the restful assurance that she is doing all her God expects of her? And would not united waiting upon God for the supply of His Spirit most certainly seem the needed blessing? We cannot doubt it.

The object of a more definite waiting upon God in our gatherings would be very much the same as in personal worship. It would mean a deeper conviction that God must and will do all; a more humble and abiding entrance into our deep helplessness, and the need of entire and unceasing dependence upon Him; a more living consciousness that the essential thing is, giving God His place of honor and of power; a confident expectation that to those who wait on Him, God will, by His Spirit, give the secret of His acceptance and presence, and then, in due time, the revelation of His saving power. The great aim would be to bring every one in a praying and worshipping company under a deep sense of God's presence, so that when they part there will be the consciousness of having met God Himself, of having left every request with Him, and of now waiting in stillness while He works out His salvation.

It is this experience that is indicated in our text. The fulfilment of the words may, at times, be in such striking interpositions of God's power that all can join in the cry, 'Lo, this is our God; this is the Lord!' They may equally become true in spiritual experience, when God's people in their waiting times become so conscious of His presence that in holy awe souls feel, 'Lo, this is our God; this is the Lord!' It is this, alas, that is too much missed in our meetings for worship. The godly minister has no more difficult, no more solemn, no more blessed task, than to lead his people out to meet God, and, before ever he preaches, to bring each one into contact with Him. 'We are now here in the presence of God' —these words of Cornelius show the way in which Peter's audience was prepared for the coming of the Holy Spirit. Waiting before God, and waiting for God, and waiting on God, are the one condition of God showing His presence.

A company of believers gathered with the one purpose, helping each other by little intervals of silence, to wait on God alone, opening the heart for whatever God may have of new discoveries of evil, of His will, of new openings in work or methods of work, would soon have reason to say, 'Lo, this is our God; we have waited for Him, He shall save us: this is the Lord; we have waited for Him, we will be glad and rejoice in His salvation.'

'My soul, wait thou only upon God!'

Day 19: As a God of Judgment.

'Yea, in the way of Thy judgments, O Lord, have we waited for Thee:... for when Thy judgments are on the earth, the inhabitants of the world learn righteousness.'
—Isa. 26:8, 9.

'The Lord is a God of judgment: blessed are all they that wait for Him.'
—Isa. 30:18.

GOD is a God of mercy and a God of judgment. Mercy and judgment are ever together in His dealings. In the flood, in the deliverance of Israel out of Egypt, in the overthrow of the Canaanites, we ever see mercy in the midst of judgment. Within the inner circle of His own people, we see it too: the judgment punishes the sin, while mercy saves the sinner. Or, rather, mercy saves the sinner, not in spite of, but by means of, the very judgment that came upon his sin. In waiting on God, we must beware of forgetting this: as we wait we must expect Him as a God of judgment.

'In the way of Thy judgments, have we waited for Thee.' That will prove true in our inner experience. If we are honest in our longing for holiness, in our prayer to be wholly the Lord's, His holy presence will stir up and discover hidden sin, and bring us very low in the bitter conviction of the evil of our nature, its opposition to God's law, its impotence to fulfil that law. The words will come true, 'Who may abide the day of His coming, for HE is like a refiner's fire.' 'O that Thou would come down, as when the melting fire burns!' In great mercy God executes, within the soul, His judgments upon sin, as He makes it feel its wickedness and guilt. Many a one tries to flee from these judgments: the soul that longs for God, and for deliverance from sin, bows under them in humility and in hope. In silence of soul it says, 'Arise, O Lord! and let Thine enemies be scattered. In the way of Thy judgments we have waited for Thee.'

Let no one who seeks to learn the blessed art of waiting on God, wonder if at first the attempt to wait on Him only discovers more of his sin and darkness. Let no one despair because unconquered sins, or evil thoughts, or great darkness appear to hide God's face. Was not, in His own Beloved Son, the gift and bearer of His mercy on Calvary, the mercy as if hidden and lost in the judgment? Oh, submit, and sink down deep under the judgment of thine every sin: judgment prepares the way, and breaks out in wonderful mercy. It is written, 'Thou shalt be redeemed with judgment.' Wait on God, in the faith that His tender mercy is working out in you His redemption in the midst of judgment: wait for Him, He will be gracious to thee.

There is another application still, one of unspeakable solemnity. We are expecting God, in the way of His judgments, to visit this earth: we are waiting for Him. What a thought! We know of these coming judgments; we know that there are tens of thousands of our professing Christians who live on in carelessness, and who, if no change come, must perish under God's hand. Oh, shall we not do our utmost to warn them, to plead with and for them, if God may have mercy on them. If we feel our want of boldness, want of zeal, want of power, shall we not begin to wait on God more definitely and persistently as a God of judgment, asking Him so to reveal Himself in the judgments that are coming on our very friends, that we may be inspired with a new fear of Him and them, and constrained to speak and pray as never yet. Verily, waiting on God is not meant to be a spiritual self-indulgence. Its object is to let God and His holiness, Christ and the love that died on Calvary, the Spirit and fire that burns in heaven and came to earth, get possession of us, to warn and rouse men with the message that we are waiting for God in the way of His judgments. O Christian! prove that you really believe in the God of judgment.

'My soul, wait thou only upon God!'

Day 20: Who Waits on Us.

'And therefore will the Lord wait, that He may be gracious unto you; and therefore will He be exalted, that He may have mercy upon you: for the Lord is a God of judgment: blessed are all they that wait for Him.' —Isa. 30:18.

WE must not only think of our waiting upon God, but also of what is more wonderful still, of God's waiting upon us. The vision of Him waiting on us, will give new impulse and inspiration to our waiting upon Him. It will give an unspeakable confidence that our waiting cannot be in vain. If He waits for us, then we may be sure that we are more than welcome; that He rejoices to find those He has been seeking for. Let us seek even now, at this moment, in the spirit of lowly waiting on God, to find out something of what it means: 'Therefore will the Lord wait, that He may be gracious unto you.' We shall accept and echo back the message: 'Blessed are all they that wait for Him.'

Look up and see the great God upon His throne. He is Love—an unceasing and inexpressible desire to communicate His own goodness and blessedness to all His creatures. He longs and delights to bless. He has inconceivably glorious purposes concerning every one of His children, by the power of His Holy Spirit, to reveal in them His love and power. He waits with all the longings of a father's heart. He waits that He may be gracious unto you. And each time you come to wait upon Him, or seek to maintain in daily life the holy habit of waiting, you may look up and see Him ready to meet you, waiting that He may be gracious unto you. Yes, connect every exercise, every breath of the life of waiting, with faith's vision of your God waiting for you.

And if you ask, how is it, if He waits to be gracious, that even after I come and wait upon Him, He does not give the help I seek, but waits on longer and longer? There is a double answer. The one is this: God is a wise husbandman, 'who waits for the precious fruit of the earth, and has long patience for it.' He cannot gather the fruit until it is ripe. He knows when we are spiritually ready to receive the blessing to our profit and His glory. Waiting in the sunshine of His love is what will ripen the soul for His blessing. Waiting under the cloud of trial, that breaks in showers of blessing, is as needful. Be assured that if God waits longer than you could wish, it is only to make the blessing doubly precious. God waited four thousand years, until the fulness of time, before He sent His Son: our times are in His hands: He will avenge His elect speedily: He will make haste for our help, and not delay one hour too long.

The other answer points to what has been said before. The giver is more than the gift; God is more than the blessing; and our being kept waiting on Him is the only way for our learning to find our life and joy in Himself. Oh, if God's children only knew what a glorious God they have, and what a privilege it is to be linked in fellowship with Himself, then they would rejoice in Him, even when He keeps them waiting. They would learn to understand better than ever; 'Therefore will the Lord wait, that He may be gracious unto you.' His waiting will be the highest proof of His graciousness.

'Blessed are all they that wait for Him.' Our queen has her ladies-in-waiting. The position is one of subordination and service, and yet it is considered one of the highest dignity and privilege, because a wise and gracious sovereign makes them companions and friends. What a dignity and blessedness to be attendants-in-waiting on the Everlasting God, ever on the watch for every indication of His will or favor, ever conscious of His nearness, His goodness, and His grace! 'The Lord is good to them that wait for Him.' 'Blessed are all they that wait for Him.' Yes, it is blessed when a waiting soul and a waiting God meet each other. God cannot do His work without His and our waiting His time: let waiting be our work, as it is His. And if His waiting be nothing but goodness and graciousness, let ours be nothing but a rejoicing in that goodness, and a confident expectancy of that grace. And let every thought of waiting become to us simply the expression of unmingled and unutterable blessedness, because it brings us to a God who waits that He may make Himself known to us perfectly as the Gracious One.

'My soul, wait thou only upon God!'

Day 21: The Almighty One.

'They that wait on the Lord shall renew their strength; they shall mount up with eagle wings; they shall run and not be weary; they shall walk and not faint.'
—Isa. 40:31.

WAITING always partakes of the character of our thoughts of the one on whom we wait. Our waiting on God will depend greatly on our faith of what He is. In our text we have the close of a passage in which God reveals Himself as the Everlasting and Almighty One. It is as that revelation enters our soul that the waiting will become the spontaneous expression of what we know Him to be—a God altogether most worthy to be waited upon.

Listen to the words: 'Why sayest thou, O Jacob, my way is hid from the Lord?' Why speakest thou as if God does not hear or help?

'Hast thou not known, hast thou not heard, that the Everlasting One, the Lord, the Creator of the ends of the earth, *fainteth not, neither is weary*?' So far from it, 'He giveth power to the faint, and to them that have no might He increaseth strength. Even the youths'—'the glory of young men is their strength'—'even the youths shall faint, and the young men shall utterly fall:' all that is accounted strong with man shall come to nought. *'But* they that wait on the Lord,' on the Everlasting One, who does not faint, neither is weary, they 'shall renew their strength; they shall mount up with wings as eagles; they shall run and,'—listen now, they shall be strong with the strength of God, and, even as He, *'shall not be weary*; they shall walk and,' even as He, *'not faint.'*

Yes, 'they shall mount up with wings as eagles.' You know what eagles' wings mean. The eagle is the king of birds, it soars the highest into the heavens. Believers are to live a heavenly life, in the very Presence and Love and Joy of God. They are to live where God lives; they need God's strength to rise there. To them that wait on Him it shall be given.

You know how the eagles' wings are obtained. Only in one way—by the eagle birth. You are born of God. You have the eagles' wings. You may not have known it: you may not have used them; but God can and will teach you to use them.

You know how the eagles are taught the use of their wings. See yonder cliff rising a thousand feet out of the sea. See high up a ledge on the rock, where there is an eagle's nest with its treasure of two young eaglets. See the mother bird come and stir up her nest, and with her beak push the timid birds over the precipice. See how they flutter and fall and sink toward the depth. See now (Deut. 32:11) 'how she fluttereth over her young, spreadeth abroad her wings, taketh them, beareth them on her wings,' and so, as they ride upon her wings, brings them to a place of safety. And so she does once and again, each time casting them out over the precipice, and then again taking and carrying them. 'So the Lord alone did lead him.' Yes, the instinct of that eagle mother was God's gift, a single ray of that love in which the Almighty trains His people to mount as on eagles' wings.

He stirs up your nest. He disappoints your hopes. He brings down your confidence. He makes you fear and tremble, as all your strength fails, and you feel utterly weary and helpless. And all the while He is spreading His strong wings for you to rest your weakness on, and offering His everlasting Creator-strength to work in you. And all He asks is that you should sink down in your weariness and wait on Him; and allow Him in His Jehovah-strength to carry you as you ride upon the wings of His Omnipotence.

Dear child of God! I pray you, lift up your eyes, and *behold your God*! Listen to Him who says that He faints not, neither is weary, who promiseth that you too shall not faint or be weary, who asketh nought but this one thing, that you should *wait on Him*. And let your answer be, With such a God, so mighty, so faithful, so tender,

'*My soul, wait thou only upon God!*'

Day 22: It Certainty of Blessing.

'*Thou shalt know that I am the Lord; for they shall not be ashamed that wait for Me.*' —Isa. 49:23.

'*Blessed are all they that wait for Him.*' —Isa. 30:18.

WHAT promises! How God seeks to draw us to waiting on Him by the most positive assurance that it never can be in vain: 'They shall not be ashamed that wait for Me.' How strange that, though we should so often have experienced it, we are yet so slow of learning that this blessed waiting must and can be as the very breath of our life, a continuous resting in God's presence and His love, an unceasing yielding of ourselves for Him to perfect His work in us. Let us once again listen and meditate, until our heart says with new conviction: 'Blessed are they that wait for Him!' In our sixth day's lesson we found in the prayer of Psalm 25: 'Let none that wait on Thee be ashamed.' The very prayer shows how we fear lest it might be. Let us listen to God's answer, until every fear is banished, and we send back to heaven the words God speaks, Yes, Lord, we believe what You say: '*All they* that wait for Me shall *not* be ashamed.' 'Blessed are *all they* that wait for Him.'

The context of each of these two passages points us to times when God's Church was in great straits, and to human eye there was no possibility of deliverance. But God interposes with His word of promise, and pledges His Almighty Power for the deliverance of His people. And it is as the God who has Himself undertaken the work of their redemption, that He invites them to wait on Him, and assures them that disappointment is impossible. We, too, are living in days in which there is much in the state of the Church, with its profession and its formalism, that is indescribably sad. Amid all we praise God for, there is, alas, much to mourn over! Were it not for God's promises we might well despair. But in His promises the Living God has given and bound Himself to us. He calls us to wait on Him. He assureth us we shall not be put to shame. Oh that our hearts might learn to wait before Him, until He Himself reveals to us what His promises mean, and in the promises reveals Himself in His hidden glory! We shall be irresistibly drawn to wait on Him alone. God increase the company of those who say, 'Our soul waiteth for the Lord: He is our Help and our Shield.'

This waiting upon God on behalf of His Church and people will depend greatly upon the place that waiting on Him has taken in our personal life. The mind may often have beautiful visions of what God has promised to do, and the lips may speak of them in stirring words, but these are not really the measure of our faith or power. No; it is what we really know of God in our personal experience, conquering the enemies within, reigning and ruling, revealing Himself in His Holiness and Power in our inmost being, —it is this will be the real measure of the spiritual blessing we expect from Him, and bring to our fellowmen. It is as we know how blessed the waiting on God has become to our own souls, that we shall confidently hope in the blessing to come on the Church around us, and the key-word of all our expectations will be; He hath said: 'All they that wait on Me shall not be ashamed.' From what He has done in us, we shall trust Him to do mighty things around us. 'Blessed are all they that wait for Him.' Yes, blessed even now in the waiting. The promised blessings, for ourselves, or for others, may tarry; the unutterable blessedness of knowing and having Him who has promised, the Divine Blesser, the Living Fountain of the coming blessings, is even now ours. Do let this truth get full possession of your souls, that waiting on God is itself the highest privilege of the creature, the highest blessedness of His redeemed child.

Even as the sunshine enters with its light and warmth, with its beauty and blessing, into every little blade of grass that rises upward out of the cold earth, so the Everlasting God meets, in the greatness and the tenderness of His love, each waiting child, to shine in his heart 'the light of the knowledge of the glory of God in the face of Jesus Christ.' Read these words again, until your heart learns to know what God waits to do to you. Who can measure the difference between the great sun and that little blade of grass? And yet the grass has all of the sun it can need or hold. Do believe that in waiting on God, His greatness and your littleness suit and meet each other most wonderfully. Just how in emptiness and poverty and utter impotence, in humility and meekness and surrender to His will, before His great glory, and be still. As you wait on Him, God draws near. He will reveal Himself as the God who will fulfil mightily His every promise. And let your heart ever again take up the song: 'Blessed are all they that wait for Him.'

'My soul, wait thou only upon God!'

Day 23: For Unlooked-for Things.

'For since the beginning of the world men have not heard, nor perceived by the ear, neither hath the eye seen, O God, beside Thee, what He hath prepared for him that waiteth for Him.' —Isa. 64:4.

THE R.V.[2] has: *'Neither hath the eye seen a God beside Thee, which worketh for him that waiteth for Him.'* In the A.V.[3] the thought is, that no eye hath seen *the thing* which God hath prepared. In the R.V. no eye hath seen a God, beside our God, who worketh for him that waiteth for Him. To both the two thoughts are common: that our place is to wait upon God, and that there will be revealed to us what the human heart cannot conceive. The difference is: in the R.V. it is *the God* who works, in the A.V. *the thing* He is to work. In 1 Cor. 2:9, the citation is in regard to the things which the Holy Spirit is to reveal, as in the A.V., and in this meditation we keep to that.

The previous verses, specially from chap. 63:15, refer to the low state of God's people. The prayer has been poured out, 'Look down from heaven.' (ver. 15.) 'Why hast Thou hardened my heart from Thy fear? Return for Thy servants' sake.' (ver. 19.) And 64:1, still more urgent, 'Oh that Thou wouldest rend[4] the heavens, that thou wouldest come down,... as when the melting fire burneth, to make Thy name known to Thy adversaries!' Then follows the plea from the past, 'When Thou didst terrible things we looked not for, Thou camest down, the mountains flowed down at Thy presence.' 'For'— this is now the faith that has been awakened by the thought of things we looked not for, He is still the same God—'eye hath not seen beside Thee, O God, what He hath prepared for him that waiteth for Him.' God alone knows what He can do for His waiting people. As Paul expounds and applies it: 'The things of God knoweth no man, save the Spirit of God.' 'But God hath revealed them to us by His Spirit.'

The need of God's people, and the call for God's interposition, is as urgent in our days as it was in the time of Isaiah. There is now, as there was then, as there has been at all times, a remnant that seek after God with their whole heart. But if we look at Christendom as a whole, at the state of the Church of Christ, there is infinite cause for beseeching God to rend the heavens and come down. Nothing but a special interposition of Almighty Power will avail. I fear we have no right conception of what the so-called Christian world is in the sight of God. Unless God comes down 'as the melting fire burneth, to make known His name to His adversaries,' our labors are comparatively fruitless. Look at the ministry—how much it is in the wisdom of man and of literary culture —how little in demonstration of the Spirit and of power. Think of the unity of the body—how little there is of the manifestation of the power of a heavenly love binding God's children into one. Think of holiness—the holiness of Christ-like humility and crucifixion to the world—how little the world sees that they have men among them who live in Christ in heaven, in whom Christ and heaven live.

What is to be done? There is but one thing. We must wait upon God. And what for? We must cry, with a cry that never rests, 'Oh that Thou wouldest rend the heavens and come down, that the mountains might flow down at Thy presence.' We must desire and believe, we must ask and expect, that God will do unlooked-for things. We must set our

---

[2] RV: Revised Version. 1885 British revision of the King James Bible
[3] AV: Authorized Version. 1611 King James Version Bible
[4] 'Rend' is to 'tear.'

faith on a God of whom men do not know what He has prepared for them that wait for Him. The wonder-doing God, who can surpass all our expectations, must be the God of our confidence.

Yes, let God's people enlarge their hearts to wait on a God able to do exceeding abundantly above what we can ask or think. Let us band ourselves together as His elect who cry day and night to Him for things men have not seen. He is able to arise and to make His people a name, and a praise in the earth. 'He will wait, that He may be gracious unto you; blessed are all they that wait for Him.'

'My soul, wait thou only upon God!'

Day 24: To Know His Goodness.

'The Lord is good unto them that wait for Him.' —Lam. 3:25.

'THERE is none good but God.' 'His goodness is in the heavens.' 'Oh how great is Thy goodness, which Thou hast laid up for them that fear Thee!' 'Oh, taste and see that the Lord is good!' And here is now the true way of entering into and rejoicing in this goodness of God—waiting upon Him. The Lord is good—even His children often do not know it, for they wait not in quietness for Him to reveal it. But to those who persevere in waiting, whose souls do wait, it will come true. One might think that it is just those who have to wait who might doubt it. But this is only when they do not wait, but grow impatient. The truly waiting ones will all have to say, 'The Lord is good to them that wait for Him.' Wouldst thou fully know the goodness of God, give thyself more than ever to a life of waiting on Him.

At our first entrance into the school of waiting upon God, the heart is chiefly set upon the blessings which we wait for. God graciously uses our need and desire for help to educate us for something higher than we were thinking of. We were seeking gifts; He, the Giver, longs to give Himself and to satisfy the soul with His goodness. It is just for this reason that He often withholds the gifts, and that the time of waiting is made so long. He is all the time seeking to win the heart of His child for Himself. He wishes that we should not only say, when He bestows the gift, How good is God! but that long ere it comes, and even if it never comes, we should all the time be experiencing: *'It is good* that a man should quietly wait': 'The Lord *is good* to them that wait for Him.'

What a blessed life the life of waiting then becomes, the continual worship of faith, adoring and trusting His goodness. As the soul learns its secret, every act or exercise of waiting just becomes a quiet entering into the goodness of God, to let it do its blessed work and satisfy our every need. And every experience of God's goodness gives the work of waiting new attractiveness, and instead of only taking refuge in time of need, there comes a great longing to wait continually and all the day. And however duties and engagements occupy the time and the mind, the soul gets more familiar with the secret art of always waiting. Waiting becomes the habit and disposition, the very second nature and breath of the soul.

Dear Christian! do you not begin to see that waiting is not one among a number of Christian virtues, to be thought of from time to time, but that it expresses that disposition which lies at the very root of the Christian life? It gives a higher value and a new power to our prayer and worship, to our faith and surrender, because it links us, in unalterable dependence, to God Himself. And it gives us the unbroken enjoyment of the goodness of God: 'The Lord is good to them that wait for Him.'

Let me press upon you once again to take time and trouble to cultivate this so much needed element of the Christian life. We get too much of religion at second hand from the teaching of men. That teaching has great value if, even as the preaching of John the Baptist sent his disciples away from himself to the Living Christ, it leads us to God Himself. What our religion needs is—*more of God*. Many of us are too much occupied with our work. As with Martha, the very service we want to render the Master separates from Him; it is neither pleasing to Him nor profitable to ourselves. The more work, the more need of waiting upon God; the doing of God's will would then, instead of exhausting, be our meat and drink, nourishment and refreshment and strength. 'The Lord is good to them that wait for Him.' How good none can tell but those who prove it in waiting on Him. How good none can fully tell but those who have proved Him to the utmost.

'My soul, wait thou only upon God!'

Day 25: Quietly.

'It is good that a man should both hope and quietly wait for the salvation of the Lord.' —Lam. 3:26.

'TAKE heed, and be quiet: fear not, neither be faint-hearted.' 'In quietness and in confidence shall be your strength.' Such words reveal to us the close connection between quietness and faith, and show us what a deep need there is of quietness, as an element of true waiting upon God. If we are to have our whole heart turned towards God, we must have it turned away from the creature, from all that occupies and interests, whether of joy or sorrow.

God is a being of such infinite greatness and glory, and our nature has become so estranged from Him, that it needs our whole heart and desires set upon Him, even in some little measure to know and receive Him. Everything that is not God, that excites our fears, or stirs our efforts, or awakens our hopes, or makes us glad, hinders us in our perfect waiting on Him. The message is one of deep meaning: 'Take heed and be quiet;' 'In quietness shall be your strength;' 'It is good that a man should quietly wait.'

How the very thought of God in His majesty and holiness should silence us, Scripture abundantly testifies.

'The Lord is in His holy temple; let all the earth keep silence before Him' (Hab. 2:20).

'Hold thy peace at the presence of the Lord God.' (Zeph. 1:7).

'Be silent, O all flesh, before the Lord; for He is raised up out of His holy habitation' (Zech. 2:13).

As long as the waiting on God is chiefly regarded as an end towards more effectual prayer, and the obtaining of our petitions, this spirit of perfect quietness will not be obtained. But when it is seen that the waiting on God is itself an unspeakable blessedness, one of the highest forms of fellowship with the Holy One, the adoration of Him in His glory will of necessity humble the soul into a holy stillness, making way for God to speak and reveal Himself. Then it comes to the fulfilment of the precious promise, that all of self and self-effort shall be humbled: 'The haughtiness of man shall be brought down, and the Lord alone shall be exalted in that day.'

Let everyone who would learn the art of waiting on God remember the lesson: 'Take heed, and be quiet;' 'It is good that a man quietly wait.' Take time to be separate from all friends and all duties, all cares and all joys; time to be still and quiet before God. Take time not only to secure stillness from man and the world, but from self and its energy. Let the Word and prayer be very precious; but remember, even these may hinder the quiet waiting. The activity of the mind in studying the Word, or giving expression to its thoughts in prayer, the activities of the heart, with its desires and hopes and fears, may so engage us that we do not come to the still waiting on the All-Glorious One; our whole being is not prostrate in silence before Him. Though at first it may appear difficult to know how thus quietly to wait, with the activities of mind and heart for a time subdued, every effort after it will be rewarded; we shall find that it grows upon us, and the little season of silent worship will bring a peace and a rest that give a blessing not only in prayer, but all the day.

'*It is good* that a man should quietly wait for the salvation of the Lord.' Yes, it is good. The quietness is the confession of our impotence, that with all our willing and running, with all our thinking and praying, it will not be done: we must receive it from God. It is the confession of our trust that our God will in His time come to our help—the quiet resting in Him alone. It is the confession of our desire to sink into our nothingness, and to let Him work and reveal Himself. Do let us wait quietly. In daily life let there be in the soul that is waiting for the great God to do His wondrous work, a quiet reverence, an abiding watching against too deep engrossment with the world, and the whole character will come to bear the beautiful stamp: Quietly waiting for the salvation of God.

'*My soul, wait thou only upon God!*'

Day 26: In Holy Expectancy.

'*Therefore will I look to the Lord; I will wait for the God of my salvation; my God will hear me.*' —Micah 7:7.

HAVE you ever read a beautiful little book, *Expectation Corner*? If not, get it; you will find in it one of the best sermons on our text. It tells of a king who prepared a city for some of his poor subjects. Not far from them were large storehouses, where everything they could need was supplied if they but sent in their requests. But on one condition—that they should be on the outlook for the answer, so that when the king's messengers came with the gifts they had desired, they should always be found waiting and ready to receive them. The sad story is told of one desponding one who never expected to get what he asked, because he was too unworthy. One day he was taken to the king's storehouses, and there, to his amazement, he saw, with his address on them, all the packages that had been made up for him, and sent. There was the garment of praise, and the oil of joy, and the eye salve, and so much more; they had been to his door, but found it closed; he was not on the outlook. From that time on he understood the lesson Micah would teach us today; 'I will look to the Lord; I will wait for the God of my salvation; my God will hear me.'

We have more than once said: Waiting for the answer to prayer is not the whole of waiting, but only a part. Today we want to take in the blessed truth: It is a part, and a very important one. When we have special petitions, in connection with which we are waiting on God, our waiting must be very definitely in the confident assurance: 'My God will hear me.' A holy, joyful expectancy is of the very essence of true waiting. And this not only in reference to the many varied requests every believer has to make, but most especially to the one great petition which ought to be the chief thing every heart seeks for itself —that The Life of God in the soul may have full sway; that Christ may be fully formed within; and that we may be filled to all the fullness of God. This is what God has promised. This is what God's people too little seek, very often because they do not believe it possible. This is what we ought to seek and dare to expect, because God is able and waiting to work it in us.

But God Himself must work it. And for this end our working must cease. We must see how entirely it is to be the faith of the operation of God who raised Jesus from the dead—just as much as the resurrection, the perfecting of God's life in our souls is to be directly His work. And waiting has to become more than ever a tarrying before God in stillness of soul, counting upon Him who raises the dead, and calls the things that are not as though they were.

Just notice how the threefold use of the name of God in our text points us to Himself as the one from whom alone is our expectation. 'I will look to The Lord; I will wait for The God of my Salvation; My God will hear me.' Everything that is salvation, everything that is good and holy, must be the direct mighty work of God Himself within us. For every moment of a life in the will of God, there must be the immediate operation of God. And the one thing I have to do is this: to look to the Lord; to wait for the God of my salvation; to hold fast the confident assurance, 'My God will hear me.'

God says: 'Be still, and know that I am God.'

There is no stillness like that of the grave. In the grave of Jesus, in the fellowship of His death, in death to self with its own will and wisdom, its own strength and energy, there is rest. As we cease from self, and our soul becomes still to God, God will arise and show Himself. 'Be still, and know,' then you shall know 'that I am God.' There is no stillness like the stillness Jesus gives when He speaks, 'Peace, be still.' In Christ, in His death, and *in His life*, in His perfected redemption, the soul may be still, and God will come in, and take possession, and do His perfect work.

'My soul, wait thou only upon God!'

Day 27: For Redemption.

'Simeon was just and devout, waiting for the consolation of Israel, and the Holy Ghost was upon him. Anna, a prophetess,… spake of Him to all then that looked for redemption in Jerusalem.' —Luke 2:25, 38.

HERE we have the mark of a waiting believer. *Just*, righteous in all his conduct; *devout*, devoted to God, ever walking as in His presence; *waiting for the consolation* of Israel, looking for the fulfilment of God's promises: *and the Holy Ghost was on him*. In the devout waiting he had been prepared for the blessing. And Simeon was not the only one. Anna spoke to all that looked for redemption in Jerusalem. This was the one mark, amid surrounding formalism and worldliness, of a godly band of men and women in Jerusalem. They were waiting on God; looking for His promised redemption.

And now that the Consolation of Israel has come, and the redemption has been accomplished, do we still need to wait? We do indeed. But will not our waiting, who look back to it as come, differ greatly from those who looked forward to it as coming? It will, especially in two aspects. We now wait on God in the full power of the redemption: and we wait for its full revelation.

Our waiting is now in the full power of the redemption. Christ spoke, 'In that day you shall know that you are in Me. Abide in Me.' The Epistles teach us to present ourselves to God 'as indeed dead to sin, and alive to God in Christ Jesus,' 'blessed with all spiritual blessings in heavenly places in Christ Jesus.' Our waiting on God may now be in the wonderful consciousness, wrought and maintained by the Holy Spirit within us, that we are accepted in the Beloved, that the love that rests on Him rests on us, that we are living in that love, in the very nearness and presence and sight of God. The old saints took their stand on the word of God, and waited, hoping on that word; we rest on the word too — but, oh! under what exceeding greater privileges, as one with Christ Jesus. In our waiting on God, let this be our confidence: in Christ we have access to the Father; how sure, therefore, may we be that our waiting cannot be vain.

Our waiting differs also in this, that while they waited for a redemption to come, we see it accomplished, and now wait for its revelation *in us*. Christ not only said, Abide in Me, but also *I in you*. The Epistles not only speak of us *in Christ*, but of Christ *in us*, as the highest mystery of redeeming love. As we maintain our place in Christ day by day, God waits to reveal Christ in us, in such a way that He is formed in us, that His mind and disposition and likeness acquire form and substance in us, so that by each it can in truth be said, 'Christ liveth in me.'

My life in Christ up there in heaven and Christ's life in me down here on earth — these two are the complement of each other. And the more my waiting on God is marked by the living faith *I in Christ*, the more the heart thirsts for and claims the CHRIST IN ME. And the waiting on God, which began with special needs and prayer, will increasingly be concentrated, as far as our personal life is concerned, on this one thing, Lord, reveal Your redemption fully in me; let Christ live in me.

Our waiting differs from that of the old saints in the place we take, and the expectations we entertain. But at root it is the same: waiting on God, from whom alone is our expectation.

Learn from Simeon and Anna one lesson. How utterly impossible it was for them to do anything towards the great redemption —towards the birth of Christ or His death. It was God's work. They could do nothing but wait. Are we as absolutely helpless as regards the revelation of Christ in us? We are indeed. God did not work out the great redemption in Christ as a whole, and leave its application in detail to us.

The secret thought that it is so lies at the root of all our feebleness. The revelation of Christ in every individual believer, and in each one the daily revelation, step by step and moment by moment, is as much the work of God's omnipotence as the birth or resurrection of Christ. Until this truth enters and fills us, and we feel that we are just as dependent upon God for each moment of our life in the enjoyment of redemption as they were in their waiting for it, our waiting upon God will not bring its full blessing. The sense of utter and absolute helplessness, the confidence that God can and will do all, —these must be the marks of our waiting as of theirs. As gloriously as God proved Himself to them the faithful and wonder-working God, He will to us also.

'My soul, wait thou only upon God!'

Day 28: For the Coming of His Son.

'Be ye yourselves like unto men that wait for their Lord.' —Luke 12:36.

'Until the appearing of our Lord Jesus Christ, which, in His own time, He shall shew, who is the blessed and only Potentate, the King of kings, and Lord of lords.' —1 Tim. 6:14, 15 (R.V.).

'Turned to God from idols to serve the living and true God, and to wait for His Son from heaven.' —1 Thess. 1:9, 10.

WAITING on God in heaven, and waiting for His Son from heaven, these two God has joined together, and no man may put them asunder. The waiting on God for His presence and power in daily life will be the only true preparation for waiting for Christ in humility and true holiness. The waiting for Christ coming from heaven to take us to heaven will give the waiting on God its true tone of hopefulness and joy. The Father who in His own time will reveal His Son from heaven, is the God who, as we wait on Him, prepares us for the revelation of His Son. The present life and the coming glory are inseparably connected in God and in us.

There is sometimes a danger of separating them. It is always easier to be engaged with the religion of the past or the future than to be faithful in the religion of today. As we look to what God has done in the past, or will do in time to come, the personal claim of present duty and present submission to His working may be escaped. Waiting on God must ever lead to waiting for Christ as the glorious consummation of His work; and waiting for Christ must ever remind us of the duty of waiting upon God, as our only proof that the waiting for Christ is in spirit and in truth. There is such a danger of our being so occupied with the things that are coming more than with Him who is to come; there is such scope in the study of coming events for imagination and reason and human ingenuity, that nothing but deeply humble waiting on God can save us from mistaking the interest and pleasure of intellectual study for the true love of Him and His appearing. All ye that say ye wait for Christ's coming, be sure that you wait on God now. All ye that seek to wait on God now to reveal His Son in you, see to it that ye do so as men waiting for the revelation of His Son from heaven. The hope of that glorious appearing will strengthen you in waiting upon God for what He is to do in you now: the same omnipotent love that is to reveal that glory is working in you even now to fit you for it.

'The blessed hope and the appearing of the glory of our great God and Savior Jesus Christ,' is one of the great bonds of union given to God's Church throughout the ages. 'He shall come to be glorified in His saints, and to be marveled at in all them that believe.' Then we shall all meet, and the unity of the body of Christ be seen in its divine glory. It will be the meeting-place and the triumph of divine love. Jesus receiving His own and presenting them to the Father. His own meeting Him and worshiping in speechless love that blessed face. His own meeting each other in the ecstasy of God's own love. Let us wait, long for, and love the appearing of our Lord and Heavenly Bridegroom. Tender love to Him and tender love to each other is the true and only bridal spirit.

I fear greatly that this is sometimes forgotten. A beloved brother in Holland was speaking about the expectancy of faith being the true sign of the bride. I ventured to express a doubt. An unworthy bride, about to be married to a prince, might only be thinking of the position and the riches that she was to receive. The expectancy of faith might be strong, and true love utterly wanting. It is love in the bridal spirit. It is not when we are most occupied with prophetic subjects, but when in humility and love we are clinging close to our Lord and His brethren, that we are in the bride's place. Jesus refuses to accept our love except as it is love to His disciples. Waiting for His coming means waiting for the glorious coming manifestation of the unity of the body, while we seek here to maintain that unity in humility and love. Those who love most are the most ready for His coming. Love to each other is the life and beauty of His bride, the Church.

And how is this to be brought about? Beloved child of God! if you would learn aright to wait for His Son from heaven, live even now waiting on God in heaven. Remember how Jesus lived ever waiting on God. He could do nothing of Himself. It was God who perfected His Son through suffering and then exalted Him. It is God alone who can give you the deep spiritual life of one who is really waiting for His Son: wait on God for it. Waiting for Christ Himself is, oh, so different from waiting for things that may come to pass! The latter any Christian can do; the former, God must work in you every day by His Holy Spirit. Therefore all you who wait on God, look to Him for grace to wait for His Son from heaven in the Spirit which is from heaven. And you who would wait for His Son, wait on God continually to reveal Christ in you.

The revelation of Christ in us as it is given to them who wait upon God is the true preparation for the full revelation of Christ in glory.

'My soul, wait thou only upon God!'

Day 29: For the Promise of the Father.

'He charged them not to depart from Jerusalem, but to wait for the promise of the Father.' —Acts 1:4.

IN speaking of the saints in Jerusalem at Christ's birth, with Simeon and Anna, we saw how, though the redemption they waited for is come, the call to waiting is no less urgent now than it was then. We wait for the full revelation in us of what came to them, but what they scarce could comprehend. Even so it is with waiting for the promise of the Father. In one sense, the fulfillment can never come again as it came at Pentecost. In another sense, and that in as deep reality as with the first disciples, we daily need to wait for the Father to fulfil His promise in us.

The Holy Spirit is not a person distinct from the Father in the way two persons on earth are distinct. The Father and the Spirit are never without or separate from each other: the Father is always in the Spirit; the Spirit works nothing but as the Father works in Him. Each moment the same Spirit that is in us, is in God too, and he who is most full of the Spirit will be the first to wait on God most earnestly, further to fulfil His promise, and still strengthen him mightily by His Spirit in the inner man. The Spirit in us is not a power at our disposal. Nor is the Spirit an independent power, acting apart from the Father and the Son. The Spirit is the real living presence and the power of the Father working in us, and therefore it is just he who knows that the Spirit is in him, who will wait on the Father for the full revelation and experience of what the Spirit's indwelling is, for His increase and abounding more and more.

See this in the apostles. They were filled with the Spirit at Pentecost. When they, not long after, on returning from the Council, where they had been forbidden to preach, prayed afresh forboldness to speak in His name—a fresh coming down of the Holy Spirit was the Father's fresh fulfillment of His promise.

At Samaria, by the word and the Spirit, many had been converted, and the whole city filled with joy. At the apostles' prayer the Father once again fulfilled the promise. Even so to the waiting company—'We are all here before God'—in Cornelius' house. And so, too, in Acts 13. It was when men, filled with the Spirit, prayed and fasted, that the promise of the Father was afresh fulfilled, and the leading of the Spirit was given from heaven: 'Separate Me Barnabas and Saul.'

So also we find Paul in Ephesians, praying for those who have been sealed with the Spirit, that God would grant them the spirit of illumination. And later on, that He would grant them, according to the riches of His glory, to be strengthened with might by the Spirit in the inner man.

The Spirit given at Pentecost was not a something that God parted with in heaven, and sent away out of heaven to earth. God does not, cannot, give away anything in that way. When He gives grace, or strength, or life, He gives it by giving Himself to work it —it is all inseparable from Himself. (See note on Law, *The Power of the Spirit*, at the end of this volume.) Much more so is the Holy Spirit. He is God, present and working in us: the true position in which we can count upon that working with an unceasing power is as we, praising for what we have, still unceasingly wait for the Father's promise to be still more mightily fulfilled.

What new meaning and promise does this give to our life of waiting! It teaches us ever to keep the place where the disciples tarried at the footstool of the Throne. It reminds us that, as helpless as they were to meet their enemies, or to preach to Christ's enemies, until they were endued with power, we, too, can only be strong in the life of faith, or the work of love, as we are in direct communication with God and Christ, and they maintain the life of the Spirit in us. It assures us that the Omnipotent God will, through the glorified Christ, work in us a power that can bring to pass things unexpected, things impossible. Oh! what will not the Church be able to do when her individual members learn to live their lives waiting on God, and when together, with all of self and the world sacrificed in the fire of love, they unite in waiting with one accord for the promise of the Father, once so gloriously fulfilled, but still unexhausted.

Come and let each of us be still in presence of the inconceivable grandeur of this prospect: the Father waiting to fill the Church with the Holy Ghost. And willing to fill me, let each one say.

With this faith let there come over the soul a hush and a holy fear, as it waits in stillness to take it all in. And let life increasingly become a deep joy in the hope of the ever fuller fulfilment of the Father's promise.

'My soul, wait thou only upon God!'

Day 30: Continually.

'Therefore turn thou to thy God: keep mercy and judgment, and wait on thy God continually.' —Hos. 12:6.

CONTINUITY is one of the essential elements of life. Interrupt it for a single hour in a man, and it is lost, he is dead. Continuity, unbroken and ceaseless, is essential to a healthy

Christian life. God wants me to be, and God waits to make me, I want to be, and I wait on Him to make me, every moment, what He expects of me, and what is well-pleasing in His sight. If waiting on God be of the essence of true religion, the maintenance of the spirit of entire dependence must be continuous. The call of God, 'Wait on your God continually,' must be accepted and obeyed. There may be times of special waiting: the disposition and habit of soul must be there unchangeably and uninterrupted.

This waiting continually is indeed a necessity. To those who are content with a feeble Christian life, it appears a luxury something beyond what is essential to being a good Christian. But all who are praying the prayer, 'Lord! make me as holy as a pardoned sinner can be made! Keep me as near to Thee as it is possible for me to be! Fill me as full of Thy love as You are willing to do!' feel at once that it is something that must be had. They feel that there can be no unbroken fellowship with God, no full abiding in Christ, no maintaining of victory over sin and readiness for service, without waiting continually on the Lord.

The waiting continually is a possibility. Many think that with the duties of life it is out of the question. They cannot be always thinking of it. Even when they wish to, they forget.

They do not understand that it is a matter of the heart, and that what the heart is full of, occupies it, even when the thoughts are otherwise engaged. A father's heart may be filled continuously with intense love and longing for a sick wife or child at a distance, even though pressing business requires all his thoughts. When the heart has learned how entirely powerless it is for one moment to keep itself or bring forth any good, when it has understood how surely and truly God will keep it, when it has, in despair of itself, accepted God's promise to do for it the impossible, it learns to rest in God, and in the midst of occupations and temptations it can wait continually.

This waiting is a promise. God's commands are enablings: gospel precepts are all promises, a revelation of what our God will do for us. When first you begin waiting on God, it is with frequent intermission and frequent failure. But do believe God is watching over you in love and secretly strengthening you in it. There are times when waiting appears to be just losing time, but it is not so. Waiting, even in darkness, is unconscious advance, because it is God you have to do with, and He is working in you. God who calls you to wait on Him, sees your feeble efforts, and works it in you. Your spiritual life is in no respect your own work: as little as you began it, can you continue it; it is God's Spirit who has begun the work in you of waiting upon God; He will enable you to wait continually.

Waiting continually will be met and rewarded by God Himself working continually. We are coming to the end of our meditations. Would that you and I might learn one lesson: God must, God will work continually. He ever does work continually, but the experience of it is hindered by unbelief. But He who by His Spirit teaches you to wait continually, will bring you to experience also how, as the Everlasting One, His work is never-ceasing. In the love and the life and the work of God there can be no break, no interruption.

Do not limit God in this by your thoughts of what may be expected. Do fix your eyes upon this one truth: in His very nature, God, as the only Giver of life, *cannot do otherwise than every moment work in His child.* Do not look only at the one side: 'If I wait continually, God will work continually.' No, look at the other side. Place God first and say, *'God works continually, every moment I may wait on Him continually.'* Take time until the vision of your God working continually, without one moment's intermission, fill your being. Your waiting continually will then come of itself. Full of trust and joy, the holy habit of the soul will be, 'On Thee do I wait *all the day*.' The Holy Spirit will keep you ever waiting.

'My soul, wait thou only upon God!'

Moment by Moment[5]

'I the Lord do keep it: I will water it every moment.'
Dying with Jesus, by death reckoned mine,
Living with Jesus a new life divine;
Looking to Jesus till glory doth shine,
Moment by moment, O Lord, I am Thine.

Chorus—Moment by moment I'm kept in His love,
Moment by moment I've life from above;
Looking to Jesus till glory doth shine;
Moment by moment, O Lord, I am Thine.

Never a battle with wrong for the right,
Never a contest that He doth not fight;
Lifting above us His banner so white,
Moment by moment I'm kept in His sight.
Chorus.

Never a trial that He is not there,
Never a burden that He doth not bear,
Never a sorrow that He does not share,
Moment by moment I'm under His care.
Chorus

Never a heartache, and never a groan,
Never a teardrop, and never a moan;
Never a danger but there on the throne
Moment by moment He thinks of His own.
Chorus.

Never a weakness that He doth not feel,
Never a sickness that He cannot heal;
Moment by moment, in woo or in weal,
Jesus, my Savior, abides with me still.
Chorus.

---

[5] Music in *Christian Endeavor Hymns* by I. D. Sankey, or on leaflet by Morgan & Scott.

Day 31: Only.

'My soul, wait thou only upon God;

For my expectation is from Him.

He only is my rock and my salvation.' —Isa. 62:5, 6.

It is possible to be waiting continually on God, but not only upon Him; there may be other secret confidences intervening and preventing the blessing that was expected. And so the word *only* must come to throw its light on the path to the fulness and certainty of blessing. 'My soul, wait thou *only* upon God. He only is my Rock.'

Yes, 'My soul, wait thou only upon God.' There is but one God, but one source of life and happiness for the heart; He *only* is my Rock; my soul, wait thou *only* upon Him. Thou desirest to be good. 'There is none good but God,' and there is no possible goodness but what is received directly from Him. Thou hast sought to be holy: 'There is none holy but the Lord,' and there is no holiness but what He by His Spirit of holiness every moment breathes in thee. Thou wouldest live and work for God and His kingdom, for men and their salvation. Hear how He says, 'The Everlasting God, the Creator of the ends of the earth. He "alone" fainteth not, neither is weary. He giveth power to the faint, and to them that have no might He increaseth strength. They that wait upon the Lord shall renew their strength.' He only is God; He only is thy Rock: 'My soul, wait thou only upon God.'

'My soul, wait thou only upon God.' Thou will not find many who can help you in this. Enough there will be of thy brethren to draw thee to put trust in churches and doctrines, in schemes and plans and human appliances, in means of grace and divine appointments. But, 'My soul, wait thou only upon God Himself.' His most sacred appointments become a snare when trusted in. The brazen serpent becomes Nehushtan;[6] the ark and the temple a vain confidence. Let the Living God alone, none and nothing but He, be thy hope.

'My soul, wait thou only upon God.' Eyes and hands and feet, mind and thought, may have to be intently engaged in the duties of this life; 'My soul, wait thou only upon God.' Thou art an immortal spirit, created not for this world but for eternity and for God. O, my soul! Realize thy destiny. Know thy privilege, and 'wait thou only upon God.' Let not the interest of religious thoughts and exercises deceive you; they very often take the place of waiting upon God. My soul, wait *thou*, thy very self, your inmost being, with all its power, 'wait thou only upon God.' God is for thee, thou art for God; wait only upon Him.

Yes, 'my soul, wait thou only upon God.' Beware of your two great enemies —the World and Self. Beware lest any earthly satisfaction or enjoyment, however innocent it appears, keep you back from saying, 'I will go to God, my exceeding joy.' Remember and study what Jesus says about denying self, 'Let a man deny himself.' Tersteegen[7] says: 'The saints deny themselves in everything.' Pleasing self in little things may be strengthening it to assert itself in greater things. 'My soul, wait thou only upon God;' let Him be all your salvation and all your desire. Say continually and with an undivided heart, 'From Him comes my expectation; He only is my Rock; I shall not be moved.' Whatever

---

[6] 2 Kings 18:4, "He removed the high places, and brake the images, and cut down the groves, and brake in pieces the brazen serpent that Moses had made: for unto those days the children of Israel did burn incense to it: and he called it Nehushtan."

[7] Gerhard Tersteegen

be thy spiritual or temporal need, whatever the desire or prayer of thy heart, whatever thy interest in connection with God's work in the Church or the world—in solitude or in the rush of the world, in public worship or other gatherings of the saints, 'My soul, wait thou *only* upon God.' Let your expectations be from Him alone. He only is your Rock.

'My soul, wait thou only upon God.' Never forget the two foundation-truths on which this blessed waiting rests. If ever you are inclined to think this 'waiting only' is too hard or too high, they will recall thee at once. They are: your absolute helplessness; and, the absolute sufficiency of thy God. Oh! enter deep into the entire sinfulness of all that is of self, and think not of letting self have anything to say one single moment. Enter deep into thy utter and unceasing impotence ever to change what is evil in thee, or to bring forth anything that is spiritually good. Enter deep into thy relation of dependence as creature on God, to receive from Him every moment what He gives. Enter deeper still into His covenant of redemption, with His promise to restore more gloriously than ever what thou hadst lost, and by His Son and Spirit to give within you unceasingly, His actual divine Presence and Power. And thus wait upon your God continually and only.

'My soul, wait thou only upon God.' No words can tell, no heart conceive, the riches of the glory of this mystery of the Father and of Christ. Our God, in the infinite tenderness and omnipotence of His love, waits to be our Life and Joy. Oh, my soul! let it be no longer needed that I repeat the words, 'Wait upon God,' but let all that is in me rise and sing: 'Truly my soul waits upon God. On Thee do I wait all the day.'

'My soul, wait thou only upon God!'

Note.

My publishers have just issued a work of William Law on the Holy Spirit.[8] In the Introduction I have said how much I owe to the book. I cannot but think that anyone who will take the trouble to read it thoughtfully will find rich spiritual profit in connection with a life of Waiting upon God.

What he puts more clearly than I have anywhere else found are these cardinal truths:—

1. That the very Nature and Being of a God, as the only Possessor and Dispenser of any life there is in the universe, imply that He must every moment communicate to every creature the power by which it exists, and therefore also much more the power by which it can do that which is good.

2. That the very Nature and Being of a creature, as owing its existence to God alone, and equally owing to Him each moment the continuation of that existence, imply that its happiness can only be found in absolute unceasing momentary dependence upon God.

3. That the great value and blessing of the gift of the Spirit at Pentecost, as the fruit of Christ's Redemption, is that it is now possible for God to take possession of His redeemed children and work in them as He did before the fall in Adam. We need to know the Holy Spirit as the Presence and Power of God in us restored to their true place.

4. That in the spiritual life our great need is the knowledge of two great lessons. The one, our entire sinfulness and helplessness, our utter impotence by any effort of our own

---

[8] The Power of the Holy Spirit: An humble earnest, and affectionate Address to the Clergy. With Additional Extracts and Introduction, by Rev. Andrew Murray. (Fleming H. Revell Company. $1.00)

to do anything towards the maintenance and increase of our inner spiritual life. The other, the infinite willingness of God's love, which is nothing but a desire to communicate Himself and His blessedness to us to meet our every need, and every moment to work us in by His Son and Spirit what we need.

5. That, therefore, the very essence of true religion, whether in heaven or upon earth, consists in an unalterable dependence upon God, because we can give God no other glory, than yielding ourselves to His love, which created us to show forth in us its glory, that it may now perfect its work in us.

I need not point out how deep down these truths go to the very root of the spiritual life, and specially the life of waiting upon God. I am confident that those who are willing to take the trouble of studying this thoughtful writer will thank me for the introduction in his book. The book referred to is The Power of the Spirit, by William Law, An Humble, Earnest and Affectionate Address to the Clergy.

The
Christian's Secret
of a
Happy Life

~ ※ ~

By *Hannah Whitall Smith*
The 1885 Edition

Preface

This is not a theological book. I frankly confess I have not been trained in theological schools, and do not understand their methods nor their terms. But the Lord has taught me experimentally and practically certain lessons out of his Word, which have greatly helped me in my Christian life, and have made it a very happy one. And I want to tell my secret, in the best way I can, in order that some others may be helped into a happy life also.

I do not seek to change the theological views of a single individual. I dare say most of my readers know far more about theology than I do myself, and perhaps may discover abundance of what will seem to be theological mistakes. But let me ask that these may be overlooked, and that my reader will try, instead, to get at the experimental point of that which I have tried to say, and if that is practical and helpful, forgive the blundering way in which it is expressed. I have tried to reach the absolute truth which lies at the foundation of all "creeds" and "views," and to bring the soul into those personal relations with God which must exist alike in every form of religion, let the expression of them differ as they may.

I have committed my book to the Lord, and have asked Him to counteract all in it that is wrong, and to let only that which is true find entrance into any heart. It is sent out in tender sympathy and yearning love for all the struggling, weary ones in the Church of Christ, and its message goes right from my heart to theirs. I have given the best I have, and could do no more. May the blessed Holy Spirit use it to teach some of my readers the true secret of a happy life!

Hannah Whitall Smith,
Germantown, Pennsylvania.

1. Introductory — God's Side and Man's Side

In introducing this subject of the life and walk of faith, I desire, at the very outset, to clear away one misunderstanding which very commonly arises in reference to the teaching of it, and which effectually hinders a clear apprehension of such teaching. This misunderstanding comes from the fact that the *two* sides of the subject are rarely kept in view at the same time. People see distinctly the way in which one side is presented, and, dwelling exclusively upon this, without even a thought of any other, it is no wonder that distorted views of the whole matter are the legitimate consequence.

Now there are two very decided and distinct sides to this subject, and, like all other subjects, it cannot be fully understood unless both of these sides are kept constantly in view. I refer, of course, to God's side and man's side; or, in other words, to God's part in the work of sanctification, and man's part. These are very distinct and even contrastive, but are not contradictory; though, to a cursory observer, they sometimes look so.

This was very strikingly illustrated to me not long ago. There were two teachers of this higher Christian life holding meetings in the same place, at alternate hours. One spoke only of God's part in the work, and the other dwelt exclusively upon man's part. They were both in perfect sympathy with one another, and realized fully that they were each teaching different sides of the same great truth; and this also was understood by a large proportion of their hearers. But with some of the hearers it was different, and one lady said to me, in the greatest perplexity, "I cannot understand it at all. Here are two preachers undertaking to teach just the same truth, and yet to me they seem flatly to contradict one another." And I felt at the time that she expressed a puzzle which really causes a great deal of difficulty in the minds of many honest inquirers after this truth.

Suppose two friends go to see some celebrated building, and return home to describe it. One has seen only the north side, and the other only the south. The first says, "The building was built in such a manner, and has such and such stories and ornaments." "Oh, no!" says the other, interrupting him, "you are altogether mistaken; I saw the building, and it was built in quite a different manner, and its ornaments and stories were so and so." A lively dispute would probably follow upon the truth of the respective descriptions, until the two friends discover that they have been describing different *sides* of the building, and then all is reconciled at once.

I would like to state as clearly as I can what I judge to be the two distinct sides in this matter; and to show how the looking at one without seeing the other, will be sure to create wrong impressions and views of the truth.

To state it in brief, I would just say that man's part is to trust and God's part is to work; and it can be seen at a glance how contrastive these two parts are, and yet not necessarily contradictory. I mean this. There is a certain *work* to be accomplished. We are to be delivered from the power of sin, and are to be made perfect in every good work to do the will of God. "Beholding as in a glass the glory of the Lord," we are to be actually "changed into the same image from glory to glory, even as by the Spirit of the Lord." We are to be transformed by the renewing of our minds, that we may prove what is that good and acceptable and perfect will of God. A real work is to be wrought in us and upon us. Besetting sins are to be conquered. Evil habits are to be overcome. Wrong dispositions and feelings are to be rooted out, and holy tempers and emotions are to be begotten. A positive transformation is to take place. So at least the Bible teaches. Now somebody must do this. Either we must do it for ourselves, or another must do it for us. We have most of us tried to do it for ourselves at first, and have grievously failed; then we discover from the Scriptures and from our own experience that it is a work we are utterly unable to do for ourselves, but that the Lord Jesus Christ has come on purpose to do it, and that He will do it for all who put themselves wholly into His hand, and trust Him to do it. Now under these circumstances, what is the part of the believer, and what is the part of the Lord? Plainly the believer can do nothing but trust; while the Lord, in whom he trusts, actually does the work entrusted to Him. *Trusting* and *doing* are certainly contrastive things, and often contradictory; but are they contradictory in this case? Manifestly not, because it is two different parties that are concerned. If we should say of one party in a transaction that he trusted his case to another, and yet attended to it himself, we should state a contradiction and an impossibility. But when we say of two parties in a transaction that one trusts the other to do something, and that that other goes to work and does it, we are making a statement that is perfectly simple and harmonious. When we say, therefore, that in this higher life, man's part is to trust, and that God does the thing entrusted to Him, we do not surely present any very difficult or puzzling problem.

The preacher who is speaking on man's part in this matter cannot speak of anything but surrender and trust, because this is positively all the man can do. We all agree about this. And yet such preachers are constantly criticized as though, in saying this, they had meant to imply there *was* no other part, and that therefore nothing but trusting is done. And the cry goes out that this doctrine of faith does away with all realities, that souls are just told to trust, and that is the end of it, and they sit down thenceforward in a sort of religious easy-chair, dreaming away a life fruitless of any actual results. All this misapprehension arises, of course, from the fact that either the preacher has neglected to state, or the hearer has failed to hear, the other side of the matter; which is, that when we trust, the Lord works, and that a great deal is done, not by us, but by Him. Actual results are reached by our trusting, because our Lord undertakes the thing trusted to Him, and accomplishes it. *We* do not do anything, but *He* does it; and it is all the more effectually done because of this. The puzzle as to the preaching of faith disappears entirely as soon as this is clearly seen.

On the other hand, the preacher who dwells on God's side of the question is criticized on a totally different ground. He does not speak of trust, for the Lord's part is not to trust, but to work. The Lord does the thing entrusted to Him. He disciplines and trains the soul by inward exercises and outward providences. He brings to bear all the resources of His wisdom and love upon the refining and purifying of that soul. He makes everything in the life and circumstances of such a one subservient to the one great purpose of making him grow in grace, and of conforming him, day by day and hour by hour, to the image of Christ. He carries him through a process of transformation, longer or shorter, as his peculiar case may require, making actual and experimental the results for which the soul has trusted. We have dared, for instance, according to the command in Rom. 6:11, by faith to reckon ourselves "dead unto sin." The Lord makes this a reality, and leads us to victory over self, by the daily and hourly discipline of His providences. Our reckoning is available only because God thus makes it real. And yet the preacher who dwells upon this practical side of the matter, and tells of God's processes for making faith's reckonings experimental realities, is accused of contradicting the preaching of faith altogether, and of declaring only a process of gradual sanctification by works, and of setting before the soul an impossible and hopeless task.

Now, sanctification is both a sudden step of faith, and also a gradual process of works. It is a step as far as we are concerned; it is a process as to God's part. By a step of faith we get into Christ; by a process we are made to grow up unto Him in all things. By a step of faith we put ourselves into the hands of the Divine Potter; by a gradual process He makes us into a vessel unto His own honor, meet for His use, and prepared to every good work.

To illustrate all this: suppose I were to be describing to a person, who was entirely ignorant of the subject, the way in which a lump of clay is made into a beautiful vessel. I tell him first the part of the clay in the matter, and all I can say about this is, that the clay is put into the potter's hands, and then lies passive there, submitting itself to all the turnings and overturnings of the potter's hands upon it. There is really nothing else to be said about the clay's part. But could my hearer argue from this that nothing else is done, because I say that this is all the clay can do? If he is an intelligent hearer, he will not dream of doing so, but will say, "I understand. This is what the clay must do; but what must the potter do?" "Ah," I answer, "now we come to the important part. The potter takes the clay thus abandoned to his working, and begins to mold and fashion it according to his own will. He kneads and works it, he tears it apart and presses it together again, he wets it and then suffers it to dry. Sometimes he works at it for hours together, sometimes he lays it aside for days and does not touch it. And then, when by all these processes he has made it perfectly pliable in his hands, he proceeds to make it up into the vessel he has purposed. He turns it upon the wheel, planes it and smooths it, and dries it in the sun, bakes it in the oven, and finally turns it out of his workshop, a vessel to his honor and fit for his use."

Will my hearer be likely now to say that I am contradicting myself; that a little while ago I had said the clay had nothing to do but lie passive in the potter's hands, and that now

I am putting upon it a great work which it is not able to perform; and that to make itself into such a vessel is an impossible and hopeless undertaking? Surely not. For he will see that, while before I was speaking of the clay's part in the matter, I am now speaking of the potter's part, and that these two are necessarily contrastive, but not in the least contradictory, and that the clay is not expected to do the potter's work, but only to yield itself up to his working.

Nothing, it seems to me, could be clearer than the perfect harmony between these two *apparently* contradictory sorts of teaching on this subject. What *can* be said about man's part in this great work, but that he must continually surrender himself and continually trust?

But when we come to God's side of the question, what is there that may not be said as to the manifold and wonderful ways in which He accomplishes the work entrusted to Him? It is here that the *growing* comes in. The lump of clay would never grow into a beautiful vessel if it stayed in the clay-pit for thousands of years. But once put into the hands of a skillful potter, and, under his fashioning, it grows rapidly into a vessel to his honor. And so the soul, abandoned to the working of the Heavenly Potter, is changed rapidly from glory to glory into the image of the Lord by His Spirit.

Having, therefore, taken the step of faith by which you have put yourself wholly and absolutely into His hands, you must now expect Him to begin to work. His way of accomplishing that which you have entrusted to Him may be different from your way. But He knows, and you must be satisfied.

I knew a lady who had entered into this life of faith with a great outpouring of the Spirit, and a wonderful flood of light and joy. She supposed, of course, this was a preparation for some great service, and expected to be put forth immediately into the Lord's harvest field. Instead of this, almost at once her husband lost all his money, and she was shut up in her own house, to attend to all sorts of domestic duties, with no time or strength left for any Gospel work at all. She accepted the discipline, and yielded herself up as heartily to sweep, and dust, and bake, and sew, as she would have done to preach, or pray or write for the Lord. And the result was that through this very training He made her into a vessel "meet for the Master's use, and prepared unto every good work."

Another lady, who had entered this life of faith under similar circumstances of wondrous blessing, and who also expected to be sent out to do some great work, was shut up with two peevish invalid nieces, to nurse, and humor, and amuse them all day long. Unlike the first lady, this one did not accept the training, but chafed and fretted, and finally rebelled, lost all her blessing, and went back into a state of sad coldness and misery. She had understood her part of trusting to begin with, but not understanding the divine process of accomplishing that for which she had trusted, she took herself out of the hands of the Heavenly Potter, and the vessel was marred on the wheel.

I believe many a vessel has been similarly marred by a want of understanding these things. The maturity of Christian experience cannot be reached in a moment, but is the result of the work of God's Holy Spirit, who, by His energizing and transforming power, causes us to grow up into Christ in all things. And we cannot hope to reach this maturity in any other way than by yielding ourselves up utterly and willingly to His mighty working. But the sanctification the Scriptures urge as a present experience upon all believers does not consist in maturity of growth, but in purity of heart, and this may be as complete in the babe in Christ as in the veteran believer.

The lump of clay, from the moment it comes under the transforming hand of the potter, is, during each day and each hour of the process, just what the potter wants it to be at that hour or on that day, and therefore pleases him. But it is very far from being matured into the vessel he intends in the future to make it.

The little babe may be all that a babe could be, or ought to be, and may therefore perfectly please its mother, and yet it is very far from being what that mother would wish it to be when the years of maturity shall come.

The apple in June is a perfect apple for June. It is the best apple that June can produce. But it is very different from the apple in October, which is a perfected apple.

God's works are perfect in every stage of their growth. Man's works are never perfect until they are in every respect complete.

All that we claim then in this life of sanctification is, that by a step of faith we put ourselves into the hands of the Lord, for Him to work in us all the good pleasure of His will; and that by a continuous exercise of faith we keep ourselves there. This is our part in the matter. And when we do it, and while we do it, we are, in the Scripture sense, truly pleasing to God, although it may require years of training and discipline to mature us into a vessel that shall be in all respects to His honor, and fitted to every good work.

Our part is the trusting, it is His to accomplish the results. And when we do our part, He never fails to do His, for no one ever trusted in the Lord and was confounded. Do not be afraid, then, that if you trust, or tell others to trust, the matter will end there. Trust is only the beginning and the continual foundation; when we trust, the Lord works, and His work is the important part of the whole matter. And this explains that apparent paradox which puzzles so many. They say, "In one breath you tell us to do nothing but trust, and in the next you tell us to do impossible things. How can you reconcile such contradictory statements?" They are to be reconciled just as we reconcile the statements concerning a saw in a carpenter's shop, when we say at one moment that the saw has sawn asunder a log, and the next moment declare that the carpenter has done it. The saw is the instrument used, the power that uses it is the carpenter's. And so we, yielding ourselves unto God, and our members as instruments of righteousness unto Him, find that He works in us to will and to do of His good pleasure; and we can say with Paul, "I labored; yet not I, but the grace of God which was with me." For we are to be His workmanship, not our own. (Eph. 2:10.) And in fact, when we come to look at it, only God, who created us at first, can re-create us, for He alone understands the "work of His own hands." All efforts after self-creating, result in the marring of the vessel, and no soul can ever reach its highest fulfillment except through the working of Him who "worketh all things after the counsel of His own will."

In this book I shall of course dwell mostly upon man's side in the matter, as I am writing for man, and in the hope of teaching believers how to fulfil their part of the great work. But I wish it to be distinctly understood all through, that unless I believed with all my heart in God's effectual working on His side, not one word of this book would ever have been written.

2. The Scripturalness of This Life

When I approach this subject of the true Christian life, that life which is hid with Christ in God, so many thoughts struggle for utterance that I am almost speechless. Where shall I begin? What is the most important thing to say? How shall I make people read and believe? The subject is so glorious, and human words seem so powerless! But something I am impelled to say. The secret must be told. For it is one concerning that victory which overcometh the world, that promised deliverance from all our enemies, for which every child of God longs and prays, but which seems so often and so generally to elude their grasp. May God grant me so to tell it, that every believer to whom this book shall come, may have his eyes opened to see the truth as it is in Jesus, and may be enabled to enter into possession of this glorious life for himself.

For sure I am that every converted soul longs for victory and rest, and nearly everyone feels instinctively, at times, that they are his birthright. Can you not remember, some of you, the shout of triumph your souls gave when you first became acquainted with the Lord Jesus, and had a glimpse of His mighty saving power? How sure you were of victory then! How easy it seemed, to be more than conquerors, through Him that loved you. Under the leadership of a Captain who had never been foiled in battle, how could you dream of defeat? And yet, to many of you, how different has been your real experience. The victories have been but few and fleeting, the defeats many and disastrous. You have not lived as you feel children of God ought to live. There has been a resting in a clear understanding of doctrinal truth, without pressing after the power and life thereof. There has been a rejoicing in the knowledge of things testified of in the Scriptures, without a living realization of the things themselves, consciously felt in the soul. Christ is believed in, talked about, and served, but He is not known as the soul's actual and very life, abiding there forever, and revealing Himself there continually in His beauty. You have found Jesus as your Savior and your Master, and you have tried to serve Him and advance the cause of His kingdom. You have carefully studied the Holy Scriptures and have gathered much precious truth therefrom, which you have endeavored faithfully to practice.

But notwithstanding all your knowledge and all your activities in the service of the Lord, your souls are secretly starving, and you cry out again and again for that bread and water of life which you saw promised in the Scriptures to all believers. In the very depths of your hearts you know that your experience is not a Scriptural experience; that, as an old writer says, your religion is "but a *talk* to what the early Christians enjoyed, possessed, and lived in." And your souls have sunk within you, as day after day, and year after year, your early visions of triumph have seemed to grow more and more dim, and you have been forced to settle down to the conviction that the best you can expect from your religion is a life of alternate failure and victory; one hour sinning, and the next repenting; and beginning again, only to fail again, and again to repent.

But *is* this all? Had the Lord Jesus only this in His mind when He laid down His precious life to deliver you from your sore and cruel bondage to sin? Did He propose to Himself only this partial deliverance? Did He intend to leave you thus struggling along under a weary consciousness of defeat and discouragement? Did He fear that a continuous victory would dishonor Him, and bring reproach on His name? When all those declarations were made concerning His coming, and the work He was to accomplish, did they mean only this that you have experienced? Was there a hidden reserve in each promise that was meant to deprive it of its complete fulfillment? Did "delivering us out of the hands of our enemies" mean only a few of them? Did "enabling us always to triumph" mean only sometimes; or being "more than conquerors through Him that love us" mean constant defeat and failure? No, no, a thousand times no! God is able to save unto the uttermost, and He means to do it. His promise, confirmed by His oath, was that "He would grant unto us, that we, being delivered out of the hand of our enemies, might serve Him without fear, in holiness and righteousness before Him, all the days of our life." It is a mighty work to do, but our Deliverer is able to do it. He came to destroy the works of the devil, and dare we dream for a moment that He is not able or not willing to accomplish His own purposes?

In the very outset, then, settle down on this one thing, that the Lord is able to save you fully, now, in this life, from the power and dominion of sin, and to deliver you altogether out of the hands of your enemies. If you do not think He is, search your Bible, and collect together every announcement or declaration concerning the purposes and object of His death on the cross. You will be astonished to find how full they are. Everywhere and always His work is said to be, to deliver us from our sins, from our bondage, from our defilement; and not a hint is given anywhere, that this deliverance was to be only the limited and partial one with which the Church so continually tries to be satisfied.

Let me give you a few texts on this subject. When the angel of the Lord appeared unto Joseph in a dream, and announced the coming birth of the Savior, he said, "And thou shalt call His name Jesus, for He shall save His people from their sins."

When Zacharias was "filled with the Holy Ghost" at the birth of his son, and "prophesied," he declared that God had visited His people in order to fulfil the promise and the oath He had made them, which promise was, "That He would grant unto us, that we, being delivered out of the hands of our enemies, might serve Him without fear, in holiness and righteousness before Him, all the days of our life."

When Peter was preaching in the porch of the Temple to the wondering Jews, he said, "Unto you first, God, having raised up His Son Jesus, sent Him to bless you in turning away every one of you from his iniquities."

When Paul was telling out to the Ephesian church the wondrous truth that Christ had loved them so much as to give Himself for them, he went on to declare, that His purpose in thus doing was, "that He might sanctify and cleanse it by the washing of water by the word, that He might present it to Himself a glorious church, not having spot or wrinkle, or any such thing; but that it should be holy and without blemish."

When Paul was seeking to instruct Titus, his own son after the common faith, concerning the grace of God, he declared that the object of that grace was to teach us "that denying ungodliness and worldly lusts, we should live soberly, righteously, and godly in this present world"; and adds, as the reason of this, that Christ "gave Himself for us that He might redeem us from all iniquity, and purify us unto Himself a peculiar people, zealous of good works."

When Peter was urging upon the Christians, to whom he was writing, a holy and Christ-like walk, he tells them that "even hereunto were ye called because Christ also suffered for us, leaving us an example that ye should follow His steps: who did no sin, neither was guile found in His mouth"; and adds, "who His own self bare our sins in His own body on the tree, that we, being dead to sins, should live unto righteousness; by whose stripes ye were healed."

When Paul was contrasting in the Ephesians the walk suitable for a Christian, with the walk of an unbeliever, he sets before them the truth in Jesus as being this, "that ye put off concerning the former conversation the old man, which is corrupt according to the deceitful lusts; and be renewed in the spirit of your mind; and that ye put on the new man, which after God is created in righteousness and true holiness."

And when, in Romans 6, he was answering forever the question as to continuing in sin, and showing how utterly foreign it was to the whole spirit and aim of the salvation of Jesus, he brings up the fact of our judicial death and resurrection with Christ as an unanswerable argument for our practical deliverance from it, and says, "God forbid. How shall we, that are dead to sin, live any longer therein? Know ye not that so many of us as were baptized into Jesus Christ were baptized into His death? Therefore we are buried with Him by baptism into death; that like as Christ was raised up from the dead by the glory of the Father, even so we also should walk in newness of life." And adds, "Knowing this, that our old man is crucified with Him, that the body of sin might be destroyed, that henceforth we should not serve sin."

Dear Christians, will you receive the testimony of Scripture on this matter? The same questions that troubled the Church in Paul's day are troubling it now: first, "Shall we continue in sin that grace may abound?" And second, "Do we then make void the law through faith?" Shall not our answer to these be Paul's emphatic "God forbid"; and his triumphant assertions that instead of making it void "we establish the law"; and that "what the law could not do, in that it was weak through the flesh, God sending His own Son in the likeness of sinful flesh, and for sin, condemned sin in the flesh: that the righteousness of the law might be fulfilled in us who walk not after the flesh, but after the Spirit"?

Can we suppose for a moment that the holy God, who hates sin in the sinner, is willing to tolerate it in the Christian, and that He has even arranged the plan of salvation in such a way as to make it impossible for those who are saved from the guilt of sin to find deliverance from its power?

As Dr. Chalmers well says, "Sin is that scandal which must be rooted out from the great spiritual household over which the Divinity rejoices… Strange administration, indeed, for sin to be so hateful to God as to lay all who had incurred it under death, and yet when readmitted into life that sin should be permitted; and that what was before the object of destroying vengeance, should now become the object of an upheld and protected toleration. Now that the penalty is taken off, think you that it is possible the unchangeable God has so given up His antipathy to sin, as that man, ruined and redeemed man, may now perseveringly indulge under the new arrangement in that which under the old destroyed him? Does not the God who loved righteousness and hated iniquity six thousand years ago, bear the same love to righteousness and hatred to iniquity still?… I now breathe the air of loving-kindness from Heaven, and can walk before God in peace and graciousness; shall I again attempt the incompatible alliance of two principles so adverse as that of an approving God and a persevering sinner? How shall we, recovered from so awful a catastrophe, continue that which first involved us in it? The cross of Christ, by the same mighty and decisive stroke wherewith it moved the curse of sin away from us, also surely moves away the power and the love of it from over us."

And not Dr. Chalmers only, but many other holy men of his generation and of our own, as well as of generations long past, have united in declaring that the redemption accomplished for us by our Lord Jesus Christ on the cross at Calvary is a redemption from the power of sin as well as from its guilt, and that He *is* able to save to the uttermost all who come unto God by Him.

A quaint old divine of the seventeenth century says: "There is nothing so contrary to God as sin, and God will not suffer sin always to rule his masterpiece, man. When we consider the infiniteness of God's power for destroying that which is contrary to Him, who can believe that the devil must always stand and prevail? I believe it is inconsistent and disagreeable with true faith for people to be Christians, and yet to believe that Christ, the eternal Son of God, to whom all power in heaven and earth is given, will suffer sin and the devil to have dominion over them.

"But you will say no man by all the power he hath can redeem himself, and no man can live without sin. We will say, Amen, to it. But if men tell us, that when God's power comes to help us and to redeem us out of sin, that it cannot be effected, then this doctrine we cannot away with; nor I hope you neither.

"Would you approve of it, if I should tell you that God puts forth His power to do such a thing, but the devil hinders Him? That it is impossible for God to do it because the devil does not like it? That it is impossible that any one should be free from sin because the devil hath got such a power in them that God cannot cast him out? This is lamentable doctrine, yet hath not this been preached? It doth in plain terms say, though God doth interpose His power, it is impossible, because the devil hath so rooted sin in the nature of man. Is not man God's creature, and cannot He new make him, and cast sin out of him? If you say sin is deeply rooted in man, I say so, too, yet not so deeply rooted but Christ Jesus hath entered so deeply into the root of the nature of man that He hath received power to destroy the devil and his works, and to recover and redeem man into righteousness and holiness. Or else it is false that 'He is able to save to the uttermost all that come unto God by Him.' We must throw away the Bible, if we say that it is impossible for God to deliver man out of sin.

"We know," he continues, "when our friends are in captivity, as in Turkey, or elsewhere, we pay our money for their redemption; but we will not pay our money if they be kept in their fetters still. Would not any one think himself cheated to pay so much money for their redemption, and the bargain be made so that he shall be *said* to be redeemed, and be *called* a redeemed captive, but he must wear his fetters still? How long? As long as he hath a day to live.

"This is for bodies, but now I am speaking of souls. Christ must be made to me redemption, and rescue me from captivity. Am I a prisoner any where? Yes, verily, verily, he that committeth sin, saith Christ, he is a servant of sin, he is a slave of sin. If thou hast sinned, thou art a slave, a captive that must be redeemed out of captivity. Who will pay a price for me? I am poor; I have nothing; I cannot redeem myself; who will pay a price for me? There is One come who hath paid a price for me. That is well; that is good news, then I hope I shall come out of my captivity. What is His name, is He called a Redeemer? So, then, I do expect the benefit of my redemption, and that I shall go out of my captivity. No, say they, you must abide in sin as long as you live. What! must we never be delivered? Must this crooked heart and perverse will always remain? Must I be a believer, and yet have no faith that reacheth to sanctification and holy living? Is there no mastery to be had, no getting victory over sin? Must it prevail over me as long as I live? What sort of a Redeemer, then, is this, or what benefit have I in this life, of my redemption?"

Similar extracts might be quoted from Marshall, Romaine, and many others, to show that this doctrine is no new one in the Church, however much it may have been lost sight of by the present generation of believers. It is the same old story that has filled with songs of triumph the daily lives of many saints of God throughout all ages; and is now afresh being sounded forth to the unspeakable joy of weary and burdened souls.

Do not reject it, then, dear reader, until you have prayerfully searched the Scriptures to see whether these things be indeed so. Ask God to open the eyes of your understanding by His Spirit, that you may "know what is the exceeding greatness of His power to us-ward who believe, according to the working of His mighty power, which He wrought in Christ, when He raised Him from the dead, and set Him at His own right hand in the heavenly places." And when you have begun to have some faint glimpses of this power, learn to look away utterly from your own weakness, and, putting your case into His hands, trust Him to deliver you.

In Psalms 8:6, we are told that God made man to "have dominion over the works of His hand." The fulfillment of this is declared in 2 Cor. 2, where the apostle cries, "Thanks be unto God which always causeth us to triumph in Christ." If the maker of a machine should declare that he had made it to accomplish a certain purpose, and if upon trial it should be found incapable of accomplishing that purpose, we would all say of that maker that he was a fraud.

Surely then we will not dare to think that it is impossible for the creature whom God has made, to accomplish the declared object for which he was created. Especially when the Scriptures are so full of the assertions that Christ has made it possible.

The only thing that can hinder is the creature's own failure to work in harmony with the plans of his Creator, and if this want of harmony can be removed, then God can work. Christ came to bring about an atonement between God and man, which should make it possible for God thus to work in man to will and to do of His good pleasure. Therefore we may be of good courage; for the work Christ has undertaken He is surely able and willing to perform. Let us then "walk in the steps of that faith of our father Abraham," who "staggered not at the promise of God through unbelief; but was strong in faith, giving glory to God; being fully persuaded that what He had promised, He was able also to perform."

3. The Life Defined

In my last chapter I tried to settle the question as to the scripturalness of the experience sometimes called the Higher Christian Life, but which to my own mind is best described in the words, the "life hid with Christ in God." I shall now, therefore, consider it as a settled point that the Scriptures do set before the believer in the Lord Jesus a life of abiding rest and of continual victory, which is very far beyond the ordinary line of Christian experience; and that in the Bible we have presented to us a Savior able to save us from the power of our sins, as really as He saves us from their guilt.

The point to be next considered is, as to what this hidden life consists in, and how it differs from every other sort of Christian experience.

And as to this, it is simply letting the Lord carry our burdens and manage our affairs for us, instead of trying to do it ourselves.

Most Christians are like a man who was toiling along the road, bending under a heavy burden, when a wagon overtook him, and the driver kindly offered to help him on his journey. He joyfully accepted the offer, but when seated, continued to bend beneath his burden, which he still kept on his shoulders. "Why do you not lay down your burden?" asked the kind-hearted driver. "Oh!" replied the man, "I feel that it is almost too much to ask you to carry me, and I could not think of letting you carry my burden too." And so Christians, who have given themselves into the care and keeping of the Lord Jesus, still continue to bend beneath the weight of their burden, and often go weary and heavy-laden throughout the whole length of their journey.

When I speak of burdens, I mean everything that troubles us, whether spiritual or temporal.

I mean, first of all, ourselves. The greatest burden we have to carry in life is self. The most difficult thing we have to manage is self. Our own daily living, our frames and feelings, our especial weaknesses and temptations, and our peculiar temperaments, our inward affairs of every kind, these are the things that perplex and worry us more than anything else, and that bring us oftenest into bondage and darkness. In laying off your burdens, therefore, the first one you must get rid of is yourself. You must hand yourself and all your inward experiences, your temptations, your temperament, your frames and feelings, all over into the care and keeping of your God, and leave them there. He made you, and therefore He understands you and knows how to manage you, and you must trust Him to do it. Say to Him, "Here, Lord, I abandon myself to thee. I have tried in every way I could think of to manage myself, and to make myself what I know I ought to be, but have always failed. Now I give it up to thee. Do thou take entire possession of me. Work in me all the good pleasure of thy will. Mold and fashion me into such a vessel as seemeth good to thee. I leave myself in thy hands, and I believe thou wilt, according to thy promise, make me into a vessel unto thine honor, 'sanctified, and meet for the Master's use, and prepared unto every good work.'" And here you must rest, trusting yourself thus to Him continually and absolutely.

Next, you must lay off every other burden,—your health, your reputation, your Christian work, your houses, your children, your business, your servants; everything, in short, that concerns you, whether inward or outward.

Christians always commit the keeping of their souls for eternity to the Lord, because they know, without a shadow of a doubt, that they cannot keep these themselves. But the things of this present life they take into their own keeping, and try to carry on their own shoulders, with the perhaps unconfessed feeling that it is a great deal to ask of the Lord to carry them, and that they cannot think of asking Him to carry their burdens too.

I knew a Christian lady who had a very heavy temporal burden. It took away her sleep and her appetite, and there was danger of her health breaking down under it. One day, when it seemed especially heavy, she noticed lying on the table near her a little tract called "Hannah's Faith." Attracted by the title, she picked it up and began to read it, little knowing, however, that it was to create a revolution in her whole experience. The story was of a poor woman who had been carried triumphantly through a life of unusual sorrow. She was giving the history of her life to a kind visitor on one occasion, and at the close the visitor said, feelingly, "O Hannah, I do not see how you could bear so much sorrow!" "I did not bear it," was the quick reply; "the Lord bore it for me." "Yes," said the visitor "that is the right way. You must take your troubles to the Lord." "Yes," replied Hannah, "but we must do more than that; we must *leave* them there. Most people," she continued, "take their burdens to Him, but they bring them away with them again, and are just as worried and unhappy as ever. But I take mine, and I leave them with Him, and come away and forget them. And if the worry comes back, I take it to Him again; I do this over and over, until at last I just forget that I have any worries, and am at perfect rest."

My friend was very much struck with this plan and resolved to try it. The circumstances of her life she could not alter, but she took them to the Lord, and handed them over into His management; and then she believed that He took it, and she left all the responsibility and the worry and anxiety with Him. As often as the anxieties returned she took them back; and the result was that, although the circumstances remained unchanged, her soul was kept in perfect peace in the midst of them. She felt that she had found out a blessed secret, and from that time she tried never again to carry her own burdens, nor to manage anything for herself.

And the secret she found so effectual in her outward affairs, she found to be still more effectual in her inward ones, which were in truth even more utterly unmanageable. She abandoned her whole self to the Lord, with all that she was and all that she had, and, believing that He took that which she had committed to Him, she ceased to fret and worry, and her life became all sunshine in the gladness of belonging to Him. And this was the Higher Christian Life! It was a very simple secret she found out. Only this, that it was possible to obey God's commandment contained in those words, "Be careful for nothing, but in everything by prayer and supplication, with thanksgiving, let your requests be made known unto God"; and that, in obeying it, the result would inevitably be, according to the promise, that the "peace of God which passeth all understanding shall keep your hearts and minds through Christ Jesus."

There are many other things to be said about this life hid with Christ in God, many details as to what the Lord Jesus does for those who thus abandon themselves to Him. But the gist of the whole matter is here stated, and the soul that has got hold of this secret has found the key that will unlock the whole treasure-house of God.

And now I do trust that I have made you hunger for this blessed life. Would you not like to get rid of your burdens? Do you not long to hand over the management of your unmanageable self into the hands of One who is able to manage you? Are you not tired and weary, and does not the rest I speak of look sweet to you?

Do you recollect the delicious sense of rest with which you have sometimes gone to bed at night, after a day of great exertion and weariness? How delightful was the sensation of relaxing every muscle, and letting your body go in a perfect abandonment of ease and comfort. The strain of the day had ceased for a few hours at least, and the work of the day had been thrown off. You no longer had to hold up an aching head or a weary back. You trusted yourself to the bed in an absolute confidence, and it held you up, without effort, or strain, or even thought on your part. You rested.

But suppose you had doubted the strength or the stability of your bed, and had dreaded each moment to find it giving away beneath you and landing you on the floor; could you have rested then? Would not every muscle have been strained in a fruitless effort to hold yourself up, and would not the weariness have been greater than not to have gone to bed at all?

Let this analogy teach you what it means to rest in the Lord. Let your souls lie down upon His sweet will, as your bodies lie down in your beds at night. Relax every strain and lay off every burden. Let yourselves go in perfect abandonment of ease and comfort, sure that when He holds you up you are perfectly safe.

Your part is simply to rest. His part is to sustain you, and He cannot fail.

Or take another analogy, which our Lord Himself has abundantly sanctioned, that of the child-life. For "Jesus called a little child unto Him, and set him in the midst of them, and said, Verily I say unto you, Except ye be converted and become as little children, ye shall not enter the kingdom of Heaven."

Now, what are the characteristics of a little child and how does he live? He lives by faith, and his chiefest characteristic is thoughtlessness. His life is one long trust from year's end to year's end. He trusts his parents, he trusts his caretakers, he trusts his teachers, he even trusts people often who are utterly unworthy of trust, because of the confidingness of his nature. And his trust is abundantly answered. He provides nothing for himself, and yet everything is provided. He takes no thought for the morrow, and forms no plans, and yet all his life is planned out for him, and he finds his paths made ready, opening out to him as he comes to them day by day, and hour by hour. He goes in and out of his father's house with an unspeakable ease and abandonment, enjoying all the good things it contains, without having spent a penny in procuring them. Pestilence may walk through the streets of his city, but he regards it not. Famine and fire and war may rage around him, but under his father's tender care he abides in utter unconcern and perfect rest. He lives in the present moment, and receives his life without question as it comes to him day by day from his father's hands.

I was visiting once in a wealthy house, where there was one only adopted child, upon whom was lavished all the love and tenderness and care that human hearts could bestow or human means procure. And as I watched that child running in and out day by day, free and light-hearted, with the happy carelessness of childhood, I thought what a picture it was of our wonderful position as children in the house of our Heavenly Father. And I said to myself, "If nothing could so grieve and wound the loving hearts around her, as to see this little child beginning to be worried or anxious about herself in any way, about whether her food and clothes would be provided for her, or how she was to get her education or her future support, how much more must the great, loving heart of our God and Father be grieved and wounded at seeing His children taking so much anxious care and thought!" And I understood why it was that our Lord had said to us so emphatically, "Take no thought for yourselves."

Who is the best cared for in every household? Is it not the little children? And does not the least of all, the helpless baby, receive the largest share? As a late writer has said, the baby "toils not, neither does he spin; and yet he is fed, and clothed, and loved, and rejoiced in," and none so much as he.

This life of faith, then, about which I am writing, consists in just this; being a child in the Father's house. And when this is said, enough is said to transform every weary, burdened life into one of blessedness and rest.

Let the ways of childish confidence and freedom from care, which so please you and win your hearts in your own little ones, teach you what should be your ways with God; and leaving yourselves in His hands, learn to be literally "careful for nothing"; and you shall find it to be a fact that "the peace of God which passeth all understanding shall keep (as in a garrison) your hearts and minds through Christ Jesus." Notice the word "nothing" in the above passage, as covering all possible grounds for anxiety, both inward and outward. We are continually tempted to think it is our duty to be anxious about some things. Perhaps our thought will be, "Oh, yes, it is quite right to give up all anxiety in a general way; and in spiritual matters of course anxiety is wrong; but there *are* things about which it would be a sin not to be anxious; about our children, for instance, or those we love, or about our church affairs and the cause of truth, or about our business matters. It would show a great want of right feeling not to be anxious about such things as these." Or else our thoughts take the other tack, and we say to ourselves, "Yes, it is quite right to commit our loved ones and all our outward affairs to the Lord, but when it comes to our inward lives, our religious experiences, our temptations, our besetting sins, our growth in grace, and all such things, these we *ought* to be anxious about; for if we are not, they will be sure to be neglected."

To such suggestions, and to all similar ones, the answer is found in our text,—

"In NOTHING be anxious."

In Matt. 6:25-34, our Lord illustrates this being without anxiety, by telling us to behold the fowls of the air and the lilies of the field, as examples of the sort of life He would have us live. As the birds rejoice in the care of their God and are fed, and as the lilies grow in His sunlight, so must we, without anxiety, and without fear. Let the sparrows speak to us:—

> *"I am only tiny sparrow,*
> *A bird of low degree;*
> *My life is of little value,*
> *But the dear Lord cares for me.*
>
> *"I have no barn nor storehouse,*
> *I neither sow nor reap;*
> *God gives me a sparrow's portion,*
> *But never a seed to keep.*
>
> *"I know there are many sparrows;*
> *All over the world they are found;*
> *But our heavenly Father knoweth*
> *When one of us falls to the ground.*
>
> *"Though small, we are never forgotten;*
> *Though weak, we are never afraid;*
> *For we know the dear Lord keepeth*
> *The life of the creatures he made.*
>
> *"I fly through the thickest forest,*
> *I light on many a spray;*
> *I have no chart nor compass,*
> *But I never lose my way.*
>
> *"And I fold my wing at twilight*
> *Wherever I happen to be;*
> *For the Father is always watching,*
> *And no harm will come to me.*
>
> *"I am only a little sparrow,*
> *A bird of low degree,*
> *But I know the Father loves me;*
> *Have you less faith than we?"*

4. How to Enter In

Having tried to settle the question as to the scripturalness of the experience of this life of full trust, and having also shown a little of what it is; the next point is as to how it is to be reached and realized.

And first, I would say that this blessed life must not be looked upon in any sense as an attainment but as an obtainment. We cannot earn it, we cannot climb up to it, we cannot win it; we can do nothing but ask for it and receive it. It is the gift of God in Christ Jesus. And where a thing is a gift, the only course left for the receiver is to take it and thank the giver. We never say of a gift, "See to what I have attained," and boast of our skill and wisdom in having attained it; but we say, "See what has been given me," and boast of the love and wealth and generosity of the giver. And everything in our salvation is a gift. From beginning to end, God is the giver and we are the receivers; and it is not to those who do great things, but to those who "receive abundance of grace, and of the gift of righteousness," that the richest promises are made.

In order, therefore, to enter into a realized experience of this interior life, the soul must be in a receptive attitude, fully recognizing the fact that it is to be God's gift in Christ Jesus, and that it cannot be gained by any efforts or works of our own. This will simplify the matter exceedingly; and the only thing left to be considered then will be to discover upon whom God bestows this gift, and how they are to receive it. And to this I would answer in short, that He bestows it only upon the fully consecrated soul, and that it is to be received by faith.

Consecration is the first thing. Not in any legal sense, not in order to purchase or deserve the blessing, but to remove the difficulties out of the way and make it possible for God to bestow it. In order for a lump of clay to be made into a beautiful vessel, it must be entirely abandoned to the potter, and must lie passive in his hands. And in order for a soul to be made into a vessel unto God's honor, "sanctified and meet for the Master's use, and prepared unto every good work," it must be entirely abandoned to Him, and must lie passive in His hands. This is manifest at the first glance.

I was once trying to explain to a physician, who had charge of a large hospital, what consecration meant, and its necessity, but he seemed unable to understand. At last I said to him, "Suppose, in going your rounds among your patients, you should meet with one man who entreated you earnestly to take his case under your especial care in order to cure him, but who should at the same time refuse to tell you all the symptoms, or to take all your prescribed remedies; and should say to you, 'I am quite willing to follow your directions as to certain things, because they commend themselves to my mind as good, but in other matters I prefer judging for myself and following my own directions.' What would you do in such a case?" I asked. "Do!" he replied with indignation,—"do! I would soon leave such a man as that to his own care. For of course," he added, "I could do nothing for him, unless he would put his whole case into my hands without any reserves, and would obey my directions implicitly." "It is necessary then," I said, "for doctors to be obeyed, if they are to have any chance to cure their patients?" "*Implicitly obeyed!*" was his emphatic reply. "And that is consecration," I continued. "God must have the whole case put into His hands without any reserves, and His directions must be implicitly followed." "I see it," he exclaimed,—"I see it! And I will do it. God shall have His own way with me from henceforth."

Perhaps to some minds the word "abandonment" might express this idea better. But whatever word we use, we mean an entire surrender of the whole being to God; spirit, soul, and body placed under His absolute control, for Him to do with us just what He pleases. We mean that the language of our soul, under all circumstances, and in view of every act, is to be, "Thy will be done." We mean the giving up of all liberty of choice. We mean a life of inevitable obedience.

To a soul ignorant of God, this may look hard. But to those who know Him, it is the happiest and most restful of lives. He is our Father, and He loves us, and He knows just what is best, and therefore, of course, His will is the very most blessed thing that can come to us under all circumstances. I do not understand how it is that Satan has succeeded in blinding the eyes of the Church to this fact. But it really would seem as if God's own children were more afraid of His will than of anything else in life; His lovely, lovable will, which only means loving-kindnesses and tender mercies, and blessings unspeakable to their souls. I wish I could only show to everyone the unfathomable sweetness of the will of God. Heaven is a place of infinite bliss because His will is perfectly done there, and our lives share in this bliss just in proportion as His will is perfectly done in them. He loves us, *loves us*, and the will of love is always blessing for its loved one. Some of us know what it is to love, and we know that could we only have our way, our beloved ones would be overwhelmed with blessings. All that is good, and sweet, and lovely in life would be poured out upon them from our lavish hands, had we but the power to carry out our will for them. And if this is the way of love with us, how much more must it be so with our God, who is love itself. Could we but for one moment get a glimpse into the mighty depths of His love, our hearts would spring out to meet His will, and embrace it as our richest treasure; and we would abandon ourselves to it with an enthusiasm of gratitude and joy, that such a wondrous privilege could be ours.

A great many Christians actually seem to think that all their Father in heaven wants is a chance to make them miserable, and to take away all their blessings, and they imagine, poor souls, that if they hold on to things in their own will, they can hinder Him from doing this. I am ashamed to write the words, and yet we must face a fact which is making wretched hundreds of lives.

A Christian lady who had this feeling, was once expressing to a friend how impossible she found it to say, "Thy will be done," and how afraid she should be to do it. She was the mother of one only little boy, who was the heir to a great fortune, and the idol of her heart. After she had stated her difficulties fully, her friend said, "Suppose your little Charley should come running to you tomorrow and say, 'Mother, I have made up my mind to let you have your own way with me from this time forward. I am always going to obey you, and I want you to do just whatever you think best with me. I know you love me, and I am going to trust myself to your love.' How would you feel towards him? Would you say to yourself, 'Ah, now I shall have a chance to make Charley miserable. I will take away all his pleasures, and fill his life with every hard and disagreeable thing I can find. I will compel him to do just the things that are the most difficult for him to do, and will give him all sorts of impossible commands.' "Oh, no, no, no!" exclaimed the indignant mother. "You know I would not. You know I would hug him to my heart and cover him with kisses, and would hasten to fill his life with all that was sweetest and best." "And are you more tender and more loving than God?" asked her friend. "Ah, no," was the reply, "I see my mistake, and I will not be afraid of saying 'Thy will be done,' to my Heavenly Father, any more than I would want my Charley to be afraid of saying it to me."

Better and sweeter than health, or friends, or money, or fame, or ease, or prosperity, is the adorable will of our God. It gilds the darkest hours with a divine halo, and sheds brightest sunshine on the gloomiest paths. He always reigns who has made it his kingdom; and nothing can go amiss to him. Surely, then, it is nothing but a glorious privilege that is opening before you when I tell you that the first step you must take in order to enter into the life hid with Christ in God, is that of entire consecration. I cannot have you look at it as a hard and stern demand. You must do it gladly, thankfully, enthusiastically. You must go in on what I call the *privilege* side of consecration; and I can assure you, from a blessed experience, that you will find it the happiest place you have ever entered yet.

Faith is the next thing. Faith is an absolutely necessary element in the reception of any gift; for let our friends give a thing to us ever so fully, it is not really ours until we believe it has been given and claim it as our own. Above all, this is true in gifts which are purely mental or spiritual. Love may be lavished upon us by another without stint or measure, but until we believe that we are loved, it never really becomes ours.

I suppose most Christians understand this principle in reference to the matter of their forgiveness. They know that the forgiveness of sins through Jesus might have been preached to them forever, but it would never have become theirs consciously until they believed this preaching, and claimed the forgiveness as their own. But when it comes to living the Christian life, they lose sight of this principle, and think that, having been saved by faith, they are now to live by works and efforts; and instead of continuing to *receive*, they are now to begin to *do*. This makes our declaration that the life hid with Christ in God is to be entered by faith, seem perfectly unintelligible to them. And yet it is plainly declared, that "as we have received Christ Jesus the Lord, so we are to walk in Him." We received Him by faith, and by faith alone; therefore we are to walk in Him by faith, and by faith alone. And the faith by which we enter into this hidden life is just the same as the faith by which we were translated out of the kingdom of darkness into the kingdom of God's dear Son, only it lays hold of a different thing. Then we believed that Jesus was our Savior from the guilt of sin, and according to our faith it was unto us. Now we must believe that He is our Savior from the power of sin, and according to our faith it shall be unto us. Then we trusted Him for our justification, and it became ours; now we must trust Him for our sanctification, and it shall become ours also. Then we took Him as a Savior in the future from the penalties of our sins; now we must take Him as a Savior in the present from the bondage of our sins. Then He was our Redeemer, now He is to be our Life. Then He lifted us out of the pit, now He is to seat us in heavenly places with Himself.

I mean all this of course experimentally and practically. Theologically and judicially I know that every believer has everything the minute he is converted. But experimentally nothing is his until by faith he claims it. "Every place that the sole of your foot shall tread upon, that have I given unto you." God "hath blessed us with all spiritual blessings in heavenly places in Christ," but until we set the foot of faith upon them they do not practically become ours. "According to our faith," is always the limit and the rule.

But this faith of which I am speaking must be a present faith. No faith that is exercised in the future tense amounts to anything. A man may believe forever that his sins will be forgiven at some future time, and he will never find peace. He has to come to the now belief, and say by faith, "My sins are now forgiven," before he can live the new life. And, similarly, no faith which looks for a future deliverance from the power of sin, will ever lead a soul into the life we are describing. The enemy delights in this future faith, for he knows it is powerless to accomplish any practical results. But he trembles and flees when the soul of the believer dares to claim a present deliverance, and to reckon itself now to be free from his power.

To sum up, then: in order to enter into this blessed interior life of rest and triumph, you have two steps to take: first, entire abandonment; and second, absolute faith. No matter what may be the complications of your peculiar experience, no matter what your difficulties or your surroundings or your associations, these two steps, definitely taken and unwaveringly persevered in, will certainly bring you out sooner or later into the green pastures and still waters of this higher Christian life. You may be sure of this. And if you will let every other consideration go, and simply devote your attention to these two points, and be very clear and definite about them, your progress will be rapid and your soul will reach its desired haven far sooner than now you can think possible.

Shall I repeat the steps, that there may be no mistake? You are a child of God, and long to please Him. You love your precious Savior, and are sick and weary of the sin that grieves Him. You long to be delivered from its power. Everything you have hitherto tried has failed to deliver you, and now in your despair you are asking if it can indeed be, as these happy people say, that the Lord is able and willing to deliver you. Surely you know in your very soul that He is; that to save you out of the hand of all your enemies is in fact just the very thing He came to do. Then trust Him. Commit your case to Him in an absolute abandonment, and believe that He undertakes it; and at once, knowing what He is and what He has said, claim that He does even now fully save. Just as you believed at first that He delivered you from the guilt of sin because He said so, believe now that He delivers you from the power of sin because He says so. Let your faith now lay hold of a new power in Christ. You have trusted Him as your dying Savior, now trust Him as your living Savior. Just as much as He came to deliver you from future punishment, did He also come to deliver you from present bondage. Just as truly as He came to bear your sins for you, has He come to live His life in you. You are as utterly powerless in the one case as in the other. You could as easily have got yourself rid of your own sins, as you could now accomplish for yourself practical righteousness. Christ, and Christ only, must do both for you, and your part in both cases is simply to give the thing to Him to do, and then believe that He does it.

A lady, now very eminent in this life of trust, when she was seeking in great darkness and perplexity to enter in, said to the friend who was trying to help her, "You all say, 'Abandon yourself, and trust, abandon yourself, and trust,' but I do not know how. I wish you would just do it out loud, so that I may see how you do it."

Shall I do it out loud for you?

"Lord Jesus, I believe that Thou art able and willing to deliver me from all the care, and unrest and bondage of my Christian life. I believe thou didst die to set me free, not only in the future, but now and here. I believe thou art stronger than Satan, and that thou canst keep me, even me, in my extreme of weakness, from falling into his snares or yielding obedience to his commands. And, Lord, I am going to trust thee to keep me. I have tried keeping myself, and have failed, and failed most grievously. I am absolutely helpless; so now I will trust thee. I will give myself to thee; I keep back no reserves. Body, soul, and spirit, I present myself to thee, a worthless lump of clay, to be made into anything thy love and thy wisdom shall choose. And now, I *am* thine. I believe thou dost accept that which I present to thee; I believe that this poor, weak, foolish heart has been taken possession of by thee, and thou hast even at this very moment begun to work in me to will and to do of thy good pleasure. I trust thee utterly, and I trust thee now!"

Are you afraid to take this step? Does it seem too sudden, too much like a leap in the dark? Do you not know that the steps of faith always "fall on the seeming void, but find the rock beneath"? A man, having to descend a well by a rope, found, to his horror, when he was a great way down, that it was too short. He had reached the end, and yet was, he estimated, about thirty feet from the bottom of the well. He knew not what to do. He had not the strength or skill to climb up the rope, and to let go was to be dashed to pieces. His arms began to fail, and at last he decided that as he could not hold on much longer, he might as well let go and meet his fate at once. He resigned himself to destruction, and loosened his grasp. He fell! To the bottom of the well it was—just three inches!

If ever your feet are to touch the "rock beneath," you must let go of every holding-place and drop into God; for there is no other way. And to do it now may save you months and even years of strain and weariness.

In all the old castles of England there used to be a place called the keep. It was always the strongest and best protected place in the castle, and in it were hidden all who were weak and helpless and unable to defend themselves in times of danger. Had you been a timid, helpless woman in such a castle during a time of siege, would it have seemed to you a leap in the dark to have hidden yourself there? Would you have been *afraid* to do it? And shall we be afraid to hide ourselves in the keeping power of our Divine Keeper, who neither slumbers nor sleeps, and who has promised to preserve our going out and our coming in, from this time forth and even forever more?

5. Difficulties Concerning Consecration

It is very important that Christians should not be ignorant of the devices of the enemy; for he stands ready to oppose every onward step of the soul's progress. And especially is he busy when he sees a believer awakened to a hunger and thirst after righteousness, and seeking to reach out to apprehend all the fulness that is in the Lord Jesus Christ for him.

One of the first difficulties he throws in the way of such a one is concerning consecration. The seeker after holiness is told that he must consecrate himself; and he endeavors to do so. But at once he meets with a difficulty. He has done it, as he thinks, and yet does not feel differently from before; nothing seems changed, as he has been led to expect it would be, and he is completely baffled, and asks the question almost despairingly, "How am I to know when I am consecrated?"

The one grand temptation which has met such a soul at this juncture is the temptation which never fails to assert itself on every possible occasion, and generally with marked success, and that is in reference to feeling. The soul cannot believe it is consecrated until it *feels* that it is; and because it does not *feel* that God has taken it in hand, it cannot believe that He has. As usual, it puts feeling first and faith second. Now, God's invariable rule is faith first and feeling second, in everything; and it is striving against the inevitable when we seek to make it different.

The way to meet this temptation, then, in reference to consecration, is simply to take God's side in the matter, and to put faith before feeling. Give yourself to the Lord definitely and fully, according to your present light, asking the Holy Spirit to show you all that is contrary to God, either in your heart or life. If He shows you anything, give it to the Lord immediately, and say in reference to it, "Thy will be done." If He shows you nothing, then you must believe that there is nothing, and must conclude that you have given Him all. Then you must believe that He takes you. You positively must not wait to *feel* either that you have given yourself or that He has taken you. You must simply believe it, and reckon it to be the case.

If you were to give an estate to a friend, you would have to give it, and he would have to receive it by faith. An estate is not a thing that can be picked up and handed over to another; the gift of it and its reception are altogether a mental transaction and therefore one of faith. Now, if you should give an estate one day to a friend, and then should go away and wonder whether you really had given it, and whether he had actually taken it and considered it his own, and should feel it necessary to go the next day and renew the gift; and if on the third day you should still feel a similar uncertainty about it, and should again go and renew the gift, and on the fourth day go through a like process, and so on, day after day for months and years, what would your friend think, and what at last would be the condition of your own mind in reference to it? Your friend certainly would begin to doubt whether you ever had intended to give it to him at all; and you yourself would be in such hopeless perplexity about it, that you would not know whether the estate was yours, or his, or whose it was.

Now, is not this very much the way in which you have been acting towards God in this matter of consecration? You have given yourself to Him over and over daily, perhaps for months, but you have invariably come away from your seasons of consecration wondering whether you really have given yourself after all, and whether He has taken you; and because you have not *felt* any differently, you have concluded at last, after many painful tossings, that the thing has not been done. Do you know, dear believer, that this sort of perplexity will last forever, unless you cut it short by faith? You must come to the point of reckoning the matter to be an accomplished and settled thing, and leaving it there, before you can possibly expect any change of feeling whatever.

The very law of offerings to the Lord settles this as a primary fact, that everything which is given to Him becomes by that very act something holy, set apart from all other things, and cannot without sacrilege be put to any other uses. "Notwithstanding, no devoted thing that a man shall devote unto the Lord of all that he hath, both of man and beast, and of the field of his possession, shall be sold or redeemed: every devoted thing is most holy unto the Lord." Having once given it to the Lord, the devoted thing henceforth was reckoned by all Israel as being the Lord's, and no one dared to stretch forth a hand to retake it. The giver might have made his offering very grudgingly and half-heartedly, but having made it, the matter was taken out of his hands altogether, and the devoted thing by God's own law became "most holy unto the Lord."

It was not the intention of the giver that made it holy, but the holiness of the receiver. "The altar sanctifies the gift." And an offering once laid upon the altar, from that moment belonged to the Lord. I can imagine an offerer who had deposited a gift, beginning to search his heart as to his sincerity and honesty in doing it, and coming back to the priest to say that he was afraid after all he had not given it right, or had not been perfectly sincere in giving it. I feel sure that the priest would have silenced him at once with saying, "As to how you gave your offering, or what were your motives in giving it, I do not know. The facts are that you did give it, and that it is the Lord's, for every devoted thing is most holy unto Him. It is too late to recall the transaction now." And not only the priest but all Israel would have been aghast at the man who, having once given his offering, should have reached out his hand to take it back. And yet, day after day, earnest-hearted Christians, who would have shuddered at such an act of sacrilege on the part of a Jew, are guilty in their own experience of a similar act, by giving themselves to the Lord in solemn consecration, and then through unbelief taking back that which they have given.

Because God is not visibly present to the eye, it is difficult to feel that a transaction with Him is real. I suppose if, when we made our acts of consecration, we could actually see Him present with us, we should feel it to be a very real thing, and would realize that we had given our word to Him and could not dare to take it back, no matter how much we might wish to do so. Such a transaction would have to us the binding power that a spoken promise to an earthly friend always has to a man of honor. And what we need is to see that God's presence is a certain fact always, and that every act of our soul is done right before Him, and that a word spoken in prayer is as really spoken to Him, as if our eyes could see Him and our hands could touch Him. Then we shall cease to have such vague conceptions of our relations with Him, and shall feel the binding force of every word we say in His presence.

I know some will say here, "Ah, yes; but if He would only speak to me, and say that He took me when I gave myself to Him, I would have no trouble then in believing it." No, of course you would not; but He does not generally say this until the soul has first proved its loyalty by believing what He has already said. It is he that *believeth* who has the witness, not he that *doubteth*. And by His very command to us to present ourselves to Him a living sacrifice, He has pledged Himself to receive us. I cannot conceive of an honorable man asking another to give him a thing which, after all, he was doubtful about taking; still less can I conceive of a loving parent acting so towards a darling child. "My son, give me thy heart," is a sure warrant for knowing that the moment the heart is given, it will be taken by the One who has commanded the gift. We may, nay we must, feel the utmost confidence then that when we surrender ourselves to the Lord, according to His own command, He does then and there receive us, and from that moment we are His. A real transaction has taken place, which cannot be violated without dishonor on our part, and which we know will not be violated by Him.

In Deut. 26:17, 18, 19, we see God's way of working under these circumstances:—

"Thou hast avouched the Lord this day to be thy God, and to walk in His ways and to keep His statutes, and His commandments, and His judgments, and to hearken unto His voice; and the Lord hath avouched thee this day to be His peculiar people, as He hath promised thee, and that thou shouldst keep all His commandments; …and that thou mayest be an holy people unto the Lord, as He hath spoken."

When we avouch the Lord to be our God, and that we *will* walk in His ways and keep His commandments, He avouches us to be His, and that we *shall* keep all His commandments. And from that moment He takes possession of us. This has always been His principle of working, and it continues to be so. "Every devoted thing is most holy to the Lord." This seems to me so plain as scarcely to admit of a question.

But if the soul still feels in doubt or difficulty, let me refer you to a New Testament declaration which approaches the subject from a different side, but which settles it, I think, quite as definitely. It is in 1 John 5:14, 15, and reads: "And this is the confidence that we have in Him, that if we ask anything according to His will, He heareth us; and if we know that He hear us, whatsoever we ask, we know that we *have* the petitions that we desired of Him." Is it according to His will that you should be entirely consecrated to Him? There can be, of course, but one answer to this, for He has *commanded* it. Is it not also according to His will that He should work in you to will and to do of His good pleasure? This question also can have but one answer, for He has declared it to be His purpose. You know, then, that these things are according to His will, therefore on God's own word you are obliged to know that He hears you; and knowing this much, you are compelled to go further and know that you have the petitions that you have desired of Him. That you have, I say, not will have, or may have, but have now in actual possession. It is thus that we "obtain promises" by faith. It is thus that we have "access by faith" into the grace that is given us in our Lord Jesus Christ. It is thus, and thus only, that we come to know our hearts are "purified by faith," and are enabled to live by faith, to stand by faith, to walk by faith.

I desire to make this subject so plain and practical that no one need have any further difficulty about it, and therefore I will repeat again just what must be the acts of your soul in order to bring you out of this difficulty about consecration.

I suppose that you have trusted the Lord Jesus for the forgiveness of your sins, and know something of what it is to belong to the family of God, and to be made an heir of God through faith in Christ. And now you feel springing up in your soul the longing to be conformed to the image of your Lord. In order for this, you know there must be an entire surrender of yourself to Him, that He may work in you all the good pleasure of His will; and you have tried over and over to do it, but hitherto without any apparent success.

At this point it is that I desire to help you. What you must do now is to come once more to Him in a surrender of your whole self to His will, as complete as you know how to make it. You must ask Him to reveal to you by His Spirit any hidden rebellion; and if He reveals nothing, then you must believe that there is nothing, and that the surrender is complete. This must, then, be considered a settled matter. You have abandoned yourself to the Lord, and from henceforth you do not in any sense belong to yourself; you must never even so much as listen to a suggestion to the contrary. If the temptation comes to wonder whether you really have completely surrendered yourself, meet it with an assertion that you have. Do not even argue the matter. Repel any such idea instantly and with decision. You meant it then, you mean it now, you have really done it. Your emotions may clamor against the surrender, but your will must hold firm. It is your purpose God looks at, not your feelings about that purpose, and your purpose, or will, is therefore the only thing you need attend to.

The surrender, then, having been made, never to be questioned or recalled, the next point is to believe that God takes that which you have surrendered, and to reckon that it is His. Not that it will be at some future time, but is now; and that He has begun to work in you to will, and to do, of His good pleasure. And here you must rest. There is nothing more for you to do, for you are the Lord's now, absolutely and entirely in His hands, and He has undertaken the whole care and management and forming of you; and will, according to His word, "work in you that which is well-pleasing in His sight through Jesus Christ." But you must hold steadily here. If you begin to question your surrender, or God's acceptance of it, then your wavering faith will produce a wavering experience, and He cannot work. But while you trust He works, and the result of His working always is to change you into the image of Christ, from glory to glory, by His mighty Spirit.

Do you, then, now at this moment surrender yourself wholly to Him? You answer, Yes. Then, my dear friend, begin at once to reckon that you are His; that He has taken you, and that He is working in you to will and to do of His good pleasure. And keep on reckoning this. You will find it a great help to put your reckoning into words, and to say over and over to yourself and to your God, "Lord, I am thine; I do yield myself up to thee entirely, and I believe that thou dost take me. I leave myself with thee. Work in me all the good pleasure of thy will, and I will only lie still in thy hands, and trust thee."

Make this a daily definite act of your will, and many times a day recur to it, as being your continual attitude before Him. Confess it to yourself. Confess it to your God. Confess it to your friends. Avouch the Lord to be your God continually and unwaveringly, and declare your purpose of walking in His ways and keeping His statutes; and you will find in practical experience that He has avouched you to be His peculiar people and that you shall keep all His commandments, and that you will be "an holy people unto the Lord, as He hath spoken."

A few simple rules may be found helpful here. I would advise the use of them in daily times of devotion, making them the definite test and attitude of the soul, until the light shines clearly on this matter.

I.   Express in definite words your faith in Christ as your Savior; and acknowledge definitely that you believe He *has* reconciled you to God; according to 2 Cor. 5:18, 19.

II.   Definitely acknowledge God as your Father, and yourself as His redeemed and forgiven child; according to Gal. 5:6.

III.   Definitely surrender yourself to be all the Lord's, body, soul, and spirit; and to obey Him in everything where His will is made known; according to Rom. 12:12.

IV.   Believe and continue to believe, against all seemings, that God takes possession of that which you thus abandon to Him, and that He will henceforth work in you to will and to do of His good pleasure, unless you consciously frustrate His grace; according to 2 Cor. 6:17, 18, and Phil. 2:13.

V.   Pay no attention to your *feelings* as a test of your relations with God, but simply attend to the state of your *will* and of your *faith*. And count all these steps you are now taking as settled, though the enemy may make it *seem* otherwise. Heb. 10:22, 23.

VI.   Never, under any circumstances, give way for one single moment to doubt or discouragement. Remember, that all discouragement is from the devil, and refuse to admit it; according to John 14:1, 27.

VII.   Cultivate the habit of expressing your faith in definite words, and repeat often, "I *am* all the Lord's and He *is* working in me now to will and to do of His good pleasure; according to Heb. 13:21.

6. Difficulties Concerning Faith

The next step after consecration, in the soul's progress out of the wilderness of Christian experience, into the land that floweth with milk and honey, is that of faith. And here, as in the first step, the enemy is very skillful in making difficulties and interposing obstacles.

The child of God, having had his eyes opened to see the fulness there is in Jesus for him, and having been made to long to appropriate that fulness to himself, is met with the assertion on the part of every teacher to whom he applies, that this fulness is only to be received by faith. But the subject of faith is involved in such a hopeless mystery in his mind, that this assertion, instead of throwing light upon the way of entrance, only seems to make it more difficult and involved than ever.

"Of course it is to be by faith," he says, "for I know that everything in the Christian life is by faith. But then, that is just what makes it so hard, for I have no faith, and I do not even know what it is, nor how to get it." And, baffled at the very outset by this insuperable difficulty, he is plunged into darkness, and almost despair.

This trouble all arises from the fact that the subject of faith is very generally misunderstood; for in reality faith is the plainest and most simple thing in the world, and the most easy of attainment.

Your idea of faith, I suppose, has been something like this. You have looked upon it as in some way a sort of *thing*, either a religious exercise of soul, or an inward gracious disposition of heart; something tangible, in fact, which, when you have got, you can look at and rejoice over, and use as a passport to God's favor, or a coin with which to purchase His gifts. And you have been praying for faith, expecting all the while to get something like this, and never having received any such thing, you are insisting upon it that you have no faith. Now faith, in fact, is not in the least this sort of thing. It is nothing at all tangible. It is simply believing God, and, like sight, it is nothing apart from its object. You might as well shut your eyes and look inside to see whether you have sight, as to look inside to discover whether you have faith. You see something, and thus know that you have sight; you believe something, and thus know that you have faith. For, as sight is only seeing, so faith is only believing. And as the only necessary thing about seeing is, that you see the thing as it is, so the only necessary thing about believing is, that you believe the thing as it is. The virtue does not lie in your believing, but in the thing you believe. If you believe the truth you are saved; if you believe a lie you are lost. The believing in both cases is the same; the things believed in are exactly opposite, and it is this which makes the mighty difference. Your salvation comes, not because your faith saves you, but because it links you on to the Savior who saves; and your believing is really nothing but the link.

I do beg of you to recognize, then, the extreme simplicity of faith; that it is nothing more nor less than just believing God when He says He either has done something for us, or will do it; and then trusting Him to do it. It is so simple that it is hard to explain. If any one asks me what it means to trust another to do a piece of work for me, I can only answer that it means letting that other one do it, and feeling it perfectly unnecessary for me to do it myself. Every one of us has trusted very important pieces of work to others in this way, and has felt perfect rest in thus trusting, because of the confidence we have had in those who have undertaken to do it. How constantly do mothers trust their most precious infants to the care of nurses, and feel no shadow of anxiety? How continually we are all of us trusting our health and our lives, without a thought of fear, to cooks and coachmen, engine drivers, railway conductors, and all sorts of paid servants, who have us completely at their mercy, and could plunge us into misery or death in a moment, if they chose to do so, or even if they failed in the necessary carefulness? All this we do, and make no fuss about it. Upon the slightest acquaintance, often, we thus put our trust in people, requiring only the general knowledge of human nature, and the common rules of human intercourse; and we never feel as if we were doing anything in the least remarkable.

You have done all this yourself, dear reader, and are doing it continually. You would not be able to live in this world and go through the customary routine of life a single day, if you could not trust your fellow-men. And it never enters into your head to say you cannot.

But yet you do not hesitate to say, continually, that you cannot trust your God!

I wish you would just now try to imagine yourself acting in your human relations as you do in your spiritual relations. Suppose you should begin tomorrow with the notion in your head that you could not trust anybody, because you had no faith. When you sat down to breakfast you would say, "I cannot eat anything on this table, for I have no faith, and I cannot believe the cook has not put poison in the coffee, or that the butcher has not sent home diseased meat." So you would go starving away. Then when you went out to your daily avocations, you would say, "I cannot ride in the railway train, for I have no faith, and therefore I cannot trust the engineer, nor the conductor, nor the builders of the carriages, nor the managers of the road." So you would be compelled to walk everywhere, and grow unutterably weary in the effort, besides being actually unable to reach many of the places you could have reached in the train. Then, when your friends met you with any statements, or your business agent with any accounts, you would say, "I am very sorry that I cannot believe you, but I have no faith, and never can believe anybody." If you opened a newspaper you would be forced to lay it down again, saying, "I really cannot believe a word this paper says, for I have no faith; I do not believe there is any such person as the queen, for I never saw her; nor any such country as Ireland, for I was never there. And I have no faith, so of course I cannot believe anything that I have not actually felt and touched myself. It is a great trial, but I cannot help it, for I have no faith."

Just picture such a day as this, and see how disastrous it would be to yourself, and what utter folly it would appear to any one who should watch you through the whole of it. Realize how your friends would feel insulted, and how your servants would refuse to serve you another day. And then ask yourself the question, if this want of faith in your fellow-men would be so dreadful, and such utter folly, what must it be when you tell God that you have no power to trust Him nor to believe His word; that "it is a great trial, but you cannot help it, for you have no faith"?

Is it possible that you can trust your fellow-men and cannot trust your God? That you can receive the "witness of men," and cannot receive the "witness of God"? That you can believe man's records, and cannot believe God's record? That you can commit your dearest earthly interests to your weak, failing fellow-creatures without a fear, and are afraid to commit your spiritual interests to the blessed Savior who shed His blood for the very purpose of saving you, and who is declared to be "able to save you to the uttermost"?

Surely, surely, dear believer, you, whose very name of believer implies that you can believe, will never again dare to excuse yourself on the plea of having no faith. For when you say this, you mean of course that you have no faith in God, since you are not asked to have faith in yourself, and you would be in a very wrong condition of soul if you had. Let me beg of you then, when you think or say these things, always to complete the sentence and say, "I have no faith in God, I cannot believe God"; and this I am sure will soon become so dreadful to you, that you will not dare to continue it.

But you say, I cannot believe without the Holy Spirit. Very well; will you conclude that your want of faith is because of the failure of the blessed Spirit to do His work? For if it is, then surely *you* are not to blame, and need feel no condemnation; and all exhortations to you to believe are useless.

But, no! Do you not see that, in taking up this position, that you have no faith and cannot believe, you are not only "making God a liar," but you are also manifesting an utter want of confidence in the Holy Spirit? For He is always ready to help our infirmities. We never have to wait for Him, He is always waiting for us. And I for my part have such absolute confidence in the blessed Holy Ghost, and in His being always ready to do his work, that I dare to say to every one of you, that you *can* believe now, at this very moment, and that if you do not, it is not the Spirit's fault, but your own.

Put your will then over on to the believing side. Say, "Lord I will believe, I do believe," and continue to say it. Insist upon believing, in the face of every suggestion of doubt with which you may be tempted. Out of your very unbelief, throw yourself headlong on to the word and promises of God, and dare to abandon yourself to the keeping and saving power of the Lord Jesus. If you have ever trusted a precious interest in the hands of any earthly friend, I conjure you, trust yourself now and all your spiritual interests in the hands of your Heavenly Friend, and never, never, NEVER allow yourself to doubt again.

And remember, there are two things which are more utterly incompatible than even oil and water, and these two are trust and worry. Would you call it trust, if you should give something into the hands of a friend to attend to for you, and then should spend your nights and days in anxious thought and worry as to whether it would be rightly and successfully done? And can you call it trust, when you have given the saving and keeping of your soul into the hands of the Lord, if day after day and night after night you are spending hours of anxious thought and questionings about the matter? When a believer really trusts anything, he ceases to worry about that thing which he has trusted. And when he worries, it is a plain proof that he does not trust. Tested by this rule how little real trust there is in the Church of Christ! No wonder our Lord asked the pathetic question, "When the Son of Man cometh shall he find faith on the earth?" He will find plenty of activity, a great deal of earnestness, and doubtless many consecrated hearts; but shall he find *faith*, the one thing He values more than all the rest? It is a solemn question, and I would that every Christian heart would ponder it well. But may the time past of our lives suffice us to have shared in the unbelief of the world; and let us everyone, who know our blessed Lord and His unspeakable trustworthiness, set to our seal that He is true, by our generous abandonment of trust in Him.

I remember, very early in my Christian life, having every tender and loyal impulse within me stirred to its depths by an appeal I met with in a volume of old sermons to all who loved the Lord Jesus, that they should show to others how worthy He was of being trusted, by the steadfastness of their own faith in Him. And I remember my soul cried out with an eager longing that I might be called to walk in paths so dark, that an utter abandonment of trust might be my blessed and glorious privilege.

"Ye have not passed this way heretofore," it may be; but today it is your happy privilege to prove, as never before, your loyal confidence in the Lord by starting out with Him on a life and walk of faith, lived moment by moment in absolute and childlike trust in Him.

You have trusted Him in a few things, and He has not failed you. Trust Him now for everything, and see if He does not do for you exceeding abundantly above all that you could ever have asked or thought; not according to your power or capacity, but according to His own mighty power, that will work in you all the good pleasure of His most blessed will.

You find no difficulty in trusting the Lord with the management of the universe and all the outward creation, and can your case be any more complex or difficult than these, that you need to be anxious or troubled about his management of it. Away with such unworthy doubtings! Take your stand on the power and trustworthiness of your God, and see how quickly all difficulties will vanish before a steadfast determination to believe. Trust in the dark, trust in the light, trust at night, and trust in the morning, and you will find that the faith, which may begin by a mighty effort, will end sooner or later by becoming the easy and natural habit of the soul.

All things are possible to God, and "all things are possible to him that believeth." Faith has, in times past, "subdued kingdoms, wrought righteousness, obtained promises, stopped the mouths of lions, quenched the violence of fire, escaped the edge of the sword, waxed valiant in fight, turned to flight the armies of the aliens"; and faith can do it again. For our Lord Himself says unto us, "If ye have faith as a grain of mustard seed, ye shall say unto this mountain, Remove hence to yonder place, and it shall remove; and nothing shall be impossible unto you."

If you are a child of God at all, you must have at least as much faith as a grain of mustard seed, and therefore you dare not say again that you cannot trust because you have no faith. Say rather, "I can trust my Lord, and I will trust Him, and not all the powers of earth or hell shall be able to make me doubt my wonderful, glorious, faithful Redeemer!"

In that greatest event of this century, the emancipation of our slaves, there is a wonderful illustration of the way of faith. The slaves received their freedom by faith, just as we must receive ours. The good news was carried to them that the government had proclaimed their freedom. As a matter of fact they were free the moment the Proclamation was issued, but as a matter of experience they did not come into actual possession of their freedom until they had heard the good news and had believed it. The fact had to come first, but the believing was necessary before the fact became available, and the feeling would follow last of all. This is the divine order always, and the order of common-sense as well. I. The fact. II. The faith. III. The feeling. But man reverses this order and says, I. The feeling. II. The faith. III. The fact.

Had the slaves followed man's order in regard to their emancipation, and refused to believe in it until they had first felt it, they might have remained in slavery a long while. I have heard of one instance where this was the case. In a little out-of-the-way Southern town a Northern lady found, about two or three years after the war was over, some slaves who had not yet taken possession of their freedom. An assertion of hers, that the North had set them free, aroused the attention of an old colored auntie, who interrupted her with the eager question,—

"O missus, *is* we free?"

"Of course you are," replied the lady.

"O missus, is you *sure?*" urged the woman, with intensest eagerness.

"Certainly, I am sure," answered the lady. "Why, is it possible you did not know it?"

"Well," said the woman, "we heered tell as how we was free, and we asked master, and he 'lowed we wasn't, and so we was afraid to go. And then we heered tell again, and we went to the cunnel, and he 'lowed we'd better stay with ole massa. And so we's just been off and on. Sometimes we'd hope we was free, and then again we'd think we wasn't. But now, missus, if you is *sure* we is free, won't you tell me all about it?"

Seeing that this was a case of real need, the lady took the pains to explain the whole thing to the poor woman; all about the war, and the Northern army, and Abraham Lincoln, and his Proclamation of Emancipation, and the present freedom.

The poor slave listened with the most intense eagerness. She heard the good news. She believed it. And when the story was ended, she walked out of the room with an air of the utmost independence, saying as she went,—

"I's free! I's ain't agoing to stay with ol massa any longer!"

She had at last received her freedom, and she had received it by faith. The government had declared her to be free long before, but this had not availed her, because she had never yet believed in this declaration. The good news had not profited her, not being "mixed with faith" in the one who heard it. But now she believed, and believing, she dared to reckon herself to be free. And this, not because of any change in herself or her surroundings, not because of any feelings of emotions of her own heart, but because she had confidence in the word of another, who had come to her proclaiming the good news of her freedom.

Need I make the application? In a hundred different messages God has declared to us our freedom, and over and over He urges us to reckon ourselves free. Let your faith then lay hold of His proclamation, and assert it to be true. Declare to yourself, to your friends, and in the secret of your soul to God, that you *are* free. Refuse to listen for a moment to the lying assertions of your old master, that you are still his slave. Let nothing discourage you, no inward feelings nor outward signs. Hold on to your reckoning in the face of all opposition, and I can promise you, on the authority of our Lord, that according to your faith it shall be unto you.

Of all the worships we can bring our God, none is so sweet to Him as this utter self-abandoning trust, and none brings Him so much glory. Therefore in every dark hour remember that "though now for a season, if need be, ye are in heaviness through manifold temptations," it is in order that "the trial of your faith, being much more precious than of gold that perisheth, though it be tried with fire, might be found unto praise, and honor, and glory, at the appearing of Jesus Christ."

7. Difficulties Concerning the Will

When the child of God has, by the way of entire abandonment and absolute trust, stepped out of himself into Christ, and has begun to know something of the blessedness of the life hid with Christ in God, there is one form of difficulty which is very likely to start up in his path. After the first emotions of peace and rest have somewhat subsided, or if, as is sometimes the case, they have never seemed to come at all, he begins to feel such an utter unreality in the things he has been passing through, that he seems to himself like a hypocrite, when he says or even thinks they are real. It seems to him that his belief does not go below the surface, that it is a mere lip-belief, and therefore of no account, and that his surrender is not a surrender of the heart, and therefore cannot be acceptable to God. He is afraid to say he is altogether the Lord's, for fear he will be telling an untruth, and yet he cannot bring himself to say he is not, because he longs for it so intensely. The difficulty is real and very disheartening.

But there is nothing here which will not be very easily overcome, when the Christian once thoroughly understands the principles of the new life, and has learned *how* to live in it. The common thought is, that this life hid with Christ in God is to be lived in the emotions, and consequently all the attention of the soul is directed towards them, and as they are satisfactory or otherwise, the soul rests or is troubled. Now the truth is that this life is not to be lived in the emotions at all, but in the will, and therefore the varying states of emotion do not in the least disturb or affect the reality of the life, if only the will is kept steadfastly abiding in its center, God's will.

To make this plain, I must enlarge a little. Fenelon says somewhere, that "pure religion resides in the will alone." By this he means that as the will is the governing power in the man's nature, if the will is set straight, all the rest of the nature must come into harmony. By the will I do not mean the wish of the man, nor even his purpose, but the choice, the deciding power, the king, to which all that is in the man must yield obedience. It is the man, in short, the "*Ego*," that which we feel to be ourselves.

It is sometimes thought that the emotions are the governing power in our nature. But, as a matter of practical experience, I think we all of us know that there is something within us, behind our emotions, and behind our wishes,—an independent self,—that after all decides everything and controls everything. Our emotions belong to us, and are suffered and enjoyed by us, but they are not ourselves; and if God is to take possession of us, it must be into this central will or personality that He shall enter. If, then, He is reigning there by the power of His Spirit, all the rest of our nature must come under His sway; and as the will is, so is the man.

The practical bearing of this truth upon the difficulty I am considering is very great. For the decisions of our will are often so directly opposed to the decisions of our emotions, that, if we are in the habit of considering our emotions as the test, we shall be very apt to feel like hypocrites in declaring those things to be real which our will alone has decided. But the moment we see that the will is king, we shall utterly disregard anything that clamors against it, and shall claim as real its decisions, let the emotions rebel as they may.

I am aware that this is a difficult subject to deal with, but it is so exceedingly practical in its bearing upon the life of faith, that I beg of you, dear reader, not to turn from it until you have mastered it.

Perhaps an illustration will help you. A young man of great intelligence, seeking to enter into this new life, was utterly discouraged at finding himself the slave to an inveterate habit of doubting. To his emotions nothing seemed true, nothing seemed real; and the more he struggled the more unreal did it all become. He was told this secret concerning the will, that if he would only put his will over on to the believing side; if he would choose to believe; if, in short, he would, in the Ego of his nature, say, "I will believe! I do believe!" he need not trouble about his emotions, for they would find themselves compelled, sooner or later, to come into harmony. "What!" he said, "do you mean to tell me that I can *choose* to believe in that way, when nothing seems true to me; and will that kind of believing be real?" "Yes," was the answer, "your part is only this,—to put your will over on God's side in this matter of believing; and when you do this, God immediately takes possession of it, and works in you to will of His good pleasure, and you will soon find that He has brought all the rest of your nature into subjection to Himself." "Well," was the answer, "I can do this. I cannot control my emotions, but I can control my will, and the new life begins to look possible to me, if it is only my will that needs to be set straight in the matter. I *can* give my will to God, and I do!"

From that moment, disregarding all the pitiful clamoring of his emotions, which continually accused him of being a wretched hypocrite, this young man held on steadily to the decision of his will, answering every accusation with the continued assertion that he chose to believe, he meant to believe, he did believe; until at the end of a few days he found himself triumphant, with every emotion and every thought brought into captivity to the mighty power of the blessed Spirit of God, who had taken possession of the will thus put into His hands. He had held fast the *profession* of his faith without wavering, although it had seemed to him that, as to real faith itself, he had none to hold fast. At times it had drained all the will power he possessed to his lips, to say that he believed, so contrary was it to all the evidence of his senses or of his emotions. But he had caught the idea that his will was, after all, himself, and that if he kept that on God's side, he was doing all *he* could do, and that God alone could change his emotions or control his being. The result has been one of the grandest Christian lives I know of, in its marvelous simplicity, directness, and power over sin.

The secret lies just here. That our will, which is the spring of all our actions, is in our natural state under the control of self, and self has been working it in us to our utter ruin and misery. Now God says, "Yield yourselves up unto Me, as those that are alive from the dead, and I will work in you to will and to do of my good pleasure." And the moment we yield ourselves, He of course takes possession of us, and does work in us "that which is well pleasing in His sight through Jesus Christ," giving us the mind that was in Christ, and transforming us into His image. (See Rom. 12:1, 2.)

Let us take another illustration. A lady, who had entered into this life hid with Christ, was confronted by a great prospective trial. Every emotion she had within her rose up in rebellion against it, and had she considered her emotions to be her king, she would have been in utter despair. But she had learned this secret of the will, and knowing that, at the bottom, she herself did really choose the will of God for her portion, she did not pay the slightest attention to her emotions, but persisted in meeting every thought concerning the trial, with the words, repeated over and over, "Thy will be done! Thy will be done!" asserting in the face of all her rebelling feelings, that she did submit her will to God's, that she chose to submit, and that His will should be and was her delight! The result was, that in an incredibly short space of time every thought was brought into captivity; and she began to find even her very emotions rejoicing in the will of God.

Again, there was a lady who had a besetting sin, which in her emotions she dearly loved, but which in her will she hated. Having believed herself to be necessarily under the control of her emotions, she had therefore thought she was unable to conquer it, unless her emotions should first be changed. But she learned this secret concerning the will, and going to her knees she said, "Lord, Thou seest that with one part of my nature I love this sin, but in my real central self I hate it. And now I put my will over on thy side in the matter. I will not do it any more. Do thou deliver me." Immediately God took possession of the will thus surrendered to Himself, and began to work in her, so that His will in the matter gained the mastery over her emotions, and she found herself delivered, not by the power of an outward commandment, but by the inward power of the Spirit of God working in her that which was well pleasing in His sight.

And now, dear Christian, let me show you how to apply this principle to your difficulties. Cease to consider your emotions, for they are only the servants; and regard simply your will, which is the real king in your being. Is that given up to God? Is that put into His hands? Does your will decide to believe? Does your will choose to obey? If this is the case, then *you* are in the Lord's hands, and you decide to believe, and you choose to obey; for your will is yourself. And the thing is done. The transaction with God is as real, where only your will acts, as when every emotion coincides. It does not seem as real to you; but in God's sight it is as real. And when you have got hold of this secret, and have discovered that you need not attend to your emotions, but simply to the state of your will, all the Scripture commands, to yield yourself to God, to present yourself a living sacrifice to Him, to abide in Christ, to walk in the light, to die to self, become possible to you; for you are conscious that, in all these, your will can act, and can take God's side: whereas, if it had been your emotions that must do it, you would sink down in despair, knowing them to be utterly uncontrollable.

When, then, this feeling of unreality or hypocrisy comes, do not be troubled by it. It is only in your emotions, and is not worth a moment's thought. Only see to it that your will is in God's hands; that your inward self is abandoned to His working; that your choice, your decision, is on His side; and there leave it. Your surging emotions, like a tossing vessel, which, by degrees, yields to the steady pull of the cable, finding themselves attached to the mighty power of God by the choice of your will, must inevitably come into captivity, and give in their allegiance to Him; and you will verify the truth of the saying that, "If any man will do His will, he shall know of the doctrine."

The will is like a wise mother in a nursery; the feelings are like a set of clamoring, crying children. The mother decides upon a certain course of action, which she believes to be right and best. The children clamor against it, and declare it shall not be. But the mother, knowing that she is mistress and not they, pursues her course calmly, unmoved by their clamors, and takes no notice of them except in trying to soothe and quiet them. The result is that the children are sooner or later compelled to yield, and fall in with the decision of the mother. Thus order and harmony are preserved. But if that mother should for a moment let in the thought that the children were the mistresses instead of herself, confusion would reign unchecked. Such instances have been known in family life! And in how many souls at this very moment is there nothing but confusion, simply because the feelings are allowed to govern, instead of the will!

Remember, then, that the real thing in your experience is what your will decides, and not the verdict of your emotions; and that you are far more in danger of hypocrisy and untruth in yielding to the assertions of your feelings, than in holding fast to the decision of your will. So that, if your will is on God's side, you are no hypocrite at this moment in claiming as your own the blessed reality of belonging altogether to Him, even though your emotions may all declare the contrary.

I am convinced that, throughout the Bible, the expressions concerning the "heart" do not mean the emotions, that which we now understand by the word "heart"; but they mean the will, the personality of the man, the man's own central self; and that the object of God's dealings with man is, that this "I" may be yielded up to Him, and this central life abandoned to His entire control. It is not the feelings of the man God wants, but the man himself.

Have you given Him yourself, dear reader? Have you abandoned your will to His working? Do you consent to surrender the very center of your being into His hands? Then, let the outposts of your nature clamor as they may, it is your right to say, even now, with the apostle, "I am crucified with Christ; nevertheless, I live; yet not I, but Christ liveth in me: and the life which I now live in the flesh, I live by the faith of the Son of God, who loved me, and gave Himself for me."

~ ※ ~

After this chapter had been enclosed to the printer, the following remarkable practical illustration of its teaching was presented by Pasteur T. Monod, of Paris. It is the experience of a Presbyterian minister, which this *pasteur* had carefully kept for many years.

Newburgh, Sept. 26, 1842.

Dear Brother,—I take a few moments of that time which I have devoted to the Lord, in writing a short epistle to you, His servant. It is sweet to feel we are wholly the Lord's, that He has received us and called us His. This is religion,—a relinquishment of the principle of self-ownership, and the adoption in full of the abiding sentiment, "I am not my own, I am bought with a price." Since I last saw you, I have been pressing forward, and yet there has been nothing remarkable in my experience of which I can speak; indeed I do not know that it is best to look for remarkable things; but *strive to be* holy, as God is holy, pressing right on toward the mark of the prize.

I do not feel myself qualified to instruct you; I can only tell you the way in which I was led. The Lord deals differently with different souls, and we ought not to attempt to copy the experience of others, yet there are certain things which must be attended to by everyone who is seeking after a clean heart.

There must be a personal consecration of all to God, a covenant made with God, that we will be wholly and forever His. This I made intellectually without any change in my feeling, with a heart full of hardness and darkness, unbelief and sin and insensibility.

I covenanted to be the Lord's, and laid all upon the altar, a living sacrifice, to the best of my ability. And after I rose from my knees, I was conscious of no change in my feeling. I was painfully conscious that there was no change. But yet I was sure that I did, with all the sincerity and honesty of purpose of which I was capable, make an entire and eternal consecration of myself to God. I did not then consider the work done by any means, but I engaged to abide in a state of entire devotion to God, a living perpetual sacrifice. And now came the effort to do this.

I knew that I must believe that God did accept me, and had come in to dwell in my heart. I was conscious I did not believe this, and yet I desired to do so. I read with much prayer John's First Epistle, and endeavored to assure my heart of God's love to me as an individual. I was sensible that my heart was full of evil. I seemed to have no power to overcome pride, or to repel evil thoughts, which I abhorred. But Christ was manifested to destroy the works of the devil, and it was clear that the sin in my heart was the work of the devil. I was enabled, therefore, to believe that God was working in me, to will and to do, while I was working out my own salvation with fear and trembling.

I was convinced of unbelief, that it was *voluntary and criminal*. I clearly saw that unbelief was an awful sin, it made the faithful God a liar. The Lord brought before me my besetting sins which had dominion over me, especially preaching myself instead of Christ, and indulging self-complacent thoughts after preaching. I was enabled to make myself of no reputation, and to seek the honor which cometh from God only. Satan struggled hard to beat me back from the Rock of Ages but thanks to God I finally hit upon the method of living by the moment, and then I found rest.

I trusted in the blood of Jesus already shed, as a sufficient atonement for all my past sins, and the future I committed wholly to the Lord, agreeing to do His will under all circumstances as He should make it known, and I saw that all I had to do was to look to Jesus for a present supply of grace, and to trust Him to cleanse my heart and keep me from sin at the present moment.

I felt shut up to a momentary dependence upon the grace of Christ. I would not permit the adversary to trouble me about the past or future, for I each moment looked for the supply for that moment. I agreed that I would be a child of Abraham, and walk by naked faith in the Word of God, and not by inward feelings and emotions: I would seek to be a Bible Christian. Since that time the Lord has given me a steady victory over sins which before enslaved me. I delight in the Lord, and in His Word. I delight in my work as a minister: my fellowship is with the Father and with His Son Jesus Christ. I am a babe in

Christ; I know my progress has been small compared with that made by many. My feelings vary, but when I have feelings, I praise God, and I trust in His word; and when I am empty and my feelings are gone, I do the same. I have covenanted to walk by faith and not by feelings.

The Lord, I think, is beginning to revive His work among my people. "Praise the Lord." May the Lord fill you with all His fulness and give you all the mind of Christ. Oh, be faithful! Walk before God and be perfect. Preach the Word. Be instant in season and out of season. The Lord loves you. He works with you. Rest your soul fully upon that promise, "Lo, I am with you alway, even unto the end of the world."

Your fellow soldier,
William Hill

There may be some who will object to this teaching, that it ignores the work of the blessed Holy Spirit. But I must refer such to the introductory chapter of this book, in which I have fully explained myself. I am not writing upon that side of the subject; I am considering man's part in the matter, and not the part of the Spirit. I realize intensely that all a man can do or try to do would be utterly useless, if the Holy Spirit did not work in that man continually. And it is only because I believe in the Spirit as a mighty power, ever present and always ready to do his work, that I can write as I do. But, like the wind that bloweth where it listeth, and thou hearest the sound thereof, but canst not tell whence it cometh, and whither it goeth, the operations of the Spirit are beyond our control, and also beyond our comprehension.

The results we know, and the steps on our part which lead to those results, but we know nothing more. And yet, like a workman in a great manufactory, who does not question the commands of his employer, and is not afraid to undertake apparent impossibilities, because he knows there is a mighty unseen power, called steam, behind his machinery, which can accomplish it all, so we dare to urge upon men that they shall simply and courageously set themselves to do that which they are commanded to do, because we know that the mighty Spirit will never fail to supply at each moment the necessary power for that moment's act. And we boldly claim that we who thus write can say from our very hearts, as earnestly and as solemnly as any other Christians, We believe in the Holy Ghost.

8. Is God In Everything?

One of the greatest obstacles to living unwaveringly this life of entire surrender is the difficulty of seeing God in everything. People say, "I can easily submit to things which come from God; but I cannot submit to man, and most of my trials and crosses come through human instrumentality." Or they say, "It is all well enough to talk of trusting; but when I commit a matter to God, man is sure to come in and disarrange it all; and while I have no difficulty in trusting God, I do see serious difficulties in the way of trusting men."

This is no imaginary trouble, but it is of vital importance, and if it cannot be met, does really make the life of faith an impossible and visionary theory. For nearly everything in life comes to us through human instrumentalities, and most of our trials are the result of somebody's failure, or ignorance, or carelessness, or sin. We know God cannot be the author of these things, and yet unless He is the agent in the matter, how can we say to Him about it, "Thy will be done"?

Besides, what good is there in trusting our affairs to God, if, after all, man is to be allowed to come in and disarrange them; and how is it possible to live by faith, if human agencies, in whom it would be wrong and foolish to trust, are to have a predominant influence in molding our lives?

Moreover, things in which we can see God's hand always have a sweetness in them which consoles while it wounds. But the trials inflicted by man are full of bitterness.

What is needed, then, is to see *God in everything*, and to receive everything directly from His hands, with no intervention of second causes. And it is just to this that we must be brought, before we can know an abiding experience of entire abandonment and perfect trust. Our abandonment must be *to God*, not to man, and our trust must be in Him, not in any arm of flesh, or we shall fail at the first trial.

The question here confronts us at once, "But *is* God in everything, and have we any warrant from the Scripture for receiving everything from His hands, without regarding the second causes which may have been instrumental in bringing it about?" I answer to this, unhesitatingly, YES. To the children of God everything comes directly from their Father's hand, no matter who or what may have been the apparent agents. There are no "second causes" for them.

The whole teaching of the Bible asserts and implies this. "Not a sparrow falls to the ground without our Father." The very hairs of our head are all numbered. We are not to be careful about anything, because our Father cares for us. We are not to avenge ourselves, because our Father has charged Himself with our defense. We are not to fear, for the Lord is on our side. No one can be against us, because He is for us. We shall not want, for He is our Shepherd. When we pass through the rivers they shall not overflow us, and when we walk through the fire we shall not be burned, because He will be with us. He shuts the mouths of lions, that they cannot hurt us. "He delivereth and rescueth." "He changeth the times and the seasons; He removeth kings and setteth up kings." A man's heart is in His hand, and, "as the river of water, He turneth it whithersoever He will." He ruleth over all the kingdoms of the heathen; and in His hand there is power and might, "so that none is able to withstand" Him. "He ruleth the raging of the sea; when the waves thereof arise, He stilleth them." He "bringeth the counsel of the heathen to naught; He maketh the devices of the people of none effect." "Whatsoever the Lord pleaseth, that does He in heaven, and in earth, in the seas, and all deep places."

"If thou seest the oppression of the poor, and violent perverting of judgment and justice in a province, marvel not at the matter; for He that is higher than the highest regardeth; and there be higher than they."

"Lo, these are a part of His ways; but how little a portion is heard of Him? But the thunder of His power who can understand?" "Hast thou not known, hast thou not heard, that the everlasting God, the Lord, the Creator of the ends of the earth, fainteth not, neither is weary? There is no searching of His understanding."

And this "God is our refuge and strength, a very present help in trouble. Therefore will not we fear, though the earth be removed, and though the mountains be carried into the midst of the sea; though the waters thereof roar and be troubled; though the mountains shake with the swelling thereof." "I will say of the Lord, He is my refuge and my fortress, my God, in Him will I trust. Surely He shall deliver thee from the snare of the fowler, and from the noisesome pestilence. He shall cover thee with His feathers, and under His wings shalt thou trust. His truth shall be thy shield and buckler. Thou shalt not be afraid for the terror by night, nor for the arrow that flieth by day, nor for the pestilence that walketh in darkness, nor for the destruction that wasteth at noonday. A thousand shall fall at thy side, and ten thousand at thy right hand; but it shall not come nigh thee." "Because thou hast made the Lord, which is my refuge, even the Most High, thy habitation, there shall no evil befall thee, neither shall any plague come nigh thy dwelling. For He shall give His angels charge over thee, to keep thee in all thy ways."

To my own mind, these Scriptures, and many others like them, settle forever the question as to the power of second causes in the life of the children of God. They are all under the control of our Father, and nothing can touch us except with His knowledge and by His permission. It may be the sin of man that originates the action, and therefore the thing itself cannot be said to be the will of God but by the time it reaches us, it has become God's will for us, and must be accepted as directly from His hands. No man or company of men, no power in earth or heaven, can touch that soul which is abiding in Christ, without first passing through Him, and receiving the seal of His permission. If God be for us, it matters not who may be against us; nothing can disturb or harm us, except He shall see that it is best for us, and shall stand aside to let it pass.

An earthly parent's care for his helpless child is a feeble illustration of this. If the child is in its father's arms, nothing can touch it without that father's consent, unless he is too weak to prevent it. And even if this should be the case, he suffers the harm first in his own person, before he allows it to reach his child. And if an earthly parent would thus care for his little helpless one, how much more will our Heavenly Father, whose love is infinitely greater, and whose strength and wisdom can never be baffled! I am afraid there are some, even of God's own children, who scarcely think that He is equal to themselves in tenderness, and love, and thoughtful care; and who in their secret thoughts, charge Him with a neglect and indifference of which they would feel themselves incapable. The truth really is, that His care is infinitely superior to any possibilities of human care; and that He who counts the very hairs of our head, and suffers not a sparrow to fall without Him, takes note of the minutest matters that can affect the lives of His children, and regulates them all according to His own sweet will, let their origin be what they may.

The instances of this are numberless. Take Joseph. What could have seemed more apparently on the face of it to be the result of sin, and utterly contrary to the will of God, than his being sold into slavery? And yet Joseph, in speaking of it, said, "As for you, ye thought evil against me: but God meant it unto good." "Now, therefore, be not grieved nor angry with yourselves, that ye sold me hither, for God did send me before you to preserve life." To the eye of sense it was surely Joseph's wicked brethren who had sent him into Egypt; and yet Joseph, looking at it with the eye of faith, could say, "God sent me." It had been undoubtedly a grievous sin in his brethren, but, by the time it had reached Joseph, it had become God's will for him, and was in truth, though at first it did not look so, the greatest blessing of his whole life. And thus we see how the Lord can make even the wrath of man to praise Him, and how all things, even the sins of others, shall work together for good to them that love Him.

I learned this lesson practically and experimentally long years before I knew the scriptural truth concerning it. I was attending a prayer-meeting held for the promotion of scriptural holiness, when a strange lady rose to speak, and I looked at her, wondering who she could be, little thinking she was to bring a message to my soul which would teach me such a grand lesson. She said she had had great difficulty in living the life of faith, on account of the second causes that seemed to her to control nearly everything that concerned her. Her perplexity became so great, that at last she began to ask God to teach her the truth about it, whether He really was in everything or not. After praying this for a few days, she had what she described as a vision. She thought she was in a perfectly dark place, and that there advanced towards her from a distance a body of light, which gradually surrounded and enveloped her and everything around her. As it approached, a voice seemed to say, "This is the presence of God; this is the presence of God." While surrounded with this presence, all the great and awful things in life seemed to pass before her,—fighting armies, wicked men, raging beasts, storms and pestilences, sin and suffering of every kind.

She shrank back at first in terror, but she soon saw that the presence of God so surrounded and enveloped each one of these, that not a lion could reach out its paw, nor a bullet fly through the air, except as His presence moved out of the way to permit it. And she saw that, let there be ever so thin a sheet, as it were, of this glorious presence between herself and the most terrible violence, not a hair of her head could be ruffled, nor anything touch her, unless the presence divided to let the evil through. Then all the small and annoying things of life passed before her, and equally she saw that these all were so enveloped in this presence of God that not a cross look, not a harsh word, nor petty trial of any kind, could reach her unless His presence moved out of the way to let them through.

Her difficulty vanished. Her question was answered forever. God was in everything; and to her henceforth there were no second causes. She saw that her life came to her day by day and hour by hour directly from His hand, let the agencies which should seem to control it be what they might. And never again had she found any difficulty in an abiding consent to His will and an unwavering trust in His care.

If we look at the seen things, we shall not be able to understand the secret of this. But the children of God are called to look, "not at the things which are seen: for the things which are seen are temporal, but the things which are not seen are eternal." Could we but see with our bodily eyes His unseen forces surrounding us on every side, we would walk through this world in an impregnable fortress, which nothing could ever overthrow or penetrate, for "the angel of the Lord encampeth round about them that fear Him, and delivereth them."

We have a striking illustration of this in the history of Elisha. The king of Syria was warring against Israel, but his evil designs were continually frustrated by the prophet; and at last he sent his army to the prophet's own city for the express purpose of taking him captive. We read, "He sent thither horses and chariots and a great host; and they came by night and compassed the city about." This was the seen thing. And the servant of the prophet, whose eyes had not yet been opened to see the unseen things, was alarmed. And we read, "And when the servant of the man of God was risen early and gone forth, behold an host compassed the city, both with horses and chariots. And his servant said unto him, Alas, my master, how shall we do?" But his master could see the unseen things, and he replied, "Fear not; for they that be with us are more than they that be with them." And then he prayed, saying, "Lord, I pray thee, open his eyes that he may see. And the Lord opened the eyes of the young man, and he saw; and behold, the mountain was full of horses and chariots of fire round about Elisha."

The presence of God is the fortress of His people. Nothing can withstand it. At His presence the wicked perish; the earth trembles; the hills melt like wax; the cities are broken down; "the heavens also dropped, and Sinai itself was moved at the presence of God." And in the secret of this presence He has promised to hide His people from the pride of man, and from the strife of tongues. "My presence shall go with thee," He says, "and I will give thee rest."

I wish it were only possible to make every Christian see this truth as plainly as I see it; for I am convinced it is the only clue to a completely restful life. Nothing else will enable a soul to live only in the present moment, as we are commanded to do, and to take no thought for the morrow. Nothing else will take all the risks and "supposes" out of a Christian's heart, and enable him to say, "Surely goodness and mercy shall follow me all the days of my life." Abiding in God's presence, we run no risks; and such a soul can triumphantly say,—

> *"I know not what it is to doubt,*
> *My heart is alway gay;*
> *I run no risks, for, come what will,*
> *God alway has His way."*

I once heard of a colored woman who earned a precarious living by daily labor, but who was a joyous, triumphant Christian. "Ah! Nancy," said a gloomy Christian lady to her one day, who almost disapproved of her constant cheerfulness, and yet envied it,— "ah! Nancy, it is all well enough to be happy now; but I should think the thoughts of your future would sober you. Only suppose, for instance, that you should have a spell of sickness and be unable to work; or suppose your present employers should move away, and no one else should give you anything to do; or suppose—" "Stop!" cried Nancy, "I never supposes. De Lord is my shepherd, and I knows I shall not want. And, honey," she added to her gloomy friend, "it's all dem *supposes* as is makin' you so miserable. You'd better give dem all up, and just trust de Lord."

There is one text that will take all the "suppose" out of a believer's life, if only it is received and acted out in a childlike faith; it is in Heb. 3:5, 6: "Be content, therefore, with such things as ye have; for He hath said I will never leave thee, nor forsake thee"; so that we may boldly say, "The Lord is my helper, and I will not fear what man shall do unto me." What if dangers of all sorts shall threaten you from every side, and the malice or foolishness or ignorance of men shall combine to do you harm? You may face every possible contingency with these triumphant words, "The Lord is my helper, and I will not fear what man shall do unto me." If the Lord is your helper, how can you fear what man may do unto you? There is no man in this world, nor company of men, that can touch you, unless your God, in whom you trust, shall please to let them. "He will not suffer thy foot to be moved: He that keepeth thee will not slumber. Behold, He that keepeth Israel shall neither slumber nor sleep. The Lord is thy keeper; the Lord is thy shade upon thy right hand. The sun shall not smite thee by day nor the moon by night. The Lord shall preserve thee from all evil: He shall preserve thy soul. The Lord shall preserve thy going out, and thy coming in, from this time forth, and even for evermore."

Nothing else but this seeing God in everything will make us loving and patient with those who annoy and trouble us. They will be to us then only the instruments for accomplishing His tender and wise purposes towards us, and we shall even find ourselves at last inwardly thanking them for the blessings they bring us.

Nothing else will completely put an end to all murmuring or rebelling thoughts. Christians often feel a liberty to murmur against man, when they would not dare to murmur against God. But this way of receiving things would make it impossible ever to murmur. If our Father permits a trial to come, it must be because that trial is the sweetest and best thing that could happen to us, and we must accept it with thanks from His dear hand. The trial itself may be hard to flesh and blood, and I do not mean that we can like or enjoy the suffering of it. But we can and must love the will of God *in* the trial, for His will is always sweet, whether it be in joy or in sorrow.

Our trials may be our chariots. We long for some victory over sin and self, and we ask God to grant it to us. His answer comes in the form of a trial which He means shall be the chariot to bear us to the longed-for triumph. We may either let it roll over us and crush us as a Juggernaut car, or we may mount into it and ride triumphantly onward. Joseph's chariots, which bore him on to the place of his exaltation, were the trials of being sold into slavery, and being cast unjustly into prison. Our chariots may be much more insignificant things than these; they may be nothing but irritating people or uncomfortable circumstances. But whatever they are, God means them to be our cars of triumph, which shall bear us onward to the victories we have prayed for. If we are impatient in our dispositions and long to be made patient, our chariot will probably be a trying person to live in the house with us, whose ways or words will rasp our very souls. If we accept the trial as from God, and bow our necks to the yoke, we shall find it just the discipline that will most effectually produce in us the very grace of patience for which we have asked.

God does not *order* the wrong thing, but He *uses* it for our blessing; just as He used the cruelty of Joseph's wicked brethren, and the false accusations of Pharaoh's wife. In short, this way of seeing our Father in everything makes life one long thanksgiving, and gives a rest of heart, and more than that, a gayety of spirit, that is unspeakable. Someone says, "God's will on earth is always joy, always tranquility." And since He must have His own way concerning His children, into what wonderful green pastures of inward rest, and beside what blessedly still waters of inward refreshment, is the soul led that learns this secret.

If the will of God is our will, and if He always has His way, then we always have our way also, and we reign in a perpetual kingdom. He who sides with God cannot fail to win in every encounter; and whether the result shall be joy or sorrow, failure or success, death or life, we may, under all circumstances, join in the apostle's shout of victory, "Thanks be unto God, which always causeth us to triumph in Christ!"

9. Growth

When the believer has been brought to the point of entire surrender and perfect trust, and finds himself dwelling and walking in a life of happy communion and perfect peace, the question naturally arises, "Is this the end?" I answer emphatically "No, it is only the beginning."

And yet this is so little understood, that one of the greatest objections made against the advocates of this life of faith, is, that they do not believe in growth in grace. They are supposed to teach that the soul arrives at a state of perfection beyond which there is no advance, and that all the exhortations in the Scripture which point towards growth and development are rendered void by this teaching.

As exactly the opposite of this is true, I have thought it important next to consider this subject carefully, that I may, if possible, fully answer such objections, and may also show what is the scriptural place to grow in, and how the soul is to grow.

The text which is most frequently quoted is 2 Pet. 3:18, "But grow in grace, and in the knowledge of our Lord and Savior Jesus Christ." Now this text exactly expresses what we believe to be God's will for us, and what also we believe He has made it possible for us to experience. We accept, in their very fullest meaning, all the commands and promises concerning our being no more children, and our growing up into Christ in all things, until we come unto a perfect man, unto the measure of the stature of the fulness of Christ. We rejoice that we need not continue always to be babes, needing milk; but that we may, by reason of use and development become such as have need of strong meat, skillful in the word of righteousness, and able to discern both good and evil. And none would grieve more than we at the thought of any finality in the Christian life beyond which there could be no advance.

But then we believe in a growing that does really produce maturity, and in a development that, as a fact, does bring forth ripe fruit. We expect to reach the aim set before us, and if we do not, we feel sure there must be some fault in our growing. No parent would be satisfied with the growth of his child, if, day after day, and year after year, it remained the same helpless babe it was in the first months of its life; and no farmer would feel comfortable under such growing of his grain as should stop short at the blade, and never produce the ear, nor the full corn in the ear. Growth, to be real, must be progressive, and the days and weeks and months must see a development and increase of maturity in the thing growing. But is this the case with a large part of that which is called growth in grace? Does not the very Christian who is the most strenuous in his longings and in his efforts after it, too often find that at the end of the year he is not as far on in his Christian experience as at the beginning, and that his zeal, and his devotedness, and his separation from the world are not as whole-souled or complete as when his Christian life first began?

I was once urging upon a company of Christians the privileges and rest of an immediate and definite step into the land of promise, when a lady of great intelligence interrupted me, with what she evidently felt to be a complete rebuttal of all I had been saying, exclaiming, "Ah! but, my dear friend, I believe in *growing* in grace." "How long have you been growing?" I asked. "About twenty-five years," was her answer. "And how much more unworldly and devoted to the Lord are you now than when you began your Christian life?" I continued. "Alas!" was the answer, "I fear I am not nearly so much so"; and with this answer her eyes were opened to see that at all events her way of growing had not been successful, but quite the reverse.

The trouble with her, and every other such case, is simply this, they are trying to grow *into* grace, instead of *in* it. They are like a rosebush which the gardener should plant in the hard, stony path, with a view to its growing *into* the flower-bed, and which would of course dwindle and wither in consequence, instead of flourishing and maturing. The children of Israel wandering in the wilderness are a perfect picture of this sort of growing. They were travelling about for forty years, taking many weary steps, and finding but little rest from their wanderings, and yet, at the end of it all, were no nearer the promised land than they were at the beginning. When they started on their wanderings at Kadesh Barnea, they were at the borders of the land, and a few steps would have taken them into it.

When they ended their wanderings in the plains of Moab, they were also at its borders; only with this great difference, that now there was a river to cross, which at first there would not have been. All their wanderings and fightings in the wilderness had not put them in possession of one inch of the promised land. In order to get possession of this land it was necessary first to be in it; and in order to grow in grace, it is necessary first to be planted in grace. But when once in the land, their conquest was very rapid; and when once planted in grace, the growth of the soul in one month will exceed that of years in any other soil. For grace is a most fruitful soil, and the plants that grow therein are plants of a marvelous growth. They are tended by a Divine Husbandman, and are warmed by the Sun of Righteousness, and watered by the dew from Heaven. Surely it is no wonder that they bring forth fruit, "some an hundred-fold, some sixty-fold, some thirty-fold."

But, it will be asked, what is meant by growing in grace? It is difficult to answer this question because so few people have any conception of what the grace of God really is. To say that it is free, unmerited favor, only expresses a little of its meaning. It is the wondrous, boundless love of God, poured out upon us without stint or measure, not according to our deserving, but according to His infinite heart of love, which passeth knowledge, so unfathomable are its heights and depths. I sometimes think we give a totally different meaning to the word "love" when it is associated with God, from that we so well understand in its human application. But if ever human love was tender and self-sacrificing and devoted; if ever it could bear and forbear; if ever it could suffer gladly for its loved ones; if ever it was willing to pour itself out in a lavish abandonment for the comfort or pleasure of its objects,—then infinitely more is Divine love tender and self-sacrificing and devoted, and glad to bear and forbear, and to suffer, and to lavish its best of gifts and blessings upon the objects of its love. Put together all the tenderest love you know of, dear reader, the deepest you have ever felt, and the strongest that has ever been poured out upon you, and heap upon it all the love of all the loving human hearts in the world, and then multiply it by infinity, and you will begin perhaps to have some faint glimpses of what the love of God in Christ Jesus is. And this is grace. And to be planted in grace is to live in the very heart of this love, to be enveloped by it, to be steeped in it, to revel in it, to know nothing else but love only and love always, to grow day by day in the knowledge of it, and in faith in it, to entrust everything to its care, and to have no shadow of a doubt but that it will surely order all things well.

To grow in grace is opposed to all self-dependence, to all self-effort, to all legality of every kind. It is to put our growing, as well as everything else, into the hands of the Lord, and leave it with Him. It is to be so satisfied with our Husbandman, and with His skill and wisdom, that not a question will cross our minds as to His modes of treatment or His plan of cultivation. It is to grow as the lilies grow, or as the babes grow, without a care and without anxiety; to grow by the power of an inward life principle that cannot help but grow; to grow because we live and therefore must grow; to grow because He who has planted us has planted a growing thing, and has made us to grow.

Surely this is what our Lord meant when He said, "Consider the lilies, how they grow; they toil not, neither do they spin: and yet I say unto you, that even Solomon in all his glory was not arrayed like one of these." Or, when He says again, "Which of you by taking thought can add one cubit unto his stature?" There is no effort in the growing of a child or of a lily. They do not toil nor spin, they do not stretch nor strain, they do not make any effort of any kind to grow; they are not conscious even that they are growing; but by an inward life principle, and through the nurturing care of God's providence, and the fostering of caretaker or gardener, by the heat of the sun and the falling of the rain, they grow and grow.

And the result is sure. Even Solomon, our Lord says, in all his glory, was not arrayed like one of these. Solomon's array cost much toiling and spinning, and gold and silver in abundance, but the lily's array costs none of these. And though we may toil and spin to make for ourselves beautiful spiritual garments, and may strain and stretch in our efforts after spiritual growth, we shall accomplish nothing; for no man by taking thought *can* add one cubit to his stature; and no array of ours can ever equal the beautiful dress with which the great Husbandman clothes the plants that grow in His garden of grace and under His fostering care.

If I could but make each one of my readers realize how utterly helpless we are in this matter of growing, I am convinced a large part of the strain would be taken out of many lives at once. Imagine a child possessed of the monomania that he would not grow unless he made some personal effort after it, and who should insist upon a combination of rope and pulleys whereby to stretch himself up to the desired height. He might, it is true, spend his days and years in a weary strain, but after all there would be no change in the inexorable fact, "No man by taking thought can add one cubit unto his stature"; and his years of labor would be only wasted, if they did not really hinder the longed-for end.

Imagine a lily trying to clothe itself in beautiful colors and graceful lines, stretching its leaves and stems to make them grow, and seeking to manage the clouds and the sunshine, that its needs might be all judiciously supplied!

And yet in these two pictures we have, I conceive, only too true a picture of what many Christians are trying to do; who, knowing they ought to grow, and feeling within them an instinct that longs for growth, yet think to accomplish it by toiling, and spinning, and stretching, and straining, and pass their lives in such a round of self-effort as is a weariness to contemplate.

Grow, dear friends, but grow, I beseech you, in God's way, which is the only effectual way. See to it that you are planted in grace, and then let the Divine Husbandman cultivate you in His own way and by His own means. Put yourselves out in the sunshine of His presence, and let the dew of heaven come down upon you, and see what will come of it. Leaves and flowers and fruit must surely come in their season, for your Husbandman is a skillful one, and He never fails in His harvesting. Only see to it that you interpose no hindrance to the shining of the Sun of Righteousness or the falling of the dew from Heaven. A very thin covering may serve to keep off the heat or the moisture, and the plant may wither even in their midst; and the slightest barrier between your soul and Christ may cause you to dwindle and fade as a plant in a cellar or under a bushel. Keep the sky clear. Open wide every avenue of your being to receive the blessed influences our Divine Husbandman may bring to bear upon you. Bask in the sunshine of His love. Drink in of the waters of His goodness. Keep your face up-turned to Him. Look, and your soul shall live.

You need make no efforts to grow; but let your efforts instead be all concentrated on this, that you abide in the Vine. The Husbandman who has the care of the vine, will care for its branches also, and will so prune and purge and water and tend them that they will grow and bring forth fruit, and their fruit shall remain; and, like the lily, they shall find themselves arrayed in apparel so glorious that that of Solomon will be as nothing to it.

What if you seem to yourselves to be planted at this moment in a desert soil where nothing can grow! Put yourself absolutely into the hands of the great Husbandman, and He will at once make that desert blossom as the rose, and will cause springs and fountains of water to start up out of its sandy wastes; for the promise is sure, that the man who trusts in the Lord "shall be as a tree planted by the waters, and that spreadeth out her roots by the river, and shall not see when heat cometh, but her leaf shall be green; and shall not be careful in the year of drought, neither shall cease from yielding fruit." It is the great prerogative of our Divine Husbandman that He is able to turn any soil, whatever it may be like, into the soil of grace, the moment we put our growing into His hands. He does not need to transplant us into a different field, but right where we are, with just the circumstances that surround us, He makes His sun to shine and His dew to fall upon us, and transforms the very things that were before our greatest hindrances into the chiefest and most blessed means of our growth. I care not what the circumstances may be, His wonder-working power can accomplish this. And we must trust Him with it all. Surely He is a Husbandman we *can* trust. And if He sends storms, or winds, or rains, or sunshine, all must be accepted at His hands with the most unwavering confidence that He who has undertaken to cultivate us, and to bring us to maturity, knows the very best way of accomplishing His end, and regulates the elements, which are all at His disposal, expressly with a view to our most rapid growth.

Let me entreat of you, then, to give up all your efforts after growing, and simply to *let* yourselves grow. Leave it all to the Husbandman, whose care it is, and who alone is able to manage it. No difficulties in your case can baffle Him. No dwarfing of your growth in years that are past, no apparent dryness of your inward springs of life, no crookedness or deformity in any of your past development, can in the least mar the perfect work that He will accomplish, if you will only put yourselves absolutely into His hands, and let Him have His own way with you. His own gracious promise to His backsliding children assures you of this. "I will heal their backslidings," He says: "I will love them freely, for mine anger is turned away from him. I will be as the dew unto Israel; he shall grow as the lily, and cast forth his roots as Lebanon. His branches shall spread, and his beauty shall be as the olive-tree, and his smell as Lebanon. They that dwell under His shadow shall return; they shall revive as the corn, and grow as the vine; the scent thereof shall be as the wine of Lebanon." And again He says, "Be not afraid, for the pastures of the wilderness do spring, for the tree beareth her fruit, the fig-tree and the vine do yield their strength. And the floors shall be full of wheat, and the fats shall overflow with wine and oil. And I will restore to you the years that the locust hath eaten; and ye shall eat in plenty and be satisfied, and praise the name of the Lord your God, who hath dealt wondrously with you; and my people shall never be ashamed."

Oh! that you could but know just what your Lord meant when He said, "Consider the lilies, *how they grow*; for they toil not, neither do they spin." Surely these words give us a picture of a life and of a growth far different from the ordinary life and growth of Christians; a life of rest, and a growth without effort; and yet a life and a growth crowned with glorious results. And to every soul that will thus become a lily in the garden of the Lord, and will grow as the lilies grow, the same glorious array will be surely given as is given them; and they will know the fulfilment of that wonderful mystical passage concerning their Beloved, that "He feedeth among the lilies."

This is the sort of growth in grace in which we who have entered into the life of full trust believe: a growth which brings the desired results, which blossoms out into flower and fruit, and becomes a tree planted by the rivers of water, that bringeth forth his fruit in his season; whose leaf also does not wither, and who prospers in whatsoever he doeth. And we rejoice to know that there are growing up now in the Lord's heritage many such plants, who, as the lilies behold the face of the sun and grow thereby, are, by beholding as in a glass the glory of the Lord, being changed into the same image from glory to glory, even as by the spirit of the Lord.

Should you ask such, how it is that they grow so rapidly and with such success, their answer would be that they are not concerned about their growing, and are hardly conscious that they do grow; that their Lord has told them to abide in Him, and has promised that if they do thus abide, they shall certainly bring forth much fruit; and that they are concerned only about the abiding, which is their part, and leave the cultivating and the growing and the training and pruning to their good Husbandman, who alone is able to manage these things or bring them about. You will find that such souls are not engaged in watching self, but in looking unto Jesus. They do not toil nor spin for their spiritual garments, but leave themselves in the hands of the Lord to be arrayed as it may please Him. Self-effort and self-dependence are at an end with them. Their interest in self is gone, transferred over into the hands of another. Self has become really nothing, and Christ alone is all in all to such as these. And the blessed result is, that not even Solomon, in all his glory, was arrayed like these shall be.

Let us look at this subject practically. We all know that growing is not a thing of effort, but is the result of an inward life, a principle of growth. All the stretching and pulling in the world could not make a dead oak grow. But a live oak grows without stretching. It is plain, therefore, that the essential thing is to get within you the growing life, and then you cannot help but grow. And this life is the life hid with Christ in God, the wonderful divine life of an indwelling Holy Ghost. Be filled with this, dear believer, and, whether you are conscious of it or not, you must grow, you cannot help growing. Do not trouble about your growing, but see to it that you have the growing life. Abide in the Vine. Let the life from Him flow through all your spiritual veins. Interpose no barrier to His mighty life-giving power, working in you all the good pleasure of His will. Yield yourself up utterly to His sweet control. Put your growing into His hands, as completely as you have put all your other affairs. Suffer Him to manage it as He will. Do not concern yourself about it, nor even think of it. Trust Him absolutely, and always. Accept each moment's dispensation as it comes to you, from His dear hands, as being the needed sunshine or dew for that moment's growth. Say a continual "Yes" to your Father's will.

Heretofore you have perhaps tried, as so many do, to be both the lily and the gardener, both the vineyard and the husbandman. You have taken upon your shoulders the burdens and responsibilities that belong only to the Divine Husbandman, and which He alone is able to bear. Henceforth consent to take your rightful place and to *be* only what you really *are*. Say to yourself, If I am the garden only, and not the gardener, if I am the vine only, and not the husbandman, it is surely essential to my right growth and well being that I should keep the place and act the part of the garden, and should not usurp the gardener's place, nor try to act the gardener's part.

Do not seek then to choose your own soil, nor the laying out of your borders; do not plant your own seeds, nor dig about, nor prune, nor watch over your own vines. Be content with what the Divine Husbandman arranges for you, and with the care He gives. Let Him choose the sort of plants and fruits He sees best to cultivate, and grow a potato as gladly as a rose, if such be His will, and homely everyday virtues as willingly as exalted fervors. Be satisfied with the seasons He sends, with the sunshine and rain He gives, with the rapidity or slowness of your growth, in short, with all His dealings and processes, no matter how little we may comprehend them.

There is infinite repose in this. As the violet rests in its little nook, receiving contentedly its daily portion satisfied to let rains fall, and suns rise, and the earth to whirl, without one anxious pang, so must we repose in the present as God gives it to us, accepting contentedly our daily portion, and with no anxiety as to all that may be whirling around us, in His great creative and redemptive plan.

The wind that blows can never kill
*   The tree God plants;*
It bloweth east, it bloweth west,
The tender leaves have little rest,
But any wind that blows is best.
*   The tree God plants*
Strikes deeper root, grows higher still,
Spreads wider boughs, for God's good-will
*   Meets all its wants.*

There is no frost hath power to blight
*   The tree God shields;*
The roots are warm beneath soft snows,
And when spring comes it surely knows,
And every bud to blossom grows.
*   The tree God shields*
Grows on apace by day and night,
Till, sweet to taste and fair to sight,
*   Its fruit it yields.*

There is no storm hath power to blast
*   The tree God knows;*
No thunder-bolt, nor beating rain,
Nor lightning flash, nor hurricane;
When they are spent it doth remain.
*   The tree God knows*
Through every tempest standeth fast,
And, from its first day to its last,
*   Still fairer grows.*

If in the soul's still garden-place
*   A seed God sows—*
A little seed—it soon will grow,
And far and near all men will know
For heavenly land He bids it blow.
*   A seed God sows,*
And up it springs by day and night;
Through life, through death, it groweth right,
*   Forever grows.*

10. Service

There is, perhaps, no part of Christian experience where a greater change is known upon entering into the life hid with Christ in God, than in the matter of service. In all the lower forms of Christian life, service is apt to have more or less of bondage in it; that is, it is one purely as a matter of duty, and often as a trial and a cross. Certain things, which at the first may have been a joy and delight, become weary tasks, performed faithfully, perhaps, but with much secret disinclination, and many confessed or unconfessed wishes that they need not be done at all, or at least that they need not be done so often. The soul finds itself saying, instead of the "May I" of love, the "Must I" of duty. The yoke, which was at first easy, begins to gall, and the burden feels heavy instead of light.

One dear Christian expressed it once to me in this way. "When I was first converted," she said, "I was so full of joy and love that I was only too glad and thankful to be allowed to do anything for my Lord, and I eagerly entered every open door. But after a while, as my early joy faded away, and my love burned less fervently, I began to wish I had not been quite so eager; for I found myself involved in lines of service which were gradually becoming very distasteful and burdensome to me. I could not very well give them up, since I had begun them, without exciting great remark, and yet I longed to do so increasingly. I was expected to visit the sick, and pray beside their beds. I was expected to attend prayer-meetings, and speak at them. I was expected to be always ready for every effort in Christian work, and the sense of these expectations bowed me down continually. At last it became so unspeakably burdensome to me to live the sort of Christian life I had entered upon, and was expected by all around me to live, that I felt as if any kind of manual labor would have been easier, and I would have preferred, infinitely, scrubbing all day on my hands and knees, to being compelled to go through the treadmill of my daily Christian work. I envied," she said, "the servants in the kitchen, and the women at the wash-tubs."

This may seem to some like a strong statement: but does it not present a vivid picture of some of your own experiences, dear Christian? Have you never gone to your work as a slave to his daily task, knowing it to be your duty, and that therefore you must do it, but rebounding like an India-rubber ball back into your real interests and pleasures the moment your work was over?

Of course you have known this was the wrong way to feel, and have been ashamed of it from the bottom of your heart, but still you have seen no way to help it. You have not *loved* your work, and, could you have done so with an easy conscience, you would have been glad to have given it up altogether.

Or, if this does not describe your case, perhaps another picture will. You do love your work in the abstract; but, in the doing of it, you find so many cares and responsibilities connected with it, so many misgivings and doubts as to your own capacity or fitness, that it becomes a very heavy burden, and you go to it bowed down and weary, before the labor has even begun. Then also you are continually distressing yourself about the results of your work, and greatly troubled if they are not just what you would like, and this of itself is a constant burden.

Now from all these forms of bondage the soul is entirely delivered that enters fully into the blessed life of faith. In the first place, service of any sort becomes delightful to it, because, having surrendered its will into the keeping of the Lord, He works in it to will and to do of His good pleasure, and the soul finds itself really *wanting* to do the things God wants it to do. It is always very pleasant to do the things we *want* to do, let them be ever so difficult of accomplishment, or involve ever so much of bodily weariness. If a man's *will* is really set on a thing, he regards with a sublime indifference the obstacles that lie in the way of his reaching it, and laughs to himself at the idea of any opposition or difficulties hindering him. How many men have gone gladly and thankfully to the ends of the world in search of worldly fortunes, or to fulfil worldly ambitions, and have scorned the thoughts of any cross connected with it! How many mothers have congratulated themselves and rejoiced over the honor done their sons in being promoted to some place of power and usefulness in their country's service, although it has involved perhaps years of separation, and a life of hardship for their dear ones? And yet these same men and these very mothers would have felt and said that they were taking up crosses too heavy almost to be borne, had the service of Christ required the same sacrifice of home, and friends, and worldly ease. It is altogether the way we look at things, whether we think they are crosses or not. And I am ashamed to think that any Christian should ever put on a long face and shed tears over doing a thing for Christ, which a worldly man would be only too glad to do for money.

What we need in the Christian life is to get believers to *want* to do God's will, as much as other people want to do their own will. And this is the idea of the Gospel. It is what God intended for us; and it is what He has promised. In describing the new covenant in Heb. 8:6-13, He says it shall no more be the old covenant made on Sinai, that is, a law given from the outside, controlling a man by force, but it shall be a law written *within* constraining a man by love. "I will put my laws," He says, "in their mind, and write them in their hearts." This can mean nothing but that we shall *love* His law, for anything written on our hearts we must love. And putting it into our minds is surely the same as God working in us to "will and to do of His good pleasure," and means that we shall will what God wills, and shall obey His sweet commands, not because it is our duty to do so, but because we ourselves want to do what He wants us to do. Nothing could possibly be conceived more effectual than this. How often have we thought when dealing with our children, "Oh, if I could only get inside of them and make them *want* to do just what I want, how easy it would be to manage them then!" And how often practically in experience we have found that, to deal with cross-grained people, we must carefully avoid suggesting our wishes to them, but must in some way induce them to suggest them themselves, sure that then there will be no opposition to contend with. And we, who are by nature a stiff-necked people, always rebel more or less against a law from outside of us, while we joyfully embrace the same law springing up within.

God's plan for us therefore is to get possession of the inside of a man, to take the control and management of his will, and to work it for him; and then obedience is easy and a delight, and service becomes perfect freedom, until the Christian is forced to exclaim, "This happy service! Who could dream earth had such liberty?"

What you need to do then, dear Christian, if you are in bondage, is to put your will over completely into the hands of your Lord, surrendering to Him the entire control of it. Say, "Yes, Lord, YES!" to everything; and trust Him so to work in you to will, as to bring your whole wishes and affections into conformity with His own sweet and lovable and most lovely will. I have seen this done over and over, in cases where it looked beforehand an utterly impossible thing. In one case, where a lady had been for years rebelling fearfully against a thing which she knew was right, but which she hated, I saw her, out of the depths of despair and without any feeling, give her will in that matter up into the hands of her Lord, and begin to say to Him, "Thy will be done; *thy will be done!*" And in one short hour that very thing began to look sweet and precious to her. It is wonderful what miracles God works in wills that are utterly surrendered to Him. He turns hard things into easy, and bitter things into sweet. It is not that He puts easy things in the place of the hard, but He actually changes the hard thing into an easy one. And this is salvation. It is grand. Do try it, you who are going about your daily Christian living as to a hard and weary task, and see if your divine Master will not transform the very life you live now as a bondage, into the most delicious liberty!

Or again, if you do love His will in the abstract, but find the doing of it hard and burdensome, from this also there is deliverance in the wonderful life of faith. For in this life no burdens are carried, nor anxieties felt. The Lord is our burden-bearer, and upon Him we must lay off every care. He says, in effect, Be careful for nothing, but just make your requests known to Me, and I will attend to them all. Be careful for *nothing*, He says, not even your service. Above all, I should think, our service, because we know ourselves to be so utterly helpless in this, that even if we were careful, it would not amount to anything. What have we to do with thinking whether we are fit or not! The Master-workman surely has a right to use any tool He pleases for His own work, and it is plainly not the business of the tool to decide whether it is the right one to be used or not. He knows; and if He chooses to use us, of course we must be fit. And in truth, if we only knew it, our chiefest fitness is in our utter helplessness. His strength can only be made perfect in our weakness. I can give you a convincing illustration of this.

I was once visiting an idiot asylum and looking at the children going through dumb-bell exercises. Now we all know that it is a very difficult thing for idiots to manage their movements. They have strength enough, generally, but no skill to use this strength, and as a consequence cannot do much. And in these dumb-bell exercises this deficiency was very apparent. They made all sorts of awkward movements. Now and then, by a happy chance, they would make a movement in harmony with the music and the teacher's directions, but for the most part all was out of harmony. One little girl, however, I noticed, who made perfect movements. Not a jar nor a break disturbed the harmony of her exercises. And the reason was, not that she had more strength than the others, but that she had no strength at all. She could not so much as close her hands over the dumb-bells, nor lift her arms, and the master had to stand behind her and do it all. She yielded up her members as instruments to him, and his strength was made perfect in her weakness. He knew how to go through those exercises, for he himself had planned them, and therefore when he did it, it was done right. She did nothing but yield herself up utterly into his hands, and he did it all. The yielding was her part, the responsibility was all his. It was not her skill that was needed to make harmonious movements, but only his. The question was not of her capacity, but of his. Her utter weakness was her greatest strength. And if this is a picture of our Christian life, it is no wonder that Paul could say, "Most gladly therefore will I rather *glory* in my infirmities, that the power of Christ may rest upon me." Who would not glory in being so utterly weak and helpless, that the Lord Jesus Christ should find no hindrance to the perfect working of His mighty power through us and in us?

Then, too, if the work is His, the responsibility is His, and we have no room left for worrying about it. Everything in reference to it is known to Him, and He can manage it all. Why not leave it all with Him then, and consent to be treated like a child and guided where to go. It is a fact that the most effectual workers I know are those who do not feel the least care or anxiety about their work, but who commit it all to their dear Master, and, asking Him to guide them moment by moment in reference to it, trust Him implicitly for each moment's needed supplies of wisdom and of strength. To see such, you would almost think perhaps that they were too free from care, where such mighty interests are at stake. But when you have learned God's secret of trusting, and see the beauty and the power of that life which is yielded up to His working, you will cease to condemn, and will begin to wonder how any of God's workers can dare to carry burdens, or assume responsibilities which He alone is able to bear.

There are one or two other bonds of service from which this life of trust delivers us. We find out that we are not responsible for all the work in the world. The commands cease to be general, and become personal and individual. The Master does not map out a general course of action for us and leave us to get along through it by our own wisdom and skill as best we may, but He leads us step by step, giving us each hour the special guidance needed for that hour. His blessed Spirit dwelling in us, brings to our remembrance *at the time* the necessary command; so that we do not need to take any thought ahead but simply to take each step as it is made known to us, following our Lord whithersoever He leads us. "The *steps* of a good man are ordered of the Lord" not his way only, but each separate step in that way. Many Christians make the mistake of expecting to receive God's commands all in a lump, as it were. They think because He tells them to give a tract to one person in a railway train, for instance, that He means them always to give tracts to everybody, and they burden themselves with an impossible command.

There was a young Christian once, who, because the Lord had sent her to speak a message to one soul whom she met in a walk, took it as a general command for always, and thought she must speak to everyone she met about their souls. This was, of course, impossible, and as a consequence she was soon in hopeless bondage about it. She became absolutely afraid to go outside of her own door, and lived in perpetual condemnation. At last she disclosed her distress to a friend who was instructed in the ways of God with His servants, and this friend told her she was making a great mistake; that the Lord had His own especial work for each especial workman, and that the servants in a well-regulated household might as well each one take it upon himself to try and do the work of all the rest, as for the Lord's servants to think they were each one under obligation to do everything. He told her just to put herself under the Lord's personal guidance as to her work, and trust Him to point out to her each particular person to whom He would have her speak, assuring her that He never puts forth His own sheep without going before them, and making a way for them Himself. She followed this advice, and laid the burden of her work on the Lord, and the result was a happy pathway of daily guidance, in which she was led into much blessed work for her Master, but was able to do it all without a care or a burden, because He led her out and prepared the way before her.

Putting ourselves into God's hands in this way, seems to me just like making the junction between the machinery and the steam engine. The power is not in the machinery, but in the steam; disconnected from the engine, the machinery is perfectly useless; but let the connection be made, and the machinery goes easily and without effort, because of the mighty power there is behind it. Thus the Christian life becomes an easy, natural life when it is the development of the divine working within. Most Christians live on a strain, because their wills are not fully in harmony with the will of God, the connection is not perfectly made at every point, and it requires an effort to move the machinery. But when once the connection is fully made, and the law of the Spirit of life in Christ Jesus can work in us with all its mighty power, we are then indeed made free from the law of sin and death, and shall know the glorious liberty of the children of God. We shall lead *frictionless* lives.

Another form of bondage as to service, from which the life of faith delivers the soul, is in reference to the after-reflections which always follow any Christian work. These self-reflections are of two sorts. Either the soul congratulates itself upon its success, and is lifted up; or it is distressed over its failure, and is utterly cast down. One of these is *sure* to come, and of the two I think the first is the more to be dreaded, although the last causes at the time the greater suffering. But in the life of trust, neither will trouble us; for, having committed ourselves and our work to the Lord, we will be satisfied to leave it to Him, and will not think about ourselves in the matter at all.

Years ago I came across this sentence in an old book: "Never indulge, at the close of an action, in any self-reflective acts of any kind, whether of self-congratulation or of self-despair. Forget the things that are behind, the moment they are past, leaving them with God." It has been of unspeakable value to me. When the temptation comes, as it always does, to indulge in these reflections, either of one sort or the other, I turn from them at once, and positively refuse to think about my work at all, leaving it with the Lord to overrule the mistakes, and to bless it as He chooses.

To sum it all up then, what is needed for happy and effectual service is simply to put your work into the Lord's hands, and leave it there. Do not take it to Him in prayer, saying, "Lord, guide me; Lord, give me wisdom; Lord, arrange for me," and then arise from your knees, and take the burden all back, and try to guide and arrange for yourself. *Leave* it with the Lord, and remember that what you trust to Him, you must not worry over nor feel anxious about. Trust and worry cannot go together. If your work is a burden, it is because you are not trusting it to Him. But if you do trust it to Him, you will surely find that the yoke He puts upon you is easy, and the burden He gives you to carry is light, and even in the midst of a life of ceaseless activity you shall find rest to your soul.

But some may say that this teaching would make us into mere puppets. I answer, No, it would simply make us into servants. It is required of a servant, not that he shall plan, or arrange, or decide, or supply the necessary material, but simply and only that he shall obey. It is for the Master to do all the rest. The servant is not responsible, either, for results. The Master alone knows what results he wished to have produced, and therefore he alone can judge of them. Intelligent service will, of course, include some degree of intelligent sympathy with the thoughts and plans of the Master, but after all there cannot be a full comprehension, and the responsibility cannot be transferred from the Master's shoulders to the servant's. And in our case, where our outlook is so limited and our ignorance so great, we can do very little more than be in harmony with the will of our Divine Master, without expecting to comprehend it very fully, and we *must* leave all the results with Him. What looks to us like failure on the seen side, is often, on the unseen side, the most glorious success; and if we allow ourselves to lament and worry, we shall often be doing the foolish and useless thing of weeping where we ought to be singing and rejoicing.

Far better is it to refuse utterly to indulge in any self-reflective acts at all; to refuse, in fact, to think about self in any way, whether for good or evil. We are not our own property, nor our own business. We belong to God, and are His instruments and His business; and since He always attends to His own business, He will of course attend to us.

I heard once of a slave who was on board a vessel in a violent storm, and who was whistling contentedly while everyone else was in an agony of terror. At last someone asked him if he was not afraid he would be drowned. He replied with a broad grin, "Well, missus, s'pose I is. I don't b'long to myself, and it will only be massa's loss any how."

Something of this spirit would deliver us from many of our perplexities and sufferings in service. And with a band of servants thus abandoned to our Master's use and to His care, what might He not accomplish? Truly one such would "chase a thousand, and two would put ten thousand to flight"; and nothing would be impossible to them. For it is nothing with the Lord "to help, whether with many or with them that have no power."

May God raise up such an army speedily!

And may you, my dear reader enroll your name in this army today and, yielding yourself unto God as one who is alive from the dead, may every one of your members be also yielded unto Him as instruments of righteousness, to be used by Him as He pleases.

11. Difficulties Concerning Guidance

You have now begun, dear reader, the life of faith. You have given yourself to the Lord to be His wholly and altogether, and He has taken you and has begun to mold and fashion you into a vessel unto His honor. Your one most earnest desire is to be very pliable in His hands, and to follow Him whithersoever He may lead you, and you are trusting Him to work in you to will and to do of His good pleasure. But you find a great difficulty here. You have not learned yet to know the voice of the Good Shepherd, and are therefore in great doubt and perplexity as to what really is His will concerning you.

Perhaps there are certain paths into which God seems to be calling you, of which your friends utterly disapprove. And these friends, it may be, are older than yourself in the Christian life, and seem to you also to be much further advanced. You can scarcely bear to differ from them or distress them; and you feel also very diffident of yielding to any seeming impressions of duty of which they do not approve. And yet you cannot get rid of these impressions, and you are plunged into great doubt and uneasiness.

There is a way out of all these difficulties, to the fully surrendered soul. I would repeat, *fully* surrendered, because if there is any reserve of will upon any point, it becomes almost impossible to find out the mind of God in reference to that point; and therefore the first thing is to be sure that you really do *purpose* to obey the Lord in every respect. If however this is the case, and your soul only needs to know the will of God in order to consent to it, then you surely cannot doubt His willingness to make His will known, and to guide you in the right paths. There are many very clear promises in reference to this. Take, for instance, John 10:3, 4: "He calleth His own sheep by name, and leadeth them out. And when He putteth forth His own sheep He goeth before them, and the sheep follow Him, for they know His voice." Or, John 14:26: "But the Comforter, which is the Holy Ghost, whom the Father will send in my name, He shall teach you all things, and bring all things to your remembrance, whatsoever I have said unto you." Or, James 1:5, 6: "If any of you lack wisdom, let Him ask of God, that giveth to all men liberally, and upbraideth not; and it shall be given him." With such passages as these, and many more like them, we must believe that Divine guidance is promised to us, and our faith must confidently look for and expect it. This is essential; for in James 1:6, 7, we are told, "Let him ask in faith nothing wavering. For he that wavereth is like a wave of the sea, driven with the wind and tossed. For let not such a man think that he shall receive anything of the Lord."

Settle this point then first of all, that Divine guidance has been promised, and that you are sure to have it, if you ask for it; and let no suggestion of doubt turn you from this.

Next, you must remember that our God has all knowledge and all wisdom, and that therefore it is very possible He may guide you into paths wherein *He* knows great blessings are awaiting you, but which to the short-sighted human eyes around you seem sure to result in confusion and loss. You must recognize the fact that God's thoughts are not as man's thoughts, nor His ways as man's ways; and that He who knows the end of things from the beginning, alone can judge of what the results of any course of action may be. You must therefore realize that His very love for you may perhaps lead you to run counter to the loving wishes of even your dearest friends. You must learn from Luke 14:26-33, and similar passages, that in order, not to be saved only, but to be a disciple or follower of your Lord, you may perhaps be called upon to forsake all that you have, and to turn your backs on even father or mother, or brother or sister, or husband or wife, or it may be your own life also. Unless the possibility of this is clearly recognized, the soul would be very likely to get into difficulty, because it often happens that the child of God who enters upon this life of obedience is sooner or later led into paths which meet with the disapproval of those he best loves; and unless he is prepared for this, and can trust the Lord through it all, he will scarcely know what to do.

All this, it will of course be understood, is perfectly in harmony with those duties of honor and love which we owe to one another in the various relations of life. The nearer we are to Christ, the more shall we be enabled to exemplify the meekness and gentleness of our Lord, and the more tender will be our consideration for those who are our natural guardians and counsellors. The Master's guidance will always manifest itself by the Master's Spirit, and where, in obedience to Him, we are led to act contrary to the advice or wishes of our friends, we shall prove that this is our motive, by the love and patience which will mark our conduct.

But this point having been settled, we come now to the question as to how God's guidance is to come to us, and how we shall be able to know His voice.

There are four especial ways in which God speaks: by the voice of Scripture, the voice of the inward impressions of the Holy Spirit, the voice of our own higher judgment, and the voice of providential circumstances.

Where these four harmonize, it is safe to say that God speaks. For I lay it down as a foundation principle, which no one can gainsay, that of course His voice will always be in harmony with itself, no matter in how many different ways He may speak. The voices may be many, the message can be but one. If God tells me in one voice to do or to leave undone anything, He cannot possibly tell me the opposite in another voice. If there is a contradiction in the voices, the speaker cannot be the same. Therefore, my rule for distinguishing the voice of God would be to bring it to the test of this harmony.

If I have an impression, therefore, I must see if it is in accordance with Scripture, and whether it commends itself to my own higher judgment, and also whether, as we Quakers say, "way opens" for its carrying out. If either one of these tests fail, it is not safe to proceed; but I must wait in quiet trust until the Lord shows me the point of harmony, which He surely will, sooner or later, if it is His voice that has spoken.

For we must not overlook the fact that there are other voices that speak to the soul. There is the loud and clamoring voice of self, that is always seeking to be heard. And there are the voices, too, of evil and deceiving spirits, who lie in wait to entrap every traveler entering these higher regions of the spiritual life. In the same epistle which tells us that we are seated in "heavenly places in Christ" (Eph. 2:6), we are also told that we shall have to fight there with spiritual enemies (Eph. 6:12). These spiritual enemies, whoever or whatever they may be, must necessarily communicate with us by means of our spiritual faculties, and their voices, therefore, will be, as the voice of God is, an inward impression made upon our spirits.

Therefore, just as the Holy Spirit may tell us, by impressions, what is the will of God concerning us, so also will these spiritual enemies tell us, by impressions, what is their will concerning us, though not of course giving it their name. It is very plain, therefore, that we must have some test or standard by which to try these inward impressions, in order that we may know whose voice it is that is speaking. And that test will always be the harmony to which I have referred. Sometimes, under a mistaken idea of exalting the Divine Spirit, earnest and honest Christians have ignored and even violated the teachings of Scripture, have disregarded the plain pointings of Providence, and have outraged their own higher judgment. God, who sees the sincerity of their hearts, can and does pity and forgive, but the consequences as to this life are often very sad.

Our first test, therefore, of the Divine authority of any voice which may seem to speak to us, must be its harmony in moral character with the mind and will of God, as revealed to us in the Gospel of Christ. Whatever is contrary to this, cannot be Divine, because God cannot contradict Himself.

Until we have found and obeyed God's will in reference to any subject, as it is revealed in the Bible, we cannot expect a separate direct personal revelation. A great many fatal mistakes are made in this matter of guidance, by the overlooking of this simple rule. Where our Father has written out for us plain directions about anything, He will not, of course, make an especial revelation to us concerning it. No man, for instance, needs or could expect any direct revelation to tell him not to steal, because God has already in the Scriptures plainly declared His will about it. This seems such an obvious thing that I would not speak of it, but that I have frequently met with Christians who have altogether overlooked it, and have gone off into fanaticism as the result. For the Scriptures are far more explicit even about details than most people think. And there are not many important affairs in life for which a clear direction may not be found in God's book. Take the matter of dress, and we have 1 Pet. 3:3, 4, and 1 Tim. 2:9, 10. Take the matter of conversation, and we have Eph. 4:29, and 5:4. Take the matter of avenging injuries and standing up for your rights, and we have Rom. 12:19, 20, 21, and Matt. 5:38-48, and 1 Pet. 2:19-21. Take the matter of forgiving one another, and we have Eph. 4:32 and Mark 11:25, 26. Take the matter of conformity to the world, and we have Rom. 12:2, and 1 John 2:15-17, and James 4:4. Take the matter of anxieties of all kind, and we have Matt. 6:25-34, and Phil. 4:6, 7.

I only give these as examples to show how very full and practical the Bible guidance is. If, therefore, you find yourself in perplexity, first of all search and see whether the Bible speaks on the point in question, asking God to make plain to you by the power of His Spirit, through the Scripture, what is His mind. And whatever shall seem to you to be plainly taught there, that you must obey.

When we read and meditate upon this record of God's mind and will, with our understandings thus illuminated by the inspiring Spirit, our obedience will be as truly an obedience to a present, living word, as though it were afresh spoken to us today by our Lord from Heaven. The Bible is not only an ancient message from God sent to us many ages ago, but it is a present message sent to us now each time we read it. "The words that I speak unto you, they are spirit, and they are life," and obedience to these words now is a living obedience to a present and personal command.

But it is essential in this connection to remember that the Bible is a book of principles, and not a book of disjointed aphorisms. Isolated texts may often be made to sanction things, to which the principles of Scripture are totally opposed. I heard not long ago of a Christian woman in a Western meeting, who, having had the text, "For we walk by faith, and not by sight," brought very vividly before her mind, felt a strong impression that it was a command to be literally obeyed in the outward; and, blindfolding her eyes, insisted on walking up and down the aisle of the meeting-house, as an illustration of the walk of faith. She very soon stumbled and fell against the stove, burning herself seriously, and then wondered at the mysterious dispensation. The *principles* of Scripture, and her own sanctified common-sense, if applied to this case, would have saved her from the delusion.

The second test, therefore, to which our impressions must be brought, is that of our own higher judgment, or common-sense.

It is as true now as in the days when Solomon wrote, that a "man of *understanding* shall attain unto wise counsels"; and his exhortation still continues binding upon us: "Wisdom is the principal thing, therefore get wisdom; and with all thy getting, get *understanding*."

As far as I can see, the Scriptures everywhere make it an essential thing for the children of God to use all the faculties which have been given them, in their journey through this world. They are to use their outward faculties for their outward walk, and their inward faculties for their inward walk. And they might as well expect to be "kept" from dashing their feet against a stone in the outward, if they walk blindfold, as to be "kept" from spiritual stumbling, if they put aside their judgment and common-sense in their interior life.

I asked a Christian of "sound mind" lately how she distinguished between the voice of false spirits and the guidance of the Holy Spirit, and she replied promptly, "I rap them over the head, and see if they have any common-sense."

Some, however, may say here, "But I thought we were not to depend on our human understanding in Divine things." I answer to this, that we are not to depend on our unenlightened human understanding, but upon our human judgment and common-sense, enlightened by the Spirit of God. That is, God will speak to us through the faculties He has Himself given us, and not independently of them. That is, just as we are to use our eyes when we walk, no matter how full of faith we may be, so also we are to use our mental faculties in our inward life.

The third and last test to which our impressions must be brought is that of providential circumstances. If a "leading" is of God, the way will always open for it. Our Lord assures us of this when He says in John 10:4, "And when He putteth forth His own sheep *He goeth before them*, and the sheep *follow* Him, for they know his voice." Notice here the expression "goeth before," and "follow." He goes before to open a way, and we are to follow in the way thus opened. It is never a sign of a Divine leading when the Christian insists on opening his own way, and riding rough-shod over all opposing things. If the Lord "goes before" us, He will open all doors for us, and we shall not need ourselves to hammer them down.

The fourth point I would make is this: that, just as our impressions must be tested, as I have shown, by the other three voices, so must these other voices be tested by our inward impressions; and if we feel a "stop in our minds" about anything, we must wait until that is removed before acting. A Christian who had advanced with unusual rapidity in the Divine life, gave me as her secret this simple receipt: "I always mind the checks." We must not ignore the voice of our inward impressions, nor ride rough-shod over them, any more than we must the other three voices of which I have spoken.

These four voices, then, will always be found to agree in any truly Divine leading, i.e., the voice of our impressions, the voice of Scripture, the voice of our own sanctified judgment, and the voice of providential circumstances; and where these four do not all agree at first, we must wait until they do.

A divine sense of "oughtness," derived from the harmony of all God's various voices, is the only safe foundation for any action.

And now I have guarded the points of danger, do permit me to let myself out for a little to the blessedness and joy of this direct communication of God's will to us. It seems to me to be the grandest of privileges. In the first place, that God should love me enough to care about the details of my life is perfectly wonderful. And then that He should be willing to tell me all about it, and to let me know just now to live and walk so as to perfectly please Him, seems almost too good to be true. We never care about the little details of people's lives unless we love them. It is a matter of indifference to us with the majority of people we meet, as to what they do or how they spend their time; but as soon as we begin to love any one, we begin at once to care. That God cares, therefore, is just a precious proof of His love; and it is most blessed to have Him speak to us about everything in our lives, about our duties, about our pleasures, about our friendships, about our occupations, about all that we do, or think, or say. You must know this in your own experience, dear reader, if you would come into the full joy and privilege of this life hid with Christ in God, for it is one of its most precious gifts!

God's promise is, that He will work in us to *will* as well as to do of His good pleasure. This, of course, means that He will take possession of our will, and work it for us, and that His suggestions will come to us, not so much commands from the outside, as desires springing up within. They will originate in our will; we shall feel as though we *wanted* to do so and so, not as though we *must*. And this makes it a service of perfect liberty; for it is always easy to do what we desire to do, let the accompanying circumstances be as difficult as they may. Every mother knows that she could secure perfect and easy obedience in her child, if she could only get into that child's will and work it for him, making him want himself to do the things she willed he should. And this is what our Father does for His children in the new dispensation; He writes His laws on our hearts and on our minds, and we love them, and are drawn to our obedience by our affections and judgment, not driven by our fears.

The way in which the Holy Spirit, therefore, usually works in His direct guidance is to impress upon the mind a wish or desire to do or leave undone certain things.

The soul when engaged, perhaps, in prayer, feels a sudden suggestion made to its inmost consciousness in reference to a certain point of duty. "I would like to do this or the other," it thinks, "I wish I could." Or perhaps the suggestion may come as question, "I wonder whether I had not better do so and so?" Or it may be only at first in the way of a conviction that such is the right and best thing to be done.

At once the matter should be committed to the Lord, with an instant consent of the will to obey Him; and if the suggestion is in accordance with the Scriptures, and a sanctified judgment, and with Providential circumstances, an immediate obedience is the safest and easiest course. At the moment when the Spirit speaks, it is always easy to obey; if the soul hesitates and begins to reason, it becomes more and more difficult continually. As a general rule, the first convictions are the right ones in a fully surrendered heart; for God is faithful in His dealings with us, and will cause His voice to be heard before any other voices. Such convictions, therefore, should never be met by reasoning. Prayer and trust are the only safe attitudes of the soul; and even these should be but momentary, as it were, lest the time for action should pass and the blessing be missed.

If, however, the suggestion does not seem quite clear enough to act upon, and doubt and perplexity ensue, especially if it is something about which one's friends hold a different opinion, then we shall need to wait for further light. The Scripture rule is, "Whatsoever is not of faith is sin"; which means plainly that we must never act in doubt. A clear conviction of right is the only safe guide. But we must wait in faith, and in an attitude of entire surrender, saying, "Yes," continually to the will of our Lord, whatever it may be. I believe the lack of a will thus surrendered lies at the root of many of our difficulties; and next to this lies the want of faith in any real Divine guidance. God's children are amazingly skeptical here. They read the promises and they feel the need, but somehow they cannot seem to believe the guidance will be given to them; as if God should want us to obey His voice, but did not know how to make us hear and understand Him. It is, therefore, very possible for God to speak, but for the soul not to hear, because it does not believe He is speaking. No earthly parent or master could possibly guide his children or servants, if they should refuse to believe he was speaking, and should not accept his voice as being really the expression of his will.

> *God, who at sundry times and in manners many,*
>   *Spake to the fathers and is speaking still,*
> *Eager to see if ever or if any*
>   *Souls will obey and hearken to His will.*

Every moment of our lives our Father is seeking to reveal Himself to us. "I that speak unto thee am He. I that speak in thy heart, I that speak in thy outward circumstances, I that speak in thy losses, I that speak in thy gains, I that speak in thy sorrows or in thy joys, I that speak everywhere and in everything, *I am He.*"

We must, therefore, have perfect confidence that the Lord's voice is speaking to us to teach and lead us, and that He will give us the wisdom needed for our right guidance; and when we have asked for light, we must accept our strongest conviction of "oughtness" as being the guidance we have sought.

A few rules will help us here.

    I.   We must believe that God will guide us.
    II.   We must surrender our own will to His guidance.
    III.   We must hearken for the Divine voice.
    IV.   We must wait for the divine harmony.
    V.   When we are sure of the guidance, we must obey without question.

> *God only is the creature's home;*
>   *Though rough and strait the rod,*
> *Yet nothing less can satisfy*
>   *The love that longs, for God.*
>
> *How little of that road, my soul!*
>   *How little hast thou gone!*
> *Take heart, and let the thought of God*
>   *Allure thee further on.*
>
> *The perfect way is hard to flesh;*
>   *It is not hard to love;*
> *If thou wert sick for want of God,*
>   *How swiftly wouldst thou move.*

Dole not thy duties out to God,
  But let thy hand be free;
Look long at Jesus, His sweet love,
  How was it dealt to thee?

And only this perfection needs
  A heart kept calm all day,
To catch the words the Spirit there,
  From hour to hour may say.

Then keep thy conscience sensitive,
  No inward token miss:
And go where grace entices thee—
  Perfection lies in this.

Be docile to thine unseen Guide,
  Love Him as He loves thee;
Time and obedience are enough,
  And thou a saint shalt be.

12. Concerning Temptation

Certain very great mistakes are made concerning this matter of temptation, in the practical working out of this life of faith.

First of all, people seem to expect that, after the soul has entered into its rest in God, temptations will cease; and to think that the promised deliverance is not only to be from yielding to temptation, but even also from being tempted. Consequently, when they find the Canaanite still in the land, and see the cities great and walled up to Heaven, they are utterly discouraged, and think they must have gone wrong in some way, and that this cannot be the true land after all.

Then, next they make the mistake of looking upon temptation as sin, and of blaming themselves for what in reality is the fault of the enemy only. This brings them into condemnation and discouragement; and discouragement, if continued in, always ends at last in actual sin. The enemy makes an easy prey of a discouraged soul; so that we fall often from the very fear of having fallen.

To meet the first of these difficulties it is only necessary to refer to the Scripture declarations, that the Christian life is to be throughout a warfare; and that, especially when seated in heavenly places in Christ Jesus, we are to wrestle against spiritual enemies there, whose power and skill to tempt us must doubtless be far superior to any we have ever heretofore encountered. As a fact, temptations generally increase in strength tenfold after we have entered into the interior life, rather than decrease; and no amount or sort of them must ever for a moment lead us to suppose we have not really found the true abiding place. Strong temptations are generally a sign of great grace, rather than of little grace. When the children of Israel had first left Egypt, the Lord did not lead them through the country of the Philistines, although that was the nearest way; for God said, "lest peradventure the people repent when they see war, and they return to Egypt." But afterwards, when they learned better how to trust Him, He permitted their enemies to attack them. Then also in their wilderness journey they met with but few enemies and fought but few battles, compared to those in the land, where they found seven great nations and thirty-one kings to be conquered, besides walled cities to be taken, and giants to be overcome.

They could not have fought with the Canaanites, or the Hittites, and the Amorites, and the Perizzites, and the Hivites, and the Jebusites, until they had gone into the land where these enemies were. And the very power of your temptations, dear Christian, therefore, may perhaps be one of the strongest proofs that you really are in the land you have been seeking to enter, because they are temptations peculiar to that land. You must never allow your temptations to cause you to question the fact of your having entered the promised "heavenly places."

The second mistake is not quite so easy to deal with. It seems hardly worth while to say that temptation is not sin, and yet most of the distress about it arises from not understanding this fact. The very suggestion of wrong seems to bring pollution with it, and the evil agency not being recognized, the poor tempted soul begins to feel as if it must be very bad indeed, and very far off from God to have had such thoughts and suggestions. It is as though a burglar should break into a man's house to steal, and, when the master of the house began to resist him and to drive him out, should turn round and accuse the owner of being himself the thief. It is the enemy's grand ruse for entrapping us. He comes and whispers suggestions of evil to us, doubts, blasphemies, jealousies, envyings, and pride; and then turns round and says, "Oh, how wicked you must be to think of such things! It is very plain that you are not trusting the Lord; for if you were, it would have been impossible for these things to have entered your heart." This reasoning sounds so very plausible that the soul often accepts it as true, and at once comes under condemnation, and is filled with discouragement; then it is easy for it to be led on into actual sin. One of the most fatal things in the life of faith is discouragement. One of the most helpful is cheerfulness. A very wise man once said that in overcoming temptations, cheerfulness was the first thing, cheerfulness the second, and cheerfulness the third. We must *expect* to conquer. That is why the Lord said so often to Joshua, "Be strong and of a good courage"; "Be not afraid, neither be thou dismayed"; "Only be thou strong and very courageous." And it is also the reason He says to us, "Let not your heart he troubled neither let it be afraid." The power of temptation is in the fainting of our own hearts. The enemy knows this well, and always begins his assaults by discouraging us, if it can in any way be accomplished.

Sometimes this discouragement arises from what we think is a righteous grief and disgust at ourselves that such things *could* be any temptation to us; but which is really a mortification arising from the fact that we have been indulging in a secret self-congratulation that our tastes were too pure, or our separation from the world was too complete for such things to tempt us. We have expected something from ourselves, and have been sorely disappointed not to find that something there, and are discouraged in consequence. This mortification and discouragement are really a far worse condition than the temptation itself, though they present an appearance of true humility, for they are nothing but the results of wounded self-love. True humility can bear to see its own utter weakness and foolishness revealed, because it never expected anything from itself, and knows that its only hope and expectation must be in God. Therefore, instead of discouraging the soul from trusting, it drives it to a deeper and more utter trust. But the counterfeit humility which springs from self, plunges the soul into the depths of a faithless discouragement, and drives it into the very sin at which it is so distressed.

I remember once hearing an allegory that illustrated this to me wonderfully. Satan called together a council of his servants to consult how they might make a good man sin. One evil spirit started up and said, "I will make him sin." "How will you do it?" asked Satan. "I will set before him the pleasures of sin," was the reply; "I will tell him of its delights and the rich rewards it brings." "Ah," said Satan, "that will not do; he has tried, it, and knows better than that." Then another spirit started up and said, "I will make him sin." "What will you do?" asked Satan. "I will tell him of the pains and sorrows of virtue. I will show him that virtue has no delights, and brings no rewards." "Ah, no!" exclaimed Satan, "that will not do at all; for he has tried it, and knows that 'wisdom's ways are ways of pleasantness and all her paths are peace.'" "Well," said another imp, starting up, "I will undertake to make him sin." "And what will you do?" asked Satan, again. "I will discourage his soul," was the short reply. "Ah, that will do," cried Satan,—"that will do! We shall conquer him now." And they did.

An old writer says, "All discouragement is from the devil"; and I wish every Christian would just take this as a pocket-piece, and never forget it. We must fly from discouragement as we would from sin.

But this is impossible if we fail to recognize the true agency in temptation. For if the temptations are our own fault, we cannot help being discouraged. But they are not. The Bible says, "Blessed is the man that endureth temptation"; and we are exhorted to "count it all joy when we fall into divers temptations." Temptation, therefore, cannot be sin; and the truth is, it is no more a sin to hear these whispers and suggestions of evil in our souls, than it is for us to hear the swearing or wicked talk of bad men as we pass along the street. The sin only comes in either case by our stopping and joining in with them. If, when the wicked suggestions come, we turn from them at once, as we would from wicked talk, and pay no more attention to them, we do not sin. But if we carry them on in our minds, and roll them under our tongues, and dwell on them with a half-consent of our will to them as true, then we sin. We may be enticed by evil a thousand times a day without sin, and we cannot help these enticings. But if the enemy can succeed in making us think that *his* enticings are *our* sin, he has accomplished half the battle, and can hardly fail to gain a complete victory.

A dear lady once came to me under great darkness, simply from not understanding this. She had been living very happily in the life of faith for some time, and had been so free from temptation as almost to begin to think she would never be tempted any more. But suddenly a very peculiar form of temptation had assailed her, which had horrified her. She found that the moment she began to pray, dreadful thoughts of all kinds would rush into her mind. She had lived a very sheltered, innocent life, and these thoughts seemed so awful to her, that she felt she must be one of the most wicked of sinners to be capable of having them. She began by thinking she could not possibly have entered into the rest of faith, and ended by concluding that she had never even been born again. Her soul was in an agony of distress. I told her that these dreadful thoughts were altogether the suggestions of the enemy, who came to her the moment she kneeled in prayer, and poured them into her mind, and that she herself was not to blame for them at all; that she could not help them any more than she could help hearing if a wicked man should pour out his blasphemies in her presence. And I urged her to recognize and treat them as from the enemy; not to blame herself or be discouraged, but to turn at once to Jesus and commit them to Him. I showed her how great an advantage the enemy had gained by making her think these thoughts were originated by herself, and plunging her into condemnation and discouragement on account of them. And I assured her she would find a speedy victory if she would pay no attention to them; but, ignoring their presence, would simply turn her back on them and look to the Lord.

She grasped the truth, and the next time these thoughts came she said to the enemy, "I have found you out now. It is you who are suggesting these dreadful thoughts to me, and I hate them, and will have nothing to do with them. The Lord is my Savior; take them to Him, and settle them in His presence." Immediately the baffled enemy, finding himself discovered, fled in confusion, and her soul was perfectly delivered.

Another thing also. The enemy knows that if a Christian recognizes a suggestion of evil as coming from him, he will recoil from it far more quickly than if it seems to be the suggestion of his own mind. If Satan prefaced each temptation with the words, "I am Satan, your relentless enemy; I have come to make you sin," I suppose we would hardly feel any desire at all to yield to his suggestions. He has to hide himself in order to make his baits attractive. And our victory will be far more easily gained if we are not ignorant of his devices, but recognize him at his very first approach.

We also make another great mistake about temptations in thinking that all time spent in combating them is lost. Hours pass, and we seem to have made no progress, because we have been so beset with temptations. But it often happens that we have been serving God far more truly during these hours, than in our times of comparative freedom from temptation. Temptation is really more the devil's wrath against God, than against us. He cannot touch our Savior, but he can wound our Savior by conquering us, and our ruin is important to him only as it accomplishes this. We are, therefore, really fighting our Lord's battles when we are fighting temptation, and hours are often worth days to us under these circumstances. We read, "Blessed is the man that *endureth* temptation"; and I am sure this means enduring the continuance of it and its frequent recurrence. Nothing so cultivates the grace of patience as the endurance of temptation, and nothing so drives the soul to an utter dependence upon the Lord Jesus as its continuance. And finally, nothing brings more praise and honor and glory to our dearest Lord Himself, than the trial of our faith which comes through manifold temptations. We are told that it is more precious than gold, though it be tried with fire, and that we, who patiently endure the trial, shall receive for our reward "the crown of life which the Lord hath promised to them that love Him."

We cannot wonder, therefore, any longer at the exhortation with which the Holy Ghost opens the Book of James: "Count it all joy when ye fall into divers temptations, knowing this, that the trying of your faith worketh patience. But let patience have her perfect work, that ye may be perfect and entire, wanting nothing."

Temptation is plainly to be the blessed instrument used by God to complete our perfection, and thus the enemy's own weapons are turned against himself, and we see how it is that all things, even temptations, can work together for good to them that love God.

As to the way of victory over temptations, it seems hardly necessary to say to those whom I am at this time especially addressing, that it is to be by faith. For this is, of course, the foundation upon which the whole interior life rests. Our one great motto is throughout, "We are nothing, Christ is all." And always and everywhere we have started out to stand, and walk, and overcome, and live by faith. We have discovered our own utter helplessness, and know that we cannot do anything for ourselves. Our only way, therefore, is to hand the temptation over to our Lord, and trust Him to conquer it for us. But when we put it into His hands we must *leave* it there. It must be as real a committing of ourselves to Him for victory, as it was at first a committing of ourselves to Him for salvation. He must do all for us in the one case, as completely as in the other. It was faith only then, and it must be faith only now.

And the victories which the Lord works in conquering the temptations of those who thus trust Him are nothing short of miracles, as thousands can testify.

But into this part of the subject I cannot go at present, as my object has been rather to present temptation in its true light, than to develop the way of victory over it. I want to deliver conscientious, faithful souls from the bondage into which they are sure to be brought, if they fail to understand the true nature and use of temptation, and confound it with sin. I want that they should not be ignorant of the fact that temptations are, after all, an invaluable part of our soul's development; and that, whatever may be their original source, they are used by God to work out in us many blessed graces of character which would otherwise be lacking. Wherever temptation is, there is God also, superintending and controlling its power. "Where wert thou, Lord I while I was being tempted?" cried the saint of the desert. "Close beside thee, my son, all the while," was the tender reply.

Temptations try us; and we are worth nothing if we are not tried. They develop our spiritual strength and courage and knowledge; and our development is the one thing God cries for. How shallow would all our spirituality be if it were not for temptations. "Blessed is the man that endureth temptation: for when he is tried he shall receive the crown of life, which the Lord hath promised to them that love Him." This "crown of life" will be worth all that it has cost of trial and endurance to obtain it; and without these it could not be attained.

An invalid lady procured once the cocoon of a very beautiful butterfly with unusually magnificent wings hoping to have the pleasure of seeing it emerge from its cocoon in her sick-chamber. She watched it eagerly as spring drew on, and finally was delighted to see the butterfly beginning to emerge. But it seemed to have great difficulty. It pushed, and strained, and struggled, and seemed to make so little headway, that she concluded it must need some help, and with a pair of delicate scissors she finally clipped the tight cord that seemed to bind in the opening of the cocoon. Immediately the cocoon opened wide, and the butterfly escaped without any further struggle. She congratulated herself on the success of her experiment, but found in a moment that something was the matter with the butterfly. It was all out of the cocoon it is true, but its great wings were lifeless and colorless, and dragged after it as a useless burden. For a few days it lived a miserable sickly life, and then died, without having once lifted its powerless wings. The lady was sorely disappointed and could not understand it. But when she related the circumstance to a naturalist, he told her that it had all been her own fault. That it required just that pushing and struggling to send the life fluid into the veins of the wings, and that her mistaken kindness in shortening the struggle, had left the wings lifeless and colorless.

Just so do our spiritual wings need the struggle and effort of our conflict with temptation and trial; and to grant us an escape from it would be to weaken the power of our soul to "mount up with wings as eagles," and would deprive us of the "crown of life" which is promised to those who endure.

13. Failures

The very title of this chapter may perhaps startle some. "Failures," they will say; "we thought there were no failures in this life of faith!"

To this I would answer that there ought not to be, and need not be; but, as a fact, there sometimes are. And we have got to deal with facts, and not with theories. No teacher of this interior life ever says that it becomes impossible to sin; they only insist that sin ceases to be a necessity, and that a possibility of uniform victory is opened before us. And there are very few who do not confess that, as to their own actual experience, they have at times been overcome by momentary temptation.

Of course, in speaking of sin here, I mean conscious, known sin. I do not touch on the subject of sins of ignorance, or what is called the inevitable sin of our nature, which are all covered by the atonement, and do not disturb our fellowship with God. I have no desire nor ability to treat of the *doctrines* concerning sin; these I will leave with the theologians to discuss and settle, while I speak only of the believer's experience in the matter. And I wish it to be fully understood that in all I shall say, I have reference simply to that which comes within the range of our consciousness.

Misunderstanding, then, on this point of known or conscious sin, opens the way for great dangers in the higher Christian life. When a believer, who has, as he trusts, entered upon the highway of holiness, finds himself surprised into sin, he is tempted either to be utterly discouraged, and to give everything up as lost; or else, in order to preserve the doctrine untouched, he feels it necessary to cover his sin up, calling it infirmity, and refusing to be honest and above-board about it. Either of these courses is equally fatal to any real growth and progress in the life of holiness. The only way is to face the sad fact at once, call the thing by its right name, and discover, if possible, the reason and the remedy. This life of union with God requires the utmost honesty with Him and with ourselves. The communion which the sin itself would only momentarily disturb, is sure to be lost by any dishonest dealing with it. A sudden failure is no reason for being discouraged and giving up all as lost. Neither is the integrity of our doctrine touched by it. We are not preaching a *state*, but a *walk*. The highway of holiness is not a place, but a way. Sanctification is not a thing to be picked up at a certain stage of our experience, and forever after possessed, but it is a life to be lived day by day, and hour by hour. We may for a moment turn aside from a path, but the path is not obliterated by our wandering, and can be instantly regained. And in this life and walk of faith, there may be momentary failures, which, although very sad and greatly to be deplored, need not, if rightly met, disturb the attitude of the soul as to entire consecration and perfect trust, nor interrupt, for more than the passing moment, its happy communion with its Lord.

The great point is an instant return to God. Our sin is no reason for ceasing to trust, but only an unanswerable argument why we must trust more fully than ever. From whatever cause we have been betrayed into failure, it is very certain that there is no remedy to be found for it in discouragement. As well might a child who is learning to walk, lie down in despair when he has fallen, and refuse to take another step; as a believer, who is seeking to learn how to live and walk by faith, give up in despair because of having fallen into sin. The only way in both cases is to get right up and try again. When the children of Israel had met with that disastrous defeat, soon after their entrance into the land, before the little city of Ai, they were all so utterly discouraged that we read:

"Wherefore the hearts of the people melted, and became as water. And Joshua rent his clothes, and fell to the earth upon his face before the ark of the Lord until the eventide, he and the elders of Israel, and put dust upon their heads. And Joshua said, Alas! O Lord God, wherefore hast Thou at all brought this people over Jordan to deliver us into the hands of the Amorites to destroy us? Would to God we had been content, and dwelt on the other side Jordan! O Lord, what shall I say, when Israel turneth their backs before their enemies? For the Canaanites and all the inhabitants of the land shall hear of it, and shall environ us round and cut off our name from the earth: and what wilt Thou do unto Thy great name?"

What a wail of despair this was! And how exactly it is repeated by many a child of God in the present day, whose heart, because of a defeat, melts and becomes as water, and who cries out, "Would to God we had been content and dwelt on the other side Jordan!" and predicts for itself further failures and even utter discomfiture before its enemies. No doubt Joshua thought then, as we are apt to think now, that discouragement and despair were the only proper and safe condition after such a failure. But God thought otherwise. "And the Lord said unto Joshua, Get thee up; wherefore liest thou upon thy face?"

The proper thing to do was not to abandon themselves thus to utter discouragement, humble as it might look, but at once to face the evil and get rid of it, and afresh and immediately to "sanctify themselves." "Up, sanctify the people," is always God's command. "Lie down and be discouraged," is always the enemy's temptation. Our feeling is that it is presumptuous, and even almost impertinent, to go at once to the Lord, after having sinned against Him. It seems as if we ought to suffer the consequences our sin first for a little while, and endure the accusings of our conscience. And we can hardly believe that the Lord can be willing at once to receive us back into loving fellowship with Himself.

A little girl once expressed the feeling to me, with a child's outspoken candor. She had asked whether the Lord Jesus always forgave us for our sins as soon as we asked Him, and I had said, "Yes, of course He does." "*Just* as soon" she repeated, doubtingly. "Yes," I replied, "the very minute we ask, He forgives us." "Well," she said deliberately, "I cannot believe that. I should think He would make us feel sorry for two or three days first. And then I should think He would make us ask Him a great many times, and in a very pretty way too, not just in common talk. And I believe that *is* the way He does, and you need not try to make me think He forgives me right at once, no matter what the Bible says." She only *said* what most Christians *think*, and, what is worse, what most Christians act on, making their discouragement and their very remorse separate them infinitely further off from God than their sin would have done. Yet it is so totally contrary to the way we like our children to act towards us, that I wonder how we ever could have conceived such an idea of God. How a mother grieves when a naughty child goes off alone in despairing remorse, and doubts her willingness to forgive; and how, on the other hand, her whole heart goes out in welcoming love to the darling who runs to her at once and begs her forgiveness! Surely our God knew this yearning love when He said to us, "Return, ye backsliding children, and I will heal your backslidings."

The fact is, that the same moment which brings the consciousness of having sinned, ought to bring also the consciousness of being forgiven. This is especially essential to an unwavering walk in the highway of holiness, for no separation from God can be tolerated here for an instant.

We can only walk in this path by looking continually unto Jesus, moment by moment; and if our eyes are taken off of Him to look upon our own sin and our own weakness, we shall leave the path at once. The believer, therefore, who has, as he trusts, entered upon this highway, if he finds himself overcome by sin, must flee with it instantly to the Lord. He must act on 1 John 1:9: "If we confess our sins, He is faithful and just to forgive us our sins, and to cleanse us from all unrighteousness." He must not hide his sin and seek to salve it over with excuses, or to push it out of his memory by the lapse of time. But he must do as the children of Israel did, rise up "*early* in the morning," and "*run*" to the place where the evil thing is hidden, and take it out of its hiding-place, and lay it "out before the Lord." He must confess his sin. And then he must stone it with stones, and burn it with fire, and utterly put it away from him, and raise over it a great heap of stones, that it may be forever hidden from his sight. And he must believe, then and there, that God *is*, according to His word, faithful and just to forgive him his sin, and that He does do it; and further, that He also cleanses him from all unrighteousness. He must claim an immediate forgiveness and an immediate cleansing by faith, and must go on trusting harder and more absolutely than ever.

As soon as Israel's sin had been brought to light and put away, at once God's word came again in a message of glorious encouragement, "Fear not, neither be thou dismayed... See, I have given into thy hand the king of Ai, and his people, and his city, and his land." Our courage must rise higher than ever, and we must abandon ourselves more completely to the Lord, that His mighty power may the more perfectly work in us all the good pleasure of His will. Moreover, we must forget our sin as soon as it is thus confessed and forgiven. We must not dwell on it, and examine it, and indulge in a luxury of distress and remorse. We must not put it on a pedestal, and then walk around it and view it on every side, and so magnify it into a mountain that hides our God from our eyes. We must follow the example of Paul, and "forgetting those things which are behind, and reaching forth unto those things which are before," we must "press toward the mark for the prize of the high calling of God in Christ Jesus."

I would like to bring up two contrastive illustrations of these things. One was an earnest Christian man, an active worker in the Church, who had been living for several months in the enjoyment of full salvation. He was suddenly overcome by a temptation to treat a brother unkindly. Not having supposed it possible that he could ever sin again, he was at once plunged into the deepest discouragement, and concluded he had been altogether mistaken, and had never entered into the life of full trust at all. Day by day his discouragement increased, until it became despair, and he concluded he had never even been born again, and gave himself up for lost. He spent three years of utter misery, going further and further away from God, and being gradually drawn off into one sin after another, until his life was a curse to himself and to all around him. His health failed under the terrible burden, and fears were entertained for his reason.

At the end of three years he met a Christian lady, who understood the truth about sin that I have been trying to explain. In a few moments' conversation she found out his trouble, and at once said, "You sinned in that act, there is no doubt about it, and I do not want you to try and excuse it. But have you never confessed it to the Lord and asked Him to forgive you?" "Confessed it!" he exclaimed, "why it seems to me I have done nothing but confess it, and entreat God to forgive me night and day for all these three dreadful years." "And you have never believed He did forgive you?" asked the lady. "No," said the poor man, "how could I, for I never felt as if He did?" "But suppose He had said He forgave you, would not that have done as well as for you to feel it?" "Oh, yes," replied the man, "if God said it, of course I would believe it." "Very well, He does say so," was the lady's answer, and she turned to the verse we have taken above 1 John 1:9) and read it aloud. "Now," she continued, "you have been all these three years confessing and confessing your sin, and all the while God's record has been declaring that He was faithful and just to forgive it and to cleanse you, and yet you have never once believed it. You have been 'making God a liar' all this while by refusing to believe His record."

The poor man saw the whole thing, and was dumb with amazement and consternation; and when the lady proposed they should kneel down, and that he should confess his past unbelief and sin, and should claim, then and there, a present forgiveness and a present cleansing, he obeyed like one in a maze. But the result was glorious. In a few moments the light broke in, and he burst out into praise at the wonderful deliverance. In three minutes his soul was enabled to traverse back by faith the whole long weary journey that he had been three years in making, and he found himself once more resting in Jesus, and rejoicing in the fulness of His salvation.

The other illustration was the case of a Christian lady who had been living in the land of promise about two weeks, and who had had a very bright and victorious experience. Suddenly, at the end of that time, she was overcome by a violent burst of anger. For a moment a flood of discouragement swept over her soul. The enemy said, "There, now, that shows it was all a mistake. Of course you have been deceived about the whole thing, and have never entered into the life of full trust at all. And now you may as well give up altogether, for you never can consecrate yourself any more entirely, nor trust any more fully, than you did this time; so it is very plain this life of holiness is not for you!" These thoughts flashed through her mind in a moment, but she was well taught in the ways of God, and she said at once, "Yes, I have sinned, and it is very sad. But the Bible says that if we confess our sins, God is faithful and just to forgive us our sins and to cleanse us from all unrighteousness, and I believe He will do it."

She did not delay a moment, but while still boiling over with anger, she ran, she could not walk, into a room where she could be alone, and kneeling down beside the bed, she said, "Lord, I confess my sin. I have sinned, I am even at this very moment sinning. I hate it, but I cannot get rid of it. I confess it with shame and confusion of face to Thee. And now I believe that, according to Thy word, Thou dost forgive and Thou dost cleanse." She said it out loud, for the inward turmoil was too great for it to be said inside. As the words "Thou dost forgive and Thou dost cleanse" passed her lips, the deliverance came. The Lord said, "Peace, be still," and there was a great calm. A flood of light and joy burst on her soul, the enemy fled, and she was more than conqueror through Him that loved her. The whole thing, the sin and the recovery from it, had occupied not five minutes, and her feet trod on more firmly than ever in the blessed highway of holiness. Thus the valley of Achor became to her a door of hope, and she sang afresh and with deeper meaning her song of deliverance, "I will sing unto the Lord, for He hath triumphed gloriously."

The truth is, the only remedy, after all in every emergency, is to trust in the Lord. And if this is all we ought to do, and all we can do, is it not better to do it at once? I have often been brought up short by the question, "Well, what can I do but trust?" And I have realized at once the folly of seeking for deliverance in any other way, by saying to myself, "I shall have to come to simple trusting in the end, and why not come to it at once now in the beginning?" It is a life and walk of *faith* we have entered upon, and if we fail in it our only recovery must lie in an increase of faith, not in a lessening of it.

Let every failure, then, if any occur, drive you instantly to the Lord, with a more complete abandonment and a more perfect trust; and you will find that, sad as they are, they will not take you out of the land of rest, nor permanently interrupt your sweet communion with Him.

And now, having shown the way of deliverance from failure, I want to say a little as to the causes of failure in this life of full salvation. The causes do not lie in the strength of the temptation nor in our own weakness, nor, above all, in any lack in the power or willingness of our Savior to save us. The promise to Israel was positive, "There shall not any man be able to stand before thee all the days of thy life." And the promise to us is equally positive. "God is faithful, who will not suffer you to be tempted above that ye are able; but will with the temptation also make a way of escape that ye may be able to bear it."

The men of Ai were "but few," and yet the people who had conquered the mighty Jericho "fled before the men of Ai." It was not the strength of their enemy, neither had God failed them. The cause of their defeat lay somewhere else, and the Lord Himself declares it, "Israel hath sinned, and they have also transgressed my covenant which I commanded them; for they have even taken of the accursed thing, and have also stolen and dissembled also, and they have put it even among their own stuff. Therefore the children of Israel could not stand before their enemies, but turned their backs upon their enemies." It was a hidden evil that conquered them. Deep down under the earth, in an obscure tent in that vast army, was hidden something against which God had a controversy, and this little hidden thing made the whole army helpless before their enemies. "There is an accursed thing in the midst of thee, O Israel; thou canst not stand before thine enemies until ye take away the accursed thing from among you."

The teaching here is simply this, that anything allowed in the heart which is contrary to the will of God, let it seem ever so insignificant, or be ever so deeply hidden, will cause us to fall before our enemies. Any root of bitterness cherished towards another, any self-seeking and harsh judgments indulged in, any slackness in obeying the voice of the Lord, any doubtful habits or surroundings, any one of these things will effectually cripple and paralyze our spiritual life. We may have hidden the evil in the most remote corner of our hearts, and may have covered it over from our sight, refusing even to recognize its existence, of which, however, we cannot help being all the time secretly aware. We may steadily ignore it, and persist in declarations of consecration and full trust, we may be more earnest than ever in our religious duties, and have the eyes of our understanding opened more and more to the truth and the beauty of the life and walk of faith. We may seem to ourselves and to others to have reached an almost impregnable position of victory, and yet we may find ourselves suffering bitter defeats. We may wonder, and question, and despair, and pray; nothing will do any good until the accursed thing is dug up from its hiding-place, brought out to the light, and laid before God. And the moment a believer who is walking in this interior life meets with a defeat, he must at once seek for the cause not in the strength of that particular enemy, but in something behind, some hidden want of consecration lying at the very center of his being. Just as a headache is not the disease itself, but only a symptom of a disease situated in some other part of the body, so the sin in such a Christian is only the symptom of an evil hidden probably in a very different part of his being.

Sometimes the evil may be hidden even in that, which at a cursory glance, would look like good. Beneath apparent zeal for the truth, may be hidden a judging spirit, or a subtle leaning to our own understanding. Beneath apparent Christian faithfulness, may be hidden an absence of Christian love. Beneath an apparently rightful care for our affairs, may be hidden a great want of trust in God. I believe our blessed Guide, the indwelling Holy Spirit, is always secretly discovering these things to us by continual little twinges and pangs of conscience, so that we are left without excuse. But it is very easy to disregard His gentle voice, and insist upon it to ourselves that all is right; and thus the fatal evil will continue hidden in our midst causing defeat in most unexpected quarters.

A capital illustration of this occurred to me once in my housekeeping. I had moved into a new house and, in looking over it to see if it was all ready for occupancy, I noticed in the cellar a very clean-looking cider-cask headed up at both ends. I debated with myself whether I should have it taken out of the cellar and opened to see what was in it, but concluded, as it seemed empty and looked nice, to leave it undisturbed, especially as it would have been quite a piece of work to get it up the stairs. I did not feel quite easy, but reasoned away my scruples and left it. Every spring and fall, when house-cleaning time came on, I would remember that cask, with a little twinge of my housewifely conscience, feeling that I could not quite rest in the thought of a perfectly cleaned house, while it remained unopened, for how did I know but under its fair exterior it contained some hidden evil. Still I managed to quiet my scruples on the subject, thinking always of the trouble it would involve to investigate it; and for two or three years the innocent-looking cask stood quietly in my cellar.

Then, most unaccountably, moths began to fill my house. I used every possible precaution against them, and made every effort to eradicate them, but in vain. They increased rapidly and threatened to ruin everything I had. I suspected my carpets as being the cause, and subjected them to a thorough cleaning. I suspected my furniture, and had it newly upholstered. I suspected all sorts of impossible things. At last the thought of the cask flashed on me. At once I had it brought up out of the cellar and the head knocked in, and I think it is safe to say that thousands of moths poured out. The previous occupant of the house must have headed it up with something in it which bred moths, and this was the cause of all my trouble.

Now I believe that, in the same way, some innocent-looking habit or indulgence, some apparently unimportant and safe thing, about which we yet have now and then little twinges of conscience, something which is not brought out fairly into the light, and investigated under the searching eye of God, lies at the root of most of the failure in this higher life. *All* is not given up. Some secret corner is kept locked against the entrance of the Lord. And therefore we cannot stand before our enemies, but find ourselves smitten down in their presence.

In order to prevent failure, or to discover its cause if we have failed, it is necessary that we should keep continually before us this prayer, "Search me, O God, and know my heart; try me and know my thoughts; and see if there be any evil way in me, and lead me in the way everlasting."

There may be something very deceptive in our sufferings over our failures. We may seem to ourselves to be wholly occupied with the glory of God, and yet in our inmost souls it may be self alone that occasions all our trouble. Our self-love is touched in a tender spot by the discovery that we are not so saintly as we thought we were; and this chagrin is often a greater sin than the original fault itself.

The only safe way to treat our failures is neither to justify nor condemn ourselves on account of them, but to lay them quietly and in simplicity before the Lord, looking at them in peace and in the spirit of love.

All the old mystic writers tell us that our progress is aided far more by a simple, peaceful turning to God, than by all our chagrin and remorse over our lapses from Him. Only be faithful, they say, in turning quietly to Him alone, the moment you perceive what you have done, and His presence will deliver you from the snares which have entrapped you. To look at self plunges you deeper into the slough, for this very slough is after all nothing but self; while the gentlest look towards God will calm and deliver your heart.

Finally, let us never forget for one moment, no matter how often we may fail, that the Lord Jesus able, according to the declaration concerning Him, to deliver us out of the hands of our enemies, that we may "serve Him without fear, in holiness and righteousness before Him all the days of our life."

Let us then pray, every one of us, day and night, "Lord, keep us from sinning, and make us living witnesses of Thy mighty power to save to the uttermost"; and let us never be satisfied until we are so pliable in His hands, and have learned so to trust Him, that He will be able to "make us perfect, in every good work to do His will, working in us that which is well-pleasing in His sight, through Jesus Christ; to whom be glory for ever and ever. Amen."

14. Doubts

A great many Christians are slaves to the habit of doubting. No drunkard was ever more utterly bound by the chains of his fatal habit than they are by theirs. Every step of their whole Christian life is taken against the fearful odds of an army of doubts, that are forever lying in wait to assail them at each favorable moment. Their lives are made wretched, their usefulness is effectually hindered, and their communion with God is continually broken by their doubts. And although the entrance of the soul upon the life of faith, of which this book treats, does in many cases take it altogether out of the region where these doubts live and flourish; yet even here it sometimes happens that the old tyrant will rise up and reassert his sway, and will cause the feet to stumble and the heart to fail, even when he cannot succeed in utterly turning the believer back into the dreary wilderness again.

We all of us remember, doubtless, the childish fascination, and yet horror, of that story of Christian's imprisonment in Doubting Castle by the wicked giant Despair, and our exultant sympathy in his escape through those massive gates and from that cruel tyrant. Little did we suspect then that we should ever find ourselves taken prisoner by the same giant, and imprisoned in the same castle. And yet I fear to every member of the Church of Christ there has been at least one such experience. Turn to the account again, if it is not fresh in your minds, and see if you do not see pictured there experiences of your own that have been very grievous to bear at the time, and very sorrowful to look back upon afterwards.

It seems strange that people, whose very name of Believers implies that their one chiefest characteristic is that they believe, should have to confess to such experiences. And yet it is such a universal habit that I feel if the majority of the Church were to be named over again, the only fitting and descriptive name that could be given them would be that of Doubters. In fact, most Christians have settled down under their doubts, as to a sort of inevitable malady, from which they suffer acutely, but to which they must try to be resigned as a part of the necessary discipline of this earthly life. And they lament over their doubts as a man might lament over his rheumatism, making themselves out as an "interesting case" of especial and peculiar trial, which requires the tenderest sympathy and the utmost consideration.

And this is too often true of believers, who are earnestly longing to enter upon the life and walk of faith, and who have made perhaps many steps towards it. They have got rid, it may be, of the old doubts that once tormented them, as to whether their sins are really forgiven, and whether they shall, after all, get safe to Heaven; but they have not got rid of doubting. They have simply shifted the habit to a higher platform. They are saying, perhaps, "Yes, I believe my sins *are* forgiven, and I *am* a child of God through faith in Jesus Christ. I dare not doubt this any more. But then—" And this "but then" includes an interminable array of doubts concerning every declaration and every promise our Father has made to His children. One after another they fight with them and refuse to believe them, until they can have some more reliable proof of their being true, than the simple word of their God. And then they wonder why they are permitted to walk in such darkness, and look upon themselves almost in the light of martyrs, and groan under the peculiar spiritual conflicts they are compelled to endure.

Spiritual conflicts! Far better would they be named did we call them spiritual rebellions! Our fight is to be a fight of faith, and the moment we doubt, our fight ceases and our rebellion begins.

I desire to put forth, if possible, one vigorous protest against this whole thing. Just as well might I join in with the lament of a drunkard and unite with him in prayer for grace to endure the discipline of his fatal indulgence, as to give way for one instant to the weak complaints of these enslaved souls, and try to console them under their slavery. To one and to the other I would dare to do nothing else but proclaim the perfect deliverance the Lord Jesus Christ has in store or them, and beseech, entreat, command them, with all the force of my whole nature, to avail themselves of it and be free. Not for one moment would I listen to their despairing excuses. You ought to be free, you *can* be free, you MUST be free!

Will you undertake to tell me that it is an inevitable necessity for God to be doubted by His children? Is it an inevitable necessity for your children to doubt you? Would you tolerate their doubts a single hour? Would you pity your son and condole with him, and feel that he was an interesting case, if he should come to you and say, "Father, I cannot believe your word, I cannot trust your love"?

I remember once seeing the indignation of a mother I knew, stirred to its very depths by a little doubting on the part of one of her children. She had brought two little girls to my house to leave them while she did some errands. One of them, with the happy confidence of childhood, abandoned herself to all the pleasures she could find in my nursery, and sang and played until her mother's return. The other one, with the wretched caution and mistrust of maturity, sat down alone in a corner to wonder whether her mother would remember to come back for her, and to fear she would be forgotten, and to imagine her mother would be glad of the chance to get rid of her anyhow, because she was such a naughty girl, and ended with working herself up into a perfect frenzy of despair. The look on that mother's face, when upon her return the weeping little girl told what was the matter with her, I shall not easily forget. Grief, wounded love, indignation, and pity, all strove together for mastery. But indignation gained the day, and I doubt if that little girl was ever so vigorously dealt with before. A hundred times in my life since has that scene come up before me with deepest teaching, and has compelled me, peremptorily, to refuse admittance to the doubts about my Heavenly Father's love, and care, and remembrance of me, that have clamored at the door of my heart for entrance.

I am convinced that to many people doubting is a real luxury, and to deny themselves from indulging in it would be to exercise the hardest piece of self-denial they have ever known. It is a luxury that, like the indulgence in all other luxuries, brings very sorrowful results; and, perhaps, looking at the sadness and misery it has brought into your own Christian experience, you may be tempted to say, "Alas! This is no luxury to me, but only a fearful trial." But pause for a moment. Try giving it up, and you will soon find out whether it is a luxury or not. Do not your doubts come trooping to your door as a company of sympathizing friends, who appreciate your hard case, and have come to condole with you? And is it no luxury to sit down with them and entertain them, and listen to their arguments, and join in with their condolences? Would it be no self-denial to turn resolutely from them, and refuse to hear a word they have to say? If you do not know, try it and see.

Have you never tasted the luxury of indulging in hard thoughts against those who have, as you think, injured you? Have you never known what a positive fascination it is to brood over their unkindnesses, and to pry into their malice, and to imagine all sorts of wrong and uncomfortable things about them? It has made you wretched, of course, but it has been a fascinating sort of wretchedness that you could not easily give up.

And just like this is the luxury of doubting. Things have gone wrong with you in your experience. Dispensations have been mysterious, temptations have been peculiar, your case has seemed different from that of any one's around you. What more natural than to conclude that for some reason God has forsaken you, and does not love you, and is indifferent to your welfare? And how irresistible is the conviction that you are too wicked for Him to care for, or too difficult for Him to manage.

You do not mean to blame Him, or accuse Him of injustice, for you feel that His indifference and rejection of you are fully deserved because of your unworthiness. And this very subterfuge leaves you at liberty to indulge in your doubts under the guise of a just and true appreciation of your own shortcomings. But all the while you are as really indulging in hard and wrong thoughts of your Lord as ever you did of a human enemy; for He says He came not to save the righteous, but sinners; and your very sinfulness and unworthiness is your chiefest claim upon His love and His care.

As well might the poor little lamb that has wandered from the flock and got lost in the wilderness say, "The shepherd does not love me, nor care for me, nor remember me, because I am lost. He only loves and cares for the lambs that never wander." As well might the ill man say, "The doctor will not come to see me, nor give me any medicines, because I am ill. He only cares for and visits well people." Jesus says, "They that are whole need not a physician, but they that are sick." And again He says, "What man of you, having an hundred sheep, if he lose one of them, doth not leave the ninety and nine in the wilderness, and go after that which is lost, until he find it?" Any thoughts of Him, therefore, which are different from what He says of Himself, are hard thoughts; and to indulge in them is far worse than to indulge in hard thoughts of any earthly friend or foe. From the beginning to the end of your Christian life it is always sinful to indulge in doubts. Doubts are all from the devil, and are always untrue. And the only way to meet them is by a direct and emphatic denial.

And this brings me to the practical part of the whole subject, as to how to get deliverance from this fatal habit. My answer would be that the deliverance from this can be by no other means than the deliverance from any other sin. It is to be found in the Lord and in Him only. You must hand your doubting over to Him, as you have learned to hand your other temptations. You must do just what you do with your temper, or your pride. You must *give it up* to the Lord. I believe myself the only effectual remedy is to take a pledge against it as you would urge a drunkard to do against drink, trusting in the Lord alone to keep you steadfast.

Like any other sin, the stronghold is in the will and the will to doubt must be surrendered exactly as you surrender the will to yield to any other temptation. God always takes possession of a surrendered will. And if we come to the point of saying that we will not doubt, and surrender this central fortress of our nature to Him, His blessed Spirit will begin at once to work in us all the good pleasure of His will, and we shall find ourselves kept from doubting by His mighty and overcoming power.

The trouble is that in this matter of doubting the soul does not always make a full surrender, but is apt to reserve to itself a little secret liberty to doubt, looking upon it as being sometimes a necessity. "I do not want to doubt any more," we will say, or, "I hope I shall not"; but it is hard to come to the point of saying, "I will not doubt again." But no surrender is effectual until it reaches the point of saying, "I will not." The liberty to doubt must be given up forever. And the soul must consent to a continuous life of inevitable trust. It is often necessary, I think, to make a definite transaction of this surrender of doubting, and to come to a point about it. I believe it is quite as necessary in the case of a doubter as in the case of a drunkard. It will not do to give it up by degrees. The total abstinence principle is the only effectual one here.

Then, the surrender once made, the soul must rest absolutely upon the Lord for deliverance in each time of temptation. It must lift up the shield of faith the moment the assault comes. It must hand the very first suggestion of doubt over to the Lord, and must tell the enemy to settle the matter with Him. It must refuse to listen to the doubt a single moment. Let it come ever so plausibly, or under whatever guise of humility, the soul must simply say, "I dare not doubt; I must trust. The Lord is good, and HE DOES love me. Jesus saves me; He saves me now." Those three little words, repeated over and over,—"Jesus saves me, Jesus saves me,"—will put to flight the greatest army of doubts that ever assaulted any soul. I have tried it times without number, and have never known it to fail. Do not stop to argue the matter out with your doubts, nor try to prove that they are wrong. Pay no attention to them whatever; treat them with the utmost contempt. Shut your door in their faces, and emphatically deny every word they say to you. Bring up some "It is written," and hurl it after them. Look right at Jesus, and tell Him you trust Him, and you mean to trust Him. Let the doubts clamor as they may, they cannot hurt you if you will not let them in.

I know it will look to you sometimes as though you were shutting the door against your best friends, and your heart will long after your doubts more than ever the Israelites longed after the flesh-pots of Egypt. But deny yourself; take up your cross in this matter, and unmercifully refuse ever to listen to a single word.

This very day a perfect army of doubts stood awaiting my awaking, and clamored at my door for admittance. Nothing seemed real, nothing seemed true; and least of all did it seem possible that I—miserable, wretched I—could be the object of the Lord's love, or care, or notice. If I only had been at liberty to let these doubts in, and invite them to take seats and make themselves at home, what a luxury I should have felt it to be! But years ago I made a pledge against doubting; and I would as soon think of violating my pledge against intoxicating liquor as to violate this one. I DARED not admit the first doubt. I therefore lifted up my shield of faith the moment I was conscious of these suggestions, and handing the whole army over to my Lord to conquer, I began to say, over and over, "The Lord *does* love me. He *is* my present and my perfect Savior; Jesus saves me, Jesus saves me *now!*" The victory was complete. The enemy had come in like a flood, but the Lord lifted up a standard against him, and he was routed and put to flight; and my soul is singing the song of Moses and the children of Israel, saying, "I will sing unto the Lord, for He hath triumphed gloriously: the horse and his rider hath He thrown into the sea. The

Lord is my strength and my song, and He is become my salvation. The Lord is a man of war; the Lord is His name."

It will help you to resist the assaults of this temptation to doubt, to see clearly that doubting is sin. It is certainly a direct disobedience to our Lord, who commands us, "Let not your heart be troubled, neither let it be afraid." And all through the Bible everywhere the commands to trust are imperative, and admit of no exceptions. Time and room would fail me to refer to one hundredth part of these, but no one can read the Psalms without being convinced that the man who trusts without a question, is the only man who pleases God and is accepted of Him. The "provocation" of Israel was that they did not trust; "anger also came up against Israel, because they believed not in God, and trusted not in His salvation." (Psalms 78:17-22.) And in contrast, we read in Isaiah concerning those who trust, "Thou wilt keep him in perfect peace whose mind is stayed on Thee, because he trusteth in Thee." Nothing grieves or wounds *our* hearts like doubting on the part of a friend, and nothing, I am convinced, grieves the heart of God more than doubting from us.

One of my children, who is now with the Lord, said to me one evening as I was tucking her up in bed, "Well, mother, I have had my first doubt." "Oh, Ray," I said, "what was it?" "Why," she replied, "Satan came to me and told me not to believe the Bible, for it was not a word of it true." "And what did thee say to him?" I asked. "Oh," she replied, triumphantly, "I just said to him, Satan, I *will* believe it. So there!" I was delighted with the child's spiritual intelligence in knowing so well how to meet doubts, and encouraged her with all my heart, explaining to her how all doubts and discouragements are from the enemy, and how he is always a liar and must not be listened to for a moment. The next night, I had forgotten all about it, however, and was surprised and startled when she said, as I was tucking her in bed, "Well, mother, Satan has been at it again." "Oh, Ray darling!" I exclaimed in dismay, "what did he say this time?" "Well," she replied, "he just told me that I was such a naughty little girl that Jesus could not love me, and I was foolish to think He did." "And what did thee say this time?" I asked. "Oh!" she replied, "I just looked at him cross and said, Satan, shut thy mouth!" And then she added, with a smile, "He can't make me unhappy one bit." A grander battle no soul ever fought than this little child had done, and no greater victory was ever won!

Dear, doubting soul, go and do likewise; and a similar victory shall be thine. As you lay down this book take up your pen and write out your determination never to doubt again. Make it a real transaction between your soul and the Lord. Give up your liberty to doubt forever. Put your will in this matter over on the Lord's side, and trust Him to keep you from falling. Tell him all about your utter weakness and your long-encouraged habits of doubt, and how helpless you are before your enemy, and commit the whole battle to Him. Tell Him you will not doubt again; and then henceforward keep your face steadfastly looking unto Jesus, away from yourself and away from your doubts, holding fast the profession of your faith without wavering, because He is faithful who has promised. And as surely as you do thus hold the beginning of your confidence steadfast unto the end, just so surely shall you find yourself in this matter made more than conqueror, through Him who loves you.

15. Practical Results in the Daily Walk and Conversation

If all that has been said concerning the life hid with Christ in God be true, its results in the practical daily walk and conversation ought to be very marked, and the people who have entered into the enjoyment of it ought to be, in very truth, a "peculiar people, zealous of good works."

My son at college once wrote to a friend to this effect: that Christians are God's witnesses necessarily, because the world will not read the Bible, but they will read our lives; and that upon the report these give will very much depend their belief in the Divine nature of the religion we profess. As we all know, this is an age of facts, and inquiries are being increasingly turned from theories to realities. If our religion is to make any headway now, it must be proved to be more than a theory, and we must present, to the investigation of the critical minds of our age, the grand facts of lives which have been actually and manifestly transformed by the mighty power of God working in us all the good pleasure of His will. Give us "forms of life," say the scientists, and we will be convinced. And when the Church is able to present to them in all its members, the form of a holy life, their last stronghold will be conquered.

I desire, therefore, before closing my book, to speak very solemnly of what I conceive to be the necessary fruits of a life of faith, such as I have been describing, and to press home to the hearts of every one of my readers their responsibility to walk worthy of the high calling wherewith they have been called.

And I would speak to some of you, at least, as personal friends, for I feel sure we have not gone this far together through this book without there having grown in your hearts, as there has in mine, a tender personal interest and longing for one another, that we may in everything show forth the praises of Him who has called us out of darkness into His marvelous light. As a friend, then, to friends, I am sure I may speak very plainly, and will be pardoned if I go into some particulars of life and character which are vital to all true Christian development.

The standard of practical holy living has been so low among Christians that any good degree of real devotedness of life and walk is looked upon with surprise, and even often with disapprobation, by a large portion of the Church. And, for the most part, the professed followers of the Lord Jesus Christ are so little like Him in character or in action, that to an outside observer there would not seem to be much harmony between them.

But we, who have heard the call of our God to a life of entire consecration and perfect trust, must do differently from all this. We must come out from the world and be separate, and must not be conformed to it in our characters nor in our purposes. We must no longer share in its spirit or its ways. Our conversation must be in Heaven, and we must seek those things that are above, where Christ sitteth on the right hand of God. We must walk through the world as Christ walked. We must have the mind that was in Him. As pilgrims and strangers we must abstain from fleshly lusts that war against the soul. As good soldiers of Jesus Christ, we must disentangle ourselves from the affairs of this life as far as possible, that we may please Him who hath chosen us to be soldiers. We must abstain from all appearance of evil. We must be kind one to another, tenderhearted, forgiving one another, even as God, for Christ's sake, hath forgiven us. We must not resent injuries or unkindness, but must return good for evil, and turn the other cheek to the hand that smites us. We must take always the lowest place among our fellowmen; and seek not our own honor, but the honor of others. We must be gentle, and meek, and yielding; not standing up for our own rights, but for the rights of others. All that we do must be done for the glory of God. And, to sum it all up, since He which hath called us is holy, so we must be holy in *all manner* of conversation; because it is written, "Be ye holy, for I am holy."

Now, dear friends, this is all exceedingly practical and means, surely, a life very different from the lives of most professors around us. It means that we do really and absolutely turn our backs on self, and on self's motives and self's aims. It means that we are a peculiar people, not only in the eyes of God, but in the eyes of the world around us; and that, wherever we go, it will be known from our Christlike lives and conversation that we are followers of the Lord Jesus Christ; and are not of the world, even as He was not of the world. We shall no longer feel that our money is our own, but the Lord's, to be used in His service. We shall not feel at liberty to use our energies exclusively in the pursuit of worldly means, but, seeking first the kingdom of God and His righteousness, shall have all needful things added unto us. We shall find ourselves forbidden to seek the highest places, or to strain after worldly advantages. We shall not be permitted to be conformed to the world in our ways of thinking or of living. We shall feel no desire to indulge in the world's frivolous pursuits. We shall find our affections set upon heavenly things, rather than upon earthly things. Our days will be spent not in serving ourselves, but in serving our Lord; and all our rightful duties will be more perfectly performed than ever, because whatever we do will be done "not with eye-service as men-pleasers, but as the servants of Christ, doing the will of God from the heart."

Into all these things we shall undoubtedly be led by the blessed Spirit of God, if we give ourselves up to His guidance. But unless we have the right standard of Christian life set before us, we shall be hindered by our ignorance from recognizing His voice; and it is for this reason I desire to be very plain and definite in my statements.

I have noticed that wherever there has been a faithful following of the Lord in a consecrated soul, several things have inevitably followed, sooner or later.

Meekness and quietness of spirit become in time the characteristics of the daily life; a submissive acceptance of the will of God, as it comes in the hourly events of each day; pliability in the hands of God to do or to suffer all the good pleasure of His will; sweetness under provocation; calmness in the midst of turmoil and bustle; yieldingness to the wishes of others, and an insensibility to slights and affronts, absence of worry or anxiety; deliverance from care and fear: all these, and many other similar graces are invariably found to be the natural outward development of that inward life which is hid with Christ in God. Then as to the habits of life: we always see such Christians sooner or later giving themselves up to some work for God and their fellowmen, willing to spend and be spent in the Master's service. They become indifferent to outward show in the furniture of their houses and the style of their living, and make all personal adornment secondary to the things of God. The voice is dedicated to God, to talk and sing for Him. The purse is placed at His disposal. The pen is dedicated to write for Him, the lips to speak for Him, the hands and the feet to do His bidding. Year after year such Christians are seen to grow more unworldly, more heavenly-minded, more transformed, more like Christ, until even their very faces express so much of the beautiful inward Divine life, that all who look at them cannot but take knowledge of them that they live with God, and are abiding in Him.

I feel sure that to each one of you have come at least some Divine intimations or foreshadowings of the life I here describe. Have you not begun to feel dimly conscious of the voice of God speaking to you in the depths of your soul about these things? Has it not been a pain and a distress to you of late to discover how much there is wrong in your life?

Has not your soul been plunged into inward trouble and doubt about certain dispositions and ways, in which you have been formerly accustomed to indulge? Have you not begun to feel uneasy with some of your habits of life, and to wish that you could do differently in these respects? Have not paths of devotedness and of service begun to open out before you, with the longing thought, "Oh, that I could walk in them"?

All these longings and doubts, and this inward distress, are the voice of the Good Shepherd in your heart seeking to call you out of all that is contrary to His will. Oh! let me entreat of you not to turn away from His gentle pleadings. You little know the secret paths into which He means to lead you by these very steps, nor the wonderful stores of blessedness that lie at their end, or you would spring forward with an eager joy to yield to every one of His requirements. The heights of Christian perfection can only be reached by faithfully following the Guide who is to lead you there, and He reveals your way to you one step at a time in the teachings and providences of your daily lives, asking only on your part that you yield yourselves up to His guidance. If, then, in anything you are convinced of sin, be sure that it is the voice of your Lord, and surrender it at once to His bidding, rejoicing with a great joy that He has begun thus to lead and guide you. Be perfectly pliable in His wise hands, go where He entices you, turn away from all from which He makes you shrink, obey Him perfectly; and He will lead you out swiftly and easily into a wonderful life of conformity to Himself, that will be a testimony to all around you, beyond what you yourself will ever know.

I knew a soul thus given up to follow the Lord whithersoever He might lead her, who in three short months travelled from the depths of darkness and despair into the realization and conscious experience of the most blessed union with the Lord Jesus Christ. Out of the midst of her darkness, she consecrated herself to the Lord, surrendering her will up altogether to Him, that He might work in her to will and to do of His own good pleasure. Immediately He began to speak to her by His Spirit in her heart, suggesting to her some little acts of service for Him, and calling her out of all un-Christlike dispositions and ways. She recognized His voice, and yielded to Him each thing He asked for, following Him whithersoever He might lead her, with no fear but the one fear of disobeying Him. He led her rapidly on, day by day conforming her more and more to His will, and making her life such a testimony to those around her, that even some who had begun by opposing and disbelieving, were forced to acknowledge that it was of God, and were won to a similar surrender. And, finally, after three short months of this faithful following, it came to pass, so swiftly had she gone, that her Lord was able to reveal to her wondering soul some of the deepest secrets of His love, and to fulfil to her the marvelous promise of Acts 1:5, baptizing her with the Holy Ghost. Think you she has ever regretted her wholehearted following of Him? Or that aught but thankfulness and joy can ever fill her soul when she reviews the steps by which her feet had been led to this place of wondrous blessedness, even though some of them may have seemed at the time hard to take? Ah! dear soul, if thou wouldst know a like blessing, abandon thyself, like her, to the guidance of the Divine Master, and shrink from no surrender for which He may call.

> "The perfect way is hard to flesh,
>   It is not hard to love;
> If thou wert sick for want of God,
>   How swiftly wouldst thou move."

Surely thou canst trust Him! And if some things may be called for which look to thee of but little moment, and not worthy thy Lord's attention, remember that He sees not as man seeth, and that things small to thee may be in His eyes the key and the clue to the deepest springs of thy being. In order to mold thee into entire conformity to His will, He must have thee pliable in his hands, and this pliability is more quickly reached by yielding in the little things than even by the greater. Thy one great desire is to follow Him fully; canst thou not say then a continual "Yes, Lord!" to all His sweet commands, whether small or great, and trust Him to lead thee by the shortest road to thy fullest blessedness?

My dear friend, this, and nothing less than this, is what thy consecration meant, whether thou knew it or not. It meant *inevitable* obedience. It meant that the will of thy God was henceforth to be thy will under all circumstances and at all times. It meant that from that moment thou surrendered thy liberty of choice, and gave thyself up utterly into the control of thy Lord. It meant an hourly following of Him whithersoever He might lead thee, without any dream of turning back.

And now I appeal to thee to make good thy word. Let everything else go, that thou mayest live out, in a practical daily walk and conversation, the Divine life thou hast dwelling within thee. Thou art united to thy Lord by a wondrous tie; walk, then, as He walked, and show to the unbelieving world the blessed reality of His mighty power to save, by letting Him save thee to the very uttermost. Thou needst not fear to consent to this, for He is thy Savior; and His power is to do it all. He is not asking thee, in thy poor weakness, to do it thyself; He only asks thee to yield thyself to Him, that He may work in thee to will and to do by His own mighty power. Thy part is to yield thyself, His part is to work; and never, never will He give thee any command which is not accompanied by ample power to obey it. Take no thought for the morrow in this matter; but abandon thyself with a generous trust to thy loving Lord, who has promised never to call His own sheep out into any path, without Himself going before them to make the way easy and safe. Take each onward step as He makes it plain to thee. Bring all thy life in each of its details to Him to regulate and guide. Follow gladly and quickly the sweet suggestions of His Spirit in thy soul. And day by day thou wilt find Him bringing thee more and more into conformity with His will in all things; molding thee and fashioning thee, as thou art able to bear it, into a vessel unto His honor, sanctified and meet for His use, and fitted to every good work. So shall be given to thee the sweet joy of being an epistle of Christ known and read of all men; and thy light shall shine so brightly that men seeing, not thee, but thy good works, shall glorify, not thee, but thy Father which is in Heaven.

We are predestined to be "conformed to the image" of God's Son. This means, of course, not a likeness of bodily presence, but a likeness of character and nature. It means a similarity of thought, of feeling, of desire, of loves, of hates. It means, that we are to think and act, according to our measure, as Christ would have thought and acted under our circumstances.

A little girl was once questioned what it meant to be a Christian. She replied, "It means to be just what Christ would be, if He was a little girl and lived in my house."

The secret of Christ's life was the pouring out of Himself for others; and if we are like Him, this will be the secret of our lives also. He saved others, but Himself He could not save. He "pleased not Himself," and therefore we are "not to please ourselves," but rather our neighbor, when it is for his good.

A thoughtful Hindoo religionist, who visited England and America lately to examine into Christianity, said, as the result of his observations, "What Christians need is a little more of Christ's Christianity, and a little less of man's."

Man's Christianity teaches sacrifice to save ourselves; Christ's Christianity teaches sacrifice to save others. Man's Christianity produces the fruitless selfishness of too much of our religion. Christ's Christianity produces the blessed unselfishness of lives that are poured out for others, as was His.

In short, then, the one practical outcome of all that our book has been teaching us, is simply this, that we are to be Christlike Christians. And all our experiences amount to nothing if they do not produce this result. For "not everyone that saith unto me, Lord, Lord, shall enter into the kingdom of heaven; but he that doeth the will of my Father which is in heaven."

16. The Joy of Obedience

I remember reading once somewhere this sentence, "Perfect obedience would be perfect happiness, if only we had perfect confidence in the power we were obeying." I remember being struck with the saying, as the revelation of a possible, although hitherto undreamed-of way of happiness; and often afterwards, through all the lawlessness and willfulness of my life, did that saying recur to me as the vision of a rest, and yet of a possible development, that would soothe and at the same time satisfy all my yearnings. Need I say that this rest has been revealed to me now, not as a vision, but as a reality; and that I have seen in the Lord Jesus, the Master to whom we may all yield up our implicit obedience, and, taking His yoke upon us, may find our perfect rest?

You little know, dear hesitating soul, of the joy you are missing. The Master has revealed Himself to you, and is calling for your complete surrender, and you shrink and hesitate. A measure of surrender you are willing to make, and think indeed it is fit and proper you should. But an *utter* abandonment, without any reserves, seems to you too much to be asked for. You are afraid of it. It involves too much, you think, and is too great a task. To be measurably obedient you desire; to be perfectly obedient appalls you.

And then, too, you see other souls who seem able to walk with easy consciences, in a far wider path than that which appears to be marked out for you, and you ask yourself why this need be. It seems strange, and perhaps hard to you, that you must do what they need not, and must leave undone what they have liberty to do.

Ah! dear Christian, this very difference between you is your privilege, though you do not yet know it. Your Lord says, "He that *hath* my commandments, and keepeth them, he it is that loveth Me; and he that loveth Me shall be loved of my Father, and I will love him, and will manifest Myself to him." You *have* His commandments; those you envy, have them not. *You* know the mind of your Lord about many things, in which, as yet, *they* are walking in darkness. Is not this a privilege? Is it a cause for regret that your soul is brought into such near and intimate relations with your Master, that He is able to tell you things which those who are further off may not know? Do you not realize what a tender degree of intimacy is implied in this?

There are many relations in life which require from the different parties only very moderate degrees of devotion. We may have really pleasant friendships with one another, and yet spend a large part of our lives in separate interests, and widely differing pursuits. When together, we may greatly enjoy one another's society, and find many congenial points; but separation is not any especial distress to us, and other and more intimate friendships do not interfere. There is not enough love between us, to give us either the right or the desire to enter into and share one another's most private affairs. A certain degree of reserve and distance is the suitable thing, we feel. But there are other relations in life where all this is changed. The friendship becomes love. The two hearts give themselves to one another, to be no longer two but one. A union of souls takes place, which makes all that belongs to one the property of the other. Separate interests and separate paths in life are no longer possible. Things which were lawful before become unlawful now, because of the nearness of the tie that binds. The reserve and distance suitable to mere friendship becomes fatal in love. Love gives all, and must have all in return. The wishes of one become binding obligations to the other, and the deepest desire of each heart is, that it may know every secret wish or longing of the other, in order that it may fly on the wings of the wind to gratify it.

Do such as these chafe under this yoke which love imposes? Do they envy the cool, calm, reasonable friendships they see around them, and regret the nearness into which their souls are brought to their beloved one, because of the obligations it creates? Do they not rather glory in these very obligations, and inwardly pity, with a tender yet exulting joy, the poor far-off ones who dare not come so near? Is not every fresh revelation of the mind of one another a fresh delight and privilege, and is any path found hard which their love compels them to travel?

Ah! dear souls, if you have ever known this even for a few hours in any earthly relation; if you have ever loved a fellow human being enough to find sacrifice and service on their behalf a joy; if a whole-souled abandonment of your will to the will of another has ever gleamed across you as a blessed and longed-for privilege, or as a sweet and precious reality, then, by all the tender longing love of your heavenly Master, would I entreat you to let it be so towards God!

He loves you with more than the love of friendship. As a bridegroom rejoices over his bride, so does He rejoice over you, and nothing but a full surrender will satisfy Him. He has given you all, and He asks for all in return. The slightest reserve will grieve Him to the heart. He spared not Himself, and how can you spare yourself? For your sake He poured out in a lavish abandonment all that He had, and for His sake you must pour out all that you have without stint or measure.

Oh, be generous in your self-surrender! Meet His measureless devotion for you, with a measureless devotion to Him. Be glad and eager to throw yourself headlong into His dear arms, and to hand over the reins of government to Him. Whatever there is of you, let Him have it all. Give up forever everything that is separate from Him. Consent to resign from this time forward all liberty of choice; and glory in the blessed nearness of union which makes this enthusiasm of devotedness not only possible but necessary. Have you never longed to lavish your love and attentions upon someone far off from you in position or circumstances, with whom you were not intimate enough for any closer approach? Have you not felt a capacity for self-surrender and devotedness, that has seemed to burn within you like a fire, and yet had no object upon which it dared to lavish itself? Have not your hands been full of alabaster boxes of ointment, very precious, which you have never been near enough to any heart to pour out? If, then, you are hearing the sweet voice of your Lord calling you into a place of nearness to Himself, which will require a separation from all else, and which will make this enthusiasm of devotedness not only possible, but necessary will you shrink or hesitate? Will you think it hard that He reveals to you more of His mind than He does to others, and that He will not allow you to be happy in anything which separates you from Himself? Do you *want* to go where He cannot go with you, or to have pursuits which He cannot share?

No! no, a thousand times, no! You will spring out to meet His dear will with an eager joy. Even His slightest wish will become a binding law to you, which it would fairly break your heart to disobey. You will glory in the very narrowness of the path He marks out for you, and will pity with an infinite pity the poor far-off ones who have missed this precious joy. The obligations of love will be to you its sweetest privileges; and the right you have acquired to lavish the uttermost abandonment of all that you have upon your Lord, will seem to lift you into a region of unspeakable glory. The perfect happiness of perfect obedience will dawn upon your soul, and you will begin to know something of what Jesus meant when He said, "I *delight* to do thy will, O my God."

And do you think the joy in this will be all on your side? Has the Lord no joy in those who have thus surrendered themselves to Him, and who love to obey Him? Ah, my friends, we are not fit to speak of this but surely the Scriptures reveal to us glimpses of the delight, the satisfaction, the joy our Lord has in us, that ravish the soul with their marvelous suggestions of blessedness. That *we* should need Him, is easy to comprehend; that *He* should need us, seems incomprehensible. That our desire should be towards Him, is a matter of course; but that His desire should be towards us, passes the bounds of human belief. And yet, over and over He says it, and what can we do but believe Him? He has made our hearts capable of this supreme, overmastering affection, and has offered Himself as the object of it. It is infinitely precious to Him, and He says, "He that loveth me shall be loved of my Father, and I will love him, and will manifest myself to him." Continually at every heart He is knocking, and asking to be taken in as the supreme object of love. "Wilt thou have me," He says to the believer, "to be thy Beloved? Wilt thou follow me into suffering and loneliness, and endure hardness for my sake, and ask for no reward but my smile of approval, and my word of praise? Wilt thou throw thyself with an utter abandonment into my will? Wilt thou give up to me the absolute control of thyself and all that thou art? Wilt thou be content with pleasing me and me only? May I have my way with thee in all things? Wilt thou come into so close a union with me as to make a separation from the world necessary? Wilt thou accept me for thy only Lord, and leave all others, to cleave only unto ME?"

In a thousand ways He makes this offer of oneness with Himself to every believer. But all do not say "Yes," to Him. Other loves and other interests seem to them too precious to be cast aside. They do not miss of Heaven because of this. But they miss an unspeakable joy.

You, however, are not one of these. From the very first your soul has cried out eagerly and gladly to all His offers, "Yes, Lord; yes!" You are more than ready to pour out upon Him all your richest treasures of love and devotedness. You have brought to Him an enthusiasm of self-surrender that perhaps may disturb and distress the more prudent and moderate Christians around you. Your love makes necessary a separation from the world, which a lower love cannot even conceive of. Sacrifices and services are possible and sweet to you, which could not come into the grasp of a more half-hearted devotedness. The life upon which you have entered gives you the right to a lavish outpouring of your *all* upon your beloved One. Services, of which more distant souls know nothing, become now your sweetest privilege. Your Lord claims from you, because of your union with Him, far more than He claims of them. What to them is lawful, love has made unlawful for you. To you

He can make known His secrets, and to you He looks for an instant response to every requirement of His love.

Oh, it is wonderful! the glorious, unspeakable privilege upon which you have entered! How little it will matter to you if men shall hate you, or shall separate you from their company, and shall reproach you and cast out your name as evil for His dear sake! You may well "rejoice in that day and leap for joy"; for behold your reward is great in Heaven, and if you are a partaker of His suffering, you shall be also of His glory.

In you He is seeing of the travail of His soul, and is satisfied. Your love and devotedness are His precious reward for all He has done for you. It is unspeakably sweet to Him. Do not be afraid then to let yourself go in a heart-whole devotedness to your Lord, that can brook no reserves. Others may not approve, but He will, and that is enough. Do not stint or measure your obedience or your service. Let your heart and your hand be as free to serve Him, as His heart and His hand were to serve you. Let Him have all there is of you, body, soul, and spirit, time, talents, voice, everything. Lay your whole life open before Him that He may control it. Say to Him each day, "Lord, how shall I regulate this day so as to please Thee? Where shall I go? what shall I do? whom shall I visit? what shall I say?" Give your intellect up into His control and say, "Lord, tell me how to think so as to please Thee?" Give Him your reading, your pursuits, your friendships, and say, "Lord, give me the insight to judge concerning all these things with Thy wisdom." Do not let there be a day nor an hour in which you are not intelligently doing His will, and following Him wholly. And this personal service to Him will give a halo to your life, and gild the most monotonous existence with a heavenly glow.

Have you ever grieved that the romance of youth is so soon lost in the hard realities of the world? Bring God thus into your life and into all its details, and a far grander enthusiasm will thrill your soul than the brightest days of youth could ever know, and nothing will seem hard or stern again. The meanest life will be glorified by this. Often, as I have watched a poor woman at her wash-tub, and have thought of all the disheartening accessories of such a life, and have been tempted to wonder why such lives need to be, there has come over me, with a thrill of joy, the recollection of this possible glorification of it, and I have said to myself, Even this life, lived in Christ, and with Christ, following Him whithersoever He may lead, would be filled with an enthusiasm that would make every hour of it glorious. And I have gone on my way comforted to know that God's most wondrous blessings thus lie in the way of the poorest and the meanest lives. "For," says our Lord Himself, "whosoever," whether they be rich or poor, old or young, bond or free, "whosoever shall do the will of God, the same is my brother, and my sister, and my mother."

Pause a moment over these simple yet amazing words. His brother, and sister, and mother! What would we not have given to have been one of these! Oh, let me entreat of you, beloved Christian, to come, taste and see for yourself how good the Lord is, and what wonderful things He has in store for those who "keep His commandments, and who do those things that are pleasing in His sight."

"And it shall come to pass, if thou shalt hearken diligently unto the voice of the Lord thy God, to observe and to do all His commandments which I command thee this day, that the Lord thy God will set thee on high, above all nations of the earth; and all these blessings shall come on thee, and overtake thee, if thou shalt hearken unto the voice of the Lord thy God.

"Blessed shalt thou be in the city, and blessed shalt thou be in the field.

"Blessed shall be the fruit of thy body, and the fruit of thy ground, and the fruit of thy cattle, the increase of thy kine, and the flocks of thy sheep.

"Blessed shall be thy basket and thy store.

"Blessed shalt thou be when thou comest in, and blessed shalt thou be when thou goest out.

"The Lord shall cause thine enemies that shall rise up against thee to be smitten before thy face; they shall come out against thee one way, and flee before thee seven ways.

"The Lord shall command the blessing upon thee in thy storehouses, and in all that thou settest thine hand unto; and He shall bless thee in the land which the Lord thy God giveth thee.

"The Lord shall establish thee an holy people unto Himself, as He hath sworn unto thee, if thou shalt keep the commandments of the Lord thy God, and walk in His ways.

"And all people of the earth shall see that thou art called by the name of the Lord, and they shall be afraid of thee.

"And the Lord shall make thee plenteous in goods, in the fruit of thy body, and in the fruit of thy cattle, in the fruit of thy ground, in the land which the Lord sware unto thy fathers to give thee.

"And the Lord shall make thee the head, and not the tail; and thou shalt be above only, and thou shalt not be beneath; if that thou hearken unto the commandments of the Lord thy God, which I command thee this day, to observe and to do them."

For the Israelites this was outward and temporal, for us it is inward and spiritual; and, as such, infinitely more glorious. May our surrendered wills leap out to embrace it in all its fulness!

17. Oneness with Christ

All the dealings of God with the soul of the believer are in order to bring him into oneness with Himself, that the prayer of our Lord may be fulfilled: "That they all may be one; as thou, Father, art in me and I in thee, that they also may be one in us."… "I in them, and thou in me, that they may be made perfect in one, and that the world may know that thou hast sent me, and hast loved them as thou hast loved me."

This soul-union was the glorious purpose in the heart of God for His people before the foundation of the world. It was the mystery hid from ages and generations. It was accomplished in the incarnation of Christ. It has been made known by the Scriptures. And it is realized as an actual experience by many of God's dear children.

But not by all. It is true of all, and God has not hidden it or made it hard, but the eyes of many are too dim and their hearts too unbelieving, and they fail to grasp it. And it is for the very purpose of bringing them into the person al and actual realization of this, that the Lord is stirring up believers everywhere at the present time to abandon themselves to Him, that He may work in them all the good pleasure of His will.

All the previous steps in the Christian life lead up to this. The Lord has made us for it; and until we have intelligently apprehended it, and have voluntarily consented to embrace it, the travail of His soul for us is not satisfied, nor have our hearts found their destined and final rest.

The usual course of Christian experience is pictured in the history of the disciples. First they were awakened to see their condition and their need, and they came to Christ and gave in their allegiance to Him. Then they followed Him, worked for Him, believed in Him; and yet, how unlike Him! seeking to be set up one above the other; running away from the cross; misunderstanding His mission and His words; forsaking their Lord in time of danger; but still sent out to preach, recognized by Him as His disciples, possessing power to work for Him. They knew Christ only "after the flesh," as outside of them, their Lord and Master, but not yet their Life.

Then came Pentecost, and these disciples came to know Him as inwardly revealed; as one with them in actual union, their very indwelling Life. Henceforth He was to them Christ within, working in them to will and to do of His good pleasure; delivering them by the law of the Spirit of His life from the bondage to the law of sin and death, under which they had been held. No longer was it between themselves and Him, a war of wills and a clashing of interest. One will alone animated them, and that was His will. One interest alone was dear to them, and that was His. They were made ONE with Him.

And surely all can recognize this picture, though perhaps as yet the final stage of it has not been fully reached. You may have left much to follow Christ, dear reader; you may have believed on him, and worked for Him, and loved Him, and yet may not be like Him. Allegiance you know, and confidence you know, but not yet union. There are two wills, two interests, two lives. You have not yet lost your own life that you may live only in His. Once it was I and not Christ; then it was I and Christ; perhaps now it is even Christ and I. But has it come yet to be Christ only, and not I at all?

Perhaps you do not understand what this oneness means. Some people think it consists in a great emotion or a wonderful *feeling* of oneness, and they turn inward to examine their emotions, thinking to decide by the state of these, what is the state of their interior union with God. But nowhere is the mistake of trusting to feelings greater than here.

Oneness with Christ must, in the very nature of things, consist in a Christ-like life and character. It is not what we *feel*, but what we *are* that settles the question. No matter how exalted or intense our emotions on the subject may be, if there is not a likeness of character with Christ, a unity of aim and purpose, a similarity of thought and of action, there can be no real oneness.

This is plain common-sense, and it is Scriptural as well.

We speak of two people being one, and we mean that their purposes, and actions, and thoughts, and desires are alike. A friend may pour out upon us enthusiastic expressions of love, and unity and oneness, but if that friend's aims, and actions, and ways of looking at things are exactly opposite to ours, we cannot feel there is any real oneness between us, notwithstanding all our affection for one another. To be truly one with another, we must have the same likes and dislikes, the same joys and sorrows, the same hopes and fears. As someone says, we must look through one another's eyes, and think with one another's brains. This is, as I said above, only plain common-sense.

And oneness with Christ can be judged by no other rule. It is out of the question to be one with Him in any other way than in the way of nature, and character, and life. Unless we are Christ-like in our thoughts and our ways, we are not one with Him, no matter how we feel.

I have seen Christians, with hardly one Christ-like attribute in their whole characters, who yet were so emotional and had such ecstatic feelings of love for Christ, as to think themselves justified in claiming the closest oneness with Him. I scarcely know a sadder sight. Surely our Lord meant to reach such cases when He said in Matt. 7:21, "Not everyone that saith unto me, Lord, Lord, shall enter into the kingdom of heaven; but he that doeth the will of my Father which is in heaven." He was not making here any arbitrary statement of God's will, but a simple announcement of the nature of things. Of course it must be so. It is like saying, "No man can enter the ranks of astronomers who is not an astronomer." Emotions will not make a man an astronomer, but life and action. He must *be* one, not merely *feel* that he is one.

There is no escape from this inexorable nature of things, and especially here. Unless we are one with Christ as to character and life and action, we cannot be one with Him in any other way, for there is no other way. We must be "partakers of His nature" or we cannot be partakers of His life, for His life and His nature are one.

But emotional souls do not always recognize this. They *feel* so near Christ and so united to Him, that they think it must be real; and overlooking the absolute necessity of Christ-likeness of character and walk, they are building their hopes and their confidence on their delightful emotions and exalted feelings, and think they must be one with Him, or they could not have such rich and holy experiences.

Now it is a psychological fact that these or similar emotions can be produced by other causes than a purely divine influence, and that they are largely dependent upon temperament and physical conditions. It is most dangerous, therefore, to make them a test of our spiritual union with Christ. It may result in just such a grievous self-deception as our Lord warns against in Luke 6:46-49, "And why call ye me, Lord, Lord, and do not the things which I say?" Our soul delights perhaps in calling Him, Lord, Lord, but are we *doing* the things which He said; for this, He tells us, is the important point, after all.

If, therefore, led by our feelings, we are saying in meetings, or among our friends, or even in our own heart before the Lord, that we are abiding in Him, let us take home to ourselves in solemn consideration these words of the Holy Ghost, "He that saith he abideth in Him, ought himself so to walk, even as He walked."

Unless we are thus walking, we cannot possibly be abiding in Him, no matter how much we may feel as if we were.

If you are really one with Christ you will be sweet to those who are cross to you; you will bear everything and make no complaints; when you are reviled you will not revile again; you will consent to be trampled on, as Christ was, and feel nothing but love in return; you will seek the honor of others rather than your own; you will take the lowest place, and be the servant of all, as Christ was; you will literally and truly love your enemies and do good to them that despitefully use you; you will, in short, live a Christ-like life, and manifest outwardly as well as feel inwardly a Christ-like spirit, and will walk among men as He walked among them. This, dear friends, is what it is to be one with Christ. And if all this is not your life according to your measure, then you are not one with Him, no matter how ecstatic or exalted your feelings may be.

To be one with Christ is too wonderful and solemn and mighty an experience to be reached by any overflow or exaltation of mere feeling. He was holy, and those who are one with Him will be holy also. There is no escape from this simple and obvious fact.

When our Lord tried to make us understand His oneness with God, He expressed it in such words as these, "I do always the things that please Him." "Whatsoever He saith unto me that I do." "The Son can do nothing of Himself, but what He seeth the Father do; for what things soever He doeth, these also doeth the Son likewise." "I can of mine own self do nothing; as I hear I judge, and my judgment is just; because I seek not mine own will, but the will of Him that sent me." "If I do not the works of my Father, believe me not. But if I do, though ye believe not me, believe the works; that ye may know and believe that the Father is in me and I in Him."

The test of oneness then, was the doing of the same works, and it is the test of oneness now. And if our Lord could say of Himself that if He did not the works of his Father, He did not ask to be believed, no matter what professions or claims He might make, surely His disciples must do no less.

It is forever true in the nature of things that "a good tree cannot bring forth evil fruit, neither can a corrupt tree bring forth good fruit." It is not that they will not, but they cannot. And a soul that is one with Christ will just as surely bring forth a Christ-like life, as a grapevine will bring forth grapes and not thistles.

Not that I would be understood to object to emotions. On the contrary, I believe they are very precious gifts, when they are from God, and are to be greatly rejoiced in. But what I do object to is the making them a test or proof of spiritual states, either in ourselves or others, and depending on them as the foundation of our faith. Let them come or let them go, just as God pleases, and make no account of them either way. But always see to it that the really vital marks of oneness with Christ, the marks of likeness in character, and life, and walk, are ours, and all will be well. For "he that saith I know Him, and keepeth not His commandments, is a liar, and the truth is not in Him. But whoso keepeth His word, in him verily is the love of God perfected: hereby know we that we are in Him."

It may be, my dear reader, that the grief of your life has been the fact that you have so few good feelings. You try your hardest to get up the feelings which you hear others talking about, but they will not come. You pray for them fervently, and are often tempted to upbraid God because He does not grant them to you. And you are filled with an almost unbearable anguish because you think your want of emotion is a sign that there is not any interior union of your soul with Christ. You judge altogether by your feelings, and think there is no other way to judge.

Now my advice to you is to let your feelings go, and pay no regard to them whatever. They really have nothing to do with the matter. They are not the indicators of your spiritual state, but are merely the indicators of your temperament, or of your present physical condition. People in very low states of grace are often the subjects of very powerful emotional experiences. We all know this from the scenes we have heard of or witnessed at camp-meetings and revivals. I myself had a colored servant once who would become unconscious under the power of her wonderful experiences, whenever there was a revival meeting at their church, who yet had hardly a token of any spiritual life about her at other times, and who was, in fact, not even moral. Now surely, if the Bible teaches nothing else, it does teach this, that a Christ-like life and walk must accompany any experience which is really born of His spirit. It could not be otherwise in the very nature of things. But I fear some Christians have separated the two things so entirely in their conceptions, as to have exalted their experiences at the expense of their walk, and have come to care far more about their emotions than about their character.

A certain colored congregation in one of the Southern States was a plague to the whole neighborhood by their open disregard of even the ordinary rules of morality; stealing, and lying, and cheating, without apparently a single prick of conscience on the subject. And yet their nightly meetings were times of the greatest emotion and "power." Someone finally spoke to the preacher about it, and begged him to preach a sermon on morality, which would lead his people to see their sins. "Ah, missus," he replied, "I knows dey's bad, but den it always brings a coldness like over de meetings when I preaches about dem things."

You are helpless as to your emotions, but character you can have if you will. You can be so filled with Christ as to be Christ-like, and if you are Christ-like, then you are one with Him in the only vital and essential way, even though your feelings may tell you that it is an impossibility.

Having thus settled what oneness with Christ really is, the next point for us to consider is how to reach it for ourselves.

We must first of all find out what are the *facts* in the case, and what is our own relation to these facts.

If you read such passages as 1 Cor. 3:16, "Know ye not that ye are the temple of God, and that the Spirit of God dwelleth in you?" and then look at the opening of the chapter to see to whom these wonderful words are spoken, even to "babes in Christ," who were "yet carnal," and walked according to man, you will see that this soul-union of which I speak, this unspeakably glorious mystery of an indwelling God is the possession of even the weakest and most failing believer in Christ. So that it is not a *new* thing you are to ask for, but only to realize that which you already have. Of every believer in the Lord Jesus it is absolutely true, that his "body is the temple of the Holy Ghost, which is in him, which he has of God."

It seems to me just in this way; as though Christ were living in a house, shut up in a far-off closet, unknown and unnoticed by the dwellers in the house, longing to make Himself known to them and be one with them in all their daily lives, and share in all their interests, but unwilling to force Himself upon their notice; as nothing but a voluntary companionship could meet or satisfy the needs of His love. The days pass by over that favored household, and they remain in ignorance of their marvelous privilege. They come and go about all their daily affairs with no thought of their wonderful Guest. Their plans are laid without reference to Him. His wisdom to guide, and His strength to protect, are all lost to them. Lonely days and weeks are spent in sadness, which might have been full of the sweetness of His presence.

But suddenly the announcement is made, "The Lord is in the house!"

How will its owner receive the intelligence? Will he call out an eager thanksgiving, and throw wide open every door for the entrance of his glorious Guest; Or will he shrink and hesitate, afraid of His presence and seek to reserve some private corner for a refuge from His all-seeing eye?

Dear friend, I make the glad announcement to thee that the Lord is in thy heart. Since the day of thy conversion He has been dwelling there, but thou hast lived on in ignorance of it. Every moment during all that time might have been passed in the sunshine of His sweet presence, and every step have been taken under His advice. But because thou knew it not, and hast never looked for Him there, thy life has been lonely and full of failure. But now that I make the announcement to thee, how wilt thou receive it? Art thou glad to have Him? Wilt thou throw wide open every door to welcome Him in? Wilt thou joyfully and thankfully give up the government of thy life into His hands? Wilt thou consult Him about everything, and let Him decide each step for thee, and mark out every path? Wilt thou invite Him to thy innermost chambers, and make Him the sharer in thy most hidden life? Wilt thou say, "YES!" to all His longing for union with thee, and with a glad and eager abandonment, hand thyself and all that concerns thee over into His hands? If thou wilt, then shall thy soul begin to know something of the joy of union with Christ.

And yet, after all, this is but a faint picture of the blessed reality. For far more glorious than it would be to have Christ a dweller in the house or in the heart, is it to be brought into such a real and actual union with Him as to be one with Him, one will, one purpose, one interest, one life. Human words cannot express such glory as this. And yet I *want* to express it. I want to make your souls so unutterably hungry to realize it, that day or night you cannot rest without it. Do you *understand* the words, one with Christ? Do you catch the slightest glimpse of their marvelous meaning? Does not your whole soul begin to exult over such a wondrous destiny? For it is a reality. It means to have no life but His life, to have no will but His will, to have no interests but His interests, to share His riches, to enter into His joys, to partake of His sorrows, to manifest His life, to have the same mind as He had, to think, and feel, and act, and walk as He did. Oh, who could have dreamed that such a destiny could have been ours!

Wilt thou have it, dear soul? Thy Lord will not force it on thee, for He wants thee as His companion and His friend, and a forced union would be incompatible with this. It must be voluntary on thy part.

The bride must say a willing "Yes," to her bridegroom, or the joy of their union is utterly wanting. Canst thou say a willing "Yes," to thy Lord?

It is such a simple transaction, and yet so real! The steps are but three. First, be convinced that the Scriptures teach this glorious indwelling of thy God; then surrender thy whole being to Him to be possessed by Him; and finally believe that He *has* taken possession, and is dwelling in thee. Begin to reckon thyself dead, and to reckon Christ as thy only life. Maintain this attitude of soul unwaveringly. Say, "I am crucified with Christ, nevertheless I live, yet not I, but Christ liveth in me," over and over day and night, until it becomes the habitual breathing of thy soul. Put off thy self-life by faith and in fact continually, and put on practically the life of Christ. Let this act become, by its constant repetition, the attitude of thy whole being. And as surely as thou dost this day by day, thou shalt find thyself continually bearing about in thy body the dying of the Lord Jesus, that the life also of Jesus may be made manifest in thy mortal flesh. Thou shalt learn to know what salvation means; and shalt have opened out to thy astonished gaze secrets of the Lord, of which thou hast hitherto hardly dreamed.

> *How have I erred! God is my home*
> *And God Himself is here.*
> *Why have I looked so far for Him,*
> *Who is nowhere but near?*
>
> *Yet God is never so far off*
> *As even to be near;*
> *He is within, our spirit is*
> *The home He holds most dear.*
>
> *So all the while I thought myself*
> *Homeless, forlorn, and weary;*
> *Missing my joy, I walked the earth,*
> *Myself God's sanctuary.*

18. "Although" and "Yet," a Lesson in the Interior Life

In many of our store windows at Christmas time there stands a most significant picture. It is a dreary, desolate winter scene. There is a dark, stormy, wintry sky, bare trees, and brown grass and dead weeds, with patches of snow over them. On a leafless tree at one side of the picture is an empty and snow-covered nest, and on a branch near sits a little bird. All is cold, and dark, and desolate enough to daunt any bird, and drive it to some fairer clime, but this bird is sitting there in an attitude of perfect contentment, and has its little head bravely lifted up towards the sky, while a winter song is evidently about to burst forth from its tiny throat.

This picture, which always stands on my shelf, has preached me many a sermon. And the test is always the same, and finds its expression in the two words that stand at the head of this article, "Although" and "Yet."

"ALTHOUGH the fig-tree shall not blossom, neither shall fruit be in the vines: the labor of the olive shall fail, and the field shall yield no meat; the flock shall be cut off from the fold, and there shall be no herd in the stall: YET I will rejoice in the Lord, I will joy in the God of my salvation."

There come times in many lives, when, like this bird in the winter, the soul finds itself bereft of every comfort both outward and inward; when all seems dark, and all seems wrong, even; when everything in which we have trusted seems to fail us; when the promises are apparently unfulfilled, and our prayers gain no response; when there seems nothing left to rest on in earth or Heaven. And it is at such times as these that the brave little bird with its message is needed. "Although" all is wrong everywhere, "yet" there is still one thing left to rejoice in, and that is God; the "God of our salvation," who changes not, but is the same good, loving, tender God yesterday, today, and forever. We can joy in *Him* always, whether we have anything else to rejoice in or not.

By rejoicing in Him, however, I do not mean rejoicing in ourselves, although I fear most people think this is really what is meant. It is *their* feelings or *their* revelations or *their* experiences that constitute the groundwork of their joy, and if none of these are satisfactory, they see no possibility of joy at all.

But the lesson the Lord is trying to teach us all the time is the lesson of self-effacement. He commands us to look away from self and all self's experiences, to crucify self and count it dead, to cease to be interested in self, and to know nothing and be interested in nothing but God.

The reason for this is that God has destined us for a higher life than the self-life. That just as He has destined the caterpillar to become the butterfly, and therefore has appointed the caterpillar life to die, in order that the butterfly life may take its place, so He has appointed our self-life to die in order that the divine life may become ours instead. The caterpillar effaces itself in its grub form, that it may evolve or develop into its butterfly form. It dies that it may live. And just so must we.

Therefore, the one most essential thing in this stage of our existence must be the death to self and the resurrection to a life only in God. And it is for this reason that the lesson of joy in the Lord, and not in self, *must* be learned. Every advancing soul *must* come sooner or later to the place where it can trust God, the bare God, if I may be allowed the expression, simply and only because of what He is in Himself, and not because of His promises or His gifts. It must learn to have its joy in Him alone, and to rejoice in Him when all else in Heaven and earth shall seem to fail.

The only way in which this place can be reached I believe, is by the soul being compelled to face in its own experience the loss of all things both inward and outward. I do not mean necessarily that all one's friends must die, or all one's money be lost: but I do mean that the soul shall find itself, from either inward or outward causes, desolate, and bereft, and empty of all consolation. It must come to the end of everything that is not God; and must have nothing else left to rest on within or without. It must experience just what the prophet meant when he wrote that "Although."

It must wade through the slough, and fall off of the precipice, and be swamped by the ocean, and at last find in the midst of them, and at the bottom of them, and behind them, the present, living, loving, omnipotent God! And then, and not until then, will it understand the prophet's exulting shout of triumph, and be able to join it: "YET I will rejoice in the Lord; I will joy in the God of my salvation."

And then, also, and not until then, will it know the full meaning of the verse that follows: "The Lord God is my strength, and He will make my feet like hind's feet, and He will make me to walk upon mine high places."

The soul often walks on what seem high places, which are, however, largely self-evolved and emotional, and have but little of God in them; and in moments of loss and failure and darkness, these high places become precipices of failure. But the high places to which the Lord brings the soul that rejoices only in Him, can be touched by no darkness or loss, for their very foundations are laid in the midst of an utter loss and death of all that is not God.

If we want an unwavering experience, therefore, we can find it only in the Lord, apart from all else; apart from His gifts, apart from His blessings, apart from all that can change or be affected by the changing conditions of our earthly life.

The prayer which is answered today, may seem to be unanswered tomorrow; the promises once so gloriously fulfilled, may cease to be a reality to us; the spiritual blessing which was at one time such a joy, may be utterly lost; and nothing of all we once trusted to and rested on may be left us, but the hungry and longing memory of it all. But when all else is gone, God is still left. Nothing changes Him. He is the same yesterday, today, and forever, and in Him is no variableness, neither shadow of turning. And the soul that finds its joy in Him alone, can suffer no wavering.

It is grand to trust in the promises, but it is grander still to trust in the Promiser. The promises may be misunderstood or misapplied, and at the moment when we are leaning all our weight upon them, they may seem utterly to fail us. But no one ever trusted in the Promiser and was confounded.

The God who is behind His promises and is infinitely greater than His promises, can never fail us in any emergency, and the soul that is stayed on Him cannot know anything but perfect peace.

The little child does not always understand its mother's promises, but it knows its mother, and its childlike trust is founded not on her word, but upon herself. And just so it is with those of us who have learned the lesson of this "Although" and "Yet." There may not be a prayer answered or a promise fulfilled to our own consciousness, but what of that? Behind the prayers and behind the promises, there is God, and He is enough. And to such a soul the simple words, GOD IS, answer every question and solve every doubt.

To the little trusting child the simple fact of the mother's existence is the answer to all its need. The mother may not make one single promise, or detail any plan, but *she is*, and that is enough for the child. The child rejoices in the mother; not in her promises, but in herself. And to the child, as to us, there is behind all that changes and can change, the one unchangeable joy of the mother's existence. While the mother lives, the child must be cared for, and the child knows this, instinctively if not intelligently, and rejoices in knowing it. And while God lives, His children must be cared for as well, and His children ought to know this, and rejoice in it as instinctively and far more intelligently than the child of human parents. For what else can God do, being what He is? Neglect, indifference, forgetfulness, ignorance, are all impossible to Him. He knows everything, He cares about everything, He can manage everything; and He loves us; and what more could we ask? Therefore, come what may, we will lift our faces to our God, like our brave little bird teacher, and, in the midst of our darkest "Althoughs," will sing our glad and triumphant "Yet."

All of God's saints in all ages have done this. Job said, out of the depths of sorrow and trial which few can equal, "*Though* He slay me *yet* will I trust in Him."

David could say in the moment of his keenest anguish, "Yea, *though* I walk through the valley of the shadow of death," *yet* "I will fear no evil; for Thou art with me." And again he could say, "God is our refuge and strength, a very present help in trouble. Therefore, will not we fear, *though* the earth be removed, and *though* the mountains be carried into the midst of the sea; *though* the waters thereof roar and be troubled; *though* the mountains shake with the swelling thereof... God is in the midst of her; she shall not be moved; God shall help her, and that right early."

Paul could say in the midst of his sorrows, "We are troubled on every side, *yet* not distressed; we are perplexed, *but* not in despair; persecuted, *but* not forsaken; cast down, *but* not destroyed... for which cause we faint not; but *though* our outward man perish, *yet* the inward man is renewed day by day. For our light affliction, which is but for a moment, worketh for us a far more exceeding and eternal weight of glory; while we look, not at the things which are seen, but at the things which are not seen; for the things which are seen are temporal; but the things which are not seen are eternal."

All this and more can the soul say that learned this lesson of rejoicing in God alone.

Spiritual joy is not a *thing*, not a lump of joy, so to speak, stored away in one's heart to be looked at and rejoiced over. Joy is only the gladness that comes from the possession of something good, or the knowledge of something pleasant. And the Christian's joy is simply his gladness in knowing Christ, and in his possession of such a God and Savior. We do not on an earthly plane rejoice in our joy, but in the thing that causes our joy. And on the heavenly plane it is the same. We are to "rejoice in the Lord, and joy in the God of our salvation"; and this joy no man nor devil can take from us, and no earthly sorrows can touch.

A writer on the interior life says, in effect, that our spiritual pathway is divided into three regions, very different from one another, and yet each one a necessary stage in the onward progress. First, there is the region of beginnings, which is a time full of sensible joys and delights, of fervent aspirations, of emotional experiences, and of many secret manifestations of God. Then comes a vast extent of wilderness, full of temptation, and trial, and conflict, of the loss of sensible manifestations, of dryness, and of inward and outward darkness and distress. And then, finally, if this desert period is faithfully traversed, there comes on the further side of it a region of mountain heights of uninterrupted union and communion with God, of superhuman detachment from everything earthly, of infinite contentment with the Divine will, and of marvelous transformation into the image of Christ.

Whether this order is true or not, I cannot here discuss, but of one thing I am very sure, that to many souls who have tasted the joy of the "region of beginnings" here set forth, there has come afterwards a period of desert experience at which they have been sorely amazed and perplexed. And I cannot but think such might, perhaps, in this explanation, find the answer to their trouble. They are being taught the lesson of detachment from all that is not God, in order that their souls may at last be brought into that interior union and oneness with Him which is set forth in the picture given of the third and last region of mountain heights of blessedness.

The soul's pathway is always through death to life. The caterpillar cannot in the nature of things become the butterfly in any other way than by dying to the one life in order to live in the other. And neither can we. Therefore, it may well be that this region of death and desolation must needs be passed through, if we would reach the calm mountain heights beyond. And if we know this, we can walk triumphantly through the darkest experience, sure that all is well, since God is God.

In the lives of many who read this paper there is, I feel sure, at least one of these desert "Althoughs," and in some lives there are many.

Dear friends, is the "Yet" there also? Have you learned the prophet's lesson? Is God enough for you? Can you sing and *mean* it,

> *"Thou, O Christ, art all I want,*
> *More than all in thee I find"?*

If not, you need the little bird to speak to you.

And the song that he sings, as he sits on that bare and leafless tree, with the winter storm howling around him, must become your song also.

> *"Though the rain may fall and the wind be blowing,*
> * And cold and chill is the wintry blast;*
> *Though the cloudier sky is still cloudier growing,*
> * And the dead leaves tell that summer is passed;*
> *Yet my face I hold to the stormy heaven,*
> * My heart is as calm as a summer sea;*
> *Glad to receive what my God hath given,*
> * Whate'er it be.*

> *"When I feel the cold, I can say, 'He sends it,'*
> * And His wind blows blessing I surely know;*
> *For I've never a want but that He attends it;*
> * And my heart beats warm, though the winds may blow*
> *The soft sweet summer was warm and glowing,*
> * Bright were the blossoms on every bough;*
> *I trusted Him when the roses were blowing,*
> * I trust Him now.*

> *"Small were my faith should it weakly falter,*
> * Now that the roses have ceased to blow;*

Frail were the trust that now should alter,
  Doubting His love when the storm-clouds grow.
If I trust Him once I must trust Him ever,
  And His way is best, though I stand or fall,
Through wind or storm He will leave me never,
  For He sends all."

19. The Baptism of the Holy Ghost

The baptism of the Holy Spirit is the crowning and vital point in all christian experience. And right views concerning it are of very great importance. It seems to be a subject beset with difficulties and errors at the present time, though evidently it was intended to be one of the simplest and most easily understood of all.

In considering it, two questions only, need to be settled: *first*, What or who is the Holy Ghost? and *second*, What is it to be baptized with the Holy Ghost?

The answer to the first question is, that the Holy Ghost or Holy Spirit is simply God's spirit. It is the life and power and nature of God, manifested in a spiritual way to man's spirit. It is in fact God Himself, as a spirit, communicating with the spiritual part of man's nature.

In John 14:16-23, we are shown this:—

"And I will pray the Father, and He shall give you another Comforter, that He may abide with you forever; even the Spirit of Truth; whom the world cannot receive, because it seeth Him not, neither knoweth Him: but ye know Him; for He dwelleth with you, and shall be in you. I will not leave you comfortless: I will come to you. Yet a little while, and the world seeth me no more; but ye see me: because I live, ye shall live also. At that day ye shall know that I am in my Father, and ye in me, and I in you. He that hath my commandments, and keepeth them, he it is that loveth me; and he that loveth me shall be loved of my Father, and I will love him, and will manifest myself to him. Judas saith unto Him (not Iscariot), Lord, how is it that thou wilt manifest thyself unto us, and not unto the world? Jesus answered and said unto him, If a man love me, he will keep my words: and my Father will love him, and we will come unto him and make our abode with him."

Here Christ speaks of His own coming and the Spirit's coming as interchangeable experiences, as though it were the same thing whether He should say, "I will come," or "the Spirit will come," or "my Father will come." He simply means that He has been with them in bodily presence, but hereafter He will be with them in spiritual presence; or in other words, that God had been manifesting Himself through the Divine Man, Christ Jesus, but hence forth He would manifest Himself in a spiritual way, through the Holy Spirit, *i.e.*, His own spirit. Consequently the Holy Spirit is called by God "my Spirit" all through the Old Testament, and also very frequently in the New Testament "the Spirit of God," and "the Spirit of Christ."

"But ye are not in the flesh, but in the Spirit, if so be that the Spirit of God dwell in you. Now if any man have not the Spirit of Christ, he is none of his. And if Christ be in you, the body is dead because of sin; but the Spirit is life because of righteousness. But if the Spirit of Him that raised up Jesus from the dead dwell in you, He that raised up Christ from the dead shall also quicken your mortal bodies by His Spirit that dwelleth in you."

The different expressions used here all mean, of course, the same thing; "the Spirit"; the "Spirit of Christ"; "Christ in you"; "the Spirit of Him that raised up Jesus"; and all mean evidently the Holy Spirit. If we substitute the words "life" or "nature" for Spirit, we shall perhaps be helped to understand just what the Holy Spirit is. As we read in Rom. 8:2, "For the law of the Spirit of life in Christ Jesus hath made me free from the law of sin and death."

The Holy Spirit therefore is the "Spirit of life in Christ Jesus," or in other words is the holy *life* or *nature* of Christ, of which we are to be made par takers; as the Scripture expresses it, "partakers of the Divine nature."

And this brings us to our second question as to what it is to be *baptized* with the Holy Ghost.

The word "baptize" means to immerse, to dip into. Baptism with anything, therefore, must mean being immersed, or dipped into, that thing. To be baptized with the Holy Ghost means to be immersed into the Spirit of God, as to character or nature. It is variously described as being "partakers of the Divine nature" (2 Pet. 1:4); having "Christ to dwell in the heart by faith" (Eph. 3:17); being a "temple of the living God" (2 Cor. 6:16); being a "habitation of God through the Spirit" (Eph. 2:22). To be filled with the Holy Ghost, therefore, means simply to be filled with God.

The word "baptize" is used in connection with the Holy Spirit eight times. Six of these cases are the announcements concerning Christ's mission as the Head of the new spiritual dispensation, the baptizer with the Holy Ghost (Matt. 3:11; Mark 1:8; Luke 3:16; John 1:26-33; Acts 1:5). Once it is used in describing the conversion of Cornelius and his household (Acts 11:16), where it was an experience that accompanied their believing the words spoken by Peter. And once it is used to declare the divine process by which every member of Christ is baptized into the one body (1 Cor. 12:13).

The same word "baptize" is also used in several places to express the same fact, but not with the actual words "Holy Ghost." As, for instance, "baptized into Jesus Christ" (Rom. 6:3); "baptized into Christ" (Gal. 3:27); "buried with Him in baptism" (Col. 2:12), etc., etc.

It is plain, therefore, that the expression "baptism of the Holy Ghost" has no exclusive meaning, but is only one way of describing the fact of out abiding in Christ and His abiding in us; in other words, "the life hid with Christ in God."

We say of an artist that he is baptized with the spirit of the old masters, and we mean, not necessarily that he had at any one time any especial or overwhelming experience, though this might be, but that he is all the time dipped into and permeated by their spirit; that he thinks like them, and paints like them, and has their views and ways. And, similarly, when we say of a man that he is baptized with the Spirit of Christ, we ought to mean that he is dipped into and permeated by the Divine Spirit and nature of Christ, as the law of his continual being.

The mistake is too often made of looking upon the "baptism of the Spirit" as an *experience* rather than a *life*; as an outpouring rather than an incoming; as an arbitrary bestowment rather than a necessary vitality. Yet the Scripture plainly teaches that the gift of the Holy Spirit is a universal gift to all believers, one without which they cannot be believers at all. It is impossible to be a child of God without the Spirit, for the new birth is distinctly declared to be a birth of the Spirit (John 3:5, 6).

Everyone, therefore, who is born of God is born of the Spirit, and has the Spirit within him as his new indwelling life. "If any man have not the Spirit of Christ, he is none of His" (Rom. 8:9) and the converse of this is necessarily true, that if any man belongs to Christ he must have the Spirit of Christ.

In Gal. 4:6, we read, "because ye are sons God hath sent forth the Spirit of His Son into your hearts." "Because ye are sons"; the very fact of sonship implies in the intrinsic nature of things the possession of the Spirit of God, for it is simply impossible to be born of God and not have God's Spirit get least in measure.

In 1 Cor. 7:13, we read, "For by one Spirit are we all baptized into one body, whether we be Jews or Gentiles, whether we be bond or free; and have been all made to drink into one Spirit." Notice the "all" twice repeated in this verse. Plainly the teaching is that everyone who belongs to the "one body" at all, belongs to it only by right of having been baptized into it by the "one Spirit."

In 1 Cor. 3:16, 17, we have another most striking declaration of this:—

"Know ye not that ye are the temple of God, and that the Spirit of God dwelleth in you? If any man defile the temple of God, him shall God destroy; for the temple of God is holy, which temple ye are."

If we refer back to the opening of this chapter we shall see that the apostle here was not writing to advanced christians, but to babes in Christ who were "yet carnal," and could not be spoken to as "spiritual," and who were not able to bear anything but the simplest milk of the Gospel (see verses 1-3). And yet to these very christians, who were "yet carnal," and who "walked as men," Paul announces the fact that even they are the temple of God, and that the Spirit of God dwelleth in them; not will dwell, but dwelleth now. And on this fact he founds his appeal to them for holiness and purity.

We must believe, therefore, that this unspeakably glorious mystery of an indwelling Holy Ghost is the possession of even the weakest and most failing child of God, whether His presence has ever yet been recognized or not, or His control acknowledged and obeyed. He *is* within each one of us, although He may not yet have been allowed to take full pos session. We *are* His temple, although we may not yet have opened every inward chamber of our hearts to His indwelling.

In seeking the baptism of the Holy Spirit, therefore, it is not a new thing you are to ask for, but simply to recognize the presence of that which you already have, and to submit fully to His possession and His control.

No one can doubt that the "well of water springing up into everlasting life," which Christ declared should be *in* the soul that came to Him to drink, is the Holy Ghost; and our Lord plainly declares that this water is already provided, and that all the soul needs is to come and drink.

"In the last day, that great day of the feast, Jesus stood and cried, saying, If any man thirst, let him come unto me and drink. He that believeth on me, as the Scripture hath said, out of his belly shall flow rivers of living water. (But this spake he of the Spirit, which they that believe on him should receive; for the Holy Ghost was not yet given; because that Jesus was not yet glorified.)"

The Holy Spirit is a gift, but the being baptized or filled with the Spirit is not a gift, but a command. Water is a gift, but the drinking of water is not a gift but our duty. The sunlight is a gift, but the let ting the sunlight into our houses is our privilege and our duty.

To be baptized with the sunlight, is merely to get into it and let it shine, and to be baptized with the Spirit is the same.

In Acts 2:33, we are told that Christ "having received of the Father the promise of the Holy Ghost, hath shed forth" this promised gift upon the church. And in Eph. 5:18, we are commanded to "be filled with the Spirit."

The Holy Spirit is like the sunlight, which forces its way into every place where there is the slightest opening to receive it. The sunlight has been shed forth upon the world; and the Holy Ghost, the promise of the Father, *hath been* shed forth upon the Church. Every man born into the world shares the world's sunlight, and may have as much or as little of it as he pleases, and every man born into the Church, (I mean, of course, the invisible Church of all believers) shares the Church's gift of the Holy Ghost, and may have as little or as much as he pleases.

If I want sunlight in my house, I do not need to ask God to give me a fresh thing shed down from the sky, but I need only to open all the doors and windows of my house to permit the entrance of the sunlight which has already been given; and if I want to be baptized with the sunshine I do not need So ask for more sunshine, but simply to go out into the sunshine and be baptized. Similarly, if I want to be filled with the Spirit, I need not ask for more of the Spirit to be given to me, but only that more of myself may be given to the Spirit. I am not to look for any fresh outpouring from God, but for a fresh incoming into me of that Spirit which has already been "shed forth" upon every believer.

The preaching of the Gospel since the coming of Christ is called, in 2 Cor. 3:8, the "ministration of the Spirit," and, in the common language of christians, we speak of the present age as being the "dispensation of the Holy Ghost." We mean by this, that the vital element of this age is the presence and power of God's Spirit as the controlling life of everything that lives.

This dispensation or "ministration of the Spirit" was prophesied of in the Old Testament in many places. (See Joel 2:28, 29.) "And it shall come to pass afterward, that I will pour out my Spirit upon all flesh"; and notice the expression "all flesh", showing it was dispensational as well as personal.

Christ reiterated this promise of the coming Spirit, and told His disciples to wait for its fulfilment.

"And being assembled together with them, com manded them that they should not depart from Jerusalem, but wait for the promise of the Father, which, saith he, ye have heard of me. For John truly baptized with water; but ye shall be baptized with the Holy Ghost not many days hence." (Acts 1:4, 5.) See also Luke 24:49; John 15:26; John 14:16, 17; John 16:7-13.

On the day of Pentecost, when the great out pouring came, declaration was made, "This is that which was spoken by the prophet Joel: and it shall come to pass in the last days, saith God, I will pour out of my Spirit upon all flesh." (Acts 2:1-4, 16-18.)

Evidently the repetition here of the prophetical expression, "upon all flesh," marks this outpouring of the Spirit as the introduction of a new dispensation, the formal instalment of the Spirit, set up in the midst of the kingdom of matter, and thenceforth to rule over and control it. The disciples were told to "tarry" and "wait for" the ushering in of this ministration or dispensation of the Spirit. But after it had been thus ushered in, there was no command henceforth to tarry, but always either an immediate bestowal, or the command to an immediate reception.

In Acts 2:38, 39, the apostle Peter, in the very first sermon preached in this new dispensation, announced that whoever believed in Christ should receive the wonderful gift, declaring to the people in the plainest words that it was their inalienable birth right: "For the promise is unto you and to your children, and to all that are afar off, even as many as the Lord our God shall call." It was to be no special gift to a few, but belonged universally to every awakened soul. See also on this point, Acts 10:44-47; Acts 11:15-17; Acts 15:8, 9. And yet, in spite of all this there were christians then as now who did not receive this filling with the Spirit. "And it came to pass that while Apollos was at Corinth, Paul having passed through the upper coasts came to Ephesus; and finding certain disciples, he said unto them, Have ye received the Holy Ghost since ye believed? And they said unto him, We have not so much as heard whether there be any Holy Ghost." (Acts 19:1, 2.)

These christians were like many in the church now; they had "not so much as heard" of their glorious possession of the Holy Ghost. The question was not, "Has God given?" but, "Have you received?" Such christians are like blind men, who do not know the sun is shining, and do not open their windows and let it in. These blind believers in Jesus kneel down in their shut-up hearts and pray for the baptism of the Spirit, when all the while this very longed-for Holy Ghost is beating upon every avenue of their being, seeking for an entrance.

If we compare Acts 18:24, 25, with Acts 19:3, we shall understand the ignorance of these Ephesian converts. Apollos, who was their teacher, could not instruct them in that of which he himself was ignorant, and as he "knew only the baptism of John," they also, of course, knew no other. There is much similar teaching of ignorance in the church to-day; and what is needed now is the same thing that was needed then, that some Aquila and Priscilla, or Paul, shall expound unto all such "the way of God more perfectly."

There are four different forces of nature used to describe the work of the Spirit:—

I.   Fire: Matt. 3:11.
II. Water: John 4:10, 14.
III. Wind: John 3:8.
IV. Light: Eph. 5:8, 9, 10, 13; John 1:4-9.

It is characteristic of all these that they force their way into every opening, let it be ever so small, and can only be kept out by erecting barriers against them. How much more true must this be of that all-pervading immanent presence of the Spirit of God, which these things are declared to typify. Therefore, if only we know it, the Holy Ghost, like the sunlight on a dome, is beating against every human heart, and streams in at the tiniest opening.

Someone has said: "Just as the atmosphere was full of electricity before we adapted the telegraph to it, before we harnessed the lightning to carry our messages, and compelled it to drive our cars, so there is an atmosphere full of spiritual electricity around us of which we have only to take hold in order to secure to ourselves its inherent powers. The fulness of God, the Spirit of God, surrounds every human soul. And the soul has only to surrender itself wholly to God, when God will stream through and into that soul with His saving power and heavenly glory."

But there is in the lives of many christians an experience of a wonderful and instantaneous baptism, which makes an epoch in their lives, and which seems to transform their characters. In the light of the above teaching, what is the explanation of this?

It is, as we have proved, an incontrovertible fact that every child of God is and must be indwelt by the Spirit of God. But it is equally a fact that not all are "filled" with this Spirit. And the definite, conscious experience, of which so many speak as the baptism of the Holy Ghost, is simply the moment when the soul, either consciously or unconsciously, surrenders itself fully to this divine incoming. The command is, "Be filled with the Spirit," and we obey this command by abandoning our whole selves to God, and opening every avenue of our being to His possession. Like sunlight, or like the wind, He enters and fills every spot that is opened to Him, The result of this, when done suddenly, is often a very emotional and overwhelming sense of His presence. But this sudden experience does not rise from the fact that anything *new* has been shed forth from God, but only that that which has been already shed forth on the day of Pentecost, eighteen hundred years ago, is now allowed to enter and take full possession.

It is not more of the Spirit the lifeless christian needs, but only that the Spirit should have more of him. And the conscious baptism is not the *coming* of the Spirit as of a thing from the outside, but the full taking possession of the whole being by the in dwelling Spirit already within. "Be filled with the Spirit," as if to say, "You have the Spirit dwelling in you, but have not yet realized His full power." You have been "sealed with that Holy Spirit of promise"; but there are doors to be unlocked, and rooms to be occupied, before it can be truly said that you are "filled with all the fulness of God."

As a late Writer has said concerning this: "Let me illustrate: I contract with a painter to paint and decorate my house. He sends a thoroughly competent man, with all necessary materials. The work man takes possession of the house; but the work progresses slowly. Why? Well, I have locked sun dry doors, and piled up lumber in the corridors, and the man cannot go on with his work. What is wanted is not that I should ask the contractor to 'send the painter,' or to let me have 'more of the painter'; not more of the painter for the house, but more of the house for the painter. Give the painter a chance. Open the barred doors, clear away the obstructing 1 amber, and he will carry on the work to a satisfactory completion, according to contract."

Like the treasures of coal under a man's field, which existed there just as really before they were known and utilized by him, as they do afterwards; so does the Holy Spirit dwell in all the children of God, whether they know it or not, waiting for them to recognize His presence and yield to His control.

His operations may be hindered and the manifestations of His presence clouded. He may be grieved and thwarted, but nevertheless it is a simple fact that the Spirit of God dwells in *all* the children of God.

In seeking for the baptism of the Holy Ghost, therefore, it is not God's attitude towards us that needs to be changed, but our attitude towards Him. He is not to give us anything new, but we are to receive in a new and far fuller sense that which He has already given.

The vital importance of this teaching will be realized by all who have, either in their own experience, or in dealing with others, known something of the extreme difficulties connected with this subject. Earnest, devoted souls have been brought into great darkness because they have not realized in their own experience the wonderful "baptism" of which others speak. They think they cannot have received the longed-for gift, because their emotions and sensations have not been like those described by others. The "fruits of the Spirit" are manifested often to a great degree in their lives, but they are afraid to attribute these fruits to the indwelling power of the Holy Ghost, for fear they may be claiming at blessing which they do not really possess. They blame themselves for not possessing this gift, and they try in every way that is suggested to obtain it; but their darkness and trouble only seem to increase, and nothing seems to come of all their seeking.

Now if it were really true that no one has received the Spirit as an indwelling guest, but those who have had some definite conscious experience of "baptism" at a certain clearly marked time, how are we to account for the "fruits of the Spirit" so beautifully developed in many devoted lives, who have known no such epoch in their experience? Dare we say these fruits have been produced by any other power, or have come from any other source, than the indwelling Spirit of God? Is not a tree to be known by its fruits, and *can* any power but the Holy Spirit produce holiness of heart and life? And on the other hand, dare we characterize all the wild fanaticism, or the many un-Christ-like self-seeking ways of some who have received a "wonderful baptism" as being the genuine fruits of that Spirit, whose essential characteristics are a Christ-like wisdom and a Christ-like spirit of meekness and self-sacrifice?

We can only conclude, therefore, that many art baptized with the Spirit of God, who can tell of no wonderful experience, and that many who have been prostrated, perhaps, by a mighty baptism, know little or nothing of the true Holy Spirit.

I have discovered by careful investigation that spiritualists have these wonderful emotional experiences quite as often as christians, and I am convinced there are emotions common to highly exalted mental states, no matter what the cause of this exaltation, whose origin is purely physical or psychical, and has nothing more to do with God's Spirit as such, than with any other source of excitation. It is of the body, and not of the spirit at all, and I fear many are sadly deceived by these experiences into thinking they must necessarily be from God, and *must* be tokens of His especial favor, who as a fact know nothing whatever of the reality of being filled with the Spirit.

To sum up the whole subject, then, we have proved the following facts:—

I.   The Holy Spirit has been shed forth on the whole church of God, as the sunlight has been shed forth on the world.

II.   All who are born into the family of God, receive the Spirit of God.

III.   To be "baptized" with the Holy Ghost means simply that the soul has surrendered itself wholly to be taken possession of in every part by this indwelling Spirit.

IV.   The "fruits" of this indwelling Spirit may or may not be strong emotions and overpowering manifestations, but they positively must be without exception Christ-like lives and characters.

V.   By the fruits you shall know the baptism.

VI.   We are not to limit the baptism of the Holy Ghost to one single motion on God's part, and one single experience on man's part. It is rather the continuous flow of the all-pervading and controlling spirit and life of God into the human soul, cleansing and consuming the darkness and sin there; and it cannot be known in its entireness and completeness until nothing is left which needs cleansing, or which the fire can consume.

VII.   It is not by believing in the Spirit, apart from God, that we receive the Holy Ghost, but by believing in and receiving God as the Spirit, and surrendering ourselves to His control.

The question next arises, How can I personally as a child of God come unto this baptism and be myself individually "filled with the Spirit"?

To this I answer that here, as in every other experience in the divine life, the things necessary on our part are surrender and faith. We must be convinced first of all that it is a fact that we as the children of God *are* indwelt by the Spirit of God. Then we must abandon ourselves wholly, body, soul, and spirit, for His full possession. We must throw wide open every chamber in our inward temple, and let the I heavenly Guest enthrone Himself in all. Then we must believe that He *does* take full possession, and that we *are* filled with the Spirit up to the measure of our capacity to receive, and we must begin from that time onward to reckon on His presence and power as a continual fact in our lives and experience. We must hold here steadfastly, regardless of all seemings, going quietly forward in a life of simple obedience to the Spirit now enthroned within, and the result will be that very soon the fruits of the Spirit will manifest themselves in a blessed abundance.

The entrance upon this life of full surrender to the control of the indwelling Holy Ghost may often be a sudden and perhaps almost overwhelming flood of emotion. But in other cases it may come, as it were, without "observation" in a quiet gladness and confidence, with a continual increasing development of spiritual power.

But however this may be, the essential *facts* are as we have seen, and the soul's part is only and always to recognize the indwelling presence of the Holy Ghost, and to yield utterly to His control. For this is the baptism of the Holy Ghost.

We sometimes see a notice up on buildings, "Room to let with power." This means that there is somewhere in the building a steam-engine, with a connection in the vacant room, and that when any one rents the room, they rent also the power of the steam-engine with which it is connected. Should a man rent such a room and put his machinery into it, he would need, of course, to make the connection between the machine and the power before he could expect his machine to go. He would not put his machinery in the room, and then go off to see the landlord and ask for the power; but he would look carefully for the point of connection with the power already provided. And just so it is with our hearts. The power of the Holy Ghost is already provided, but we need to make the connection, and this connection can only be made on our part by surrender and faith.

Everything is provided on God's side always, and what we want is simply adjustment to his plans.

I once passed through a large linen manufactory on a Sabbath day. There was one vast room full of the most beautiful and complicated machinery, all standing perfectly still and doing no work. Every wheel and spindle and thread was in its right position for use, and all was in perfect order; but nothing could be done because the power was wanting. The connection with the steam-engine had been cut off. And as I recall it I cannot but think how like those great silent rows of looms were to the silent rows of grand christian men and women who are so divinely gifted for the Master's work, but who are useless, because the connection with the mighty power of the Holy Ghost has not been fully made.

In Luke 11:9-13, we have the strongest expression possible of the utter freedom of this gift:—

"And I say unto you, Ask, and it shall be given you; seek, and ye shall find; knock, and it shall be opened unto you. For everyone that asketh receiveth; and he that seeketh findeth; and to him that knocketh it shall be opened. If a son shall ask bread of any of you that is a father, will he give him a stone? or if he ask a fish, will he for a fish give him a serpent? Or if he shall ask an egg, will he offer him a scorpion? If ye then, being evil, know how to give good gifts unto your children, how much more shall your heavenly Father give the Holy Spirit to them that ask Him."

We have only to ask, and at once we receive, for asking and receiving go together. Moreover, what stronger figure could be used than that of the parent and the hungry child. What parent is there who is not eager to give bread to the child that needs it? Yet notice the "how much more," in reference to God.

The whole process, then, is summed up in 1 John 5:14, 15:—

"And this is the confidence that we have in Him, that, if we ask anything according to His will, He heareth us: and if we know that He hear us, what soever we ask, we know that we have the petitions that we desired of Him."

Come out then, dear Christian, into the full sunlight of this truth we have been teaching concerning the Holy Ghost, and let the wonderful "promise of the Father" baptize you, as a man is baptized with sun shine who stands in the full blaze of the natural sun. Do not stay shut up in your unbelief and questioning, and cry for the baptism, but open wide every avenue of your being and let the all-environing Spirit of God pour in and flood your surrendered soul.

The world is full of sunlight; but if I shut my plant up in a dark cellar, it will dwindle and die for want of it. In such a case I might pray forever, "O Lord, pour out thy sunlight on my plant," but none would come. In the nature of things, none could come. But if I take the plant out of the cellar and place it in the sunlight, it is flooded at once.

The Holy Ghost is my soul's sunlight, and the world is full of it. I have only to get out of the cellar of my unbelief and put myself "in the light," and I too shall be flooded at once.

20. Kings and their Kingdoms; Or, How to Reign in the Interior Life

"And when he was demanded of the Pharisees when the kingdom of God should come, he answered them and said, The kingdom of God cometh not with observation: neither shall they say, lo here! or, lo there! for, behold, the kingdom of God is within you."

The expressions "kingdom of God" and "kingdom of Heaven" are used in Scripture concerning the divine life in the soul. They mean simply the place or condition where God rules, and where His will is done. It is an interior kingdom, not an exterior one. Its thrones are not outward thrones of human pomp and glory, but inward thrones of dominion and supremacy over the things of time and sense. Its kings are not clothed in royal robes of purple and fine linen, but with the interior garments of purity and truth. And its reign is not in outward show, but in inward power. Neither is it in one place rather than another, nor in one form of things above another. It is not, lo here, nor lo there, not in this mountain nor yet at Jerusalem, that we are to find Christ, and enter into His kingdom. It is not a matter of place at all, but one of condition. And in every place and under every name, and through every form, all who seek God and work righteousness shall find His kingdom within them.

But this is very little understood. In our childish fashion of literalism we have too much imbibed the idea that a kingdom must necessarily be in a particular place and with outward observation; and have therefore expected that the kingdom of heaven would mean for us an outward victory of heaven over earth in some particular place, or under some especial form; and that to sit on a throne with Christ, would be to have an outward uplifting in power and glory before the face of all around us.

But as the inner sense of Scripture unfolds to us, we see that this would be but a poor and superficial fulfilling of the real meaning of these wonderful symbols. And the vision of their true significance grows and strengthens before the "eyes that see," until at last we know that our Lord's words were truer than ever we had dreamed before, that the "kingdom of God cometh not with observation; neither shall they say, lo here! or, lo there! for, behold, the kingdom of God is within you."

In Daniel 2:44, we have the announcement of the kingdom, and in Isaiah 9:6, 7, the announcement of the King:—

"The God of heaven shall set up a kingdom which shall never be destroyed; and the kingdom shall not be left to other people, but it shall break in pieces and consume all these kingdoms, and it shall stand forever."

"For unto us a child is born, unto us a son is given: and the government shall be upon His shoulder; and His name shall be called Wonderful, Counsellor, the mighty God, the everlasting Father, the Prince of Peace. Of the increase of His government and peace there shall be no end, upon the throne of David, and upon His kingdom, to order it, and to establish it with judgment and with justice from henceforth even forever. The zeal of the Lord of hosts will perform this."

This kingdom is to break in pieces and consume all other kingdoms by right of the law by which the inward always rules the outward. If there is peace within, no outward turmoil can affect the soul; but outward peace can never quiet an inward tempest. A happy heart can walk in triumphant indifference through a sea of external trouble; while internal anguish cannot find happiness in the most favorable surroundings. What a man is within himself, makes or unmakes his joy, and not what he possesses outside of himself.

Someone said to Diogenes, "The king has degraded you." "Yes" replied Diogenes, triumphantly, "but I am not degraded!" No act of kings or emperors can degrade a soul that retains its own dignity; no tyrant can enslave a man who is inwardly free.

Therefore to have this divine kingdom set up within, means that all other powers to conquer or enslave are broken, and the soul reigns triumphant over them all. Men and devils may try to hold such a one in bondage, but they are powerless before the might of this interior kingdom. No longer will fashion, or conventionality, or the fear of man, or the love of ease, or any other of the many tyrants to which Christians cringe and bow, rule a soul that has been raised to a throne in this inward kingdom. No sin or temptation can overcome, no sorrow can crush, no discouragement can hinder. Let a man or woman have been bound in ever so tyrannical chains of sinful habits, this kingdom will set them free. Circumstances make men kings in the outward life, but in this hidden life men become kings over circumstances. And the soul that has aforetime been the slave of a thousand outward things, finds itself here utterly independent of them, everyone.

For the King in this kingdom is One whom no circumstances can affect or baffle. He it is indeed who makes circumstances. And since the government is upon His shoulders, we cannot doubt that He will order the kingdom with a judgment and justice that will leave nothing for any subject in His kingdom to desire.

In the expression "the government shall be upon His shoulder," we have the whole secret of this wonderful kingdom. Upon *His* shoulder, not upon *ours*. The care is His, the burdens are His, the responsibility belongs to Him, the protection rests upon Him, the planning, and providing, and controlling, and guiding, all are in His hands. No one can question as to His perfect fulfilment of every requirement of His kingship. Therefore those who are in His kingdom, are utterly delivered from any need to be anxious, or burdened, or perplexed, or troubled. And by this deliverance they become kings. The government is not upon their shoulders, and they have no business to interfere with it. Their King has assumed the whole responsibility, and if He can but see His subjects happy and prosperous, He is content Himself to bear all the weight and care of kingship. How often we speak of the responsibilities of earthly kings, and pity them for the burdens that kingship imposes. We recognize, even on an earthly plane, that to be a king means, or ought to mean, the bearing of the burdens of even the meanest of his subject. And even now, as I write, many hearts are aching with sympathy for the new Czar, who has assumed the grievous burden of the mighty Russian Empire.

From this instinctive sense of every human heart as to the rightful duties and responsibilities of kingship, we may learn what it means to be in a kingdom over which God is King, and where He has himself declared all things shall be ordered with judgment and justice from henceforth and even forever. Surely no care or anxiety can ever enter here, if the heart but knows its kingdom and its King!

In John 18:36, our King tells us the tactics of His kingdom: "Jesus answered, My kingdom is not of this world: if my kingdom were of this world then would my servants fight, that I should not be delivered to the Jews; but now is my kingdom not from hence."

Earthly kings and earthly kingdoms gain and keep their supremacy by outward conflict; God's kingdom conquers by inward power. Earthly kings subdue enemies; God subdues enmity. His victories must be interior before they can be exterior. He does not subjugate, but he conquers. Even we, on our earthly plane, know something of this principle, and do not value any victory over another which only reaches the body and has not subdued the heart. No true mother cares for an outward obedience merely; nothing will satisfy her but the inward surrender. Unless the citadel of the heart is conquered, the conquest seem worthless. And with God how much more will this be the case, since we are told that "He seeth not as man seeth; for man looketh on the outward appearance, but the Lord looketh on the heart." We speak of "subduing hearts," and we mean, not that they are overpowered or forced into an unwilling and compulsory surrender, but that they are conquered by being won, and are willingly yielded up to another's control. And it is after this fashion and no other that God subdues. So that to read that "His kingdom ruleth over all," means that all hearts are won to His service in a glad and willing surrender.

For again I repeat, His reign must be inward before it can be outward. And in truth it is no reign at all, unless it is within. If we think of it a moment we shall see that this must be so in the very nature of things, and that it is impossible to conceive of God reigning in a kingdom where the subduing reaches no further than the outside actions of His subjects. His kingdom is not of this world, but is in a spiritual sphere, where its power is over the souls and not the bodies of men; and therefore only when the soul is conquered, can it be set up.

Understood in this light, how full of love and blessing do all those declarations and prophecies become, which tell us that God is to subdue His enemies under His feet, and is to rule them in righteousness and power! And how glorious with hope does the voice of that great multitude heard by John sound out, saying, "Alleluia! for the Lord God omnipotent reigneth!"

In confirmation of all this we have two passages descriptive of this kingdom, in Rom. 14:17, and 1 Cor. 4:20: "For the kingdom of God is not meat and drink, but righteousness and peace and joy in the Holy Ghost." "For the kingdom of God is not in word, but in power."

Not outward things, but inward. Not what a man eats and drinks, not where he lives, nor what is his nationality, nor the customs of his race, not even what he thinks nor what he says; but what are the inward characteristics of his nature, and the inward power of his spiritual life. For these alone constitute this kingdom of God. Not what I do, but what I am, is to decide whether I belong to it or not. And only as inward righteousness, and inward peace, and inward joy, and inward power are bestowed and experienced, can this kingdom be set up. Therefore no outward subjugation can accomplish results like these, but only the interior work of the all-subduing spirit of God.

I have been greatly instructed by the story of Ulysses, when he was sailing past the islands of the sirens. These sirens had the power of charming by their songs all who listened to them, and of inducing them to leap into the sea. To avert this danger, Ulysses filled the ears of his crew with wax, that they might not hear the fatal music, and bound himself to the mast with knotted cords; and thus they passed the isle in safety. But when Orpheus was obliged to sail by the same island, he gained a better victory, for he himself made sweeter music than that of the sirens, and enchanted his crew with more alluring songs; so that they passed the dangerous charmers not only with safety, but with disdain. Wax and knotted cords kept Ulysses and his crew from making the fatal leap; but inward delights enabled Orpheus and his crew to reign triumphant over the very source of temptation itself. And just so is it with the kingdom of which we speak. It needs no outward law to bind it, but reigns by right of its inward life. So that it is said of those who have entered it, "Against such there is no law."

For it is a kingdom of kings. The song we shall one day sing, nay, that we ought to be singing even now and here in this life, declare this: "Unto Him that loved us, and washed us from our sins in His own blood, and hath made us kings and priests unto God and His Father; to Him be glory and dominion for ever and ever. Amen." (Rev. 1:5, 6.)

We who have entered this kingdom, or, rather, in whom this kingdom is set up, sit upon the throne with our King and share His dominion. The world was His footstool, and it becomes our footstool also. Over the things of time and sense He reigned triumphant by the power of a life lived in a plane above them and superior to them, and so may we. We are all of us familiar with the expression that such or such a person "rises superior to his surroundings," and we mean that there is in that soul a hidden power that controls its surroundings, instead of being controlled by them. Our King essentially rose superior to His surroundings; and it is given to us who are reigning with Him to do the same.

But, just as He was not a king in outward appearance, but only in inward power, so shall we be. He reigned, not in this, that He had all the treasures and riches of the world at His command, but that He had none of them, and could do without them. And so shall our reigning be. We shall not have all men bowing down to us, and all things bending to our will; but with all men opposing and all things adverse, we shall walk in a royal triumph of soul through the midst of them. We shall suffer the loss of all things, and by that loss be set forever free from their power to bind. We shall hide ourselves in the impregnable fortress of the will of our King, and shall reign there in a perpetual kingdom.

All this is contrary to man's thought of kingship. The only idea the human heart can compass, is, that outward circumstances must bend and bow to the soul that is seated on a throne with Christ. Friends must approve, enemies must be silenced, obstacles must be overcome, affairs must prosper, or there can be no reigning. If man had had the ordering of Daniel's business, or of that matter of the three Hebrew children in the burning fiery furnace, he would have said the only way of victory would be for the minds of the kings to have been so changed that Daniel should not have been cast into the den of lions, and the Hebrew children should have been kept out of the furnace. But God's way was infinitely grander. He suffered Daniel to be cast among the lions, in order that he might reign triumphant over them when in their very midst, and He allowed Shadrach, Meshach, and Abednego to be cast into the burning, fiery furnace, in order that they might walk through it without so much as the smell of fire upon them. He tells us, not that we shall walk in paths where there are no dragons and adders, but that we shall walk through the midst of dragons and adders, and shall "tread them under our feet."

And how much more glorious a kingdom is this than any outward rule or control could be! To be inwardly a king, while outwardly a slave, is one of the grandest heights of triumph of which our hearts can conceive. To be destitute, afflicted, tormented, to be stoned and torn asunder, and slain with the sword; to wander in sheepskins and goatskins, and in deserts and mountains, and in dens and caves of the earth, and yet to be through it all, kings in interior kingdoms of righteousness, peace and joy in the Holy Ghost, is surely a kingdom that none but God could give, and none but God-like souls receive.

A few such kings we have at some time or other seen or heard of in this world of ours, and all hearts have acknowledged their unconscious sway. One I read of among the brethren of the monastery of St. Cyr. Because of their piety, these brethren incurred the hatred of the monasteries around them, and the anger of their superiors, and were cast out as evil from their community. One of them was sent as prisoner to a monastery where his chief enemies dwelt, and was there subjected to the most cruel and degrading treatment. Although he was of gentle birth, and had been an abbot in the community he had left, he was compelled to do the most menial work, was forced to carry a noisome burden on his back, and was driven out to beg with a placard on his bosom declaring him to be the vilest of the vile. But through it all the spirit of the saint reigned triumphant, and nothing disturbed his calm, or soured for a moment his Christ-like sweetness. For his persecutors he never had anything but words of kindness and smiles of love. And at last by the mighty power of the divine kingdom in which he lived, he subdued all hearts around him to himself, and became the trusted friend and adviser, and the beloved ruler over the very enemies who had once so delighted to persecute and revile him. "Blessed are the meek, for they shall inherit the earth." By his meekness he conquered and became king.

At one time a dangerous criminal was sent to the monastery for imprisonment. He was so violent that no bonds sufficed to bind him, and no strength could control him. At last he was taken to the cell of this brother from St. Cyr, and they were shut up together; even the stolid monks themselves recognizing in that divine meekness a power to conquer that surpassed all the powers with which they were acquainted. The saint received the violent man as a beloved brother, and smiled upon him with heavenly kindness. But the criminal returned it with abuse and violence. He broke the monk's furniture and destroyed his bed, he kicked him, and beat him, and tore his hair, and spat upon him. He exhausted himself in his violence against him. Through it all the monk made no resistance, and said no word but words of love; and when at length the criminal, worn out with his fury, paused to take breath, the beaten and outraged man looked upon his persecutor with a smile of ineffable love and tender compassion, as though he would gather him to his bosom and comfort him for his misery. It was more than the criminal could bear. Hatred, and revenge, and anger he could repay in kind, but against love and meekness like this he had no weapons, and his heart was conquered. He fell at the feet of the saint and washed them with his tears, as he entreated forgiveness for his cruelty, and vowed a lifelong loyalty to his service. And from that moment all trouble with that criminal was over. He followed the saint about like a loving and faithful dog, eager to do or to be anything the other might desire. And when the time of his imprisonment was over, and the gates of his prison were opened for his release, he could not be induced to go, because he could not bear to leave the man who had saved him by love.

Of such a nature is kingship in this kingdom of heaven.

Each soul can make the application for itself, without need of comment from me.

In Matt. 5, 6, and 7, we have the King of this kingdom describing the characteristics of His kingdom and giving the laws for His subjects. "Blessed are the poor in spirit," He says, "for theirs is the kingdom of heaven." Not the rich, or great, or wise, or learned, but the poor in spirit, the meek, the merciful, the pure in heart, those who mourn, and those who hunger and thirst, those who are persecuted, and reviled, and spoken evil against, all such belong to this kingdom. Gentleness, yieldingness, meekness, charity, are the characteristics of these kings, and they reign in the power of them.

One Christian asked another, "How can I make people respect me?" "I would *command* their respect," was the reply. And this meant, not that he should stand up and say in tones of authority, "Now I command you all to respect me," but that he should so act, and live, and be, that no one could help respecting him. Men sometimes win an outward show of respect and submission by an over-bearing tyranny, but he who would rule the heart of his subjects must try other methods.

Our Lord developed this thought to some who wished to share His throne. He called them to Him, and said, "Ye know that they which are accounted to rule over the Gentiles exercise lordship over them; and their great ones exercise authority upon them. But so shall it not be among you: but whosoever will be great among you, shall be your minister: and whosoever of you will be the chiefest shall be servant of all. For even the Son of man came not to be ministered unto, but to minister, and to give his life a ransom for many."

From the human standpoint, that man alone reigns who is able to exercise lordship over those around him. From the divine standpoint the soul that serves is the soul that reigns. Not he who demands most, receives this inward crowning, but he who gives up most.

What grander kingship can be conceived of than that which Christ sets forth in the sermon on the mount, "But I say unto you, that ye resist not evil; but whosoever shall smite thee on thy right cheek, turn to him the other also. And if any man will sue thee at the law and take away thy coat, let him have thy cloak also. And whosoever shall compel thee to go a mile, go with him twain."

Surely only a soul that is in harmony with God can mount such a throne of dominion as this!

But this is our destiny. We are made for this purpose. We are born of a kingly race, and are heirs to this ineffable kingdom; "heirs of God and joint heirs with Christ."

Would that we could realize this; and could see in every act of service or surrender to which we might find ourselves called, an upward step in the pathway that leads us to our kingdom and our throne!

I mean this in a very practical sense. I mean that the homely services of our daily lives, and the little sacrifices which each day demands, will be, if faithfully fulfilled, actual rounds in the ladder by which we are mounting to our thrones. I mean that if we are faithful over the "few things" of our earthly kingdom, we shall be made ruler over the "many things" of the heavenly kingdom.

He that follows Christ in this ministry of service and of suffering, will reign with Him in the glory of supreme self-sacrifice, and will be the "chiefest" in His divine kingdom of love. Knowing this, who would hesitate to "turn the other cheek," since by the turning a kingdom is to be won and a throne is to be gained?

Joseph was a type of all this. In slavery and in prison he reigned a king, as truly as when seated on Pharaoh's throne or riding in Pharaoh's chariot. (See Gen. 39:6, 22, 23.) He became the greatest by being the least, the chiefest by being servant of all.

Dear reader, art thou reigning after this fashion, and in this sort of a kingdom? Art thou the greatest in thy little world of home, or church, or social circle by being the least, and chiefest by being the servant of all? If not, thy kingdom is not Christ's kingdom, and thy throne is not one shared by Him.

To enter into the secrets of this interior kingdom and to partake of its heavenly power, is no notional victory, no fancied supremacy. It is a real and actual reigning, which will cause thee as a matter of fact to "rise superior" to the world and the things of it, and to walk through it independent of its smiles or frowns, dwelling in a region of heavenly peace and heavenly triumph which earth can neither give nor take away. "For the kingdom of God is not in word but in power." It is not a talk but a fact; and those who are in it recognize their kingship and prove it by reigning.

But perhaps thou wilt say, "How can I enter into this kingdom, if I am not already in?" Let our Lord himself answer thee: "At the same time came the disciples unto Jesus, saying, Who is the greatest in the kingdom of heaven? And Jesus called a little child unto him, and set him in the midst of them, and said, Verily I say unto you, Except ye be converted, and become as little children, ye shall not enter into the kingdom of heaven. Whosoever therefore shall humble himself as this little child, the same is greatest in the kingdom of heaven."

It is a kingdom of childlike hearts, and only such can enter it.

To be a "little child" means simply to *be* one. I cannot describe it better than this. We all have known little children in our lives, and have delighted ourselves in their simplicity and their trustfulness, their light-hearted carelessness, and their unquestioning obedience to those in authority over them. And to be the greatest in this divine kingdom means to have the most of this guileless, tender, trustful, self-forgetting, obedient heart of the child.

"Not everyone that saith unto me, Lord, Lord, shall enter into the kingdom of heaven; but he that doeth the will of my Father which is in heaven."

It is not saying, but doing, that will avail us here. We must be a child, or we cannot sit on the child's throne. And to be a child means to do the Father's will, since the very essence of true childhood is the spirit of obedience united to the spirit of trust.

Become a little child, then, by laying aside all thy greatness, all thy self-assertion, all thy self-dependence, all thy wisdom, and all thy strength, and consenting to die to thy own self-life, be born again into the kingdom of God. The only way out of one life into another is by a death to one and a new birth into the other. It is the old story, therefore, reiterated so often and in so many different ways, of through death to life. Die, then, that you my live. Lose your own life that you may find Christ's life. The caterpillar can only enter into the butterfly's kingdom by dying to its caterpillar life, and emerging into the resurrection life of the butterfly; and just so can we also only enter into the kingdom of God by the way of a death out of the kingdom of self, and an emergence into the resurrection life of Christ. Let everything go, then, that belongs to the natural; all your own notions, and plans, and ways, and thoughts; and accept in their stead God's plans, and ways, and thoughts. Do this faithfully and do it persistently, and you shall come at last to sit on His throne, and to reign with Him in an interior kingdom which shall break in pieces and consume all other kingdoms, and shall stand for ever and ever.

There is no other way. This kingdom cannot be entered by pomp, and show, and greatness, and strength; but by littleness, and helplessness, and childlikeness, and babyhood, and death. He that humbleth himself, and he only, shall be exalted here; and to mount the throne with Christ requires that we shall first have followed Him in the suffering, and loss, and crucifixion. If we suffer with him, we shall also reign with Him. Not as an arbitrary reward for our suffering, but as the result that will follow in the very nature of things. Christ's loss must necessarily bring Christ's gain, Christ's death must bring Christ's resurrection, and to follow Him in the regeneration, will surely and inevitably bring the soul that follows to His crown and His throne.

In a volume of sermons for children I have found a vivid illustration of this royal kingdom:—

"A little fellow from one of the Refuges in England had risked his life to save one of his comrades, and England's Queen had sent him a medal by the hand of one of England's earls. The little fellow was held forward by his comrades to receive it, for he was shy and nervous and tried to sidle away.

"Look at the noble chairman; he had driven down from his proper place in the House of Lords, where were gathered earls and dukes, and the men who had done well as lawyers, and judges, and statesmen, and warriors, and the Princes of the royal blood. Yet, all peer though he was, he was moved to the sincerest depths of his being as he murmured, 'I have the honor,' and pinned the life-saving medal on the child's jacket. His heart was full. He paused to swallow down something that would rise in his throat before he could go on.

"There is the 'glory and honor' of successful statesmen, and warriors, and lawyers, but the glory of self-forgetful saving of life is a glory that excelleth, and that was the wondrous glory won by this boy. He had plunged into the stream and shared a drowning boy's risk, and that little hand, look at it there, steadying him by holding the table, had come out holding the saved.

"Why has self-forgetfulness such mighty power? How was it that a twelve-year-old boy could bow down an audience of grown men before him? What gave to that brow, that its stubby crown of carroty hair, a glory and honor more than the luster of gold and jewels? Why was it that that small body in its little breeches and jacket, wiping its tears on the rough little sleeve, could grip thousands of hearts and hold them all, and make them for the time loyal members of his kingdom?

"Why was all this so?

"It was so because that little boy in his measure had been like Christ, in the self-forgetful spirit of sacrifice for others. He had a bit of the same beauty we are all made on purpose to worship; the glory before which angels give a great shout, and all the company of heaven fall down and adore, saying with a loud voice, 'Worthy is the Lamb that was slain!'"

The "Lamb that was slain" is the mightiest King the world has ever known, and all who partake of His spirit share in His kingdom.

And since this kingdom is not a *place*, but is *character*, those who have not the character cannot by any possibility be in it.

We pray daily, "Thy kingdom come." Do we know what we are praying for? Do we comprehend the change it will make in us if it comes in us? Are we willing to be so changed?

What is the kingdom of God but the rule of God? And what is the rule of God but the will of God? Therefore when we pray, "Thy will be done on earth as it is in heaven," we have touched the secret of it all.

A horde of savages might conquer a civilized kingdom by sheer brute force; but if they would conquer the civilization of that kingdom, they could only do so by submitting to its control. And just so is it with the kingdom of heaven. It yields its scepter to none but those who render obedience to its laws.

"To him that overcometh will I give to sit with me in my throne, even as I also overcame and am set down with my Father in his throne."

"He always reigns who sides with God," says an old writer. And again, "He who perfectly accepts the will of God, dwells in a perpetual kingdom."

Art thou reigning after this fashion and in this sort of a kingdom?

Art thou the "chiefest" by being the "servant of all"?

Art thou a king over thy circumstances, or do thy circumstances reign over thee?

Dost thou triumph over thy temptations, or do they triumph over thee?

Canst thou sit on an inward throne in the midst of outward defeat and loss?

Canst thou conquer by yielding, and become the greatest by being the least?

If thou canst answer Yes to all these questions, then thou art come into thy kingdom; and whatever thy outward lot may be, or the estimation in which men may hold thee, thou art in very truth among the number of those concerning whom our Lord declares "the same shall be called greatest in the kingdom of heaven."

21. The Chariots of God

FOUNDATION TEXT.—Psalm 68:17.

Chariots are for conveyance and progress. Earthly chariots carry the bodies of those who ride in them over all intervening distances or obstacles to the place of their destination, and God's chariots carry their souls. No words can express the glorious places to which that soul shall arrive who travels in the chariots of God. And our verse tells us they are "very many." All around us on every side they wait for us; but we, alas! we do not always see them. Earth's chariots are always visible, but God's chariots are invisible.

2 Kings 6:14-17.

The king of Syria came up against the man of God with horses and chariots that were visible to everyone, but God had chariots that could be seen by none save the eye of faith. The servant of the prophet could only see the outward and visible, and he cried, as so many have done since, "Alas, my Master! how shall we do?" But the prophet himself sat calmly within his house without fear, because his eyes were opened to see the invisible. And all that he asked for his servant was, "Lord, I pray thee open his eyes that he may see."

This is the prayer we need to pray for ourselves and for one another, "Lord, open our eyes that we may see." For the world all around us is full of God's horses and chariots, waiting to carry us to places of glorious victory.

But they do not look like chariots. They look instead like enemies, sufferings, trials, defeats, misunderstandings, disappointments, unkindnesses. They look like Juggernaut cars of misery and wretchedness, that are only waiting to roll over us and crush us into the earth; but they really are chariots of triumph in which we may ride to those very heights of victory for which our souls have been longing and praying.

Deut. 32:12, 13.

If we would "ride on the high places of the earth" we must get into the chariots that can take us there; and only the "chariots of God" are equal to such lofty riding as this.

Isa. 58:14.

We may make out of each event in our lives either a Juggernaut car to crush us, or a chariot in which to ride to heights of victory. It all depends upon how we take them; whether we lie down under our trials and let them roll over and crush us, or whether we climb up into them as into a chariot, and make them carry us triumphantly onward and upward.

2 Kings 2:11, 12.

Whenever we mount into God's chariots the same thing happens to us spiritually that happened to Elisha. We shall have a translation. Not into the heavens above us, as Elisha did, but into the heaven within us, which after all is almost a grander translation than his. We shall be carried up away from the low earthly groveling plane of life, where everything hurts and everything is unhappy, up into the "heavenly places in Christ Jesus," where we shall ride in triumph over all below.

Eph. 2:6.

These "heavenly places" are interior, not exterior, and the road that leads to them is interior also. But the chariot that carries the soul over this road is generally some outward loss, or trial or disappointment; some chastening that does not indeed seem for the present to be joyous, but grievous; but that nevertheless afterward yieldeth the peaceable fruits of righteousness to them that are exercised thereby.

Heb. 12:5-11.

Look upon these chastenings, no matter how grievous they may be for the present, as God's chariots sent to carry your souls into the "high places" of spiritual achievement and uplifting, and you will find that they are after all "paved with love."

Canticles 3:9, 10.

Your own individual chariot may look very unlovely. It may be a cross-grained relative or friend; it may be the result of human malice, or cruelty, or neglect; but every chariot sent by God must necessarily be paved with love, since God is love, and God's love is the sweetest, softest, tenderest thing to rest one's self upon that was ever found by any soul anywhere. It is His love indeed that sends the chariot.

Hab. 3:8, 12, 13.

Here the prophet tells us that it was God's displeasure against the obstacles which beset the path of His people that made Him come to their rescue, riding in His "chariots of salvation." Everything becomes a "chariot of salvation" when God rides upon it.

The "clouds" that darken our skies and seem to shut out the shining of the sun of righteousness are, after all, if we only knew it, His chariots, into which we may mount with Him, and "ride prosperously" over all the darkness.

Ps. 45:3, 4; Ps. 18:10; Deut. 33:26.

A late writer has said that we cannot, by even the most vigorous and toilsome efforts, sweep away the clouds, but we can climb so high above them as to reach the clear atmosphere overhead; and he who rides with God rides upon the heavens far above all earth-born clouds.

Ps. 68:32-34.

This may sound fanciful, but it is really exceedingly practical when we begin to act it out in our daily lives.

I knew a lady who had a very slow servant. She was an excellent girl in every other respect, and very valuable in the household, but her slowness was a constant source of irritation to her mistress, who was naturally quick, and who always chafed at slowness. The lady would consequently get out of temper with the girl twenty times a day, and twenty times a day would repent of her anger, and resolve to conquer it, but in vain. Her life was made miserable by the conflict. One day it occurred to her that she had for a long while been praying for patience, and that perhaps this slow servant was the very chariot the Lord had sent to carry her soul over into patience. She immediately accepted it as such, and from that time used the slowness of her servant as a chariot for her soul. And the result was a victory of patience that no slowness of anybody was ever after able to disturb.

Another instance: I knew a sister at one of our conventions who was put to sleep in a room with two others on account of the crowd. *She* wanted to sleep, but *they* wanted to talk, and the first night she was greatly disturbed, and lay there fretting and fuming long after the others had hushed and she might have slept. But the next day she heard something about God's chariots, and that night she accepted these talking sisters as her chariots to carry her over into sweetness and patience, and she lay there feeling peaceful and at rest. When, however, it grew very late, and she knew they all ought to be sleeping, she ventured to say slyly, "Sisters, I am lying here riding in a chariot," and the effect was instantaneous in producing perfect quiet. Her chariot had carried her over to victory, not only inwardly, but at last outwardly as well.

If we would ride in God's chariots, instead of in our own, we should find this to be the case continually.

Isa. 31:1-3; Ps. 20:7, 8.

Our constant temptation is to trust in the "chariots of Egypt." We can *see* them; they are tangible and real, and they look so substantial; while God's chariots are invisible and intangible, and it is hard to believe they are there. Our eyes are not opened to see them.

2 Kings 19:23.

We try to reach the high places with the "multitude of our chariots." We depend first on one thing, and then on another, to advance our spiritual condition and to gain our spiritual victories. We "go down to Egypt for help." And God is obliged often to destroy all our own chariots before he can bring us to the point of mounting into His.

Micah 5:10; Hag. 2:22.

We lean too much upon a dear friend to help us onward in the spiritual life, and the Lord is obliged to separate us from that friend. We feel that all our spiritual prosperity depends on our continuance under the ministry of a favorite preacher, and we are mysteriously removed. We look upon our prayer-meeting or our Bible-class as the chief source of our spiritual strength, and we are shut up from attending it. And the "chariot of God," which alone can carry us to the places where we hoped to be taken by the instrumentalities upon which we have been depending, is to be found in the very deprivations we have so mourned over. God must burn up with the fire of His love every chariot of our own that stands in the way of our mounting into His.

Isa. 66:15, 16.

Let us be thankful, then, for every trial that will help to destroy our chariots, and will compel us to take refuge in the chariot of God, which stands ready and waiting beside us.

Ps. 62:5-8.

We have to be brought to the place where all other refuges fail us, before we can say, "He only." We say, "He *and*—something else." "He, and my experience," or "He, and my church relationships," or "He, and my Christian work"; and all that comes after the "and" must be taken away from us, or must be proved useless before we can come to the "He only." As long as visible chariots are at hand, the soul will not mount into the invisible ones.

Ps. 68:4.

If we want to ride with God "upon the heavens," we have to be brought to an end of all riding upon the earth.

Ps. 68:24.

To see God's "goings," we must get into the "sanctuary" of his presence; and to share in His "goings" and "go" with Him, we must abandon all earthly "goings."

Prov. 20:24; Ps. 17:5; Ps. 40:1, 2.

When we mount into God's chariot our goings are "established," for no obstacles can hinder its triumphal course. All losses therefore are gains that bring us to this.

Phil. 3:7-9.

Paul understood this, and he gloried in the losses which brought him such unspeakable gain.

2 Cor. 12:7-10.

Even the "thorn in the flesh," the messenger of Satan sent to buffet him, became only a chariot to his willing soul, that carried him to heights of triumph which he could have reached in no other way. To "take pleasure" in one's trials, what is this but turning them into the grandest of chariots?

Joseph had a revelation of his future triumphs and reigning, but the chariots that carried him there looked to the eye of sense like the bitterest failures and defeats. It was a strange road to a kingdom, through slavery and a prison, and yet by no other road could Joseph have reached his triumph.

His dream, Gen. 37:5-10; His chariots, Gen. 37:19, 20, 27, 28; 39:19, 20; How he rode in his chariots, Gen. 39:1-6, 21-23; His triumph, Gen. 43:38-43.

And now a word as to how one is to mount into these chariots.

My answer would be simply this: Find out where God is in each one of them, and hide yourself in Him. Or, in other words, do what the little child does when trouble comest, who finds its mother and hides in her arms. The real chariot after all that takes us through triumphantly is the carrying of God.

Isa. 46:4.

The baby carried in the chariot of its mother's arms rides triumphantly through the hardest places, and does not even know they are hard.

Isa. 63:9.

And how much more we, who are carried in the chariot of the "arms of God"!

Get into your chariot, then. Take each thing that is wrong in your lives as God's chariot for you. No matter who the builder of the wrong may be, whether men or devils, by the time it reaches your side it is God's chariot for you, and is meant to carry you to a heavenly place of triumph. Shut out all the second causes, and find the Lord in it. Say, "Lord, open my eyes that I may see, not the visible enemy, but thy unseen chariots of deliverance."

Accept His will in the trial, whatever it may be, and hide yourself in His arms of love. Say, "Thy will be done; Thy will be done!" over and over. Shut out every other thought but the one thought of submission to His will and of trust in His love. Make your trial thus your chariot, and you will find your soul "riding upon the heavens" with God in a way you never dreamed could be.

I have not a shadow of doubt that if all our eyes were opened today we would see our homes, and our places of business, and the streets we traverse, filled with the "chariots of God." There is no need for any one of us to walk for lack of chariots. That cross inmate of your household, who has hitherto made life a burden to you, and who has been the Juggernaut car to crush your soul into the dust, may henceforth be a glorious chariot to carry you to the heights of heavenly patience and longsuffering. That misunderstanding, that mortification, that unkindness, that disappointment, that loss, that defeat, all these are chariots waiting to carry you to the very heights of victory you have so longed to reach.

Mount into them, then, with thankful hearts, and lose sight of all second causes in the shining of His love who will "carry you in His arms" safely and triumphantly over it all.

22. Without Me Ye Can Do Nothing

Concerning the Life of Divine Union in its Practical Aspects.

Not long ago I was driving with a Quaker preacher through our beautiful Philadelphia Park, when our conversation turned on the apparent fruitlessness of a great deal of the preaching in the church at the present time. We had spoken, of course, of the foundation cause in the absence of the power of the Holy Ghost, but we still felt that this could not account for it all, as we both of us knew many preachers really baptized with the Spirit, who yet seemed to have no fruit to their ministry. And then I suggested that one reason might be in the fact that so many ministers, when preaching or talking on religious subjects, put on a different tone and manner from the one they ordinarily use, and by this very manner remove religion so far from the range of ordinary life, as to fail of gaining any real hold on the hearts of the men and women whose whole lives are lived on the plane of ordinary and homely pleasures and duties. "Now, for instance," I said, "if in thy preaching from the Friends' gallery thee could use the same tone and manner as thy present one, how much more effectual and convincing thy preaching would be." "Oh, but I could not do *that*," was the reply, "because the preacher's gallery is so much more solemn a place than this."

"But why is it more solemn?" I asked. "Is it not the presence of God only that makes the gallery or the pulpit solemn, and have we not the presence of God equally here? Is it not just as solemn to live in our everyday life as it is to preach, and ought we not to do the one to His glory just as much as the other?" And then I added, as the subject seemed to open out before me, "I verily believe a large part of the difficulty lies in the unscriptural and unnatural divorce that has been brought about between our so-called religious life and our so-called temporal life; as if our religion were something apart from ourselves, a sort of outside garment that was to be put on and off according to our circumstances and purposes. On Sundays, for instance, and in church, our purpose is to seek God, and worship and serve Him, and therefore on Sundays we bring out our religious life and put it on in a suitably solemn manner, and live it with a strained gravity and decorum which deprives it of half its power. But on Mondays our purpose is to seek our own interests and serve them, and so we bring out our temporal life and put it on with a sense of relief, as from an unnatural bondage, and live it with ease and naturalness, and consequently with far more power."

The thoughts thus started remained with me and gathered strength. Not long afterward I was present at a meeting where the leader opened with reading John 15, and the words, "Without me ye can do nothing," struck me with amazement. Hundreds of times before I had read those words, and had thought that I understood them thoroughly. But now it seemed almost as though they must have been newly inserted in the Bible, so ablaze were they with wondrous meaning.

"There it is," I said to myself, "Jesus himself said so, that apart from Him we have no real life of any kind, whether we call it temporal or spiritual, and that, therefore, all living or doing that is without Him is of such a nature that God, who sees into the realities of things, calls it 'nothing.'" And then the question forced itself upon me as to whether any soul really believed this statement to be true; or, if believing it theoretically, whether any one made it practical in their daily walk and life. And I saw, as in a flash almost, that the real secret of divine union lay quite as much in this practical aspect of it as in any interior revealings or experiences. For if I do nothing, literally nothing, apart from Christ, I am of course united to Him in a continual oneness that cannot be questioned or gainsaid; while if I live a large part of my daily life and perform a large part of my daily work apart from Him, I have no real union, no matter how exalted and delightful my emotions concerning it may be.

It is to consider this aspect of the subject, therefore, that the present paper is written. For I am very sure that the wide divorce made between things spiritual and things temporal, of which I have spoken, has done more than almost anything else to hinder a realized interior union with God, and to put all religion so outside of the pale of common life as to make it an almost unattainable thing to the ordinary mass of mankind. Moreover it has introduced an unnatural constraint and stiltedness into the experience of Christians that seems to shut them out from much of the free, happy, childlike ease that belongs of right to the children of God.

I feel, therefore, that it is of vital importance for us to understand the truth of this matter.

And the thought that makes it clearest to me is this, that the fact of our oneness with Christ contains the whole thing in a nutshell. If we are one with Him, then of course in the very nature of things we can do nothing without Him. For that which is one cannot act as being two. And if I therefore do anything without Christ, then I am not one with Him in that thing, and like a branch severed from the vine I am withered and worthless. It is as if the branch should recognize its connection with and dependence upon the vine for most of its growth, and fruit-bearing, and climbing, but should feel a capacity in itself to grow and climb over a certain fence or around the trunk of a certain tree, and should therefore sever its connection with the vine for this part of its living. Of course that which thus sought an independent life would wither and die in the very nature of things. And just so is it with us who are branches of Christ the true vine. No independent action, whether small or great, is possible to us without withering and death, any more than to the branch of the natural vine.

This will show us at once how fatal to the realized oneness with Christ, for which our souls hunger, is the divorce I have spoken of. We have all realized, more or less, that without Him we cannot live our religious life, but when it comes to living our so-called temporal life, to keeping house or transacting business, or making calls, or darning stockings, or sweeping a room, or trimming a bonnet, or entertaining company, who is there that even theoretically thinks such things as these are to be done for Christ, and can only be rightly done as we abide in Him and do them in His strength?

But if it is Christ working in the Christian who is to lead the prayer-meeting, then, since Christ and the Christian are one, it must be also Christ working in and through the Christian who is to keep the house and make the bargain; and one duty is therefore in the very essence of things as religious as the other. It is the man that makes the action, not the action the man. And as much solemnity and sweetness will thus be brought into our everyday domestic and social affairs as into the so-called religious occasions of life, if we will only "acknowledge God in all our ways," and do whatever we do, even if it be only eating and drinking, to His glory.

If our religion is really our life, and not merely something extraneous tacked on to our life, it must necessarily go into everything in which we live; and no act, however human or natural it may be, can be taken out of its control and guidance.

If God is with us *always*, then He is just as much with us in our business times and our social times as in our religious times, and one moment is as solemn with His presence as another.

If it is a fact that in Him we "live and move and have our being," then it is also a fact, whether we know it or not, that without Him we cannot do anything. And facts are stubborn things, thank God, and do not alter for all our feelings.

In Psalm 127:1, 2, we have a very striking illustration of this truth. The Psalmist says, "Except the Lord build the house, they labor in vain that build it: except the Lord keep the city, the watchman waketh but in vain. It is vain for you to rise up early, to sit up late, to eat the bread of sorrows; for so He giveth His beloved sleep." The two things here spoken of as being done in vain, unless the Lord is in the doing of them, are purely secular things, so called; simple business matters on the human plane of life. And whatever spiritual lesson they were intended to teach gains its impressiveness only from this, that these statements concerning God's presence in temporal things were statements of patent and incontrovertible facts.

In truth the Bible is full of this fact, and the only wonder is how any believer in the Bible could have overlooked it. From the building of cities down to the numbering of the hairs of our head and the noting of a sparrow's fall, throughout the whole range of homely daily living, God is declared to be present and to be the mainspring of it all. Whatever we do, even if it be such a purely physical thing as eating and drinking, we are to do for Him and to His glory, and we are exhorted to so live and so walk in the light in everything, as to have it made manifest of *all* our works, temporal as well as spiritual, that "they are wrought in God."

There is unspeakable comfort in this for every loving Christian heart, in that it turns all of life into a sacrament, and makes the kitchen, or the workshop, or the nursery, or the parlor, as sweet and solemn a place of service to the Lord, and as real a means of union with Him, as the prayer-meeting, or the mission board, or the charitable visitation.

A dear young Christian mother and housekeeper came to me once with a sorely grieved heart, because of her engrossing temporal life. "There seems," she said, "to be nothing spiritual about my life from one week's end to the other. My large family of little children are so engrossing that day after day passes without my having a single moment for anything but simply attendance on them and on my necessary household duties, and I go to bed night after night sick at heart because I have felt separated from my Lord all day long, and have not been able to do anything for Him." I told her of what I have written above, and assured her that all would be changed if she would only see and acknowledge God in all these homely duties, and would recognize her utter dependence upon Him for the doing of them. Her heart received the good news with gladness, and months afterward she told me that from that moment life had become a transformed and glorified thing, with the abiding presence of the Lord, and with the sweetness of continual service to Him.

Another Christian, a young lady in a fashionable family, came to me also in similar grief that in so much of her life she was separated from God and had no sense of His presence. I told her she ought never to do anything that could cause such a separation; but she assured me that it was impossible to avoid it, as the things she meant were none of them wrong things. "For instance," she said, "it is plainly my duty to pay calls with my mother, and yet nothing seems to separate me so much from God as paying calls." "But how would it be," I asked, "if you paid the calls as service to the Lord and for His glory?" "What!" she exclaimed, "pay calls for God! I never heard of such a thing." "But why not?"

I asked; "if it is right to pay calls at all it ought to be done for God, for we are commanded whatsoever we do to do it for His glory, and if it is not right you ought not to do it. As a Christian," I continued, "you must not do anything that you cannot do for Him." "I see! I see!" she exclaimed, after a little pause, "and it makes all life look so different! Nothing can separate me from Him that is not sin, but each act done to His glory, whatever it may be, will only draw me closer and make His presence more real."

These two instances will illustrate my meaning. And I feel sure there are thousands of other burdened and weary lives that would be similarly transformed if these truths were but realized and acted on.

An old spiritual writer says something to this effect, that in order to become a saint it is not always necessary to change our works, but only to put an interior purpose towards God in them all; that we must begin to do for His glory and in His strength that which before we did for self and in self's capacity; which means, after all, just what our Lord meant when He said, "Without me ye can do nothing."

There is another side of this truth also which is full of comfort, and which the Psalmist develops in the verses I have quoted. "It is vain," he says, "to rise up early, to sit up late, to eat the bread of sorrows." Or, in other words, "What is the use of all this worry and strain? For the work will after all amount to nothing unless God is in it, and if He *is* in it, what folly to fret or be burdened, since He of course, by the very fact of His presence, assumes the care and responsibility of it all."

Ah, it is vain indeed, and I would that all God's children knew it!

We mothers at least ought to know it, for our own ways with our children would teach us something of it every day we live, if we had but the "eyes to see."

How many mothers have risen early, and sat up, late, and eaten the bread of sorrows, just that they might give sleep to their beloved children. And how grieved their hearts would have been if, after all their pains, the children had refused to rest. I can appeal to some mother hearts, I am sure, as thoroughly understanding my meaning. Memories will arise of the flushed and rosy boy coming in at night, tired with his play or his work, with knees out and coat torn, and of the patient, loving toil to patch and mend it all, sitting up late and rising early, that the dearly loved cause of all the mischief might rest undisturbed in childhood's happy sleep. How "vain," and worse than vain, would it have been for that loved and cared-for darling to have himself also sat up late, and risen early, and eaten the bread of sorrows, when all the while his mother was doing it for him just that he might not have it to do.

And if this is true of mothers, how much more true must it be of Him who made the mothers, and who came among us in bodily form to bear our burdens, and carry our sorrows, and do our work, just that we might "enter into His rest."

Beloved, *have* we entered into this rest?

"For he that is entered into his rest, he also hath ceased from his own works as God did from His." That is, he has learned at last the lesson that without Christ or apart from Him he can do nothing, but that he can do all things through Christ strengthening him; and therefore he has laid aside all self-effort, and has abandoned himself to God that He may work in him both to will and to do of His good pleasure. This and this only is the rest that remaineth for the people of God.

Scientific men are seeking to resolve all forces in nature into one primal force. Unity of origin is the present cry of science. Light, heat, sound are all said to be the products of one force differently applied, and that force is motion. All things, say the scientists, can be resolved back to this. Whether they are right or wrong I cannot say; but the Bible reveals to us one grand primal force which is behind motion itself, and that is God-force. God is at the source of everything, God is the origin of everything, God is the explanation of everything. Without Him was not anything made that was made, and without Him is not anything done that is done.

Surely, then, it is not the announcement of any mystery, but the simple statement of a simple fact, when our Lord says, "Without me ye can do nothing."

Even of Himself He said, "I can of mine own self do nothing," and He meant that He and His Father were so one that any independent action was impossible. Surely it is the revelation of a glorious necessity existing between our souls and Christ that He should say we could do nothing without Him; for it means that He has made us so one with Himself that independent action is as impossible with us as towards Him, as it was with Him as towards His Father.

Dear Christian, dost thou not catch a glimpse here of a region of wondrous glory?

Let us believe, then, that without Him we can literally do nothing. We *must* believe it, for it is true. But let us recognize its truth, and act on it from this time forward. Let us make a hearty renunciation of all living apart from Christ, and let us begin from this moment to acknowledge Him in all our ways, and do everything, whatsoever we do, as service to Him and for His glory, depending upon Him alone for wisdom, and strength, and sweetness, and patience, and everything else that is necessary for the right accomplishing of all our living.

As I said before, it is not so much a change of acts that will be necessary, as a change of motive and of dependence. The house will be kept, or the children cared for, or the business transacted, perhaps, just the same as before as to the outward, but inwardly God will be acknowledged, and depended on, and served; and there will be all the difference between a life lived at ease in the glory of His presence, and a life lived painfully and with effort apart from Him. There will result also from this bringing of God into our affairs a wonderful accession of divine wisdom in the conduct of them, and a far greater quickness and dispatch in their accomplishment, a surprising increase in the fertility of resource, an ease in apprehending the true nature and bearing of things, and an enlargement on every side that will amaze the hitherto cramped and cabined soul.

I mean this literally. I mean that the house will be kept more nicely and with greater ease, the children will be trained more swiftly, the stockings will be darned more swiftly, the guest will be entertained more comfortably, the servants will be managed more easily, the bargain will be made more satisfactorily, and all life will move with far more sweetness and harmony. For God will be in every moment of it, and where He is all *must* go well.

Moreover the soul itself, in this natural and simple way, will acquire such a holy habit of "abiding in Christ" that at last His presence will become the most real thing in life to our consciousness, and an habitual, silent, and secret conversation with Him will be carried on that will yield a continual joy.

Sometimes the child of God asks eagerly and hungrily, "What is the shortest and quickest way by which I can reach the highest degree of union and communion with God, possible to human beings in this life?" No shorter or quicker way can be found than the one I have been declaring. By the homely path of everyday duties done thus in God and for God, the sublimest heights are reached. Not as a reward, however, but as an inevitable and natural result, for if we thus abide in Him and refuse to leave Him, where He is there shall we also be, and all that He is will be ours.

If, then, thou wouldst know, beloved reader, the interior divine union realized in thy soul, begin from this very day to put it outwardly in practice as I have suggested. Offer each moment of thy living and each act of thy doing to God, and say to Him continually, "Lord, I am doing this in Thee and for Thy glory. Thou art my strength, and my wisdom, and my all-sufficient supply for every need. I depend only upon Thee." Refuse utterly to live for a single moment or to perform a single act apart from Him. Persist in this until it becomes the established habit of thy soul. And sooner or later thou shalt surely know the longings of thy soul satisfied in the abiding presence of Christ, thy indwelling Life.

23. God With Us; Or, the 139th Psalm

"Thus doth thy hospitable greatness lie
Around us like a boundless sea;
We cannot lose ourselves where all is home,
Nor drift away from Thee."

Very few of us understand the full meaning of the words in Matt. 1:23, "They shall call His name Emmanuel; which being interpreted is, God with us." In this short sentence is revealed to us the grandest fact the world can ever know; that God, the Almighty God, the Creator of Heaven and earth, is not a far-off Deity, dwelling in a Heaven of unapproachable glory, but is living with us right here in this world, in the midst of our poor, ignorant, helpless lives, as close to us as we are to ourselves. This seems so incredible to the human heart that we are very slow to believe it; but that the Bible teaches it as a fact, from cover to cover, cannot be denied by any honest mind. In the very beginning of Genesis we read of the "presence of the Lord God amongst the trees of the garden." And from that time on He is revealed to us always as in the most familiar and daily intercourse with His people everywhere.

In Exodus we find Him asking them to make Him a "sanctuary, that He might dwell among them." He is recorded as having "walked" with them in the wilderness, and as "taking up His abode" with them in the promised land. He taught them to rely on Him as an ever-present Friend and Helper, to consult Him about all their affairs, and to abandon the whole management of their lives to Him. And finally He came in Christ in bodily form and dwelt in the world as a man among men, making Himself bone of our bone and flesh of our flesh, taking upon Him our nature, and revealing to us, in the most tangible and real way possible, the grand, and blessed, and incomprehensible fact that He intended to be with us always, even unto the end of the world.

Whoever will believe this fact with all their hearts will find in it the solution of every difficulty of their lives.

I remember when I was a little girl and found myself in any trouble or perplexity, the coming in of my father or mother on the scene would always bring me immediate relief. The moment I heard the voice of one of them saying, "Daughter, I am here," that moment every burden dropped off and every anxiety was stilled. It was their simple presence that did it. They did not need to promise to relieve me, they did not need to tell me their plans of relief; the simple fact of their presence was all the assurance I required that everything now would be set straight and all would go well for me, and my only interest after their arrival was simply to see *how* they would do it all. Perhaps they were exceptional parents, to have created such confidence in their children's hearts. I think myself they were. But as our God is certainly an exceptional God, the application has absolute force, and His presence is literally all we need. It would be enough for us, even if we had not a single promise nor a single revelation of His plans. How often in the Bible He has stilled all questions and all fears by the simple announcement, "I will be with thee"; and who can doubt that in these words He meant to assure us that all His wisdom, and love, and omnipotent power would therefore, of course, be engaged on our side? Over and over again in my childhood have the magic words, "Oh, there is mother!" brought me immediate relief and comfort; and over and over again in my later years have almost the same words reverently spoken, "Oh, there is God!" brought me a far more blessed deliverance. With Him present, what could I have to fear? Since He has said, "I will never leave thee nor forsake thee," surely I may boldly say, "The Lord is my helper, and I will not fear what man shall do unto me." I remember to this day the inspiring sense of utter security that used to come to me with my earthly father's presence. I never feared anything when he was by. And surely with my Heavenly Father by, there can be no possible room for fear.

It is because of its practical help and comfort, therefore, that I desire to make this wonderful fact of "Emmanuel, God with us," clear and definite, for I am very sure but few, even of God's own children, really believe it. They may say they do, they may repeat a thousand times in the conventional, pious tone considered suitable to such a sentiment, "Oh, yes, we know that God is always present with us, but—" And in this "but" the whole story is told. There are no "buts" in the vocabulary of the soul that accepts His presence as a literal fact. Such a soul is joyously triumphant over every suggestion of fear or of doubt. It has God, and that is enough for it. His presence is its certain security and supply, always, and for everything.

Let me, then, beg my readers to turn with me for a while to the 139th Psalm, where we shall find a most blessed revelation of this truth.

The central thought of the Psalm is to be found in verses 7 to 12, "Whither shall I go from thy Spirit? or whither shall I flee from thy presence? If I ascend up into heaven, thou art there: if I make my bed in hell, behold, thou art there. If I take the wings of the morning, and dwell in the uttermost parts of the sea; even there shall thy hand lead me, and thy right hand shall hold me. If I say, Surely the darkness shall cover me; even the night shall be light about me. Yea, the darkness hideth not from thee; but the night shineth as the day: the darkness and the light are both alike to thee. For thou hast possessed my reins: thou hast covered me in my mother's womb."

I cannot conceive of a more definite or sweeping declaration of His continual presence with us, wherever we may be or whatever we may do, than is contained in this passage. People talk about seeking to get into the presence of the Lord, but here we see that they cannot get out of it; that there is no place in the whole universe where He is not present; neither heaven, nor hell, nor the uttermost parts of the sea; and no darkness so great as to hide for one moment from Him. And the reason of this is, that He "has possessed our reins," which means that He is not only with us, but within us, and consequently must accompany us wherever we ourselves go.

We must accept it as true, therefore, that the words of our Lord, "Lo, I am with you alway, even unto the end of the world," were the expression, not of a beautiful sentiment merely, but of an incontrovertible fact. He *is* with us, and we cannot get away from Him.

We may be in such thick darkness as to be utterly unable to see Him, and may think, probably often have thought, that, therefore, He does not see us. But our Psalm assures us that the darkness hideth not from Him, and that, in fact, darkness and light are both alike to Him. We are as present to His view and as plainly seen when our own souls are in the depths of spiritual darkness, as when they are basking in the brightest light. The darkness may hide Him from us, but it does not hide us from Him. Neither does any apparent spiritual distance or wandering take us out of His presence; not even if we go into the depths of sin in our wandering. In the uttermost parts of the sea, or wherever we may be, He is ever present to hold and to lead us. There is not a moment nor a place where we can be left without His care.

There are times in our lives when delirium makes us utterly unaware of the presence of our most careful and tender nurses. A child in delirium will cry out in anguish for its mother, and will harrow her heart by its piteous lamentations and appeals, when all the while she is holding its fevered hand, and bathing its aching head, and caring for it with all the untold tenderness of a mother's love. The darkness of disease has hidden the mother from the child, but has not hidden the child from the mother.

And just so it is with our God and us. The darkness of our doubts or our fears, of our sorrows or our despair, or even of our sins, cannot hide us from Him, although it may, and often does, hide Him from us. He has told us that the darkness and the light are both alike to Him; and if our faith will only lay hold of this as a fact, we will be enabled to pass through the darkest seasons in quiet trust, sure that all the while, though we cannot see nor feel Him, our God *is* caring for us, and will never leave nor forsake us.

Whether, however, this abiding presence of our God will be a joy to us or a sorrow, will depend upon what we know about Him. If we think of Him as a stern tyrant, intent only on His own glory, we shall be afraid of His continual presence. If we think of Him as a tender, loving Father, intent only on our blessing and happiness, we shall be glad and thankful to have Him thus ever with us. For the presence and the care of love can never mean anything but good to the one beloved.

The Psalm we are considering shows us that the presence of our God is the presence of love, and that it brings us an infinitude of comfort and rest. He says in verses 1 to 5, "O Lord, thou hast searched me, and known me. Thou knowest my downsitting and mine uprising; thou understandest my thought afar off. Thou compassest my path and my lying down, and art acquainted with all my ways. For there is not a word in my tongue, but lo, O Lord, thou knowest it altogether. Thou hast beset me behind and before, and laid thine hand upon me."

Our God knows us and understands us, and is acquainted with all our ways. No one else in all the world understands us. Our actions are misinterpreted, it may be, and our motives misjudged. Our natural characteristics are not taken into account, nor our inherited tendencies considered. No one makes allowances for our ill health; no one realizes how much we have to contend with. But our Father knows it all. He *understands* us, and His judgment of us takes into account every element, conscious or unconscious, that goes to make up our character and to control our actions. Only an all-comprehending love can be just, and our God is just. No wonder Faber can say:—

There is no place where earth's sorrows
Are more felt than up in Heaven;
There is no place where earth's failings
Have such kindly judgment given."

Some of you have been afraid of His justice, perhaps, because you thought it would be against you. But do you not see now that it is all on your side, just as a mother's justice is, because "He knoweth our frame and remembereth that we are dust"? No human judge can ever do this; and to me this comprehension of God is one of my most blessed comforts. Often I do not understand myself; all within looks confused and hopelessly tangled. But then I remember that He has searched me, and that He knows me and understands the thoughts which so perplex me, and that, therefore, I may just leave the whole miserable tangle to Him to unravel. And my soul sinks down at once, as on downy pillows, into a place of the most blissful rest.

Then further, because of this complete knowledge and understanding of our needs, what comfort it is to be told that He knows our downsitting and our uprising; that He compasses our path, and takes note of our lying down. Just what a mother does for her foolish, careless, ignorant, but dearly loved little ones, this very thing does our God for us. When a mother is with her children she thinks of their comfort and well-being always before her own. *They* must have comfortable seats where no draught can reach them, no matter what amount of discomfort she may herself be compelled to endure. Their beds must be soft and their blankets warm, let hers be what they may. Their paths must be smooth and safe, even though she is obliged herself to walk in rough and dangerous ways. Her own comfort, as compared with that of her children, is of no account in a loving mother's eyes. And surely our God has not made the mothers in this world more capable of a self-sacrificing love than He is Himself. He *must* be better and greater on the line of love and self-sacrifice than any mother He ever made.

Then, since He has assured us that He knows our downsitting and our uprising, that He compasses our path and our lying down, we may be perfectly and blessedly sure that in even these little details of our lives we get the very best that His love, and wisdom, and power can compass. I mean this in a very literal sense. I mean that He cares for our literal seats and our literal beds, and sees that we, each one, have just that sort of a seat or that sort of a bed which is best for us and for our highest development. And just on this last point is where He is so much better than any mother can be. His love is a wise love, that sees the outcome of things, and cares more for our highest good than for that which is lower. So that, while a mother's weak love cannot see beyond the child's present comfort, and cannot bear to inflict or allow any discomfort, the strong, wise love of our God can bear to permit the present discomfort, for the sake of the future glory that is to result therefrom.

At home and abroad, therefore, let us commit the choosing of our seats, and of our beds, and of all the other little homely circumstances of our daily lives and surroundings, to the God who has thus assured us that He knows all about every one of them.

For we are told in our Psalm that He "besets" our path. We have some of us known what it was to be "beset" by unwelcome and unpleasant people or things. But we never have thought, perhaps, that we were beset by God, that He loves us so that He cannot leave us alone, and that no coldness nor rebuffs on our parts can drive Him away. Yet it is gloriously true! And, moreover, He besets us "behind" as well as before. Just as a mother does. She goes after her children and picks up all they have dropped, and clears away all the rubbish they have left behind them. We mothers begin this in the nursery with the blocks and playthings, and we go on with it all our lives long; seeking continually to set straight that which our children have left crooked behind them; often at the cost of much toil and trouble, but always with a love that makes the toil and trouble nothing in comparison to caring for the children we love. What good mother ever turned away the poor little tearful darling who came with a tangled knot for her unraveling, or refused to help the eager rosy boy to unwind his kite-strings? Suppose it has been their own fault that the knots and tangles have come, still her love can sympathize with and pity the very faults themselves, and all the more does she seek to atone for them.

All this and more does our God do for us from our earliest infancy, long even before we know enough to be conscious of it, until the very end of our earthly lives. We have seen Him before *us* perhaps, but we have never thought of Him as *behind* us as well. Yet it is a blessed fact that He is behind us all the time, longing to make crooked things straight, to untangle our tangled skeins, and to atone continually for the wrong we have done and the mistakes we have made. If any of us, therefore, have that in our past which has caused us anxiety or remorse, let us lift up our heads in a happy confidence from henceforth, that the God who is behind us will set it all straight somehow, if we will but commit it to Him, and can even make our very mistakes and misdoings work together for good. Ah! it is a grand thing to be "beset" by God.

Then again what depths of comfort there are in verses 14 to 16: "I will praise thee; for I am fearfully and wonderfully made: marvelous are Thy works; and that my soul knoweth right well. My substance was not hid from thee, when I was made in secret, and curiously wrought in the lowest parts of the earth. Thine eyes did see my substance, yet being unperfect; and in thy book all my members were written, which in continuance were fashioned, when as yet there was none of them."

One of the things which often troubles us more than we care to confess, is our dislike of the way we have been put together. Our mental or moral "make-up" does not suit us. We think if we had only been created with less of this or more of that, if we were less impulsive or more enthusiastic, if we had been made more like someone else whom we admire, that then our chances of success would have been far greater; that we could have served God far more acceptably; and could have been more satisfactory in every way to ourselves and to Him. And we are tempted sometimes to think that with our miserable make-up, it is hopeless to expect to please Him.

If we really realized that God Himself had made us, we should see the folly of all this at once, but we secretly feel as if somehow He had not had much hand in the matter, but as if we had been put together in a haphazard sort of way, that had left our characters very much to chance. We believe in creation in the general, but not in the particular, when it comes to ourselves. But in this Psalm we see that God has presided over the creation of each one of us, superintending the smallest details; even, to speak figuratively, writing down what each "member" was to be, when as yet there was none of them. Therefore we, just as we are naturally, with just the characteristics that inhere in us by birth, are precisely what God would have us to be, and were planned out by His own hand to do the especial work that He has prepared for our doing. I mean, of course, our natural characteristics, not the perversion of them by sin on our parts.

There is something very glorifying to the Creator in this way of looking at it. Genius always seeks expression, and seeks, too, to express itself in as great a variety of forms and ways as possible. No true artist repeats himself, but each picture he paints, or statue he carves, is a new expression of his creative power. When we go to an exhibition of pictures, we should feel it a lowering of art if two were exactly alike; and just so is it with us who are "God's workmanship." His creative power is expressed differently in each one of us. And in the individual "make-up" which sometimes so troubles us, there is a manifestation of this power different from every other, and without which the day of exhibition, when we are, each one, to be to the praise of His glory, would be incomplete. All He asks of us is that, as He has had the making of us, so He may also have the managing, since He alone understands us, and is, therefore, the only one who can do it.

The man who makes an intricate machine is the best one to manage it and repair it; any one else who meddles with it is apt to spoil it. And when we think of the intricacy of our inward machinery and the continual failure of our own management of it, we may well be thankful to hand it all over to the One who created it, and to leave it in His hands. We may be sure He will then make the best out of us that can be made, and that we, even we, with our "peculiar temperaments," and our apparently unfortunate characteristics, will be made vessels unto honor, sanctified and meet for the Master's use, and fitted to every good work.

I met once with a saying in an old Quaker writer which I have never forgotten: "Be content to be just what thy God has made thee." It has helped me to understand the point upon which I am dwelling; and I feel sure contentment with our own "make-up" is as essential a part of our submission to God as contentment with any other of the circumstances of our daily life. If we did not each one of us exist just as we are by nature, then one expression of God's creative power would be missing, and one part of His work would be left undone. And besides, to complain of ourselves is to complain of the One who has made us, and cannot but grieve Him. Let us be content, then, and only see to it that we let the Divine Potter make out of us the very best He can, and use us according to His own good pleasure.

Verses 17 and 18 bring out another view of God's continual presence with us, and that is, that He is always thinking about us, and that His thoughts are kind and loving thoughts, for the Psalmist calls them precious. "How precious also are thy thoughts unto me, O God! How great is the sum of them! If I should count them, they are more in number than the sand: when I awake, I am still with thee."

So many people are tempted to think that God is not paying any attention to them. They think that their interests and their affairs are altogether beneath His notice, and that they are too unworthy to hope for His attention. But they wrong Him grievously by such thoughts. A mother pays as much attention to her smallest infant as to her oldest children, and is as much interested in its little needs and pleasures as in theirs. I am not sure but she is more. Her thoughts dwell around the one who needs them most; and He who made the mother's heart will not Himself be less attentive to the needs and pleasures of the meanest and most helpless of His creatures. He even hears the young lions when they cry, and not a sparrow can fall to the ground without Him; therefore, we, who are of more value than many sparrows, need not be afraid of a moment's neglect.

In fact, the responsibilities of creating anything require an unintermitting care of it on the part of the Creator; and it is the glory of omnipotence that it can attend at once to the smallest details and to the grandest operations as well.

> *"For greatness which is infinite makes room*
> *For all things in its lap to lie;*
> *We should be crushed by a magnificence*
> *Short of infinity."*

I do not know why it is that we consider a man or woman weak who attends to large affairs to the neglect of little details, and then turn around and accuse our God of doing this very thing. But if any of my readers have hitherto been guilty of this folly, let it end now and here, and let each one from henceforth believe, without any questioning, that always and everywhere the "Lord thinketh upon me."

The remainder of the Psalm develops the perfect accord of thought between the soul and God, where this life of simple faith has been entered upon. Having learned the transforming fact of God's continual presence and unceasing care, the soul is brought into so profound a union with Him as to love what He loves, and hate what He hates; and eagerly appeals to Him to search it, and try it, that there may be no spot left anywhere in all its being which is out of harmony with Him.

In the sunlight of His presence darkness must flee, and the heart will soon feel that it cannot endure to have any corner shut away from His shining; for in His presence is "fulness of joy," and at His right hand "there are pleasures forevermore."

An old woman, living in a rather desolate part of England, made considerable money by selling ale and beer to chance travelers who passed her lonely cottage. But her conscience troubled her about it. She wanted to be a Christian and to go to Heaven when she died, but she had an inward feeling that if she did become a Christian she would have to give up her profitable business, and this she thought would be more than she could do; so that between the two things she was brought into great conflict.

But one night, at the meeting she attended, a preacher from a distance told about the sweet and blessed fact of God's continual presence with us, and of the joy this was sure to bring when it was known. Her soul was enraptured at the thought of such a possibility for her, and forgetting all about the beer, she began at once with a very simple faith to claim it as a blessed reality. Over and over again she exclaimed in her heart, as the preacher went on with his sermon, "Why, Lord Jesus, I didn't know as thee wast always with me! Why, Lord, how good it is to know that I have got thee all the time to live with me and take care of me! Why, Lord, I sha'n't never be lonely no more!" And when the meeting closed and she took her way home across the moors, all the time the happy refrain went on, "Ah, Lord Jesus, thee art going home with me tonight. Never mind, Lord Jesus, old Betty won't never let thee go again now, I knows I have got thee!"

As her faith thus laid hold of the fact of His presence she began to rejoice in it more and more, until finally, when she had reached her cottage door, her soul was full of delight. As she opened the door, the first object her eyes rested upon was a great pot of ale on the table ready for selling. At once it flashed into her mind, "The Lord will not like to have that ale in the house where He lives," and her whole heart responded eagerly, "That ale shall go." She knew the pot was heavy, and she kneeled beside it saying, "Lord, thee hast come home with me, and thee art going to live with me always in this cottage, and I know thee don't like this ale. Please give me strength to tip it over into the road." Strength was given, and the ale was soon running down the lane. Then the old woman came back into her cottage, and kneeling down again thanked the Lord for the strength given, and added,

"Now, Lord, if there is anything else in this cottage that thee does not like, show it to me, and it shall be tipped out too."

Is not this a perfect illustration of the close of our Psalm? "Do not I hate them, O Lord, that hate thee? and am not I grieved with those that rise up against thee? I hate them with a perfect hatred; I count them mine enemies. Search me, O God, and know my heart; try me, and know my thoughts; and see if there be any wicked way in me, and lead me in the way everlasting."

Just as light drives out darkness, so does the realized presence of God drive out sin, and the soul that by faith abides in His presence knows a very real and wonderful deliverance.

And now I trust that some will ask, "How can I find this presence to be real to myself?" I will close, therefore, with a few practical directions.

First, convince yourself from the Scriptures that it is a fact. Facts must always be the foundation of our experiences, or the experiences are worthless. It is not the feeling that causes the fact, but the fact that produces the feeling. And what every soul needs in this case first of all, is to be convinced beyond question, from God's own words about it, that His continual presence with us is an unalterable *fact*.

Then, this point having been settled, the next thing to do is to make it real to ourselves by "practicing His presence," as an old writer expresses it, always and everywhere, and in everything.[1] This means simply that you are to obey the Scripture command, and "in all your ways acknowledge Him," by saying over each hour and moment, "The Lord is here," and by doing everything you do, even if only eating and drinking, in His presence and for Him. Literally, "whether, therefore, ye eat or drink, or *whatsoever* ye do, do all to the glory of God."

By this continual "practice of His presence," the soul at last acquires a *habit* of faith; and it becomes, finally, as difficult to doubt His presence as it was at first to believe it.

No great effort is required for this, but simply an unwavering faith. It is not studied reasonings or elaborate meditations that will help you here. The soul must recognize, by an act of simple faith, that God *is* present, and must then accustom itself to a continual conversation with Him about all its affairs, in freedom and simplicity. He does not require great things of us. A little remembrance of His presence, a few words of love and confidence, a momentary lifting of the heart to Him from time to time as we go about our daily affairs, a constant appeal to Him in everything as to a present and loving friend and helper, an endeavor to live in a continual sense of His presence, and a letting of our hearts "dwell at ease" because of it,—this is all He asks; the least little remembrance is welcome to Him, and helps to make His presence real to us.

Whoever will be faithful in this exercise will soon be led into a blessed realization of all I have been trying to tell in this book, and of far more that I cannot tell; and will understand in a way beyond telling, those wonderful words concerning our Lord, "They shall call His name Emmanuel, which being interpreted is, God with us."

---

[1] "The Practice of the Presence of God." A little book I would strongly recommend.

The Practice of the Presence of God

The Best Rule of Holy Life
being Conversations and Letters
of Brother Lawrence

*Good
when He gives,*

supremely good;

*Nor less
when He denies:*

Afflictions,

*from His sovereign
hand,*

*Are blessings
in disguise.*

By *Brother Lawrence*

Preface

This book consists of notes of several conversations had with, and letters written by Nicholas Herman, of Lorraine, a lowly and unlearned man, who, after having been a footman and soldier, was admitted a Lay Brother among the barefooted Carmelites at Paris in 1666, and was afterwards known as "Brother Lawrence."

His conversion, which took place when he was about eighteen years old, was the result, under God, of the mere sight in midwinter, of a dry and leafless tree, and of the reflections it stirred respecting the change the coming spring would bring. From that time he grew eminently in the knowledge and love of GOD, endeavoring constantly to walk *"as in His presence."* No wilderness wanderings seem to have intervened between the Red Sea and the Jordan of his experience. A wholly consecrated man, he lived his Christian life through as a pilgrim—as a steward and not as an owner, and died at the age of eighty, leaving a name which has been as "ointment poured forth."

The "Conversations" are supposed to have been written by M. Beaufort, Grand Vicar to M. de Chalons, formerly Cardinal de Noailles, by whose recommendation the letters were first published.

The book has, within a short time, gone through repeated English and American editions, and has been a means of blessing to many souls. It contains very much of that wisdom which only lips the Lord has touched can express, and which only hearts He has made teachable can receive.

May this edition also be blessed by GOD, and redound to the praise of the glory of His grace.

FIRST CONVERSATION.

The first time I saw *Brother Lawrence*, was upon the 3d of August, 1666. He told me that GOD had done him a singular favor, in his conversion at the age of eighteen.

That in the winter, seeing a tree stripped of its leaves, and considering that within a little time the leaves would be renewed and after that the flowers and fruit appear, he received a high view of the Providence and Power of GOD, which has never since been effaced from his soul. That this view had perfectly set him loose from the world, and kindled in him such a love for GOD, that he could not tell whether it had increased during the more than forty years he had lived since.

That he had been footman to M. Fieubert, the treasurer, and that he was a great awkward fellow who broke everything.

That he had desired to be received into a monastery, thinking that he would there be made to smart for his awkwardness and the faults he should commit, and so he should sacrifice to GOD his life, with its pleasures: but that God had disappointed him, he having met with nothing but satisfaction in that state.

That we should establish ourselves in a sense of GOD'S Presence, by continually conversing with Him. That it was a shameful thing to quit His conversation, to think of trifles and fooleries.

That we should feed and nourish our souls with high notions of GOD; which would yield us great joy in being devoted to Him.

That we ought to *quicken*, i.e., *to enliven, our faith*. That it was lamentable we had so little; and that instead of taking *faith* for the rule of their conduct, men amused themselves with trivial devotions, which changed daily. That the way of Faith was the spirit of the Church, and that it was sufficient to bring us to a high degree of perfection.

That we ought to give ourselves up to GOD, with regard both to things temporal and spiritual, and seek our satisfaction only in the fulfilling of His will, whether he lead us by suffering or by consolation, for all would lie equal to a soul truly resigned. That there needed fidelity in those dryness, or insensibilities and irksomenesses in prayer, by which GOD tries our love to him; that *then* was the time for us to make good and effectual acts of resignation, whereof one alone would oftentimes very much promote our spiritual advancement.

That as for the miseries and sins he heard of daily in the world, he was so far from wondering at them, that, on the contrary, he was surprised that there were not more, considering the malice sinners were capable of; that for his part he prayed for them; but knowing that GOD could remedy the mischiefs they did when He pleased, he gave himself no farther trouble.

That to arrive at such resignation as GOD requires, we should watch attentively over all the passions which mingle as well in spiritual things as in those of a grosser nature; that GOD would give light concerning those passions to those who truly desire to serve Him. That if this was my design, viz., sincerely to serve GOD, I might come to him (B. Lawrence) as often as I pleased, without any Fear of being troublesome; but if not, that I ought no more to visit him.

SECOND CONVERSATION.

That he had always been governed by love, without selfish views; and that having resolved to make the love of GOD the *end* of all his actions, he had found reasons to be well satisfied with his method. That he was pleased when he could take up a straw from the ground for the love of GOD, seeking Him only, and nothing else, not even His gifts.

That he had been long troubled in mind from a certain belief that he should be damned; that all the men in the world could not have persuaded him to the contrary; but that he had thus reasoned with himself about it: *I engaged in a religious life only for the love of* GOD, *and I have endeavored to act only for Him; whatever becomes of me, whether I be lost or saved, I will always continue to act purely for the love of* GOD. *I shall have this good at least, that till death I shall have done all that is in me to love Him.*

That this trouble of mind had lasted four years; during which time he had suffered much. But that at last he had seen that this trouble arose from want of faith; and that since then he had passed his life in perfect liberty and continual joy. That he had placed his sins betwixt him and GOD, as it were, to tell Him that he did not deserve His favors, but that GOD still continued to bestow them in abundance.

That in order to form a habit of conversing with GOD continually, and referring all we do to Him, we must at first apply to Him with some diligence: but that after a little care we should find His love inwardly excite us to it without any difficulty.

That he expected after the pleasant days GOD had given him, he should have his turn of pain and suffering; but that he was not uneasy about it, knowing very well, that as he could do nothing of himself, GOD would not fail to give him the strength to bear it.

That when an occasion of practicing some virtue offered, he addressed himself to GOD, saying, LORD, *I cannot do this unless Thou enablest me*: and that then he received strength more than sufficient.

That when he had failed in his duty, he only confessed his fault, saying to GOD, *I shall never do otherwise, if You leave me to myself; it is You who must hinder my falling, and mend what is amiss*. That after this, he gave himself no further uneasiness about it.

That we ought to act with GOD in the greatest simplicity, speaking to Him frankly and plainly, and imploring His assistance in our affairs, just as they happen. That GOD never failed to grant it, as he had often experienced.

That he had been lately sent into Burgundy, to buy the provision of wine for the society, which was a very unwelcome task for him, because he had no turn for business, and because he was lame and could not go about the boat but by rolling himself over the casks. That however he gave himself no uneasiness about it, nor about the purchase of the wine. That he said to GOD, *It was His business he was about*, and that he afterwards found it very well performed. That he had been sent into Auvergne, the year before, upon the same account; that he could not tell how the matter passed, but that it proved very well.

So, likewise, in his business in the kitchen (to which he had naturally a great aversion), having accustomed himself to do everything there for the love of GOD, and with prayer, upon all occasions, for His grace to do his work well, he had found everything easy, during fifteen years that he had been employed there.

That he was very well pleased with the post he was now in; but that he was as ready to quit that as the former, since he was always pleasing himself in every condition, by doing little things for the love of GOD.

That with him the set times of prayer were not different from other times; that he retired to pray, according to the directions of his Superior, but that he did not want such retirement, nor ask for it, because his greatest business did not divert him from GOD.

That as he knew his obligation to love GOD in all things, and as he endeavored so to do, he had no need of a director to advise him, but that he needed much a Confessor to absolve him. That he was very sensible of his faults, but not discouraged by them; that he confessed them to GOD, but did not plead against Him to excuse them. When he had so done, he peaceably resumed his usual practice of love and adoration.

That in his trouble of mind, he had consulted nobody, but knowing only by the light of faith that GOD was present, he contented himself with directing all his actions to Him, *i.e.*, doing them with a desire to please Him, let what would come of it.

That useless thoughts spoil all: that the mischief began there; but that we ought to reject them, as soon as we perceived their impertinence to the matter in hand, or our salvation; and return to our communion with GOD.

That at the beginning he had often passed his time appointed for prayer, in rejecting wandering thoughts, and falling back into them. That he could never regulate his devotion by certain methods as some do. That nevertheless, at first he had *meditated* for some time, but afterwards that went off, in a manner he could give no account of.

That all bodily mortifications and other exercises are useless, except as they serve to arrive at the union with GOD by love; that he had well considered this, and found it the shortest way to go straight to Him by a continual exercise of love, and doing all things for His sake.

That we ought to make a great difference between the acts of the *understanding* and those of the *will*: that the first were comparatively of little value, and the others, all. That our only business was to love and delight ourselves in GOD.

That all possible kinds of mortification, if they were void of the love of GOD, could not efface a single sin. That we ought, without anxiety, to expect the pardon of our sins from the Blood of JESUS CHRIST, only endeavoring to love Him with all our hearts. That GOD seemed to have granted the greatest favors to the greatest sinners, as more signal monuments of his mercy.

That the greatest pains or pleasures of this world, were not to be compared with what he had experienced of both kinds in a spiritual state: so that he was careful for nothing and feared nothing, desiring only one thing of GOD, viz., that he might not offend Him.

That he had no scruples; for, said he, when I *fail* in my duty, I readily acknowledge it, saying, *I am used to do so: I shall never do otherwise, if I am left to myself.* I fail not, then I give GOD thanks, acknowledging the strength comes from Him.

THIRD CONVERSATION.

He told me that the *foundation of the spiritual life* in *him*, had been a high notion and esteem of GOD in faith; which when he had once well conceived, he had no other care at first, but faithfully to reject every other thought, *that he might perform all his actions for the love of* GOD. That when sometimes he had not thought of GOD for a good while, he did not disquiet himself for it; but after having acknowledged his wretchedness to GOD, he returned to Him with so much the greater trust in Him, as he had found himself wretched through forgetting Him.

That the trust we put in GOD, honors Him much, and draws down great graces.

That it was impossible, not only that GOD should deceive, hut also that He should long let a soul suffer which is perfectly resigned to Him, and resolved to endure everything for His sake.

That he had so often experienced the ready succors of Divine Grace upon all occasions, that from the same experience, when he had business to do, he did not think of it beforehand; but when it was time to do it, he found in GOD, as in a clear mirror, all that was fit for him to do. That of late he had acted thus, without anticipating care; but before the experience above mentioned, he had used it in his affairs.

When outward business diverted him a little from the thought of GOD, a fresh remembrance coming from GOD invested his soul, and so inflamed and transported him that it was difficult for him to contain himself.

That he was more united to GOD in his outward employments, than when he left them for devotion in retirement.

That he expected hereafter some great pain of body or mind; that the worst that could happen to him was, to lose that sense of GOD which he had enjoyed so long; but that the goodness of GOD assured him He would not forsake him utterly, and that He would give him strength to bear whatever evil He permitted to happen to him; and therefore that he feared nothing, and had no occasion to consult with anybody about his state. That when he had attempted to do it, he had always come away more perplexed; and that as he was conscious of his readiness to lay down his life for the love of GOD, he had no apprehension of danger. That perfect resignation to GOD was a sure way to heaven, a way in which we had always sufficient light for our conduct.

That in the beginning of the spiritual life, we ought to be faithful in doing our duty and denying ourselves; but after that, unspeakable pleasures followed; that in difficulties we need only have recourse to JESUS CHRIST, and beg his grace; with that everything became easy.

That many do not advance in the Christian progress because they stick in penances, and particular exercises, while they neglect the love of GOD, which is the *end*. That this appeared plainly by their works, and was the *reason* why we see so little solid virtue.

That there needed neither art nor science for going to GOD, but only a heart resolutely determined to apply itself to nothing but Him, or for *His* sake, and to love him only.

FOURTH CONVERSATION.

He discoursed with me very frequently, and with great openness of heart concerning his manner of *going* to GOD, whereof some part is related already.

He told me that all consists *in one hearty renunciation* of everything which we are sensible does not lead to GOD; that we might accustom ourselves to a continual conversation with Him, with freedom and in simplicity. That we need only to recognize GOD intimately present with us, to address ourselves to Him every moment, that we may beg His assistance for knowing His will in things doubtful, and for rightly performing those which we plainly see he requires of us, offering them to Him before we do them, and giving Him thanks when we have done.

That in this conversation with God, we are also employed in praising, adoring and loving Him incessantly, for His infinite goodness and perfection.

That, without being discouraged on account of our sins, we should pray for His grace with a perfect confidence, as relying upon the infinite merits of our LORD JESUS CHRIST. That GOD never failed offering us His grace at each action; that he distinctly perceived it, and never failed of it, unless when his thoughts had wandered from a sense of GOD'S Presence, or he had forgotten to ask His assistance.

That GOD always gave us light in our doubts, when we had no other design but ask to please Him.

That our sanctification did not depend upon *changing* our works, but in doing that for GOD's sake, which we commonly do for our own. That it was lamentable to see how many people mistook the means for the end, addicting themselves to certain works, which they performed very imperfectly, by reason of their human or selfish regards.

That the most excellent method he had found of going to GOD, was that of doing our common business without any view of pleasing men,[1] and (as far as we are capable) purely for the love of GOD.

That it was a great delusion to think that the times of prayer ought to differ from other times: that we are as strictly obliged to adhere to GOD by action in the time of action, as by prayer in the season of prayer.

That his prayer was nothing else but a sense of the presence of GOD, his soul being at that time insensible to everything but Divine love: and that when the appointed times

[1] Gal. i, 10; Eph. vi, 5, 6.

of prayer were past, he found no difference, because he still continued with GOD, praising and blessing Him with all his might, so that he passed his life in continual joy; yet hoped that GOD would give him somewhat to suffer, when he should grow stronger.

That we ought, once for all, heartily to put our whole trust in GOD, and make a total surrender of ourselves to Him, secure that He would not deceive us.

That we ought not to be weary of doing little things for the love of GOD, who regards not the greatness of the work, but the love with which it is performed. That we should not wonder if, in the beginning, we often failed in our endeavors, but that at last we should gain a habit, which will naturally produce its acts in us, without our care, and to our exceeding great delight.

That the whole substance of religion was faith, hope and charity; by the practice of which we become united to the will of GOD: that all besides is indifferent, and to be used as a means that we may arrive at our end, and be swallowed up therein, by faith and charity.

That all things are possible to him who *believes*—that they are less difficult to him who *hopes*—that they are more easy to him who *loves*, and still more easy to him who perseveres in the practice of these three virtues.

That the end we ought to propose to ourselves is to become, in this life, the most perfect worshippers of GOD we can possibly be, as we hope to be through all eternity.

That when we enter upon the spiritual life, we should consider, and examine to the bottom, what we are. And then we should find ourselves worthy of all contempt, and not deserving indeed the name of Christians: subject to all kinds of misery and numberless accidents, which trouble us and cause perpetual vicissitudes in our health, in our humors, in our internal and external dispositions; in fine, persons whom GOD would humble by many pains and labors, as well within as without. After this we should not wonder that troubles, temptations, oppositions and contradictions happen to us from men. We ought, on the contrary, to submit ourselves to them, and bear them as long as GOD pleases, as things highly advantageous to us.

That the greater perfection a soul aspires after, the more dependent it is upon Divine grace.

Being questioned by one of his own society[2] (to whom he was obliged to open himself) by what means he had attained such an habitual sense of GOD, he told him that, since his first coming to the monastery, he had considered GOD as the end of all his thoughts and desires, as the mark to which they should tend, and in which they should terminate.

That in the beginning of his novitiate, he spent the hours appointed for private prayer in thinking of GOD, so as to convince his mind of, and to impress deeply upon his heart, the Divine existence, rather by devout sentiments, and submission to the lights of faith, than by studied reasonings and elaborate meditations. That by this short and sure method, he exercised himself in the knowledge and love of GOD, resolving to use his utmost endeavor to live, in a continual sense of His Presence, and if possible, never to forget Him more.

That when he had thus in prayer filled his mind with great sentiments of that infinite Being, he went to his work appointed in the kitchen (for he was cook to the society); there

---

[2] The particulars which follow are collected from other accounts of Brother Lawrence.

having first considered severally the things his office required, and when and how each thing was to be done, he spent all the intervals of his time, as well before as after his work, in prayer.

That when he began his business, he said to GOD, with a filial trust in Him, "O my GOD, since Thou art with me, and I must now, in obedience to Thy commands, apply my mind to these outward things, I beseech Thee to grant me the grace to continue in Thy Presence; and to this end do Thou prosper me with Thy assistance, receive all my works, and possess all my affections."

As he proceeded in his work, he continued his familiar conversation with his Maker, —imploring His grace, and offering to Him all his actions.

When he had finished, he examined himself how he had discharged his duty; if he found *well*, he returned thanks to GOD; if otherwise, he asked pardon; and without being discouraged, he set his mind right again, and continued his exercise of the *presence* of GOD, as if he had never deviated from it. "Thus," said he, "by rising after my falls, and by frequently renewed acts of faith and love, I am come to a state wherein it would be as difficult for me not to think of GOD as it was at first to accustom myself to it."

As brother Lawrence had found such an advantage in walking in the presence of GOD, it was natural for him to recommend it earnestly to others; but his example was a stronger inducement than any arguments he could propose. His very countenance was edifying, such a sweet and calm devotion appearing in it as could not but effect the beholders. And it was observed that in the greatest hurry of business in the kitchen, he still preserved his recollection and heavenly-mindedness. He was never hasty nor loitering, but did each thing in its season, with an even, uninterrupted composure and tranquility of spirit. "The time of business," said he, "does not with me differ from the time of prayer; and in the noise and clatter of my kitchen, while several persons are at the same time calling for different things, I possess GOD in as great tranquility as if I were upon my knees at the blessed sacrament."

FIRST LETTER.

Since you desire so earnestly that I should communicate to you the method by which I arrived at that *habitual sense of* GOD'S *Presence*, which our LORD, of His mercy, has been pleased to vouch-safe to me, I must tell you that it is with great difficulty that I am prevailed on by your importunities; and now I do it only upon the terms that you show my letter to nobody. If I knew that you should let it be seen, all the desire that I have for your advancement would not be able to determine me to it. The account I can give you is:

Having found in many books different methods of going to GOD, and divers practices of the spiritual life, I thought this would serve rather to puzzle me than facilitate what I sought after, which was nothing but how to become wholly GOD'S. This made me resolve to give the all for the all; so after having given myself wholly to GOD, that He might take away my sin, *I renounced, for the love of Him, everything that was not He; and I began to live as if there was none but He and I in the world.* Sometimes I considered myself before Him as a poor criminal at the feet of his judge; at other times I beheld Him in my heart as my FATHER, as my GOD: I worshipped Him the oftenest that I could, keeping my mind in His holy Presence, and recalling it as often as I found it wandered from Him. I found no small pain in this exercise, and yet I continued it, notwithstanding all the difficulties that occurred, without troubling or disquieting myself when my mind had wandered involuntarily. I made this my business as much all the day long as at the appointed times of prayer; for at all times, every hour, every minute, even in the height of my business, I drove away from my mind everything that was capable of interrupting my thought of GOD.

Such has been my common practice ever since I entered in religion; and, though I have done it very imperfectly, yet I have found great advantages by it. These, I well know, are to be imputed to the mere mercy and goodness of GOD, because we can do nothing without Him; and *I* still less than any. But when we are faithful to keep ourselves in His holy Presence, and set Him always before us, this not only hinders our offending Him, and doing anything that may displease Him, at least wilfully, but it also begets in us a holy freedom, and, if I may so speak, a familiarity with GOD, wherewith we ask, and that successfully, the graces we stand in need of. In fine, by often repeating these acts, they become *habitual*, and the presence of GOD rendered as it were *natural to* us Give Him thanks, if you please, with me, for His great goodness towards me, which I can never sufficiently admire, for the many favors He has done to so miserable a sinner as I am. May all things praise Him. Amen.

I am, in our LORD, yours, &c.

SECOND LETTER.

To the Reverend—

Not finding my manner of life in books, although I have no difficulty about it, yet, for greater security, I shall be glad to know your thoughts concerning it.

In a conversation some days since with a person of piety, he told me the spiritual life was a life of grace, which begins with servile fear, which is increased by hope of eternal life, and which is consummated by pure love. That each of these states had its different stages, by which one arrives at last at that blessed consummation.

I have not followed all these methods. On the contrary, from I know not what instincts, I found they discouraged me. This was the reason why, at my entrance into religion, I took a resolution to give myself up to GOD, as the best return I could make for His love; and, for the love of Him, to renounce all besides.

For the first year I commonly employed myself during the time set apart for devotion with the thought of death, judgment, heaven, hell, and my sins, Thus continued some years, applying my mind carefully the rest of the day, and even in the midst of my business, *to the presence of* GOD, whom I considered always as *with* me, often as *in* me.

At length I came insensibly to do the same thing during my set time of prayer, which caused in me great delight and consolation. This practice produced in me so high an esteem for GOD, that *faith* alone was capable to satisfy me in that point.[3]

Such was my beginning; and yet I must tell you that for the first ten years I suffered much: the apprehension that I was not devoted to GOD as I wished to be, my past sins always present to my mind, and the great unmerited favors which GOD did me, were the matter and source of my sufferings. During this time I fell often, and rose again presently.

---

[3] *I suppose he means* that all distinct notions he could form of GOD, were unsatisfactory, because he perceived them to be unworthy of GOD; and therefore his mind was not to be satisfied but by the views of *faith*, which apprehend GOD as infinite and incomprehensible, as He is in Himself, and not as He can be conceived by human ideas.

It seemed to me that all creatures, reason, and GOD Himself were against me; and *faith* alone for me. I was troubled sometimes with thoughts that to believe I had received such favors was an effect of my presumption, which pretended to be *at once* where others arrive with difficulty; at other times that it was a wilful delusion, and that there was no salvation for me.

When I thought of nothing but to end my days in these troubles (which did not at all diminish the trust I had in GOD, and which served only to increase my faith), I found myself changed all at once; and my soul, which, till that time, was in trouble, felt a profound inward peace, as if she were in her centre and place of rest.

Ever since that time I walk before GOD simply, in faith, with humility and with love; and I apply myself diligently to do nothing and think nothing which may displease Him. I hope that when I have done what I can, He will do with me what He pleases.

As for what passes in me at present, I cannot express it. I have no pain or difficulty about my state, because I have no will but that of GOD, which I endeavor to accomplish in all things, and to which I am so resigned that I would not take up a straw from the ground against His order, or from any other motive than purely that of love to Him.

I have quitted all forms of devotion and set prayers but those to which my state obliges me. And I make it my business only to persevere in His holy presence, wherein I keep myself by a simple attention, and a general fond regard to GOD, which I may call an *actual presence of* GOD; or, to speak better, an habitual, silent and secret conversation of the soul with GOD, which often causes me joys and raptures inwardly, and sometimes also outwardly, so great, that I am forced to use means to moderate them and prevent their appearance to others.

In short, I am assured beyond all doubt that my soul has been with GOD above these thirty years. I pass over many things that I may not be tedious to you, yet I think it proper to inform you after what manner I consider myself before GOD, whom I behold as my King.

I consider myself as the most wretched of men, full of sores and corruption, and who has committed all sorts of crimes against his King; touched with a sensible regret, I confess to him all my wickedness, I ask His forgiveness, I abandon myself in His hands that He may do what he pleases with me. The King, full of mercy and goodness, very far from chastising me, embraces me with love, makes me eat at His table, serves me with His own hands, gives me the key of His treasures; He converses and delights Himself with me incessantly, in a thousand and a thousand ways, and treats me in all respects as His favorite. It is thus I consider myself from time to time in His holy presence.

My most useful method is this simple attention, and such a general passionate regard to GOD; to whom I find myself often attached with greater sweetness and delight than that of an infant at the mother's breast; so that, if I dare use the expression, I should choose to call this state the bosom, of GOD, for the inexpressible sweetness which I taste and experience there.

If sometimes my thoughts wander from it by necessity or infirmity, I am presently recalled by inward motions so charming and delicious that I am ashamed to mention them. I desire your reverence to reflect rather upon my great wretchedness, of which you are fully informed, than upon the great favors which GOD does me, all unworthy and ungrateful as I am.

As for my set hours of prayer, they are only a continuation of the same exercise. Sometimes I consider myself there as a stone before a carver, whereof he is to make a statue; presenting myself thus before GOD, I desire Him to form His perfect image in my soul, and make me entirely like Himself.

At other times, when I apply myself to prayer, I feel all my spirit and all my soul lift itself up without any care or effort of mine, and it continues as it were suspended and firmly fixed in GOD, as in its centre and place of rest.

I know that some charge this state with inactivity, delusion and self-love. I confess that it is a holy inactivity, and would be a happy self-love, if the soul in that state were capable of it; because, in effect, while she is in this repose, she cannot be disturbed by such acts as she was formerly accustomed to, and which were then her support, but which would now rather hinder than assist her.

Yet I cannot bear that this should be called delusion; because the soul which thus enjoys GOD desires herein nothing but Him. If this be delusion in me, it belongs to GOD to remedy it. Let Him do what He pleases with me; I desire only Him, and to be wholly devoted to Him. You will, however, oblige me in sending me your opinion, to which I always pay a great deference, for I have a singular esteem for your reverence, and am in our LORD,

Yours, &c.

THIRD LETTER.

We have a GOD who is infinitely gracious and knows all our wants. I always thought that He would reduce you to extremity. He will come in His own time, and when you least expect it. Hope in Him more than ever; thank Him with me for the favors he does you, particularly for the fortitude and patience which He gives you in your afflictions. It is a plain mark of the care He takes of you. Comfort yourself, then, with Him, and give thanks for all.

I admire also the fortitude and bravery of Mr. ——. God has given him a good disposition and a good will; but there is in him still a little of the world, and a great deal of youth. I hope the affliction which GOD has sent him will prove a wholesome remedy to him, and make him enter into himself. It is an accident which should engage him to put all his trust in *Him* who accompanies him everywhere. Let him think of Him as often as he can, especially in the greatest dangers. A little lifting up of the heart suffices. A little remembrance of GOD, one act of inward worship, though upon a march, and a sword in hand, are prayers, which, however short, are nevertheless very acceptable to GOD; and far from lessening a soldier's courage in occasions of danger, they best serve to fortify it.

Let him then think of GOD the most he can. Let him accustom himself, by degrees, to this small but holy exercise. No one will notice it, and nothing is easier than to repeat often in the day these little internal adorations. Recommend to him, if you please, that he think of GOD the most he can, in the manner here directed. It is very fit and most necessary for a soldier, who is daily exposed to the dangers of life. I hope that GOD will assist him and all the family, to whom I present my service, being theirs and Yours, &c.

FOURTH LETTER.

I have taken this opportunity to communicate to you the sentiments of one of our society, concerning the admirable effects and continual assistances which he receives from *the presence of* GOD. Let you and me both profit by them.

You must know his continual care has been, for about forty years past that he has spent in religion, to be *always with* GOD, and to do nothing, say nothing, and think nothing which may displease Him; and this without any other view than purely for the love of Him, and because he deserves infinitely more.

He is now so accustomed to that *Divine Presence*, that he receives from it continual succors upon all occasions. For about thirty years, his soul has been filled with joys so continual, and sometimes so great, that he is forced to use means to moderate them, and to hinder their appearing outwardly.

If sometimes he is a little too much absent from that *Divine Presence*, GOD presently makes Himself to be felt in his soul to recall him, which often happens when he is most engaged in his outward business. He answers with exact fidelity to these inward drawings, either by an elevation of his heart towards GOD, or by a meek and fond regard to Him, or by such words as love forms upon these occasions, as for instance, *My God, here I am all devoted to Thee*: LORD, *make me according to Thy heart*. And then it seems to him (as in effect he feels it) that this GOD of love, satisfied with such few words, reposes again, and rests in the fund and centre of his soul. The experience of these things gives him such an assurance that GOD is always in the fund or bottom of his soul, that it renders him incapable of doubting it upon any account whatever.

Judge by this what content and satisfaction he enjoys while he continually finds in himself so great a treasure. He is no longer in an anxious search after it, but has it open before him, and may take what he pleases of it.

He complains much of our blindness, and cries often that we are to be pitied who content ourselves with so little. GOD, saith he, *has infinite treasure to bestow, and we take up with a little sensible devotion, which passes in a moment. Blind as we are, we hinder GOD, and stop the current of His graces. But when He finds a soul penetrated with a lively faith, He pours into it His graces and favors plentifully: there they flow like a torrent, which, after being forcibly stopped against its ordinary course, when it has found a passage, spreads itself with impetuosity and abundance.*

Yes, we often stop this torrent by the little value we set upon it. But let us stop it no more; let us enter into ourselves and break down the bank which hinders it. Let us make way for grace; let us redeem the lost time, for perhaps we have but little left. Death follows us close; let us be well prepared for it: for we die but once; and a miscarriage *there* is irretrievable.

I say again, let us enter into ourselves. The time presses, there is no room for delay: our souls are at stake. I believe you have taken such effectual measures that you will not be surprised. I commend you for it; it is the one thing necessary. We must, nevertheless, always work at it, because not to advance in the spiritual life is to go back. But those who have the gale of the HOLY SPIRIT go forward even in sleep. If the vessel of our soul is still tossed with winds and storms, let us awake the LORD, who reposes in it, and He will quickly calm the sea.

I have taken the liberty to impart to you these good sentiments, that you may compare them with your own. It will serve again to kindle and inflame them, if by misfortune (which GOD forbid, for it would be indeed a great misfortune) they should be, though never so little, cooled. Let us then *both* recall our first fervors. Let us profit by the example and the sentiments of this brother, who is little known of the world, but known of GOD, and extremely caressed by Him. I will pray for you; do you pray instantly for me, who am, in our LORD.

Yours, &c.

FIFTH LETTER.

I received this day two books and a letter from Sister ——, who is preparing to make her profession, and upon that account desires the prayers of your holy society, and yours in particular. I perceive that she reckons much upon them; pray do not disappoint her. Beg of GOD that she may make her sacrifice in the view of His love alone, and with a firm resolution to be wholly devoted to Him. I will send you one of these books which treat of *the presence of* GOD; a subject which, in my opinion, contains the whole spiritual life; and it seems to me that whoever duly practices it will soon become spiritual.

I know that for the right practice of it, the heart must be empty of all other things; because GOD will possess the heart *alone*; and as He cannot possess it *alone* without emptying it of all besides, so neither can He act *there*, and do in it what He pleases, unless it be left vacant to Him.

There is not in the world a kind of life more sweet and delightful than that of a continual conversation with GOD. Those only can comprehend it who practice and experience it; yet I do not advise you to do it from that motive. It is not pleasure which we ought to seek in this exercise; but let us do it from a principle of love, and because GOD would have us.

Were I a preacher, I should, above all other things, preach the practice of *the presence of* GOD; and, were I a director, I should advise all the world to do it, so necessary do I think it, and so easy too.

Ah! knew we but the want we have of the grace and assistance of GOD, we should never lose sight of Him, no, not for a moment. Believe me; make immediately a holy and firm resolution never more wilfully to forget Him, and to spend the rest of your days in His sacred presence, deprived for the love of Him, if He thinks fit, of all consolations.

Set heartily about this work, and if you do it as you ought, be assured that you will soon find the effects of it. I will assist you with my prayers, poor as they are. I recommend myself earnestly to yours and those of your holy society being theirs, and more particularly

Yours, &c.

SIXTH LETTER.

To the Same.

I have received from Mrs. ——, the things which you gave her for me. I wonder that you have not given me your thoughts of the little book I sent to you, and which you must have received. Pray set heartily about the practice of it in your old age: it is better late than never.

I cannot imagine how religious persons can live satisfied without the practice of *the presence of* GOD. For my part, I keep myself retired with Him in the fund or centre of my soul as much as I can; and while I am so with Him I fear nothing, but the least turning from Him is insupportable.

This exercise does not much fatigue the body; it is, however, proper to deprive it sometimes, nay often; of many little pleasures which are innocent and lawful, for GOD will not permit that a soul which desires to be devoted entirely to Him should take other pleasures than with Him: that is more than reasonable.

I do not say that therefore we must put any violent constraint upon ourselves. No, we must serve GOD in a holy freedom; we must do our business faithfully; without trouble or disquiet, recalling our mind to GOD mildly, and with tranquility, as often as we find it wandering from Him.

It is, however, necessary to put our whole trust in GOD, laying aside all other cares, and even some particular forms of devotion, though very good in themselves, yet such as one often engages in unreasonably, because these devotions are only means to attain to the end. So when by this exercise of *the presence of* GOD we are *with Him* who is our end, it is then useless to return to the means; but we may continue with Him our commerce of love, persevering in His holy presence, one while by an act of praise, of adoration or of desire; one while by an act of resignation or thanksgiving; and in all the ways which our spirit can invent.

Be not discouraged by the repugnance which you may find in it from nature; you must do yourself violence. At the first one often thinks it lost time, but you must go on, and resolve to persevere in it to death, notwithstanding all the difficulties that may occur. I recommend myself to the prayers of your holy society, and yours in particular. I am, in our LORD,

Yours, &c.

SEVENTH LETTER.

I pity you much. It will be of great importance if you can leave the care of your affairs to ——, and spend the remainder of your life only in worshiping GOD. He requires no great matters of us; a little remembrance of Him from time to time; a little adoration; sometimes to pray for His grace, sometimes to offer Him your sufferings, and sometimes to return Him thanks for the favors He has given you, and still gives you, in the midst of your troubles, and to console yourself with Him the oftenest you can. Lift up your heart to Him, sometimes even at your meals, and when you are in company: the least little remembrance will always be acceptable to Him. You need not cry very loud; He is nearer to us than we are aware of.

It is not necessary for being with GOD to be always at church: we may make an oratory of our heart wherein to retire from time to time to converse with Him in meekness, humility and love. Every one is capable of such familiar conversation with GOD, some more, some less: He knows what we can do. Let us begin, then. Perhaps He expects but one generous resolution on our part. Have courage. We have but little time to live; you are near sixty-four, and I am almost eighty. Let us live and die with GOD. Sufferings will be sweet and pleasant to us while we are with Him; and the greatest pleasures will be, without Him, a cruel punishment to us. May He be blessed for all. Amen.

Accustom yourself, then, by degrees thus to worship Him, to beg His grace, to offer Him your heart from time to time in the midst of your business, even every moment, if you can. Do not always scrupulously confine yourself to certain rules, or particular forms of devotion, but act with a general confidence in GOD, with love and humility. You may assure —— of my poor prayers, and that I am their servant, and particularly

Yours in our LORD, &c.

EIGHTH LETTER.

(Concerning wandering thoughts in Prayer.)

You tell me nothing new; you are not the only one that is troubled with wandering thoughts. Our mind is extremely roving; but, as the will is mistress of all our faculties, she must recall them, and carry them to GOD as their last end.

When the mind, for want of being sufficiently reduced by recollection at our first engaging in devotion, has contracted certain bad habits of wandering and dissipation, they are difficult to overcome, and commonly draw us, even against our wills, to the things of the earth.

I believe one remedy for this is to confess our faults, and to humble ourselves before GOD. I do not advise you to use multiplicity of words in prayer: many words and long discourses being often the occasions of wandering. Hold yourself in prayer before GOD, like a dumb or paralytic beggar at a rich man's gate. Let it be *your* business to keep your mind in the presence of the LORD. If it sometimes wander and withdraw itself from Him, do not much disquiet yourself for that: trouble and disquiet serve rather to distract the mind than to re-collect it: the will must bring it back in tranquility. If you persevere in this manner, GOD will have pity on you.

One way to re-collect the mind easily in the time of prayer, and preserve it more in tranquility, is *not to let it wander too far at other times*: you should keep it strictly in the presence of GOD; and being accustomed to think of Him often, you will find it easy to keep your mind calm in the time of prayer, or at least to recall it from its wanderings.

I have told you already at large, in my former letters, of the advantages we may draw from this practice of the presence of GOD: let us set about it seriously, and pray for one another.

Yours, &c.

NINTH LETTER.

The enclosed is an answer to that which I received from ——; pray deliver it to her. She seems to me full of good will, but she would go faster than grace. One does not become holy all at once. I recommend her to you: we ought to help one another by our advice, and yet more by our good examples. You will oblige me to let me hear of her from time to time, and whether she be very fervent and very obedient.

Let us thus think often that our only business in this life is to please GOD, and that all besides is but folly and vanity. You and I have lived about forty years in religion (*i.e.*, a monastic life). Have we employed them in loving and serving GOD, who by His mercy has called us to this state and for that very end? I am filled with shame and confusion when I reflect on one hand upon the great favors which GOD has done, and incessantly continues to do me; and on the other, upon the ill use I have made of them, and my small advancement in the way of perfection.

Since by His mercy He gives us still a little time, let us begin in earnest: let us repair the lost time: let us return with a full assurance to that FATHER of mercies, who is always ready to receive us affectionately. Let us renounce, let us generously renounce, for the love of Him, all that is not Himself; He deserves infinitely more. Let us think of Him perpetually. Let us put all our trust in Him. I doubt not but we shall soon find the effects of it in receiving the abundance of His grace, with which we can do all things, and without which we can do nothing but sin.

We cannot escape the dangers which abound in life without the actual and *continual* help of GOD: let us then pray to Him for it *continually*. How can we pray to Him without being with Him? How can we be with Him but in thinking of Him often? And how can we often think of Him, but by a holy habit which we should form of it? You will tell me that I am always saying the same thing. It is true, for this is the best and easiest method I know; and as I use no other, I advise all the world to do it. We must *know* before we can *love*. In order to *know* GOD, we must often *think* of Him; and when we come to *love* Him, we shall then also think of Him often, for our heart will be with our treasure. This is an argument which well deserves your consideration.

I am, Yours, &c.

TENTH LETTER.

I have had a good deal of difficulty to bring myself to write to Mr. ——, and I do it now purely because you and Madam —— desire me. Pray write the directions and send it to him. I am very well pleased with the trust which you have in GOD: I wish that He may increase it in you more and more. We cannot have too much in so good and faithful a Friend, who will never fail us in this world nor in the next.

If Mr. —— makes his advantage of the loss he has had, and puts all his confidence in GOD, He will soon give him another friend, more powerful and more inclined to serve him. He disposes of hearts as He pleases. Perhaps Mr. —— was too much attached to him he has lost. We ought to love our friends, but without encroaching upon the love due to GOD, which must be the principal.

Pray remember what I have recommended to you, which is, to think often on GOD, by day, by night, in your business, and even in your diversions. He is always near you and with you: leave Him not alone. You would think it rude to leave a friend alone who came to visit you: why then must GOD be neglected? Do not then forget Him, but think on Him often, adore Him continually, live and die with Him; this is the glorious employment of a Christian. In a word, this is our profession; if we do not know it, we must learn it. I will endeavor to help you with my prayers, and am, in our LORD, Yours, &c.

ELEVENTH LETTER.

I do not pray that you may be delivered from your pains, but I pray GOD earnestly that He would give you strength and patience to bear them as long as He pleases. Comfort yourself with Him who holds you fastened to the cross. He will loose you when He thinks fit. Happy those who suffer with Him: accustom yourself to suffer in that manner, and seek from Him the strength to endure as much, and as long, as He shall judge to be necessary for you. The men of the world do not comprehend these truths, nor is it to be wondered at, since they suffer like what they are, and not like Christians. They consider sickness as a pain to nature, and not as a favor from GOD; and seeing it only in that light, they find nothing in it but grief and distress. But those who consider sickness as coming from the hand of GOD, as the effect of His mercy, and the means which He employs for their salvation—such, commonly find in it great sweetness and sensible consolation.

I wish you could convince yourself that GOD is often (in some sense) nearer to us, and more effectually present with us, in sickness than in health. Rely upon no other Physician; for, according to my apprehension, He reserves your cure to Himself. Put, then, all your trust in Him, and you will soon find the effects of it in your recovery, which we often retard by putting greater confidence in physic than in GOD.

Whatever remedies you make use of, they will succeed only so far as He permits. When pains come from GOD, He only can cure them. He often sends diseases of the body to cure those of the soul. Comfort yourself with the sovereign Physician both of the soul and body.

Be satisfied with the condition in which GOD places you: however happy you may think me, I envy you. Pains and sufferings would be a paradise to me while I should suffer with my GOD; and the greatest pleasures would be hell to me if I could relish them without Him. All my consolation would be to suffer something for His sake.

I must, in a little time, go to GOD. What comforts me in this life is, that I now see Him *by faith*; and I see Him in such a manner as might make me say sometimes, *I believe no more, but I see*. I feel what faith teaches us, and in that assurance and that practice of faith, I will live and die with Him.

Continue then always with GOD: it is the only support and comfort for your affliction. I shall beseech Him to be with you. I present my service.

Yours, &c.

TWELFTH LETTER.

If we were well accustomed to the exercise of *the presence of* GOD, all bodily diseases would be much alleviated thereby. GOD often permits that we should suffer a little to purify our souls and oblige us to continue *with* Him.

Take courage: offer Him your pains incessantly: pray to Him for strength to endure them. Above all, get a habit of entertaining yourself often with GOD, and forget Him the least you can. Adore Him in your infirmities, offer yourself to Him from time to time, and in the height of your sufferings, beseech Him humbly and affectionately (as a child his father) to make you conformable to His holy-will. I shall endeavor to assist you with my poor prayers.

GOD has many ways of drawing us to Himself. He sometimes hides Himself from us, but *faith* alone, which will not fail us in time of need, ought to be our support, and the foundation of our confidence, which must be all in GOD.

I know not how GOD will dispose of me. I am always happy. All the world suffer; and I, who deserve the severest discipline, feel joys so continual and so great that I can scarce contain them.

I would willingly ask of GOD a part of your sufferings, but that I know my weakness, which is so great, that if He left me one moment to myself I should be the most wretched man alive. And yet I know not how He can leave me alone, because faith gives me as strong a conviction as sense can do, that He never forsakes us until we have first forsaken

Him. Let us fear to leave Him. Let us be always with Him. Let us live and die in His presence. Do you pray for me, as I for you.

I am, Yours, &c.

THIRTEENTH LETTER.

To the Same.

I am in pain to see you suffer so long. What gives me some ease and sweetens the feelings I have for your griefs is, that they are proofs of GOD'S love towards you. See them in that view and you will bear them more easily. As your case is, it is my opinion that you should leave off human remedies, and resign yourself entirely to the providence of GOD: perhaps He stays only for that resignation and a perfect trust in Him to cure you. Since, notwithstanding all your cares, physic has hitherto proved unsuccessful, and your malady still increases, it will not be tempting GOD to abandon yourself in His hands, and expect all from Him.

I told you in my last that He sometimes permits bodily diseases to cure the distempers of the soul. Have courage then: make a virtue of necessity. Ask of GOD, not deliverance from your pains, but strength to bear resolutely, for the love of Him, all that He should please, and as long as He shall please.

Such prayers, indeed, are a little hard to nature, but most acceptable to GOD, and sweet to those that love Him. Love sweetens pains; and when one loves GOD, one suffers for His sake with joy and courage. Do you so, I beseech you: comfort yourself with Him, who is the only Physician of all our maladies. He is the FATHER of the afflicted, always ready to help us. He loves us infinitely more than we imagine. Love Him, then, and seek no consolation elsewhere. I hope you will soon receive it. Adieu. I will help you with my prayers, poor as they are, and shall always be, in our LORD Yours, &c.

FOURTEENTH LETTER.

To the Same.

I render thanks to our LORD for having relieved you a little, according to your desire. I have been often near expiring, but I never was so much satisfied as then. Accordingly, I did not pray for any relief, but I prayed for strength to suffer with courage, humility and love. Ah, how sweet it is to suffer with GOD! However great the sufferings may be, receive them with love. It is paradise to suffer and be with Him; so that if in this life we would enjoy the peace of paradise we must accustom ourselves to a familiar, humble, affectionate conversation with Him. We must hinder our spirits wandering from Him upon any occasion. We must make our heart a spiritual temple, wherein to adore Him incessantly. We must watch continually over ourselves, that we may not do, nor say, nor think anything that may displease Him. When our minds are thus employed about GOD, suffering will become full of unction and consolation.

I know that to arrive at this state the beginning is very difficult, for we must act purely in faith. But though it is difficult, we know also that we can do all things with the grace of GOD, which He never refuses to them who ask it earnestly. Knock, persevere in knocking, and I answer for it that He will open to you in His due time, and grant you all at once what He has deferred during many years. Adieu! Pray to Him for me, as I pray to Him for you. I hope to see Him quickly.

I am, Yours, &c.

FIFTEENTH LETTER.

To the Same.

GOD knoweth best what is needful for us, and all that He does is for our good. If we knew how much He loves us, we should always be ready to receive equally and with indifference from His Hand the sweet and the bitter: all would please that came from Him. The sorest afflictions never appear intolerable, except when we see them in the wrong light. When we see them as dispensed by the hand of GOD, when we know that it is our loving FATHER who abases and distresses us, our sufferings will lose their bitterness, and become even matter of consolation.

Let all our employment be to *know* GOD: the more one *knows* Him, the more one *desires* to know Him. And as *knowledge* is commonly the measure of *love*, the deeper and more extensive our *knowledge* shall be, the greater will be our *love*: and if our love of GOD were great, we should love Him equally in pains and pleasures.

Let us not content ourselves with loving GOD for the mere sensible favors, how elevated soever, which he has done, or may do us. Such favors, though never so great, cannot bring us so near to Him as faith does in one simple act. Let us seek Him often by faith. He is within us: seek Him not elsewhere. If we do love Him alone, are we not rude, and do we not deserve blame, if we busy ourselves about trifles which do not please and perhaps offend Him. It is to be feared these *trifles* will one day cost us dear.

Let us begin to be devoted to Him in good earnest. Let us cast everything besides out of our hearts. He would possess them alone. Beg this favor of Him. If we do what we can on our parts, we shall soon see that change wrought in us which we aspire after. I cannot thank Him sufficiently for the relaxation He has vouchsafed you. I hope from His mercy the favor to see Him within a few days.[4] Let us pray for one another.

I am, in our LORD, Yours, &c.

f i n i s

---

[4] He took to his bed two days after, and died within the week.

Absolute Surrender
and Other Addresses
~ ※ ~

By *Andrew Murray*
"I am thine and all that I have." (1 Kings 20:1-4).

Absolute Surrender

"And Ben-hadad the king of Syria gathered all his host together: and there were thirty and two kings with him, and horses, and chariots: and he went up and besieged Samaria, and warred against it. And he sent messengers to Ahab king of Israel into the city, and said unto him, "Thus saith Ben-hadad, Thy silver and thy gold is mine; thy wives also and thy children, even the goodliest, are mine. And the king of Israel answered and said, My lord, O king, according to thy saying, I am thine and all that I have." (1 Kings 20:1-4).

What Ben Hadad asked was *absolute surrender*; and what Ahab gave was what was asked of him—*absolute surrender*. I want to use these words: "My lord, O king, according to thy saying, I am thine, and all that I have," as the words of absolute surrender with which every child of God ought to yield himself to his Father. We have heard it before, but we need to hear it very definitely—the condition of God's blessing is absolute surrender of all into His hands. Praise God! If our hearts are willing for that, there is no end to what God will do for us, and to the blessing God will bestow.

Absolute surrender—let me tell you where I got those words. I used them myself often, and you have heard them numberless times. But in Scotland once I was in a company where we were talking about the condition of Christ's Church, and what the great need of the Church and of believers is; and there was in our company a godly worker who has much to do in training workers, and I asked him what he would say was the great need of the Church, and the message that ought to be preached. He answered very quietly and simply and determinedly:

"Absolute surrender to God is the one thing."

The words struck me as never before. And that man began to tell how, in the workers with whom he had to deal, he finds that if they are sound on that point, even though they be backward, they are willing to be taught and helped, and they always improve; whereas others who are not sound there very often go back and leave the work. The condition for obtaining God's full blessing is *absolute surrender* to Him.

And now, I desire by God's grace to give to you this message—that your God in Heaven answers the prayers which you have offered for blessing on yourselves and for blessing on those around you by this one demand: *Are you willing to surrender yourselves absolutely into His hands?* What is our answer to be? God knows there are hundreds of hearts who have said it, and there are hundreds more who long to say it but hardly dare to do so. And there are hearts who have said it, but who have yet miserably failed, and who feel themselves condemned because they did not find the secret of the power to live that life. May God have a word for all!

Let me say, first of all, that God claims it from us.

God Expects Your Surrender

Yes, it has its foundation in the very nature of God. God cannot do otherwise. Who is God? He is the Fountain of life, the only Source of existence and power and goodness, and throughout the universe there is nothing good but what God works. God has created the sun, and the moon, and the stars, and the flowers, and the trees, and the grass; and are they not all absolutely surrendered to God? Do they not allow God to work in them just what He pleases? When God clothes the lily with its beauty, is it not yielded up, surrendered, given over to God as He works in its beauty? And God's redeemed children, oh, can you think that God can work His work if there is only half or a part of them surrendered? God cannot do it. God is life, and love, and blessing, and power, and infinite beauty, and God delights to communicate Himself to every child who is prepared to receive Him; but ah! this one lack of absolute surrender is just the thing that hinders God. And now He comes, and as God, He claims it.

You know in daily life what absolute surrender is. You know that everything has to be given up to its special, definite object and service. I have a pen in my pocket, and that pen is absolutely surrendered to the one work of writing, and that pen must be absolutely surrendered to my hand if I am to write properly with it. If another holds it partly, I cannot write properly. This coat is absolutely given up to me to cover my body. This building is entirely given up to religious services. And now, do you expect that in your immortal being, in the divine nature that you have received by regeneration, God can work His work, every day and every hour, unless you are entirely given up to Him? God cannot. The Temple of Solomon was absolutely surrendered to God when it was dedicated to Him. And every one of us is a temple of God, in which God will dwell and work mightily on one condition—absolute surrender to Him. God claims it, God is worthy of it, and without it God cannot work His blessed work in us.

God not only claims it, but God will work it Himself.

God Accomplishes Your Surrender

I am sure there is many a heart that says: "Ah, but that absolute surrender implies so much!" Someone says: "Oh, I have passed through so much trial and suffering, and there is so much of the self-life still remaining, and I dare not face the entire giving of it up, because I know it will cause so much trouble and agony."

Alas! alas! that God's children have such thoughts of Him, such cruel thoughts. Oh, I come to you with a message, fearful and anxious one. God does not ask you to give the perfect surrender in your strength, or by the power of your will; God is willing to work it in you. Do we not read: "It is God that worketh in us, both to will and to do of his good pleasure" (Phil. 2:13)? And that is what we should seek for—to go on our faces before God, until our hearts learn to believe that the everlasting God Himself will come in to turn out what is wrong, to conquer what is evil, and to work what is well-pleasing in His blessed sight. God Himself will work it in you.

Look at the men in the Old Testament, like Abraham. Do you think it was by accident that God found that man, the father of the faithful and the Friend of God, and that it was Abraham himself, apart from God, who had such faith and such obedience and such devotion? You know it is not so. God raised him up and prepared him as an instrument for His glory.

Did not God say to Pharaoh: "For this cause have I raised thee up, for to show in thee my power" (Ex. 9:16)?

And if God said that of him, will not God say it far more of every child of His?

Oh, I want to encourage you, and I want you to cast away every fear. Come with that feeble desire; and if there is the fear which says: "Oh, my desire is not strong enough, I am not willing for everything that may come, I do not feel bold enough to say I can conquer everything"—I pray you, learn to know and trust your God now. Say: "My God, I am willing that Thou shouldst make me willing." If there is anything holding you back, or any sacrifice you are afraid of making, come to God now, and prove how gracious your God is, and be not afraid that He will command from you what He will not bestow.

God comes and offers to work this absolute surrender in you. All these searchings and hungerings and longings that are in your heart, I tell you they are the drawings of the divine magnet, Christ Jesus. He lived a life of absolute surrender, He has possession of you; He is living in your heart by His Holy Spirit. You have hindered and hindered Him terribly, but He desires to help you to get hold of Him entirely. And He comes and draws you now by His message and words. Will you not come and trust God to work in you that absolute surrender to Himself? Yes, blessed be God, He can do it, and He will do it.

God not only claims it and works it, but God accepts it when we bring it to Him.

God Accepts Your Surrender

God works it in the secret of our heart, God urges us by the hidden power of His Holy Spirit to come and speak it out, and we have to bring and to yield to Him that absolute surrender. But remember, when you come and bring God that absolute surrender, it may, as far as your feelings or your consciousness go, be a thing of great imperfection, and you may doubt and hesitate and say:

"Is it absolute?"

But, oh, remember there was once a man to whom Christ had said:

"If thou canst believe, all things are possible to him that believeth" (Mark 9:23).

And his heart was afraid, and he cried out:

"Lord, I believe, help thou mine unbelief" (Mark 9:24).

That was a faith that triumphed over the Devil, and the evil spirit was cast out. And if you come and say: "Lord, I yield myself in absolute surrender to my God," even though it be with a trembling heart and with the consciousness: "I do not feel the power, I do not feel the determination, I do not feel the assurance," it will succeed. Be not afraid, but come just as you are, and even in the midst of your trembling the power of the Holy Spirit will work.

Have you never yet learned the lesson that the Holy Spirit works with mighty power, while on the human side everything appears feeble? Look at the Lord Jesus Christ in Gethsemane. We read that He, "through the eternal Spirit" (Heb. 9:14), offered Himself a sacrifice unto God. The Almighty Spirit of God was enabling Him to do it. And yet what agony and fear and exceeding sorrow came over Him, and how He prayed! Externally, you can see no sign of the mighty power of the Spirit, but the Spirit of God was there. And even so, while you are feeble and fighting and trembling, in faith in the hidden work of God's Spirit do not fear, but yield yourself.

And when you do yield yourself in absolute surrender, let it be in the faith that God does now accept of it. That is the great point, and that is what we so often miss—that believers should be thus occupied with God in this matter of surrender. I pray you, be occupied with God. We want to get help, every one of us, so that in our daily life God shall be clearer to us, God shall have the right place, and be "all in all." And if we are to have that through life, let us begin now and look away from ourselves, and look up to God. Let each believe—while I, a poor worm on earth and a trembling child of God, full of failure and sin and fear, bow here, and no one knows what passes through my heart, and while I in simplicity say, O God, I accept Thy terms; I have pleaded for blessing on myself and others, I have accepted Thy terms of absolute surrender—while your heart says that in deep silence, remember there is a God present that takes note of it, and writes it down in His book, and there is a God present who at that very moment takes possession of you. You may not feel it, you may not realize it, but God takes possession if you will trust Him.

God not only claims it, and works it, and accepts it when I bring it, but God maintains it.

God Maintains Your Surrender

That is the great difficulty with many. People say: "I have often been stirred at a meeting, or at a convention, and I have consecrated myself to God, but it has passed away. I know it may last for a week or for a month, but away it fades, and after a time it is all gone."

But listen! It is because you do not believe what I am now going to tell you and remind you of. When God has begun the work of absolute surrender in you, and when God has accepted your surrender, then God holds Himself bound to care for it and to keep it. Will you believe that?

In this matter of surrender there are two: God and I—I a worm, God the everlasting and omnipotent Jehovah. Worm, will you be afraid to trust yourself to this mighty God now? God is willing. Do you not believe that He can keep you continually, day by day, and moment by moment?

Moment by moment I'm kept in His love;

Moment by moment I've life from above.

If God allows the sun to shine upon you moment by moment, without intermission, will not God let His life shine upon you every moment? And why have you not experienced it? Because you have not trusted God for it, and you do not surrender yourself absolutely to God in that trust.

A life of absolute surrender has its difficulties. I do not deny that. Yes, it has something far more than difficulties: it is a life that with men is absolutely impossible. But by the grace of God, by the power of God, by the power of the Holy Spirit dwelling in us, it is a life to which we are destined, and a life that is possible for us, praise God! Let us believe that God will maintain it.

Some of you have read the words of that aged saint who, on his ninetieth birthday, told of all God's goodness to him—I mean George Muller. What did he say he believed to be the secret of his happiness, and of all the blessing which God had given him? He said he believed there were two reasons. The one was that he had been enabled by grace to maintain a good conscience before God day by day; the other was, that he was a lover of God's Word. Ah, yes, a good conscience is complete obedience to God day by day, and fellowship with God every day in His Word, and prayer—that is a life of absolute surrender.

Such a life has two sides—on the one side, absolute surrender to work what God wants *you* to do; on the other side, to let God work what *He* wants to do.

First, *to do what God wants* you *to do.*

Give up yourselves absolutely to the will of God. You know something of that will; not enough, far from all. But say absolutely to the Lord God: "By Thy grace I desire to do Thy will in everything, every moment of every day." Say: "Lord God, not a word upon my tongue but for Thy glory, not a movement of my temper but for Thy glory, not an affection of love or hate in my heart but for Thy glory, and according to Thy blessed will."

Someone says: "Do you think that possible?"

I ask, What has God promised you, and what can God do to fill a vessel absolutely surrendered to Him? Oh, God wants to bless you in a way beyond what you expect. From the beginning, ear hath not heard, neither hath the eye seen, what God hath prepared for them that wait for Him (1 Cor. 2:9). God has prepared unheard-of things, blessings much more wonderful than you can imagine, more mighty than you can conceive. They are divine blessings. Oh, say now:

"I give myself absolutely to God, to His will, to do only what God wants."

It is God who will enable you to carry out the surrender.

And, on the other side, come and say: "I give myself absolutely to God, *to let Him work in me to will and to do of His good pleasure,* as He has promised to do."

Yes, the living God wants to work in His children in a way that we cannot understand, but that God's Word has revealed, and He wants to work in us every moment of the day. God is willing to maintain our life. Only let our absolute surrender be one of simple, childlike, and unbounded trust.

God Blesses When You Surrender

This absolute surrender to God will wonderfully bless.

What Ahab said to his enemy, King Ben-hadad—"My lord, O king, according to thy word I am thine, and all that I have"—shall we not say to our God and loving Father? If we do say it, God's blessing will come upon us. God wants us to be separate from the world; we are called to come out from the world that hates God. Come out for God, and say: "Lord, anything for Thee." If you say that with prayer, and speak that into God's ear, He will accept it, and He will teach you what it means.

I say again, God will bless you. You have been praying for blessing. But do remember, there must be absolute surrender. At every tea-table you see it. Why is tea poured into that cup? Because it is empty, and given up for the tea. But put ink, or vinegar, or wine into it, and will they pour the tea into the vessel? And can God fill you, can God bless you if you are not absolutely surrendered to Him? He cannot. Let us believe God has wonderful blessings for us, if we will but stand up for God, and say, be it with a trembling will, yet with a believing heart:

"O God, I accept Thy demands. I am thine and all that I have. Absolute surrender is what my soul yields to Thee by divine grace."

You may not have such strong and clear feelings of deliverances as you would desire to have, but humble yourselves in His sight, and acknowledge that you have grieved the Holy Spirit by your self-will, self-confidence, and self-effort. Bow humbly before him in the confession of that, and ask him to break the heart and to bring you into the dust before Him. Then, as you bow before Him, just accept God's teaching that in your flesh "there dwelleth no good thing" (Rom. 7:18), and that nothing will help you except another life which must come in. You must deny self once for all. Denying self must every moment be the power of your life, and then Christ will come in and take possession of you.

When was Peter delivered? When was the change accomplished? The change began with Peter weeping, and the Holy Spirit came down and filled his heart.

God the Father loves to give us the power of the Spirit. We have the Spirit of God dwelling within us. We come to God confessing that, and praising God for it, and yet confessing how we have grieved the Spirit. And then we bow our knees to the Father to ask that He would strengthen us with all might by the Spirit in the inner man, and that He would fill us with His mighty power. And as the Spirit reveals Christ to us, Christ comes to live in our hearts forever, and the self-life is cast out.

Let us bow before God in humility, and in that humility confess before Him the state of the whole Church. No words can tell the sad state of the Church of Christ on earth. I wish I had words to speak what I sometimes feel about it. Just think of the Christians around you. I do not speak of nominal Christians, or of professing Christians, but I speak of hundreds and thousands of honest, earnest Christians who are not living a life in the power of God or to His glory. So little power, so little devotion or consecration to God, so little perception of the truth that a Christian is a man utterly surrendered to God's will! Oh, we want to confess the sins of God's people around us, and to humble ourselves. We are members of that sickly body, and the sickliness of the body will hinder us, and break us down, unless we come to God, and in confession separate ourselves from partnership with worldliness, with coldness toward each other, unless we give up ourselves to be entirely and wholly for God.

How much Christian work is being done in the spirit of the flesh and in the power of self! How much work, day by day, in which human energy—our will and our thoughts about the work—is continually manifested, and in which there is but little of waiting upon God, and upon the power of the Holy Spirit! Let us make confession. But as we confess the state of the Church and the feebleness and sinfulness of work for God among us, let us come back to ourselves. Who is there who truly longs to be delivered from the power of the self-life, who truly acknowledges that it is the power of self and the flesh, and who is willing to cast all at the feet of Christ? There is deliverance.

I heard of one who had been an earnest Christian, and who spoke about the "cruel" thought of separation and death. But you do not think that, do you? What are we to think of separation and death? This: death was the path to glory for Christ. For the joy set before Him He endured the cross. The cross was the birthplace of His everlasting glory. Do you love Christ? Do you long to be in Christ, and not like Him? Let death be to you the most desirable thing on earth—death to self, and fellowship with Christ. Separation—do you think it a hard thing to be called to be entirely free from the world, and by that separation to be united to God and His love, by separation to become prepared for living and walking with God every day? Surely one ought to say:

"Anything to bring me to separation, to death, for a life of full fellowship with God and Christ."

Come and cast this self-life and flesh-life at the feet of Jesus. Then trust Him. Do not worry yourselves with trying to understand all about it, but come in the living faith that Christ will come into you with the power of His death and the power of His life; and then the Holy Spirit will bring the whole Christ—Christ crucified and risen and living in glory—into your heart.

"The Fruit of the Spirit is Love"

I want to look at the fact of a life filled with the Holy Spirit more from the practical side, and to show how this life will show itself in our daily walk and conduct.

Under the Old Testament you know the Holy Spirit often came upon men as a divine Spirit of revelation to reveal the mysteries of God, or for power to do the work of God. But He did not then dwell in them. Now, many just want the Old Testament gift of power for work, but know very little of the New Testament gift of the indwelling Spirit, animating and renewing the whole life. When God gives the Holy Spirit, His great object is the formation of a holy character. It is a gift of a holy mind and spiritual disposition, and what we need above everything else, is to say:

"I must have the Holy Spirit sanctifying my whole inner life if I am really to live for God's glory."

You might say that when Christ promised the Spirit to the disciples, He did so that they might have power to be witnesses. True, but then they received the Holy Spirit in such heavenly power and reality that He took possession of their whole being at once and so fitted them as holy men for doing the work with power as they had to do it. Christ spoke of power to the disciples, but it was the Spirit filling their whole being that worked the power.

I wish now to dwell upon the passage found in Gal. 5:22:

"The fruit of the Spirit is love."

We read that "Love is the fulfilling of the law" (Rom. 13:10), and my desire is to speak on love as a fruit of the Spirit with a twofold object. One is that this word may be a searchlight in our hearts, and give us a test by which to try all our thoughts about the Holy Spirit and all our experience of the holy life. Let us try ourselves by this word. Has this been our daily habit, to seek to be filled with the Holy Spirit as the Spirit of love? "The fruit of the Spirit is love." Has it been our experience that the more we have of the Holy Spirit the more loving we become? In claiming the Holy Spirit we should make this the first object of our expectation. The Holy Spirit comes as a Spirit of love.

Oh, if this were true in the Church of Christ how different her state would be! May God help us to get hold of this simple, heavenly truth that the fruit of the Spirit is a love which appears in the life, and that just as the Holy Spirit gets real possession of the life, the heart will be filled with real, divine, universal love.

One of the great causes why God cannot bless His Church is *the want of love*. When the body is divided, there cannot be strength. In the time of their great religious wars, when

Holland stood out so nobly against Spain, one of their mottoes was: "Unity gives strength." It is only when God's people stand as one body, one before God in the fellowship of love, one toward another in deep affection, one before the world in a love that the world can see—it is only then that they will have power to secure the blessing which they ask of God. Remember that if a vessel that ought to be one whole is cracked into many pieces, it cannot be filled. You can take a potsherd, one part of a vessel, and dip out a little water into that, but if you want the vessel full, the vessel must be whole. That is literally true of Christ's Church, and if there is one thing we must pray for still, it is this: Lord, melt us together into one by the power of the Holy Spirit; let the Holy Spirit, who at Pentecost made them all of one heart and one soul, do His blessed work among us. Praise God, we can love each other in a divine love, for "the fruit of the Spirit is love." Give yourselves up to love, and the Holy Spirit will come; receive the Spirit, and He will teach you to love more.

God Is Love

Now, why is it that the fruit of the Spirit is love? *Because God is love* (1 John 4:8).

And what does that mean?

It is the very nature and being of God to delight in communicating Himself. God has no selfishness, God keeps nothing to Himself. God's nature is to be always giving. In the sun and the moon and the stars, in every flower you see it, in every bird in the air, in every fish in the sea. God communicates life to His creatures. And the angels around His throne, the seraphim and cherubim who are flames of fire—whence have they their glory? It is because God is love, and He imparts to them of His brightness and His blessedness. And we, His redeemed children—God delights to pour His love into us. And why? Because, as I said, God keeps nothing for Himself. From eternity God had His only begotten Son, and the Father gave Him all things, and nothing that God had was kept back. "God is love."

One of the old Church fathers said that we cannot better understand the Trinity than as a revelation of divine love—the Father, the loving One, the Fountain of love; the Son, the beloved one, the Reservoir of love, in whom the love was poured out; and the Spirit, the living love that united both and then overflowed into this world. The Spirit of Pentecost, the Spirit of the Father, and the Spirit of the Son is love. And when the Holy Spirit comes to us and to other men, will He be less a Spirit of love than He is in God? It cannot be; He cannot change His nature. The Spirit of God is love, and "the fruit of the Spirit is love."

Mankind Needs Love

Why is that so? That was the one great need of mankind, that was the thing which Christ's redemption came to accomplish: *to restore love to this world.*

When man sinned, why was it that he sinned? Selfishness triumphed—he sought self instead of God. And just look! Adam at once begins to accuse the woman of having led him astray. Love to God had gone, love to man was lost. Look again: of the first two children of Adam the one becomes a murderer of his brother.

Does not that teach us that sin had robbed the world of love? Ah! what a proof the history of the world has been of love having been lost! There may have been beautiful examples of love even among the heathen, but only as a little remnant of what was lost. One of the worst things sin did for man was to make him selfish, for selfishness cannot love.

The Lord Jesus Christ came down from Heaven as the Son of God's love. "God so loved the world that He gave His only begotten Son" (John 3:16). God's Son came to show what love is, and He lived a life of love here upon earth in fellowship with His disciples, in compassion over the poor and miserable, in love even to His enemies, and He died the death of love. And when He went to Heaven, whom did He send down? The Spirit of love, to come and banish selfishness and envy and pride, and bring the love of God into the hearts of men. "The fruit of the Spirit is love."

And what was the preparation for the promise of the Holy Spirit? You know that promise as found in the fourteenth chapter of John's Gospel. But remember what precedes in the thirteenth chapter. Before Christ promised the Holy Spirit, He gave a new commandment, and about that new commandment He said wonderful things. One thing was: "Even as I have loved you, so love ye one another." To them His dying love was to be the only law of their conduct and intercourse with each other. What a message to those fishermen, to those men full of pride and selfishness! "Learn to love each other," said Christ, "as I have loved you." And by the grace of God they did it. When Pentecost came, they were of one heart and one soul. Christ did it for them.

And now He calls us to dwell and to walk in love. He demands that though a man hate you, still you love him. True love cannot be conquered by anything in Heaven or upon the earth. The more hatred there is, the more love triumphs through it all and shows its true nature. This is the love that Christ commanded His disciples to exercise.

What more did He say? "By this shall all men know that ye are my disciples, if ye have love one to another" (John 13:35).

You all know what it is to wear a badge. And Christ said to His disciples in effect: "I give you a badge, and that badge is love. That is to be your mark. It is the only thing in Heaven or on earth by which men can know me."

Do we not begin to fear that love has fled from the earth? That if we were to ask the world: "Have you seen us wear the badge of love?" the world would say: "No; what we have heard of the Church of Christ is that there is not a place where there is no quarreling and separation." Let us ask God with one heart that we may wear the badge of Jesus' love. God is able to give it.

Love Conquers Selfishness

"The fruit of the Spirit is love." Why? Because *nothing but love can expel and conquer our selfishness.*

Self is the great curse, whether in its relation to God, or to our fellow-men in general, or to fellow-Christians, thinking of ourselves and seeking our own. Self is our greatest curse. But, praise God, Christ came to redeem us from self. We sometimes talk about deliverance from the self-life—and thank God for every word that can be said about it to help us—but I am afraid some people think deliverance from the self-life means that now they are going to have no longer any trouble in serving God; and they forget that deliverance from self-life means to be a vessel overflowing with love to everybody all the day.

And there you have the reason why many people pray for the power of the Holy Spirit, and they get something, but oh, so little! because they prayed for power for work, and power for blessing, but they have not prayed for power for full deliverance from self. That means not only the righteous self in intercourse with God, but the unloving self in intercourse with men. And there is deliverance. "The fruit of the Spirit is love." I bring you the glorious promise of Christ that He is able to fill our hearts with love.

A great many of us try hard at times to love. We try to force ourselves to love, and I do not say that is wrong; it is better than nothing. But the end of it is always very sad. "I fail continually," such a one must confess. And what is the reason? The reason is simply this: Because they have never learned to believe and accept the truth that the Holy Spirit can pour God's love into their heart. That blessed text; often it has been limited!—"The love of God is shed abroad in our hearts" (Rom. 5:5). It has often been understood in this sense: It means the love of God *to me*. Oh, what a limitation! That is only the beginning. The love of God is always the love of God in its entirety, in its fullness as an indwelling power, a love of God to me that leaps back to Him in love, and overflows to my fellow-men in love—God's love to me, and my love to God, and my love to my fellow-men. The three are one; you cannot separate them.

Do believe that the love of God can be shed abroad in your heart and mine so that we can love all the day.

"Ah!" you say, "how little I have understood that!"

Why is a lamb always gentle? Because that is its nature. Does it cost the lamb any trouble to be gentle? No. Why not? It is so beautiful and gentle. Has a lamb to study to be gentle? No. Why does that come so easy? It is its nature. And a wolf—why does it cost a wolf no trouble to be cruel, and to put its fangs into the poor lamb or sheep? Because that is its nature. It has not to summon up its courage; the wolf-nature is there.

And how can I learn to love? Never until the Spirit of God fills my heart with God's love, and I begin to long for God's love in a very different sense from which I have sought it so selfishly, as a comfort and a joy and a happiness and a pleasure to myself; never until I begin to learn that "God is love," and to claim it, and receive it as an indwelling power for self-sacrifice; never until I begin to see that my glory, my blessedness, is to be like God and like Christ, in giving up everything in myself for my fellow-men. May God teach us that! Oh, the divine blessedness of the love with which the Holy Spirit can fill our hearts! "The fruit of the Spirit is love."

Love Is God's Gift

Once again I ask, Why must this be so? And my answer is: *Without this we cannot live the daily life of love.*

How often, when we speak about the consecrated life, we have to speak about *temper*, and some people have sometimes said:

"You make too much of temper."

I do not think we can make too much of it. Think for a moment of a clock and of what its hands mean. The hands tell me what is within the clock, and if I see that the hands stand still, or that the hands point wrong, or that the clock is slow or fast, I say that something inside the clock is not working properly. And temper is just like the revelation that the clock gives of what is within. Temper is a proof whether the love of Christ is filling the heart, or not. How many there are who find it easier in church, or in prayer-meeting, or in work for the Lord—diligent, earnest work—to be holy and happy than in the daily life with wife and children; easier to be holy and happy outside the home than in it! Where is the love of God? In Christ. God has prepared for us a wonderful redemption in Christ, and He longs to make something supernatural of us. Have we learned to long for it, and ask for it, and expect it in its fullness?

Then there is the *tongue!* We sometimes speak of the tongue when we talk of the better life, and the restful life, but just think what liberty many Christians give to their tongues. They say:

"I have a right to think what I like."

When they speak about each other, when they speak about their neighbors, when they speak about other Christians, how often there are sharp remarks! God keep me from saying anything that would be unloving; God shut my mouth if I am not to speak in tender love. But what I am saying is a fact. How often there are found among Christians who are banded together in work, sharp criticism, sharp judgment, hasty opinion, unloving words, secret contempt of each other, secret condemnation of each other! Oh, just as a mother's love covers her children and delights in them and has the tenderest compassion with their foibles or failures, so there ought to be in the heart of every believer a motherly love toward every brother and sister in Christ. Have you aimed at that? Have you sought it? Have you ever pleaded for it? Jesus Christ said: "As I have loved you . . . love one another" (John 13:34). And He did not put that among the other commandments, but He said in effect:

"That is a new commandment, the one commandment: Love one another as I have loved you" (John 13:34).

It is in our daily life and conduct that the fruit of the Spirit is love. From that there comes all the graces and virtues in which love is manifested: joy, peace, longsuffering, gentleness, goodness; no sharpness or hardness in your tone, no unkindness or selfishness; meekness before God and man. You see that all these are the gentler virtues. I have often thought as I read those words in Colossians, "Put on therefore as the elect of God, holy and beloved, bowels of mercies, kindness, humbleness of mind, meekness, longsuffering" (Col. 3:12), that if we had written this, we should have put in the foreground the manly virtues, such as zeal, courage, and diligence; but we need to see how the gentler, the most womanly virtues are especially connected with dependence upon the Holy Spirit. These are indeed heavenly graces. They never were found in the heathen world. Christ was needed to come from Heaven to teach us. Your blessedness is longsuffering, meekness, kindness; your glory is humility before God. The fruit of the Spirit that He brought from Heaven out of the heart of the crucified Christ, and that He gives in our heart, is first and foremost—love.

You know what John says: "No man hath seen God at any time. If we love one another, God dwelleth in us" (1 John 4:12). That is, I cannot see God, but as a compensation I can see my brother, and if I love him, God dwells in me. Is that really true? That I cannot see God, but I must love my brother, and God will dwell in me? Loving my brother is the way to real fellowship with God. You know what John further says in that most solemn test, "If a man say, I love God, and hateth his brother, he is a liar; for he that loveth not his brother whom he hath seen, how can he love God whom he hath not seen?" (1 John 4:20). There is a brother, a most unlovable man. He worries you every time you meet him. He is of the very opposite disposition to yours. You are a careful businessman, and you have to do with him in your business. He is most untidy, unbusiness-like. You say:

"I cannot love him."

Oh, friend, you have not learned the lesson that Christ wanted to teach above everything. Let a man be what he will, you are to love him. Love is to be the fruit of the Spirit all the day and every day. Yes, listen! If a man loves not his brother whom he hath seen—if you don't love that unlovable man whom you have seen, how can you love God whom you have not seen? You can deceive yourself with beautiful thoughts about loving God. You must prove your love to God by your love to your brother; that is the one standard by which God will judge your love to Him. If the love of God is in your heart you will love your brother. The fruit of the Spirit is love.

And what is the reason that God's Holy Spirit cannot come in power? Is it not possible?

You remember the comparison I used in speaking of the vessel. I can dip a little water into a potsherd, a bit of a vessel; but if a vessel is to be full, it must be unbroken. And the children of God, wherever they come together, to whatever church or mission or society they belong, must love each other intensely, or the Spirit of God cannot do His work. We talk about grieving the Spirit of God by worldliness and ritualism and formality and error and indifference, but, I tell you, the one thing above everything that grieves God's Spirit is this lack of love. Let every heart search itself, and ask that God may search it.

Our Love Shows God's Power

Why are we taught that "the fruit of the Spirit is love*"? Because the Spirit of God has come to make our daily life an exhibition of divine power and a revelation of what God can do for His children.*

In the second and the fourth chapters of Acts we read that the disciples were of one heart and of one soul. During the three years they had walked with Christ they never had been in that spirit. All Christ's teaching could not make them of one heart and one soul. But the Holy Spirit came from Heaven and shed the love of God in their hearts, and they were of one heart and one soul. The same Holy Spirit that brought the love of Heaven into their hearts must fill us too. Nothing less will do. Even as Christ did, one might preach love for three years with the tongue of an angel, but that would not teach any man to love unless the power of the Holy Spirit should come upon him to bring the love of Heaven into his heart.

Think of the church at large. What divisions! Think of the different bodies. Take the question of holiness, take the question of the cleansing blood, take the question of the baptism of the Spirit—what differences are caused among dear believers by such questions! That there are differences of opinion does not trouble me. We do not have the same constitution and temperament and mind. But how often hate, bitterness, contempt, separation, unlovingness are caused by the holiest truths of God's Word! Our doctrines, our creeds, have been more important than love. We often think we are valiant for the truth and we forget God's command to speak the truth *in love*. And it was so in the time of the Reformation between the Lutheran and Calvinistic churches. What bitterness there was then in regard to the Holy Supper, which was meant to be the bond of union among all believers! And so, down the ages, the very dearest truths of God have become mountains that have separated us.

If we want to pray in power, and if we want to expect the Holy Spirit to come down in power, and if we want indeed that God shall pour out His Spirit, we must enter into a covenant with God that we love one another with a heavenly love.

Are you ready for that? Only that is true love that is large enough to take in all God's children, the most unloving and unlovable, and unworthy, and unbearable, and trying. If my vow—absolute surrender to God—was true, then it must mean absolute surrender to the divine love to fill me; to be a servant of love to love every child of God around me. "The fruit of the Spirit is love."

Oh, God did something wonderful when He gave Christ, at His right hand, the Holy Spirit to come down out of the heart of the Father and His everlasting love. And how we have degraded the Holy Spirit into a mere power by which we have to do our work! God forgive us! Oh, that the Holy Spirit might be held in honor as a power to fill us with the very life and nature of God and of Christ!

Christian Work Requires Love

"The fruit of the Spirit is love." I ask once again, Why is it so? And the answer comes: *That is the only power in which Christians really can do their work.*

Yes, it is that we need. We want not only love that is to bind us to each other, but we want a divine love in our work for the lost around us. Oh, do we not often undertake a great deal of work, just as men undertake work of philanthropy, from a natural spirit of compassion for our fellow-men? Do we not often undertake Christian work because our minister or friend calls us to it? And do we not often perform Christian work with a certain zeal but without having had a baptism of love?

People often ask: "What is the baptism of fire?"

I have answered more than once: I know no fire like the fire of God, the fire of everlasting love that consumed the sacrifice on Calvary. The baptism of love is what the Church needs, and to get that we must begin at once to get down upon our faces before God in confession, and plead:

"Lord, let love from Heaven flow down into my heart. I am giving up my life to pray and live as one who has given himself up for the everlasting love to dwell in and fill him."

Ah, yes, if the love of God were in our hearts, what a difference it would make! There are hundreds of believers who say:

"I work for Christ, and I feel I could work much harder, but I have not the gift. I do not know how or where to begin. I do not know what I can do."

Brother, sister, ask God to baptize you with the Spirit of love, and love will find its way. Love is a fire that will burn through every difficulty. You may be a shy, hesitating man, who cannot speak well, but love can burn through everything. God fill us with love! We need it for our work.

You have read many a touching story of love expressed, and you have said, How beautiful! I heard one not long ago. A lady had been asked to speak at a Rescue Home where there were a number of poor women. As she arrived there and got to the window with the matron, she saw outside a wretched object sitting, and asked: "Who is that?"

The matron answered: "She has been into the house thirty or forty times, and she has always gone away again. Nothing can be done with her, she is so low and hard."

But the lady said: "She must come in."

The matron then said: "We have been waiting for you, and the company is assembled, and you have only an hour for the address."

The lady replied: "No, this is of more importance"; and she went outside where the woman was sitting and said: "My sister, what is the matter?"

"I am not your sister," was the reply.

Then the lady laid her hand on her, and said: "Yes, I am your sister, and I love you"; and so she spoke until the heart of the poor woman was touched.

The conversation lasted some time, and the company were waiting patiently. Ultimately the lady brought the woman into the room. There was the poor wretched, degraded creature, full of shame. She would not sit on a chair, but sat down on a stool beside the speaker's seat, and she let her lean against her, with her arms around the poor woman's neck, while she spoke to the assembled people. And that love touched the woman's heart; she had found one who really loved her, and that love gave access to the love of Jesus.

Praise God! there is love upon earth in the hearts of God's children; but oh, that there were more!

O God, baptize our ministers with a tender love, and our missionaries, and our Bible-readers, and our workers, and our young men's and young women's associations. Oh, that God would begin with us now, and baptize us with heavenly love!

Love Inspires Intercession

Once again. *It is only love that can fit us for the work of intercession.*

I have said that love must fit us for our work. Do you know what the hardest and the most important work is that has to be done for this sinful world? It is the work of intercession, the work of going to God and taking time to lay hold on Him.

A man may be an earnest Christian, an earnest minister, and a man may do good, but alas! how often he has to confess that he knows but little of what it is to tarry with God. May God give us the great gift of an intercessory spirit, a spirit of prayer and supplication! Let me ask you in the name of Jesus not to let a day pass without praying for all saints, and for all God's people.

I find there are Christians who think little of that. I find there are prayer unions where they pray for the members, and not for all believers. I pray you, take time to pray for the Church of Christ. It is right to pray for the heathen, as I have already said. God help us to pray more for them. It is right to pray for missionaries and for evangelistic work, and for the unconverted. But Paul did not tell people to pray for the heathen or the unconverted. Paul told them to pray for believers. Do make this your first prayer every day: "Lord, bless Thy saints everywhere."

The state of Christ's Church is indescribably low. Plead for God's people that He would visit them, plead for each other, plead for all believers who are trying to work for God. Let love fill your heart. Ask Christ to pour it out afresh into you every day. Try to get it into you by the Holy Spirit of God: I am separated unto the Holy Spirit, and the fruit of the Spirit is love. God help us to understand it.

May God grant that we learn day by day to wait more quietly upon Him. Do not wait upon God only for ourselves, or the power to do so will soon be lost; but give ourselves up to the ministry and the love of intercession, and pray more for God's people, for God's people round about us, for the Spirit of love in ourselves and in them, and for the work of God we are connected with; and the answer will surely come, and our waiting upon God will be a source of untold blessing and power. "The fruit of the Spirit is love."

Have you a lack of love to confess before God? Then make confession and say before Him, "O Lord, my lack of heart, my lack of love—I confess it." And then, as you cast that lack at His feet, believe that the blood cleanses you, that Jesus comes in His mighty, cleansing, saving power to deliver you, and that He will give His Holy Spirit.

"The fruit of the Spirit is love."

Separated unto the Holy Spirit

"Now there were in the church that was at Antioch certain prophets and teachers; as Barnabas, and Simeon that was called Niger, and Lucius of Cyrene, and Manaen . . . and Saul.

"As they ministered to the Lord, and fasted, the Holy Spirit said, Separate me Barnabas and Saul for the work whereunto I have called them.

"And when they had fasted and prayed, and laid their hands on them, they sent them away. So they, being sent forth by the Holy Spirit, departed unto Seleucia" (Acts 13:1-4).

In the story of our text we shall find some precious thoughts to guide us as to what God would have of us, and what God would do for us. The great lesson of the verses quoted is this: *The Holy Spirit is the director of the work of God upon the earth.* And what we should do if we are to work rightly for God, and if God is to bless our work, is to see that we stand in a right relation to the Holy Spirit, that we give Him every day the place of honor that belongs to Him, and that in all our work and (what is more) in all our private inner life, the Holy Spirit shall always have the first place. Let me point out to you some of the precious thoughts our passage suggests.

First of all, we see that *God has His own plans with regard to His kingdom.*

His church at Antioch had been established. God had certain plans and intentions with regard to Asia, and with regard to Europe. He had conceived them; they were His, and He made them known to His servants.

Our great Commander organizes every campaign, and His generals and officers do not always know the great plans. They often receive sealed orders, and they have to wait on Him for what He gives them as orders. God in Heaven has wishes, and a will, in regard to any work that ought to be done, and to the way in which it has to be done. Blessed is the man who gets into God's secrets and works under God.

Some years ago, at Wellington, South Africa, where I live, we opened a Mission Institute—what is counted there a fine large building. At our opening services the principal said something that I have never forgotten. He remarked:

"Last year we gathered here to lay the foundation-stone, and what was there then to be seen? Nothing but rubbish, and stones, and bricks, and ruins of an old building that had been pulled down. There we laid the foundation-stone, and very few knew what the building was that was to rise. No one knew it perfectly in every detail except one man, the architect. In his mind it was all clear, and as the contractor and the mason and the carpenter came to their work they took their orders from him, and the humblest laborer had to be obedient to orders, and the structure rose, and this beautiful building has been completed. And just so," he added, "this building that we open today is but laying the foundation of a work of which only God knows what is to become."

But God has His workers and His plans clearly mapped out, and our position is to wait, that God should communicate to us as much of His will as each time is needful.

We have simply to be faithful in obedience, carrying out His orders. God has a plan for His Church upon earth. But alas! we too often make our plan, and we think that we know what ought to be done. We ask God first to bless our feeble efforts, instead of absolutely refusing to go unless God goes before us. God has planned for the work and the extension of His kingdom. The Holy Spirit has had that work given in charge to Him. "The work whereunto I have called them." May God, therefore, help us all to be afraid of touching "the ark of God" except as we are led by the Holy Spirit.

Then the *second* thought—*God is willing and able to reveal to His servants what His will is.*

Yes, blessed be God, communications still come down from Heaven! As we read here what the Holy Spirit said, so the Holy Spirit will still speak to His Church and His people. In these later days He has often done it. He has come to individual men, and by His divine teaching He has led them out into fields of labor that others could not at first understand or approve, into ways and methods that did not recommend themselves to the majority. But the Holy Spirit does still in our time teach His people. Thank God, in our foreign missionary societies and in our home missions, and in a thousand forms of work, the guiding of the Holy Spirit is known, but (we are all ready, I think, to confess) *too little* known. We have not learned enough to wait upon Him, and so we should make a solemn declaration before God: O God, we want to wait more for Thee to show us Thy Will.

Do not ask God only for power. Many a Christian has his own plan of working, but God must send the power. The man works in his own will, and God must give the grace—the one reason why God often gives so little grace and so little success. But let us all take our place before God and say:

"What is done in the will of God, the strength of God will not be withheld from it; what is done in the will of God must have the mighty blessing of God."

And so let our first desire be to have the will of God revealed.

If you ask me, Is it an easy thing to get these communications from Heaven, and to understand them? I can give you the answer. It is easy to those who are in right fellowship with Heaven, and who understand the art of waiting upon God in prayer.

How often we ask: How can a person know the will of God? And people want, when they are in perplexity, to pray very earnestly that God should answer them at once. But God can only reveal His will to a heart that is humble and tender and empty. God can only reveal His will in perplexities and special difficulties to a heart that has learned to obey and honor Him loyally in little things and in daily life.

That brings me to the *third* thought—*Note the disposition to which the Spirit reveals God's will.*

What do we read here? There were a number of men ministering to the Lord and fasting, and the Holy Spirit came and spoke to them. Some people understand this passage very much as they would in reference to a missionary committee of our day. We see there is an open field, and we have had our missions in other fields, and we are going to get on to that field. We have virtually settled that, and we pray about it. But the position was a very different one in those former days. I doubt whether any of them thought of Europe, for later on even Paul himself tried to go back into Asia, till the night vision called him by the will of God. Look at those men. God had done wonders. He had extended the Church to Antioch, and He had given rich and large blessing. Now, here were these men ministering to the Lord, serving Him with prayer and fasting. What a deep conviction they have—"It must all come direct from Heaven. We are in fellowship with the risen Lord; we must have a close union with Him, and somehow He will let us know what He wants." And there they were, empty, ignorant, helpless, glad and joyful, but deeply humbled.

"O Lord," they seem to say, "we are Thy servants, and in fasting and prayer we wait upon Thee. What is Thy will for us?"

Was it not the same with Peter? He was on the housetop, fasting and praying, and little did he think of the vision and the command to go to Caesarea. He was ignorant of what his work might be.

It is in hearts entirely surrendered to the Lord Jesus, in hearts separating themselves from the world, and even from ordinary religious exercises, and giving themselves up in intense prayer to look to their Lord—it is in such hearts that the heavenly will of God will be made manifest.

You know that word *fasting* occurs a second time (in the third verse): "They fasted and prayed." When you pray, you love to go into your closet, according to the command of Jesus, and shut the door. You shut out business and company and pleasure and anything that can distract, and you want to be alone with God. But in one way even the material world follows you there. You must eat. These men wanted to shut themselves out from the influences of the material and the visible, and they fasted. What they ate was simply enough to supply the wants of nature, and in the intensity of their souls they thought to give expression to their letting go of everything on earth in their fasting before God. Oh, may God give us that intensity of desire, that separation from everything, because we want to wait upon God, that the Holy Spirit may reveal to us God's blessed will.

The *fourth* thought—*What is now the will of God as the Holy Spirit reveals it?* It is contained in one phrase: *Separation unto the Holy Spirit.* That is the <u>keynote of the message from Heaven.</u>

"Separate me Barnabas and Saul for the work whereunto I have called them. The work is mine, and I care for it, and I have chosen these men and called them, and I want you who represent the Church of Christ upon earth to set them apart unto me."

Look at this heavenly message in its twofold aspect. The men were to be *set apart* to the Holy Spirit, and *the Church was to do this separating work.* The Holy Spirit could trust these men to do it in a right spirit. There they were abiding in fellowship with the heavenly, and the Holy Spirit could say to them, "Do the work of separating these men." And these were the men the Holy Spirit had prepared, and He could say of them, "Let them be separated unto me."

Here we come to the very root, to the very life of the need of Christian workers. The question is: What is needed that the power of God should rest upon us more mightily, that the blessing of God should be poured out more abundantly among those poor, wretched people and perishing sinners among whom we labor? And the answer from Heaven is:

"I want men separated unto the Holy Spirit."

What does that imply? You know that there are two spirits on earth. Christ said, when He spoke about the Holy Spirit: "The world cannot receive him" (John 14:17). Paul said: "We have received not the spirit of the world, but the Spirit that is of God" (1 Cor. 2:12). That is the great want in every worker—the spirit of the world going out, and the Spirit of God coming in to take possession of the inner life and of the whole being.

I am sure there are workers who often cry to God for the Holy Spirit to come upon them as a Spirit of power for their work, and when they feel that measure of power, and get blessing, they thank God for it. But God wants something more and something higher. God wants us to seek for the Holy Spirit as a Spirit of power in our own heart and life, to conquer self and cast out sin, and to work the blessed and beautiful image of Jesus into us.

There is a difference between the power of the Spirit as a gift, and the power of the Spirit for the grace of a holy life. A man may often have a measure of the power of the Spirit, but if there is not a large measure of the Spirit as the Spirit of grace and holiness, the defect will be manifest in his work. He may be made the means of conversion, but he never will help people on to a higher standard of spiritual life, and when he passes away, a great deal of his work may pass away too. But a man who is separated unto the Holy Spirit is a man who is given up to say:

"Father, let the Holy Spirit have full dominion over me, in my home, in my temper, in every word of my tongue, in every thought of my heart, in every feeling toward my fellow men; let the Holy Spirit have entire possession."

Is that what has been the longing and the covenant of your heart with your God—to be a man or a woman separated and given up unto the Holy Spirit? I pray you listen to the voice of Heaven. "Separate me," said the Holy Spirit. Yes, *separated* unto the Holy Spirit. May God grant that the Word may enter into the very depths of our being to search us, and if we discover that we have not come out from the world entirely, if God reveals to us that the self-life, self-will, self-exaltation are there, let us humble ourselves before Him.

Man, woman, brother, sister, you are a worker separated unto the Holy Spirit. Is that true? Has that been your longing desire? Has that been your surrender? Has that been what you have expected through faith in the power of our risen and almighty Lord Jesus? If not, here is the call of faith, and here is the key of blessing—*separated unto the Holy Spirit.* God write the word in our hearts!

I said the Holy Spirit spoke to that church as a church capable of doing that work. The Holy Spirit trusted them. God grant that our churches, our missionary societies, and our workers' unions, that all our directors and councils and committees may be men and women who are *fit for the work of separating workers unto the Holy Spirit.* We can ask God for that too.

Then comes my *fifth* thought, and it is this—*This holy partnership with the Holy Spirit in this work becomes a matter of consciousness and of action.*

These men, what did they do? They set apart Paul and Barnabas, and then it is written of the two that they, being sent forth by the Holy Spirit, went down to Seleucia. Oh, what fellowship! The Holy Spirit in Heaven doing part of the work, men on earth doing the other part. After the ordination of the men upon earth, it is written in God's inspired Word that they were sent forth by the Holy Spirit.

And see how this partnership calls to new prayer and fasting. They had for a certain time been ministering to the Lord and fasting, perhaps days; and the Holy Spirit speaks, and they have to do the work and to enter into partnership, and at once they come together for more prayer and fasting. That is the spirit in which they obey the command of their Lord. And that teaches us that it is not only in the beginning of our Christian work, but all along that we need to have our strength in prayer. If there is one thought with regard to the Church of Christ, which at times comes to me with overwhelming sorrow; if there is one thought in regard to my own life of which I am ashamed; if there is one thought of which I feel that the Church of Christ has not accepted it and not grasped it; if there is one thought which makes me pray to God: "Oh, teach us by Thy grace, new things"—it is the _wonderful power that prayer is meant to have in the kingdom_. We have so little availed ourselves of it.

We have all read the expression of Christian in Bunyan's great work, when he found he had the key in his breast that should unlock the dungeon. We have the key that can unlock the dungeon of atheism and of heathendom. But, oh! we are far more occupied with our work than we are with prayer. We believe more in speaking to men than we believe in speaking to God. Learn from these men that the work which the Holy Spirit commands must call us to new fasting and prayer, to new separation from the spirit and the pleasures of the world, to new consecration to God and to His fellowship. Those men gave themselves up to fasting and prayer, and if in all our ordinary Christian work there were more prayer, there would be more blessing in our own inner life. If we felt and proved and testified to the world that our only strength lay in keeping every minute in contact with Christ, every minute allowing God to work in us—if that were our spirit, would not, by the grace of God, our lives be holier? Would not they be more abundantly fruitful?

I hardly know a more solemn warning in God's Word than that which we find in the third chapter of Galatians, where Paul asked:

"Having begun in the Spirit, are ye now made perfect by the flesh?" (Gal. 3:3).

Do you understand what that means? A terrible danger in Christian work, just as in a Christian life that is begun with much prayer, begun in the Holy Spirit, is that it may be gradually shunted off on to the lines of the flesh; and the word comes: "Having begun in the Spirit, are ye now made perfect by the flesh?" In the time of our first perplexity and helplessness we prayed much to God, and God answered and God blessed, and our organization became perfected, and our band of workers became large; but gradually the organization and the work and the rush have so taken possession of us that the power of the Spirit, in which we began when we were a small company, has almost been lost. Oh, I pray you, note it well! It was with new prayer and fasting, with more prayer and fasting, that this company of disciples carried out the command of the Holy Spirit, "My soul, wait thou only upon God." That is our highest and most important work. The Holy Spirit comes in answer to believing prayer.

You know when the exalted Jesus had ascended to the throne, for ten days the footstool of the throne was the place where His waiting disciples cried to Him. And that is the law of the kingdom—the King upon the throne, the servants upon the footstool. May God find us there unceasingly!

Then comes the *last* thought—*What a wonderful blessing comes when the Holy Spirit is allowed to lead and to direct the work, and when it is carried on in obedience to Him!*

You know the story of the mission on which Barnabas and Saul were sent out. You know what power there was with them. The Holy Spirit sent them, and they went on from place to place with large blessing. The Holy Spirit was their leader further on. You recollect how it was by the Spirit that Paul was hindered from going again into Asia, and was led away over to Europe. Oh, the blessing that rested upon that little company of men, and upon their ministry unto the Lord!

I pray you, let us learn to believe that God has a blessing for us. The Holy Spirit, into whose hands God has put the work, has been called "the executive of the Holy Trinity." The Holy Spirit has not only power, but He has the Spirit of love. He is brooding over this dark world and every sphere of work in it, and He is willing to bless. And why is there not more blessing? There can be but one answer. We have not honored the Holy Spirit as we should have done. Is there one who can say that that is not true? Is not every thoughtful heart ready to cry: "God forgive me that I have not honored the Holy Spirit as I should have done, that I have grieved Him, that I have allowed self and the flesh and my own will to work where the Holy Spirit should have been honored! May God forgive me that I have allowed self and the flesh and the will actually to have the place that God wanted the Holy Spirit to have."

Oh, the sin is greater than we know! No wonder that there is so much feebleness and failure in the Church of Christ!

Peter's Repentance

"And the Lord turned, and looked upon Peter. And Peter remembered the word of the Lord, how he had said unto him, Before the cock crow, thou shalt deny me thrice. And Peter went out, and wept bitterly" (Luke 22:61, 62).

That was the turning-point in the history of Peter. Christ had said to him: "Thou canst not follow me now" (John 13:36). Peter was not in a fit state to follow Christ, because he had not been brought to an end of himself; he did not know himself, and he therefore could not follow Christ. But when he went out and wept bitterly, then came the great change. Christ previously said to him: "When thou art converted, strengthen thy brethren." Here is the point where Peter was converted from self to Christ.

I thank God for the story of Peter. I do not know a man in the Bible who gives us greater comfort. When we look at his character, so full of failures, and at what Christ made him by the power of the Holy Spirit, there is hope for every one of us. But remember, before Christ could fill Peter with the Holy Spirit and make a new man of him, he had to go out and weep bitterly; he had to be humbled. If we want to understand this, I think there are four points that we must look at. First, let us look at *Peter the devoted disciple of Jesus*; next, at *Peter as he lived the life of self*; then at *Peter in his repentance*; and last, at *what Christ made of Peter by the Holy Spirit*.

Peter the Devoted Disciple of Christ

Christ called Peter to forsake his nets, and follow Him. Peter did it at once, and he afterward could say rightly to the Lord:

"We have forsaken all and followed thee" (Matt. 19:27).

Peter was a man of *absolute surrender*; he gave up all to follow Jesus. Peter was also a man of *ready obedience.* You remember Christ said to him, "Launch out into the deep, and let down the net." Peter the fisherman knew there were no fish there, for they had been toiling all night and had caught nothing; but he said: "At thy word I will let down the net" (Luke 5:4, 5). He submitted to the word of Jesus. Further, he was a man *of great faith.* When he saw Christ walking on the sea, he said: "Lord, if it be thou, bid me come unto thee" (Matt. 14:28); and at the voice of Christ he stepped out of the boat and walked upon the water.

And Peter was a man of *spiritual insight.* When Christ asked the disciples: "Whom do ye say that I am?" Peter was able to answer: "Thou art the Christ, the Son of the living God." And Christ said: "Blessed art thou, Simon Barjona; for flesh and blood hath not revealed it unto thee, but my Father which is in heaven." And Christ spoke of him as the *rock* man, and of his having the keys of the kingdom. Peter was a splendid man, a devoted disciple of Jesus, and if he were living nowadays, everyone would say that he was an advanced Christian. And yet how much there was wanting in Peter!

Peter Living the Life of Self

You recollect that just after Christ had said to him: "Flesh and blood hath not revealed it unto thee, but my Father which is in heaven," Christ began to speak about His sufferings, and Peter dared to say: "Be it far from thee, Lord; this shall not be unto thee." Then Christ had to say:

"Get thee behind me, Satan; for thou savorest not the things that be of God, but those that be of men" (Matt. 16:22-23).

There was Peter in his self-will, trusting his own wisdom, and actually forbidding Christ to go and die. Whence did that come? Peter trusted in himself and his own thoughts about divine things. We see later on, more than once, that among the disciples there was a questioning who should be the greatest, and Peter was one of them, and he thought he had a right to the very first place. He sought his own honor even above the others. It was the life of self strong in Peter. He had left his boats and his nets, but not his old self.

When Christ had spoken to him about His sufferings, and said: "Get thee behind me, Satan," He followed it up by saying: "If any man will come after me, let him deny himself, and take up his cross, and follow me" (Matt. 16:24). No man can follow Him unless he do that. Self must be utterly denied. What does that mean? When Peter denied Christ, we read that he said three times: "I do not know the man"; in other words: "I have nothing to do with Him; He and I are no friends; I deny having any connection with Him." Christ told Peter that he must deny self. Self must be ignored, and its every claim rejected. That is the root of true discipleship; but Peter did not understand it, and could not obey it. And what happened? When the last night came, Christ said to him:

"Before the cock crow twice thou shalt deny me thrice."

But with what self-confidence Peter said:

"Though all should forsake thee, yet will not I. I am ready to go with thee, to prison and to death" (Mark 14:29; Luke 22:33).

Peter meant it honestly, and Peter really intended to do it; but Peter did not know himself. He did not believe he was as bad as Jesus said he was.

We perhaps think of individual sins that come between us and God, but what are we to do with that self-life which is all unclean—our very nature? What are we to do with that flesh that is entirely under the power of sin? Deliverance from that is what we need. Peter knew it not, and therefore it was that in his self-confidence he went forth and denied his Lord.

Notice how Christ uses that word *deny* twice. He said to Peter the first time, "*Deny self*"; He said to Peter the second time, "*Thou wilt deny me.*" It is either of the two. There is no choice for us; we must either deny self or deny Christ. There are two great powers fighting each other—the self-nature in the power of sin, and Christ in the power of God. Either of these must rule within us.

It was self that made the Devil. He was an angel of God, but he wanted to exalt self. He became a Devil in hell. Self was the cause of the fall of man. Eve wanted something for herself, and so our first parents fell into all the wretchedness of sin. We their children have inherited an awful nature of sin.

Peter's Repentance

Peter denied his Lord thrice, and then the Lord looked upon him; and that look of Jesus broke the heart of Peter, and all at once there opened up before him the terrible sin that he had committed, the terrible failure that had come, and the depth into which he had fallen, and "Peter went out and wept bitterly."

Oh! who can tell what that repentance must have been? During the following hours of that night, and the next day, when he saw Christ crucified and buried, and the next day, the Sabbath—oh, in what hopeless despair and shame he must have spent that day!

"My Lord is gone, my hope is gone, and I denied my Lord. After that life of love, after that blessed fellowship of three years, I denied my Lord. God have mercy upon me!"

I do not think we can realize into what a depth of humiliation Peter sank then. But that was the turning point and the change; and on the first day of the week Christ was seen of Peter, and in the evening He met him with the others. Later on at the Lake of Galilee He asked him: "Lovest thou me?" until Peter was made sad by the thought that the Lord reminded him of having denied Him thrice; and said in sorrow, but in uprightness:

"Lord, thou knowest all things; thou knowest that I love thee" (John 21:17).

Peter Transformed

Now Peter was prepared for deliverance from self, and that is my last thought. You know Christ took him with others to the footstool of the throne, and bade them wait there; and then on the day of Pentecost the Holy Spirit came, and Peter was a changed man. I do not want you to think only of the change in Peter, in that boldness, and that power, and that insight into the Scriptures, and that blessing with which he preached that day. Thank

God for that. But there was something for Peter deeper and better. Peter's whole nature was changed. The work that Christ began in Peter when He looked upon him, was perfected when he was filled with the Holy Spirit.

If you want to see that, read the First Epistle of Peter. You know wherein Peter's failings lay. When he said to Christ, in effect: "Thou never canst suffer; it cannot be"—it showed he had not a conception of what it was to pass through death into life. Christ said: "*Deny thyself*," and in spite of that he denied his Lord. When Christ warned him: "Thou shalt deny me," and he insisted that he never would, Peter showed how little he understood what there was in himself. But when I read his epistle and hear him say: "If ye be reproached for the name of Christ, happy are ye, for the Spirit of God and of glory resteth upon you" (1 Pet. 4:14), then I say that it is not the old Peter, but that is the very Spirit of Christ breathing and speaking within him.

I read again how he says: "Hereunto ye are called, to suffer, even as Christ suffered" (1 Pet. 2:21). I understand what a change had come over Peter. Instead of denying Christ, he found joy and pleasure in having self denied and crucified and given up to the death. And therefore it is in the Acts we read that, when he was called before the Council, he could boldly say: "We must obey God rather than men" (Acts 5:29), and that he could return with the other disciples and rejoice that they were counted worthy to suffer for Christ's name.

You remember his self-exaltation; but now he has found out that "the ornament of a meek and quiet spirit is in the sight of God of great price." Again he tells us to be "subject one to another, and be clothed with humility" (1 Pet. 5:5).

Dear friend, I beseech you, look at Peter utterly changed—the self-pleasing, the self-trusting, the self-seeking Peter, full of sin, continually getting into trouble, foolish and impetuous, but now filled with the Spirit and the life of Jesus. Christ had done it for him by the Holy Spirit.

And now, what is my object in having thus very briefly pointed to the story of Peter? That story must be the history of every believer who is really to be made a blessing by God. That story is a prophecy of what everyone can receive from God in Heaven.

Now let us just glance hurriedly at what these lessons teach us.

The *first lesson* is this—You may be a very earnest, godly, devoted believer, in whom the power of the flesh is yet very strong.

That is a very solemn truth. Peter, before he denied Christ, had cast out devils and had healed the sick; and yet the flesh had power, and the flesh had room in him. Oh, beloved, we have to realize that it is just because there is so much of that self-life in us that the power of God cannot work in us as mightily as God is willing that it should work. Do you realize that the great God is longing to double His blessing, to give tenfold blessing through us? But there is something hindering Him, and that something is a proof of nothing but the self-life. We talk about the pride of Peter, and the impetuosity of Peter, and the self-confidence of Peter. It all rooted in that one word, *self*. Christ had said, "Deny self," and Peter had never understood, and never obeyed; and every failing came out of that.

What a solemn thought, and what an urgent plea for us to cry: O God, do reveal this to us, that none of us may be living the self-life! It has happened to many a one who had been a Christian for years, who had perhaps occupied a prominent position, that God found him out and taught him to find himself out, and he became utterly ashamed, falling down broken before God. Oh, the bitter shame and sorrow and pain and agony that came to him, until at last he found that there was deliverance! Peter went out and wept bitterly, and there may be many a godly one in whom the power of the flesh still rules.

And then my *second lesson* is—It is the work of our blessed Lord Jesus to reveal the power of self.

How was it that Peter, the carnal Peter, self-willed Peter, Peter with the strong self-love, ever became a man of Pentecost and the writer of his epistles? It was because Christ had him in charge, and Christ watched over him, and Christ taught and blessed him. The warnings that Christ had given him were part of the training; and last of all there came that look of love. In His suffering Christ did not forget him, but turned round and looked upon him, and "Peter went out and wept bitterly." And the Christ who led Peter to Pentecost is waiting today to take charge of every heart that is willing to surrender itself to Him.

Are there not some saying: "Ah! that is the mischief with me; it is always the self-life, and self-comfort, and self-consciousness, and self-pleasing, and self-will; how am I to get rid of it?"

My answer is: It is Christ Jesus who can rid you of it; none else but Christ Jesus can give deliverance from the power of self. And what does He ask you to do? He asks that you should humble yourself before Him.

Impossible with Man, Possible with God

"And he said, The things which are impossible with men are possible with God" (Luke 18:27).

Christ had said to the rich young ruler, "Sell all that thou hast . . . and come, follow me." The young man went away sorrowful. Christ then turned to the disciples, and said: "How hardly shall they that have riches enter into the kingdom of God!" The disciples, we read, were greatly astonished, and answered: "If it is so difficult to enter the kingdom, who, then, can be saved?" And Christ gave this blessed answer:

"The things which are impossible with men are possible with God."

The text contains two thoughts—that *in religion, in the question of salvation and of following Christ by a holy life, it is impossible for man to do it.* And then alongside that is the thought—*What is impossible with man is possible with God.*

The two thoughts mark the two great lessons that man has to learn in the religious life. It often takes a long time to learn the first lesson, that in religion man can do nothing, that salvation is impossible to man. And often a man learns that, and yet he does not learn the second lesson—what has been impossible to him is possible with God. Blessed is the man who learns both lessons! The learning of them marks stages in the Christian's life.

Man Cannot

The one stage is when a man is trying to do his utmost and fails, when a man tries to do better and fails again, when a man tries much more and always fails. And yet very often he does not even then learn the lesson: *With man it is impossible to serve God and Christ.* Peter spent three years in Christ's school, and he never learned that, *It is impossible,* until he had denied his Lord and went out and wept bitterly. Then he learned it.

Just look for a moment at a man who is learning this lesson. At first he fights against it; then he submits to it, but reluctantly and in despair; at last he accepts it willingly and rejoices in it. At the beginning of the Christian life the young convert has no conception of this truth. He has been converted, he has the joy of the Lord in his heart, he begins to run the race and fight the battle; he is sure he can conquer, for he is earnest and honest, and God will help him. Yet, somehow, very soon he fails where he did not expect it, and sin gets the better of him. He is disappointed; but he thinks: "I was not watchful enough, I did not make my resolutions strong enough." And again he vows, and again he prays, and yet he fails. He thought: "Am I not a regenerate man? Have I not the life of God within me?" And he thinks again: "Yes, and I have Christ to help me, I can live the holy life."

At a later period he comes to another state of mind. He begins to see such a life is impossible, but he does not accept it. There are multitudes of Christians who come to this point: "I cannot"; and then think God never expected them to do what they cannot do. If you tell them that God does expect it, it appears to them a mystery. A good many Christians are living a low life, a life of failure and of sin, instead of rest and victory, because they began to see: "I cannot, it is impossible." And yet they do not understand it fully, and so, under the impression, I cannot, they give way to despair. They will do their best, but they never expect to get on very far.

But God leads His children on to a third stage, when a man comes to take that, *It is impossible,* in its full truth, and yet at the same time says: "I must do it, and I will do it— it is impossible for man, and yet I must do it"; when the renewed will begins to exercise its whole power, and in intense longing and prayer begins to cry to God: "Lord, what is the meaning of this?—how am I to be freed from the power of sin?"

It is the state of the regenerate man in Romans 7. There you will find the Christian man trying his very utmost to live a holy life. God's law has been revealed to him as reaching down into the very depth of the desires of the heart, and the man can dare to say:

"I delight in the law of God after the inward man. To will what is good is present with me. My heart loves the law of God, and my will has chosen that law."

Can a man like that fail, with his heart full of delight in God's law and with his will determined to do what is right? Yes. That is what Romans 7 teaches us. There is something more needed. Not only must I delight in the law of God after the inward man, and will what God wills, but I need a divine omnipotence to work it in me. And that is what the apostle Paul teaches in Philippians 2:13:

"It is God which worketh in you, both to will and to do."

Note the contrast. In Romans 7, the regenerate man says: "To will is present with me, but to do—I find I cannot do. I will, but I cannot perform." But in Philippians 2, you have a man who has been led on farther, a man who understands that when God has worked the renewed will, God will give the power to accomplish what that will desires. Let us receive this as the first great lesson in the spiritual life: "It is impossible for me, my God;

let there be an end of the flesh and all its powers, an end of self, and let it be my glory to be helpless."

Praise God for the divine teaching that makes us helpless!

When you thought of absolute surrender to God were you not brought to an end of yourself, and to feel that you could see how you actually could live as a man absolutely surrendered to God every moment of the day—at your table, in your house, in your business, in the midst of trials and temptations? I pray you learn the lesson now. If you felt you could not do it, you are on the right road, if you let yourselves be led. Accept that position, and maintain it before God: "My heart's desire and delight, O God, is absolute surrender, but I cannot perform it. It is impossible for me to live that life. It is beyond me." Fall down and learn that when you are utterly helpless, God will come to work in you not only to will, but also to do.

God Can

Now comes the second lesson. "The things which *are impossible with men are possible with God.*"

I said a little while ago that there is many a man who has learned the lesson, *It is impossible with men,* and then he gives up in helpless despair, and lives a wretched Christian life, without joy, or strength, or victory. And why? Because he does not humble himself to learn that other lesson: *With God all things are possible.*

Your religious life is every day to be a proof that God works impossibilities; your religious life is to be a series of impossibilities made possible and actual by God's almighty power. That is what the Christian needs. He has an almighty God that he worships, and he must learn to understand that he does not need a little of God's power, but he needs—with reverence be it said—the whole of God's omnipotence to keep him right, and to live like a Christian.

The whole of Christianity is a work of God's omnipotence. Look at the birth of Christ Jesus. That was a miracle of divine power, and it was said to Mary: "With God nothing shall be impossible." It was the omnipotence of God. Look at Christ's resurrection. We are taught that it was according to the exceeding greatness of His mighty power that God raised Christ from the dead.

Every tree must grow on the root from which it springs. An oak tree three hundred years old grows all the time on the one root from which it had its beginning. Christianity had its beginning in the omnipotence of God, and in every soul it must have its continuance in that omnipotence. All the possibilities of the higher Christian life have their origin in a new apprehension of Christ's power to work all God's will in us.

I want to call upon you now to come and worship an almighty God. Have you learned to do it? Have you learned to deal so closely with an almighty God that you know omnipotence is working in you? In outward appearance there is often so little sign of it. The apostle Paul said: "I was with you in weakness and in fear and in much trembling, and . . . my preaching was . . . in demonstration of the Spirit and of power." From the human side there was feebleness, from the divine side there was divine omnipotence. And that is true of every godly life; and if we would only learn that lesson better, and give a wholehearted, undivided surrender to it, we should learn what blessedness there is in dwelling every hour and every moment with an almighty God. Have you ever studied in the Bible the attribute of God's omnipotence? You know that it was God's omnipotence that created the world, and created light out of darkness, and created man. But have you studied God's omnipotence in the works of redemption?

Look at Abraham. When God called him to be the father of that people out of which Christ was to be born, God said to him: "I am God Almighty, walk before me and be thou perfect." And God trained Abraham to trust Him as the omnipotent One; and whether it was his going out to a land that he knew not, or his faith as a pilgrim midst the thousands of Canaanites—his faith said: This is my land—or whether it was his faith in waiting twenty-five years for a son in his old age, against all hope, or whether it was the raising up of Isaac from the dead on Mount Moriah when he was going to sacrifice him—Abraham believed God. He was strong in faith, giving glory to God, because he accounted Him who had promised able to perform.

The cause of the weakness of your Christian life is that you want to work it out partly, and to let God help you. And that cannot be. You must come to be utterly helpless, to let God work, and God will work gloriously. It is this that we need if we are indeed to be workers for God. I could go through Scripture and prove to you how Moses, when he led Israel out of Egypt; how Joshua, when he brought them into the land of Canaan; how all God's servants in the Old Testament counted upon the omnipotence of God doing impossibilities. And this God lives today, and this God is the God of every child of His. And yet we are some of us wanting God to give us a little help while we do our best, instead of coming to understand what God wants, and to say: "I can do nothing. God must and will do all." Have you said: "In worship, in work, in sanctification, in obedience to God, I can do nothing of myself, and so my place is to worship the omnipotent God, and to believe that He will work in me every moment"? Oh, may God teach us this! Oh, that God would by His grace show you what a God you have, and to what a God you have entrusted yourself—an omnipotent God, willing with His whole omnipotence to place Himself at the disposal of every child of His! Shall we not take the lesson of the Lord Jesus and say: "Amen; the things which are impossible with men are possible with God"?

Remember what we have said about Peter, his self-confidence, self-power, self-will, and how he came to deny his Lord. You feel, "Ah! there is the self-life, there is the flesh-life that rules in me!" And now, have you believed that there is deliverance from that? Have you believed that Almighty God is able so to reveal Christ in your heart, so to let the Holy Spirit rule in you, that the self-life shall not have power or dominion over you? Have you coupled the two together, and with tears of penitence and with deep humiliation and feebleness, cried out: "O God, it is impossible to me; man cannot do it, but, glory to Thy name, it is possible with God"? Have you claimed deliverance? Do it now. Put yourself afresh in absolute surrender into the hands of a God of infinite love; and as infinite as His love is His power to do it.

God Works in Man

But again, we came to the question of absolute surrender, and felt that that is the want in the Church of Christ, and that is why the Holy Spirit cannot fill us, and why we cannot live as people entirely separated unto the Holy Spirit; that is why the flesh and the self-life cannot be conquered. We have never understood what it is to be absolutely surrendered to God as Jesus was. I know that many a one earnestly and honestly says: "Amen, I accept the message of absolute surrender to God"; and yet thinks: "Will that ever be mine? Can

I count upon God to make me one of whom it shall be said in Heaven and on earth and in Hell, he lives in absolute surrender to God?" Brother, sister, "the things which are impossible with men are possible with God." Do believe that when He takes charge of you in Christ, it is possible for God to make you a man of absolute surrender. And God is able to maintain that. He is able to let you rise from bed every morning of the week with that blessed thought directly or indirectly: "I am in God's charge. My God is working out my life for me."

Some are weary of thinking about sanctification. You pray, you have longed and cried for it, and yet it appeared so far off! The holiness and humility of Jesus—you are so conscious of how distant it is. Beloved friends, the one doctrine of sanctification that is scriptural and real and effectual is: "The things which are impossible with men are possible with God." God can sanctify men, and by His almighty and sanctifying power every moment God can keep them. Oh, that we might get a step nearer to our God now! Oh, that the light of God might shine, and that we might know our God better!

I could go on to speak about the life of Christ in us—living like Christ, taking Christ as our Savior from sin, and as our life and strength. It is God in Heaven who can reveal that in you. What does that prayer of the apostle Paul say: "That he would grant you according to riches of his glory"—it is sure to be something very wonderful if it is according to the riches of His glory—"to be strengthened with might by his Spirit in the inner man"? Do you not see that it is an omnipotent God working by His omnipotence in the heart of His believing children, so that Christ can become an indwelling Savior? You have tried to grasp it and to seize it, and you have tried to believe it, and it would not come. It was because you had not been brought to believe that "the things which are impossible with men are possible with God."

And so, I trust that the word spoken about love may have brought many to see that we must have an inflowing of love in quite a new way; our heart must be filled with life from above, from the Fountain of everlasting love, if it is going to overflow all the day; then it will be just as natural for us to love our fellow men as it is natural for the lamb to be gentle and the wolf to be cruel. Until I am brought to such a state that the more a man hates and speaks evil of me, the more unlikable and unlovable a man is, I shall love him all the more; until I am brought to such a state that the more the obstacles and hatred and ingratitude, the more can the power of love triumph in me—until I am brought to see that, I am not saying: "It is impossible with men." But if you have been led to say: "This message has spoken to me about a love utterly beyond my power; it is absolutely impossible"—then we can come to God and say: "It is possible with Thee."

Some are crying to God for a great revival. I can say that that is the prayer of my heart unceasingly. Oh, if God would only revive His believing people! I cannot think in the first place of the unconverted formalists of the Church, or of the infidels and skeptics, or of all the wretched and perishing around me, my heart prays in the first place: "My God, revive Thy Church and people." It is not for nothing that there are in thousands of hearts yearnings after holiness and consecration: it is a forerunner of God's power. God works *to will* and then He works *to do.* These yearnings are a witness and a proof that God has worked *to will.* Oh, let us in faith believe that the omnipotent God will work *to do* among His people more than we can ask. "Unto him," Paul said, "who is able to do exceeding abundantly above all that we ask or think. . . . unto him be glory." Let our hearts say that. Glory to God, the omnipotent One, who can do above what we dare to ask or think!

"The things which are impossible with men are possible with God." All around you there is a world of sin and sorrow, and the Devil is there. But remember, Christ is on the throne, Christ is stronger, Christ has conquered, and Christ will conquer. But wait on God. My text casts us down: "The things which are *impossible with men*"; but it ultimately lifts us up high—"are *possible with God.*" Get linked to God. Adore and trust Him as the omnipotent One, not only for your own life, but for all the souls that are entrusted to you. Never pray without adoring His omnipotence, saying: *"Mighty God, I claim Thine almightiness."* And the answer to the prayer will come, and like Abraham you will become strong in faith, giving glory to God, because you account Him who hath promised able to perform.

"O Wretched Man that I am!"

"O wretched man that I am! who shall deliver me from the body of this death? I thank God through Jesus Christ our Lord" (Romans 7:24, 25).

You know the wonderful place that this text has in the wonderful epistle to the Romans. It stands here at the end of the seventh chapter as the gateway into the eighth. In the first sixteen verses of the eighth chapter the name of the Holy Spirit is found sixteen times; you have there the description and promise of the life that a child of God can live in the power of the Holy Spirit. This begins in the second verse: "The law of the Spirit of life in Christ Jesus hath made me free from the law of sin and death" (Rom. 8:12). From that Paul goes on to speak of the great privileges of the child of God, who is to be led by the Spirit of God. The gateway into all this is in the twenty-fourth verse of the seventh chapter:

"O wretched man that I am!"

There you have the words of a man who has come to the end of himself. He has in the previous verses described how he had struggled and wrestled in his own power to obey the holy law of God, and had failed. But in answer to his own question he now finds the true answer and cries out: "I thank God through Jesus Christ our Lord." From that he goes on to speak of what that deliverance is that he has found.

I want from these words to describe the path by which a man can be led out of the spirit of bondage into the spirit of liberty. You know how distinctly it is said: "Ye have not received the spirit of bondage again to fear." We are continually warned that this is the great danger of the Christian life, to go again into bondage; and I want to describe the path by which a man can get out of bondage into the glorious liberty of the children of God. Rather, I want to describe the man himself.

First, these words are the language of a *regenerate* man; *second,* of an *impotent* man; *third,* of a *wretched* man; and *fourth,* of a man *on the borders of complete liberty.*

The Regenerate Man

There is much evidence of regeneration from the fourteenth verse of the chapter on to the twenty-third. "It is no more I that do it, but sin that dwelleth in me" (Rom. 7:17): that is the language of a regenerate man, a man who knows that his heart and nature have been renewed, and that sin is now a power in him that is not himself. "I delight in the law of the Lord after the inward man" (Rom. 7:22): that again is the language of a regenerate man. He dares to say when he does evil: "It is no more I that do it, but sin that dwelleth in me." It is of great importance to understand this.

In the first two great sections of the epistle, Paul deals with justification and sanctification. In dealing with justification, he lays the foundation of the doctrine in the teaching about sin, not in the singular, *sin*, but in the plural, *sins*—the actual transgressions. In the second part of the fifth chapter he begins to deal with sin, not as actual transgression, but as a power. Just imagine what a loss it would have been to us if we had not this second half of the seventh chapter of the Epistle to the Romans, if Paul had omitted in his teaching this vital question of the sinfulness of the believer. We should have missed the question we all want answered as to sin in the believer. What is the answer? The regenerate man is one in whom the will has been renewed, and who can say: "I delight in the law of God after the inward man."

The Impotent Man

Here is the great mistake made by many Christian people: they think that when there is a renewed will, it is enough; but that is not the case. This regenerate man tells us: *"I will to do what is good, but the power to perform I find not."* How often people tell us that if you set yourself determinedly, you can perform what you will! But this man was as determined as any man can be, and yet he made the confession: "To will is present with me; but how to perform that which is good, I find not" (Rom. 7:18).

But, you ask: "How is it God makes a regenerate man utter such a confession, with a right will, with a heart that longs to do good, and longs to do its very utmost to love God?"

Let us look at this question. What has God given us our will for? Had the angels who fell, in their own will, the strength to stand? Surely not. The will of the creature is nothing but an empty vessel in which the power of God is to be made manifest. The creature must seek in God all that it is to be. You have it in the second chapter of the epistle to the Philippians, and you have it here also, that God's work is to work in us both *to will* and *to do* of His good pleasure. Here is a man who appears to say: "God has not worked *to do* in me." But we are taught that God works both to will and to do. How is the apparent contradiction to be reconciled?

You will find that in this passage (Rom. 7:6-25) the name of the Holy Spirit does not occur once, nor does the name of Christ occur. The man is wrestling and struggling to fulfill God's law. Instead of the Holy Spirit and of Christ, the law is mentioned nearly twenty times. In this chapter, it shows a believer doing his very best to obey the law of God with his regenerate will. Not only this; but you will find the little words, *I, me, my,* occur more than forty times. It is the regenerate *I* in its impotence seeking to obey the law without being filled with the Spirit. This is the experience of almost every saint. After conversion a man begins to do his best, and he fails; but if we are brought into the full light, we need fail no longer. Nor need we fail at all if we have received the Spirit in His fullness at conversion.

God allows that failure that the regenerate man should be taught his own utter impotence. It is in the course of this struggle that there comes to us this sense of our utter sinfulness. It is God's way of dealing with us. He allows that man to strive to fulfill the law that, as he strives and wrestles, he may be brought to this: "I am a regenerate child of

God, but I am utterly helpless to obey His law." See what strong words are used all through the chapter to describe this condition: "I am carnal, sold under sin" (Rom. 7:14); "I see another law in my members bringing me into captivity" (Rom. 7:23); and last of all, "O wretched man that I am! who shall deliver me from the body of this death?" (Rom. 7:24). This believer who bows here in deep contrition is utterly unable to obey the law of God.

The Wretched Man

Not only is the man who makes this confession a regenerate and an impotent man, but he is also a wretched man. He is utterly unhappy and miserable; and what is it that makes him so utterly miserable? It is because God has given him a nature that loves Himself. He is deeply wretched because he feels he is not obeying his God. He says, with brokenness of heart: "It is not I that do it, but I am under the awful power of sin, which is holding me down. It is I, and yet not I: alas! alas! it is myself; so closely am I bound up with it, and so closely is it intertwined with my very nature." Blessed be God when a man learns to say: "O wretched man that I am!" from the depth of his heart. He is on the way to the eighth chapter of Romans.

There are many who make this confession a pillow for sin. They say that if Paul had to confess his weakness and helplessness in this way, what are they that they should try to do better? So the call to holiness is quietly set aside. Would God that every one of us had learned to say these words in the very spirit in which they are written here! When we hear sin spoken of as the abominable thing that God hates, do not many of us wince before the word? Would that all Christians who go on sinning and sinning would take this verse to heart. If ever you utter a sharp word say: "O wretched man that I am!" And every time you lose your temper, kneel down and understand that it never was meant by God that this was to be the state in which His child should remain. Would God that we would take this word into our daily life, and say it every time we are touched about our own honor, and every time we say sharp things, and every time we sin against the Lord God, and against the Lord Jesus Christ in His humility, and in His obedience, and in His self-sacrifice! Would to God you could forget everything else, and cry out: "O wretched man that I am! who shall deliver me from the body of this death?"

Why should you say this whenever you commit sin? Because it is when a man is brought to this confession that deliverance is at hand.

And remember it was not only the sense of being impotent and taken captive that made him wretched, but it was above all the sense of sinning against his God. The law was doing its work, making sin *exceedingly sinful* in his sight. The thought of continually grieving God became utterly unbearable—it was this that brought forth the piercing cry: "O wretched man!" As long as we talk and reason about our impotence and our failure, and only try to find out what Romans 7 means, it will profit us but little; but when once *every sin* gives new intensity to the sense of wretchedness, and we feel our whole state as one of not only helplessness, but actual exceeding sinfulness, we shall be pressed not only to ask: "Who shall deliver us?" but to cry: "I thank God through Jesus Christ my Lord."

The Almost-Delivered Man

The man has tried to obey the beautiful law of God. He has loved it, he has wept over his sin, he has tried to conquer, he has tried to overcome fault after fault, but every time he has ended in failure.

What did he mean by "the body of this death"? Did he mean, my body when I die? Surely not. In the eighth chapter you have the answer to this question in the words: "If ye through the Spirit do mortify the deeds of the body, ye shall live." *That* is the body of death from which he is seeking deliverance.

And now he is on the brink of deliverance! In the twenty-third verse of the seventh chapter we have the words: "I see another law in my members, warring against the law of my mind, and bringing me into *captivity* to the law of sin which is in my members." It is a *captive* that cries: "O wretched man that I am! who shall deliver me from the body of this death?" He is a man who feels himself bound. But look to the contrast in the second verse of the eighth chapter: "The law of the Spirit of life in Christ Jesus hath *made me free* from the law of sin and death." That is the deliverance through Jesus Christ our Lord; the *liberty* to the captive which the Spirit brings. Can you keep captive any longer a man made free by the "law of the Spirit of life in Christ Jesus"?

But you say, the regenerate man, had not he the Spirit of Jesus when he spoke in the sixth chapter? Yes, *but he did not know what the Holy Spirit could do for him.*

God does not work by His Spirit as He works by a blind force in nature. He leads His people on as reasonable, intelligent beings, and therefore when He wants to give us that Holy Spirit whom He has promised, He brings us first to the end of self, to the conviction that though we have been striving to obey the law, we have failed. When we have come to the end of that, then He shows us that in the Holy Spirit we have the power of obedience, the power of victory, and the power of real holiness.

God works *to will*, and He is ready to work *to do*, but, alas! many Christians misunderstand this. They think because they have the will, it is enough, and that now they are able to do. This is not so. The new will is a permanent gift, an attribute of the new nature. The power to do is not a permanent gift, but must be each moment received from the Holy Spirit. It is the man who is conscious *of his own impotence as a believer* who will learn that by the Holy Spirit *he can live a holy life.* This man is on the brink of that great deliverance; the way has been prepared for the glorious eighth chapter. I now ask this solemn question: Where are you living? Is it with you, "O wretched man that I am! who shall deliver me?" with now and then a little experience of the power of the Holy Spirit? or is it, "I thank God through Jesus Christ! The law of the Spirit hath set me free from the law of sin and of death"?

What the Holy Spirit does is to give the victory. "If ye through the Spirit do mortify the deeds of the flesh, ye shall live" (Rom. 8:13). It is the Holy Spirit who does this—the third Person of the Godhead. He it is who, when the heart is opened wide to receive Him, comes in and reigns there, and mortifies the deeds of the body, day by day, hour by hour, and moment by moment.

I want to bring this to a point. Remember, dear friend, what we need is to come to decision and action. There are in Scripture two very different sorts of Christians. The Bible speaks in *Romans, Corinthians* and *Galatians* about yielding to the flesh; and that is the life of tens of thousands of believers. All their lack of joy in the Holy Spirit, and their lack of the liberty He gives, is just owing to the flesh. The Spirit is within them, but the flesh rules the life. To be led by the Spirit of God is what they need. Would God that I could make every child of His realize what it means that the everlasting God has given His dear Son, Christ Jesus, to watch over you every day, and that what you have to do is to trust; and that the work of the Holy Spirit is to enable you every moment to remember Jesus, and to trust Him! The Spirit has come to keep the link with Him unbroken every moment. Praise God for the Holy Spirit! We are so accustomed to think of the Holy Spirit as a luxury, for special times, or for special ministers and men. But the Holy Spirit is necessary for every believer, every moment of the day. Praise God you have Him, and that He gives you the full experience of the deliverance in Christ, as He makes you free from the power of sin.

Who longs to have the power and the liberty of the Holy Spirit? Oh, brother, bow before God in one final cry of despair:

"O God, must I go on sinning this way forever? Who shall deliver me, O wretched man that I am! from the body of this death?"

Are you ready to sink before God in that cry and seek the power of Jesus to dwell and work in you? Are you ready to say: "I thank God through Jesus Christ"?

What good does it do that we go to church or attend conventions, that we study our Bibles and pray, unless our lives are filled with the Holy Spirit? That is what God wants; and nothing else will enable us to live a life of power and peace. You know that when a minister or parent is using the catechism, when a question is asked an answer is expected. Alas! how many Christians are content with the question put here: "O wretched man that I am! who shall deliver me from the body of this death?" but never give the answer. Instead of answering, they are silent. Instead of saying: "I thank God through Jesus Christ our Lord," they are forever repeating the question without the answer. If you want the path to the full deliverance of Christ, and the liberty of the Spirit, the glorious liberty of the children of God, take it through the seventh chapter of Romans; and then say: "I thank God through Jesus Christ our Lord." Be not content to remain ever groaning, but say: "I, a wretched man, thank God, through Jesus Christ. Even though I do not see it all, I am going to praise God."

There is deliverance, there is the liberty of the Holy Spirit. The kingdom of God is "joy in the Holy Spirit" (Rom. 14:17).

"Having Begun in the Spirit"

The words from which I wish to address you, you will find in the epistle to the Galatians, the third chapter, the third verse; let us read the second verse also: "This only would I learn of you, Received ye the Spirit by the works of the law, or by the hearing of faith? Are ye so foolish?" And then comes my text—"Having begun in the Spirit, are ye now made perfect by the flesh?"

When we speak of the quickening or the deepening or the strengthening of the spiritual life, we are thinking of something that is feeble and wrong and sinful; and it is a great thing to take our place before God with the confession:

"Oh, God, our spiritual life is not what it should be!"

May God work that in your heart, reader.

As we look round about on the church we see so many indications of feebleness and of failure, and of sin, and of shortcoming, that we are compelled to ask: Why is it? Is there any necessity for the church of Christ to be living in such a low state? Or is it actually possible that God's people should be living always in the joy and strength of their God?

Every believing heart must answer: It *is* possible.

Then comes the great question: Why is it, how is it to be accounted for, that God's church as a whole is so feeble, and that the great majority of Christians are not living up to their privileges? There must be a reason for it. Has God not given Christ His Almighty Son to be the Keeper of every believer, to make Christ an ever-present reality, and to impart and communicate to us all that we have in Christ? God has given His Son, and God has given His Spirit. How is it that believers do not live up to their privileges?

We find in more than one of the epistles a very solemn answer to that question. There are epistles, such as the first to the Thessalonians, where Paul writes to the Christians, in effect: "I want you to grow, to abound, to increase more and more." They were young, and there were things lacking in their faith, but their state was so far satisfactory, and gave him great joy, and he writes time after time: "I pray God that you may abound more and more; I write to you to increase more and more" (1 Thes. 4:1,10). But there are other epistles where he takes a very different tone, especially the epistles to the Corinthians and to the Galatians, and he tells them in many different ways what the one reason was, that they were not living as Christians ought to live; many were under the power of the flesh. My text is one example. He reminds them that by the preaching of faith they had received the Holy Spirit. He had preached Christ to them; they had accepted that Christ and had received the Holy Spirit in power. But what happened? Having begun in the Spirit, they tried to perfect the work that the Spirit had begun in the flesh by their own effort. We find the same teaching in the epistle to the Corinthians.

Now, we have here a solemn discovery of what the great want is in the church of Christ. God has called the church of Christ to live in the power of the Holy Spirit, and the church is living for the most part in the power of human flesh, and of will and energy and effort apart from the Spirit of God. I doubt not that that is the case with many individual believers; and oh, if God will use me to give you a message from Him, my one message will be this: "If the church will return to acknowledge that the Holy Spirit is her strength and her help, and if the church will return to give up everything, and wait upon God to be filled with the Spirit, her days of beauty and gladness will return, and we shall see the glory of God revealed among us." This is my message to every individual believer: "Nothing will help you unless you come to understand that you must live every day under the power of the Holy Spirit."

God wants you to be a living vessel in whom the power of the Spirit is to be manifested every hour and every moment of your life, and God will enable you to be that.

Now let us try to learn that this word to the Galatians teaches us—some very simple thoughts. It shows us how (1) *the beginning of the Christian life is receiving the Holy Spirit.* It shows us (2) *what great danger there is of forgetting that we are to live by the Spirit, and not live after the flesh.* It shows us (3) *what are the fruits and the proofs of our seeking perfection in the flesh.* And then it suggests to us (4) *the way of deliverance from this state.*

Receiving the Holy Spirit

First of all, Paul says: *"Having begun in the Spirit."* Remember, the apostle not only preached justification by faith, but he preached something more. He preached this—the epistle is full of it—that justified men cannot live but by the Holy Spirit, and that therefore God gives to every justified man the Holy Spirit to seal him. The apostle says to them in effect more than once:

"How did you receive the Holy Spirit? Was it by the preaching of the law, or by the preaching of faith?"

He could point back to that time when there had been a mighty revival under his teaching. The power of God had been manifested, and the Galatians were compelled to confess:

"Yes, we have got the Holy Spirit: accepting Christ by faith, by faith we received the Holy Spirit."

Now, it is to be feared that there are many Christians who hardly know that when they believed, they received the Holy Spirit. A great many Christians can say: "I received pardon and I received peace." But if you were to ask them: "Have you received the Holy Spirit?" they would hesitate, and many, if they were to say Yes, would say it with hesitation; and they would tell you that they hardly knew what it was, since that time, to walk in the power of the Holy Spirit. Let us try and take hold of this great truth: The beginning of the true Christian life is to receive the Holy Spirit. And the work of every Christian minister is that which was the work of Paul—to remind his people that they received the Holy Spirit, and must live according to His guidance and in His power.

If those Galatians who received the Holy Spirit in power were tempted to go astray by that terrible danger of perfecting in the flesh what had been begun in the Spirit, how much more danger do those Christians run who hardly ever know that they have received the Holy Spirit, or who, if they know it as a matter of belief, hardly ever think of it and hardly ever praise God for it!

Neglecting the Holy Spirit

But now look, in the second place, at *the great danger.*

You all know what shunting is on a railway. A locomotive with its train may be run in a certain direction, and the points at some place may not be properly opened or closed, and unobservingly it is shunted off to the right or to the left. And if that takes place, for instance, on a dark night, the train goes in the wrong direction, and the people might never know it until they have gone some distance.

And just so God gives Christians the Holy Spirit with this intention, that every day all their life should be lived in the power of the Spirit. A man cannot live one hour a godly life unless by the power of the Holy Spirit. He may live a proper, consistent life, as people call it, an irreproachable life, a life of virtue and diligent service; but to live a life acceptable to God, in the enjoyment of God's salvation and God's love, to live and walk in the power of the new life—he cannot do it unless he be guided by the Holy Spirit every day and every hour.

But now listen to the danger. The Galatians received the Holy Spirit, but what was begun by the Spirit they tried to perfect in the flesh. How? They fell back again under

Judaizing teachers who told them they must be circumcised. They began to seek their religion in external observances. And so Paul uses that expression about those teachers who had them circumcised, that "they sought to glory in their flesh" (Gal. 6:13).

You sometimes hear the expression used, *religious flesh*. What is meant by that? It is simply an expression made to give utterance to this thought: My human nature and my human will and my human effort can be very active in religion, and after being converted, and after receiving the Holy Spirit, I may begin in my own strength to try to serve God.

I may be very diligent and doing a great deal, and yet all the time it is more the work of human flesh than of God's Spirit. What a solemn thought, that man can, without noticing it, be shunted off from the line of the Holy Spirit on to the line of the flesh; that he can be most diligent and make great sacrifices, and yet it is all in the power of the human will! Ah, the great question for us to ask of God in self-examination is that we may be shown whether our religious life is lived more in the power of the flesh than in the power of the Holy Spirit. A man may be a preacher, he may work most diligently in his ministry, a man may be a Christian worker, and others may tell of him that he makes great sacrifices, and yet you can feel there is a want about it. You feel that he is not a spiritual man; there is no spirituality about his life. How many Christians there are about whom no one would ever think of saying: "What a spiritual man he is!" Ah! there is the weakness of the Church of Christ. It is all in that one word—*flesh*.

Now, the flesh may manifest itself in many ways. It may be manifested in fleshly wisdom. My mind may be most active about religion. I may preach or write or think or meditate, and delight in being occupied with things in God's Book and in God's Kingdom; and yet the power of the Holy Spirit may be markedly absent. I fear that if you take the preaching throughout the Church of Christ and ask why there is, alas! so little converting power in the preaching of the Word, why there is so much work and often so little result for eternity, why the Word has so little power to build up believers in holiness and in consecration—the answer will come: It is the absence of the power of the Holy Spirit. And why is this? There can be no other reason but that the flesh and human energy have taken the place that the Holy Spirit ought to have. That was true of the Galatians, it was true of the Corinthians. You know Paul said to them: "I cannot speak to you as to spiritual men; you ought to be spiritual men, but you are carnal." And you know how often in the course of his epistles he had to reprove and condemn them for strife and for divisions.

Lacking the Fruit of the Holy Spirit

A third thought: *What are the proofs or indications that a church like the Galatians, or a Christian, is serving God in the power of the flesh—is perfecting in the flesh what was begun in the Spirit?*

The answer is very easy. Religious self-effort always ends in sinful flesh. What was the state of those Galatians? Striving to be justified by the works of the law. And yet they were quarreling and in danger of devouring one another. Count up the expressions that the apostle uses to indicate their want of love, and you will find more than twelve—envy, jealousy, bitterness, strife, and all sorts of expressions. Read in the fourth and fifth chapters what he says about that. You see how they tried to serve God in their own strength, and they failed utterly. All this religious effort resulted in failure. The power of sin and the sinful flesh got the better of them, and their whole condition was one of the saddest that could be thought of.

This comes to us with unspeakable solemnity. There is a complaint everywhere in the Christian Church of the want of a high standard of integrity and godliness, even among the professing members of Christian churches. I remember a sermon which I heard preached on commercial morality. And, oh, if we speak not only of the commercial morality or immorality, but if we go into the homes of Christians, and if we think of the life to which God has called His children, and which He enables them to live by the Holy Spirit, and if we think of how much, nevertheless, there is of unlovingness and temper and sharpness and bitterness, and if we think how much there is very often of strife among the members of churches, and how much there is of envy and jealousy and sensitiveness and pride, then we are compelled to say: "Where are marks of the presence of the Spirit of the Lamb of God?" Wanting, sadly wanting!

Many people speak of these things as though they were the natural result of our feebleness and cannot well be helped. Many people speak of these things as sins, yet have given up the hope of conquering them. Many people speak of these things in the church around them, and do not see the least prospect of ever having the things changed. There is no prospect until there comes a radical change, until the Church of God begins to see that every sin in the believer comes from the flesh, from a fleshly life midst our religious activities, from a striving in self-effort to serve God. Until we learn to make confession, and until we begin to see, we must somehow or other get God's Spirit in power back to His Church, we must fail. Where did the Church begin in Pentecost? There they began in the Spirit. But, alas, how the Church of the next century went off into the flesh! They thought to perfect the Church in the flesh.

Do not let us think, because the blessed Reformation restored the great doctrine of justification by faith, that the power of the Holy Spirit was then fully restored. If it is our faith that God is going to have mercy on His Church in these last ages, it will be because the doctrine and the truth about the Holy Spirit will not only be studied, but sought after with a whole heart; and not only because that truth will be sought after, but because ministers and congregations will be found bowing before God in deep abasement with one cry: "We have grieved God's Spirit; we have tried to be Christian churches with as little as possible of God's Spirit; we have not sought to be churches filled with the Holy Spirit."

All the feebleness in the Church is owing to the refusal of the Church to obey its God.

And why is that so? I know your answer. You say: "We are too feeble and too helpless, and we try to obey, and we vow to obey, but somehow we fail."

Ah, yes, *you fail because you do not accept the strength of God.* God alone can work out His will in you. You cannot work out God's will, but His Holy Spirit can; and until the Church, until believers grasp this, and cease trying by human effort to do God's will, and wait upon the Holy Spirit to come with all His omnipotent and enabling power, the Church will never be what God wants her to be, and what God is willing to make of her.

Yielding to the Holy Spirit

I come now to my last thought, the question: *What is the way to restoration?*

Beloved friend, the answer is simple and easy. If that train has been shunted off, there is nothing for it but to come back to the point at which it was led away. The Galatians had no other way in returning but to come back to where they had gone wrong, to come back from all religious effort in their own strength, and from seeking anything by their own work, and to yield themselves humbly to the Holy Spirit. There is no other way for us as individuals.

Is there any brother or sister whose heart is conscious: "Alas! my life knows but little of the power of the Holy Spirit"? I come to you with God's message that you can have no conception of what your life would be in the power of the Holy Spirit. It is too high and too blessed and too wonderful, but I bring you the message that just as truly as the everlasting Son of God came to this world and wrought His wonderful works, that just as truly as on Calvary He died and wrought out your redemption by His precious blood, so, just as truly, can the Holy Spirit come into your heart that with His divine power He may sanctify you and enable you to do God's blessed will, and fill your heart with joy and with strength. But, alas! we have forgotten, we have grieved, we have dishonored the Holy Spirit, and He has not been able to do His work. But I bring you the message: The Father in Heaven loves to fill His children with His Holy Spirit. God longs to give each one individually, separately, the power of the Holy Spirit for daily life. The command comes to us individually, unitedly. God wants us as His children to arise and place our sins before Him, and to call upon Him for mercy. Oh, are ye so foolish? Having begun in the Spirit, are ye perfecting in the flesh that which was begun in the Spirit? Let us bow in shame, and confess before God how our fleshly religion, our self-effort, and self-confidence, have been the cause of every failure.

I have often been asked by young Christians: "Why is it that I fail so? I did so solemnly vow with my whole heart, and did desire to serve God; why have I failed?"

To such I always give the one answer: "My dear friend, you are trying to do in your own strength what Christ alone can do in you."

And when they tell me: "I am sure I knew Christ alone could do it, I was not trusting in myself," my answer always is:

"You were trusting in yourself or you could not have failed. If you had trusted Christ, He could not fail."

Oh, this perfecting in the flesh what was begun in the Spirit runs far deeper through us than we know. Let us ask God to reveal to us that it is only when we are brought to utter shame and emptiness that we shall be prepared to receive the blessing that comes from on high.

And so I come with these two questions. Are you living, beloved brother-minister— I ask it of every minister of the Gospel—are you living under the power of the Holy Spirit? Are you living as an anointed, Spirit-filled man in your ministry and your life before God? O brethren, our place is an awful one. We have to show people what God will do for us, not in our words and teaching, but in our life. God help us to do it!

I ask it of every member of Christ's Church and of every believer: Are you living a life under the power of the Holy Spirit day by day, or are you attempting to live without that? Remember you cannot. Are you consecrated, given up to the Spirit to work in you and to live in you? Oh, come and confess every failure of temper, every failure of tongue however small, every failure owing to the absence of the Holy Spirit and the presence of the power of self. Are you consecrated, are you given up to the Holy Spirit?

If your answer is No, then I come with a second question—Are you *willing* to be consecrated? Are you willing to give up yourself to the power of the Holy Spirit?

You well know that the human side of consecration will not help you. I may consecrate myself a hundred times with all the intensity of my being, and that will not help me. What will help me is this—that God from Heaven accepts and seals the consecration.

And now are you willing to give yourselves up to the Holy Spirit? You can do it now. A great deal may still be dark and dim, and beyond what we understand, and you may feel nothing; but come. God alone can effect the change. God alone, who gave us the Holy Spirit, can restore the Holy Spirit in power into our life. God alone can "strengthen us with might by his Spirit in the inner man." And to every waiting heart that will make the sacrifice, and give up everything, and give time to cry and pray to God, the answer will come. The blessing is not far off. Our God delights to help us. He will enable us to perfect, not in the flesh, but in the Spirit, what was begun in the Spirit.

Kept by the Power of God

The words from which I speak, you will find in 1 Peter 1:5. The third, fourth and fifth verses are: "Blessed be the God and Father of our Lord Jesus Christ, which . . . hath begotten us again unto a lively hope by the resurrection of Jesus Christ from the dead, to an inheritance incorruptible . . . reserved in heaven for you, who are kept by the power of God through faith unto salvation." The words of my text are: "Kept by the power of God through faith."

There we have two wonderful, blessed truths about the keeping by which a believer is kept unto salvation. One truth is, *Kept by the power of God*; and the other truth is, *Kept through faith.* We should look at the two sides—at God's side and His almighty power, offered to us to be our Keeper every moment of the day; and at the human side, we having nothing to do but in faith to let God do His keeping work. We are begotten again to an inheritance kept in Heaven for us; and we are kept here on earth by the power of God. We see there is a double keeping—*the inheritance kept for me in Heaven,* and *I on earth kept for the inheritance* there.

Now, as to the first part of this keeping, there is no doubt and no question. God keeps the inheritance in Heaven very wonderfully and perfectly, and it is waiting there safely. And the same God keeps me for the inheritance. That is what I want to understand.

You know it is very foolish of a father to take great trouble to have an inheritance for his children, and to keep it for them, if he does not keep them for it. What would you think of a man spending his whole time and making every sacrifice to amass money, and as he gets his tens of thousands, you ask him why it is that he sacrifices himself so, and his answer is: "I want to leave my children a large inheritance, and I am keeping it for them"— if you were then to hear that that man takes no trouble to educate his children, that he allows them to run upon the street wild, and to go on in paths of sin and ignorance and folly, what would you think of him? Would not you say: "Poor man! he is keeping an inheritance for his children, but he is not keeping or preparing his children for the inheritance"! And there are so many Christians who think: "My God is keeping the inheritance for me"; but they cannot believe: "My God is keeping me for that inheritance." The same power, the same love, the same God doing the double work.

Now, I want to speak about a work God does upon us—keeping us for the inheritance. I have already said that we have two very simple truths: the one the divine side—*we are kept by the power of God*; the other, the human side—*we are kept through faith.*

Kept by the Power of God

Look at the divine side: Christians are kept by the power of God.

Keeping Includes All

Think, first of all, that *this keeping is all-inclusive.*

What is kept? *You* are kept. How much of you? The whole being. Does God keep one part of you and not another? No. Some people have an idea that this is a sort of vague, general keeping, and that God will keep them in such a way that when they die they will get to Heaven. But they do not apply that word kept to everything in their being and nature. And yet that is what God wants.

Here I have a watch. Suppose that this watch had been borrowed from a friend, and he said to me: "When you go to Europe, I will let you take it with you, but mind you keep it safely and bring it back."

And suppose I damaged the watch, and had the hands broken, and the face defaced, and some of the wheels and springs spoiled, and took it back in that condition, and handed it to my friend; he would say: "Ah, but I gave you that watch on condition that you would keep it."

"Have I not kept it? There is the watch."

"But I did not want you to keep it in that general way, so that you should bring me back only the shell of the watch, or the remains. I expected you to keep every part of it."

And so God does not want to keep us in this general way, so that at the last, somehow or other, we shall be saved as by fire, and just get into Heaven. But the keeping power and the love of God applies to every particular of our being.

There are some people who think God will keep them in spiritual things, but not in temporal things. This latter, they say, lies outside of His line. Now, God sends you to work in the world, but He did not say: "I must now leave you to go and earn your own money, and to get your livelihood for yourself." He knows you are not able to keep yourself. But God says: "My child, there is no work you are to do, and no business in which you are engaged, and not a cent which you are to spend, but I, your Father, will take that up into my keeping." God not only cares for the spiritual, but for the temporal also. The greater part of the life of many people must be spent, sometimes eight or nine or ten hours a day, amid the temptations and distractions of business; but God will care for you there. The keeping of God includes all.

There are other people who think: "Ah! in time of trial God keeps me, but in times of prosperity I do not need His keeping; then I forget Him and let Him go." Others, again, think the very opposite. They think: "In time of prosperity, when things are smooth and quiet, I am able to cling to God, but when heavy trials come, somehow or other my will rebels, and God does not keep me then."

Now, I bring you the message that in prosperity as in adversity, in the sunshine as in the dark, your God is ready to keep you all the time.

Then again, there are others who think of this keeping thus: "God will keep me from doing very great wickedness, but there are small sins I cannot expect God to keep me from. There is the sin of temper. I cannot expect God to conquer that."

When you hear of some man who has been tempted and gone astray or fallen into drunkenness or murder, you thank God for His keeping power.

"I might have done the same as that man," you say, "if God had not kept me." And you believe He kept you from drunkenness and murder.

And why do you not need believe that God can keep you from outbreaks of temper? You thought that this was of less importance; you did not remember that the great commandment of the New Testament is—"Love one another as I have loved you" (John 13:34). And when your temper and hasty judgment and sharp words came out, you sinned against the highest law—the law of God's love. And yet you say: "God will not, God cannot"—no, you will not say, God cannot; but you say, "God does not keep me from that." You perhaps say: "He can; but there is something in me that cannot attain to it, and which God does not take away."

I want to ask you, Can believers live a holier life than is generally lived? Can believers experience the keeping power of God all the day, to keep them from sin? Can believers be kept in fellowship with God? And I bring you a message from the Word of God, in these words: *Kept by the power of God.* There is no qualifying clause to them. The meaning is, that if you will entrust yourself entirely and absolutely to the omnipotence of God, He will delight to keep you.

Some people think that they never can get so far as that every word of their mouth should be to the glory of God. But it is what God wants of them, it is what God expects of them. God is willing to set a watch at the door of their mouth, and if God will do that, cannot He keep their tongue and their lips? He can; and that is what God is going to do for them that trust Him. God's keeping is all-inclusive, and let everyone who longs to live a holy life think out all their needs, and all their weaknesses, and all their shortcomings, and all their sins, and say deliberately: "Is there any sin that my God cannot keep me from?" And the heart will have to answer: "No; God can keep me from every sin."

Keeping Requires Power

Second, if you want to understand this keeping, remember that it is not only an all-inclusive keeping, but it is an almighty keeping.

I want to get that truth burned into my soul; I want to worship God until my whole heart is filled with the thought of His omnipotence. God is almighty, and the Almighty God offers Himself to work in my heart, to do the work of keeping me; and I want to get linked with Omnipotence, or rather, linked to the Omnipotent One, to the living God, and to have my place in the hollow of His hand. You read the Psalms, and you think of the wonderful thoughts in many of the expressions that David uses; as, for instance, when he speaks about God being *our God, our Fortress, our Refuge, our strong Tower, our Strength* and *our Salvation.* David had very wonderful views of how the everlasting God is Himself the hiding place of the believing soul, and of how He takes the believer and keeps him in the very hollow of His hand, in the secret of His pavilion, under the shadow of His wings, under His very feathers. And there David lived. And oh, we who are the children of Pentecost, we who have known Christ and His blood and the Holy Spirit sent down from Heaven, why is it we know so little of what it is to walk tremblingly step by step with the Almighty God as our Keeper?

Have you ever thought that in every action of grace in your heart you have the whole omnipotence of God engaged to bless you? When I come to a man and he bestows upon me a gift of money, I get it and go away with it. He has given me something of his; the rest he keeps for himself. But that is not the way with the power of God. God can part with nothing of His own power, and therefore I can experience the power and goodness of God only so far as I am in contact and fellowship with Himself; and when I come into contact and fellowship with Himself, I come into contact and fellowship with the whole omnipotence of God, and have the omnipotence of God to help me every day.

A son has, perhaps, a very rich father, and as the former is about to commence business the father says: "You can have as much money as you want for your undertaking." All the father has is at the disposal of the son. And that is the way with God, your Almighty God. You can hardly take it in; you feel yourself such a little worm. His omnipotence needed to keep a little worm! Yes, His omnipotence is needed to keep every little worm that lives in the dust, and also to keep the universe, and therefore His omnipotence is much more needed in keeping your soul and mine from the power of sin.

Oh, if you want to grow in grace, do learn to begin here. In all your judgings and meditations and thoughts and deeds and questionings and studies and prayers, learn to be kept by your Almighty God. What is Almighty God not going to do for the child that trusts Him? The Bible says: "Above all that we can ask or think" (Eph. 3:20). It is Omnipotence you must learn to know and trust, and then you will live as a Christian ought to live. How little we have learned to study God, and to understand that a godly life is a life full of God, a life that loves God and waits on Him, and trusts Him, and allows Him to bless it! We cannot do the will of God except by the power of God. God gives us the first experience of His power to prepare us to long for more, and to come and claim all that He can do. God help us to trust Him every day.

Keeping Is Continuous

Another thought. This keeping is not only all-inclusive and omnipotent, but also continuous and unbroken.

People sometimes say: "For a week or a month God has kept me very wonderfully: I have lived in the light of His countenance, and I cannot say what joy I have not had in fellowship with Him. He has blessed me in my work for others. He has given me souls, and at times I felt as if I were carried heavenward on eagle wings. But it did not continue. It was too good; it could not last." And some say: "It was necessary that I should fall to keep me humble." And others say: "I know it was my own fault; but somehow you cannot always live up in the heights."

Oh, beloved, why is it? Can there be any reason why the keeping of God should not be continuous and unbroken? Just think. All life is in unbroken continuity. If my life were stopped for half an hour I would be dead, and my life gone. Life is a continuous thing, and the life of God is the life of His Church, and the life of God is His almighty power working in us. And God comes to us as the Almighty One, and without any condition He offers to be my Keeper, and His keeping means that day by day, moment by moment, God is going to keep us.

If I were to ask you the question: "Do you think God is able to keep you one day from actual transgression?" you would answer: "I not only know He is able to do it, but I think He has done it. There have been days in which He has kept my heart in His holy presence, when, though I have always had a sinful nature within me, He has kept me from conscious, actual transgression."

Now, if He can do that for an hour or a day, why not for two days? Oh! let us make God's omnipotence as revealed in His Word the measure of our expectations. Has God not said in His Word: "I, the Lord, do keep it, and will water it every moment" (Isa. 27:3)? What can that mean? Does "every moment" *mean* every moment? Did God promise of that vineyard or red wine that *every moment* He would water it so that the heat of the sun and the scorching wind might never dry it up? Yes. In South Africa they sometimes make a graft, and above it they tie a bottle of water, so that now and then there shall be a drop to saturate what they have put about it. And so the moisture is kept there unceasingly until the graft has had time to stroke, and resist the heat of the sun.

Will our God, in His tenderhearted love toward us, not keep us every moment when He has promised to do so? Oh! if we once got hold of the thought: Our whole spiritual life is to be God's doing—"It is God that worketh in us to will and to do of his good pleasure" (Phil. 2:13)—when once we get faith to expect that from God, God will do all for us.

The keeping is to be continuous. Every morning God will meet you as you wake. It is not a question: If I forgot to wake in the morning with the thought of Him, what will come of it? If you trust your waking to God, God will meet you in the morning as you wake with His divine sunshine and love, and He will give you the consciousness that through the day you have got God to take charge of you continuously with His almighty power. And God will meet you the next day and every day; and never mind if in the practice of fellowship there comes failure sometimes. If you maintain your position and say: "Lord, I am going to expect Thee to do Thy utmost, and I am going to trust Thee day by day to keep me absolutely," your faith will grow stronger and stronger, and you will know the keeping power of God in unbrokenness.

Kept Through Faith

And now the other side—*Believing.* "Kept by the power of God *through faith.*" How must we look at this faith?

Faith Implies Helplessness

Let me say, first of all, that this faith means utter impotence and helplessness before God.

At the bottom of all faith there is a feeling of helplessness. If I have a bit of business to transact, perhaps to buy a house, the lawyer must do the work of getting the transfer of the property in my name and making all the arrangements. I cannot do that work, and in trusting that agent I confess I cannot do it. And so faith always means helplessness. In many cases it means: I can do it with a great deal of trouble, but another can do it better. But in most cases it is utter helplessness; another must do it for me. And that is the secret of the spiritual life. A man must learn to say: "I give up everything; I have tried and longed and thought and prayed, but failure has come. God has blessed me and helped me, but still, in the long run, there has been so much of sin and sadness." What a change comes when a man is thus broken down into utter helplessness and self-despair, and says: "I can do nothing!"

Remember Paul. He was living a blessed life, and he had been taken up into the third Heaven, and then the thorn in the flesh came, "a messenger of Satan to buffet me." And what happened? Paul could not understand it, and he prayed the Lord three times to take it away; but the Lord said, in effect:

"No; it is possible that you might exalt yourself, and therefore I have sent you this trial to keep you weak and humble."

And Paul then learned a lesson that he never forgot, and that was—to rejoice in his infirmities. He said that the weaker he was the better it was for him, for when he was weak, he was strong in his Lord Christ.

Do you want to enter what people call "the higher life"? Then go a step lower down. I remember Dr. Boardman telling how that once he was invited by a gentleman to go to see a factory where they made fine shot, and I believe the workmen did so by pouring down molten lead from a great height. This gentleman wanted to take Dr. Boardman up to the top of the tower to see how the work was done. The doctor came to the tower, he entered by the door, and began going upstairs; but when he had gone a few steps the gentleman called out:

"That is the wrong way. You must come down this way; that stair is locked up."

The gentleman took him downstairs a good many steps, and there an elevator was ready to take him to the top; and he said:

"I have learned a lesson that going down is often the best way to get up."

Ah, yes, God will have to bring us very low down; there will have to come upon us a sense of emptiness and despair and nothingness. It is when we sink down in utter helplessness that the everlasting God will reveal Himself in His power, and that our hearts will learn to trust God alone.

What is it that keeps us from trusting Him perfectly?

Many a one says: "I believe what you say, but there is one difficulty. If my trust were perfect and always abiding, all would come right, for I know God will honor trust. But how am I to get that trust?"

My answer is: "By the death of self. The great hindrance to trust is self-effort. So long as you have got your own wisdom and thoughts and strength, you cannot fully trust God. But when God breaks you down, when everything begins to grow dim before your eyes, and you see that you understand nothing, then God is coming near, and if you will bow down in nothingness and wait upon God, He will become all."

As long as we are something, God cannot be all, and His omnipotence cannot do its full work. That is the beginning of faith—utter despair of self, a ceasing from man and everything on earth, and finding our hope in God alone.

Faith Is Rest

And then, next, we must understand that faith is rest.

In the beginning of the faith-life, faith is struggling; but as long as faith is struggling, faith has not attained its strength. But when faith in its struggling gets to the end of itself, and just throws itself upon God and rests on Him, then comes joy and victory.

Perhaps I can make it plainer if I tell the story of how the Keswick Convention began. Canon Battersby was an evangelical clergyman of the Church of England for more than twenty years, a man of deep and tender godliness, but he had not the consciousness of rest and victory over sin, and often was deeply sad at the thought of stumbling and failure and sin. When he heard about the possibility of victory, he felt it was desirable, but it was as if he could not attain it. On one occasion, he heard an address on "Rest and Faith" from the story of the nobleman who came from Capernaum to Cana to ask Christ to heal his child. In the address it was shown that the nobleman believed that Christ could help him in a general way, but he came to Jesus a good deal by way of an experiment. He hoped

Christ would help him, but he had not any assurance of that help. But what happened? When Christ said to him: "Go thy way, for thy child liveth," that man believed the word that Jesus spoke; he rested in that word. He had no proof that his child was well again, and he had to walk back seven hours' journey to Capernaum. He walked back, and on the way met his servant, and got the first news that the child was well, that at one o'clock on the afternoon of the previous day, at the very time that Jesus spoke to him, the fever left the child. That father rested upon the word of Jesus and His work, and he went down to Capernaum and found his child well; and he praised God, and became with his whole house a believer and disciple of Jesus.

Oh, friends, that is faith! When God comes to me with the promise of His keeping, and I have nothing on earth to trust in, I say to God: "Thy word is enough; kept by the power of God." That is faith, that is rest.

When Canon Battersby heard that address, he went home that night, and in the darkness of the night found rest. He rested on the word of Jesus. And the next morning, in the streets of Oxford, he said to a friend: "I have found it!" Then he went and told others, and asked that the Keswick Convention might be begun, and those at the convention with himself should testify simply what God had done.

It is a great thing when a man comes to rest on God's almighty power for every moment of his life, in prospect of temptations to temper and haste and anger and unlovingness and pride and sin. It is a great thing in prospect of these to enter into a covenant with the omnipotent Jehovah, not on account of anything that any man says, or of anything that my heart feels, but on the strength of the Word of God: "Kept by the power of God through faith."

Oh, let us say to God that we are going to test Him to the very uttermost. Let us say: We ask Thee for nothing more than Thou canst give, but we want nothing less. Let us say: My God, let my life be a proof of what the omnipotent God can do. Let these be the two dispositions of our souls every day—deep helplessness, and simple, childlike rest.

Faith Needs Fellowship

That brings me to just one more thought in regard to faith—faith implies fellowship with God.

Many people want to take the Word and believe that, and they find they cannot believe it. Ah, no! you cannot separate God from His Word. No goodness or power can be received separate from God, and if you want to get into this life of godliness, you *must* take time for fellowship with God.

People sometimes tell me: "My life is one of such scurry and bustle that I have no time for fellowship with God." A dear missionary said to me: "People do not know how we missionaries are tempted. I get up at five o'clock in the morning, and there are the natives waiting for their orders for work. Then I have to go to the school and spend hours there; and then there is other work, and sixteen hours rush along, and I hardly get time to be alone with God."

Ah! there is the lack. I pray you, remember two things. I have not told you to trust the omnipotence of God as a thing, and I have not told you to trust the Word of God as a written book, but I have told you to go to the God of omnipotence and the God of the Word. Deal with God as that nobleman dealt with the living Christ. Why was he able to believe the word that Christ spoke to him? Because in the very eyes and tones and voice of Jesus, the Son of God, he saw and heard something which made him feel that he could trust Him. And that is what Christ can do for you and me. Do not try to stir and arouse faith from within. How often I have tried to do that, and made a fool of myself! You cannot stir up faith from the depths of your heart. Leave your heart, and look into the face of Christ, and listen to what He tells you about how He will keep you. Look up into the face of your loving Father, and take time every day with Him, and begin a new life with the deep emptiness and poverty of a man who has got nothing, and who wants to get everything from Him—with the deep restfulness of a man who rests on the living God, the omnipotent Jehovah—and try God, and prove Him if He will not open the windows of Heaven and pour out a blessing that there shall not be room to receive it.

I close by asking if you are willing to experience to the very full the heavenly keeping for the heavenly inheritance? Robert Murray M'Cheyne says, somewhere: "Oh, God, make me as holy as a pardoned sinner can be made." And if that prayer is in your heart, come now, and let us enter into a covenant with the everlasting and omnipotent Jehovah afresh, and in great helplessness, but in great restfulness place ourselves in His hands. And then as we enter into our covenant, let us have the one prayer—that we may believe fully that the everlasting God is going to be our Companion, holding our hand every moment of the day; our Keeper, watching over us without a moment's interval; our Father, delighting to reveal Himself in our souls always. He has the power to let the sunshine of His love be with us all the day. Do not be afraid because you have got your business that you cannot have God with you always. Learn the lesson that the natural sun shines upon you all the day, and you enjoy its light, and wherever you are you have got the sun; God takes care that it shines upon you. And God will take care that His own divine light shines upon you, and that you shall abide in that light, if you will only trust Him for it. Let us trust God to do that with a great and entire trust.

Here is the omnipotence of God, and here is faith reaching out to the measure of that omnipotence. Shall we not say: "All that that omnipotence can do, I am going to trust my God for"? Are not the two sides of this heavenly life wonderful? God's omnipotence covers me, and my will in its littleness rests in that omnipotence, and rejoices in it!

> *Moment by moment, I'm kept in His love;*
> *Moment by moment, I've life from above;*
> *Looking to Jesus, the glory doth shine;*
> *Moment by moment, Oh, Lord, I am Thine!*

"Ye are the Branches"

An Address to Christian Workers

Everything depends on our being right ourselves in Christ. If I want good apples, I must have a good apple tree; and if I care for the health of the apple tree, the apple tree will give me good apples. And it is just so with our Christian life and work. *If our life with Christ be right,* all will come right. There may be the need of instruction and suggestion and help and training in the different departments of the work; all that has value. But in the long run, the greatest essential is to have the full life in Christ—in other words, to have Christ in us, working through us. I know how much there often is to disturb us, or to cause anxious questionings; but the Master has such a blessing for every one of us, and such perfect peace and rest, and such joy and strength, if we can only come into, and be kept in, the right attitude toward Him.

I will take my text from the parable of the Vine and the Branches, in John 15:5: "I am the vine, ye are the branches." Especially these words: "Ye are the branches."

What a simple thing it is to be a branch, the branch of a tree, or the branch of a vine! The branch grows out of the vine, or out of the tree, and there it lives and grows, and in due time, bears fruit. It has no responsibility except just to receive from the root and stem sap and nourishment. And if we only by the Holy Spirit knew our relationship to Jesus Christ, our work would be changed into the brightest and most heavenly thing upon earth. Instead of there ever being soul-weariness or exhaustion, our work would be like a new experience, linking us to Jesus as nothing else can. For, alas! is it not often true that our work comes between us and Jesus? What folly! The very work that He has to do in me, and I for Him, I take up in such a way that it separates me from Christ. Many a laborer in the vineyard has complained that he has too much work, and not time for close communion with Jesus, and that his usual work weakens his inclination for prayer, and that his too much intercourse with men darkens the spiritual life. Sad thought, that the bearing of fruit should separate the branch from the vine! That must be because we have looked upon our work as something other than the branch bearing fruit. May God deliver us from every false thought about the Christian life.

Now, just a few thoughts about this blessed branch-life.

Absolute Dependence

In the first place, it is a life of absolute dependence. The branch has nothing; it just depends upon the vine for everything. *Absolute dependence* is one of the most solemn and precious of thoughts. A great German theologian wrote two large volumes some years ago to show that the whole of Calvin's theology is summed up in that one principle of *absolute dependence* upon God; and he was right. Another great writer has said that *absolute, unalterable dependence upon God* alone is the essence of the religion of angels, and should be that of men also. God is everything to the angels, and He is willing to be everything to the Christian. If I can learn every moment of the day to depend upon God, everything will come right. You will get the higher life if you depend absolutely upon God.

Now, here we find it with the vine and the branches. Every vine you ever see, or every bunch of grapes that comes upon your table, let it remind you that the branch is absolutely dependent on the vine. The vine has to do the work, and the branch enjoys the fruit of it.

What has the vine to do? It has to do a great work. It has to send its roots out into the soil and hunt under the ground—the roots often extend a long way out—for nourishment, and to drink in the moisture. Put certain elements of manure in certain directions, and the vine sends its roots there, and then in its roots or stems it turns the moisture and manure into that special sap which is to make the fruit that is borne. The vine does the work, and the branch has just to receive from the vine the sap, which is changed into grapes. I have been told that at Hampton Court, London, there is a vine that sometimes bore a couple of thousand bunches of grapes, and people were astonished at its large growth and rich fruitage. Afterward it was discovered what was the cause of it. Not so very far away runs the River Thames, and the vine had stretched its roots away hundreds of yards under the ground, until it had come to the riverside, and there in all the rich slime of the riverbed it had found rich nourishment, and obtained moisture, and the roots had drawn the sap all that distance up and up into the vine, and as a result there was the abundant, rich harvest. The vine had the work to do, and the branches had just to depend upon the vine, and receive what it gave.

Is that literally true of my Lord Jesus? Must I understand that when I have to work, when I have to preach a sermon, or address a Bible class, or to go out and visit the poor, neglected ones, that all the responsibility of the work is on Christ?

That is exactly what Christ wants you to understand. Christ wants that in all your work, the very foundation should be the simple, blessed consciousness: Christ must care for all.

And how does He fulfill the trust of that dependence? He does it by sending down the Holy Spirit—not now and then only as a special gift, for remember the relationship between the vine and the branches is such that hourly, daily, unceasingly there is the living connection maintained. The sap does not flow for a time, and then stop, and then flow again, but from moment to moment the sap flows from the vine to the branches. And just so, my Lord Jesus wants me to take that blessed position as a worker, and morning by morning and day by day and hour by hour and step by step, in every work I have to go out to just to abide before Him in the simple utter helplessness of one who knows nothing, and is nothing, and can do nothing. Oh, beloved workers, study that word *nothing.* You sometimes sing: "Oh, to be nothing, nothing"; but have you really studied that word and prayed every day, and worshiped God, in the light of it? Do you know the blessedness of that word *nothing*?

If I am something, then God is not everything; but when I become *nothing,* God can become *all*, and the everlasting God in Christ can reveal Himself fully. That is the higher life. We need to become nothing. Someone has well said that the seraphim and cherubim are flames of fire because they know they are nothing, and they allow God to put His fullness and His glory and brightness into them. Oh, become nothing in deep reality, and, as a worker, study only one thing—to become poorer and lower and more helpless, that Christ may work all in you.

Workers, here is your first lesson: learn to be nothing, learn to be helpless. The man who has got something is not absolutely dependent; but the man who has got nothing is absolutely dependent. Absolute dependence upon God is the secret of all power in work. The branch has nothing but what it gets from the vine, and you and I can have nothing but what we get from Jesus.

Deep Restfulness

But second, the life of the branch is not only a life of entire dependence, but of deep restfulness.

That little branch, if it could think, and if it could feel, and if it could speak—that branch away in Hampton Court vine, or on some of the million vines that we have in South Africa, in our sunny land—if we could have a little branch here today to talk to us, and if we could say: "Come, branch of the vine, I want to learn from you how I can be a true branch of the living Vine," what would it answer? The little branch would whisper:

"Man, I hear that you are wise, and I know that you can do a great many wonderful things. I know you have much strength and wisdom given to you but I have one lesson for you. With all your hurry and effort in Christ's work you never prosper. The first thing you need is to come and rest in your Lord Jesus. That is what I do. Since I grew out of that vine I have spent years and years, and all I have done is just to rest in the vine. When the time of spring came I had no anxious thought or care. The vine began to pour its sap into me, and to give the bud and leaf. And when the time of summer came I had no care, and in the great heat I trusted the vine to bring moisture to keep me fresh. And in the time of harvest, when the owner came to pluck the grapes, I had no care. If there was anything in the grapes not good, the owner never blamed the branch, the blame was always on the vine. And if you would be a true branch of Christ, the living Vine, just rest on Him. Let Christ bear the responsibility."

You say: "Won't that make me slothful?"

I tell you it will not. No one who learns to rest upon the living Christ can become slothful, for the closer your contact with Christ the more of the Spirit of His zeal and love will be borne in upon you. But, oh, begin to work in the midst of your entire dependence by adding to that *deep restfulness*. A man sometimes tries and tries to be dependent upon Christ, but he worries himself about this absolute dependence; he tries and he cannot get it. But let him sink down into entire restfulness every day.

> *In Thy strong hand I lay me down.*
> *So shall the work be done;*
> *For who can work so wondrously*
> *As the Almighty One?*

Worker, take your place every day at the feet of Jesus, in the blessed peace and rest that come from the knowledge —

> *I have no care, my cares are His!*
> *I have no fear, He cares for all my fears.*

Come, children of God, and understand that it is the Lord Jesus who wants to work through you. You complain of the lack of fervent love. It will come from Jesus. He will give the divine love in your heart with which you can love people. That is the meaning of the assurance: "The love of God is shed abroad in our hearts by the Holy Spirit" (Rom. 5:5); and of that other word: "The love of Christ constraineth us" (2 Cor. 5:14). Christ can give you a fountain of love, so that you cannot help loving the most wretched and the most ungrateful, or those who have wearied you hitherto. Rest in Christ, who can give wisdom and strength, and you do not know how that restfulness will often prove to be the very best part of your message. You plead with people and you argue, and they get the idea: "There is a man arguing and striving with me." They only feel: "Here are two men dealing with each other." But if you will let the deep rest of God come over you, the rest in Christ Jesus, the peace and rest and holiness of Heaven, that restfulness will bring a blessing to the heart, even more than the words you speak.

Much Fruitfulness

But third, the branch teaches a lesson of much fruitfulness.

The Lord Jesus Christ repeated that word *fruit* often in that parable. He spoke, first, of *fruit,* and then of *more fruit,* and then of *much fruit*. Yes, you are ordained not only to bear fruit, but to bear *much fruit*. "Herein is my Father glorified, *that ye bear much fruit*"

(John 15:8). In the first place, Christ said: "I am the Vine, and my Father is the Husbandman. My Father is the Husbandman who has charge of me and you." He who will watch over the connection between Christ and the branches is God; and it is in the power of God through Christ we are to bear fruit.

Oh, Christians, you know this world is perishing for the want of workers. And it lacks not only more workers—the workers are saying, some more earnestly than others: "We need not only more workers, but we need our workers to have a new power, a different life; that we workers should be able to bring more blessing." Children of God, I appeal to you. You know what trouble you take, say, in a case of sickness. You have a beloved friend apparently in danger of death, and nothing can refresh that friend so much as a few grapes, and they are out of season; but what trouble you will take to get the grapes that are to be the nourishment of this dying friend! And, oh, there are around you people who never go to church, and so many who go to church, but do not know Christ. And yet the heavenly grapes, the grapes of the heavenly Vine, are not to be had at any price, except as the child of God bears them out of his inner life in fellowship with Christ. Except the children of God are filled with the sap of the heavenly Vine, except they are filled with the Holy Spirit and the love of Jesus, they cannot bear much of the real heavenly grape. We all confess there is a great deal of work, a great deal of preaching and teaching and visiting, a great deal of machinery, a great deal of earnest effort of every kind; but there is not much manifestation of the power of God in it.

What is lacking? There is lacking the close connection between the worker and the heavenly Vine. Christ, the heavenly Vine, has blessings that He could pour on tens of thousands who are perishing. Christ, the heavenly Vine, has power to provide the heavenly grapes. But "Ye are the branches," and you cannot bear heavenly fruit unless you are in close connection with Jesus Christ.

Do not confound *work* and *fruit.* There may be a good deal of work for Christ that is not the fruit of the heavenly Vine. Do not seek for work only. Oh! study this question of fruit-bearing. It means the very life and the very power and the very spirit and the very love within the heart of the Son of God—it means the heavenly Vine Himself coming into your heart and mine.

You know there are different sorts of grapes, each with a different name, and every vine provides exactly that peculiar aroma and juice which gives the grape its particular flavor and taste. Just so, there is in the heart of Christ Jesus a life, and a love, and a Spirit, and a blessing, and a power for men, that are entirely heavenly and divine, and that will come down into our hearts. Stand in close connection with the heavenly Vine and say:

"Lord Jesus, nothing less than the sap that flows through Thyself, nothing less than the Spirit of Thy divine life is what we ask. Lord Jesus, I pray Thee let Thy Spirit flow through me in all my work for Thee."

I tell you again that the sap of the heavenly Vine is nothing but the Holy Spirit. The Holy Spirit is the life of the heavenly Vine, and what you must get from Christ is nothing less than a strong inflow of the Holy Spirit. You need it exceedingly, and you want nothing more than that. Remember that. Do not expect Christ to give a bit of strength here, and a bit of blessing yonder, and a bit of help over there. As the vine does its work in giving its own peculiar sap to the branch, so expect Christ to give His own Holy Spirit into your heart, and then you will bear much fruit. And if you have only begun to bear fruit, and are listening to the word of Christ in the parable, "more fruit," "much fruit," remember that in order that you should bear more fruit you just require more of Jesus in your life and heart.

We ministers of the Gospel, how we are in danger of getting into a condition of work, work, work! And we pray over it, but the freshness and buoyancy and joy of the heavenly life are not always present. Let us seek to understand that the life of the branch is a life of much fruit, because it is a life rooted in Christ, the living, heavenly Vine.

Close Communion

And fourth, the life of the branch is a life of close communion.

Let us again ask: What has the branch to do? You know that precious, inexhaustible word that Christ used: Abide. Your life is to be an abiding life. And how is the abiding to be? It is to be just like the branch in the vine, abiding every minute of the day. There are the branches, in close communion, in unbroken communion, with the vine, from January to December. And cannot I live every day—it is to me an almost terrible thing that we should ask the question—cannot I live in abiding communion with the heavenly Vine?

You say: "But I am so much occupied with other things."

You may have ten hours' hard work daily, during which your brain has to be occupied with temporal things; God orders it so. But the abiding work is the work of the heart, not of the brain, the work of the heart clinging to and resting in Jesus, a work in which the Holy Spirit links us to Christ Jesus. Oh, do believe that deeper down than the brain, deep down in the inner life, you can abide in Christ, so that every moment you are free the consciousness will come:

"Blessed Jesus, I am still in Thee."

If you will learn for a time to put aside other work and to get into this abiding contact with the heavenly Vine, you will find that fruit will come.

What is the application to our life of this abiding communion? What does it mean?

It means *close fellowship with Christ in secret prayer.* I am sure there are Christians who do long for the higher life, and who sometimes have got a great blessing, and have at times found a great inflow of heavenly joy and a great outflow of heavenly gladness; and yet after a time it has passed away. They have not understood that close personal actual communion with Christ is an absolute necessity for daily life. Take time to be alone with Christ. Nothing in Heaven or earth can free you from the necessity for that, if you are to be happy and holy Christians.

Oh! how many Christians look upon it as a burden and a tax, and a duty, and a difficulty to be often alone with God! That is the great hindrance to our Christian life everywhere. We need more quiet fellowship with God, and I tell you in the name of the heavenly Vine that you cannot be healthy branches, branches into which the heavenly sap can flow, unless you take plenty of time for communion with God. If you are not willing to sacrifice time to get alone with Him, and to give Him time every day to work in you, and to keep up the link of connection between you and Himself, He cannot give you that blessing of His unbroken fellowship. Jesus Christ asks you to live in close communion with Him. Let every heart say: "O, Christ, it is this I long for, it is this I choose." And He will gladly give it to you.

Absolute Surrender

And then finally, the life of the branch is a life of absolute surrender.

This word, absolute surrender, is a great and solemn word, and I believe we do not understand its meaning. But yet the little branch preaches it.

"Have you anything to do, little branch, besides bearing grapes?"

"No, *nothing.*"

"Are you fit for nothing?"

Fit for nothing! The Bible says that a bit of vine cannot even be used as a pen; it is fit for nothing but to be burned.

"And now, what do you understand, little branch, about your relationship to the vine?"

"My relationship is just this: I am utterly given up to the vine, and the vine can give me as much or as little sap as it chooses. Here I am at its disposal and the vine can do with me what it likes."

Oh, friends, we need this absolute surrender to the Lord Jesus Christ. The more I speak, the more I feel that this is one of the most difficult points to make clear, and one of the most important and needful points to explain—what this absolute surrender is. It is often an easy thing for a man or a number of men to come out and offer themselves up to God for entire consecration, and to say: "Lord, it is my desire to give up myself entirely to Thee." That is of great value, and often brings very rich blessing. But the one question I ought to study quietly is What is meant by *absolute surrender*?

It means that, as literally as Christ was given up entirely to God, I am given up entirely to Christ. Is that too strong? Some think so. Some think that never can be; that just as entirely and absolutely as Christ gave up His life to do nothing but seek the Father's pleasure, and depend on the Father absolutely and entirely, I am to do nothing but to seek the pleasure of Christ. But that is actually true. Christ Jesus came to breathe His own Spirit into us, to make us find our very highest happiness in living entirely for God, just as He did. Oh, beloved brethren, if that is the case, then I ought to say:

"Yes, as true as it is of that little branch of the vine, so true, by God's grace, I would have it to be of me. I would live day by day that Christ may be able to do with me what He will."

Ah! here comes the terrible mistake that lies at the bottom of so much of our own religion. A man thinks:

"I have my business and family duties, and my relationships as a citizen, and all this I cannot change. And now alongside all this I am to take in religion and the service of God, as something that will keep me from sin. God help me to perform my duties properly!"

This is not right. When Christ came, He came and bought the sinner with His blood. If there was a slave market here and I were to buy a slave, I should take that slave away to my own house from his old surroundings, and he would live at my house as my personal property, and I could order him about all the day. And if he were a faithful slave, he would live as having no will and no interests of his own, his one care being to promote the well-being and honor of his master. And in like manner I, who have been bought with the blood of Christ, have been bought to live every day with the one thought—How can I please my Master?

Oh, we find the Christian life so difficult because we seek for God's blessing while we live in our own will. We should be glad to live the Christian life according to our own liking. We make our own plans and choose our own work, and then we ask the Lord Jesus to come in and take care that sin shall not conquer us too much, and that we shall not go too far wrong; we ask Him to come in and give us so much of His blessing. But our relationship to Jesus ought to be such that we are entirely at His disposal, and every day come to Him humbly and straightforwardly and say:

"Lord, is there anything in me that is not according to Thy will, that has not been ordered by Thee, or that is not entirely given up to Thee?"

Oh, if we would wait and wait patiently, I tell you what the result would be. There would spring up a relationship between us and Christ so close and so tender that we should afterward be amazed at how we formerly could have lived with the idea: "I am surrendered to Christ." We should feel how far distant our intercourse with Him had previously been, and that He can, and does indeed, come and take actual possession of us, and gives unbroken fellowship all the day. The branch calls us to absolute surrender.

I do not speak now so much about the giving up of sins. There are people who need that, people who have got violent tempers, bad habits, and actual sins which they from time to time commit, and which they have never given up into the very bosom of the Lamb of God. I pray you, if you are branches of the living Vine, do not keep one sin back. I know there are a great many difficulties about this question of holiness. I know that all do not think exactly the same with regard to it. That would be to me a matter of comparative indifference if I could see that all are honestly longing to be free from every sin. But I am afraid that unconsciously there are in hearts often compromises with the idea that we cannot be without sin, we must sin a little every day; we cannot help it. Oh, that people would actually cry to God: "Lord, do keep me from sin!" Give yourself utterly to Jesus, and ask Him to do His very utmost for you in keeping you from sin.

There is a great deal in our work, in our church and our surroundings that we found in the world when we were born into it, and it has grown all around us, and we think that it is all right, it cannot be changed. We do not come to the Lord Jesus and ask Him about it. Oh! I advise you, Christians, *bring everything into relationship with Jesus* and say:

"Lord, everything in my life has to be in most complete harmony with my position as a branch of Thee, the blessed Vine."

Let your surrender to Christ be absolute. I do not understand that word *surrender* fully; it gets new meanings every now and then; it enlarges immensely from time to time. But I advise you to speak it out: "Absolute surrender to Thee, O Christ, is what I have chosen." And Christ will show you what is not according to His mind, and lead you on to deeper and higher blessedness.

In conclusion, let me gather up all in one sentence. Christ Jesus said: "I am the Vine, ye are the branches." In other words: "I, the living One who have so completely given myself to you, am the Vine. You cannot trust me *too much*. I am the Almighty Worker, full of a divine life and power." You are the branches of the Lord Jesus Christ. If there is in your heart the consciousness that you are not a strong, healthy, fruit-bearing branch, not closely linked with Jesus, not living in Him as you should be—then listen to Him say: "I am the Vine, I will receive you, I will draw you to myself, I will bless you, I will strengthen you, I will fill you with my Spirit. I, the Vine, have taken you to be my branches, I have given myself utterly to you; children, give yourselves utterly to me. I have surrendered myself as God absolutely to you; I became man and died for you that I might be entirely yours. Come and surrender yourselves entirely to be mine."

What shall our answer be? Oh, let it be a prayer from the depths of our heart, that the living Christ may take each one of us and link us close to Himself. Let our prayer be that He, the living Vine, shall so link each of us to Himself that we shall go away with our hearts singing: "He is my Vine, and I am His branches—I want nothing more—now I have the everlasting Vine." Then, when you get alone with Him, worship and adore Him, praise and trust Him, love Him and wait for His love. "Thou art my Vine, and I am Thy branch. It is enough, my soul is satisfied."

Glory to His blessed name!

Other Books on Victorious Living

And there are also many other things which Jesus did, the which, if they should be written every one, I suppose that even the world itself could not contain the books that should be written. Amen. — John 21:25

Abandoned to Christ by L. E. Maxwell

Andrew Murray Four Book Treasury (ISBN 9781640322318)

Christian Omnibus Vol. 1 - Eight Books on Prayer (ISBN 9781640323087)

In His Steps: What Would Jesus Do? by Charles M. Sheldon (ISBN 9781640322493)

Man: The Dwelling Place of God by A. Z. Tozer

Not I, But Christ by Stephen F. Olford

R. A. Torrey Five Book Set (ISBN 9781640322738)

The Indwelling Life of Christ: All of Him in All of Me by Ian Major Thomas

The Normal Christian Life by Watchman Nee (ISBN 9781640322196)

Victorious Living by E. Stanley Jones

Victory in Christ by Charles Trumbull

9 781640 323117